John's Gospel
A Discipleship Journey with Jesus

and Bible Study Commentary for Personal Devotional Use, Small Groups or
Sunday School Classes, and Sermon Preparation for Pastors and Teachers

JesusWalk® Bible Study Series

by Dr. Ralph F. Wilson
Director, Joyful Heart Renewal Ministries

Additional books, and reprint licenses are available at:
www.jesuswalk.com/books/john.htm

Free Participant Guide handout sheets are available at:
http://www.jesuswalk.com/john/john-lesson-handouts.pdf

JesusWalk® Publications
Loomis, California

Paperback

ISBN-13: 978-0-9962025-0-3
ISBN-10: 0996202501

Library of Congress subject headings:
    Bible – N.T – John – Commentaries

Suggested Classifications
    Library of Congress – BS 2615
    Dewey Decimal – 226.5

Published by JesusWalk® Publications, P.O. Box 565, Loomis, CA 95650-0565, USA.

JesusWalk is a registered trademark and Joyful Heart is a trademark of Joyful Heart Renewal Ministries.

Unless otherwise noted, all the Bible verses quoted are from the New International Version (International Bible Society, 1973, 1978), used by permission.

Lesson 2 is adapted from my book *Lamb of God: Jesus' Atonement for Sin* (third edition, JesusWalk, 2011). Lesson 6 is adapted from my book *Jesus and the Kingdom of God: Discipleship Lessons* (JesusWalk, 2010). Lessons 13, 30, and 31 contain elements adapted from my book *JesusWalk: Discipleship Training in Luke's Gospel* (JesusWalk, 2010). Lesson 14 is adapted from my book *Lord's Supper: Meditations for Disciples on the Eucharist or Communion* (JesusWalk, 2006, 2011). Lesson 30 contains sections adapted from my book, *Seven Last Words of Christ from the Cross* (JesusWalk, 2009). Lesson 31 contains elements adapted from my book *Resurrection and Easter Faith* (JesusWalk, 2007, 2011).

150406

I dedicate this book to our Lord Jesus Christ, in the humble hope that I have accurately interpreted his teachings to my generation.

I also dedicate this to my wife Jean, who has enjoyed with me many, many discussions of John's Gospel over the nine months of this project.

Finally, I dedicate this to the men of my Tuesday Morning Men's Discipleship Group, who have poured over the words of John's Gospel with me in an attempt to understand them and help them to guide our thoughts and lives as disciples today. Thank you Steve Dunlap, Steve Winther, and Paul Johnson – my friends.

Preface

I love John's Gospel, and I hope that you will love it too! St. Augustine once said about the Gospel of John, that,

> "It is shallow enough for a child not to drown, yet deep enough for an elephant to swim in it."

The most memorized verse in the New Testament is found in the Fourth Gospel:

> "For God so loved the world, that he gave his only begotten Son, that whoever believes in him should not perish but have eternal life." (John 3:16, ESV)

Some of the greatest truths of the Christian faith are taught in the Fourth Gospel, perhaps more than in any New Testament book. For example:

- Jesus Christ is the only-begotten, fully divine, Son of God;
- The Holy Spirit, the Paraclete, guides, teaches, and empowers us to carry on Jesus' miraculous ministry;
- The Father loves us as He does Jesus;
- Eternal life vs. the wrath of God;
- And much more....

Good Shepherd, stained glass window at All Saints Church, Alburgh, Norfolk, UK, by Powell of London (1872). Photo © by Simon Knott. Used by permission.

John shares some of the same incidents that we find in Matthew, Mark, and Luke (the Synoptic Gospels) and offers his own insightful perspective from the point of view of one close to Jesus, a perspective that helps us understand the deeper significance of these events. But John's Gospel also contains a lot of material not found in the other Gospels – among others:

- Changing the water into wine (2:1-11),
- The woman at the well of Sychar (4:1-26)
- Healing of the invalid at the Pool of Bethesda (5:1-15)
- "I am the Bread of Life" (6:25-51)
- The woman taken in adultery (8:1-11)
- "I am the light of the world" (8:12)
- "The truth shall set you free" (8:32)
- Healing the man born blind (8:48-9:41)
- "I am the Good Shepherd" (10:1-42)
- Raising Lazarus from the dead (11:1-44)
- Washing the disciples feet (13:1-38)
- "I am the Way, the Truth, and the Life" (14:6)
- "I am the vine, you are the branches" (15:1-17)
- Jesus' "High Priestly" prayer (chapter 17)
- "As the Father sent me, so send I you" (20:19-31)

I'm sure you've read the Gospel of John before – perhaps many times – but with these lessons I've prepared, I hope this time we can study it with special depth and mine its riches for ourselves – you and I together. It is a long study. John's Gospel itself spans 21 chapters of rich material. My focus will be on how we can learn to be better disciples and walk more closely with Jesus.

I look forward to studying John's Gospel with you.

> Yours in Christ,
> Dr. Ralph F. Wilson
> Loomis, California
> Resurrection Day, 2015

Table of Contents

Table of Contents

References and Abbreviations

Barrett   C.K. Barrett, *The Gospel According to St. John* (Second Edition; Westminster, 1978)

BDAG   Walter Bauer and Frederick William Danker, *A Greek-English Lexicon of the New Testament and Other Early Christian Literature* (Third Edition; based on previous English editions by W.F. Arndt, F.W. Gingrich, and F.W. Danker; University of Chicago Press, 1957, 1979, 2000)

Beasley-Murray George R. Beasley-Murray, *John* (Word Biblical Commentary 36; Word, 1987)

Brown, *Death* Raymond E. Brown, *The Death of the Messiah: From Gethsemane to the Grave* (Doubleday, 1994).

Brown, *John* Raymond E. Brown, *The Gospel According to John* (Anchor Bible; Doubleday; Part 1, John I-XII, 1966; Part 2, John XIII-XXII,

Carson   D. A. Carson, *The Gospel According to John* (Pillar New Testament Commentary; Eerdmans, 1991)

DJG   Joel B. Green, Scot McKnight, and I. Howard Marshall (editors), *Dictionary of Jesus and the Gospels* (InterVarsity Press, 1992)

DJG[2]   Joel B. Green, Jeannine K. Brown, and Nicholas Perrin (editors), *Dictionary of Jesus and the Gospels* (second edition, InterVarsity Press, 2013)

ESV   English Standard Version (Crossway, 2001)

Green, *Luke* Joel B. Green, *The Gospel of Luke* (The New International Commentary on the New Testament; Eerdmans, 1997)

Grudem, *Systematic Theology* Wayne Grudem, *Systematic Theology: An Introduction to Biblical Doctrine* (Zondervan, 1994, 2000)

Hengel, *Crucifixion* Martin Hengel (translator John Bowden), *Crucifixion in the Ancient World and the Folly of the Message of the Cross* (German edition 1976; English edition: Fortress Press/SCM Press, 1977)

ISBE   Geoffrey W. Bromiley (general editor), *The International Standard Bible Encyclopedia* (Eerdmans, 1979-1988; fully revised from the 1915 edition)

Jeremias   Joachim Jeremias, *Jerusalem in the Time of Jesus* (translated from the third German edition of 1965; Fortress/SCM Press, 1969)

Jesus &   James H. Charlesworth (editor), *Jesus and Archaeology* (Eerdmans, 2006)
Archaeology

KJV   King James Version (Authorized Version, 1611)

Kruse   Colin G. Kruse, *John* (Tyndale New Testament Commentaries; Eerdmans, 2003)

Ladd   George Eldon Ladd, *A Theology of the New Testament* (Eerdmans, 1974), especially his section on "The Fourth Gospel," pp. 213-308

Liddell-Scott   Henry George Liddell. Robert Scott, *A Greek-English Lexicon* (revised and augmented throughout by Sir Henry Stuart Jones with the assistance of. Roderick McKenzie; Oxford, Clarendon Press, 1940, Perseus Project online edition)

Marshall, *Luke*   I. Howard Marshall, *Commentary on Luke* (New International Greek Testament Commentary; Eerdmans, 1978)

Metzger   Bruce M. Metzger, *A Textual Commentary on the Greek New Testament* (United Bible Societies, 1971)

Morris, *John*   Leon Morris, *The Gospel According to John* (New International Commentary of the New Testament; Eerdmans, 1971)

Morris, *Studies*   Leon Morris, *Studies in the Fourth Gospel* (Eerdmans, 1969)

Morris, *Theology*   Leon Morris, *Gospel of Life: Theology in the Fourth Gospel* (Hendrickson, 1991)

NASB   New American Standard Bible (The Lockman Foundation, 1960-1988)

NIDNTT   Colin Brown (editor), *New International Dictionary of New Testament Theology* (Zondervan, 1975-1978) translated with additions and revisions from *Theologisches Begriffslexikon zum Neuen Testament*, Coenen, Beyreuther, and Bitenhard, editors)

NIV   New International Version (International Bible Society, 1973, 1978)

NJB   New Jerusalem Bible (Darton, Longman & Todd Ltd, 1985)

NRSV   New Revised Standard Version (Division of Christian Education of the
                          National Council of Churches of Christ, USA, 1989)

Robertson   Archibald Thomas Robertson, *Word Pictures in the New Testament* (Sunday
                          School Board of the Southern Baptist Convention, 1932, 1960)

Strack and   Hermann L. Strack and Paul Billerbeck, *Kommentar zum Neuen Testament aus
Billerbeck   Talmud und Midrasch* (München: Beck, 1922)

TDNT   Gerhard Kittel and Gerhard Friedrich (editors), Geoffrey W. Bromiley
                          (translator and editor), *Theological Dictionary of the New Testament* (Eerdmans,
                          1964-1976; translated from *Theologisches Wörterbuch zum Neuen Testament*, ten
                          volume edition)

TWOT   R. Laird Harris, Gleason L. Archer, Jr., and Bruce K. Waltke, (editors), *Theological
                          Wordbook of the Old Testament* (2 volumes, Moody Press, 1980)

Reprint Guidelines

Copying the Handouts. In some cases, small groups or Sunday school classes would like to use these notes to study this material. That's great. An appendix provides copies of handouts designed for classes and small groups. There is no charge whatsoever to print out as many copies of the handouts as you need for participants.

Free Participant Guide handout sheets are available at:

www.jesuswalk.com/john/john-lesson-handouts.pdf

All charts and notes are copyrighted and must bear the line:

"Copyright © 2014-15, Ralph F. Wilson. All rights reserved. Reprinted by permission."

You may not resell these notes to other groups or individuals outside your congregation. You may, however, charge people in your group enough to cover your copying costs.

Copying the book (or the majority of it) in your congregation or group, you are requested to purchase a reprint license for each book. A Reprint License, $2.50 for each copy is available for purchase at

www.jesuswalk.com/books/john.htm

Or you may send a check to:

> Dr. Ralph F. Wilson
> JesusWalk Publications
> PO Box 565
> Loomis, CA 95650, USA

The Scripture says,

> "The laborer is worthy of his hire" (Luke 10:7) and "Anyone who receives instruction in the word must share all good things with his instructor." (Galatians 6:6)

However, if you are from a third world country or an area where it is difficult to transmit money, please make a small contribution instead to help the poor in your community.

Introduction to John's Gospel

John's Gospel is dramatically different than the Synoptic Gospels (meaning *similar* Gospels, "presenting the same view") – Matthew, Mark, and Luke. These first three Gospels share, to some degree, a similar source, and often have passages that seem almost the same word-for-word as in the others.

But John's Gospel is in a class by itself. It draws upon a separate, independent gospel tradition. It's as if the Synoptic Gospels tell the story of Jesus' life, miracles, parables, and teaching, letting readers draw their own conclusions. But John is very selective in the events he includes. And when he does include a miracle, he often leads us to ponder its meaning in a discourse. John's Gospel, written late in the apostle's life, is full of thoughtful, theological reflection.[1]

John Calvin said about the four Gospels:

> "As all of them had the same object in view, to point out Christ, the three former exhibit his body, if we may be permitted to use the expression, but John exhibits his soul."[2]

A great deal has been written about John's Gospel, for it is deep and complex for the scholar. For a more thorough introduction, consult one of the technical commentaries. However, here are some of the basics that will help you as you begin to study.

James J. Tissot, 'St. John the Evangelist' (1886-94) gouache on paper, 13.6x9.7". Brooklyn Museum, New York.

Authorship

The nearly unanimous tradition of the early church is that John the Apostle, son of Zebedee, is the author of the Gospel that bears his name. The first clear reference is by Irenaeus (died 202 AD). Irenaeus knew personally Polycarp (69 to c. 160 AD), who in turn had been a personal disciple of the Apostle John. Irenaeus wrote:

---

[1] This is not intended to deny that each of the Synoptic Gospel writers came from his own particular theological perspective and focus on a particular audience.

[2] John Calvin, *Commentary on the Gospel of John*, The Argument.

> "John, the disciple of the Lord, who also had leaned upon His breast, did himself publish a Gospel during his residence at Ephesus in Asia."[3]

Eusebius quotes Clement of Alexandria (c. 150-215 AD) as saying:

> "But John, last of all, conscious that the outward facts had been set forth in the Gospels, was urged on by his disciples, and, divinely moved by the Spirit, composed a spiritual gospel."[4]

I could go on. By the end of the second century AD there is virtual agreement in the Church as to the authority, canonicity, and authorship of the Gospel of John.

This remained so until the mid-nineteenth century, the rise of the Enlightenment. The question of whether the Apostle John was the author of this Gospel has raged hot in the twentieth century. Many place its authorship within the "Johannine Community," written perhaps by a disciple of John.

However, I believe there are strong reasons to accept John the Apostle, son of Zebedee, as the author of the Gospel of John. Chief of these is the testimony of an editor at the end of the Gospel itself about "the disciple that Jesus loved."

> "Peter turned and saw that **the disciple whom Jesus loved**[5] was following them. (This was the one who had leaned back against Jesus at the supper and had said, 'Lord, who is going to betray you?') ... This is the disciple who testifies to these things and who wrote them down. We know that his testimony is true." (21:20, 24)

It is clear that this Beloved Disciple was close to Jesus (13:23, 24), trusted by Jesus with the care of his mother (19:26-27), was the only disciple who remained at the cross when Jesus died (19:34-35), the disciple who raced Peter to the tomb (20:2-5, 8), and the one who recognized Jesus on the shore after the resurrection (21:7). It is the Beloved Disciple who Jesus hinted might outlive St. Peter (21:20ff). Of course, the term "the disciple that Jesus loved," is a strange way to indentify oneself. But it is also a strange way to identify someone else! There are clear evidences of eyewitness testimony, and much more.

From both external sources and internal evidence, the strongest case can be made for John as the author of this Gospel. The case for any other author is much weaker.

---

[3] Irenaeus, *Against Heresies*, xxx, 1, 2. There is a clear reference to the "beloved disciple" in John 13:23.

[4] Clement, quoted by Eusebius, *Ecclesiastical History*, VI, xiv, 7. Cited by Carson, *John*, pp. 27-28.

[5] Based on John 11:3, some have presumed that Lazarus is to be understood here.

Date and Place

So John is the author. But when and where was the Gospel written? While there is little evidence, most scholars see the date of John's Gospel as comparatively late, probably in the 90s AD, though some evangelical scholars see it as written somewhat earlier.[6]

John's Gospel can't have been written much later than 100 AD. The earliest known fragment of a New Testament document is Papyrus 52, from Egypt dating from about 130 AD. It contains portions of John 18:31-33. Other early portions of John come from the second century AD (Papyri 66 and 75) and the early third century (Papyrus 45).

Papyrus 52, a fragment of the Gospel of John (18:31-33) in the John Rylands Library, is dated from about 130 AD in Egypt.

The 90s AD is considerably later than the proposed date for Mark, usually seen as the earliest of the Synoptic Gospels, written probably in the 60s AD. John seems to assume that his readers are acquainted with the facts of Jesus as given in the Synoptic Gospels (1:40; 3:24; 4:44; 6:67, 71; 11:1-2).

There are several early traditions that place the Apostle John as Bishop of Ephesus. Revelation 1:9 places John, author of Revelation, in exile on the Island of Patmos, off the coast of Asia Minor near Ephesus. Irenaeus (cited above) refers to John's residence in Ephesus.[7] Justin Martyr (in 135 AD) places John at Ephesus.[8] While there, John probably penned his Gospel.

Purpose

While many reasons have been suggested for why John wrote his Gospel, the most straightforward is the purpose stated in the Gospel itself:

> "Jesus did many other miraculous signs in the presence of his disciples, which are not recorded in this book. But these are written that you may believe that Jesus is the Christ, the Son of God, and that by believing you may have life in his name." (John 20:30-31)

While the Synoptics give many more incidents in Jesus' life, and the instruction of many parables and sayings, John seems to have an evangelistic purpose that guides his selection of material. He wants his readers to be convinced that Jesus is the promised Messiah and the divine Son of God, to the end that they might experience his Life. Perhaps this is why John is a favorite gospel to give to inquirers and new Christians.

John probably wrote to convince unbelieving Greek-speaking Jews to believe in Jesus as the Christ, the Messiah. But since he often explains Jewish customs in Palestine, he probably has Gentile unbelievers in mind as well.

---

[6] Morris (John, p. 35), sees a date "prior to 70 AD," the fall of Jerusalem. Carson (John, p. 82) holds a tentative date of 80 AD.

[7] Irenaeus, *Against Heresies*, xxx, 1, 2.

[8] Justin Martyr, *Dialogue with Trypho*, 81.4.

John and the Synoptics

It seems clear that while John was *aware* of the Synoptic Gospels, there is no evidence of literary dependence upon them. John represents a unique, eyewitness gospel tradition.

There are, of course, some similarities between John and the Synoptics – they all focus on the life of Jesus of Nazareth – but there are many differences. For example, John tends to:

- Record longer discourses, rather than parables and brief sayings.
- A focus on eternal life more than on the Kingdom of God.
- Fewer miracles, but an emphasis on them as "signs" of who Jesus is.[9]
- A strongly theological prologue, that begins by telling us just who Jesus is.
- No Christian baptism or sacraments mentioned.
- Ministry primarily in Judea and Jerusalem, with less on his Galilean ministry.
- A focus on Jewish feasts, especially on the Passover.
- An emphasis on the tragedy of Jesus' rejection by his own people and their leaders.

Theology

John is an intensely theological book. Some of the strongest themes include:

- The Word/Logos.
- God as Father.
- The "I Am" sayings.[10]
- Jesus as Son of God.
- Jesus as the Christ.
- Miracle signs and their relationship to true faith.
- Salvation.
- Life – especially eternal life.
- The Holy Spirit as Paraclete.

We'll be exploring these in the lessons to come.

Style

John's writing style is different. If you're especially observant, you may spot some of these characteristics:

- Quasi-poetic, solemn style of Jesus' discourses.
- Purposeful twofold or double meanings. For example, in 3:16 the Greek adverb anōthen can mean both "from above" and "again."
- Misunderstanding, where Jesus is speaking on the heavenly level, but he is misunderstood as speaking to a material or earthly situation. Examples: water and bread, his body as the temple.
- Irony. Derogatory statements of Jesus' enemies are often ironic in the sense that they say more than they know they are saying.

---

[9] See Appendix 5. "Signs" in John's Gospel.
[10] Appendix 4. The "I Am" Passages in John's Gospel.

- Explanatory notes are common, to explain names, symbols, and customs to make sure readers in a different place and culture understand the references.

Summary

Many mature Christians find the Gospel of John to be their "favorite" Gospel, one that they go back to again and again. It is rich. It is cosmic in its view of the Christ. And it is convincing in its explanation of who Jesus is and what he has done for us.

John contains perhaps the most-often memorized verse in the entire Bible, loved by all because it seems to contain the scope of the Gospel in a single sentence.

"For God so loved the world, that he gave his only Son, that whoever believes in him should not perish but have eternal life." (3:16, ESV)

It is my prayer that by a deep study of John's Gospel your faith will be deepened, and that you will find many opportunities to point others to Christ, that they too might find eternal life.

Prayer

Father, thank you for this wonderful Gospel. I pray that you would help my brothers and sisters persist through the many lessons that comprise this study – that they won't let circumstances force them to drop out and leave many passages unstudied and unappropriated for their lives. Enrich us as we study. May your Holy Spirit work within us as we study so that Christ may be formed in us. In Jesus' holy name we pray. Amen.

Section I – Prologue (1:1-18)

John's Gospel begins with a flourish, with a powerful prologue that makes huge claims about who Jesus is and his cosmic significance. The stated purpose of John's Gospel is:

> "These are written that you may believe that Jesus is the Christ, the Son of God, and that by believing you may have life in his name." (20:31)

The remainder of the Gospel goes about demonstrating the truth of these claims by what Jesus said and did on earth, as well as documenting his resurrection from the dead.

Gerard (Gerrit) van Honthorst (1590-1656), 'Adoration of the Children' (1620), Uffizi Gallery, Florence. Italy.

1. The Word Became Flesh (1:1-18)

The Word Was God (1:1-3)

The Bible begins with the well-known verse:

> "In the beginning God created the heavens and the earth." (Genesis 1:1)

The Bible traces all beginnings to God, who is omnipresent, and is present at the creation. John begins his Gospel with the same startling three words – "In the beginning" – but introduces Jesus Christ as "the Word," as God himself, as co-Creator with the Father.

> "¹ In the beginning was the Word, and the Word was with God, and the Word was God. ² He was with God in the beginning. ³ Through him all things were made; without him nothing was made that has been made." (1:1-3)

"Word" is the extremely common Greek noun *logos*, "word," a communication by which the mind finds utterance. It can have a wide range of meanings, depending on the context, such as "statement, assertion, message, declaration." Another use is as "computation, reckoning." But the use in John 1:1 is unique. Here *logos* is "the independent personified expression of God." You see hints of this in other Johannine books:

"That which was from the beginning, which we have heard, which we have seen with our eyes, which we have looked at and our hands have touched – this we proclaim concerning the **Word of life**." (1 John 1:1)

"He is dressed in a robe dipped in blood, and his name is the **Word of God**." (Revelation 19:13)

John is purposely drawing analogies to Genesis 1, so the idea of the "Word" or *Logos* of God no doubt refers to God speaking and creating, such as:

"And God said, 'Let there be light,' and there was light." (Genesis 1:3)

Another major teaching of 1:1-3, 14 – and indeed John's whole Gospel – is the preexistence of Jesus. He is with God in the beginning of creation. He became flesh (1:14), but that is not the beginning of his existence.[11] Jesus' self-awareness of and teaching of his preexistence is also seen in his taking the title Son of Man based on Daniel 7:13-14. This is summed up in our passage by the term *logos*, "Word."[12]

A great deal has been written about John's use of *logos* here, but essentially, in verse 1 John is saying that Jesus in the flesh is the very Expression of God Himself, and that this Jesus IS God himself – a very bold statement indeed to begin John's Gospel. Another verse in this prologue to the Gospel makes a similarly bold statement of Jesus' full divinity, which we'll discuss in due course.

"No one has ever seen God, but God the One and Only, who is at the Father's side, has made him known." (1:18)

Jehovah Witnesses, who deny the concept of the Trinity,[13] have mistranslated verse 1 to conform to their doctrine that Jesus is not Jehovah or God himself, but a created being – divine, yes, but lesser than Jehovah.

"In the beginning was the Word, and the Word was with God, and the Word was **a god**." (1:1, New World Translation, 1950)

The Jehovah's Witness translators added the indefinite article "a" to indicate that Jesus was a divine being, one among other divine beings. The problem with their translation is that there is no indefinite article in the Greek text or suggested by Greek grammar – they've added it![14]

It is quite clear, however, that the Apostle John sees Jesus as fully divine – on the same level of divinity as the Father!

To help you internalize and apply what you're learning from John's Gospel, I've included several Discussion Questions in each lesson. These are designed to help you think about and ponder the most important points. Don't skip this. It's best to write them out. You can post your

---

[11] See 1:30; 6:33-38, 46, 50-51, 62; 8:23, 38; etc. Paul taught Jesus' preexistence also: Romans 1:4; Philippians 2:6ff.; Colossians 1:16; cf. 1 Corinthians 8:6.

[12] Kittel observes: "The distinctive thing in John 1:1ff. is that preexistence is now put thematically at the head and expressed in the term *logos*" (Gerhard Kittel, *logos, ktl.*, TDNT 4:100-143).

[13] For more on the doctrine of the Trinity, see my article, "Four Reasons Why I Believe in the Trinity," http://www.joyfulheart.com/scholar/trinity.htm

[14] The Greek grammar here gets very technical. For more information, consult a critical commentary. See, for example, Bruce M. Metzger, "On the Translation of John 1:1," *Expository Times*, LXIII (1951-52), 125 f., But suffice it to say, the Jehovah's Witness translation breaks the well-established rules of Greek grammar, because, when properly translated, John 1:1 indicates something that their doctrine denies – that Jesus is God at the same level as the Father.

answers – and read what others have written – by going to the online forum by clicking on the URL below each question. (Before you can post your answer the first time, you'll need to register. You can find instructions at http://www.joyfulheart.com/forums/instructions.htm

Q1. (John 1:1-3) According to the Apostle John, is Jesus fully God? What does it mean that Jesus is the "Word"? What does this say about him and his ministry?
http://www.joyfulheart.com/forums/topic/1387-q1-fully-god/

Light and Life (1:4-5)

In Genesis 1:3, light is created by *God's Word*:

"And God *said*, 'Let there be light,' and there was light." (Genesis 1:3)

Indeed, light characterizes God's glory, as we'll see when we examine 1:14. In John's Gospel, Jesus, the Logos, the co-Creator, is the Bringer of Light to all humankind.

"4 In him was life, and that life was the light of men. 5 The light shines in the darkness, but the darkness has not understood it." (1:4-5)

Here, John introduces the theme of a war between spiritual light and darkness that pervades his Gospel (John 1:4-5, 7-9; 3:19-21; 8:12; 9:5; 11:9-10; 12:35-36, 46). Here, Christ's light represents and brings life. Light is brimming with inextinguishable Life. The Light actively attacks the darkness (1:5a).

"The reason the Son of God appeared was to destroy the devil's work." (1 John 3:8)

"Darkness" in verse 5 seems almost to be darkness personified in both the prince of darkness, Satan, as well as all those who live in spiritual darkness. Light is shining but they haven't "understood it" (NIV), "overcome it" (NRSV, ESV), "comprehended it" (KJV). The Greek word *katalambanō*, which has the basic meaning of "to seize, lay hold of," could refer to gaining a mental or spiritual grasp ("understood" or "comprehend") or it could mean, "seize with hostile intent, overtake, come upon" ("overcome").[15] The NIV offers the alternate translation in its footnote.

Though the concept of recognizing the Christ is present a few verses later (1:10b), I think that the predominant concept here is one of spiritual warfare as reflected in the NRSV and ESV. The light has come and shines boldly in the darkness to dispel it. And even though darkness combats the light and tries to overcome it, darkness does not prevail. The light is infinitely stronger.

One of the frustrating – and intriguing – characteristics of John's style is that he often uses words ambiguously, words that can be taken two ways. So John may well have meant for us to see both aspects of *katalambanō* – "comprehend" as well as "overcome."

John's Witness to the Light (1:6-8)

John introduces John the Baptist here, then picks him up again later in the chapter. The Synoptic Gospels give us background about John the Baptist. He was, for example:

---

[15] *Katalambanō*, BDAG 520, meanings 1, 2, and 3.

- Jesus' cousin, just about six months older than Jesus (Luke 1:36-66).
- Lived in the desert (Luke 1:80; 3:2).
- Ministered along the Jordan River east of Jerusalem "preaching a baptism of repentance for the forgiveness of sins" (Luke 3:3).
- Attracted a large following from Jerusalem and Judea (Matthew 3:5; Mark 1:5).
- Denounced the religious hypocrites (Luke 3:7-8).
- Demanded love and justice of those who sought baptism (Luke 3:10-14).
- Proclaimed that one who came after him would baptize with the Holy Spirit and fire (Luke 3:16-17).
- Rebuked Herod Antipas, Tetrarch of Galilee and Perea, for adultery and incest, and was imprisoned (Luke 3:19-20) and later beheaded because of the tetrarch's wife Herodias's anger at John's rebuke (Matthew 14:3-12).
- Baptized Jesus (Luke 3:21).
- Was widely considered to be a prophet (Mark 11:32), and declared to be one by Jesus (Matthew 11:9).
- A Nazirite (Luke 1:15; Matthew 11:18).
- A righteous and holy man (Mark 6:20).
- Jesus said that he fulfilled the prophecy that Elijah should return (Matthew 17:12-13; Mark 9:13).

The Apostle John assumes that his readers already know what the Synoptics taught about John. Instead of rehearsing this material, he goes for the *meaning* of John's ministry.

"⁶ There came a man who was sent from God; his name was John. ⁷ He came as **a witness to testify** concerning that light, so that through him all men might believe. ⁸ He himself was not the light; he came only as a **witness** to the light." (1:6-8)

We learn from the Apostle John that John the Baptist:
- Is sent from God.
- Is a witness to testify regarding Jesus the Light.

The noun is "witness" (*martyria*), from the verb "testify/bear witness" (*martyreō*), and has a legal flavor: "to confirm or attest something on the basis of personal knowledge or belief, bear witness, be a witness."[16] We get our English word "martyr" from this root.[17]

The Apostle seems to be referring to John the Baptist's testimony concerning Jesus later in this chapter:
- "He was before me" (1:15), where the word "testify" occurs.
- "The Lamb of God who takes away the sin of the world" (1:29, 36).
- "The Son of God" (1:34), where John uses the phrase, "I have seen and testify...."

Q2. (John 1:7-8) What did it mean that John was sent to "testify" to the light? In what sense are you put here with the purpose of "testifying" to the light? How are you doing in this regard?

[16] *Martyreō*, BDAG 617, 1aα.

[17] Martyr – "a person who voluntarily suffers death as the penalty of witnessing to and refusing to renounce a religion" (*Webster's 11th Collegiate Dictionary*).

What happened to John the Baptist? What might happen to you if you testify clearly? What might happen to the people to whom you testify?
http://www.joyfulheart.com/forums/topic/1388-q2-testifying-to-the-light/

The Light Is Not Recognized or Received by All (1:9-13)

God has sent people to testify to the Light, but not all accept this testimony or receive the Light as God.

"The true light that gives light to every man was coming into the world." (1:9)

John develops the theme of light and darkness in 3:19-21. Later, Jesus declares, "I am the light of the world" (8:12; 9:5). In what sense does Jesus "give light to every man"? I think in the sense that those who hear about him and believe in him don't have to walk in darkness any longer (12:46). But it still incumbent upon us to tell others. As the old Gospel hymn put it:

Send the light, the blessed gospel light,
Let it shine, from shore to shore...."[18]

Now John continues, explaining that though the light was present in the world, it was rejected by a blind world – his own world!

"[10] He was in the world, and though the world was made through him, the world did not recognize him. [11] He came to that which was his own, but his own did not receive him." (1:9-10)

These verses reflect the sadness of the gospel record that though Jesus was a Jew, the Jewish leaders, as a whole, rejected Jesus as coming from God – to the extent that they even crucified him! Indeed, Jesus' mission was exclusively directed towards the "lost sheep of the house of Israel" (Matthew 15:24; 10:6). John seems to echo God's sadness in Isaiah:

"I revealed myself to those who did not ask for me;
I was found by those who did not seek me.
To a nation that did not call on my name,
I said, 'Here am I, here am I.'
All day long I have held out my hands to an obstinate people,
who walk in ways not good,
pursuing their own imaginations–
a people who continually provoke me to my very face...."
(Isaiah 65:1-3a; cf. Romans 10:21)

We sense this same sadness in Jesus as he enters the Holy City on Palm Sunday:

"O Jerusalem, Jerusalem, you who kill the prophets and stone those sent to you, how often I have longed to gather your children together, as a hen gathers her chicks under her wings, but you were not willing!" (Luke 13:34)

---

[18] Words by Charles H. Gabriel, 1890.

Those Who Believed and Received Jesus (1:12-13)

But not all rejected him. One of the wonders of the New Testament is that his grace was extended to the Gentiles, many of whom *did* receive him.

"[12] Yet to all[19] who received him, to those who believed in his name, he gave the right to become children of God – [13] children born not of natural descent, nor of human decision or a husband's will, but born of God." (1:12-13)

These two verses are extremely important in helping us understand elements of the "new birth" that Jesus treats more fully in his encounter with Nicodemus in John 3. In theological terms, the "new birth" is called regeneration.

Notice three learnings from this passage – and I hope you'll commit John 1:12 to memory:

1. Rejection. Not all people who hear about Jesus trust him. It seems crazy to us that the Son of God could come among men and be rejected, but that is exactly what happened. Pharisees could see him perform miracles and then conclude that he must be killed. Not all your friends or even your family may really trust Jesus. In other words, not all people believed in him, but to those who did came an amazing privilege.

2. Personal belief. The new birth requires personal openness and trust in Jesus. I say "personal" because not all respond in this way to Jesus. The response that produces a "new birth" is described in two ways:

a. **Receiving.** The Greek word is the extremely common verb *lambanō*, with the basic meaning, "take hold of, grasp." Here, it has the connotation, "to include someone in an experience, take up, receive," specifically, "receive someone in the sense of recognizing the other's authority."[20]

b. **Believing.** *Pisteuō* means, "to consider something to be true and therefore worthy of one's trust, believe." Here it has the connotation, "to entrust oneself to an entity in complete confidence, believe (in), trust, with the implication of total commitment to the one who is trusted."[21] In John we often see the phrase "believe in his name." This phrase carries the idea of, "believe in the Son and accept what his name proclaims him to be."[22] We'll explore this idea of "the name" later in our study.

Note that "believe" here isn't in terms of intellectual assent only – though it includes that. To "believe in Jesus" means to trust oneself fully to him. As the Amplified Bible rightly renders it: "believe in – adhere to, trust in, and rely on."[23]

3. Spiritual birth as God's children. Those who receive Jesus' authority and trust in him this way are the recipients of a wonderful gift: "He gave the right to become children of God" (1:12c). "Right"

---

[19] Verse 12 opens with the Greek pronoun *hosos*, "as much (many) as," pertaining to a comparative quantity or number of objects or events (BDAG 729, 2).

[20] *Lambanō*, BDAG 584, meanings 5 and 7. There is similar usage elsewhere in John (John 5:43; 13:20). The closely related idea, "accept as true, receive someone's words," is found in both John (12:48; 17:8) and the Synoptics. In Matthew 13:20 and Mark 4:16 Jesus describes in the Parable of the Sower those on rocky places who initially receive the word with joy, only to fall away in times of persecution.

[21] *Pisteuō*, BDAG 2aβ. See also 2:23; 3:18c; and 1 John 5:13; cf. 1 John 3:23.

[22] *Pisteuō*, BDAG 817, 2aα.

[23] John 1:12b, *Amplified Bible* (Lockman Foundation/Zondervan, 1954, 1965).

(NIV, ESV), "power" (NRSV, KJV) is *exousia*, "authority," here, "capability, might, power."[24] Paul develops the similar idea of "adoption as sons" in his letters (Romans 8:15; Ephesians 1:5; Galatians 4:5). But here the image is birth, since John contrasts it with natural birth in 1:13.

The implications of these verses are astounding. All may be "children of God" in the sense of creation (Acts 17:28-29), but not all are his children in a spiritual sense – only those who receive Jesus as God's son and wrap their lives around him. Without the new birth we can't claim "authority" to be called God's children, in the same sense that without legal adoption papers we can't claim to be someone's child. Sonship, that is a privilege bestowed by Jesus himself. Jesus said something similar to Nicodemus, a highly religious man:

> "I tell you the truth, no one can see the kingdom of God unless he is born again." (3:3)

Q3 (John 1:12-13) What does it mean to "receive" Jesus? What does it imply to "believe in" Jesus? What is the spiritual relationship to God of those who receive and believe in Jesus? Of those who do not?
http://www.joyfulheart.com/forums/topic/1389-q3-receiving-and-believing-children/

The Word Became Flesh (1:14a)

Verses 14-18 are astounding in their clear statement of Jesus' full divinity while in the flesh. While Matthew 1 and Luke 2 give a narrative view of the incarnation, John gives a theological view, spelling out the implications of Jesus' coming as a man. Let's look at each of these statements carefully, for they lie at the very bedrock of the Christian faith.

> "The Word became flesh and made his dwelling among us." (1:14a)

John has already identified this Word (*Logos*) with God in verses 1-2, with creation in verse 3, and with light and life in verses 4 and 5. Now John tells us in verse 14, that this Word, the very expression of God, "became flesh and made his dwelling among us."

For Jews, with their belief in the One Invisible God, such a statement would be deemed blasphemous. For the Greeks, with their sharp dualism between flesh (evil) and spirit (good), the idea that a holy god, a spirit, could become flesh wouldn't make sense.

But that is what John says with jolting clarity: "The Word became[25] flesh and made his dwelling[26] among us" (1:14a). Luke conveys to us the angel's proclamation,

> "Do not be afraid. I bring you good news of great joy that will be for all the people. Today in the town of David a Savior has been born to you; he is Christ the Lord." (Luke 2:10-11)

---

[24] *Exousia*, BDAG 353, 2.

[25] "Became" is the common verb *ginomai*, "to come into existence, become" here, "to experience a change in nature and so indicate entry into a new condition, become something" (BDAG 198, 5a). This is in the Aorist tense, so the emphasis isn't on a continuing process, but on a one-time event.

[26] "Made his dwelling" (NIV), "lived" (NRSV), "dwelt" (KJV) is the verb *skēnoō*, "live, settle, take up residence," from *skēnos*, "tent, lodging," a temporary abode as opposed to a permanent structure (BDAG 929). This also is in the Aorist tense, speaking of an event that took place in the past.

Paul describes it poetically in his letter to the Philippians:

> "Who, being in very nature God,
> did not consider equality with God something to be grasped,
> but made himself nothing,
> taking the very nature of a servant,
> being made in human likeness.
> And being found in appearance as a man,
> he humbled himself
> and became obedient to death –
> even death on a cross!" (Philippians 2:6-8)

This is worthy of much meditation – usually exercised during the Christmas season – of God sending his Son to be born a baby to a poor family in the ancestral home of King David. The Son, the Creator, becoming flesh and blood for a time so that he might save us.... It is amazing, remarkable!

Glory of the 'Only-Begotten' (1:14b)

John continues,

> "We have seen his glory, the glory of the One and Only, who came from the Father, full of grace and truth." (1:14b)

This sentence contains several huge concepts that we need to examine.

First, Uniqueness is expressed in three words: *monogenous para patros*, literally, "only son from father." "One and Only" (NIV), "only Son" (ESV, NRSV), "only begotten" (KJV) is the adjective *monogenēs*, "pertaining to being the only one of its kind within a specific relationship, one and only, only." [27] Here, "pertaining to being the only one of its kind or class, unique (in kind)," of something that is the only example of its category.[28,29] Jesus is utterly unique. He is not just another created human being. He is unique from the Father.

John uses *monogenēs* to describe Jesus three additional times in his writings:

> "No one has ever seen God, but **God the One and Only**, who is at the Father's side, has made him known." (1:18)

> "For God so loved the world that he gave **his one and only Son**, that whoever believes in him shall not perish but have eternal life." (3:16)

> "This is how God showed his love among us: He sent **his one and only Son** into the world that we might live through him." (1 John 4:9)

We'll consider the startling words in 1:18 shortly.

---

[27] It is used in the New Testament as "only son" (of Abraham, Hebrews 11:17; of the widow of Nain, Luke 7:12; of the man with the demon-possessed son, Luke 9:38) and "only daughter" (of Jairus, Luke 8:42). In the Septuagint you see it with Jephthah's daughter, an only child (Judges 11:34).

[28] *Monogenēs*, BDAG 658, 2.

[29] We shouldn't overly stress the idea of begetting, since the word derives from the verb *ginomai*, "be born, become," rather than *gennaō*, "beget," (Morris, *John*, p. 105, fn. 93), (though used with "from the Father," begetting would be implied).

John's prologue and the word *monogenēs* have had a very strong influence on orthodox Christology, as evidenced in the Nicene Creed (325, 381 AD), though the Church Fathers understood *monogenēs* in the sense of "begotten" rather than "unique":

> "We believe ... in one Lord Jesus Christ, the **only-begotten**[30] Son of God, **begotten**[31] of the Father before all worlds, Light of Light, very God of very God, **begotten, not made**, being of one substance with the Father; by whom all things were made...."

Second, Glory. Throughout the Old Testament we read about the "glory of God," which was sometimes manifested in fire and brightness, what the Jews called the "Shekinah," the dwelling or settling of the divine presence. In Hebrew "glory" is *kābôd*, from *kābēd*—"to be heavy," hence "wealth, honor, dignity, power," etc. In the New Testament, *kābôd* is translated by *doxa*, "reputation." Yahweh sometimes manifests himself in fire and in a cloud. Yahweh is the epitome of light itself.

> "You are clothed with splendor and majesty.
> He wraps himself in light as with a garment." (Psalm 104:1b-2a)

> "His splendor was like the sunrise;
> rays flashed from his hand,
> where his power was hidden." (Habakkuk 3:4)

> "He ... dwells in unapproachable light" (1 Timothy 6:16).[32]

John himself had seen that very Shekinah glory upon Jesus during the transfiguration, and, with Peter and James, "were eyewitnesses of his majesty" (2 Peter 1:16-18).

> "After six days Jesus took with him Peter, James and John the brother of James, and led them up a high mountain by themselves. There he was transfigured before them. His face shone like the sun, and his clothes became as white as the light." (Matthew 17:1-2).[33]

Third, Grace. Jesus is "full of grace and truth." "Grace," a word thoroughly developed by the Apostle Paul in his letters, is *charis*, "favor." It is important to understand that this favor is not based upon our worthiness, rather, it is unilateral. Though we don't see the word again in John's writings (except in 1:16), the concept is often expressed in other terms, such as:

> "For God so loved the world that he gave his one and only Son, that whoever believes in him shall not perish but have eternal life." (John 3:16)

> "We love him, because he first loved us." (1 John 4:19)

God doesn't love us (that is, show favor to us) because we are deserving. His grace or favor doesn't have anything to do with our worthiness. Jesus took our sins upon him to make us worthy.

Fourth, Truth. "Truth" is a word that appears often in the Gospel. Jesus often prefaces his important assertions with the phrase, "I tell you the truth..." (NIV), or "Verily, verily I say unto you..." (KJV).[34] Jesus is the truth-teller to the world. He tells good news and exposes as lies the so-called truths

---

[30] *Monogenēs*.

[31] *Gennaō*. The very Father-Son relationship supports the idea of "begetting" vs. "making."

[32] Also Exodus 34:29; Revelation 22:5; 1 John 1:5; etc.

[33] See more in Appendix 6. "Glory" and "Glorify" in John's Gospel.

[34] John 1:51; 3:3, 5, 11; 5:19, 24, 25; 6:26, 32, 47, 53; 8:34, 45; 10:1, 7; 12:24; 13:16, 20, 21, 38; 14:12; 16:7, 20, 23; 21:18. Also frequently in Matthew; less so in Mark and Luke.

that people have been clinging to. Jesus insists that people worship God "in spirit and in truth" (4:23-24). He declares:

> "If you hold to my teaching, you are really my disciples. Then you will know the truth, and the truth will set you free." (John 8:31b-32)

Because Jesus tells them the truth, his enemies want to kill him (8:40). The devil is the polar opposite: "a liar and the father of lies," and "there is no truth in him" (8:44). After his departure, Jesus promises to send to his disciples the Holy Spirit, whom he calls three times, "the Spirit of truth" (14:17; 15:26; 16:13). Jesus calls on the Father to sanctify the disciples by his truth, his word (17:17, 19). And finally, he appears before Pilate to speak the truth:

> "'You are a king, then!' said Pilate.
> Jesus answered, 'You are right in saying I am a king. In fact, for this reason I was born, and for this I came into the world, to testify to the truth. Everyone on the side of truth listens to me.'
> 'What is truth?' Pilate asked." (John 18:37-38a)

Part of John's core testimony is that Jesus is himself God's truth for us – and his truth is as inescapable for us as it was for Pilate.

> "I am the way, and the truth, and the life.
> No one comes to the Father except through me." (14:6)

Q4. (John 1:14) Why is the idea of God "becoming flesh" so important to the basis of the Christian faith? What would Christ's life, crucifixion, and resurrection mean if he were only pretending to "become flesh"? In what ways have you personally experienced his grace? In what ways has his truth changed your life from what it was?
http://www.joyfulheart.com/forums/topic/1390-q4-becoming-flesh/

Making the Father Known (1:15-18)

John's prologue concludes with several additional assertions about Jesus' identity and ministry that help the reader understand Jesus' significance.

> "[15] John testifies concerning him. He cries out, saying, 'This was he of whom I said, "He who comes after me has surpassed me because he was before me."' [16] From the fullness of his grace we have all received one blessing after another. [17] For the law was given through Moses; grace and truth came through Jesus Christ. [18] No one has ever seen God, but God the One and Only, who is at the Father's side, has made him known." (John 1:15-18)

In these verses, John makes three major points:

1. **Christ Surpasses John the Baptist** (1:15). Jesus both surpasses and predates John the Baptist. With his characteristic ambiguity, John is making the point that though John the Baptist first appears on the scene (and was, indeed, born before Jesus, Luke 1), Jesus ranks ahead of him

because he, in actuality, predates John.[35] It is a reference to the preexistence of Christ, to which Jesus alludes when he says, "Before Abraham was, I am" (8:58).

2. **Christ Surpasses Moses** (1:16-17). While Moses was rightfully honored among the Jews, John notes that Christ surpasses even Moses. Moses brought the Law, but Jesus brought grace ("God's underserved favor") and truth, and Jesus has brought many blessings that continue to flow to us.

3. **Christ reveals the Father (1:18).** No one has seen God, but the pre-existent Christ has been at the Father's side throughout eternity. Christ predates them all.

The Only-Begotten God (1:18)

"No one has ever seen God, but God the One and Only, who is at the Father's side, has made him known." (1:18)

We can't leave John's Prologue without noting the amazing title that John bestows on Jesus. Here it is in various translations.

"God the One and Only" (NIV)
"God the Only Son" (NRSV)
"The Only God" (ESV)
"The Only Begotten God" (NRSV)
"The only-begotten Son" (KJV, NKJV)

What makes this so remarkable is that John seems to refer to Jesus as fully God "at the Father's side." He distinguishes between Jesus and the Father, but calls Jesus, "the Only Begotten God." Wow!

However, not all translations render this bold statement thus. While the earliest Greek manuscripts read "only-begotten God," the KJV, NKJV, and the New Jerusalem Bible (in the tradition of the Latin Vulgate) use the word "Son" instead of "God," following the majority of Greek manuscripts (though not the earliest).[36]

Whatever the original text in this particular verse, John clearly places Jesus right next to God as fully divine (John 1:1-3, etc.).

---

[35] "Surpassed" (NIV), "ranks ahead" (NRSV), "is preferred before" (KJV) is two words: the verb *erchomai*, "come" and the adverb *emprosthen*, "in front, ahead." *Emprosthen* here is a bit ambiguous because it can refer to time as well as rank (BDAG 324). The adjective *prōtos* is also a bit ambiguous, since it can mean "first" of a sequence as well as "first" in prominence (BDAG 894).

[36] "Only begotten God" is found in a substantial number of the earliest texts (P66,75 Aleph1.*, B C*, L, etc.), as well as in quotations from early Fathers such as Irenaeus, Origin, Didymus of Alexandria. "Only begotten Son" is found in A, C3, Θ, Ψ, f1.13, and the Byzantine texts, and Latin and Syriac translations. Clearly, the majority of Greek manuscripts support "only-begotten Son," but it seems that among the earliest Greek manuscripts more support "only-begotten God." You would expect it to read "only-begotten Son," because the phrase is used elsewhere (John 3:16, 18; 4:9; Hebrews 11:17). You wouldn't expect "only-begotten God." The field of Textual Criticism seeks to determine the original text from several principles. The original text is likely to have the strongest "external support" from the early Greek manuscripts. The original text is likely to be the "hardest reading," since you'd expect scribes to change a less-expected text to a more-expected text. For these reasons most modern translations agree with the majority of Editorial Committee of the United Bible Societies' Greek New Testament, which gives "only-begotten God" a {B} or "some degree of doubt" rating, on a scale of A to D (Metzger, *Textual Commentary*, p. 198).

Q5. (John 1:18) What does it mean that Jesus is the "Only God" or the "Only Begotten God"? Does the Apostle John seem to make a distinction between God the Father and God the Son? What does all this mean for our understanding of the Trinity?
http://www.joyfulheart.com/forums/topic/1391-q5-only-begotten-god/

Lessons for Disciples

John's Prologue gives us a great deal of information about who Jesus is. Here are just some of our learnings:

1. Jesus is fully divine. He is God (1:1).
2. Jesus is the full expression of God the Father (1:1).
3. Jesus is not a created being, rather he was delegated the task of creation (1:2-3).
4. Jesus is the source of life and truth for mankind (1:4).
5. Jesus was rejected by his own people (1:11).
6. Only those who believe and receive Jesus have "authority" to be called God's children (1:12).
7. Jesus (the Word) became human (flesh) and showed us God's glory (1:14).
8. Jesus brings grace and truth (1:14, 17).
9. Jesus is the One and Only God (1:18).

Sometimes we're so busy doing and being obedient that we don't take time to reflect and bask in the glory of who Jesus is. Take that time!

John has begun his Gospel by displaying word pictures of the glory and magnificence of Jesus Christ. When you try to take it all in, it's almost mind-boggling. But what it comes down to for you and me is that, according to John 1:12, if we believe in Jesus as the Son of God, and receive him into our lives as our Lord and Savior, then we become children of God. I pray that you have done this, or will do so very soon.

Prayer

Father, thank you for the immense privilege of being children of God, through faith in Jesus Christ. We certainly don't deserve this privilege, nor do we take it for granted. But we bask in it. Thank you. Help us to let our world know that Jesus is the Only Begotten God come to earth. In Jesus' glorious name, we pray. Amen.

Key Verses

"In the beginning was the Word, and the Word was with God, and the Word was God. He was with God in the beginning. Through him all things were made; without him nothing was made that has been made." (John 1:1-3, NIV)

"He came to that which was his own, but his own did not receive him. Yet to all who received him, to those who believed in his name, he gave the right to become children of God – children born not of natural descent, nor of human decision or a husband's will, but born of God." (John 1:11-13, NIV)

"The Word became flesh and made his dwelling among us. We have seen his glory, the glory of the One and Only, who came from the Father, full of grace and truth." (John 1:14, NIV)

"No one has ever seen God, but God the One and Only, who is at the Father's side, has made him known." (John 1:18, NIV)

Section II. The Signs and Public Discourses of Jesus (1:19 - 12:50)

We've begun the second major section of John's Gospel. After the Prologue (1:1-18), John carefully selects incidents in Jesus' life that tell us Jesus' significance, who Jesus is. Who he *really* is. Remember John's purpose:

> "Jesus did many other **miraculous signs** (*sēmeion*) in the presence of his disciples, which are not recorded in this book. But these are written **that you may believe** that Jesus is the Christ, the Son of God, and **that by believing you may have life** in his name." (20:30-31)

Many commentators call 1:19-12:50 the Book of Signs, followed by the Book of Glory (13:1-20:31), where Jesus glory is seen in his death and resurrection.

One of the characteristic words for miracle or healing in John's Gospel is "sign." The term "miraculous signs" (NIV), "signs" (NRSV), "miracles" (KJV) is the plural of *sēmeion*, "a sign or distinguishing mark whereby something is known, sign, token, indication." Here, "an event that is an indication or confirmation of intervention by transcendent powers, miracle, portent."[37] For John, these wonders are not just miracles, but signs that point to who Jesus actually is.

"Feeding the Multitude" window (2000-2001), St. Andrews Episcopal Church, Ayer, Massachusetts, under the direction of Scott McDaniel, Art Director, Stained Glass Resources, Hamden, MA.

In the early part of his Gospel, John numbers two of his signs (2:11; 4:54). If you were to number all the signs about which John gives considerable space, you could come up with Seven Signs:

1. Changing the Water into Wine (2:1-11)
2. Healing of the Nobleman's Son (4:46-54)
3. Healing at the Pool of Bethesda (5:1-9)
4. Feeding the Multitude (6:1-14)
5. Walking on the Water (6:15-25)
6. Healing the Man Born Blind (9:1-8)
7. Raising Lazarus from the Dead (11:1-46)

---

[37] *Sēmeion*, BDAG 920, 2aα.

Unlike the Synoptic Gospels that include many teaching parables about the Kingdom of God, John's Gospel displays Jesus' teaching in a series of discourses, many of which follow miraculous sings. If you were to number the major discourses in the Book of Signs you could come up with Seven Discourses:

1. The New Birth (3:1-36)
2. The Water of Life (4:1-42)
3. The Divine Son (5:19-47)
4. The Bread of Life (6:22-66)
5. The Life-Giving Spirit (7:1-52)
6. The Light of the World (8:12-59)
7. The Good Shepherd (10:1-42)

Whether John planned his Gospel to be divided so neatly into two Books, Seven Signs and Seven Discourses, is debatable. However, it provides the modern reader with some structure within which to understand Jesus' ministry.

2. John the Baptist's Witness to the Lamb of God (1:19-34)

Before we meet Jesus, we meet John the Baptist, who reveals him to Israel.

The Significance of John the Baptist for the Jews

Notice that the author assumes that we know who John the Baptist is. The Apostle John probably wrote his Gospel rather late, in the 90s AD. The Synoptic Gospels (Matthew, Mark, and Luke) that told John the Baptist's story had probably been in circulation among the churches for at least a decade or two. Furthermore, John the Baptist seems to have

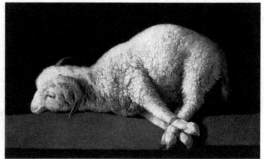

Francisco de Zurburan (1598-1664), 'Agnus Dei' (1635-40), oil on canvas 38 x 62 cm., Museo Nacional del Prado, Madrid

been well known in Jewish circles as a revivalist. He was a rough country preacher who was drawing great crowds and baptizing in the Jordan River.

Josephus records several paragraphs about him.

> "John, that was called the Baptist ... who was a good man, and commanded the Jews to exercise virtue, both as to righteousness towards one another, and piety towards God, and so to come to baptism; for that the washing [with water] would be acceptable to him, if they made use of it, not in order to the putting away [or the remission] of some sins [only], but for the purification of the body; supposing still that the soul was thoroughly purified beforehand by righteousness...."[38]

Peter refers to John the Baptist as he preaches about Jesus in the Roman city of Caesarea. Paul speaks of him in a synagogue in Pisidian Antioch on his first missionary journey (Acts 13:24). Even as far away as Ephesus in about 52 AD, Paul finds a zealous Jew from Alexandria who "knows only the baptism of John" (Acts 18:25).

John's preaching made a huge impact on the Jewish world – and produced a reaction among the Jewish leaders in Jerusalem, who sent a delegation down to the Jordan where he was baptizing to interrogate him.

> "Now this was John's testimony when the Jews of Jerusalem sent priests and Levites to ask him who he was." (1:19)

In our text, there seem to be two groups sent to investigate and interrogate John – (1) priests and Levites from Jerusalem (1:19), the power elite of the Temple who tended to be Sadducees; and (2)

---

[38] Josephus, *Antiquities*, xviii. 5.2.

Pharisees (1:24), who were especially strict in their adherence to the commandments in the Law of Moses.[39]

Who Are You, John? (1:19-21)

In response to his questioners from Jerusalem, John the Baptist is forthright and humble.

> "²⁰ He did not fail to confess, but confessed freely, 'I am not the Christ.' ²¹ They asked him, 'Then who are you? Are you Elijah?' He said, 'I am not.' 'Are you the Prophet?' He answered, 'No.'" (1:20-21)

John records that John the Baptist made no pretentions about who he was. The Jewish leaders inquired if he were one of the three figures whom the Jews expected to return in the Last Days.

1. **The Messiah or Christ**.
2. **Elijah**. Malachi's prophecy says,

   > "See, I will send you the prophet Elijah before that great and dreadful day of the LORD comes." (Malachi 4:5)

3. **The Prophet**. This figure was referred to by Moses:

   > "The LORD your God will raise up for you a prophet like me from among your own brothers. You must listen to him." (Deuteronomy 18:15)

John was not Elijah himself, but prophecy given by his father Zechariah indicated that he did come "in the spirit and power of Elijah" (Luke 1:17). Jesus said that John had fulfilled the prophecy about Elijah's coming (Matthew 7:11-13).

At any rate, John the Baptist himself didn't see himself as any of these figures, so he categorically denied being any of them.

James J. Tissot, 'The Voice in the Desert' (1886-94), gouache on paper, 11.5x6.7", Brooklyn Museum, New York.

The Voice Crying in the Wilderness (1:22-23)

John had told him who he wasn't. Now they ask him who he is on his own terms.

> "²² Finally they said, 'Who are you? Give us an answer to take back to those who sent us. What do you say about yourself?' ²³ John replied in the words of Isaiah the prophet, 'I am the voice of one calling in the desert, "Make straight the way for the Lord."'" (1:22-23)

John's answer was that he was the voice in the wilderness mentioned in Isaiah 40:3-5 calling people to prepare a highway on which Yahweh would come. Building a highway requires both cutting high spots and filling low spots to create a level roadbed, figurative of the repentance that God requires in our lives.

> "³ A voice of one calling:
> "In the desert prepare the way for the LORD;

---

[39] See Appendix 2. "The Jews" in John's Gospel, and Appendix 3. Religious Leaders in Jesus' Day.

make straight in the wilderness a highway for our God.

"⁴ Every valley shall be raised up,

every mountain and hill made low;

the rough ground shall become level,

the rugged places a plain.

⁵ And the glory of the LORD will be revealed,

and all mankind together will see it.

For the mouth of the LORD has spoken." (Isaiah 40:3-5)

John came proclaiming that the Kingdom of God is at hand, repent (Matthew 3:1-2) and called for baptism for the forgiveness of sins (Mark 1:4). He was that voice prophesied from old to prepare for the Messiah, the Son of God, "to prepare the way of the Lord."

> **Q1. (John 1:19-23) Why do you think John the Baptist was being hassled by the religious leaders from Jerusalem? What were they afraid of? How did John understand his own mission? How much conflict do you think could be expected from John's mission?**
> **http://www.joyfulheart.com/forums/topic/1392-q1-hassling-john-the-baptist/**

John's Baptism and the One Who Comes After (1:24-28)

"This all happened at Bethany on the other side of the Jordan, where John was baptizing." (1:28)

John was baptizing east of the Jordan River at a place called Bethany, a location we can't pinpoint twenty centuries later, though it may well be near the Hajlah ford across the Jordan from Jericho. [40]

"²⁴ Now some Pharisees who had been sent ²⁵ questioned him, 'Why then do you baptize if you are not the Christ, nor Elijah, nor the Prophet?'" (1:24-25)

---

[40] "Bethabara" (KJV) is a textual variant of "Bethany" in 1:18, though the best manuscripts read "Bethany." Bethabara was the only location known to Origin (185-254 AD). We can't be sure of its location, but since it was known to origin, that would explain the textual variant as scribes sought to correct it (Ralph Earl, Bethabara, ISBE 1:463). The Byzantines built a church to commemorate it at a site across from Jericho at Beth-nimrah. Other traditions identify it with Qasr el-Yehud, west of Jordan; with Makhadet 'Abara, just north of the Harrod Valley, and other locations. J. Carl Laney ("The Identification of Bethany Beyond the Jordan," from *Selective Geographical Problems in the Life of Christ*, a doctoral dissertation by (Dallas Theological Seminary, 1977), who has looked all the possibilities notes that reliable ancient tradition does appear to associate Bethany near the Hajlah ford in the vicinity of Wadi el-Kharrar, east of Jericho. Urban C. Von Wahlde ("Archaeology and John's Gospel," in *Jesus & Archaeology*, pp. 528-33) doesn't see enough evidence to make any firm conclusion.

The Pharisees, legalists that they are[41], don't seem impressed with John's response. If you're not one of the three figures expected in the Last Day, just who do think you are to take it on yourself to baptize? they ask.

What's your authority to baptize? The verb *baptizō* was used in Classical Greek to mean "to put or go under water" in a variety of senses. It could be translated, "plunge, dip, wash, baptize."[42] The origins of John's baptism are difficult to discern precisely. We know that the Community at Qumran (in John's desert "territory," certainly) practiced repeated ritual washings,[43] but John's baptism seems different – an act of purification and forgiveness that can be looked back upon as a single event (Acts 19:3-4). Probably, the antecedent for John's baptism is the first century practice of Jewish proselyte baptism, a ritual bath by which a Gentile convert to Judaism was cleansed from moral and religious impurity.[44]

But John wasn't baptizing proselytes to the Jewish faith; he was baptizing Jews! What authority do you have to do this? the Pharisees demand.

John gives the only answer he has. He repeats his call from God.

> "[26] 'I baptize with water,' John replied, 'but among you stands[45] one you do not know. [27] He is the one who comes after me, the thongs of whose sandals I am not worthy to untie.'" (1:26-27)

This personage John speaks of is of such high rank that John feels unworthy to untie his sandal-thongs, the task of a house-slave. This person is among you now, John says, though John doesn't seem to know yet who it is.

Q2. (John 1:26-27) Why did John baptize? What is the meaning of the baptism he was performing? What do you think baptism represents to those John baptized?
http://www.joyfulheart.com/forums/topic/1393-q2-meaning-of-johns-baptism/

Q3. (John 1:19-27) How does John the Baptist show humility? How can a person see himself as the fulfillment of a passage from Isaiah and still be humble about it? How does John see himself in relation to the coming Messiah? How can a person be such a strong revivalist preacher and still remain humble? Can humility and powerful, confident speech co-exist?
http://www.joyfulheart.com/forums/topic/1394-q3-johns-humility/

---

[41] Appendix 3. Religious Leaders in Jesus' Day.

[42] *Baptizō*, BDAG 164, 2.

[43] *Manual of Discipline* 1QS 3:4-9; 6:14-23. See also D.S. Dockery, "Baptism," in DJG, p. 56, who thinks the Qumran washings are the most probable antecedent for John's baptism.

[44] G.R. Beasley-Murray, *Baptism in the New Testament* (Eerdmans, 1962, 1973), pp. 23ff.

[45] *Histēmi*, "to stand," perfect tense, that is, a past action that continues to the present.

Behold, the Lamb of God (1:29)

The day after the interrogation by the Pharisees, John the Baptist sees Jesus coming towards him and it is supernaturally revealed to him just who he is.

> "The next day John saw Jesus coming toward him and said, 'Look, the Lamb of God, who takes away the sin of the world!'" (1:29)

John repeats this saying a little later in 1:36. The context of these verses doesn't tell us a great deal about what John the Baptist actually meant when he said this. So let's examine the words themselves.

"Behold" (KJV) is the Greek particle *ide*, which can be taken two ways. (1) to point out something to which the speaker wishes to draw attention – "Look! See!" and (2) to indicate a place or individual, "Here is (are)" so-and-so.[46] Hence the translations, "Look!" (NIV), "Here is...." (NRSV), "Behold!" (KJV). John draws attention to Jesus and indicates that Jesus is the focus of his words that follow.

"Lamb," the Greek noun *amnos*, refers to a young sheep, including at least up to one year old.[47] We'll come back to this word.

"Of God" can mean either "sent from God" or perhaps "owned by God." John says that Jesus is in some way *like* a lamb sent from or provided by God himself.

"Sin" is the common Greek noun *harmartia*. Originally it meant "to miss the mark, be mistaken." In the New Testament it occurs 173 times as a comprehensive expression of everything opposed to God.[48] Sin and forgiveness of sin are major themes of the Bible, both Old and New Testaments. Our modern society really doesn't like the concept of sin at all – though dealing with guilt is a major psychological problem that plagues people of all religions and no religion.

"Of the world" employs the Greek noun *kosmos*, which refers here to "humanity in general."[49] Jesus doesn't come to deal with just a single person, or the sin of just the Jewish people for that year, but for the sins of everyone in the whole world for all time.

"Take away" describes what the Lamb will do with sin, employing the Greek verb *airō*, which means generally "to lift up and move from one place to another." Here it means "to take away, remove, blot out."[50]

> "Behold, the Lamb of God, who takes away the sin of the world." (1:29)

The Sacrificial Lamb

What specific lamb is John the Baptist referring to? It could be a sacrificial Passover Lamb or the lamb described in Isaiah 53, or perhaps he is using it in a general way.[51] Clearly, John indicates that

---

[46] *Ide*, BDAG 446.

[47] *Amnos*, BDAG 54.

[48] Walther Günther, "Sin," NIDNTT 3:573-583.

[49] *Kosmos*, BDAG 562.

[50] *Airō*, BDAG 28. Joachim Jeremias, "*airō*," TDNT 1:185-186, indicates that *airo* can refer here to either the substitutionary bearing of penalty (if the Suffering Servant of Isaiah 53 is in mind) or "the setting aside of sin by the expiatory power of the death of Jesus." Jeremias prefers the latter approach.

[51] George R. Beasley-Murray, *John: Word Biblical Commentary 36* (Word, 1987), pp. 24-25; Raymond E. Brown, *The Gospel According to John* (Anchor Bible vol. 29; Doubleday, 1966), 1:58-63; C.K. Barrett, *The Gospel According to St. John* (Second Edition; Westminster Press, 1978), 175-177.

Jesus is the Lamb of God in some sacrificial sense, since lambs were commonly used by the Jews for sacrifices to obtain forgiveness for sin (Exodus 27; Leviticus 1-7). God provides animal sacrifice as a way that justice can be done, that men's and women's sins can be atoned for, and that they can approach God once more. The taking of any life affects us as it affected the Israelites – blood indicates taking of life. And taking life, even to eat, is never a trivial thing. God tells Moses:

> "For the life of a creature is in the blood, and I have given it to you to make atonement for yourselves on the altar; it is the blood that makes atonement for one's life." (Leviticus 17:11)

"Atonement" in Hebrew seems to mean, "to wipe clean, purge," a sacrifice that cleanses from sin.[52]

> "When anyone is guilty in any of these ways, he must **confess** in what way he has sinned and, as a penalty for the sin he has committed, he must bring to the LORD a female lamb or goat from the flock as a sin offering; and the priest shall make **atonement** for him for his sin." (Leviticus 5:5-6)

The amazing prophecy of Isaiah 53 describes this ministry of atonement and sacrifice that Jesus took upon himself by divine appointment:

> "He was pierced for our transgressions,
> he was crushed for our iniquities;
> the punishment that brought us peace was upon him,
> and by his wounds we are healed.
> We all, like sheep, have gone astray,
> each of us has turned to his own way;
> and the LORD has laid on him the iniquity of us all." (Isaiah 53:5-6)

Sacrifice for sin is the context from which John the Baptist speaks when he says, "Behold, the Lamb of God who takes away the sin of the world" (1:29). Jesus is greater than our analogies, of course. But there is a sense in which the analogy of the sacrificial Lamb fits Jesus accurately, since he, as Son of God and Son of Man is the only One perfect and great enough to actually atone for sin and, at the same time, represent and substitute for all men in this atonement – once and for all.

Look! This is the Lamb of God, who takes away the sin of the world!

Q4. (John 1:29) What does the title "Lamb of God" tell us about Jesus' ministry? According to 1:29, whose sins did he come to take away? In what ways did Jesus fulfill Isaiah 53? http://www.joyfulheart.com/forums/topic/1395-q4-lamb-of-god/

---

[52] The word translated "atonement" here is the Hebrew verb *kāpar, kipper*, "to make an atonement, make reconciliation, purge." An equivalent Arabic root means "cover" or "conceal," but evidence that the Hebrew root means "to cover over sin" is weak. Rather, the root idea of *kipper* seems to be "to purge," related to an Akkadian cognate *kuppuru* meaning "to wipe clean" (Richard E. Averbeck, "Sacrifices and Offerings," DOTP 706-732, especially p. 710; R. Laird Harris, *kāpar*, TWOT #1023). Our English word "atonement" comes from the Middle English "at-one-ment" or "reconciliation," which expresses the result of an atoning sacrifice.

John Came to Reveal Jesus to Israel (1:30-31)

Now John the Baptist identifies Jesus with the person he had described to the Pharisees the day before (1:26-27), and the person he had previously proclaimed who would surpass him (1:15). He is the One who is the Lamb of God.

> "30 This is the one I meant when I said, 'A man who comes after me has surpassed me because he was before me. 31 I myself did not know him, but the reason I came baptizing with water was that he might be revealed to Israel.'" (1:30-31)

It's interesting that John begins to understand more why God called him. John had known that he was to be a voice in the wilderness proclaiming the coming of the king. He was doubtless aware of the angel's word to his father Zechariah that John was "to make ready a people prepared for the Lord" (Luke 1:17). He knew his father's prophecy at his birth:

> "And you, my child, will be called a prophet of the Most High;
> for you will go on before the Lord to prepare the way for him." (Luke 1:76)

But now he realizes that he has been given the awesome privilege of introducing the Messiah to Israel! His life's work has been fulfilled in this moment![53]

The Spirit as a Dove (1:32-34)

The Synoptic Gospels give the incident of the dove in the context of Jesus' baptism by John the Baptist. For example, Luke writes:

> "When all the people were being baptized, Jesus was baptized too. And as he was praying, heaven was opened and the Holy Spirit descended on him in bodily form like a dove. And a voice came from heaven: 'You are my Son, whom I love; with you I am well pleased.'" (Luke 3:21-22)

But in characteristic fashion the Apostle John truncates the story narrative to get to the point of John the Baptist's testimony about who Jesus is:

> "32 Then John gave this testimony: 'I saw the Spirit come down from heaven as a dove and remain on him. 33 I would not have known him, except that the one who sent me to baptize with water told me, "The man on whom you see the Spirit come down and remain is he who will baptize with the Holy Spirit." 34 I have seen and I testify that this is the Son of God.'" (1:32-34)

John's clear message about Jesus is: "This is the Son of God!" which accords precisely with the purpose of John's Gospel:

> "... that you may believe that Jesus is the Christ, the Son of God, and that by believing you may have life in his name." (20:31)

Baptize with the Holy Spirit (1:33)

The Holy Spirit plays a large part in Jesus' teaching in John's Gospel – far more than in the Synoptics. And this promise of the coming of the Holy Spirit to those who believe is a major theme of the Gospel.

---

[53] Later, of course, John in prison has a moment of doubt (Luke 7:18-23), but there beside the Jordan it was all clear, and even his moment of doubt does not diminish his greatness (Luke 7:24-28).

"The one who sent me to baptize with water told me, 'The man on whom you see the Spirit come down and remain is he who will baptize with the Holy Spirit.'" (1:33)

What does it mean that Jesus "will baptize with the Holy Spirit"? This is very controversial. Pentecostals and some other groups see the "baptism of the Holy Spirit" as a "second work of grace," separate from regeneration or new birth by the Spirit.

This is probably the case because many Pentecostals have an experience with the Holy Spirit that includes speaking in tongues that happens *after* their conversion. There is also the example of the Holy Spirit falling upon the church on the Day of Pentecost, *after* the disciples had believed (though see John's "Pentecost" in 20:22), and some experiences in the early church (8:15-17; 10:44-47; 11:15-17; 19:4-7). I myself had an experience that Pentecostals would term the "baptism of the Holy Spirit" when I was eighteen years old that was life-changing, long after I had received Christ as my Savior at age nine. It helped introduce me to a spiritual world in which I believe God can do anything!

While I believe my experience, and that of many Pentecostals, is valid, I think we have misnamed it. It is certainly a *filling* of the Holy Spirit, like the early believers experienced in Acts 4:31. If we're walking close to the Lord we can expect many fillings.

I believe that the New Testament – and John's Gospel in particular – uses a number of analogies to express what the Holy Spirit does in our lives. And I believe that many of these analogies are functional equivalents of each other. Consider how John describes the coming of the Holy Spirit in different analogies and figures:

- "Born of the Spirit" (3:6, 8), "born from above/again" (3:6).
- Worship "in Spirit and in truth" (4:24).
- "Rivers of living water" flowing out of one's heart (7:38-39), offered to "whoever believes in me."
- "The Spirit of truth," who is with you and will be in you (14:16-17) – another Counselor (Greek *Paraklētos*), the indwelling Spirit.
- The Spirit (*Paraklētos*) who will teach and remind believers of what Jesus said (14:26).
- The Spirit (*Paraklētos*) who testifies of Jesus (15:26).
- The Spirit (*Paraklētos*) who will guide us into all truth (16:13-15), and who will convict the world of sin (16:8-11).
- The Spirit Whom Jesus breathed upon his disciples – "Receive the Holy Spirit" (20:22).

It makes more sense to me that John and Jesus are talking about many of the same experiences, but with different terminologies – though I know that will upset some of my dear Pentecostal brothers and sisters.

We don't need a watered-down, low-power Christianity, however. God forbid! We need the full power of the Holy Spirit to come upon us – by whatever terminology – and fill us and keep us full so that we might fulfill Jesus' mission here on earth (Acts 1:8). When the Spirit possesses fully, many people won't understand, but that doesn't really matter so much as pleasing God and receiving his bountiful gifts! O Baptizer in the Holy Spirit, dunk us again in your Spirit's waters![54]

---

[54] For more on how I understand the Baptism in the Holy Spirit, see my article, "Spirit Baptism, the New Birth, and Speaking in Tongues" (http://www.joyfulheart.com/scholar/spirit-baptism.htm).

Devout Christians differ on the baptism of the Holy Spirit. As you discuss this, make sure that your attitude is one of love for your brothers and sisters, even if you might disagree with some things they believe.

Q5. (John 1:33) How does John the Baptist's baptism differ from the baptism that Jesus brings? Baptism is a word that means "immerse, plunge under water." What does a "baptism of the Holy Spirit" imply about this event?
http://www.joyfulheart.com/forums/topic/1396-q5-baptism-of-the-holy-spirit/

Lessons for Disciples

What should we learn from these verses? I see several things.

1. John humbly and faithfully fulfilled his mission, which he saw clearly enough, even though he may not have fully understood how he fit into God's plan (1:23).
2. Jesus is the "Lamb of God," God's sacrifice for our sins, prophesied in Isaiah 53 and fulfilled on the cross. Jesus' mission was to take away our sins (1:29).
3. John realizes that his job is to reveal Christ to Israel – and he's okay about that, even though he doesn't get to take the glory for himself (1:30).
4. Jesus baptizes with the Holy Spirit, that is, he floods people with his Holy Spirit (1:33).
5. Jesus is the Son of God (1:34).

In this lesson, John the Baptist has testified about God's words to him and how they were fulfilled. This last of the Old Testament prophets has declared Jesus to be the Lamb of God – God's sacrifice to atone for all our sins – and to be the Son of God, who sends the Holy Spirit. In the next lesson we'll examine how Jesus began to gather disciples for this new chapter in the unfolding of the Kingdom of God of whom John was the herald.

Prayer

Father, thank you for sending to us Jesus, the Lamb of God, who takes away all our sins. I pray that you would forgive us for our foolish joking that undermines the solemnity of this awesome role that led to the cross. Work in us true reverence – and holy joy. And flood us afresh with the Holy Spirit that Jesus was sent to baptize us with. In Jesus' holy name, we pray. Amen.

Key Verses

"'I baptize with water,' John replied, 'but among you stands one you do not know. He is the one who comes after me, the thongs of whose sandals I am not worthy to untie.'" (John 1:26-27, NIV)

"The next day John saw Jesus coming toward him and said, 'Look, the Lamb of God, who takes away the sin of the world!'" (John 1:29, NIV)

"I have seen and I testify that this is the Son of God." (John 1:34, NIV)

3. Disciples Direct Friends to Jesus (1:35-51)

This passage gives us some examples of how Jesus gathers disciples – and notice, Jesus' disciples do some of that disciple-gathering too.

The Synoptic Gospels relate later seaside callings of the fishermen and Levi (Matthew) the tax collector. But John shares an intimate encounter that probably took place at the Jordan where Jesus had just been baptized and proclaimed as the Lamb of God (1:43).

Perhaps more than any place in the Bible, this passage illustrates how people come to Christ by personal recommendation of a person they know and respect.

This incident seems to take place in Judea. But a number of Galileans have come to John's "revival meetings." Perhaps they had all come down from Galilee together to Passover in Jerusalem, and then down to the Jordan to hear John's message. Many of them know each other from Galilee.

Ottavio Vannini (1585-c. 1643), 'Saint John showing Christ to Saint Andrew' (17th century), oil on canvas, San Gaetano, Florence.

John's Disciples Begin to Follow Jesus (1:35-37)

"[35] The next day John was there again with two of his disciples. [36] When he saw Jesus passing by, he said, 'Look, the Lamb of God!' [37] When the two disciples heard him say this, they followed Jesus." (1:35-37)

As a great preacher of his time, John the Baptist has attracted disciples, men who hang out with him to learn from him. The word is *mathētēs*, generally, "learner, pupil, disciple." In particular, "one who is rather constantly associated with someone who has a pedagogical reputation or a particular set of views, disciple, adherent."[55]

Here is the first example of John's later words, "He must increase, but I must decrease" (3:30). It takes a great man or great woman to encourage your followers to follow someone greater than you. Even so, we know that John continued to attract disciples until his death and beyond.[56]

But these two begin to follow Jesus. This term "follow" is *akoloutheō*, literally "to come after." But it also has a specific figurative sense that we see in the Four Gospels, "to follow someone as a disciple, be a disciple, follow."[57] Jesus uses this word when he calls out to people: "Follow me!"

---

[55] *Mathētēs*, BDAG 609, 2a.

[56] John the Baptist's disciples are mentioned in Matthew 9:14a; 11:2; 14:12; Mark 2:18ab; 6:29; Luke 5:33; 7:18f; 11:1; John 1:35, 37; 3:25; Acts 18:25; 19:3.

Q1. (John 1:35-37) Upon whose recommendation did Andrew and another person start following Jesus? What did this recommendation cost the recommender in this case?
http://www.joyfulheart.com/forums/topic/1397-q1-recommending-jesus/

"Come and See" (1:38-39)

Whenever I read these verses I am fascinated – and amused – by how Jesus engages these inquirers.

> "[38] Turning around, Jesus saw them following and asked, 'What do you want?'
> They said, 'Rabbi' (which means Teacher), 'where are you staying?'
> [39] 'Come,' he replied, 'and you will see.'
>
> So they went and saw where he was staying, and spent that day with him. It was about the tenth hour[58]." (1:38-39)

Note that these two are following, but it is Jesus who initiates the conversation. Jesus turns around and sees them. He asks what they want. They don't really answer his question, but suggest that they would like to talk further, so they ask where he is staying. I love Jesus' answer: "Come and see." He doesn't give them an address or make an appointment. He invites them to come along with him and walk with him.

This seems characteristic of Jesus today. He doesn't answer all our questions, but he invites us to journey along with him. Following him – and in the process, learning from him – is the essence of what it means to be a disciple. Mark's Gospel tells us of the Twelve:

> "He appointed twelve – designating them apostles – **that they might be with him** and that he might send them out to preach and to have authority to drive out demons." (Mark 3:14-15)

If we want to become close-following disciples of Jesus, we must "hang out with him," spend time with him so we can learn from him and pattern our lives after him.

Q2. (John 1:38-39) Why doesn't Jesus tell his inquirers where he is staying? Why was it important for disciples to "be with" Jesus? What does "being with" Jesus mean today?
http://www.joyfulheart.com/forums/topic/1398-q2-being-with-jesus/

---

[57] *Akoloutheō*, BDAG 36, 3. It is derived from a-, a particle of union, + *keleuthos*, "a road," properly, "to be in the same way with, that is, to accompany, specifically as a disciple.

[58] The "tenth hour" using the Jewish reckoning, means that it was about 4 pm. This makes more sense than trying to refer to the Roman reckoning at about 10 am, which doesn't seem likely. See the extended discussion in Morris, *John*, pp. 158, fn. 90.

Jesus Calls Peter (1:40-42)

The two disciples who have begun to follow Jesus aren't quiet about their discovery. They tell their friends. We don't know the identity of the unnamed companion – he may be John himself. But the other is Andrew.

> "⁴⁰ Andrew, Simon Peter's brother, was one of the two who heard what John had said and who had followed Jesus. ⁴¹ The first thing Andrew did was to find his brother Simon and tell him, 'We have found the Messiah' (that is, the Christ). ⁴² And he brought him to Jesus. Jesus looked at him and said, 'You are Simon son of John. You will be called Cephas' (which, when translated, is Peter)." (1:40-42)

Bible teachers have long drawn attention to Andrew's reaction to his time with Jesus.

> "**The first thing Andrew did** was to find his brother Simon and tell him...." (1:41a)

This is the basis of the popular "Operation Andrew" program, used by Billy Graham Crusades and many others, which involves listing your friends and acquaintances, praying for them, and inviting them to attend a meeting with you. It's a great program, easily understood by people.

James J. Tissot, 'The Calling of Saint John and Saint Andrew' (1886-94), gouache on paper, 9.7x6", Brooklyn Museum.

But notice that Andrew doesn't invite his brother Peter to a meeting or a "program." He invites him to meet Jesus. In Andrew's day this was a social act. But in our day, since Jesus doesn't walk in the flesh, it is an intensely spiritual act. Usually prayer is the way we introduce people to Jesus.

I've found that especially when people are hurting, I tell them how Jesus can help. If they are willing, I begin to pray and in my prayer introduce them to Jesus. I might say something like, "Jesus, this is Joe. He needs your help...." Then I ask Joe to tell Jesus what he's told me. Most of the time in that context, I've found that people will begin to pray rather naturally. You've modeled prayer for them, and you may have to coach them a bit to get them talking to God. It may seem kind of bold, but when a person is ready, this seems like a very natural way to introduce someone to Jesus.

The content of Andrew's message to his brother is, "We have found the Messiah." For a very long time, Jews had been expecting the Messiah, the descendant of David, to return and deliver Israel. Andrew tells Peter that they have found this person! Incidentally, "Messiah" is a transliteration of the Hebrew word *māshîah*, "anointed," from the Hebrew custom of pouring oil upon the head of one who is set apart for a particular office of king or priest. The Greek equivalent is *christos*, "smeared, anointed."

When Peter comes to Jesus, the Master looks at him and says, "You are Simon son of John. You will be called Cephas." Cephas is the Aramaic word for "rock." *Petros* (Peter) is the Greek word for "rock." Jesus seems to be prophesying to Peter of his future as the rock, the foundation, by his faith, of the new Christian movement. Later, when Peter confesses Jesus to be "the Christ, the Son of the Living God," Jesus says:

"And I tell you that you are Peter, and on this rock I will build my church, and the gates of Hades will not overcome it." (Matthew 16:1)

I wonder what "new name" Jesus has for you? What future does he have for you to live into?

Q3. (John 1:40-42) What role does Andrew play in Simon Peter's conversion? Today, why do so many Christians substitute bringing a person to Jesus with bringing them to church? What might be the similarities? What might be the differences?
http://www.joyfulheart.com/forums/topic/1399-q3-bringing-a-friend-to-jesus/

Jesus Calls Philip (1:43-44)

"⁴³ The next day Jesus decided to leave for Galilee. Finding Philip, he said to him, 'Follow me.' ⁴⁴ Philip, like Andrew and Peter, was from the town of Bethsaida." (1:43-44)

About to leave the Jordan in Judea to go to Galilee, Jesus seeks out Philip. This is the first time we meet Philip in John's Gospel, but he may have been the other unnamed disciple of John the Baptist who had begun to follow Jesus (1:37) – we just don't know for sure.

Notice the variation. In the case of Andrew and his brother Peter, Andrew brings Peter. But in the case of Philip, Jesus seeks him out. People come to faith in Christ in many ways – there isn't a single formula.

Verse 44 says that Philip, Andrew, and Peter are all from the town of Bethsaida. See Lesson 13 for more about this town.

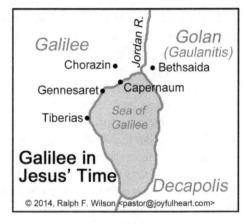

Philip Introduces Nathanael to Jesus (1:45-50)

But Philip doesn't just come along by himself. He tells someone else! (Are you sensing a pattern here?)

"⁴⁵ Philip found Nathanael and told him, 'We have found the one Moses wrote about in the Law, and about whom the prophets also wrote – Jesus of Nazareth, the son of Joseph.'
⁴⁶ 'Nazareth! Can anything good come from there?' Nathanael asked.
'Come and see,' said Philip.
⁴⁷ When Jesus saw Nathanael approaching, he said of him, 'Here is a true Israelite, in whom there is nothing false.'
⁴⁸ 'How do you know me?' Nathanael asked.
Jesus answered, 'I saw you while you were still under the fig tree before Philip called you.' ⁴⁹ Then Nathanael declared, 'Rabbi, you are the Son of God; you are the King of Israel.' ⁵⁰ Jesus said, 'You believe because I told you I saw you under the fig tree. You shall see greater things than that.'" (1:45-50)

Nathanael, whose name means "God has given," is a skeptic. Philip extols Jesus to him as the "prophet" that Moses said would come (Deuteronomy 18:15) and the Messiah/Deliverer that the prophets foretold (Micah 5:2 and many others). But when Philip mentions that Jesus is from Nazareth, his natural prejudice comes out:

"Nazareth! Can anything good come from there?" (1:46a)

Perhaps Nathanael knows Micah 5:2 that says the Messiah will be born in Bethlehem. Or maybe he disdains Nazareth as an inconsequential town. Philip doesn't argue with him. Rather, he invites him to see for himself. When dealing with skeptics, invite them to try Jesus for themselves. To try praying an honest prayer to him, "Jesus, if you are real, please show me."

Nathanael does come with Philip, and when Jesus sees him he says something that seemed all too familiar to Nathanael:

Jesus: "Here is a true Israelite, in whom there is nothing false."
Nathanael: "How do you know me?"

Then Jesus refers to some incident that Nathanael experienced "under the fig tree." There are a lot of fig trees in Israel, so being under a fig tree wouldn't be remarkable in and of itself. It is something else that Jesus knows – and Nathanael knows he knows! Nathanael responds with instant faith in response to this prophetic insight:

"Rabbi, you are the Son of God; you are the King of Israel." (1:49)

This confession, "You are the Son of God," seems very similar to John the Baptist's confession in 1:34. "King of Israel" is another way of saying that Jesus is the Messiah, the promised son of David (2 Samuel 7:11-16) who would restore the throne of Israel once again. Jesus' prophetic insight about the Samaritan woman at the well prompts similar faith. Her response to her townspeople is,

"Come, see a man who told me everything I ever did. Could this be the Christ?" (4:29)

Jesus seems to have been exercising what is sometimes referred to as the "word of knowledge" (1 Corinthians 12:8), some kind of supernatural prophetic insight into a person's life or needs, something like an ancient "seer" might have. This gift in our day can result in faith and salvation. Let's honor it in our churches and not neglect it. Jesus is our exemplar in this. We'll talk more about this in Lesson 8 regarding the Samaritan woman at the well of Sychar.

Q4. (John 1:45-50) How does Jesus deal with Nathanael's skepticism? What was the nature of the miracle? Upon coming to faith, what title does Nathanael bestow upon Jesus?
http://www.joyfulheart.com/forums/topic/1400-q4-skepticism-and-faith/

Jesus as the Heavenly Son of Man (1:50-51)

Jesus commends Nathanael's faith, but promises even more. It's like we might say in American vernacular, "You ain't seen nothing yet!"

"[50] Jesus said, 'You believe because I told you I saw you under the fig tree. You shall see greater things than that.' [51] He then added, 'I tell you the truth, you shall see heaven open, and the angels of God ascending and descending on the Son of Man.'" (1:50-51)

Here's the first instance of Jesus' characteristic "I tell you the truth" (NIV), "very truly" (NRSV), "truly, truly" (ESV), "verily, verily" (KJV). In Greek it is *amēn amēn*, doubled for emphasis. The word indicates strong affirmation of what is stated, an assertive particle, "truly."[59]

By saying "Amen, amen," Jesus is giving all possible emphasis to a radical prediction:

"You shall see heaven open, and the angels of God ascending and descending on the Son of Man." (1:51b)

"Son of Man" seems to be Jesus' favorite self-title, especially in the Synoptic Gospels.[60] Jesus is referring to a passage from Daniel describing the heavenly Son of Man:

"In my vision at night I looked, and there before me was **one like a son of man, coming with the clouds of heaven**. He approached the Ancient of Days and was led into his presence. He was given authority, glory and sovereign power; all peoples, nations and men of every language worshiped him. His dominion is an everlasting dominion that will not pass away, and his kingdom is one that will never be destroyed." (Daniel 7:13-14)

Jesus is saying that Nathanael is just beginning to see the full extent of Jesus' glory. Yes, perhaps some of the disciples saw heaven open and the dove of the Holy Spirit alight upon Jesus at his baptism (Matthew 3:16). Peter, James, and John saw Jesus transfigured before them (Matthew 17:2). The martyr Stephen at his death saw "heaven open and the Son of Man standing at the right hand of God" (Acts 7:56). But the final fulfillment of Jesus' prediction is still in the future, awaiting his coming.

"... They will see the Son of Man coming on the clouds of the sky, with power and great glory. And he will send his angels with a loud trumpet call, and they will gather his elect from the four winds, from one end of the heavens to the other." (Matthew 24:30b-31)

Come soon, Lord Jesus!

Q5. (John 1:50-51) Which aspects of Daniel's prophecy in Daniel 7:13-14 does Jesus apply to his title as Son of Man? When will the Son of Man complete his ministry?
http://www.joyfulheart.com/forums/topic/1401-q5-son-of-man/

Lessons for Disciples

Our lessons from the passage are primarily about reaching out to those we know. Here are some lessons for disciples:

---

[59] With this usage, in the New Testament *amēn* is always used with the verb *legō*, "say," and is only found in the mouth of Jesus. The doubled *amēn* is also found elsewhere in John: 3:3, 5, 11; 5:19, 24, 25; 6:26, 32, 47, 53; 8:34, 51, 58; 10:1, 7; 12:24; 13:16, 20, 21, 38; 14:12; 16:20, 23; 21:18. In the Synoptic Gospels, the phrase has just a single *amēn*. Greek *amēn* is a transliteration of the Hebrew 'āmēn, from the verb 'āman, "to be firm or certain" (BDAG, 53, 1b).

[60] The title "Son of Man" is used twelve times in John (1:51; 3:13, 14; 5:27, 6:27, 53, 62; 8:28; 12:23, 34; 13:31), but more often in the Synoptic Gospels (Matthew, 28 times; Mark, 13 times; Luke, 25 times).

1. Friends often become disciples by being pointed to Jesus by their friends. It is a natural way of becoming a disciple. We must trust our friends to Jesus, rather than keep them for ourselves without "ruining" a friendship by mentioning "religion."
2. Jesus is called by several titles in this passage: Messiah (Christ, 1:41), Son of God (1:49), King of Israel (1:49), and Son of Man (1:51).
3. Jesus exercises the "spiritual gift" of the "word of knowledge" (1 Corinthians 12:8) to convince people of who he is. We need to draw on spiritual gifts to convince people of who Jesus is.
4. Jesus gives Peter a "new name" that signifies what his future role will be. God may have some role for you that is far beyond what you can imagine.

Prayer

Father, thank you for the examples of people becoming disciples. Help me to spend more time with you so I might become a better disciple. Show me how – and make me willing – to point my friends to Jesus. Open me to the gifts of your Spirit so I might be more effective. In Jesus' name, I pray. Amen.

Key Verses

"When the two disciples heard him say this, they followed Jesus. Turning around, Jesus saw them following and asked, 'What do you want?' They said, 'Rabbi' (which means Teacher), 'where are you staying?' 'Come,' he replied, 'and you will see.'" (John 1:37-39a, NIV)

"The first thing Andrew did was to find his brother Simon and tell him, 'We have found the Messiah' (that is, the Christ). And he brought him to Jesus." (John 1:41-42a, NIV)

"Jesus looked at him and said, 'You are Simon son of John. You will be called Cephas' (which, when translated, is Peter)." (John 1:42b, NIV)

"I tell you the truth, you shall see heaven open, and the angels of God ascending and descending on the Son of Man." (John 1:51, NIV)

4. Changing the Water into Wine (2:1-12)

Jesus has been in Judea. Now the scene shifts from Judea in the south to the north in Galilee, the region in which Jesus grew up. Jesus is at a wedding in Cana, with his disciples and his mother. It is a "big deal," with many guests and festivities planned to last for days celebrating the new couple.

John selects this incident, not found in the other Gospels, to begin to reveal who Jesus is.

Invited to the Wedding (2:1-2)

"¹ On the third day a wedding took place at Cana in Galilee. Jesus' mother was there, ² and Jesus and his disciples had also been invited to the wedding." (2:1-2)

Apparently, Jesus' family was friends (or relatives) of the bride or groom, because Jesus' mother and brothers (2:12) were there; Jesus and his disciples were also invited.

James J. Tissot, 'The Marriage at Cana' (1886-94), gouache on paper, 9x7.8", Brooklyn Museum, New York.

Cana in Galilee

Cana (literally "place of reeds") is in the hills of Galilee (2:1), though the exact location isn't certain. Church tradition identifies it as Kefr Kanna, about four miles northeast of Nazareth on the road to Tiberius on the Sea of Galilee, but perhaps the most likely site is Khirbet Kana, an ancient ruin about 8 miles northeast of Nazareth, which served as the military headquarters for a time of Jewish historian and general Josephus [61] (see map) Jesus probably came to Cana accompanied by Nathanael, since it is Nathanael's home village.

---

[61] Josephus, *Vita*, 16, 41. Josephus described the spot as "Plain of Asochis, that is the Bet Netufa Valley," which would suit Khirbet Kana. Robert H. Mounce, "Cana," ISBE 1:585. Urban C. von Wahlde ("Archaeology and John's Gospel," in *Jesus & Archaeology*, pp. 538-542) sees the issue as yet unresolved, while Peter Richardson ("Khirbet Qana and other Villages as a Context for Jesus," in *Jesus & Archaeology*, pp. 120-144) sees scholarly opinion as shifted to Khirbet Qana as the New Testament Cana, and cites extensive excavations there since 1998.

Marriage Customs in Jesus' Day

Marriage in Jesus' day begins with a betrothal up to a year before the marriage celebration. The man and woman enter into a binding agreement to marry, more binding than our "engagement" in the West. The man gives the bride's father a bridal gift, a form of compensation to the father (some of which becomes a dowry the father gives to the daughter at the marriage to help provide economic stability to the marriage bond). The couple doesn't live together or consummate the marriage at their betrothal, though they are considered husband and wife, and the bond cannot be broken without divorce.

A marriage in this culture is a celebration. The groom and his friends go to the bride's home, and then escort the bride in a festive procession to the groom's home, where a grand celebration takes place. There is probably an exchange of vows and some kind of religious ceremony, though none of these details survive from the first century AD. The groom gives his bride gifts. After the marriage feast, the bride and groom enter the nuptial chamber and the marriage is consummated.

The festivities go on, however, sometimes for a week or more, if the groom's family can afford it. Friends and family will be coming from afar, so weddings are occasions where family connections are renewed over food and drink.

The New Testament has a number of references to weddings and wedding feasts.[62] Indeed, the concept of the Church as the Bride of Christ is hinted at in the Gospels and fulfilled at the Marriage Supper of the Lamb in Revelation 19:6-9.

Q1. (John 2:1-2) Why are we sometimes "too busy" to spend time with friends and relatives? What does Jesus' attendance at this wedding tell us about him? How can we apply that learning in our own personal lives?
http://www.joyfulheart.com/forums/topic/1402-q1-time-for-friends/

They Run Out of Wine (2:3)

The wedding Jesus and his disciples are attending, however, has a serious problem. They had wine enough to begin the festivities – but before long they run out of wine!

"When the wine was gone, Jesus' mother said to him, 'They have no more wine.'" (2:3)

---

[62] The Parable of the Wedding Banquet (Matthew 22:1-14; cf. Luke 14:15-24), the Parable of the Ten Virgins (Matthew 25:1-13), and Jesus teaching at a luncheon about humility (Luke 14:1-14) and the reference to a master delayed in returning from a wedding feast (Luke 12:36).

We might not appreciate the problem. A small loan perhaps and a quick trip to the store might solve the problem without any fuss.

But enough wine for days of festivities would require a great deal of wine, and there is no way to get enough quickly. And to supply only water for the festivities would be considered a severe social embarrassment for the groom's family – especially at a time when the groom's ability to be a good provider is so clearly in view. This is a crisis!

Mary Asks Jesus to Solve the Problem (2:4-5)

Mary, who is perhaps especially close to the groom's family, and thus sensitive to their need, not only mentions it to Jesus, but suggests that he solve their problem.

> "[3b] Jesus' mother said to him, 'They have no more wine.'
> [4] 'Dear woman, why do you involve me?' Jesus replied. 'My time has not yet come.'
> [5] His mother said to the servants, 'Do whatever he tells you.'" (2:3b-5)

Jesus addresses her as "woman" (NRSV, KJV), which the NIV rightly softens a bit to, "dear woman." You'd expect him to address her as "Mother," but he doesn't. Jesus uses this same expression from the cross, when he assigns the care of his mother into the hands of the Apostle John (19:26). Perhaps this term "woman" (which was not nearly so cold or unkind as it might sound in English) was designed to separate his family responsibilities from his ministry responsibilities. You see Jesus doing something similar when his mother and brothers seem to impose upon him by interrupting him while he is teaching a crowd of people (Mark 3:31-35).

Jesus answers with a question: "Why do you involve me?" (NIV), or, more literally, "What concern is that to you and to me?" (NRSV).[63]

You might wonder why Mary is motivated to involve Jesus in this way. Though the text doesn't tell us, she probably knows that Jesus can help. She has lived with him for thirty years and knows that he is not only resourceful in practical matters, but probably has seen him perform miracles in the context of the family. She knows Jesus is the Christ, the Son of God. And perhaps she wants to show him off, a bit – who knows? At any rate, she specifically mentions the problem to Jesus in a way that leaves him no doubt that she expects him to take care of it.

Jesus explains, "My time[64] has not yet come" (NIV) or "My hour has not yet come" (NRSV, KJV). Jesus has a clear sense throughout his ministry of the particular "hour" or "time," at which point he is to fulfill his purpose as the sacrifice for the sins of all. We see this phrase, either on his lips or by the narrator, several times: "his time had not yet come" (John 7:6, *kairos*; 30; 8:20). At the end of his ministry, the hour has arrived for him "to be glorified" (12:23; 17:1), as he put it, for him "to leave this world and go to the Father" (13:1).[65]

---

[63] *Tis* is an interrogative pronoun, referring to someone or something – "Who? Which (one)? What?" Literally the phrase means, "What is it to me and to thee?" (Robertson, *Word Pictures*).

[64] The noun is *hōra*, "hour," here in the figurative sense of "a point of time as an occasion for an event, time" (BDAG 1103, 3).

[65] The Synoptics bring another "hour," the period "when darkness reigns" (Luke 22:53). It began in the Garden of Gethsemane, "Look, the hour is near, and the Son of Man is betrayed into the hands of sinners" (Matthew 26:45).

Throughout the Gospels, we see Jesus' clear awareness that he must not plunge into fame too quickly. That is why he tells people on certain occasions not to tell everybody about their miracle (Mark 1:43-45; 7:36) or that he is the Messiah (Mark 8:29-30 = Matthew 16:20; Mark 9:9 = Luke 9:36 = Matthew 17:9). His hour had not yet come, and manipulating publicity would force that "hour" to come before he can train his disciples for their Kingdom work. Jesus' eyes were clearly on his chief purpose, but he isn't in a hurry. There is no rush.

Here, at the very beginning of his ministry, is the same concern that the spectacular not overtake his true path. So he tells his mother, "My time has not yet come" (2:4).

It's almost like his mother isn't listening or heeding what he is saying, for she pushes right ahead in her quest to rescue the wedding party from disgrace.

> "His mother said to the servants, 'Do whatever he tells you.'" (2:5)

As I read this, I ask myself: How many times I have pushed through my own goals without heeding Jesus' cautions?

Nevertheless, Jesus accedes to her wishes. Perhaps to be a dutiful son, and perhaps because he senses that the Father has a purpose in it.

> **Q2. (John 2:3-5) Why do you think Mary pushes Jesus to solve the wedding host's problem? Are her words to Jesus appropriate? Would you categorize Jesus' reply as a rebuke? If so, why does he go ahead with the miracle?**
> http://www.joyfulheart.com/forums/topic/1403-q2-marys-nudge/

Six Stone Jars (2:6)

> "Nearby stood six stone water jars, the kind used by the Jews for ceremonial washing, each holding from twenty to thirty gallons."[66] (2:6)

I can imagine pottery water jars, like the woman at the well used to carry water into town. But the jars described here are not pottery, but stone. Nobody was carrying water in these. Such stone jars have been found in Israel. In the so-called "Burnt House" in the Jewish Quarter of the Old City of Jerusalem, archaeologists found several stone water jars from the first century AD. They are 2 to 2.5 feet high (65-80 cm.), shaped from limestone on some kind of very large lathe. They held about 17 gallons (80 liters), and were covered by a flat piece of stone. In Capernaum, several stone jars from the fourth century AD have been found in the synagogue there.

John notes that such jars were used to hold water for ceremonial washing or purification.[67] Before a meal, servants (or perhaps the host) would pour water over the hands of each of the guests. Mark explains the custom:

[66] "Gallons" (NIV, NRSV), "firkins" (KJV) is *metrētēs*, a liquid measure of about 40 liters, "measure." It is similar to the Hebrew *bath*, containing 72 sextarii or pints = 39.39 liters, or about nine gallons (BDAG 643). The British firkin was one-fourth of a barrel.

[67] "Ceremonial washing" (NIV), "rites of purification" (NRSV), "purifying" (KJV) is *katharismos*, "cleansing from cultic impurity, purification" (BDAG 489, 1).

"The Pharisees and all the Jews do not eat unless they give their hands a ceremonial washing, holding to the tradition of the elders. When they come from the marketplace they do not eat unless they wash. And they observe many other traditions, such as the washing of cups, pitchers and kettles." (Mark 7:3-4)

While the strict Pharisees practiced this, not all of Jesus' disciples were so scrupulous (Mark 7:2, 5; John 3:25). This was not something required by Scripture[68], but a "tradition of the elders."[69] Nevertheless, the home where the wedding is being held, has on hand six stone jars (probably some borrowed from neighbors for the occasion), so that not even the strictest Jews will be offended.

Full to the Brim (2:7)

Our story picks up part-way into the multi-day festivities, so quite a bit of water has already been drawn from the jars to rinse the hands of guests at each meal.

"Jesus said to the servants, 'Fill the jars with water'; so they filled them to the brim." (2:7)

To refill six stone jars, each of which could hold 20 to 30 gallons would require the servants to make many, many trips to the town well and back, considering that their smaller water jars might hold a gallon or two. When they finish, they report back to Jesus for further instructions.

Water to Wine (2:8-9a)

It may have taken several hours for them to comply with Jesus' somewhat strange request.

"[8] Then he told them, 'Now draw some out and take it to the master of the banquet.' They did so, [9] and the master of the banquet tasted the water that had been turned into wine. He did not realize where it had come from, though the servants who had drawn the water knew." (2:8-9a)

When did the miracle occur? Probably between the time the servants had filled the water jars and the time the chief servant drew some to take to the master of the banquet.

Saved the Best for Last (2:9b-10)

Who is the "master of the banquet"?[70] In classical Greek this was the "the slave who was responsible for managing a banquet," in which case we might term him the "head waiter, butler." But since he doesn't seem to be aware of the wine shortage situation nor the actions of the other servants – *and* he is able to summon the bridegroom – I think it's likely that he was one of the guests who was appointed toastmaster or "president of the banquet."[71]

Here I indulge my imagination a bit. The master of the banquet breathes in the wine in the cup he has been given. Ah, excellent bouquet! Then he tastes the wine, sloshes it around in his mouth, then

[68] The only things Scripture says is that Aaron and the priests were required to wash their hands and feet before serving in the temple (Exodus 30:19-21; 40:31).

[69] The Mishnah (which contains these traditions) includes a tractate "*Yadayim* (hands)" with four chapters on the purification of hands.

[70] *Architriklinos*, BDAG 139.

[71] Liddell-Scott. So Morris, *John*, pp. 183-184. Perhaps here the *architriklinos* is the same as the *sumposiarchos* as described in *Wisdom of Sirach* 32:1.

swallows, detecting the smooth finish. Amazing wine! Then he goes to the bridegroom, takes him aside, and speaks to him quietly.

> "9b Then he called the bridegroom aside 10 and said, 'Everyone brings out the choice wine first and then the cheaper wine after the guests have had too much to drink; but you have saved the best till now.'" (2:9b-10)

The normal time for fine wine would be at the beginning of the party when people haven't eaten and drunk much, when their palates are "fresh" – and when they aren't too drunk to notice! The master of the feast is a keen observer of normal human behavior, and is surprised to get such good wine so late in the feast.

The last line of the narrative gives the punch line – "You have saved the best till now" (2:10b). The point, of course, is that the wine Jesus has created is not only abundant – 150 gallons or so – but the finest of wine!

Q3. (John 2:6-10) Why do you think alcoholics are quick to point out this miracle? Which is wrong: drinking wine or drunkenness? How can we avoid excesses and still enjoy God's good gifts?
http://www.joyfulheart.com/forums/topic/1404-q3-drinking-vs-drunkenness/

Q4. (John 2:6-10) Why did Jesus perform this miracle behind-the-scenes? Who was he trying to protect? What does the quantity of the wine tell us about Jesus' glory? What does the quality of the wine tell us about Jesus' glory?
http://www.joyfulheart.com/forums/topic/1405-q4-quiet-miracle/

The Meaning of this "Sign" (2:11)

> "This, the first of his miraculous signs, Jesus performed at Cana in Galilee. He thus revealed his glory, and his disciples put their faith in him." (2:11)

"Miraculous signs" (NIV), "signs" (NRSV), "miracles" (KJV) is the plural of *sēmeion*, "a sign or distinguishing mark whereby something is known, sign, token, indication." Here, "an event that is an indication or confirmation of intervention by transcendent powers, miracle, portent."[72] For John, these wonders are not just miracles, but signs that point to who Jesus actually is. According to verse 11 this sign had two functions:

1. **Reveals his glory**. The teacher is more than he seems, and every so often the massive Shekinah glory of God shines out. See more in Appendix 6. "Glory" and "Glorify" in John's Gospel.
2. **Inspires faith**. It's important to observe that in his disciples, the miracles inspired faith, but in his enemies they inspired only a determination to eliminate him (Mark 3:6; Matthew 12:14).

---

[72] *Sēmeion*, BDAG 920, 2aα.

Toward the end of his Gospel, John explains,

> "[30] Jesus did many other miraculous signs in the presence of his disciples, which are not recorded in this book. [31] But these are written that you may believe that Jesus is the Christ, the Son of God, and that by believing you may have life in his name." (20:30-31)

Sēmeion is one of the characteristic words used in John (2:11, 18; 4:54; 6:2, 14, 26, 30; 7:31; 9:16; 10:41; 11:47; 12:18, 37; 20:30). In the early part of his Gospel, John designates Seven Signs, of which this is the first:

1. Changing the Water into Wine (2:1-11)
2. Healing of the Nobleman's Son (4:46-54)
3. Healing at the Pool of Bethesda (5:1-9)
4. Feeding the Multitude (6:1-14)
5. Walking on the Water (6:15-25)
6. Healing the Man Born Blind (9:1-8)
7. Raising Lazarus from the Dead (11:1-46)[73]

On to Capernaum (2:12)

The narrative of the changing the water into wine concludes with a transitional verse:

> "After this he went down to Capernaum with his mother and brothers and his disciples. There they stayed for a few days." (2:12)

Jesus goes to Capernaum not only with his disciples, but with his whole family. From the Synoptics we learn that Jesus has moved from Nazareth to Capernaum (Matthew 4:13) and considers it his home (Matthew 9:1). Apparently, some of the disciples who were originally from Bethsaida (1:44) now live in Capernaum (Mark 1:29), a fishing village on the northwest shore of the Sea of Galilee.[74]

"Spiritual" Interpretations

The simplest explanation of the changing of the water into wine is given in 2:11, that Jesus' miracle shows his glory and inspires faith. It is a "sign" pointing to who he is. That would be the literal interpretation.

However, there is a different approach to interpretation that dominated the Church for many centuries, known as "spiritual interpretation," that seeks to find the inner, hidden meaning in Jesus' parables and miracles.[75] To illustrate the extremes of this approach, here are a few "deeper" interpretations:

- The marriage represents the wedding of Christ and his bride, the church.
- The six stone water jars represent the Jewish traditions. Six is the number of incompleteness, but seven is the number of completeness and perfection.[76]

---

[73] See Appendix 5. "Signs" in John's Gospel.

[74] The exact location of Capernaum has been debated. The most likely location is Tell Ḥûm, a site which contains the ruins of a fourth century synagogue (R.H. Mounce, "Capernaum," ISBE 1:610).

[75] "Spiritual interpretation" takes its cue from early Christian philosopher and theologian Origen of Alexandria (184-253 BC). In this spiritual interpretation approach, a narrative, a parable, a teaching is an allegory of a deeper truth.

[76] Of course, the story doesn't end with seven – so this probably has nothing to do with six and imperfection.

> "This incident illustrates at once the poverty of the old dispensation with its merely ceremonial cleansing and the richness of the new, in which the blood of Christ is available for both cleansing and drink."[77]

Yes, perhaps it *illustrates* those things, but did John *intend* it so? I doubt it.

Lessons for Disciples

These are the some of the things I think we disciples can learn from this story.

1. Celebrations with family and friends are important to Jesus – and should be to us. We shouldn't feel ourselves too spiritual or too busy for such earthly joys and responsibilities.
2. It's possible to try to push God into acting on our behalf. It's best to be less pushy than Jesus' mother, or we may be rebuked like she was.
3. Jesus is not against wine. It's drunkenness that is wrong, the misuse of God's gifts, not wine itself.
4. Miracles need not be showy or even trumpeted to others. To meet the need is enough. Jesus was not a showman.

Jesus' ministry is now underway with an almost behind-the-scenes glimpse at his glory. The bulk of Jesus' ministry in Galilee is chronicled by the Synoptic Gospels, while John focuses more on Jesus' Judean ministry that we'll see in the next lesson.

Prayer

Thank you, Lord, for allowing me to see this amazing behind-the-scenes ministry of Jesus to meet very human needs. Please give me a compassion for ministry in everyday life so that I can emulate him. In Jesus' name, I pray. Amen.

Key Verses

> "When the wine was gone, Jesus' mother said to him, 'They have no more wine.' 'Dear woman, why do you involve me?' Jesus replied. 'My time has not yet come.' His mother said to the servants, 'Do whatever he tells you.'" (John 2:3-5, NIV)

> "Everyone brings out the choice wine first and then the cheaper wine after the guests have had too much to drink; but you have saved the best till now." (John 2:10, NIV)

---

[77] Barrett, *John*, p. 192.

5. Cleansing the Temple (2:13-25)

While the turning of water into wine was the first sign of Jesus' ministry, according to John, the first *public* act of his ministry is to cleanse the temple.

Jesus had been to the temple many times as a boy and as a young man, but now he comes as Messiah. And what has bothered him on his previous visits, he is determined to change.

James J. Tissot, 'The Merchants Chased from the Temple' (1886-94), gouache on paper, 7.25x11.6, Brooklyn Museum.

The Temple in Jerusalem

The first temple was built by Solomon on Mount Moriah in Jerusalem about 950 BC to replace the tabernacle that had been Israel's portable place of worship, first in the wilderness at Sinai and for the next several hundred years at Shiloh. Solomon's Temple was destroyed in 587 BC when Nebuchadnezzar's army destroyed Jerusalem. The next temple was built when the Jews returned from exile under Zerubbabel in about 515 BC. It was damaged, plundered, and desecrated by Greek conqueror Antiochus Epiphanes in 167 BC and later by Roman generals Pompey in 63 BC and Crassus in 54 BC. Herod the Great destroyed some of the temple walls as he stormed Jerusalem in 37 BC.

Herod the Great, now King of the Jews under the Romans, began to rebuild the temple in 20-19 BC, a process that continued for most of the next decade, with further ornamentation continuing perhaps through the 60s AD (cf. 2:20). Since Herod's Temple was constructed over the foundation of the temple built under Zerubbabel in 515 BC (though greatly expanded), it is known by Jews today as the Second Temple. Remnants of this temple are still visible today in the Wailing Wall at the base of its Western Wall.

1:50 scale model of Herod's Temple, constructed by Israeli archeologist and historian Michael Avi-Yonah (1904-1974) at the Holyland Hotel, now at the Israel Museum, Jerusalem.

The temple grounds consisted of several courts surrounding the central temple structure itself.

Court of the Gentiles was the outermost court, paved with stone and surrounded on three sides by porticos, each about 45 feet wide supported by two rows of marble columns some 37 feet high. Jesus and his disciples – and later the early church – met under Solomon's Porch on the east side of the temple complex (10:23; Acts 3:11; 5:12). Gentiles as well as Jews were allowed to be there. This was the location where sacrificial animals were sold and money exchanged.

Court of Women was divided from the Court of the Gentiles by a stone balustrade, perhaps 4.5 feet high, where women, but not Gentiles, could come and pray.

Courts of Israel and of the Priests were accessible from the Nicanor Gate on the west side of the Court of Women. Within the Court of the Priests were the altar, laver, various chambers, and the Temple building itself.

Temple Building. The front of the temple building was 150 feet wide and high, a gilded spectacle that was the wonder of all. The Second Temple

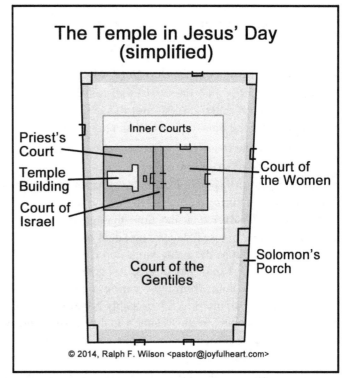

The Temple in Jesus' Day (simplified)

Inner Courts

Priest's Court

Temple Building

Court of Israel

Court of the Women

Solomon's Porch

Court of the Gentiles

© 2014, Ralph F. Wilson <pastor@joyfulheart.com>

as finally destroyed by the Romans under Titus in 70 AD, and has not been rebuilt. Later the Romans built palaces and a Temple of Jupiter, and the Byzantines a church, on the site. The present Dome of the Rock was built on the site by Muslim conquerors between 687-691 AD and the last remnants of the Second Temple were removed.[78]

Passover and other Jewish Festivals (2:13)

According to the Mosaic Law, all Jews were to come to Jerusalem for three festivals each year:

"Three times a year all your men must appear before the LORD your God at the place he will choose: at the Feast of Unleavened Bread, the Feast of Weeks and the Feast of Tabernacles." (Deuteronomy 16:16; Exodus 23:14-17)

John's Gospel includes mentions of at least three Passovers (2:13, 23; 6:4; and 11:55, etc.). He also mentions Jesus' attendance at the Feast of Tabernacles (7:2-14), the Feast of Dedication (Hanukkah, 10:22), and another feast which isn't specified (5:1).

The incident of Jesus' cleansing of the temple took place at Passover.

"When it was almost time for the Jewish Passover, Jesus went up[79] to Jerusalem." (2:13)

---

[78] Accessible sources on the temple include: Stephen Westerholm, "Temple," ISBE 1:759-776. Another source of information is Alfred Edersheim, *The Temple: Its Ministry and Services As they Were at the Time of Christ* (1874; reprinted by Eerdmans, 1958); B. Chilton, P.W. Comfort, and M.O. Wise, "Temple, Jewish," in Craig A. Evans and Stanley E. Porter (editors), *Dictionary of New Testament Background* (InterVarsity Press, 2000), pp. 1167-1183; M.O. Wise, "Temple," DJG, pp. 811-817.

Passover is a celebration of God delivering the Jewish people from Egypt. In remembrance of the Passover lambs sacrificed on the first Passover (Exodus 13), lambs were sacrificed in Jerusalem each Passover.

Desecration of the Temple Courts (2:14)

This wasn't Jesus' first Passover in Jerusalem, by any means. He had doubtless been many times from childhood on (Luke 2:41-50). But this is the first time he has come to Passover during his public ministry. Now is the time for him to begin to call people to repentance in the very center of Judaism:

> "In the temple courts he found men selling cattle, sheep and doves, and others sitting at tables exchanging money." (2:14)

Jews came to the Temple from all over Israel, indeed from all over the known world. Most of the time, they couldn't bring animals with them to sacrifice.

Moreover, Passover was the time that people paid the annual temple tax (Matthew 17:24-27; Exodus 30:13, 26). In Jesus' day, many kinds of coinage were circulating. The Romans, of course, had their own coins, but so did many kings and city-states across the empire. The various Herodian kings issued coins, as did the Phoenicians, Aegeans, Corinthians, and Persians. If these were voluntary offerings, perhaps, coins from these various countries and kingdoms might have been accepted. But this was a tax, not an offering. So, probably because of its exact weight and good alloy, Tyrian coinage (from Tyre) is specified in the Mishnah as the only coinage acceptable for the temple tax.[80] Of course, there was a fee to exchange one's coins for the Tyrian coins. The chief priest controlled the entire enterprise of money-changing and sale of sacrificial animals – and got his percentage of the gross.

The sacrificial animals and money-changing tables were located in the Court of the Gentiles within the temple grounds. So the place designated for believing Gentiles to pray and worship was cluttered with the clink of coins, the braying of animals, and the sounds of commerce – hardly a place of peace wherein to seek the Lord.

Driving Out the Animals and Moneychangers (2:15-17)

Jesus was outraged.

> "[15] So he made a whip out of cords[81], and drove all from the temple area, both sheep and cattle; he scattered the coins of the money changers and overturned their tables. [16] To those who sold doves he said, 'Get these out of here! How dare you turn my Father's house into a market!' [17] His disciples remembered that it is written: 'Zeal for your house will consume me.'" (2:15-17)

Jesus was offended, not that pilgrims needed to purchase sacrificial animals – cattle, sheep, goats, doves/pigeons, etc. – but that God's house had become perverted from its main function as a house of

---

[79] Jerusalem is always "up," since it is at a higher elevation than nearly all of the territory of Israel.

[80] *Bekhorot* 8:7. Some have contended that the reason for the money-changers was to only accept coins without heathen symbols on them. However, the Tyrian coins did bear heathen symbols (Morris, *John*, p. 194; citing Israel Abrahams, *Studies in Pharisaism and the Gospels*, I (Cambridge, 1917), pp. 83f).

[81] "Whip" (NIV, NRSV), "scourge" (KJV) is *phragellion*, "whip, lash" made of ropes (far less lethal than the penal 'flagellum' (BDAG 1064). "Cords" is *schoinion*, "rope or cord" (originally of rushes, then generally of other material) (BDAG 982).

prayer, and turned into something resembling a market, at which everyone brought their produce, set up stalls, and crowds came to do their shopping.[82]

The verbs are strong – drove, scattered, overturned! You shall not make....![83] Jesus is obviously angry. So is anger okay? Yes, some anger is appropriate. There are times when the lack of anger at a great injustice shows a disengagement with reality. It's not anger that is the evil, but what that anger causes us to do that is unrighteous (Ephesians 4:6). So we must control our anger so that our actions are appropriate.

For the Son of God to return his Father's House to its rightful state was entirely appropriate, if not "politically correct."

This is the first instance in John's Gospel where Jesus uses this term, "Father." After this, we see it often in this Gospel.[84] The Jewish leaders were highly offended by this because it seemed too intimate, not formal and distant enough. To them it seemed like heresy – and it would have been if it weren't true.

> "For this reason the Jews[85] tried all the harder to kill him; not only was he breaking the Sabbath,
> but he was even calling God his own Father, making himself equal with God." (5:18)

Jesus uses the phrase "in my Father's house" of the temple here and on the occasion when he is found in the temple as a boy (Luke 2:49). Later, he uses "in my Father's house" of heavenly dwellings (14:2).[86] Here the phrase is used almost as one's ancestral home might be called "the old home place."

His disciples later compared Jesus' passion for his Father's house to David's words in Psalm 69:

> "I endure scorn for your sake,
> and shame covers my face.
> I am a stranger to my brothers,
> an alien to my own mother's sons;
> for **zeal for your house consumes me**,
> and the insults of those who insult you fall on me." (Psalm 69:7-9)

Jesus has so identified with his Father, that he sees the merchandising as an insult to his Father, and thus to him. He takes it personally!

Q1. (John 2:14-17) What was going on in the temple? Why was Jesus offended by it? What action did Jesus take?
http://www.joyfulheart.com/forums/topic/1406-q1-offense-in-the-temple/

---

[82] "Market(place) (NIV, NRSV) is literally a "house of merchandise" (KJV). The noun is *emporion* (from which we get our "emporium"), "place where business is carried on, market, marketplace" (BDAG 325).

[83] "Drove" is a rather violent word: *ekballō*, "force to leave, drive out, expel" (BDAG 299, 1). "Scattered" (NIV), "poured out" (NRSV, KJV) is *ekcheō*, "cause to be emitted in quantity, pour out," of coins, "scatter" (BDAG 312, 1b). "Over-turned/overthrew" is *anastrephō*, "to overturn completely, upset, overturn" (BDAG 72, 1). The NIV's wording, "How dare you" gets the idea, but the wording is literally a command: "Do not make...."

[84] John 1:14, 18; 3:35; 4:21, 23; 5:17-26, 36-37, 43, 45, etc.

[85] For John's use of "the Jews" to refer to Jewish leaders, see Appendix 2. "The Jews" in John's Gospel.

[86] In the parable of the Rich Man and Lazarus, the rich man pleads to Abraham to go to "my father's house" and warn his five brothers (Luke 16:27).

Q2 (John 2:11-17) Apparently, Jesus was angry. Was his anger justified? Why? Is anger good or bad? What about anger gets us into trouble?
http://www.joyfulheart.com/forums/topic/1407-q2-jesus-anger/

One Cleansing or Two?

While John's Gospel places the cleansing of the temple at the beginning of Jesus' ministry, the Synoptics place it during the last week of his ministry, the precipitating event that caused the Jewish rulers to arrest him. This raises the question of whether there was one cleansing or two.

While the Synoptic account of the cleansing is quite similar to John's, Jesus' comment and the Scripture quoted are different. Matthew wrote:

> "Jesus entered the temple area and drove out all who were buying and selling there. He overturned the tables of the money changers and the benches of those selling doves. 'It is written,' he said to them, '"My house will be called a house of prayer," but you are making it a "den of robbers."'" (Matthew 21:12-13)

In Matthew 21:13 Jesus alludes to two verses from the prophets – different than what we see in John's Gospel:

> "... My house will be called a house of prayer for all nations." (Isaiah 56:7)

> "Has this house, which bears my Name, become a den of robbers to you? But I have been watching! declares the LORD." (Jeremiah 7:11)

How should we understand the differences between John and the Synoptics? There are three main possibilities.

1. John's chronology is correct. The Synoptics placed the cleansing at the end because they didn't record the events at the previous feasts and Passovers as did John.

2. Synoptic chronology is correct, though John placed the cleansing first for theological or literary reasons. This is the position of the majority of scholars. After all, Luke seems to put Jesus' visit to Nazareth right after Jesus' wilderness temptation for literary and theological reasons (Luke 4:14-30), compared to later in Matthew and Mark (Matthew 13:54-58; Mark 6:2-5).

3. There were two cleansings, one at the beginning and the other at the end of Jesus' ministry. Jesus' comments at the cleansing and the verses quoted are different in the Synoptics and John. It is not unlikely that animals and moneychangers would return to the temple within a short period of time, requiring Jesus to repeat his earlier action. [87]

I'm not sure which view is correct. It is clear that John is both aware of the Synoptic witness to Jesus – and is, for the most part, independent of the Synoptics in the way he presents Jesus' life and teaching. However, for the purposes of studying John's Gospel, we do well to seek to understand *why* he includes this particular incident – and leaves out many others (20:30-31).

---

[87] Arguments for two cleansings are presented in Morris, *John*, pp. 188-192.

Destroy the Temple, Raise It Again in Three Days (2:18-22)

Now we come to a saying of Jesus that is missing in the Synoptics, but alluded to there. After Jesus cleanses the temple, the Jewish leaders challenge his authority to do so.

"Then the Jews[88] demanded of him, 'What miraculous sign can you show us to prove your authority to do all this?'" (2:18)

Apparently, they are saying: If you were a prophet you might have authority to do what you did. Prove to us by some miracle that you are a prophet of God. Though Jesus was entirely capable of doing so, instead he offers them a cryptic saying as a "sign" of his Messiahship, rather than an immediate miracle.

[19] Jesus answered them, 'Destroy this temple, and I will raise it again in three days.' [20] The Jews replied, 'It has taken forty-six years to build this temple, and you are going to raise it in three days?' [21] But the temple he had spoken of was his body. [22] After he was raised from the dead, his disciples recalled what he had said. Then they believed the Scripture and the words that Jesus had spoken." (2:18-22)

The Jewish leaders obviously thought he was referring to Herod's temple. After all, his presence in this temple seems to be the context of Jesus' statement. His enemies used a somewhat garbled account of these words against him at his trial.

"Then some stood up and gave this false testimony against him: 'We heard him say, "I will destroy this man-made temple and in **three days** will build another, not made by man."' Yet even then their testimony did not agree." (Mark 14:57-59; cf. Matthew 26:60-61)

Why would Jesus answer his enemies in this way? I think it's similar to the reason he spoke in parables – so that the spiritually obtuse, those who wouldn't believe no matter what he said, wouldn't understand, but that his disciples would be able to learn.

The bottom line is that no sign would have convinced his enemies, except perhaps his death and resurrection from the dead – which is the very sign he offers them! He gives his enemies a similar cryptic sign later in his ministry – the sign of Jonah.

"Then some of the Pharisees and teachers of the law[89] said to him, 'Teacher, we want to see a miraculous sign from you.' He answered, 'A wicked and adulterous generation asks for a miraculous sign! But none will be given it except the sign of the prophet Jonah. For as Jonah was three days and three nights in the belly of a huge fish, so the Son of Man will be **three days** and three nights in the heart of the earth.'" (Matthew 12:38-40)

Jesus' disciples didn't understand either of these sayings when they were given, but after the resurrection they remembered them and it increased their faith, since they realized that Jesus had foreseen both his death and resurrection.

---

[88] For John's use of "the Jews" to refer to Jewish leaders, see Appendix 2. 'The Jews' in John's Gospel.
[89] See Appendix 3. Religious Leaders in Jesus' Day.

Did Not Entrust Himself to Followers (2:23-25)

"²³ Now while he was in Jerusalem at the Passover Feast, many people saw the miraculous signs he was doing and believed in his name. ²⁴ But Jesus would not entrust himself to them, for he knew all men. ²⁵ He did not need man's testimony about man, for he knew what was in a man." (2:23-25)

We're not told all of the miracles that Jesus did in Jerusalem that Passover, but they must have been considerable. Seeing the miracles prompted initial faith in many people (the verb is *pisteuō*, "to believe") – and that was good, so far as it went. But faith that rests on miracles alone, and doesn't mature to embrace Jesus and follow him, is shallow and fickle. Thus, our text says that Jesus didn't "entrust" (NIV, NRSV) or "commit" (KJV) himself to them. The verb again is *pisteuō*, this time with the connotation of "to entrust oneself to an entity in complete confidence, believe (in), trust, with implication of total commitment to the one who is trusted."[90]

If Jesus *had* trusted himself to the people, they would have tried to make him king (see 6:15). All around him people were trying to use him for their own purposes – and continue to do so to this day!

Jesus didn't need to hear people's testimonies and protestations about how much they believed in him. He knew our weaknesses and shallow faith all too well.

What amazes me is that he trusted himself to his twelve disciples. Yes, their faith was growing, but still weak and vacillating. And, ultimately, one of his own disciples betrayed him. Yet, he trusts into our hands his mission on earth, the witness to his person and glory, yes, his very reputation. In spite of our weaknesses, he has placed in us, his people, a great and precious trust. Let us live up to his trust!

Q3. (John 2:23-25) What is the problem with faith that rests solely on miracles? Is it true faith? What is necessary for it to develop into true faith? Did Jesus see these problems as a reason not to perform miracles?
http://www.joyfulheart.com/forums/topic/1408-q3-miracles-and-faith/

Lessons for Disciples

There are several things we can learn from this incident.

1. Jesus is upset when his place of worship is desecrated. God cares what goes on inside our congregations. Though our buildings are ministry structures, not sacred temples in the sense of the Jerusalem temple, there are appropriate behaviors there. These behaviors should not be controlled by our traditions so much as moral issues -- what is right and wrong. Many church members have desecrated Christ's church by their gossip, backbiting, and rebellion against authority.
2. There is such a thing as appropriate anger. But we must still control our actions, not justify them with the term "righteous indignation."

---

[90] *Pisteuō*, BDAG 817, 2aα.

3. Any action we take to bring holiness within a group of people or a building will be met with opposition by those who are called to account.

4. Jesus didn't trust himself to everyone. Openness towards others doesn't mean allowing them to determine our future or orchestrate our actions. These rather we trust into the hands of God only.

Prayer

Father, thank you for an example of Jesus' moral outrage and cleansing of the temple. Help us to stand strong against wrongs. And, Lord, cleanse the temples of our hearts, no matter how much we might be offended and upset, so that our hearts might be holy places that welcome you. In Jesus' name, we pray. Amen.

Key Verses

"In the temple courts he found men selling cattle, sheep and doves, and others sitting at tables exchanging money. So he made a whip out of cords, and drove all from the temple area, both sheep and cattle; he scattered the coins of the money changers and overturned their tables. To those who sold doves he said, 'Get these out of here! How dare you turn my Father's house into a market!'" (John 3:14-16, NIV)

"Jesus answered them, 'Destroy this temple, and I will raise it again in three days.' ... But the temple he had spoken of was his body." (John 2:19, 21, NIV)

"But Jesus would not entrust himself to them, for he knew all men. He did not need man's testimony about man, for he knew what was in a man." (John 2:24-25, NIV)

6. You Must Be Born Again (3:1-21)

Celebrities often attract people for the wrong reasons. People want to be close to glamour and fame, hoping that some of it will rub off. People want to be able to say they saw so-and-so, since it adds to their own status. And if the person is a performer, people are attracted by the act. In Jesus' case, many were attracted by his actions, his miracles, and, sadly, many went no deeper. This account is of one man who did go deeper.

James J. Tissot, detail of "The Interview between Jesus and Nicodemus" (1886-94), gouache on paper, 9-1/8 x 7", Brooklyn Museum, New York.

Nicodemus the Pharisee (3:1)

Jesus is still in Jerusalem during the Passover. While there, he receives a nocturnal visit from a very important man.

> "Now there was a man of the Pharisees named Nicodemus, a member of the Jewish ruling council." (3:1)

"Nicodemus" is a Greek name (*Nikodēmos*, from *nikos*, "victorious" + *dēmos*, "public, people") that means "conqueror of the people." The name was found among both Jews and Greeks. Perhaps he was a member of the Greek-speaking synagogue that met in Jerusalem (Acts 6:9; 9:29). We just don't know.[91]

However, we learn several things about Nicodemus here and in the two other passages where he is mentioned. First, he was a minor celebrity in his own right as one of the 70 Jewish rulers[92] who served on Jerusalem's Great Sanhedrin, the body that made decisions for the country – under Roman rule, of course.[93]

He was also a Pharisee, that is, a strict observer of the law (7:50-51). What's more, he was an expert in Jewish law, a scribe, since Jesus calls him "Israel's teacher" (3:10). He was probably wealthy, both to be considered to be a member of the Sanhedrin and because he assisted Joseph of Arimathea in Jesus' burial, both physically and financially (19:39).

---

[91] TalBab *Taanith* 20a speaks of a wealthy and generous man in Jerusalem prior to 70 AD named Naqdimon ben Gurion (or Bunai), but he probably isn't the same person (Brown, *John* 1:130).

[92] Nicodemus was an *archōn*, "one who has administrative authority, leader, official." *Archōn*, BDAG 140, 2a.

[93] The Jewish Sanhedrin, the highest Jewish governing body in Palestine, was "made up of priests (Sadducees), scribes (Pharisees) and lay elders of the aristocracy. Its seventy members were presided over by the high priest" (Brown, *John* 1:30). See more in Appendix 3. Religious Leaders in Jesus' Day.

Nicodemus the Seeker (3:2)

But there is something different about Nicodemus from the other members of the Sanhedrin: he is spiritually hungry.

> "He came to Jesus at night and said, 'Rabbi, we know you are a teacher who has come from God. For no one could perform the miraculous signs you are doing if God were not with him.'" (3:2)

Twice, the Gospel of John tells us that he came to Jesus at night (3:2; 19:39). Why the nocturnal visit? There are several possibilities:

1. **Fear.** We're told that fellow Sanhedrin member Joseph of Arimathea hadn't publicly identified himself with Jesus "because he feared the Jews[94]" (19:38). Was Nicodemus afraid too? Perhaps, but he seemed bolder, since he stood up for Jesus in a meeting of the Sanhedrin (7:51).
2. **Caution.** Probably caution fits Nicodemus. He doesn't want to be seen endorsing the teachings of this new Galilean teacher until he is sure. That's wise, it seems to me.
3. **Accessibility.** Perhaps the best reason for seeking out Jesus at night is the ability to engage him in a longer conversation and ask earnest questions without interruption.[95] Nighttime was probably a good choice for an earnest seeker.

Notice what this esteemed Bible scholar acknowledges when he meets Jesus.

1. Rabbi, which means in Hebrew, "great one." Nicodemus acknowledges the legitimacy of Jesus' teaching role, though Jesus hasn't been educated in the finest schools under the best rabbis, as had Paul, for example (Acts 22:3). Jesus *had,* of course, impressed the temple teachers as a boy of twelve (Luke 2:46-47), and had, no doubt, studied Hebrew and the Holy Scriptures under a local rabbi at his own synagogue when growing up. Nicodemus is impressed by him as a teacher, which is high praise coming from a well-known teacher like Nicodemus.

2. A teacher come from God. Unlike some of his fellow Pharisees who claimed that Jesus cast out demons by the devil himself (Mark 3:22), Nicodemus recognizes the divine origin of Jesus' miracles.

I used to think that Nicodemus was just being polite when he said: "Rabbi, we know you are a teacher who has come from God" (3:2a). But I think I was wrong. Nicodemus is just being honest. It is these miracles that make Nicodemus so curious.

Lots of people had seen Jesus' miracles and been attracted to him.

> "While [Jesus] was in Jerusalem at the Passover Feast, many people saw the miraculous signs he was doing and believed in his name." (2:23)

Nicodemus is one of these. He isn't a full believer yet, but the miracles cause him to recognize that God is behind Jesus' miracles. I know that the first time I saw a miracle first-hand, it exploded my world-view. Unlike most of his fellow Pharisees, instead of rejecting Jesus' miracles or signs, he sees them as an indication of God's hand. Now he has come to learn more.

---

[94] For John's use of "the Jews" to refer to Jewish leaders, see Appendix 2. 'The Jews' in John's Gospel.
[95] Beasley-Murray, *John,* p. 47.

Discerning the Kingdom of God (3:3-5)

Now Jesus begins to teach about the spiritual nature of the Kingdom of God.

"[3] In reply Jesus declared, 'I tell you the truth, no one can see[96] the **kingdom of God** unless he is born again.'

[4] 'How can a man be born when he is old?' Nicodemus asked. 'Surely he cannot enter a second time into his mother's womb to be born!'

[5] Jesus answered, 'I tell you the truth, no one can enter the **kingdom of God** unless he is born of water and the Spirit.'" (3:3-5)

I've always thought that Jesus' reply to Nicodemus' statement seems rather abrupt and off-topic. Nicodemus is talking about miracles and Jesus is discussing the Kingdom of God. Then I realized that Nicodemus' own presence that night with the miracle-worker is powerful testimony that he is seeking the Kingdom of God to which the miracles attest.[97] Nicodemus is hungry to see and understand the Kingdom.

We're often so eager to understand what it means to be "born again" that we miss what Jesus is saying about the Kingdom. The prevailing Jewish expectation was that the Messiah would come as a military leader to deliver them from Roman oppression, perhaps in the way that Judas Maccabeus and his family had led a rebellion to deliver Israel from the control of the pagan Greek king Antiochus Epiphanes less than two centuries before.

Jesus tells us two things about the Kingdom:

1. **The Kingdom is spiritually discerned**, that is, you can't see it or grasp it spiritually unless you are "born from above," unless God enables you to see it.
2. **The Kingdom is spiritually entered**, that is, you can't enter into the Kingdom, which is a synonym for inheriting eternal life, unless you are changed spiritually.

James J. Tissot, "Nicodemus" (1886-94), Watercolor, The Brooklyn Museum, New York.

Recall with me a couple of verses. Jesus has this dialog with Pontius Pilate:

"Pilate … summoned Jesus and asked him, 'Are you the king of the Jews?'
… Jesus said, **'My kingdom is not of this world.** If it were, my servants would fight to prevent my arrest by the Jews. But now my kingdom is from another place.'
'You are a **king**, then!' said Pilate.
Jesus answered, 'You are right in saying **I am a king**. In fact, for this reason I was born, and for this I came into the world, to testify to the truth….'" (18:33, 36-37)

---

[96] "See" is *eidōn*, an obsolete form of the present tense, of *horaō*, "to catch sight of." Here it is used figuratively in the sense of "to be mentally or spiritually perceptive, perceive" (BDAG 719, 4).

[97] Edersheim (*Life and Times*, 1:383) put it this way: "His errand was soon told: one sentence, that which admitted the Divine Teachership of Jesus, implied all the questions he could wish to ask. Nay, his very presence there spoke them."

And another teaching, this time about the hiddenness of the Kingdom.

"No one knows the Son except the Father, and no one knows the Father except the Son and those to whom the Son **chooses to reveal** him." (Matthew 11:27)

"No one can come to me unless the Father who sent me **draws** him." (John 6:44)

The parables of the Kingdom are hidden from the unbelievers, too.

> "The disciples came to him and asked, 'Why do you speak to the people in parables?' He replied, 'The knowledge of the secrets of the kingdom of heaven has been given to you, but not to them. Whoever has will be given more, and he will have an abundance. Whoever does not have, even what he has will be taken from him.'" (Matthew 13:10-12)

The Kingdom of God is hidden from unbelievers.

> "The god of this age has blinded the minds of unbelievers, so that they cannot see the light of the gospel of the glory of Christ, who is the image of God." (2 Corinthians 4:4)

Unbelievers can see that the Kingdom might be present from the signs or miracles that result, and this may cause them, like Nicodemus, to search further. But unaided, they can't see or discern the Kingdom, much less enter it. It is God's prerogative to reveal.

At one level, this may not seem quite fair. After all, seeing spiritual things is a right, isn't it? No! We are blind, unless God graciously rescues us, saves us. There is a spiritual war going on. Salvation is costly. So costly that it can only be a gift.

Does this sound like the sovereignty of God and predestination? Yes, that is what it is. But as we'll see shortly, there is something that man can and must do to prepare himself to receive the gift.

> **Q1. (John 3:3, 5) What does Jesus teach here about the nature of the Kingdom of God? Do you think Nicodemus understands him? Why or why not?**
> http://www.joyfulheart.com/forums/topic/1409-q1-seeing-the-kingdom/

Begotten or Born? (3:3-5)

Now let's explore this heavenly birth that Jesus teaches:

> "³ In reply Jesus declared, 'I tell you the truth, no one can see the kingdom of God unless he is **born again**.'
> ⁴ 'How can a man be **born** when he is old?' Nicodemus asked. 'Surely he cannot enter a second time into his mother's womb to be **born**!'
> ⁵ Jesus answered, 'I tell you the truth, no one can enter the kingdom of God unless he is **born of water and the Spirit**.'" (3:3-5)

The word "born" is *gennaō*, "become the parent of, beget" by procreation.[98] The passive can mean either, "born," as by a mother, or "begotten," as by a father.[99] Nicodemus takes the word in its

---

[98] *Gennaō*, BDAG 194, 1a.

[99] The same meanings are possible for the Hebrew root *yld* (Brown *John*,1:130).

feminine sense of being in one's mother's womb. But elsewhere, the idea seems to be "beget" in the masculine sense:[100]

Look at places where this concept of being born/begotten is used elsewhere in the New Testament.

"Yet to all who received him, to those who believed in his name, he gave the right to become children of God – children born not of natural descent, nor of human decision or a husband's will, but **born of God**." (1:12-13)

"No one who is **born of God** will continue to sin, because **God's seed** (*sperma*[101]) remains in him; he cannot go on sinning, because he has been born of God." (1 John 3:9)

"Everyone who believes that Jesus is the Christ is **born of God**, and everyone who loves the father loves his child as well." (1 John 5:1)

"For you have been **born again**, not of **perishable seed** (*spora*[102]), but of imperishable, through the living and enduring word of God." (1 Peter 1:23)

"Again" or "from Above" (3:3, 5, 7)

There's another issue to examine as we try to understand Jesus' teaching as accurately as possible. The adverb modifying "born/beget" in verses 3 and 5 is *anōthen*. The Greek word can have both the meaning "from above" (which is most common) as well as "again, anew" (less common).[103]

1. Argument for "from above"

Most modern commentators[104] take the primary meaning here as "from above," since that is how the adverb is used three other times in this gospel (3:31; 19:11, 23). In addition, John's writings contain the idea of "born of God" in several verses, which is the same idea as "born from above" (as seen in the previous paragraph – 1 John 3:9; 4:7; 5:1, 4; 5:18). A.T. Robertson observes that though Nicodemus took the word in the sense of "again," "the misapprehension of Nicodemus does not prove the meaning of Jesus."[105] The translation "from above" is contained in the NRSV and NJB.

2. Argument for "again, anew"

I believe a strong case can be made for the translation "again, anew." First, the possibility of two meanings of the word is possible in Greek only, not in the Aramaic that Jesus would have spoken.[106] Second, Nicodemus clearly took it in the sense of "again" when he pictured a person crawling back

---

[100] "Despite the fact that the Spirit, mentioned in vs. 5 as the agent of this birth or begetting, is feminine in Hebrew (neuter in Greek), the primary meaning seems to be 'begotten'" (Brown, *John* 1:130).

[101] *Sperma*, "'seed,' male seed or semen" (BDAG 937, 1b).

[102] *Spora*, "primarily 'the activity of sowing' and figuratively 'procreation,' then by metonymy, 'that which is sown, seed'" (BDAG 939). We get our word "spore" from this word.

[103] "In extension from a source that is above, from above" ... "at a subsequent point of time involving repetition, again, anew" (BDAG 92, 1 and 4).

[104] Brown, *John* 1:130-131; C.K. Barrett, *The Gospel According to St. John* (Second Edition; Westminster Press, 1955, 1978), p. 206; Beasley-Murray, *John*, p. 45.

[105] A.T. Robertson, *Word Pictures, in loc.*

[106] Brown (John 1:130) observes, "Such a misunderstanding is possible only in Greek; we know of no Hebrew or Aramaic word of similar meaning which would have this spatial and temporal ambiguity."

into his mother's womb "a second time"[107] to be born. Third, Jesus seems to have taught something similar in Matthew:

> "I tell you the truth, unless you change[108] and **become like little children**, you will never enter the kingdom of heaven." (Matthew 18:3)

We also clearly see the idea of being "born anew" elsewhere in the New Testament:

> "He saved us, not because of righteous things we had done, but because of his mercy. He saved us through the washing of **rebirth** (*palingenesia*[109]) and **renewal** (*anakainōsis*[110]) by the Holy Spirit." (Titus 3:5)

> "In his great mercy he has **given us new birth** (*anagennaō*[111]) into a living hope...." (1 Peter 1:3)

> "For you have been **born again** (*anagennaō*), not of perishable seed, but of imperishable, through the living and enduring word of God." (1 Peter 1:23)

For these reasons, I think that the translation "born anew" reflects Jesus' meaning here.[112] Indeed, a number of commentators support this view.[113] The NIV and ESV translations use "born anew/again." Jesus intends this to be understood as not a repetition of a previous birth, but clearly a "new" kind of birth brought about by the Spirit.

Having said that, commentators agree that John deliberately used the ambiguous adverb *anōthen* so that both ideas of "anew" and "from above" would be considered, since the spiritual birth is both "anew" *and* "from above."

Q2. (John 3:3-5) What does "entering the Kingdom" have to do with being "born anew"? Which do you think is the best translation here: "born again," "born anew," or "born from above"? Defend your reasoning.
http://www.joyfulheart.com/forums/topic/1410-q2-born-anew-again-from-above/

---

[107] *Deuteros*, "second" ... "for the second time" (BDAG 220, 2).

[108] *Strephō*, "turn around," here figuratively, "to experience an inward change, turn, change" (BDAG 948, 5), "be converted" (KJV).

[109] "Rebirth" (NIV, NRSV), "regeneration" (KJV) is *palingenesia*, from *palin*, "again, once more, anew" + *genesis*, "birth," meaning "experience of a complete change of life, rebirth" of a redeemed person (BDAG 752, 2).

[110] *Anakainōsis*, "renewal" (BDAG 64) is found here and in Romans 12:2, "the renewal of your minds." It is a compound word from *ana-*, "repetition, renewal" (equivalent to *denuo*, 'anew, over again," Thayer p. 34) + *kainos*, "new, fresh."

[111] *Anagennaō*, "beget again, cause to be born again" (BDAG 59).

[112] Edersheim (*Life and Times*, 1:384) explains that the term "new-born" was used in rabbinical literature to refer to both Gentile proselytes, as well as "the bridegroom on his marriage, the Chief of the academy on his promotion, the king on his enthronement.... The expression, therefore, was not only common, but, so to speak, fluid...."

[113] Morris (*John*, p. 213, fn. 13) cites Edwin A Abbott, *Johannine Grammar* (London, 1906); Strack and Billerbeck 2:420f; and Brook Foss Westcott, *The Gospel according to St. John* (Grand Rapids, 1954) 1:136. Rudolf Bultmann (*Das Evangelium des Johannes* (Göttigen, 1956), p. 135) also favors this view (as cited by Beasley-Murray, *John*, p. 45).

Born of Water and Spirit (3:5-7)

Jesus has explained the concept of being "born anew." Nicodemus responds with a repetition of one's physical birth. It's not clear whether Nicodemus is making fun of the idea or just struggling to grasp it. But Jesus continues on instructing the earnest man.

> "5 Jesus answered, 'I tell you the truth, no one can enter the kingdom of God unless he is born of water and the Spirit. 6 Flesh gives birth to flesh, but the Spirit gives birth to spirit. 7 You should not be surprised at my saying, "You must be born again."'" (3:5-7)

It's pretty clear that Jesus is differentiating this as a spiritual birth in distinction from a physical birth (as Nicodemus had understood it). What isn't so clear is what he means by "born of water and the Spirit." We understand the idea of being born of the Spirit in the sense of Jesus' conception (Matthew 1:20). But it's the reference to the water that is confusing to us.

Morris recites the various interpretations of water in the passage.

1. **Christian Baptism**. John must have known that water would be associated by his readers with Christian baptism. Indeed, some groups have used this passage to teach a doctrine of baptismal regeneration, that a person cannot be saved without being baptized. However, Nicodemus could not have understood such a reference to a not-yet-existent sacrament. This explanation doesn't make sense to me.

2. **Procreation**. Since Jesus contrasts physical birth with spiritual birth, some see the water as a reference to either semen or bag of waters in the womb. Though such ideas may seem offensive to modern ears, there are many references in Rabbinic, Mandaean, and Hermetic sources that use terms like "water," "rain," "dew," and "drop" in the sense of male semen. Moreover, Hellenistic mystery religions made use of the terminology of re-birth.[114] I see water as referring to procreation as a *possibility*.

3. **Repentance and Purification**. Dipping in water naturally suggests washing and cleansing. If we look at the context of John's Gospel as far as chapter 3, the only water we've seen is the water of John's baptism and the water that Jesus turned to wine in Cana. Therefore, I think the most natural interpretation is to take "water and Spirit" to refer to the ministry of John the Baptist who preached "a baptism of repentance for the forgiveness of sins" (Mark 1:4). His baptism with water was also contrasted with the baptism of the Holy Spirit (Mark 1:8; John 1:33).

As we saw earlier, since John's baptism was probably viewed in the light of a baptism required of Jewish proselytes in the first century, it would take a real heart of humility for a Jew to submit to it, especially those who already considered themselves religiously pure, such as the Pharisees. Many of Nicodemus' colleagues bristled at the thought of *them* being baptized. Luke reports,

> "The Pharisees and experts in the law rejected God's purpose for themselves, because they had not been baptized by John." (Luke 7:30)

---

[114] H. Odeberg (*The Fourth Gospel Interpreted in Its Relation to Contemporaneous Religious Currents in Palestine and the Hellenistic-Oriental World* (Uppsala, 1929)) argues that the water stands for the celestial waters, viewed in mystical Judaism as corresponding to the semen of the fleshly being. Thus to be born of water and the Spirit means a rebirth by means of spiritual seed as in 1 John 3:9.

We don't need to be cleansed like some new proselyte, they would assert proudly. We are Abraham's direct descendants! John the Baptist's response was sharp. He called them a brood of vipers:

> "Produce fruit in keeping with repentance. And do not think you can say to yourselves, 'We have Abraham as our father.' I tell you that out of these stones God can raise up children for Abraham." (Matthew 3:8-9)

So, in this context, I believe Jesus is saying to Nicodemus: You must be born anew by your own repentance and humbling yourself before God *and* the Holy Spirit's divine regenerative work within you. You can't enter the Kingdom of God by your own effort. You must surrender yourself to God! Only God can bring about this new creation in you.

> **Q3. (John 3:5-7) What does it mean to be "born of water and the Spirit"? What do you think "water" refers to? Why have you come to this conclusion? How, then, would you paraphrase "born of water and the Spirit" to best bring out the full meaning?**
> **http://www.joyfulheart.com/forums/topic/1411-q3-water-and-the-spirit/**

The Wind of the Spirit (3:8)

Jesus reinforces this by emphasizing that the Holy Spirit cannot be manipulated. He is out of man's control and entirely directed by God:

> "The wind (*pneuma*) blows wherever it pleases. You hear its sound, but you cannot tell where it comes from or where it is going. So it is with everyone born of the Spirit (*pneuma*)." (3:8)

"Wind" is *pneuma*, the breath of God, the same word that is translated "Spirit" at the end of the verse. People who have been born of the Spirit, Jesus is saying, are motivated and moved by an unseen but powerful force beyond themselves. The life of the Spirit is a new level of spiritual existence, a different plane entirely. Only people who have been born of the Spirit can perceive and enter the Kingdom of God.

The Witness of the Son of Man (3:9-13)

Nicodemus is mystified. He hasn't heard anything like this before. He asks a somewhat arrogant question: How can this be true if I don't know about it?

> "[9] 'How can this be?' Nicodemus asked.
> [10] 'You are Israel's teacher,' said Jesus, 'and do you not understand these things? [11] I tell you the truth, we speak of what we know, and we testify to what we have seen, but still you people do not accept our testimony.'" (3:9-11)

Jesus responds to Nicodemus with a gentle rebuke. In his answer you see a couple of key words that appear again and again in John's Gospel – testify/testimony and truth. Jesus is claiming to be an eyewitness to heavenly things. Now he makes an amazing claim:

"¹² I have spoken to you of earthly things and you do not believe; how then will you believe if I speak of heavenly things? ¹³ No one has ever gone into heaven except the one who came from heaven – the Son of Man.'" (3:12-13)

As we discussed previously, Jesus' self-descriptive title of "Son of Man" is taken from a passage in Daniel that discusses the heavenly nature of this figure:

"I saw in the night visions, and behold, with the **clouds of heaven** there came one like a **son of man**, and he came to the Ancient of Days and was presented before him. And to him was given dominion and glory and a kingdom, that all peoples, nations, and languages should serve him; his dominion is an everlasting dominion, which shall not pass away, and his kingdom one that shall not be destroyed." (Daniel 7:13-14)

When Jesus made claim to be the Son of Man quoting this passage at his trial (Mark 14:61-64), the High Priest declared the statement blasphemy. Nicodemus, the strict Pharisee, the "teacher of Israel," must have pondered these words deeply.

The Son of Man Must Be Lifted Up (3:14-15)

Now Jesus now refers to a curious image from the Old Testament.

"¹⁴ Just as Moses lifted up the snake in the desert, so the Son of Man must be lifted up, ¹⁵ that everyone who believes in him may have eternal life." (3:14-15)

Jesus is teaching Nicodemus about the relationship of faith and life. Jesus calls attention to an incident that took place during the Israelite's sojourn in the desert after the exodus from Egypt. Many of them had been bitten by poisonous snakes, and Moses asked God what to do.

"The LORD said to Moses, 'Make a snake and put it up on a pole; anyone who is bitten can look at it and live.' So Moses made a bronze snake and put it up on a pole. Then when anyone was bitten by a snake and looked at the bronze snake, he lived." (Numbers 21:8-9)

James J. Tissot, detail of "The Brazen Serpent" (1896-1904), watercolor, The Jewish Museum, New York City, NY.

A bronze snake was lifted up on a pole[115] for people to look at in faith, and in looking they were healed.

Jesus is saying that in the same way that people looked with belief upon the bronze snake that was lifted up, so must they look with belief upon the Son of Man, who will be lifted up. Nicodemus can't know what this means fully, but in hindsight we see that Jesus was lifted up on the cross, raised from the dead, and finally ascended to glory.

---

[115] *Nēs*, "standard, ensign, signal, sign," then "standard," as pole. (BDB 652, 2). This "standard-bearing pole," is literally the word for "sign" both in the Masoretic text and in the Septuagint (Brown, *John* 1:133).

This phrase "lifted up" is found three times in John.

"Just as Moses lifted up the snake in the desert, so the Son of Man must be **lifted up**, that everyone who believes in him may have eternal life." (3:14-15)

"When you have **lifted up** the Son of Man, then you will know that I am [the one I claim to be]...." (8:28a)

"'But I, when I am **lifted up** from the earth, will draw all men to myself.' He said this to show the kind of death he was going to die." (12:32-33)

Even early in his ministry, Jesus knew that it would end on the cross, the precursor to the resurrection. See more in Appendix 6. "Glory" and "Glorify" in John's Gospel.

For God So Loved the World that He Gave (3:16)

What we've been discussing is the context for the most famous verse in the Bible:

"For God so loved the world that he gave his one and only Son, that whoever believes in him shall not perish but have eternal life." (3:16)

Let's examine the verse phrase by phrase so we can understand it fully. The speaker[116] attributes two actions to God: God loved and God gave. Both are in the Aorist indicative tense, which indicates a particular point in past time that God so loved and therefore gave (presumably, gave on the cross):

"Loved" is *agapaō*, the word used in the New Testament for the highest form of love, "to have a warm regard for and interest in another, cherish, have affection for, love."[117] "Loved" is modified by the adverb "so," which indicates an intense degree of love.[118]

The object of love is "the world," the *kosmos*, a broad word that here refers to "humanity in general, the world."[119] This verse doesn't limit God's love only to the Jewish people or to believers, but to all of humanity.[120] Thus he loved us while were still his enemies (Romans 5:8). In his first letter, John writes:

"He is the atoning sacrifice for our sins, and not only for ours but also for the sins of the whole **world** (*kosmos*)." (1 John 2:2)

"God was reconciling the **world** (*kosmos*) to himself in Christ, not counting men's sins against them." (2 Corinthians 5:19)

"We have put our hope in the living God, who is the Savior of **all men**, and especially of those who believe." (1 Timothy 4:10)[121]

---

[116] Some scholars see a change of speakers at verse 13 or verse 16 because the last "you" is in verse 12 and there is shift to the third person in verses 13 and following. But this is not unusual in John's Gospel and there is no indication that Jesus has stopped speaking. Brown rejects this theory of a change in speakers. He says: "All Jesus' words come to us through the channels of the evangelist's understanding and rethinking, but the Gospel presents Jesus as speaking and not the evangelist" (Brown, *John* 1:149).

[117] *Agapaō*, BDAG 5, 1bα.

[118] "So" is the adverb *houtō*," here a marker of a relative high degree, "so." Before a verb, it intensifies the verb, "so intensely," here and in 1 John 4:11, "Dear friends, since God *so loved* us, we also ought to love one another" (BDAG 742, 3).

[119] *Kosmos*, BDAG 562, 6b.

[120] I know that 5-point Calvinism limits Christ's atonement to the elect only, but John 3:16 doesn't support such an interpretation.

Gave in John 3:16 is the common verb *didōmi*, "to give." It echoes the related verb *paradidomai* in Isaiah 53:12 (Septuagint), "He was given up for their sins." The verb in 3:16 isn't "sent," but "gave," emphasizing the idea of sacrifice.[122]

Jesus, God's Unique Son (*monogenēs*)

Let's pause here to consider how the speaker describes Jesus as God's "one and only Son" (NIV), "only Son" (NRSV, NJB), "only begotten Son" (KJV, NASB). The word modifying Son is *monogenēs* (which we saw in 1:14, 18), "pertaining to being the only one of its kind or class, unique (in kind) of something that is the only example of its category."[123] This compound word is formed from *monos*, "sole, single" + *genos*, "kind." Brown comments, "Although *genos* is distantly related to *gennaō*, 'to beget,' there is little Greek justification for the translation of *monogenēs* as 'only begotten.'"[124]

This verse points clearly to Jesus as God's unique Son, one of a kind. We become sons and daughters of God by spiritual birth or adoption (depending upon which analogy you choose). Praise God! What a privilege this is! However, though we resemble Jesus, he is unique in his relationship to God, since he is the Son from eternity, the Second Person of the Trinity.

Results and Purposes of God's Love (3:16)

We've been moving word by word through John 3:16. Now we're at the second half. Take another look:

> "For God so loved the world **that** he gave his one and only Son, **that** whoever believes in him shall not perish but have eternal life." (3:16)

Notice the two "thats" in the verse:

1. **Result**. The first "that" (*hōste*[125]) indicates *result* in verse 16a. God's intense love *resulted* in him giving/sacrificing his Son.
2. **Purpose**. The second "that" (*hina*[126]) indicates *purpose* in verse 16b. God's love resulted in giving or sacrificing his Son *for the purpose* of (a) preventing us from perishing, but rather (b) having eternal life.

---

[121] Strict Calvinists affirm a doctrine called the "Limited Atonement" (the L in TULIP), which says that Jesus died for only the elect. I find this doctrine both contrary to the spirit of the verses cited here, and somewhat unnecessary. Of course, Jesus died that the elect might be saved! But his heart is the salvation of "all men," of "whosoever believes," of "the world." As St. Peter put it, "He is patient with you, not wanting anyone to perish, but everyone to come to repentance" (2 Peter 3:9).

[122] Vincent, *Word Studies*, in loc.

[123] *Monogenēs*, BDAG 658, 2.

[124] Brown, *John* 1:13. He says, "*Monogenēs* describes a quality of Jesus, his uniqueness, not what is called in Trinitarian theology his 'procession.'"

[125] "That" is *hōste*, which introduces a dependent clause of the actual result, "so that" (BDAG 110, 2aα). "The result clause is in the indicative.... The classical use of this construction is for the purpose of stressing the reality of the result: 'that he actually gave the only Son'" (Brown, *John* 1:134).

[126] *Hina* is a marker to denote purpose, aim, or goal, "in order that, that," in the final sense (BDAG 475, 1).

Not Perish (3:16b)

God's purpose is for us who believe to have eternal life. But to clarify this, we are given both the positive purpose, *to have eternal life,* and the flip side, the negative way of stating the same thing, *to avoid perishing.*

In our day, there's a lot of resistance to the idea of hell. Even Evangelical Christians seem to be moving towards the Jehovah's Witness position that hell is a sudden extinguishing of life into nothingness, not eternal punishment in the fires of hell. After all, how could a God of love allow people to suffer, even wicked people?

What does it mean to perish? The verb is *apollymi,* "to cause or experience destruction." In the middle voice as here, it means, "perish, be ruined." This word encompasses dying by storm at sea, by the sword, killed by snakes, and especially of eternal death.[127] This Greek word is often used of missing out on eternal life – both in the Old Testament Greek Bible (the Septuagint)[128] as well as in the New Testament.[129, 130] New Testament scholar Albrecht Oepke concludes, "In view is not just physical destruction but a hopeless destiny of eternal death."[131]

Jesus' Teaching on Hell

Though in John's Gospel words for "hell" don't appear[132], in the Synoptics, Jesus uses two Greek words that have been translated "hell" in the KJV.

Hadēs, "(originally a proper noun, god of the underworld), then the nether world, Hades as place of the dead."[133] Jesus taught that unbelievers would "go down to the depths" (Matthew 11:23; Luke 10:15), identified the "gates of Hades" (Matthew 16:18) as the enemy of the church, and the opposite of Abraham's bosom, a place where the rich man asks to have Lazarus "dip the tip of his finger in water and cool my tongue, because I am in agony in this fire" (Luke 16:23-24).

Gehenna, "Valley of the Sons of Hinnom," a ravine south of Jerusalem. There, according to later Jewish popular belief, God's final judgment was to take place.[134]

---

[127] *Apollymi,* BDAG 110, 1bα.

[128] Psalms 9:5-6; 37:20; 68:2; 73:27; 83:17; Isaiah 41:11.

[129] John 3:16; 10:28; 17:12; Romans 2:12; 1 Corinthians 1:18; 8:11; 15:18; 2 Corinthians 2:15; 4:3; 2 Thessalonians 2:10.

[130] *Apollymi* is often translated "lost" in the New Testament. This word is at the core of Jesus' teaching on his mission to "the lost sheep of the house of Israel" (Matthew 10:6; 15:24), as well as Jesus' Parables of the Lost Sheep (Matthew 18:10-14; Luke 15:3-7), the Lost Coin (Luke 15:8-10), the Lost Son (Luke 15:11-32).

[131] Albrecht Oepke, *apollumi, ktl.,* TDNT 1:394-397.

[132] *Hadēs* does appear in Revelation 1:18; 6:8; 20:13-14, where you also find the concept of "the lake of fire" (Revelation 20:14).

[133] *Hadēs,* BDAG 19.

[134] Here, in the Valley of the Sons of Hinnom, children had been burned to death as sacrifices to the false god Molech (2 Chronicles 28:3). "The fire" was identified early with the Valley of Hinnom. It was also a place where the prophets Jeremiah pronounced terrible curses of God's judgment and slaughter of the wicked (Jeremiah 7:31-32; 19:1-6). Isaiah saw the judgment of the wicked in terms of burning: "And they will go out and look upon the dead bodies of those who rebelled against me; their worm will not die, nor will their fire be quenched, and they will be loathsome to all mankind" (Isaiah 66:24). By the second century B.C., the Valley of Hinnom had come to be equated with the hell of the last judgment (Joachim Jeremias, *gehenna,* TDNT 1:657-658). There is some evidence that the Valley of Hinnom was the refuse dump of Jerusalem. The Prophet Jeremiah identifies the location of the Valley of Hinnom as "near the entrance of the Potsherd Gate" (Jeremiah 19:2), that is, the place where broken pots were discarded. New Testament scholar

In the Gospels, Ghenna is the place of punishment in the next life, "hell."[135] Jesus speaks of the "fire of hell" (Matthew 5:22: 18:9), being "thrown into hell" (Matthew 5:29-30), the place "where the fire never goes out" (Mark 9:43, 45, 47), "condemned to hell" (Matthew 23:33).

Some of the most graphic images of hell are in the last book of the Bible, being "thrown into the lake of burning sulfur … tormented day and night for ever and ever" (Revelation 20:10).

Finally, Jesus also talked about being "cast out into outer darkness" where "there shall be weeping and gnashing of teeth" (Matthew 8:12; cf. 13:42, 50; 22:13, 51; 25:30).

Of course, these descriptions are all symbolic rather than literal – aren't they? And if they *are* symbolic, the reality must be terrible beyond anything we can imagine.

Why do we ruin the discussion of such a pretty verse as John 3:16 by talking about a literal hell? Because, if we don't understand what it means *not to perish*, we don't understand the greatness of the alternative – *everlasting life*.

But Have Everlasting Life (3:16b)

"Eternal life" (NIV, NRSV, NASB), "everlasting life" (KJV) is made up of two words:

1. **Zōē** (from which we get our words, "zoo" and "zoology") means, "life," especially "transcendent life."[136] In the New Testament, it is the word used for eternal life, rather than the other word for life, *bios* (from which we get our word "biology"). *Bios* refers particularly to life in its appearance and manifestations, distinguished from *zōē*, the condition of being alive.[137]

2. **Aiōnios**, from the noun *aiōn*, "an extended period of time, age." *Aiōnios* means here, "pertaining to a period of unending duration, without end."[138]

"Eternal life" was used in the Judaism of Jesus' time as a synonym of entering or inheriting the Kingdom of God. You can see these terms used as synonyms in Jesus' encounter with the rich young ruler, who asks what he must do to "inherit eternal life" (Mark 10:17, cf. verse 30). When the rich young ruler is unwilling to obey the Master, Jesus says to his disciples, "How hard it is for the rich to enter the kingdom of God!" (verse 23).

Our passage in John 3 begins with Jesus' statement that a spiritual birth is necessary to "enter the kingdom of God" (3:5). Here faith is required to receive eternal life (3:16).

Joachim Jeremias observes, "It was still in modern times the place for rubbish, carrion, and all kinds of refuse" (*Jerusalem*, p. 17). Jeremias also cites an ancient Jewish document that identifies the Dung Gate as leading to the Valley of Hinnom (*Jerusalem*, p. 310). It is logical, then, that it was a place where garbage burned continually. Both David John Wieand ("Hinnom, Valley of," ISBE 2:717, citing Lightfoot) and Leon Morris (*Matthew* (Eerdmans, 1992), p. 115) see this as a possibility.

[135] *Gehenna*, BDAG 190-191.
[136] *Zōē*, BDAG 430, 2bβ.
[137] *Bios*, BDAG 176.
[138] *Aiōnios*, BDAG 33, 3.

Q4. (John 3:16) Why is this verse so famous? What does it teach us about God? What does it teach us about salvation? Since "entering eternal life" is a synonym for "entering the Kingdom of God," what does this verse teach us about our destiny?
http://www.joyfulheart.com/forums/topic/1412-q4-john-316/

Not to Condemn, but to Save (3:17-19)

Our passage concludes with two sayings, the first about condemnation and the second about light.

"[17] For God did not send[139] his Son into the world to condemn the world, but to save the world through him. [18] Whoever believes in him is not condemned, but whoever does not believe stands condemned already because he has not believed in the name of God's one and only Son." (3:17-19)

This passage helps fill out the meaning of verse 16:

- "to save the world" (verse 17) corresponds to "have eternal life" (verse 16)
- "to condemn the world" (verse 17) corresponds to "perish" (verse 16)

Note that "has not believed" is perfect tense, indicating a continuing disbelief. This is not a momentary lapse, but a determined unbelief.

Drawn to the Light of the Gospel (3:19-21)

John concludes this section with a teaching about light and darkness:

"[19] This is the verdict: Light has come into the world, but men loved darkness instead of light because their deeds were evil. [20] Everyone who does[140] evil hates the light, and will not come into the light for fear that his deeds will be exposed.[141] [21] But whoever lives by the truth comes into the light, so that it may be seen plainly[142] that what he has done has been done through God." (3:19-21)

We first saw this conflict between the light and darkness at the beginning of John's Gospel.

"[4] In him was life, and that life was the light of men. [5] The light shines in the darkness, but the darkness has not understood it." (1:4-5)

Why do evil people prefer darkness rather than light? Why do they try to hide their sinful actions? Because when non-believers see degradation and corruption with clarity, they will likely condemn it. No wonder Jesus developed enemies, because he shed a strong light on hypocritical, unethical, and downright wicked practices – and because of his light, they could no longer hide. When we live good, honest, and righteous lives – even when we don't loudly criticize others' lifestyles – our lives often cause a negative reaction in those who don't believe, since our righteousness casts a light on their

---

[139] "Sent" (*apostellō*) is parallel to "gave" in verse 16. Both are in the Aorist tense. *Apostellō* means, "to dispatch someone for the achievement of some objective, send away/out" (BDAG 120, 1b).

[140] *Prassō*, "do, accomplish" (BDAG 860, 1a). It carries the idea of "to practice" in the present tense.

[141] *Elenchō*, "to scrutinize or examine carefully, bring to light, expose, set forth" (BDAG 315, 1).

[142] *Phaneroō*, "reveal, expose publicly," here, "become public knowledge, be disclosed, become known" (BDAG 1048, 2aβ).

unrighteousness. Jesus said, "No servant is greater than his master. If they persecuted me, they will persecute you also" (John 15:20).

Lessons for Disciples

This passage tells us some very basic things about the Kingdom of God.

1. It is a spiritual kingdom. The very finest religious person doesn't have a clue what the real Kingdom of God is about unless he has been born by the Spirit of God. Remember your parents saying, "When you're older you'll understand"? You couldn't understand then because you lacked the basic life experience and understanding that was needed to decipher what you were seeing. The Kingdom is spiritually discerned.

2. Heart belief in Jesus is the key to this spiritual kingdom. Sometimes we confuse new birth with a radical conversion experience. Often conversion is sudden and radical, but sometimes it is gradual. Sometimes we confuse the new birth with saying the "sinner's prayer." That's an entry door for many, but many have prayed that prayer from unprepared hearts and come away with hearts still unlit by the Spirit. It comes back to our attitude towards Jesus. Do we "believe in him"?

3. All men and women are lost and need rescuing. This truth cuts very clearly across a culture that desperately resists absolute truth, absolute right and wrong, and vocally attacks any kind of judgment on its lifestyle. "Man is basically good, and just needs a little moral direction." No! To prove this, all you need to do is look at the environment, economic disparity, the apathetic consciences of the privileged, and the mess that many have made of their lives. Jesus teaches in this passage that man is basically blind, and lost, and perishing. The Kingdom is essentially God's rescue mission to a doomed planet.

> "For God so loved the world that he gave his one and only Son, that whoever believes in him shall not perish but have eternal life." (3:16)

Nicodemus came seeking truth from Jesus one night and got more than he bargained for. We have no record of a conversion that night. But on reckoning day, Nicodemus and Joseph of Arimathea, buried the King as best they could. Out of the fog of Nicodemus' understanding, the shape of Jesus began to emerge and then sharpen in focus. One day, Nicodemus would come to believe in Jesus so much, that where a prudent leader would distance himself from an executed criminal, Nicodemus instead cradled Jesus in his arms, washed his body, and tenderly anointed and wrapped it for burial. Did he believe in the end? O yes, he believed. He could now see the Kingdom beyond the grave.

Prayer

Thank you, God, for your patience with us. So often we have been too busy to listen, too self-absorbed to recognize you. Thank you for coming to rescue us from our blindness. For taking us by the hand, and teaching us, and opening our eyes to your Kingdom, and flooding us with your Spirit. Thank you, King Jesus. Amen.

Key Verses

"I tell you the truth, no one can see the kingdom of God unless he is born again." (John 3:3, NIV)

"I tell you the truth, no one can enter the kingdom of God unless he is born of water and the Spirit. Flesh gives birth to flesh, but the Spirit gives birth to spirit. You should not be surprised at my saying, 'You must be born again.'" (John 3:5-7, NIV)

"For God so loved the world that he gave his one and only Son, that whoever believes in him shall not perish but have eternal life." (John 3:16, NIV)

7. He Must Increase (3:22-4:3)

John's narrative now moves from Jerusalem at Passover to the countryside where both Jesus and John the Baptist are ministering in different areas.

Spending Time with Disciples (3:22)

"After this, Jesus and his disciples went out into the Judean countryside[143], where he spent some time with them, and baptized." (3:22)

Two things were on Jesus' agenda:

1. Spending time with his disciples, and

2. Baptizing.

We'll come to baptizing in a moment, but I don't want you to miss the vital importance Jesus saw in just spending time with[144] or "hanging out" with his disciples.

How do you disciple a man or woman? Can you structure it into a weekly class for one hour? Jesus didn't.

Jesus' typical call was, "Follow me!" Come with me. Listen to my teaching 20 or 30 times as I repeat it in village after village. Get to know me intimately. Live alongside me. Watch how I engage needy people. Observe how I pray for them, how I touch them, how I

Matthias Grünewald, detail of the John the Baptist panel in the Isenheim Altarpiece (1512–1516). Oil on panel. Unterlinden Museum, Colmar, Alsace.

heal them. See my love in action so it becomes your highest value also. Learn my way of looking at all sorts of situations.

And assist me. Be an active apprentice in ministry. Help the crowd get seated comfortably and keep some order as thousands of people gather to hear me. And let me rebuke and correct you when you are overzealous in preventing little children to come near me.

Later, Jesus will increase their responsibilities. He sends them on missionary trips two by two, and then debriefs them carefully so they learn the important things from their encounters.

Effective discipling requires a great deal of time between the discipler and the disciple. Jesus knew this, so he set aside time to do just that. To us who always have to be doing something, we'll misunderstand. Quiet time with Jesus is vital to learning to be a disciple!

---

[143] "Countryside" (NIV, NRSV), "land" (KJV) is *gē*, "portions or regions of the earth, region, country" (BDAG 196, 3).

[144] "Spent some time" (NIV) is *diatribō*, "to remain or stay in a place, spend time," usually rendered stay in sense of duration, especially when associated with place or person (BDAG 238).

Jesus also baptized during this time – which means that lots of people were coming to him out in the country, believing his message, repenting from their sins, and were being baptized for the forgiveness of sins (Mark 1:15). We'll come to that later in this lesson.

> **Q1. (John 3:22) What is the importance of Jesus spending time with his disciples? What is his strategy? How does Jesus make disciples today? Where is our time with the Discipler? How important is your time as a discipler, "hanging out" with people God puts on your heart to disciple?**
> http://www.joyfulheart.com/forums/topic/1413-q1-hanging-out-with-jesus/

John the Baptist Ministers West of the Jordan (3:23-24)

While Jesus begins to baptize, his mentor John the Baptist continues his ministry. Their ministries overlap.

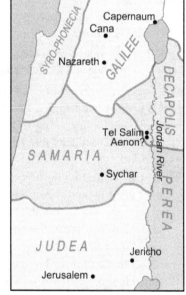

> "23 Now John also was baptizing at Aenon near Salim, because there was plenty of water, and people were constantly coming to be baptized. 24 (This was before John was put in prison.)" (3:23-24)

The Gospel of John tells us that John had moved his ministry from "beyond Jordan," that is, on the east side of the Jordan River (1:28; 3:26; 10:40), to "Aenon near Salim," on the west side of Jordan. Aenon means "springs" in Aramaic, and was a place where there was a lot of water for baptizing (a verse that Baptists love to quote).

Various locations have been proposed for Aenon, but perhaps the best possibility is the springs at Tel Salim (identified as such by Eusebius and Jerome), about seven miles south of Beth Shan).[145]

Just as people had streamed to John the Baptist in his earlier ministry in Judea, the flow of people continues[146] in this new location.

John's note, "This was before John was put in prison," is quite interesting. Nowhere in John's Gospel is the story of John's imprisonment and subsequent execution given. John assumes that his readers are familiar with the story, however, no doubt from the accounts in the Synoptic Gospels, which, by the time John wrote, were circulating widely in the churches. John's purpose is not to tell

---

[145] Another possibility for Salim is about three miles east of Shechem. We may never know the exact location (Urban C. von Wahlde, "Archaeology and John's Gospel," in *Jesus & Archaeology*, pp. 555-556; W. Ewing, "Aenon," ISBE 1:60).

[146] The words "coming" (*paraginomai*) and "baptizing" (*baptizō*) are in the imperfect tense, which means that an event occurs and continues to occur in the past.

the same story in the same way, but to reflect on various aspects of the story that point out Jesus as the Son of God and build faith in his readers (20:31).

He Must Become Greater (3:25-30)

John introduces baptism to tell a story that has John the Baptist pointing to Jesus once again.

"An argument developed between some of John's disciples and a certain Jew over the matter of ceremonial washing[147]." (3:25)

Strict Jews were quite adamant about a ceremonial rinsing of their hands before a meal – not for hygiene, nor from a direct commandment of Scripture, but to fulfill the "oral law," the tradition of the rabbis. You'll recall the stone water jars at the wedding at Cana that contained water for this purpose (2:6). And you may remember a dispute between Jesus and the Pharisees about hand-rinsing (Matthew 15:2).

When you think about it, baptism itself is a Jewish rite of purification. Converts to Judaism were required to be circumcised, offer a sacrifice, and be baptized (undergo ritual ablution).[148] So the controversy between a Jew and John's disciples about purification was to be expected. However, this Jew apparently brought reports of Jesus' success at baptizing. So these disciples came to John the Baptist with the report.

"They came to John and said to him, 'Rabbi, that man who was with you on the other side of the Jordan – the one you testified about – well, he is baptizing, and everyone is going to him.'" (3:26)

You can sense resentment in John's disciples. After all, baptism was what John himself was known for. Now this upstart is upstaging him and "everyone is going to him." No doubt this was an exaggeration; people were still coming to John the Baptist. But clearly, more were now coming to Jesus to be baptized. John 4:2 explains that Jesus wasn't baptizing people himself; he had delegated this ministry to his disciples.

Those that bring this news to John sound like reporters framing a question in a such a way that they might elicit a candid response. John the Baptist's reply surprises them. They expect anger and hurt. But John the Baptist doesn't respond with anger and hurt. He makes four points:

1. God directs our lives, not ambition.
2. I am not the Christ.
3. I find fulfillment in the bridegroom's joy.
4. He must increase, I must decrease.

John the Baptist's reply is remarkable. Edersheim says of it,

---

[147] "Ceremonial cleansing" (NIV), "purification, purifying" (NRSV, KJV) is *katharismos*, "cleansing from cultic impurity, purification" (BDAG 489). We saw this word referring to the stone jars used for purification in the incident of changing the water into wine.

[148] "According to rabbinical teachings, which dominated even during the existence of the Temple (*Pes.* viii. 8), Baptism, next to circumcision and sacrifice, was an absolutely necessary condition to be fulfilled by a proselyte to Judaism (Talmud: *Yebamoth* 46b, 47b; *Ker.* 9a; *'Ab. Zarah* 57a; *Shab.* 135a; *Yer. Kid.* iii. 14, 64d. "Baptism," *Jewish Encyclopedia*, 1908).

"The answer which the Baptist made may be said to mark the high point of his life and witness. Never before was he so tender, almost sad; never before more humble and self-denying, more earnest and faithful."[149]

1. God directs our lives, not our ambitions (3:27)

It's so easy to define ourselves in terms of success, and feel hurt when others succeed while we fail. John the Baptist's comment is insightful:

"A man can receive only what is given him from heaven." (3:27)

The Jews often used words such as "heaven" to avoid using the divine name. John the Baptist's point is that our lives are in God's hands. We don't call the shots. God directs our affairs. We must be obedient, of course, and make the most of what we are given – that is our responsibility. But when we judge ourselves on human standards we err.

> Q2. (John 3:26) Have you ever resented "larger churches" that attracted people from "your" church? What is wrong with this kind of possessiveness? Is it self-pity or something else? http://www.joyfulheart.com/forums/topic/1414-q2-possessiveness/

2. I am not the Christ (3:28)

John's second point is that he had already told his disciples that he isn't the Messiah, but a fore-runner (1:20-27).

"You yourselves can testify that I said, 'I am not the Christ but am sent ahead[150] of him.'" (3:28)

3. I find fulfillment in the bridegroom's joy (3:29)

John's third point carries this further. I am the bridegroom's friend, not the bridegroom himself.

"The bride belongs to the bridegroom. The friend who attends the bridegroom waits and listens for him, and is full of joy when he hears the bridegroom's voice. That joy is mine, and it is now complete." (3:29)

The allusion is to a wedding. The "friend of the bridegroom" – we would say, the "best man," the traditional Jewish *shosh^ebin* – acts as an agent for the groom and takes care of arranging for the wedding. He works behind the scenes to prepare for the celebration, but he isn't the focus of the day. The focus, of course, is on the bridegroom and his bride. The best man receives his joy when he hears the groom conversing with the bride. "It's not about me," John insists. "It is about the Messiah."

Of course, using such a wedding analogy carries with it the overtones from the Old Testament of Israel as the bride of God (Isaiah 62:4-5; Jeremiah 2:2; 3:20; Ezekiel 16:8; 23:4; Hosea 2:19-20), which the

---

[149] Edersheim, *Life and Times*, 3:396.

[150] "Sent ahead of" (NIV, NRSV), "sent before" (KJV) is two words, the verb *apostellō*, "to send," and the adverb *emprosthen*, "pertaining to a position in front of an object," as marker of something that is relatively removed in distance, "in front, ahead" (BDAG 325, 1a).

New Testament carries forward to the Church as the bride of Christ (2 Corinthians 11:2; Ephesians 5:25-32; Revelation 19:7-8; 21:2; 22:17).

> **Q3. (John 3:29) How does John the Baptist find joy in Jesus' success? Do you find joy in the success of others who could be seen as competing with your ministry – in your church or in your community or in your denomination? Why do you think some pastors seem to compete with each other?**
>
> **http://www.joyfulheart.com/forums/topic/1415-q3-rejoicing-in-anothers-success/**

4. He must increase, I must decrease (3:30)

"He must become greater[151]; I must become less.[152]" (3:30, NIV)
"He must increase, but I must decrease." (KJV, NRSV)

John the Baptist models for us here humility and obedience. John recognizes that he has already reached the zenith of his arc and is on the way down, while Jesus' arc is just beginning and will greatly surpass his. John was alright with this. In fact, he sees it as a necessity; the Greek verb is *dei*, "to be under necessity of happening, it is necessary, one must, one has to," denoting compulsion of any kind.[153]

This is also an important concept for you and me to grasp in our relationship to Jesus. "He *must* increase, but I *must* decrease." Your goal, my goal is not self-actualization, self-fulfillment, but letting Christ make us all he has made us to be. When he is greater in your life, you live in God's full power, but when you try to do it yourself, you are limited by your own weaknesses. In the last six months or year, has Christ increased in your life? Has your control decreased? It is "necessary" that this happen in your life and in mine!

> **Q4. (John 3:30) In what sense, in order to be successful in your Christian life, must you decrease and Christ increase? How can you facilitate the shift necessary for this change to occur? What steps might help you do this?**
>
> **http://www.joyfulheart.com/forums/topic/1416-q4-he-must-increase/**

Believing Jesus' Eyewitness Testimony (3:31-33)

As in Jesus' discourse with Nicodemus, it is difficult here to tell when John the Baptist's words end and where John the Apostle's reflections begin. I think that John the Apostle's words begin at verse 31 – but there are no quotation marks in Greek to tell us.

---

[151] "Become greater" (NIV), "increase" (NRSV, KJV) is *auxanō*, "to become greater, grow, increase" (BDAG 151, 2b).

[152] "Become less" (NIV), "decrease" (NRSV, KJV) is *elattoō*, "make lower," here, "to become less important, diminish, become less" (BDAG 314, 3).

[153] *Dei*, BDAG 214, 1a.

"31 The one who comes from above is above[154] all; the one who is from the earth belongs to the earth, and speaks as one from the earth. The one who comes from heaven is above all. 32 He testifies to what he has seen and heard, but no one accepts his testimony. 33 The man who has accepted it has certified that God is truthful." (3:31-33)

John points out that Jesus' superiority comes from the fact that he is the Heavenly Man who has come down to earth. He is not merely a human prophet as John the Baptist is. Jesus is an eyewitness to heaven! As he told Nicodemus:

"We speak of what we know, and we testify to what we have seen, but still you people do not accept our testimony." (3:11)

The sad fact is that most people judge Jesus from their merely human perspective and thus miss out (2 Corinthians 5:16). What arrogance we humans possess! If we don't know or understand something, then we think it must not be true. As we read at the beginning of John's Gospel:

"Though the world was made through him, the world did not recognize him." (1:10)

It comes down to whether or not we will accept Jesus' words as accurate and truthful. John the Apostle is pushing his readers to put their faith in Jesus:

"The one who has accepted [Jesus' testimony] has certified[155] that God is truthful." (3:33)

Verse 33 uses the analogy of placing one's unique seal on a document to verify its authenticity. If you believe Jesus, then you show that you believe God who sent him.

The Father, the Son, and the Spirit (3:34-35)

The narrator continues to spell out the implications of Jesus' testimony in a passage that puts Father, Son, and Spirit in a single verse.

"34 For the one whom God has sent speaks the words of God, for God[156] gives the Spirit without limit. 35 The Father loves the Son and has placed everything in his hands." (3:34-35)

Verse 35 seems to explain verse 34, that is, that the Father's boundless[157] giving of the Spirit to the Son is another way of saying that he places everything into his hands.[158] Thus we are to trust him completely. He speaks God's words and he wields all power.

---

[154] "Above" is *epanō*, a word of relative position, "above, over," but here, figuratively, "pertaining to being superior in status, above, over, something" (BDAG 359, 3).

[155] "Certified" (NIV, NRSV), "set to his seal" (KJV) is *sphragizō*, "to seal," here, by extension, "to certify that something is so, attest, certify, acknowledge" (as a seal does on a document) (BDAG 980, 4).

[156] The KJV uses "God gives" based on the Textus Receptus, following A C² D Θ Ψ lat etc. Newer translations follow the more ambiguous reading of "he gives" without the subject, following P⁵⁵, ⁷⁵ Aleph B² C* L W *f*¹, etc.

[157] "Without limit" (NIV) is a phrase of three words, *ouk*, "not", *ek*, "from", and *metron*, "a measure," then, "quantity, number." Though the phrase is not found elsewhere in Greek, from context it must mean, "not from a measure, without (using a) measure" (BDAG 644, 1b).

[158] It is grammatically possible to see the Son as giving the Spirit without limit to believers here, but it has two problems: (1) The context would indicate that, if verses 34 and 35 are parallel, as would be expected, then the Father is the subject of the giving. (2) "Grace was given to each one of us according to the measure of Christ's gift" (Ephesians 4:7) seems to indicate that the Spirit isn't given without measure to us.

Eternal Life vs. God's Wrath (3:36)

Because Jesus represents God fully, then to reject the Son is to reject the Father.

"Whoever believes in the Son has eternal life, but whoever rejects the Son will not see life, for God's wrath remains on him." (3:36)

This verse is a key one in John that discusses a major theme – eternal life to those who believe. We see this several times in the early chapters of John:

"Yet to all who received him, to **those who believed** in his name, he gave the right to become children of God." (1:12)

"For God so loved the world that he gave his one and only Son, that **whoever believes** in him shall not perish but have eternal life." (3:16)

"I tell you the truth, whoever hears my word and **believes him who sent me** has eternal life and will not be condemned; he has crossed over from death to life." (5:24)

"My Father's will is that everyone who looks to the Son and **believes in him** shall have eternal life, and I will raise him up at the last day." (6:40)

"I tell you the truth, **he who believes** has everlasting life." (6:47)

As we discovered when we studied 1:12, this Greek word *pisteuō* means much more than intellectual assent. It is an active verb that means "to entrust oneself to an entity in complete confidence, believe (in), trust, with the implication of total commitment to the one who is trusted."[159] Those who believe in Jesus enough to follow him, to commit their lives to him, are promised eternal life. Notice that the verb here is not future tense, "will have," but present tense, "has" now! (see 5:24)

But the flip side of believing the Son is rejecting or disobeying the Son. "Rejects" (NIV), "disobeys" (NRSV), "does not obey" (ESV), "believeth not" (KJV) is *apeitheō*, "disobey, be disobedient."[160] John isn't teaching some kind of "works righteousness" here, that if you don't obey all the time and in every matter, that you will be condemned. We know from his first epistle that he doesn't believe that (1 John 2:1-2). What he is saying is that those who believe in Jesus will see an effect in their lives – they'll start to follow him and to obey his teachings. As the Sunday school song goes:

"If you're saved and you know it,
Then your life will surely show it."

Unfortunately, there are many who would call themselves Christians who have no interest in obeying Christ. They aren't his followers, they just identify themselves with the Christian religion. There is no eternal life for those who don't embrace Christ with their lives. All who teach otherwise, by their doctrine make a mockery of the clear teaching of Scripture. Dear friend, do you believe in Christ? Have you embraced him with your life? Do you seek to obey him? If so, eternal life is yours, beginning now and extending to eternity!

But for those who don't believe, and who disobey Christ as a result of this lack of commitment, they have a terrible fate – the wrath of God.

[159] *Pisteuō*, BDAG 2aβ.
[160] *Apeitheō*, BDAG 99, from *a-*, "not" + *peithō*, "persuade, be convinced."

Wrath of God

"Whoever believes in the Son has eternal life, but **whoever rejects the Son will not see life, for God's wrath remains on him.**" (3:36)

The word "wrath," here, is *orgē*, "anger," especially, "strong indignation directed at wrongdoing, with focus on retribution, wrath," referring to God's future punitive judgment.[161]

In our day, to talk about the "wrath of God" is pretty unpopular – with unbelievers as well as believers. As a post-Christian culture, we've thoroughly rejected a preaching of hellfire and brimstone that characterized the preaching of previous eras. We have "advanced"! We believe in a God of love, not of anger. God is compassionate and forgiving, not stern and angry. Or so we think. But the Bible (contrary to our culture) makes it abundantly clear that God's wrath and punishment for sin is very real. The God of the Bible has both love for sinners who repent, and terrible judgment for those who don't repent. Consider, for example, these New Testament verses:

"The **wrath of God** is being revealed from heaven against all the godlessness and wickedness of men who suppress the truth by their wickedness." (Romans 1:18)

"Since we have now been justified by his blood, how much more shall we be saved from **God's wrath** through him!" (Romans 5:9)

"Let no one deceive you with empty words, for because of such things **God's wrath** comes on those who are disobedient." (Ephesians 5:6)

"Put to death, therefore, whatever belongs to your earthly nature: sexual immorality, impurity, lust, evil desires and greed, which is idolatry. Because of these, the **wrath of God** is coming." (Colossians 3:5-6)

"... They always heap up their sins to the limit. The **wrath of God** has come upon them at last." (1 Thessalonians 2:16)

"[We] wait for his Son from heaven, whom he raised from the dead – Jesus, who rescues us from **the coming wrath.**" (1 Thessalonians 1:10)

"They called to the mountains and the rocks, 'Fall on us and hide us from the face of him who sits on the throne and from **the wrath of the Lamb!** For **the great day of their wrath** has come, and who can stand?'" (Revelation 6:16-17)

"Then one of the four living creatures gave to the seven angels seven golden bowls filled with the **wrath of God**, who lives for ever and ever." (Revelation 15:7)

"He treads the winepress of **the fury of the wrath of God Almighty**. On his robe and on his thigh he has this name written: KING OF KINGS AND LORD OF LORDS." (Revelation 19:15-16)

Anyone who discards the wrath of God as old fashioned and unbiblical is clearly misrepresenting the truth as we find it in the New Testament.

Look at our verse again:

"Whoever believes in the Son has eternal life, but **whoever rejects the Son will not see life, for God's wrath remains on him.**" (3:36)

---

[161] *Orgē*, BDAG 721, 2b.

It teaches us that though God loves us and doesn't want us to perish (3:16), God's righteous wrath and judgment "remains"[162] on us if we don't believe. It continues as it was before. In other words, our natural state without Christ is devoid of eternal life – "will not see life" – and under judgment, subject to the wrath of God. It's the same truth as taught in John 3:16 – that without Christ we'll "perish." God's desire is for us to believe and have eternal life, but since he is a just God, our end without Christ is judgment.

> "He is patient with you, not wanting anyone to perish, but everyone to come to repentance." (2 Peter 3:9b)

Q5. (John 3:36) Is it possible to believe in God's love and God's wrath at the same time? How does God's justice allow salvation, when what we deserve is punishment for our sin and unbelief? (Hint: the "substitutionary atonement.")
http://www.joyfulheart.com/forums/topic/1417-q5-love-and-wrath/

Jesus Returns to Galilee (4:1-3)

This lesson concludes with the Pharisees becoming more aware of Jesus' increase in popularity.

> "¹ The Pharisees heard that Jesus was gaining[163] and baptizing more disciples than John, ² although in fact it was not Jesus who baptized, but his disciples. ³ When the Lord learned of this, he left Judea and went back once more to Galilee." (4:1-3)

Apparently, Jesus felt that it was safer for now to minister in Galilee, farther away from the center of power for the Jerusalem Pharisees who were hardening their resistance to him.

Lessons for Disciples

1. Discipline means spending time, the discipler with the disciple.
2. God directs our lives; we are not in competition.
3. We are to take joy in one another's successes.
4. Our control of our lives must decrease so Jesus' control of us can increase.
5. The wrath of God, eternal punishment, is a person's destiny without Jesus' life.

As Jesus' disciples we are absorbing and embracing a heavenly perspective on spiritual things, not the mistaken view of our culture.

Prayer

Father, when I look at my own heart, how I have hurt when others succeeded, how I have so often been competitive, I thank you for your grace in forgiving me. Continue to cause my sinful pride to

---

[162] "Remains" (NIV, ESV), "must endure" (NRSV), "abideth" (KJV) is *menō*, "remain, stay," here, in a transferred sense, of someone who does not leave a certain realm or sphere: "remain, continue, abide" (BDAG 631, 1aβ).

[163] "Gaining" (NIV), "making/made" (NRSV, KJV) is *poieō*, "do, make," here, "get or gain something for oneself, provide oneself with something" (BDAG 481, 5a).

decrease, so Jesus' life and direction can increase in me, so He can be easily be seen in me. Please! In Jesus' name, I pray. Amen.

Key Verses

"He must become greater; I must become less." (John 3:30, NIV)

"Whoever believes in the Son has eternal life, but whoever rejects the Son will not see life, for God's wrath remains on him." (John 3:36, NIV)

8. The Samaritan Woman at the Well (4:4-26)

John has a way of teaching us who Jesus is and what faith looks like, by giving us a glimpse into Jesus' encounters with various people – John the Baptist, Nicodemus, and surprisingly, a Samaritan woman who is shunned by her own townspeople for her immoral behavior.

C. Michael Dudash, "Living Water." Copyrighted by the artist. Permission requested.

Jesus Travels to Galilee through Samaria (4:1-4)

Jesus has been in Judea, ministering with his disciples. But the Pharisees in Jerusalem have been closely monitoring the revival meetings taking place near the Judean capital. More and more people are flocking to Jesus, so the religious protectors of the status quo are making it more dangerous for Jesus in Judea. It is time to return to his native Galilee.

> "¹ The Pharisees heard that Jesus was gaining and baptizing more disciples than John, ² although in fact it was not Jesus who baptized, but his disciples. ³ When the Lord learned of this, he left Judea and went back once more to Galilee. ⁴ Now he had to go through Samaria." (4:1-4)

There were three routes between Galilee and Jerusalem. (1) Along the coast, (2) along the Jordan valley, or (3) along the central ridge road that wound north through the passes in the mountains. The latter was the fastest and most direct, though it required travelling through Samaria. Antagonism between the Jews and Samaritans sometimes caused tension along this route (Luke 9:52), but, because of its speed, it was the route taken by most Jews going to Jerusalem,[1] except, perhaps, the strictest Jews who avoided the route to prevent contracting some kind of ceremonial uncleanness.

Our text says, however, that Jesus "had to" (NIV, NRSV) or "must needs" (KJV) take this route – perhaps because it was faster, but surely because Jesus had a divine appointment with a woman at Jacob's well outside of Sychar.

The Town of Sychar (4:5-6)

> "⁵ So he came to a town in Samaria called Sychar, near the plot of ground Jacob had given to his son Joseph. ⁶ Jacob's well was there and Jesus, tired as he was from the journey, sat down by the well. It was about the sixth hour." (4:5-6)

---

[1] Josephus, *Life*, 269; *Antiquities* 10:118.

Sychar, probably on the site of the present-day town of Aschar, is near the ancient ruins of Shechem.[2] The site lies on the ridge road between Galilee and Jerusalem in the narrow pass between two mountains, Mt. Ebal to the north (3,080 feet elevation) and Mt. Gerizim to the south (2,890 feet elevation).

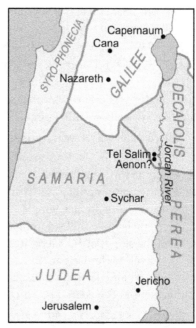

Jacob's well still exists there, fed by springs and dug out to a depth of more than 100 feet. Though the Bible doesn't tell of its initial construction, it was doubtless dug on the land Jacob purchased from the leader of the nearby city of Shechem (Genesis 33:18-20).[3]

As it was right alongside the main road, Jesus stopped there to rest at noon ("the sixth hour") while his disciples went into town to buy some food (4:8).

Jesus Is Tired (4:5)

John observes that Jesus is "tired from the journey" (4:5). Though John is very clear that Jesus is the Son of God, even "God the One and Only" who is at the Father's side (1:18), yet in his physical body, Jesus becomes tired like everyone else. John is not portraying a superman, some kind of super-hero, but a fully human man in whom the Spirit and Presence of God dwell fully. This is the mystery of the incarnation, what theologians refer to as a "hypostatic union" of two natures in one person.[4] Our best understanding of this union of two natures was carefully stated by the Council of Chalcedon in 451 AD, when church leaders gathered in order to clearly lay out the teaching of Scripture about the dual nature of Christ in order to defend it from various misunderstandings and heresies.[5]

Jesus Asks the Samaritan Woman for a Drink (4:7, 9)

A tired Jesus is sitting at the well, waiting for the disciples, when a woman appears.

[2] Urban C. von Wahlde, "Archaeology and John's Gospel," *Jesus & Archaeology*, pp. 556-559.

[3] W. Ewing and D.J. Wieand, "Jacob's Well," ISBE 2:955.

[4] The Greek noun *hypostasis* means "the essential or basic structure/nature of an entity, substantial nature, essence, actual being, reality" (the underlying structure, often in contrast to what merely seems to be, BDAG 1040, 1). So "hypostatic union" refers to the union of Christ's two natures at the substance or essential nature of his person. He was not a man pretending to be God, or God pretending to be man.

[5] The Chaldonian Definition in part, states about Christ that he is: "... acknowledged in Two Natures unconfusedly, unchangeably, indivisibly, inseparably; the difference of the Natures being in no way removed because of the Union, but rather the properties of each Nature being preserved, and (both) concurring into One Person and One Hypostasis; not as though He were parted or divided into Two Persons, but One and the Self-same Son and Only-begotten God, Word, Lord, Jesus Christ."

"7 When a Samaritan woman came to draw water, Jesus said to her, 'Will you give me a drink?' ...
9 The Samaritan woman said to him, 'You are a Jew and I am a Samaritan woman. How can you ask me for a drink?' (For Jews do not associate with Samaritans.)" (4:7, 9)

Jesus' request for a drink of water was strange at several levels.

1. Gender difference. In that culture men didn't usually initiate a conversation with women they didn't know.

"His disciples ... were surprised[6] to find him talking with a woman." (4:27)

2. Religious difference, as the woman herself observes (4:9). Jews considered Samaritans to be unclean, half-breed Jews who refused to worship in the temple at Jerusalem, but rather had developed their own hybrid religion. They had even built a temple on the slopes of Mt. Gerizim to the south so they wouldn't have to travel to Jerusalem, though it had been destroyed a century and a half before. So to use a Samaritan's vessel for water would have been considered by strict Jews to make them unclean.

"Jews do not associate with[7] Samaritans." (4:9b)

3. The Woman's Status. As the story develops, we find that the woman had had five men and was living with a sixth. Most of the time women got water from the well in the evening, not in the heat of the day. But about noon is the time the woman in our story appears, perhaps so she wouldn't have to be subject to the constant abuse from the women in the town who despise her as a home-breaker.

Detail from Polish painter Henryk Siemiradzki, 'Christ and the Samaritan Woman' (1890) 106.5×184 cm, Lviv National Art Gallery, Ukraine.

Nevertheless, Jesus asks her for a drink, and, though she doesn't refuse, she wonders aloud why he would go against the social norms to ask her for a drink.

Q1. (John 4:7-9) Why do you think Jesus went against the social norms to communicate with the woman? Why do we hesitate to go against social norms to share the good news? How do we balance our need to obey God and our need to live peaceably in our culture?
http://www.joyfulheart.com/forums/topic/1418-q1-good-news-and-social-norms/

[6] "Were surprised" (NIV), "were astonished" (NRSV), "marveled" (KJV, KJV) is *thaumazō*, "to be extraordinarily impressed or disturbed by something, wonder, marvel, be astonished" (BDAG 444, 1aγ).
[7] "Do not associate with" (NIV), "do not share things in common" (NRSV), "have no dealings with" (ESV, KJV) is the negative particle and the verb *synchraomai*, generally, "to avail oneself of something, make use of," here, "to associate on friendly terms with, have dealings with" (BDAG 953, 2), from *syn-*, "with" + *chraomai*, "make use of, employ."

My sister-in-law sometimes wears a feminist t-shirt that says, "Well-behaved women seldom make history."[8] Maybe that applies to disciples as well.

Living Water (4:10-12)

Now Jesus says something provocative, something designed to provoke a response, a religious conversation.

> "¹⁰ Jesus answered her, 'If you knew the gift of God and who it is that asks you for a drink, you would have asked him and he would have given you living water.'
> ¹¹ 'Sir,' the woman said, 'you have nothing to draw with and the well is deep. Where can you get this living water? ¹² Are you greater than our father Jacob, who gave us the well and drank from it himself, as did also his sons and his flocks and herds?'" (4:10-12)

Jesus' reply draws the woman's attention to two things: (1) his gift, and (2) his person.

"Gift" in verse 10 is *dōrea*, "that which is given or transferred freely by one person to another, gift, bounty," a word that stresses the freeness of a gift.[9]

Jesus mentions "living water." This phrase normally referred to flowing water from a river or stream, as opposed to standing water from a pond or well. But Jesus uses the word ambiguously (as is common in John's Gospel), giving the word a deeper meaning, water that imparts life, and, as we see in verse 14, a gift that imparts *eternal* life.

Though the woman probably didn't know it (because the Samaritans only recognized the authority of the Pentateuch, not the Prophets), Jesus is calling upon a Biblical metaphor. Yahweh refers to himself as "the spring of living water" (Jeremiah 2:13; 17:13), his people will drink from his "river of delights," and he offers the "fountain of life" (Psalm 36:8-9). As we'll see, Jesus uses the metaphor of living water to refer to the gift of the Spirit in 7:37-39. And the metaphor appears as a symbol of eternal life in Revelation (7:17; 22:1, 17). The phrase "gift (*dōrea*) of the Holy Spirit" appears in Acts 2:38 and 10:45. "Heavenly gift (*dōrea*) is found in Hebrews 6:4.

> "If you knew the gift of God and who it is that asks you for a drink, you would have asked him and he would have given you living water." (4:10)

Jesus is obviously speaking metaphorically, but the woman seems to take it literally, perhaps of the underground spring that fed the well deep below where they were. She points out that he doesn't have any way to draw water from the well, and that somehow Jesus is exalting himself over the patriarch Jacob who dug the well.

A Spring of Water Welling up to Eternal Life (4:13-15)

Jesus ignores her lack of understanding, but continues to explain the gift he is talking about. He compares literal water with spiritual water.

---

[8] The phrase originated with Harvard history professor Laurel Thatcher Ulrich, in her article, "Vertuous Women Found: New England Ministerial Literature, 1668-1735," *American Quarterly*, Volume 28, Number 1, Spring 1976, p. 20. In 2007 she wrote a book titled with the quote, published by Alfred A. Knopf. Ulrich is active in the LDS.

[9] *Dōrea*, BDAG 266.

"13 Jesus answered, 'Everyone who drinks this water will be thirsty again, 14 but whoever drinks the water I give him will never thirst. Indeed, the water I give him will become in him a spring of water welling up to eternal life.'

15 The woman said to him, 'Sir, give me this water so that I won't get thirsty and have to keep coming here to draw water.'" (4:13-15)

The woman still doesn't seem to understand.

Jesus makes two claims for those who drink this Living Water.

1. They will never thirst.
2. They will have eternal life.

We will never thirst in the sense that we will always be in touch with God through the Spirit, in the flow of God's eternal supply. We will have eternal life because the Holy Spirit who "seals" us (as Paul would say), preserves us until the coming of Christ. And that eternal life begins when we receive the Holy Spirit – everything becomes new. The expression in verse 14b is of a "spring welling up to eternal life." "Welling up" (NIV, ESV), "gushing up" (NRSV), "springing up" (KJV) is *hallomai*, literally, "to make a quick leaping movement, leap, spring up," here used figuratively of the quick movement of inanimate things, "to spring up from a source," of water, "well up, bubble up."[10]

It is clear that Jesus is speaking here of the gift of the Holy Spirit, as he does in a variety of ways elsewhere in John:

- "Baptize with the Holy Spirit." (1:33b)
- "Born of the Spirit." (3:8b)
- "In him a spring of water welling up to eternal life." (4:14)
- "Streams of living water will flow from within him." (7:38)
- "Another Counselor (*paraklētos*) to be with you forever." (14:16)
- "The Counselor, the Holy Spirit, whom the Father will send in my name." (14:26)
- "The Counselor ... whom I will send to you from the Father, the Spirit of truth." (15:26; 16:7)
- "Receive the Holy Spirit." (20:22)

Of all the Gospels, John has the most developed teaching – by far – concerning the difference the Holy Spirit makes in the life of a believer.

The Spirit in us is an active, powerful, life-giving spring flowing with amazing "water pressure," and – if we will follow his leading – will enable and propel us to do things far beyond our ability. And this Spirit, birth of this Spirit, moves us from the temporal to the eternal plane. Our "eternal life" begins when we are born by this Spirit!

Q2. (John 4:9-15) Jesus' words to the woman in verses 10-13 seem to imply that all people are spiritually thirsty. What has been your experience? Does the woman seem spiritually thirsty at this point? What caused her deep thirst to surface? What does this teach us about our own witness?
http://www.joyfulheart.com/forums/topic/1419-q2-spiritual-thirst/

---

[10] *Hallomai*, BDAG 46, 2.

Note: Believing Christians disagree about some of these issues. Be gentle and loving as you respond to one another.

Q3. (John 4:9-15) What does the "gift of God" and the "living water" (4:9) refer to? What does receiving this gift result in (4:14)? Does this gift differ from or is another way of saying the "baptism with the Spirit" that John the Baptist spoke about in 1:33?
http://www.joyfulheart.com/forums/topic/1420-q3-the-gift-of-god/

The Woman's Five Husbands (4:16-19)

Back to the conversation between Jesus and the woman. They have been talking about water and getting a drink. So far, the woman hasn't understood what Jesus is saying on the spiritual level. So he engages her attention in a different way. It is important to understand that the Greek word *anēr* can mean both "man, adult male" *and* "husband," just as the Hebrew *'îsh* can mean both "man" and "husband."

"¹⁶ He told her, 'Go, call your husband and come back.'

¹⁷ 'I have no husband,' she replied.

Jesus said to her, 'You are right when you say you have no husband. ¹⁸ The fact is, you have had five husbands, and the man you now have is not your husband. What you have just said is quite true.'

¹⁹ 'Sir,' the woman said, 'I can see that you are a prophet.'" (4:16-19)

Can you imagine what the woman felt when Jesus told her this? Everyone in Sychar knew, of course. It was a small town. But for a complete stranger to tell her the embarrassing truth about her history with men would have shaken her! These are the possibilities:

1. She could have had five actual husbands who had either died or divorced her.
2. She could have had five lovers among the men in town, who, like her current "man," wasn't hers in the sense of being her husband.

She wasn't a prostitute, apparently, who had sex for money. But she was the loose woman, the town home-wrecker who went from man to man looking for something that didn't belong to her.

The Source of Jesus' Knowledge

How did Jesus know this about the woman? Or Nathanael sitting under the fig tree (1:48), for that matter?

1. Gossip. He was familiar with the village scuttle-but at Sychar. Unlikely, because Jews didn't mingle with Samaritans. And the woman attributed it to him as being a prophet.

2. Divinity. He was God so He knew everything. It is true that Jesus was and is God. Some people explain all Jesus' miracles on this basis. But in some sense, Jesus "emptied himself" (Philippians 2:7), divested himself not of his divinity, but of some of the attributes of his divinity – his manifest glory, for example. Luke says that he "grew[11] in wisdom and stature, and in favor with God and men" (Luke 2:52).

3. Holy Spirit. Though many would see Jesus' divinity as the source of Jesus' special knowledge on this occasion, I believe it came from the anointing of the Holy Spirit that he was given when he began his ministry (1:33; Acts 10:38; Luke 3:22; 4:1, 14). Jesus is rather clear that he doesn't act on his own volition. He operates by listening to and emulating the Father (5:19), and that when he goes he will send the Holy Spirit who will empower believers to "do what I have been doing. He will do even greater things than these, because I am going to the Father" (14:12). I believe that Jesus is our exemplar for ministry. Subject to God's direction, we can do what he did through the Holy Spirit's gifts (1 Corinthians 12:1-11).

There are some believers today to whom the Holy Spirit will give a prophetic "word" for a person, or will have special knowledge of a person's condition to increase their faith so God might work in them. Sometimes this "word of knowledge" can work in tandem with "gifts of healings." Often, though not always, of course.

> **Q4. (John 4:16-19) What was the effect of Jesus' special knowledge of the woman's history with men? What effect did it have on her faith? How can such gifts of the Spirit work today to bring people to faith or deepen their faith?**
> **http://www.joyfulheart.com/forums/topic/1421-q4-a-word-of-knowledge/**

Worship on Mt. Gerizim or in Jerusalem (4:19-22)

"'Sir,' the woman said, 'I can see that you are a prophet." (4:19)

Though the woman had been profoundly shaken by Jesus' revelation of her history with men, her immediate response seems to be to engage him in a long-standing religious controversy between the Samaritan and Jewish religions.

A bit of history will help clarify the situation. Samaria was part of the Northern Kingdom that had rebelled against the Assyrians in 722 BC. In order to quell rebellious provinces, it was their practice to exile the leaders to areas of Assyria and then, in their place, resettle people on their land from other areas of the realm. So far as we are told, few, if any, people exiled from the Northern Kingdom ever returned to their land. The result was that, while the area of Samaria retained a belief in Yahweh and the Pentateuch, they rejected the rest of the Old Testament. The Jews considered them heretics and apostates, and had nothing to do with them.

Like their forefathers in the Northern Kingdom, they refused to recognize Jerusalem as the center of worship. Rather, in the fourth century BC, the Samaritans had built a temple on the slopes of Mt. Gerizim. It was destroyed in 128 BC by Hyrcanus, a Jewish king. Nevertheless, the Samaritans

---

[11] "Grew" (NIV), "increased" (NRSV, KJV) is *prokoptō*, "to move forward to an improved state, progress, advance" (BDAG 871, 2).

maintained that Mt. Gerizim was the proper place to worship, while the Jews insisted on worshipping in Jerusalem (4:20).[12]

So when the woman recognized that Jesus was a prophet she said:

"'20 Our fathers worshiped on this mountain, but you Jews claim that the place where we must worship is in Jerusalem.'

21 Jesus declared, 'Believe me, woman, a time is coming when you will worship the Father neither on this mountain nor in Jerusalem. 22 You Samaritans worship what you do not know; we worship what we do know, for salvation is from the Jews." (4:20-22)

Jesus affirmed that "salvation is from the Jews," that the Jewish understanding of where to worship was correct. But he quickly stated that it would soon become obsolete! No doubt he foresaw the destruction of the Jerusalem temple by the Romans in 70 AD, after which Jerusalem was no longer the center of Judaism – until the second half of the twentieth century!

Q5. (John 4:19-22) What motives cause the woman to bring up a religious controversy to Jesus? Why do people today try to generate religious controversies with us? What are their motives?
http://www.joyfulheart.com/forums/topic/1422-q5-provoking-controversy/

Worship in Spirit and in Truth (4:23-24)

Jesus looks forward to a new era of worship.

"'23 Yet a time is coming and has now come when the true worshipers will worship the Father in spirit and truth, for they are the kind of worshipers the Father seeks. 24 God is spirit, and his worshipers must worship in spirit and in truth.'" (4:23-24)

Let's break these verses into their important phrases:

A New Era (4:23a)

"... A time[13] is coming[14] and has now come[15]...." (4:23a)

Jesus is ushering in a new age, the Age of the Kingdom. Following John the Baptist's lead, Jesus began his ministry preaching:

"The time has come. The kingdom of God is near.[16] Repent and believe the good news!" (Mark 1:15)

---

[12] R.T. Anderson, "Samaritans," ISBE 4:303-308; H.F. Vos, "Gerizim, Mount," ISBE 2:448-449.

[13] "Time" (NIV), "hour" (NRSV, ESV, KJV) is *hōra*, "hour," here, "a point of time as an occasion for an event, time" (BDAG 1103, 3).

[14] The verb is *erchomai*, "to come," here with the idea of "to take place" (BDAG 394, 4aα) The first occurrence is in the present, active sense, which suggests that its coming is still going on a Jesus speaks.

[15] "Has now come" (NIV), "is now here" (NRSV, ESV) or "now is" (KJV) is the temporal adverb of time *nyn*, "now" (BDAG 681, 1aα aleph), plus the verb *eimi*, "to be," here probably "to take place as a phenomenon or event, take place, occur, become, be, be in" (BDAG 285, 6). The tense of *eimi* is the present, active tense, going on as Jesus speaks.

With Jesus comes the long-prophesied Kingdom of God. It is both present as he declares it, and will come in its fullness when he returns in glory. Jesus is saying to the Samaritan woman that the time of spiritual worship of God's people has fully arrived, (and will be clear to all when the temple has been destroyed).

True Worshipers (4:23b)

"The true worshipers will worship the Father in spirit and truth, for they are the kind of worshipers the Father seeks." (4:23)

In John's Gospel, we frequently see the adjective "true" in the sense of, "pertaining to being real, genuine, authentic."[17]

- "The true light" (1:9)
- "True worshippers" (4:23)
- "True bread from heaven" (6:32)
- "True vine" (15:1)
- "Only true God" (17:3; cf. 7:28)

But John's use of "true" sometimes goes beyond the idea of "authentic" to the idea of "ultimate," reflecting the ultimate revelation of God's truth[18] – the ultimate Light, the ultimate Manna/Bread, the ultimate Vine. Jesus is looking forward to the "true worshipers," who are not tied to a race or religion, but worship the Father "in spirit and truth."

God Is Spirit (4:24a)

But what does "in spirit and truth" mean? First we must ask what it means that "God is spirit..." (4:24). The text shouldn't read "God is a spirit," as in the KJV, suggesting he is one among many; there is no article. "God is spirit" doesn't mean only that God is incorporeal, invisible, though it does mean that (in contrast to LDS teaching that God has a corporeal body[19]). Spirit in the Old Testament includes the ideas of renovative, creative, life-giving, so saying "God is spirit" suggests those concepts as well. Of course, "God is spirit" doesn't completely describe God, any more than "God is light" (1 John 1:5) and "God is love" (1 John 4:8) describe all his attributes.

But here John seems to be focusing on the idea that God is invisible and omnipresent, not to be represented by any kind of physical object nor confined to any single place.

---

[16] The time (*kairos*, "right time, opportune time") has arrived (*plēroō*, "to complete a period of time, fill (up), complete" (BDAG 828, 2). "Has come" is in the perfect tense, denoting a past action and affirming an existing result, which is standing at the present time. "Is near" (NIV), "has come near" (NRSV), "is at hand" (KJV, ESV) is *engizō*, draw near, come near, approach," in a temporal sense (BDAG 270, 2). It, too, is in the perfect tense, denoting a past action that is true up to the present time.

[17] *Alēthinos*, BDAG 43, 3b.

[18] Carson, *John*, p. 122.

[19] See http://www.mormon.org/faq/nature-of-god/

Worship in Spirit and in Truth (4:23c-24)

"23 Yet a time is coming and has now come when the true worshipers will worship the Father in spirit and truth, for they are the kind of worshipers the Father seeks. 24 God is spirit, and his worshipers must worship in spirit and in truth." (4:23-24)

Worship "in spirit" can be taken at more than one level – as is typical of John's Gospel. It refers to worship that is spiritual, rather merely physical, such as going though the physical motions of worship (showing up, sacrificing, bringing gifts, kneeling, lifting hands, etc.) in some holy place – whether Jerusalem or Mt. Gerizim or elsewhere. But since Jesus has taught that only those who are born by the Holy Spirit are in the Kingdom, these "true worshipers" must also approach God by means of the Holy Spirit within them. Unless they are born by the Spirit, they can't truly worship God.

Worship "in truth" can also be taken at two levels. First, Jesus has just affirmed the superiority of the Jews' understanding of proper worship vs. the Samaritans (4:22). *Alētheia*, "truth," can refer to "the content of what is true," proper doctrine, embracing Jesus' teachings. But it can also refer to "an actual event or state, reality" as opposed to mere appearance, in the sense that we find in John's First Epistle:

"Dear children, let us not love with words or tongue but with actions and in truth." (1 John 3:18)

It is quite possible for us believers to gather on Sunday – or in our daily devotions – and just go through the motions of worship, with our mind and heart elsewhere, perhaps even half-asleep. To be a true worshiper that the Father seeks, we must enter into worship by the Holy Spirit, with our heart and intent to be focused on him. He is seeking authentic, genuine worship, not just lip-service.

Q6. (John 4:23-24) What does it mean that "God is spirit"? What does it mean to worship in spirit and in truth? Have you ever "gone through the motions" of worship without worshipping? How can you worship in a way more pleasing to God?
http://www.joyfulheart.com/forums/topic/1423-q6-spiritual-worship/

I Am the Christ (4:25-26)

Jesus' encounter at the well of Samaria ends with the woman's growing awareness that Jesus is more than just "a prophet" but "*the* Prophet" whom the Samaritans (and Jews) saw as the Messiah who was coming (Deuteronomy 18:15-18).

"25 The woman said, 'I know that Messiah' (called Christ) 'is coming. When he comes, he will explain everything to us.'

26 Then Jesus declared, 'I who speak to you am he.'" (4:25-26)

Rarely is Jesus so open with anyone at this stage of his ministry, that he is indeed the Messiah (Matthew 16:20; Mark 8:30). But here in Samaria, Jesus has little to fear that word will travel to his enemies in Jerusalem that he has declared himself the Messiah, so Jesus tells her openly: "I who speak to you am he!" This thirsty Samaritan woman is beginning to understand her deep need for salvation and wholeness – and Jesus is her answer.

We'll examine the rest of the story – the result of the woman's faith – in the next lesson (4:27-42)

Lessons for Disciples

But first let's consider what we have learned so far in this passage that can help us grow as disciples.

1.   Jesus gets tired. His is human – *and* divine.
2.   Jesus is willing to break social norms to minister to people.
3.   Jesus offers truth a bit at a time to tantalize the woman into asking for more.
4.   The gift of the Holy Spirit brings eternal life.
5.   Jesus uses prophetic insight, perhaps the spiritual gift of the "word of knowledge," to get the woman's attention.
6.   Jesus looks forward to worship not tied to place, but by the Holy Spirit, and in reality – real spiritual worship.

Prayer

Father, thank you that Jesus doesn't leave us at the surface, but probes until he can lead us deeper. Help us to drink deeply at the well of your Living Water! Help us never take your Holy Spirit for granted. Thank you for your incredible grace that brings us to faith and sustains us unto eternal life. In Jesus' name, we pray. Amen.

Key Verses

"If you knew the gift of God and who it is that asks you for a drink, you would have asked him and he would have given you living water." (John 4:10, NIV)

"Everyone who drinks this water will be thirsty again, but whoever drinks the water I give him will never thirst. Indeed, the water I give him will become in him a spring of water welling up to eternal life." (John 4:13-14, NIV)

"A time is coming and has now come when the true worshipers will worship the Father in spirit and truth, for they are the kind of worshipers the Father seeks. God is spirit, and his worshipers must worship in spirit and in truth." (John 4:23-24, NIV)

"The woman said, 'I know that Messiah' (called Christ) 'is coming. When he comes, he will explain everything to us.' Then Jesus declared, 'I who speak to you am he.'" (John 4:25-26, NIV)

9. The Fields Are Ripe for Harvest (4:27-42)

We are so often blind to the people – both to their spiritual needs and to their readiness and openness to Jesus. We see their lifestyle and sometimes hard attitudes, and forget that God is able to work powerfully in them when the time is right. This is a lesson about taking the blinders off regarding the people around us.

We met the woman at the well in Lesson 8. But her story continues as it opens up a whole Samaritan village to faith and leads Jesus' band of disciples to develop new eyes to see the harvest.

The fields are ripe for harvest.

The Disciples' Return and the Woman Testifies (4:27-30)

Verses 27-30 are transitional. Jesus' disciples return and the woman returns to town.

"27 Just then his disciples returned and were surprised to find him talking with a woman. But no one asked, 'What do you want?' or 'Why are you talking with her?'
28 Then, leaving her water jar, the woman went back to the town and said to the people, 29 'Come, see a man who told me everything I ever did. Could this be the Christ?'
30 They came out of the town and made their way toward him." (4:27-30)

Notice that woman left her water jar at the well. Why? She is in such a hurry to tell her neighbors about the One she has discovered, that she leaves everything behind to rush back to the town.

She doesn't even like her neighbors probably – they are so mean to her! But she can't help herself. She rushes back to tell them anyway!

"Come, see a man who told me everything I ever did. Could this be the Christ?" (4:29)

She's exaggerating, of course, like we do when we're excited. Jesus, through the Holy Spirit, had put his finger on the sore, festering, defining sin of her life. He saw into her life and loved her anyway. He offered her living water, eternal life. She had to tell!

She reminds me of John the Baptist who has to tell his disciples, "Look, the Lamb of God!" (1:36), and Andrew, who "first thing" has to tell his brother Simon Peter (1:41), and Philip who had to tell his friend Nathanael (1:45).

"He can't be the Messiah, can he?" the Samaritan woman says to her neighbors.[183]

Her neighbors – especially the wives – don't like this particular Samaritan woman, but they can't help but see that something is different about her. Her encounter with the man whom she is telling them about has changed her. That is clear.

---

[183] The sentence, "could this be the Christ?" begins with *mēti*, a marker that invites a negative response to the question that it introduces (BDAG 649). The NRSV gets the sense of the Greek: "He cannot be the Messiah, can he?"

So they begin to leave what they're doing in town and make their way to the well outside of town. The verbs in verse 30 are both present tense, suggesting continuing action. While Jesus is talking with his disciples and talking about food and the white harvest, there is a steady stream of people leaving the city and beginning to approach Jesus.

Food You Don't Understand (4:31-34)

"Meanwhile" – while these people are coming – Jesus' disciples are trying to get him to eat the food they've bought in town.

> "31 Meanwhile his disciples urged him, 'Rabbi, eat[184] something.' 32 But he said to them, 'I have food to eat that you know nothing about.' 33 Then his disciples said to each other, 'Could someone have brought him food?' 34 'My food,' said Jesus, 'is to do the will of him who sent me and to finish his work.'" (4:31-34)

I can imagine Jesus' disciples pressing him to eat. "Jesus, you're tired! You're hungry! Eat something! But Jesus replies cryptically:

> "I have food[185] to eat that you know nothing about." (4:32)

It's clear now that he is using the concept of "food" in a figurative way as he does elsewhere in this Gospel – just as he used "water" figuratively and confused the woman at the well (4:10-14).

> "Do not work for food that spoils, but for food that endures to eternal life, which the Son of Man will give you. " (6:27a)

> "For my flesh is real food and my blood is real drink." (6:55)

What does he mean in our passage? He is saying: "What gives me energy, what motivates me, what 'gets my juices flowing' is to do my Father's work!" It's like he said in another context, quoting from Deuteronomy 8:3 –

> "Man does not live on bread alone, but on every word that comes from the mouth of God." (Matthew 4:4)

Yes, we need physical food. But there are things more important than food! If we spend all our energies on our own maintenance, we don't have time for the Father's work.

Dear friend, how much of your energy do you spend on doing the work the Father has assigned to you? Oh, I don't have any assignment, you might say. Yes you do!

What are you personally doing about the desperate spiritual need of your neighbors and in your neighborhood? What are you doing about the desperate spiritual need you see in your family members or grandchildren,

James J. Tissot, "The Sower" (1886-94), watercolor, Brooklyn Museum, New York.

---

[184] "Eat" is *esthiō*, "to take something in through the mouth, usually solids, but also liquids, eat" (BDAG 396, 1a).

[185] "Food" (NIV, NRSV), "meat" (KJV) in verse 32 is *brōsis*, "eating," then what is eaten, "food," here used figuratively (BDAG 185, 3b). "Food" (NIV, NRSV), "meat" (KJV) in verse 34 is *brōma*, "that which is eaten, food," here figuratively, "nourishment of a transcendent nature, means of sustenance, food" (BDAG 184, 2).

nieces and nephews. They are your assignment! God has put you there. You must find out from the Lord *how* to minister to them, since they are your responsibility, your "field" to work. Jesus is seeking to teach his disciples about the urgency of doing the Father's work.

> **Q1. (John 4:31-34) What does Jesus mean by "food" in these verses? What was his passion? What is your passion? What will it take so that your passion, your goal in life, is to do the Father's work? In your life, what do you think that might look like?**
> **http://www.joyfulheart.com/forums/topic/1424-q1-jesus-passion/**

Fields Are Ripe for Harvest (4:35)

As he is speaking, I believe that Jesus turns and extends his hand towards the crowd of Samaritan townspeople who are approaching him, and says,

> "Do you not say, 'Four months more and then the harvest'? I tell you, open your eyes and look at the fields! They are ripe[186] for harvest." (4:35)

The phrase "Four months more and then the harvest," may have been rural proverb about the time between the last of sowing in the fall and harvest in the spring – about four months. It shouldn't be used to date this incident which seems to have taken place shortly after Passover in March or April. Jesus seems to be saying: Normally there's a time span between sowing and harvest. But he has barely begun to sow (to the Samaritan woman) and immediately comes the harvest of people coming to faith in Christ.

Jesus is comparing an agricultural harvest to a spiritual harvest. When he says, "look at the fields" (4:35b), he has in mind – and perhaps is pointing to the crowd of Samaritans coming up the path as he is speaking. And when he says "harvest" he is talking about bringing people from unbelief to faith and from sin and destruction to eternal life.[187] This accords with John's purpose in writing this Gospel:

> "... that you may believe that Jesus is the Christ, the Son of God, and that by believing you may have life in his name." (20:31)

Jesus tells his disciples, "open your eyes" (NIV), "look around you" (NRSV), "lift up your eyes" (ESV, KJV). So often we are blind to the spiritual state of others, such as their state of readiness to receive Christ. Jesus tells his disciples to become alert to the readiness of the harvest.

On another occasion, Jesus looks out at the crowds and talks about the enormity of the task of the harvest:

> "When he saw the crowds, he had compassion on them, because they were harassed and helpless, like sheep without a shepherd. Then he said to his disciples, 'The harvest is plentiful but the

---

[186] "Ripe" (NIV, NRSV), "white" (ESV, KJV) is interesting. "White" clearly means "ripe" here, but few crops are "white" when they are ready to harvest. Perhaps it should be translated "bright, shining, gleaming" rather than green (*leukos*, BDAG 593, 1). Some have thought that "white" refers to the clothing of the Samaritans who are coming towards Jesus (Morris, *John*, p. 279, fn. 85).

[187] A number of Christian hymns use this kind of language, such as "Bringing in the Sheaves" and "Come Ye Thankful People Come."

workers are few. Ask the Lord of the harvest, therefore, to send out workers into his harvest field.'" (Matthew 9:36-38)

Q2. (John 4:35) What caused the harvest to ripen so rapidly in Sychar? How likely is it that the testimony of one, discredited woman could make such a huge impact? What might God do with your testimony if you were to share it? Why is it necessary to "open our eyes" to see the potential spiritual harvest?
http://www.joyfulheart.com/forums/topic/1425-q2-eyes-for-the-harvest/

Sowers and Reapers (4:36-38)

We see this kind of agricultural analogy of sowing and reaping in several of Jesus' other parables, such as:

- The Parable of the Sower (Matthew 13:3-9, 18-23)

- The Parable of the Weeds or Tares (Matthew 13:24-30, 36-43)

- The Seed Growing Secretly (Mark 4:26-29)

In our passage, Jesus continues:

"³⁶ Even now the reaper draws his wages, even now he harvests the crop for eternal life, so that the sower and the reaper may be glad together. ³⁷ Thus the saying 'One sows and another reaps' is true. ³⁸ I sent you to reap what you have not worked for. Others have done the hard work, and you have reaped the benefits of their labor." (4:36-38)

Sickles were used to harvest gain as far back as the Neolithic era. Illustrator unknown.

Jesus seems to base his spiritual metaphor concerning sowers and reapers on a popular proverb of the day: "One sows and another reaps." He is almost ready to reap a harvest, that is, bring to salvation, a whole Samaritan town. In the analogy, both sower and reaper are glad, because when the harvest comes in, the sower (usually the farmer himself) and the reapers (often temporary workers hired to get in the harvest quickly) get paid.

Who sowed the seed that resulted in the spiritual harvest of this Samaritan town? Perhaps the Old Testament prophets or the Father, who prepared them for this hour.

Jesus alludes to his disciples' successful ministry as well:

"I sent you to reap what you have not worked for. Others have done the hard work, and you have reaped the benefits of their labor." (4:38)

In the West, we have a similar metaphor of dwarfs standing on the shoulders of giants, meaning that we discover new truths by building on previous discoveries.[188] We should take appropriate pride in doing our own work well, but we must never forget that it isn't all about us. Jesus' own ministry

---

[188] The quotation is attributed to a 1676 letter of Isaac Newton, though it goes back at least to Bernard of Chartres in the twelfth century.

built on that of John the Baptist, who stood in a long line of prophets who had preached repentance and faith even before him.

To the Corinthian church that was denigrating one preacher and exalting another, the Apostle Paul used a similar analogy:

> "What, after all, is Apollos? And what is Paul? Only servants, through whom you came to believe – as the Lord has assigned to each his task. I planted the seed, Apollos watered it, but God made it grow. So neither he who plants nor he who waters is anything, but only God, who makes things grow. The man who plants and the man who waters have one purpose, and each will be rewarded according to his own labor." (1 Corinthians 3:5-8)

Whether your ministry is primarily to sow (share your faith, testify, preach), to water (disciple-ship), or to reap (lead people to Christ), all are important – and when the harvest comes in, everyone will "get paid."

But, Paul, reminds us, as he shifts his analogy from sowing and reaping to building:

> "Each one should be careful how he builds." (1 Corinthians 3:10)

Each of us is responsible for the quality of our work. We can't be lazy or sloppy! That dishonors the "Lord of the harvest" who calls us (Matthew 9:38).

Q3. (John 4:36-38) Sowers and reapers usually got "paid" when the crop was harvested. According to this analogy, what will Christian workers receive at the end of the age when the final harvest takes place and Christ comes?
http://www.joyfulheart.com/forums/topic/1426-q3-rewards-for-workers/

The Samaritans Believed (4:39-42)

Notice the remarkable result of one woman's testimony – and a despised woman at that!

> "³⁹ Many of the Samaritans from that town believed in him because of the woman's testimony, 'He told me everything I ever did.' ⁴⁰ So when the Samaritans came to him, they urged him to stay with them, and he stayed two days. ⁴¹ And because of his words many more became believers. ⁴² They said to the woman, 'We no longer believe just because of what you said; now we have heard for ourselves, and we know that this man really is the Savior of the world.'" (4:39-42)

The progression is clear. Many believed because of the woman's testimony – that is, they believed enough to seek out Jesus themselves and came to a greater, more complete faith. Others who didn't come out initially became believers when Jesus and his disciples stayed in the village for two additional days!

It's our job to bring people to a place where they can listen to Jesus for themselves. Ultimately, it is Jesus' own words that they will believe or disbelieve.

Changing His Ministry Plan (4:40)

It is quite remarkable that Jesus stayed in this Samaritan town for two days. Many strict Jews would have considered him disgusting, unclean by his voluntary social contact with the Samaritans. I expect that it was difficult for the disciples themselves to adapt this way. It went against everything they had always believed and all their prejudices.

Indeed, on other occasions Jesus hesitated to preach outside of Israel (Mark 7:24-30) and instructed his disciples:

> "Do not go among the Gentiles or enter any town of the Samaritans. Go rather to the lost sheep of Israel." (Matthew 10:5-6)

But this was a special case, an exception to the rule. We know that Jesus didn't let men's traditions keep him from his ministry – even though it upset the Pharisees. Here, he didn't let his own "rules" prevent him from ministering to the Samaritans, even though that wasn't the main focus of his ministry.

Savior of the World (4:42b)

This extended section on Jesus' ministry in Samaria concludes with the Samaritans' words:

> "We know that this man really is the Savior of the world.[189]" (4:42b)

Though this story isn't included by the other Gospel writers, John includes it to underscore Jesus' ministry outside of Israel, such as the Gentiles the Apostle John is ministering to in Ephesus and elsewhere. A number of verses in John's writings allude to Christ being Savior of the World:

> "Look, the Lamb of God, who **takes away the sin of the world**!" (1:29)

> "For **God so loved the world** that he gave his one and only Son, that whoever believes in him shall not perish but have eternal life. For God did not send his Son **into the world** to condemn the world, but to save the world through him." (3:16-17)

> "I did not come to **judge the world**, but to save it." (12:47b)

> "And we have seen and testify that the Father has sent his Son to be the **Savior of the world.**" (1 John 4:14)

> "He is the atoning sacrifice for our sins, and not only for ours but also for **the sins of the whole world.**" (1 John 2:2)

We also see this emphasis elsewhere in the New Testament, for example:

> "I bring you good news of great joy that will be for **all the people.**" (Luke 2:10)

> "'**Anyone** who trusts in him will never be put to shame.' For there is no difference between Jew and Gentile.... 'Everyone who calls on the name of the Lord will be saved.'" (Romans 10:11, 13)

Jesus is not a Jewish Messiah only – or a Messiah to twenty-first century Americans. He is the Savior of the whole world. And because this is true, his commission to us is to take the gospel to the whole world.

> "Therefore go and make disciples of all nations...." (Matthew 28:19a)

---

[189] "World" is *kosmos*, "world," here of humanity in general (BDAG 562, 6b).

"You will receive power when the Holy Spirit comes on you; and you will be my witnesses in Jerusalem, and in all Judea and Samaria, and to the ends of the earth." (Acts 1:8)

What began in Israel, spread to Samaria. When Philip came to Samaria a decade or so later, many people responded to his ministry there – Jesus had sown the seed. And the gospel spread to Asia Minor and to Europe. To India and Asia and the British Isles and to the Americas. Our prayer is that someday:

"The earth will be full of the knowledge of the LORD
as the waters cover the sea." (Isaiah 11:9)

"that at the name of Jesus every knee should bow,
in heaven and on earth and under the earth,
and every tongue confess that Jesus Christ is Lord,
to the glory of God the Father." (Philippians 2:10-11)

Come soon, oh Savior of the World!

Q4. (John 4:39-42). Why do you think Jesus stayed two days in Samaria, when elsewhere he instructed his disciples not to preach in Samaritan villages? What does it mean that Jesus is the Savior of the whole world? What are its implications for our lives? For your church's mission? http://www.joyfulheart.com/forums/topic/1427-q4-savior-of-the-world/

Lessons for Disciples

What are the lessons we can learn from this passage as disciples?

1. The testimony of a transformed person is extremely powerful in drawing friends and acquaintances to Christ.
2. Jesus' mission was the focus of his life and passion, and what energized him far more than food. Does our mission energize us?
3. A spiritual harvest can happen any time when God prepares people – even seemingly hardened people. We need to look at people as if God is working in them, not as impossible cases.
4. We will be rewarded for our labors when Christ returns and "reaps the final harvest."
5. Jesus is the Savior of the world.
6. Jesus altered his normal ministry parameters temporarily when the Father opened new doors.

Prayer

O Lord, take away our prejudices of race and upbringing, of what part of town a person lives in or how much money others have. Forgive us for our parochialism and narrowness and selfishness. Give us a world vision of the world-wide harvest that you are seeking in our day. Give us eyes to see the magnitude of this harvest and to volunteer to be your hands extended. Give us zeal so that our passion is not for gourmet food and selfish luxuries, but that our food is to do your work. Help us to find our satisfaction in you! In Jesus' name, we pray. Amen.

Key Verses

"His disciples urged him, 'Rabbi, eat something.' But he said to them, 'I have food to eat that you know nothing about.' Then his disciples said to each other, 'Could someone have brought him food?' 'My food,' said Jesus, 'is to do the will of him who sent me and to finish his work.'" (John 4:31-34, NIV)

"Do you not say, 'Four months more and then the harvest'? I tell you, open your eyes and look at the fields! They are ripe for harvest." (John 4:35, NIV)

"They said to the woman, 'We no longer believe just because of what you said; now we have heard for ourselves, and we know that this man really is the Savior of the world.'" (John 4: 42, NIV)

10. Healing the Royal Official's Son (4:43-54)

On his way to Galilee from Judea, Jesus had an encounter with a woman at the well of Sychar, and spent two days in Samaria. And in Sychar he had an unexpectedly positive reception. Now he resumes his travel north to Galilee and arrives in Cana.

This lesson is relatively short, but contains some important lessons in faith.

Jesus Travels to Galilee (4:43-46a)

"[43] After the two days he left for Galilee. [44] (Now Jesus himself had pointed out that a prophet has no honor in his own country.) [45] When he arrived in Galilee, the Galileans welcomed him. They had seen all that he had done in Jerusalem at the Passover Feast, for they also had been there. [46] Once more he visited Cana in Galilee, where he had turned the water into wine." (4:43-46a)

From Sychar Jesus moves into the southern districts of Galilee and arrives at Cana.

At first glance it seems strange that in verse 44 John recalls Jesus' comment that a prophet has no honor in his own country (*patris*[190]), and in the very next sentence says that the Galileans welcomed him.

The royal official implores Jesus to heal his son. Illustrator unknown.

In John's Gospel, Jesus has seen growing opposition in Judea (4:1-3), prompting him to travel to his home area of Galilee. But John is warning the reader not to expect sudden acceptance even in Galilee. It won't be like the acceptance he had experienced in Sychar. As we'll see in verse 48, the Galilean's belief in him was largely based on his miraculous signs, not in recognizing who he was. Just because Jesus is a Galilean doesn't mean they'll see Jesus for who he is, any more than the Judeans had. Nevertheless, Jesus initial welcome in Galilee was quite positive, since the Galileans knew of the miracles Jesus had performed in Jerusalem at Passover.

---

[190] *Patris*, literally, "of one's fathers" can refer to "a relatively large geographical area associated with one's familial connections and personal life, fatherland, homeland," or to the locale of one's immediate family, "hometown, one's own part of the country" (BDAG 788, 1). In the Synoptic Gospels, the context of this saying is in Jesus' hometown of Nazareth, though the same word (*patris*) occurs in both John and the Synoptics.

The Royal Official's Son (4:46b-47)

John has set the scene. Now he introduces the desperate need that Jesus meets in Cana. A man's son is burning up of a fever and is nearly dead.

> "And there was a certain royal official whose son[191] lay sick at Capernaum. [47] When this man heard that Jesus had arrived in Galilee from Judea, he went to him and begged him to come and heal his son, who was close to death." (4:46b-47)

Jesus has been in Cana for several days – long enough for word to reach Capernaum that Jesus was back in Galilee. Immediately upon hearing that Jesus is in Cana, an important man with a dying son rushes up the road from Capernaum to Cana, a distance of about 20 miles, and a rise from the Sea of Galilee of about 1,250 feet (382 meters), a good two days' journey on foot – probably less on horseback, since this man was a wealthy official. He would probably have gone south west from Capernaum along the lake, then at Tiberius up the road into the mountains to Cana.[192]

This resident of Capernaum is an official in service of Herod Antipas (reigned 4 BC to 39 AD), tetrarch of Galilee and Perea, and considered a king or "royal" by the populace.[193] Herod Antipas was a builder, and during his long reign had built his capital of Tiberius, on the western shore of the Sea of Galilee.[194]   We know of two early believers who had

James J. Tissot, 'Herod' (1886-94), gouache on board, 6-3/16x3-3/16 inches, Brooklyn Museum, NY.

connections with Herod: Joanna, whose husband Chuza managed Herod's household (Luke 8:3) and Manaen, who had been brought up with Herod (Acts 13:1). Perhaps one of these is the "royal official" whose son Jesus healed – we just don't know.

The Faith of the Royal Official (4:47-50)

The royal official had probably heard Jesus when he had come to Capernaum previously (2:12). He has seen him do miracles of healing there (Luke 4:23; Matthew 11:23). He is desperate! He knows Jesus can heal his son, but he must find the Master. His faith is based on the miracles he has seen, but it is strong enough to sustain him on a two-day mountainous journey.

---

[191] "Son" in verses 46 and 47 is not the word for child, but *paidion*, a term more expressive of affection, as Barclay puts it, "my little lad" (Morris, *John*, p. 291, fn. 114).

[192] Kafr Kanna is about 343 m. elevation. Capernaum at Galilee is -39 m., a difference of 382 m. or 1,250 feet elevation.

[193] "Royal official" (NIV, NRSV), "official" (ESV), "nobleman" (KJV), is *basilikos*, "royal." The "royal" of John 4:46, 49 could be a relative of the royal (Herodian) family. (BDAG 170).

[194] He also had major building projects at Sepphoris and Betharamphtha. He was given the fortified palace at Machaerus, built by Herod the Great, on the east side of the Dead Sea, where Josephus says that John the Baptist was imprisoned and later executed.

So now he comes to Jesus and implores him to help.

> "He ... begged[195] him to come[196] and heal[197] his son, who was close to death." (4:47b)

The verb is in the imperfect tense, which means that he asked and kept on asking. He didn't stop or take "No" for an answer.

Jesus' first response is a rebuke not just of the official's faith, but of all the Galileans, who were more interested in signs and wonders rather than in who Jesus actually was.

> "Unless you people[198] see miraculous signs and wonders,' Jesus told him, 'you will never believe.'" (4:48)

But the man refuses to be denied. He is persistent.

> "[49] The royal official said, 'Sir, come down before my child dies.'
> [50] Jesus replied, 'You may go. Your son will live.' The man took Jesus at his word and departed." (4:49-50)

Jesus responds with a command and a statement: "Go, your son lives," which is more accurate than most translations that say "will live." The present imperative emphasizes a word of power, a healing word, and underscores the continuing power of life that Jesus brings.[199]

The man's response shows his faith. Instead of pestering Jesus to come with him, he believes that Jesus has already healed his son. "He took Jesus at his word" (NIV) is an English idiom for the more literal, "He believed the word that Jesus spoke to him" (NRSV, ESV).

Q1. (John 4:43-48) Many of the Galileans believe mainly because they have seen miracles. In what ways do miracles help build faith? Why does only seeing miracles not build a mature faith? Why does Jesus rebuke the Galileans in 4:48?
http://www.joyfulheart.com/forums/topic/1428-q1-maturing-faith/

Q2. (John 4:43-50) What do we learn about the royal official's faith from his actions? Why did he travel 20 miles from Capernaum to Cana? What does this say about his faith? When he departs for home and "takes Jesus at his word," what does this tell us about his faith?
http://www.joyfulheart.com/forums/topic/1429-q2-royal-officials-faith/

---

[195] "Begged" (NIV, NRSV), "besought" (KJV), "asked" (ESV) is *erōtaō*, "ask a question," then "to ask for something, ask, request." (BDAG 395, 2). It is in the imperfect tense – past tense continuing action.

[196] "Come" is *katabainō*, "to move downward, come/go/climb down" (BDAG 514, 1aβ).

[197] "Heal" is *iaomai*, "to restore someone to health after a physical malady, heal, cure" (BDAG 465, 1).

[198] *Oida*, "to see" is in the plural, translated by the NIV "you people."

[199] "Will live" (NIV, NRSV, ESV) is more accurately, "lives" (KJV), present tense.

Confirmation of the Time (4:51-54)

So the official heads down the mountain to return to Capernaum, and while on his way home, meets some of his servants who bring a joyous message.

> "[51] While he was still on the way, his servants met him with the news that his boy was living. [52] When he inquired as to the time when his son got better, they said to him, 'The fever[200] left him yesterday at the seventh hour.' [53] Then the father realized that this was the exact time at which Jesus had said to him, 'Your son will live.' So he and all his household believed." (4:51-53)

When this father gets over his initial shock that his son is healed, he finds out that the time of the boy's healing – about 1 pm – was just the time that Jesus had spoken the word of healing.

As a result, the man and all his extended household (*oikia*[201]) – immediate family, extended family, and servants – become believers. His faith had begun with seeing miracles, but it has gone deeper. He believes Jesus' word and later sees the results.

I don't doubt that Jesus (and John) got the full story when they arrived in Capernaum later on this trip to Galilee, and John recalled it decades later to include in his Gospel.

John saw special significance in this healing, as a sign pointing to who Jesus is – the man who can heal at a distance by only a word. The first sign John pointed out was the changing of the water into wine (2:11) – also in Cana.

> "This was the second miraculous sign[202] that Jesus performed, having come from Judea to Galilee." (4:54)

Q3. (John 4:53) What are the factors that caused the royal official's household (immediate family, extended family, and servants) to believe? How mature was this faith initially? How do you think the royal official was able to nurture it beyond mere "miracles faith"?
http://www.joyfulheart.com/forums/topic/1430-q3-household-faith/

Parallels with the Healing of the Centurion's Servant

Some scholars have concluded that John's account of the healing of the official's son is another version of the Synoptic's account of the healing of the centurion's servant (Matthew 8:5-13; Luke 7:2-10). In both accounts, you have an official personage who has faith for healing from a distance.

However, the stories have a number of differences:
- The centurion was a Gentile, the royal official likely a Jew.
- The centurion's slave was paralyzed, while the son had a fever.
- The centurion meets Jesus in Capernaum, while the royal official finds him in Cana.
- The centurion's faith is praised by Jesus, while the royal official's faith is rebuked as deficient.

[200] "Fever" is *pyretos*, "fiery heat," here, "fever" (BDAG 899).
[201] *Oikia*, "social unit within a dwelling, household, family" (BDAG 695, 2).
[202] See Appendix 5. "Signs" in John's Gospel.

- The centurion urges Jesus *not* to come, while the royal official does urge Jesus to come.

I think it's fair to say that strong evidence suggests that the healing of the royal official's son is a different healing than that of the centurion's slave.

Lessons for Disciples

What are we supposed to learn from this account? I think there are several lessons:

1. You can't expect your closest family, friends, or countrymen to appreciate you as a godly leader – "a prophet has no honor in his own country" (4:44).
2. Faith based on miracles alone is deficient (4:45, 48). Faith that is praise-worthy is based on who Jesus actually is: faith in his word and authority.
3. We must sometimes take Jesus at his word and act before seeing the result.

Q4. Have you read of miracles accompanying a great harvest of new believers on the missions fields in our day? What place do miracles have in evangelism today – both in your country and abroad? Why do some denominations in our day deemphasize miracles or claim that they were only for the early church? Why do some denominations emphasize miracles? Which of these types of denominations tend to grow faster? What kind of "discipling" is necessary for those who come to Christ primarily on the basis of miracles?
http://www.joyfulheart.com/forums/topic/1431-q4-miracles-and-evangelism/

Prayer

Father, thank you that you even honor a small amount of faith. Help us to believe you for more than we do now. Grow our faith. Help us to learn to take you at your word and take actions even when we don't see immediate results. Grow us up in you. We pray in Jesus' name. Amen.

Key Verses

"Jesus replied, 'You may go. Your son will live.' The man took Jesus at his word and departed. While he was still on the way, his servants met him with the news that his boy was living." (John 4:50-51, NIV)

11. Healing at the Pool of Bethesda (5:1-16)

Of the many incidents of Jesus healing people that John had observed as a disciple, he selected only a very few to include in his Gospel. He apparently assumed that his readers had access to one or more of the Synoptic Gospels. So we have to assume that his selections were intended to teach important things about what who Jesus is and what it means to believe in him.

Nathan Greene, "At the Pool of Bethesda," oil on canvas, 40x30. Copyrighted, permission requested.

From Samaria to Galilee to Jerusalem (5:1)

After Jesus' ministry in Samaria, we know from the Synoptic Gospels that he spent considerable time ministering in Galilee, though John only records the healing of the royal official's son. Now John takes us back to Jerusalem, to a remarkable healing at the Pool of Bethesda.

> "Some time later[203], Jesus went up to Jerusalem for a feast of the Jews." (5:1)

We're not told what feast Jesus had come to Jerusalem for, so it's probably not too important, except to clarify that this was an historical event.[204]

The Pool of Bethesda (5:2)

John describes the scene as you would expect an eyewitness to do for readers who hadn't been to Jerusalem.

> "Now there is in Jerusalem near the Sheep Gate a pool, which in Aramaic is called Bethesda and which is surrounded by five covered colonnades." (5:2)

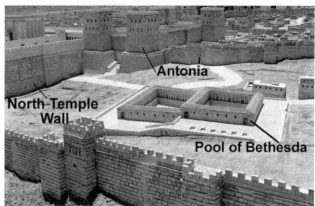

Photo of the Pool of Bethesda in a 1:50 scale model of Jerusalem in the period of the Second Temple, constructed by Israeli archeologist and historian Michael Avi-Yonah (1904-1974) at the Holyland Hotel, now at the Israel Museum, Jerusalem.

---

[203] "Some time later" (NIV) is a bit of an over-translation. It's more accurately translated, "after this" (NRSV, KJV, ESV).The Greek is *meta tauta. Meta* with the accusative is a "marker of time after another point of time, after" (BDAG 637, B2c).

[204] John does specify that Jesus went to Jerusalem for the Feast of the Unleavened Bread and Passover (4:45; 6:4; 13:1; 11:56; 12:12, 20) and the Festival of Tabernacles or Booths (7:2, 8, 10, 14, 37).

The Sheep Gate was doubtless the gate through which the sheep traveled on their way to be sacrificed in the temple. The Pool of Bethesda was nearby, just north of the temple precincts.

In the early manuscripts there are a number of spellings for the name of the pool. Most English translations give it as "Bethesda," which means "House of Mercy." This seems to be supported by a reference in the Copper Scroll discovered at Qumran.[205] In this lesson I'll be using the familiar name "Bethesda."

The pool of Bethesda was discovered in the 19th century under the ruins of a Byzantine church. The archaeological evidence shows a pool shaped like a trapezoid, varying from 165 to 200 feet (50 to 60 meters) wide by 315 feet (96 meters) long, divided into two pools by a central partition. The southern pool had broad steps with landings, indicating that it was a *mikveh*, or ritual bath (similar to the Pool of Siloam at the south end of the city), where Jerusalem's pilgrims would gather to purify themselves for cleansing prior to a feast, for example. The northern pool provided a reservoir to continually replenish and re-purify the southern pool with fresh water flowing south through the dam between them.[206] Water probably came from runoff in the city and some underground springs.

John describes "five covered colonnades," (NIV, ESV), "porticos" (NRSV), "porches" (KJV). The word means, "a roofed colonnade open normally on one side, portico,"[207] that is, a series of columns set at regular intervals and usually supporting the base of a roof structure.[208] Weather permitting, people could sit or lie during the day under these covered porches to be sheltered from the sun.

Troubling of the Waters (5:3-4)

But pilgrims to the city were not the only ones who came to the Pool of Bethesda. It was also a center for healing. John explains:

> "Here a great number of disabled people[209] used to lie – the blind, the lame[210], the paralyzed.[211]" (5:3)

Why they were there is explained by a gloss, or explanation by an early scribe trying to make the reason for the gathering clear for the readers. It is included in the footnotes of modern translations, but

---

[205] "Bethesda" (NIV, ESV, NASB, NJB, KJV) is attested by A C Θ 078 f¹, ¹³ Byzantine texts. "Beth-zatha" (NRSV, RSV) is also well-supported by early manuscripts (Aleph 33 Eusebius L D it), and was selected as "the least unsatisfactory reading" by the Editorial Committee of the United Bible Societies, which gives it a {D} or "doubtful" designation. Metzger, *Textual Commentary*, p. 208.

[206] Brown, *John* 1:207; Urban C. von Wahlde, "Archaeology and John's Gospel," in Charlesworth, *Jesus & Archaeology*, p. 560-566. See also Urban C. Von Wahlde, "The Puzzling Pool of Bethesda," *Biblical Archaeology Review* September-ber/October 2011 (Vol. 37, No. 5), pp. 40-47, 65.

[207] *Stoa*, BDAG 945.

[208] *Merriam-Webster's 11th Collegiate Dictionary*.

[209] "Disabled people"(NIV), "invalids" (NRSV), "impotent folk" (KJV) is the participle of *astheneō*, "to suffer a debilitating illness, be sick" (BDAG 142, 1), also in verse 7.

[210] "Lame" is *chōlos*, "lame, crippled" (BDAG 1093).

[211] "Paralyzed" (NIV, NRSV), withered" (KJV) is *xēros*, "dry, withered up," figuratively, "pertaining to being shrunken or withered and therefore immobile because of disease, withered, shrunken, paralyzed" (BDAG 685, 2).

it clearly was not part of the earliest Greek manuscripts, thus not part of Holy Scripture, though it explains the situation clearly enough.[212]

> "[3b] and they waited for the moving of the waters. [4] From time to time an angel of the Lord would come down and stir up the waters. The first one into the pool after each such disturbance would be cured of whatever disease he had." (5:3b-4)

This explanation of healing from an angel stirring up the waters was believed by many of the sick and infirm in the city. The stirring doubtless had a physical cause – some bubbling up of an intermittent spring, perhaps. But that an angel troubled the waters seems to have been a popular superstition among the populace, much like the superstitions that have surrounded "holy wells" and mineral springs back to Babylonian times.[213] Instead of seeking out the Healer who had come to Jerusalem to heal and save, they huddled around this pool and pinned their hopes on the chance that they might be the first into the waters.

We're not told how many invalids might be gathered on a given day, but I imagine there were scores, perhaps hundreds.

An Invalid for 38 Years (5:5-9)

Now John introduces us to the subject of Jesus' healing that day. Of all the wretched people gathered at poolside that day, Jesus selected this one man.

> "[5] One who was there had been an invalid for thirty-eight years. [6] When Jesus saw him lying there and learned that he had been in this condition for a long time, he asked him, 'Do you want to get well?'
> [7] 'Sir,' the invalid replied, 'I have no one to help me into the pool when the water is stirred[214]. While I am trying to get in, someone else goes down ahead of me.'
> [8] Then Jesus said to him, 'Get up! Pick up your mat and walk.'
> [9] At once the man was cured; he picked up his mat and walked. (5:5-9)

We're not told of the man's particular problem. He is referred to as an "invalid" (NIV, ESV), one "who had been ill" (NRSV), "had an infirmity" (KJV). The word is a general word referring to "a state of debilitating illness, sickness, disease."[215]

I assume that he was not merely lame, making his way on crutches, but paralyzed, since he was lying on a mat and couldn't get into the water very easily by himself. I'm guessing that some people, perhaps relatives or neighbors, carried him to the pool every morning and home every night. But during the day they would need to work to support themselves and him, and there was no one he could rely on to help him. No friend.

---

[212] Verses 3b-4 are missing on the earliest and most important manuscripts, including, p[56,75] Aleph B C* D W[a]. The Editorial Committee of the United Bible Societies, Greek New Testament gave the omission an {A} or "virtually certain" rating (Metzger, *Textual Commentary*, p. 209).

[213] Edersheim, *Life and Times*, 3:466.

[214] "Stirred" (NIV), "troubled" is *tarassō*, "to cause movement by shaking or stirring, shake together, stir up," of water (in verses 3, 4, and 7).

[215] *Astheneia*, BDAG 142, 1.

Jesus has learned – probably from talking with the man himself – that he has been an invalid for 38 years. I can almost hear him recite to Jesus his litany of complaint about his sad and miserable life.

The Invalid's Character and the Grace of God

From John's brief account, we begin to get some hints about the invalid's character. Though we'll look deeper at some of these in a moment, it's helpful to list them in one place.

1. **Old**. If the life expectancy in those days was maybe 35, and if this man had been afflicted during his childhood, he might have been 40 or 50 by this time – an old man (5:5).
2. **Dependent**. He probably relies on others to bring him, take him home, and support him (5:7). If he couldn't take care of himself well, he was probably dirty and smelly too – a smelly old man.
3. **Complainer**. He complains about how long he's been an invalid. He complains that he doesn't have anyone to help him into the pool (5:5, 7)
4. **Blamer**. When confronted by the Jews for carrying his pallet on the Sabbath he blames the person who told him to carry it (5:10-13).
5. **Sinner** (5:14), serious enough for Jesus to confront him in the temple.
6. **Ungrateful and disloyal**. When he learns Jesus' name, he reports it to the religious leaders. He "tattles" on Jesus rather than being thankful for his healing and loyal to his healer (5:15).
7. **Unrepentant** (5:14-15). There's no indication that he accepted and acted on Jesus' rebuke about his sin; rather John tells us that he reports Jesus to the authorities.

Why did Jesus choose to heal this man of all those gathered at the Pool of Bethesda that day? I can only conclude that it was the Father's clear direction (see 5:19) and utter grace! Clearly, this man didn't deserve what he received – nor did he seem to appreciate it at any depth.

> **Q1. (John 5:1-16) How would you describe the invalid's character? The invalid's faith? How does Jesus' healing here demonstrate the grace of God? Why do we humans find it difficult to accept grace when it is offered to us? Why do we resist the concept that God's gifts are entirely by grace?**
> **http://www.joyfulheart.com/forums/topic/1432-q1-character-and-grace/**

"Do you want to get well?" (5:6)

> "When Jesus saw him lying there and learned that he had been in this condition for a long time, he asked him, 'Do you want to get well[216]?'" (5:6)

I've pondered Jesus' question. Why in the world would you ask a seriously ill person if he wants to get well? "Yes!" seems like the obvious answer! But I think Jesus wanted more than a Yes or No answer. He wanted to assess desire and faith.

---

[216] "Get well" (NIV), "healed" (ESV), "made well" (NRSV), "made whole" (KJV) is two words, *ginomai*, "to become" and *hygiēs* (from which root we get our word "hygiene"), "pertaining to being physically well or sound, 'healthy, sound.'" The adjective *hygiēs* occurs in verses 4, 6, 9, 14, as well as 5:11, 15; 7:23 (BDAG 102, 1a).

John Wimber, founder of the Vineyard Fellowship movement and teacher in a class called "Signs, Wonders and Church Growth" (MC510) at Fuller Theological Seminary in the early 1980s, taught students to question those who came to them for healing. Too often we assume that a person wants one thing, while they just aren't where we imagine them to be. Since I learned this, when people come to me for prayer or come forward in a service, I usually ask, "What do you want God to do for you?" It helps me discern how to pray for them. And as I pray to God for wisdom, occasionally I get guidance on how to pray also.

Not all sick people really want to be healed – or to surrender their lives to Christ – even though that is their true need. Sometimes their sickness puts them in a place where they get lots of attention, for example. Jesus set the ministry example for us: Ask!

The invalid in our story didn't exactly answer the question. Rather he explained why he hadn't been healed. As mentioned above, his answer tells us something about his character and his faith.

Q2. (John 5:6) Why do you think Jesus asked the invalid if he wanted to get well? Why is it important for us not to make assumptions, but to seek discernment about people's needs before we pray for them?
http://www.joyfulheart.com/forums/topic/1433-q2-inquiry-and-prayer/

Get up! Walk! (5:8-9)

Jesus doesn't pray for the man. He commands him with a word of power.

"⁸ Then Jesus said to him, 'Get up! Pick up your mat and walk.'
⁹ At once the man was cured; he picked up his mat and walked." (5:8-9)

We see this command to "get up" (NIV, ESV), "stand up" (NRSV), "rise" (KJV) a number of places in the Gospels. The word means, "awaken," then, "rise, get up," here, in a command to evoke movement from a fixed position "get up!, come!"[217] We see it with the paralytic when the ceiling of a home was broken up (Matthew 9:5-6; Mark 2:9, 11; Luke 5:23-24), a man in the synagogue with a shriveled hand (Mark 3:3; Luke 6:8), Jairus's daughter who is raised from dead (Mark 5:41; Luke 8:54), blind Bartimaeus (Mark 10:49), and the crippled man at the Beautiful Gate of the Temple (Acts 3:6).

Is the man obedient to Jesus' command? I'm not sure. He certainly got on his feet "at once" or "immediately,"[218] picked up his pallet, and began to walk. I think (but can't prove) that when Jesus spoke, his legs suddenly strengthened and he found himself standing. It wasn't so much a matter of obedience or faith, but an instinctive response to a sudden healing and the realization – as he began to stand – that he indeed had the strength to do so. Hallelujah! Perhaps his attempt to stand was even the trigger for the healing. We read about the 10 lepers who were healed:

"He said, 'Go, show yourselves to the priests.'
And **as they went**, they were cleansed." (Luke 17:14)

[217] *Egeirō*, BDAG 272, 13a.
[218] "At once" (NIV, NRSV), "immediately" (KJV) is *eutheōs*, "at once, immediately" (BDAG 405).

The two other elements of the healing were to pick up[219] his mat and walk. The mat or pallet could have been a bed or couch, or perhaps a stretcher on which friends carried him.[220] The man didn't need to be there any longer, so he took up his pallet and began to walk home – and that's where he got into trouble.

Trouble with the "Sabbath Police" (5:9b-13)

We read in the news that in certain Middle Eastern countries there are self-appointed men who police how women must cover themselves – or even drive a car themselves.

John tells us that this healing took place on a Sabbath. Apparently, in Jerusalem some of the strict Jews, probably Pharisees who interpreted the Law quite strictly, saw this man carrying his pallet home, and took it upon themselves to confront him.

> "9b The day on which this took place was a Sabbath, 10 and so the Jews said to the man who had been healed, 'It is the Sabbath; the law forbids you to carry your mat.'" (5:9-10)

The law indeed was clear about observing the Sabbath. The Fourth Commandment says:

> "Remember the Sabbath day by keeping it holy. Six days you shall labor and do all your work, but the seventh day is a Sabbath to the LORD your God." (Exodus 20:8-10a)

Of course, the intent was that God's people should rest on the Sabbath and not pursue their normal work. But then the lawyers took over. There is a large tractate in the Mishnah that details just what is allowed and disallowed on the Sabbath. Accordingly it was allowable to carry a man on a bed on the Sabbath, but not to carry a bed without a man on it.[221]

As you may recall, Jesus was severely criticized for healing on the Sabbath (Luke 12:14; John 5:16; 9:14-16; etc.) and allowing his disciples to eat heads of grain they plucked as they walked ("harvesting," Matthew 12:2). Yes, carrying loads for your work was indeed prohibited (Jeremiah 17:21-22; Mark 11:16), but a healed man carrying home his pallet? That's not work!

The healed man's defense is to shift blame from himself to Jesus. "He told me to do it!"

> "11 But he replied, 'The man who made me well said to me, "Pick up your mat and walk."'
> 12 So they asked him, "Who is this fellow who told you to pick it up and walk?"
> 13 The man who was healed had no idea who it was, for Jesus had slipped away into the crowd that was there." (5:11-13)

It's interesting that the healed man didn't learn Jesus' name. You would think that he would have been exceedingly grateful and thank Jesus. But, apparently, his only thought was his own healing. He didn't turn to Jesus with thanksgiving.

The text says that Jesus "slipped away" (NIV), "disappeared" (NRSV), "conveyed himself away" (KJV) "had withdrawn" (ESV), translating the verb *ekneuō*, "to draw away from, turn aside,

---

[219] "Pick/take up" is *airō*, "to lift up and move from one place to another," here, "carry away, remove" (BDAG 28, 2b).

[220] "Mat" (NIV, NRSV), "bed" (ESV, KJV) is *krabbatos*, "mattress, pallet" (BDAG 563) (Mark 2:4, 9, 11; 6:55). In Acts 5:15 the sick are laid on "beds (*klinē*) and mats (*krabbatos*)". There "bed" is *klinē*, "bed, couch," or "pallet, stretcher" on which a sick man was carried, probably not differentiated from "bed" (Matthew 9:2, 6; Luke 5:18; BDAG 549, 1).

[221] Beasley-Murray, *John*, p. 70, cites Strack and Billerbeck, 1:454-461.

withdraw."[222] This is in keeping with Jesus' style of not trying to use the spectacular to promote himself. He often told people not to tell anyone about a miracle (Matthew 8:4; 17:9; Mark 1:43; 3:12; 5:43; 7:36; etc.), and told his disciples not to reveal that he was the Messiah (Matthew 16:20).

How unlike him we often are! We seek the praise of men (5:41) and the free publicity that comes with the spectacular. We want to exploit the public relations value of anything we can. On the other hand, we do know that God often uses miracles to draw people to Christ. Many mass-healing campaigns overseas have swelled from word-of-mouth testimony and many have come to Christ as a result. My point is to check our motive. If it's pride – and this is often one of our hidden motives – we're not emulating Christ. God help us!

> **Q3. (John 5:9-13) Why are the "sabbath police" (the Pharisees) so upset at the man who is healed? How can a person be so intent on rules that they miss what God is doing? Have you ever caught yourself doing that? Has someone in your church been so intent on "how we do things here" that they couldn't see God at work? What is the sin of the Pharisees here?**
> **http://www.joyfulheart.com/forums/topic/1434-q3-spiritual-blindness/**

Stop Sinning (5:14)

Later, perhaps that day or the next[223] – we're not told – Jesus sees the healed man in the temple. Perhaps he has come to offer a thank offering for his healing.

> "[14] Later Jesus found him at the temple and said to him, 'See, you are well again. Stop sinning or something worse may happen to you.' [15] The man went away and told the Jews that it was Jesus who had made him well." (5:14-15)

Notice that Jesus spots[224] the man in the temple, not the other way around, even though there was probably a crowd of people around Jesus.

Jesus goes to the man and confronts him about his sin. We don't know what his sin was – slander, cheating, sexual sin. We're not told. But it doesn't seem to be some kind of garden-variety weakness, but serious sin. Jesus commands him to stop sinning.[225] The verb is in the present imperative, suggesting that the man is continuing to sin – it's not just a slip or single occurrence. It is his way of life.

Jesus tells him of the consequence if he doesn't stop sinning. "... Lest something worse may happen to you" (5:14b).[226]

---

[222] *Ekneuō*, BDAG 307.

[223] "Later" (NIV, NRSV), "afterward" (KJV, ESV) is, literally, "after (*meta*) these things." We're not told the interval of time.

[224] The verb is *heuriskō*, "to come upon something either through purposeful search or accidentally, find" (BDAG 411, 1b).

[225] "Stop sinning" (NIV), "do not sin any more" (NRSV), "sin no more" (KJV, ESV) is two words: *mēketi*, "no longer, not from now on" (BDAG 647, fα), and *hamartanō* in the imperative present tense, "to commit a wrong, to sin" (in the sense 'transgress' against divinity, custom, or law (BDAG 49, 1a).

[226] This future is not certain, for the verb is in the subjunctive rather than the future tense.

You might ask, What would be worse[227] than being crippled for 38 years? Hell – forever and throughout eternity, that is what Jesus is doubtless referring to.

Repentance

Both John the Baptist and Jesus preached, "Repent, for the Kingdom of heaven is at hand" (Matthew 3:2; 4:17). It is very clear that repentance from sin is necessary to believe in Christ (Matthew 11:20; 21:32; Mark 6:12). The only reason we find this shocking is that we have embraced a gospel of grace *without* repentance. Just pray the sinner's prayer and be forgiven, we tell people. But faith without repentance is an oxymoron. It isn't biblical!

This doesn't mean we don't sometimes fall into sin. That we're not sometimes rebellious. That we don't need continual forgiveness purchased at great cost by the sacrifice of Jesus Christ for our sins (1 John 1:8-10; 2:1-2). We do. But we must repent from a lifestyle of sin. St. Paul is very clear that if we don't repent of sinful lifestyles, we are kidding ourselves if we think we're going to heaven (1 Corinthians 6:9-11; Galatians 5:19-21). Jesus required this man – and the woman taken in adultery (John 8:11) – to stop sinning, to repent and to begin to live a different way.

The story of the healing of the man at the Pool of Bethesda is all of grace – he didn't deserve anything, in fact, he wasn't a very good man to start with. But it is all about repentance also. If we try to separate grace from repentance we severely distort the gospel that Jesus and the apostles taught.

Former slave ship captain John Newton penned these immortal words:

"Amazing grace, how sweet the sound,
That saved a wretch like me.
I once was lost, but now I'm found,
Was blind, but now I see."

It follows, that if we can now "see," then we now avoid the things we used to be blind to and blunder into.

Sin and Sickness (5:14)

Verse 14 implies that there can be a relationship between sin and sickness.

"Later Jesus found him at the temple and said to him, 'See, you are well again. Stop sinning or something worse may happen to you.'" (5:14)

A number of times in the Bible we find instances where God *does* afflict people with sickness as a punishment.[228] With the paralytic let down by his friends into the house where Jesus was speaking, Jesus linked sin with illness (Mark 2:9). Does that mean that all sickness is a result of sin? No. We shouldn't generalize. Clearly, most of the time, Satan and demons bring illness (Luke 13:10-13). And with the man born blind, Jesus specifically states an instance where a man's sickness was absolutely not the result of sin at all (9:2-3).

---

[227] "Worse" is *cheirōn*, "worse, more severe" (BDAG 1083).

[228] Some instances of God afflicting people with sickness as a punishment are: disobedient Israelites, Deuteronomy 28:59; 29:22; Nabal, 1 Samuel 25:38; Gehazi, 2 Kings 5:27; Uzziah, 2 Chronicles 26:19-20.

The Healed Man Tattles on Jesus (5:15)

Did the healed man heed Jesus' rebuke to "stop sinning"? I don't think so. John records what happened next:

> "The man went away and told the Jews that it was Jesus who had made him well." (5:15)

Is it possible that the man repented later on? Yes, it's possible. But here his actions don't show belief in the Healer, but passing on blame and persecution to Jesus so he can avoid it himself, hardly the mark of a disciple. There's another such sad story in the Gospels, that of the rich young ruler. The man had a problem with a love of money Jesus had to confront that he might be saved:

> "Jesus looked at him and loved him. 'One thing you lack,' he said. 'Go, sell everything you have and give to the poor, and you will have treasure in heaven. Then come, follow me.' 22 At this the man's face fell. He went away sad, because he had great wealth." (Mark 10:21-22)

This kind of story makes us both sad and uncomfortable. The fact is, that we do what we believe is in our greatest interest at the time. Will you repent, my friend, or only pretend that you truly "believe."

> **Q4. (John 5:14-15) Is it possible to be blessed outwardly, but lost inwardly? Why did Jesus confront the healed man in the temple with his sin? How was this necessary for a full healing, his salvation? Does the man seem to respond with faith to Jesus' rebuke?**
> **http://www.joyfulheart.com/forums/topic/1435-q4-inner-and-outer-healing/**

Conflict with the Jewish Leaders and Pharisees (5:16-18)

Our passage closes by explaining that Jesus' death was due to the same kind of blind legalism that the Pharisees often exhibited.

> "16 So, because Jesus was doing these things on the Sabbath, the Jews[229] persecuted him. 17 Jesus said to them, "My Father is always at his work to this very day, and I, too, am working." 18 For this reason the Jews tried all the harder to kill him; not only was he breaking the Sabbath, but he was even calling God his own Father, making himself equal with God." (5:16-18)

They could see an astounding miracle, but criticize Jesus for not obeying their interpretation of the law.

The discourse that follows, explaining Jesus' relation to the Father is closely related to the story of the healing of the man at the Pool of Bethesda, but we'll consider it by itself in the next lesson.

Lessons for Disciples

There are several clear lessons for disciples found in our text:

1. **God's grace**. God can work miracles without any bit of merit, earning, or deserving on our part.

---

[229] For John's use of "the Jews" to refer to Jewish leaders, see Appendix 2. 'The Jews' in John's Gospel.

2. **Outward blessing**, can accompany **inner death**. Paradoxically, the man at the pool of Bethesda is healed outwardly, but apparently is never healed inwardly, because he shows no evidence of repentance when Jesus calls him to it.

3. **Ask a discerning question** (verse 6). When you pray, ask what people want, in order to assess their needs and desires.

4. **God-awareness** (verses 16-18). Some people, like the Pharisees, are so obsessed with their rules that they miss the miracle.

5. **Jesus expects repentance** (verse 14). It is possible to repent and turn from our sins. We can change and improve, even if we don't become perfect in this life.

This story is about healing. Even if you aren't suffering from a chronic physical ailment like the man at the pool, we all need healing. As Matthew Henry put it:

"We are all by nature impotent folk in spiritual things, blind, halt, and withered; but full provision is made for our cure, if we attend to it."

Prayer

Father, we are such spiritually dull people sometimes. We receive bountiful blessings from you and yet respond so ungratefully. It's not just the healed man in our story, but it's us! Forgive us. Change our hearts. Put in us faith and gratitude, we pray. And thank you for your grace that covers all our sins. In Jesus' name, we pray. Amen.

Key Verses

"[Jesus] asked him, 'Do you want to get well?'" (John 5:6, NIV)

"Later Jesus found him at the temple and said to him, 'See, you are well again. Stop sinning or something worse may happen to you.'" (John 5:14, NIV)

12. Life in the Son (5:17-47)

John's Gospel probably contains the deepest insights of any other any other book in the Bible concerning who Jesus is and how he relates to the Father. And in this passage we're examining, Jesus' light shines brightly.

The context of 5:17-47 follows on the heels of Jesus' healing of the man at the Pool of Bethesda, and the Jews' criticism of him carrying his pallet on the Sabbath Day – and Jesus' healing on the Sabbath for that matter.

My Father Is Always at His Work (5:16-18a)

"[16] So, because Jesus was doing these things on the Sabbath, the Jews[230] persecuted him. [17] Jesus said to them, 'My Father is always at his work to this very day, and I, too, am working.' [18] For this reason the Jews tried all the harder to kill him; not only was he breaking the Sabbath...." (5:16-18a)

Detail of 'Resurrection' stained glass window, Co-Cathedral of the Sacred Heart, Houston, 2008, full size is 40ft x 20ft. Designed and constructed by Mellini Art Glass and Mosaics in Florence, Italy. Photo © Lea McNulty. Used by permission.

Observance of the Sabbath was one of the chief characteristics of Judaism. And rightly so.

Jesus, too, observed the Fourth Commandment: "Remember the Sabbath day by keeping it holy" (Exodus 20:8). He made it a point to be in the synagogue each Sabbath (Luke 4:16, 31, 44) and encouraged his disciples to keep every part of the Law – better than the scribes and Pharisees (Matthew 5:17-20). Pharisees were extreme legalists, following all the interpretations of rabbis before them – "the tradition of the elders" (Matthew 15:2) the oral law, finally written down in the Mishnah about 180-220 AD. They defined "work" on the Sabbath day with extreme rigor. Thus healing (the work of a physician) was prohibited. So was harvesting. And so on. As a result, Jesus had many conflicts with the Pharisees over Sabbath observance.

Jesus, on the other hand, sought to fulfill the spirit of the Law. He saw the Sabbath as God's blessing to man, not the other way around.

"The Sabbath was made for man, not man for the Sabbath. So the Son of Man is Lord even of the Sabbath." (Mark 2:27-28)

In our text he gives another basis for his more dynamic understanding of Sabbath observance. While the Pharisees were fixated on "work" as the antithesis of the Sabbath, Jesus said,

"My Father is always at his work to this very day, and I, too, am working." (5:17)

---

[230] For John's use of "the Jews" to refer to Jewish leaders, see Appendix 2. 'The Jews' in John's Gospel.

This wasn't an entirely new idea in Judaism; Jesus was just bringing it to their attention. All the rabbis in Jesus' day acknowledged that God works on the Sabbath, otherwise providence itself "would weekly go into abeyance."[231] Jesus point is: If the Father works on the Sabbath, then I can do his works on the Sabbath. As you'll see, in this passage several times Jesus mentions his aim to "complete the work" that the Father assigned him (5:35; 14:10; 17:4).

Making Himself Equal with God (5:18)

The Jewish leaders probably agreed with the concept that God continues to work, but they strenuously disagreed with the way Jesus expressed it – "My Father ...." It sounded way too personal for them. It sounded like blasphemy.

> "For this reason the Jews[232] tried all the harder to kill him; not only was he breaking the Sabbath, but he was even calling God his own Father, making himself **equal with God**." (5:18)

The question revolved about being "equal with God." "Equal" is *isos*, "pertaining to being equivalent in number, size, quality, equal."[233] We see the word *isos* one other time in the New Testament in this context.

> "Who, being in very nature God,
> did not consider **equality with God** something to be grasped,
> but made himself nothing,
> taking the very nature of a servant,
> being made in human likeness." (Philippians 2:6-7)

In the following verses, Jesus explains what this equality entails and what it does not entail.

Jesus Does What He Sees His Father Doing (5:19-20)

> "19 Jesus gave them this answer: 'I tell you the truth, the Son can do nothing by himself; he can do only what he sees his Father doing, because whatever the Father does the Son also does. 20 For the Father loves the Son and shows him all he does. Yes, to your amazement he will show him even greater things than these.'" (5:19-20)

Verse 30 is a companion to verse 19:

> "By myself I can do nothing; I judge only as I hear...." (5:30)

Look at what we learn about the relationship in these amazing verses:
1.   The Son doesn't operate independently of the Father.
2.   The Son is in constant touch with the Father.
3.   The Son does what he discerns the Father is doing.
4.   The Father loves the Son and shows him everything he is doing.

---

[231] Carson, *John*, p. 247.
[232] For John's use of "the Jews" to refer to Jewish leaders, see Appendix 2. 'The Jews' in John's Gospel.
[233] *Isos*, BDAG 480.

Then there's what's called a "teaser" in the broadcast industry, a hint at "even greater things than these." In other words, Jesus has been in touch with the Father and working miracles in tandem with the Father already. But to come is an even greater phenomenon – the resurrection of the dead (5:21).

The key to Jesus' Sonship is constant communication with and obedience to the Father. Thus he is the perfect expression of the Father here on earth. The Word (*Logos*) of chapter 1.

"No one has ever seen God, but God the One and Only, who is at the Father's side, has made him known." (1:18)

There's a fascinating interchange between Jesus and Philip later in the Gospel that helps explain what Jesus is saying in 5:19.

> "[8] Philip said, 'Lord, **show us the Father** and that will be enough for us.'
> [9] Jesus answered: 'Don't you know me, Philip, even after I have been among you such a long time? **Anyone who has seen me has seen the Father.** How can you say, "Show us the Father"?
> [10] Don't you believe that I am in the Father, and that the Father is in me? **The words I say to you are not just my own. Rather, it is the Father, living in me, who is doing his work.** [11] Believe me when I say that I am in the Father and the Father is in me; or at least believe on the evidence of the miracles themselves. [12] **I tell you the truth, anyone who has faith in me will do what I have been doing. He will do even greater things than these, because I am going to the Father.** (John 14:8-12)

Notice that this close communication with and obedience to the Father is not just for Jesus, but also for his disciples – "anyone who has faith in me will do what I have been doing...."

We are Jesus' disciples. We must learn from Jesus how to listen to the Father and then follow his instructions here on earth. In fact, if we attempt to operate independently of the Father – just doing religious things that we've learned to do them from others – we will be powerless and ineffective.

No wonder Jesus' disciples were called "Christians" – little christs (Acts 11:26). They had learned the secret of listening and obeying.

Later in our passage, Jesus talks about searching the Scriptures to find eternal life (5:39-14). The life is found in the Person of Christ to whom the Scriptures point. No wonder we have "dead orthodoxy" in our day. No wonder we have powerless Christianity! We have relied on ourselves rather than on the Living God.

Q1. (John 5:19-20) Are we intended to emulate Jesus' listening to the Father, or is knowing the Bible a modern-day substitute for this? Why don't churches teach more about hearing the voice of God? What would happen in our generation if we would learn to dynamically hear God and then obey what he is saying to us?
http://www.joyfulheart.com/forums/topic/1436-q1-listening-to-the-father/

The Son Is Given the Father's Attributes (5:21-23)

Now Jesus tells the Jewish leaders of two divine attributes that he has been granted, that have been delegated to him. They must have been beside themselves with anger!

"21 For just as the Father raises the dead and gives them life, even so the Son gives life to whom he is pleased to give it. 22 Moreover, the Father judges no one, but has entrusted all judgment to the Son, 23 that all may honor the Son just as they honor the Father. He who does not honor the Son does not honor the Father, who sent him." (5:21-23)

The attributes Jesus claims are:

1. Granting life (5:21). God has given all living creatures the "breath of life" (Genesis 1:30, etc.). Job said, "In his hand is the life of every creature and the breath of all mankind" (Job 12:10). Yahweh creates the earth, and "gives breath to its people, and life to those who walk on it" (Isaiah 42:5). The Father "raises the dead and gives them life" in the Age to Come. Now the Son has been given this authority.

2. Granting judgment (5:22). In the Old Testament, Yahweh is called "the Judge of all the earth." (Genesis 18:25; cf. Psalm 94:2; 1 Samuel 2:10; etc.). But the Messiah's right to judge is clearly prophesied in Isaiah 11:1-4, and as Son of Man he is giving authority and dominion over the Kingdom of God.

The purpose of these grants is that people might honor Jesus the Son in the same way as they honor the Father. Wow! In fact, if people don't honor the Son, then they insult the Father who sent him.

Did Jesus indeed claim to be equal with God, as the Jewish leaders claim? Yes, indeed! Though exactly what that meant was different than what they thought.

Crossed Over from Death to Life (5:24)

In a paragraph of seemingly audacious statements, Jesus makes another – one of the most memorable verses about eternal life in the Bible, and well worth memorizing. This verse combines both of Jesus' claims – to giving life and to judgment of all.

" I tell you the truth, whoever hears my word and believes him who sent me has[234] eternal life and will not be condemned; he has crossed over from death to life." (5:24)

Let's look at this verse in detail:

Introduction. Jesus begins with his "Truly, truly I say to you" formula which emphasizes the solemnity of this statement.

Qualification. Next, he gives the qualifications of those who are eligible to receive this wonderful promise.

"Whoever hears my word and believes him who sent me...."

In other words, the promise is for those who believe God sent Jesus and gave him authority of Messiah and Son of God.

Promises: (a) has eternal life, and (b) will not be condemned. Let's probe a bit deeper.

(a) **Eternal life**. In the phrase, "has eternal life," the verb "has" is *echō*, "have," here, "to possess or contain, have, own," in the sense of "to have within oneself."[235] It doesn't say "will have eternal life," but *has* eternal life now (present tense). And to emphasize this fact, Jesus says that the believer *has*

---

[234] "Has" in verse 24a is the common verb *echō*, "have," in the sense of "to possess or contain, have, own," here "to have within oneself" (BDAG 420, 1d).

[235] *Echō*, BDAG 420, 1d.

(present tense) "crossed over from death to life. "Crossed over" (NIV), "passed" (NRSV, ESV, KJV) is *metabainō*, "to transfer from one place to another, go/pass over," then by extension, "to change from one state or condition to another state, pass, pass on."[236] Eternal life is not just future. It begins now with a relationship with Jesus, and will become even more intense when Christ returns. In that sense, the Kingdom is both present and future.

(b) **No condemnation**. The phrase, "will not be condemned" (NIV), is literally, "does not come under judgment" (NRSV). "Condemned" (NIV), "judgment" (NRSV), "condemnation" (KJV) is *krisis* (from which we get our English word "crisis"), "legal process of judgment, judging." The word often (as in our verse and the sentence that follows) means judgment that goes against a person, "condemnation."[237] This doesn't mean that we won't appear before Jesus for judgment. Paul says, "We will all stand before God's judgment seat" (Romans 14:10) and "We must all appear before the judgment seat of Christ...." (2 Corinthians 5:10). Indeed, we will all appear at the Great White Throne Judgment of Revelation:[238]

> "And I saw the dead, great and small, standing before the throne, and books were opened. Another book was opened, which is the book of life." (Revelation 20:12)

What is different about us on that Day is that the judgment has already been made for eternal life – and our names are already written in the "Lamb's book of life" (Revelation 13:8). We have already been transferred from death into life. Judgment Day will only proclaim what has already taken place.

Yes, we will stand before Christ for judging the quality our deeds, but the judgment regarding life or death has already been given. We've been written in God's Book as "pardoned" through the precious blood of Christ! (1 John 2:1-2; 1 Peter 1:18-19). Hallelujah!

Paul rejoices over this fact in Romans:

> "Therefore, there is now **no condemnation** for those who are in Christ Jesus, because through Christ Jesus the law of the Spirit of life set me free from the law of sin and death." (Romans 8:1-2)

Q2. (John 5:21-24) According to John 5:24, when does eternal life begin? What is our default position without Christ – life or death? How can people come to eternal life if they never "hear my word"? How do your friends and neighbors normally hear Jesus' word? What might be your role in seeing that they hear his word?
http://www.joyfulheart.com/forums/topic/1437-q2-passing-from-death-to-life/

---

[236] *Metabainō*, BDAG 638, 2. The idea also appears in 1 John: "We know that we have passed from death to life, because we love our brothers" (1 John 3:14).

[237] *Krisis*, BDAG 569, 1aβ.

[238] Some have taught that the Judgment Seat of Christ is different from the Great White Throne Judgment. I disagree. The simplest way to understand this is that all appear before the Great White Throne Judgment, but that since our names are written in the Lamb's book of Life, we are treated differently than the unbelievers.

Life in the Son

Sometimes our understanding of the gift of eternal life gets distorted. Some see this using the analogy of a transaction. Others as a Christmas gift that the recipient now "owns" and "controls." Our passage gives another analogy that I think clears up some of these misunderstandings. Life is in the Son himself, and not separate from him. When we put our trust in Christ, we receive his New Life and are now "in Christ," united to him, our righteousness now being his righteousness.

John sums up this concept well in his First Epistle:

> "And this is the testimony: God has given us eternal life, and **this life is in his Son. He who has the Son has life**; he who does not have the Son of God does not have life." (1 John 5:11-12)

You can't have eternal life unless you are united to the Son by faith – they come as one inseparable package.

The Dead Who Hear Will Live (5:25-26)

Now Jesus tells of something that is happening as he speaks and will happen in the future – "a time is coming and has now come":

> "25 I tell you the truth, a time is coming and has now come when the dead will hear the voice of the Son of God and those who hear will live. 26 For as the Father has life in himself, so he has granted the Son to have life in himself." (5:25-26)

Jesus is speaking on two different levels – as he often does in John's Gospel. Here is an example of what theologians call "realized eschatology," the Kingdom of God being both present and future, both "now" and "not yet."

	Time Coming	Has now come
"Dead"	Physically dead	Spiritually dead
"Dead who hear"	Called to resurrection by the Messiah	Those who hear and believe
"Will live"	Raised from the dead on the Last Day	Receive salvation and eternal life

The reason that Jesus can do this is explained in verse 26:

> "For as the Father has life in himself, so he has granted[239] the Son to have life in himself." (5:26)

This is an echo of the first few verses of John. God the Creator, the Life-Giver of Genesis gives life to and through his Son.

---

[239] "Granted" (NIV, NRSV), "given" (KJV) is common *didōmi*, "to give," here with the connotation, "to grant by formal action, grant, allow" (BDAG 242, 13).

"All things were made by him; and without him was not anything made that was made. **In him was life**; and the life was the light of men." (1:3-4)

Authority to Judge (5:27)

As we saw in verses 21 and 22, the Father has granted the Son the divine prerogative of "life in himself." He also has granted him "authority to judge."

"And he has given him authority to judge because he is the Son of Man." (5:27)

With the title "Son of Man" (Jesus' preferred title), Jesus is recalling a Messianic passage from Daniel:

> 13 "In my vision at night I looked, and there before me was one like a **son of man**, coming with the clouds of heaven. He approached the Ancient of Days and was led into his presence. 14 **He was given authority, glory and sovereign power**; all peoples, nations and men of every language worshiped him. His dominion is an **everlasting dominion** that will not pass away, and his kingdom is one that **will never be destroyed**." (Daniel 7:13-14)

Because Jesus is both the heavenly Son of Man and the Son of God, he has all authority.

> "... that at the name of Jesus every knee should bow,
> in heaven and on earth and under the earth,
> and every tongue confess that Jesus Christ is Lord,
> to the glory of God the Father." (Philippians 2:10-11)

Judgment at the Resurrection (5:28-29)

This authority to judge *and* to offer life will be exercised at the resurrection of the dead:

> "28 Do not be amazed at this, for a time is coming when all who are in their graves will hear his voice 29 and come out – those who have done good will rise to live, and those who have done evil will rise to be condemned. (5:28-29)

These words also recalled Daniel's prophecies of the Last Day that speaks of a resurrection of both the just and the unjust.

> "Multitudes who sleep in the dust of the earth will awake: some to everlasting life, others to shame and everlasting contempt." (Daniel 12:2)

The same idea is found on Paul's lips proclaiming before Felix the Governor in Caesarea his agreement with the Pharisees concerning the resurrection:

> "I have the same hope in God as these men, that there will be a resurrection of both the righteous and the wicked." (Acts 24:15)

"By Myself I Can Do Nothing" – Subordination of the Son to the Father (5:30)

Again, as in 5:19, Jesus states his complete dependence upon the Father.

> "By myself I can do nothing; I judge only as I hear, and my judgment is just, for I seek not to please myself but him who sent me." (5:30)

The Son is not independent of the Father, but rather dependent and working in concert. Jesus listens to the Father and speaks the Father's words, declares the Father's judgment. He and the Father are inseparable.

The doctrine of the Trinity affirms that the Father and Son and Holy Spirit are eternally equal in Person, but acknowledges that the Son and Holy Spirit are subordinate in role – "ontological equality, but economic subordination," that is, "equal in being, but subordinate in role." That understanding of equality and subordination in role is apparent in the very words "Father" and "Son."[240]

If you and I would follow this same example of submission by constantly listening to the voice of the Spirit, rather than forging ahead in our own wisdom, we would be much farther along in fulfilling God's plan for our own lives.

> **Q3. (John 5:30) Why is Jesus so dependent upon the Father for wisdom? How dependent are you upon your culture to approve of your way of life and validate your wisdom? To what degree do you depend upon God for wisdom?**
> http://www.joyfulheart.com/forums/topic/1438-q3-wisdom-from-the-father/

1. John the Baptist's Testimony Concerning Jesus (5:31-35)

So far Jesus has explained his relationship as a Son to the Father. But now he shifts to a very Jewish concern – the validity of one's statements. According to Jewish jurisprudence, everything had to be established on the basis of two or three credible witnesses, based on Deuteronomy 17:6 and 19:15-19.[241] One's own testimony about oneself wasn't considered valid. It needed to be confirmed by other testimony.

Jesus' first collaborating testimony is John the Baptist.

> "31 If I testify about myself, my testimony is not valid. 32 There is another who testifies in my favor, and I know that his testimony about me is valid. 33 You have sent to John and he has testi-fied to the truth. 34 Not that I accept human testimony; but I mention it that you may be saved. 35 John was a lamp that burned and gave light, and you chose for a time to enjoy his light." (5:31-35)

2. Testimony of Jesus' Miracles (5:36-37a)

Jesus' second collaborating witness is God the Father.

> "I have testimony weightier than that of John. For the very work that the Father has given me to finish, and which I am doing, testifies that the Father has sent me." (5:36)

Jesus makes the claim that his own miracles are testimony of God's confirmation. As Nicodemus said to Jesus:

---

[240] Wayne Grudem, *Systematic Theology*, pp. 351-352. See also my article, "Four Reasons Why I Believe in the Trinity" (www.joyfulheart.com/scholar/trinity.htm).

[241] See Matthew 18:16; 26:60; 2 Corinthians 13:1; 1 Timothy 5:19; Hebrews 10:28.

"Rabbi, we know you are a teacher who has come from God. For no one could perform the miraculous signs you are doing if God were not with him." (3:2)

Later, the man born blind whom Jesus heals, states the obvious syllogism or logical argument to Jesus' enemies:

"We know that God does not listen to sinners. He listens to the godly man who does his will. Nobody has ever heard of opening the eyes of a man born blind. If this man were not from God, he could do nothing." (9:31-33)

Again:

"The miracles I do in my Father's name speak for me.... even though you do not believe me, believe the miracles." (10:25, 38)

"... At least believe on the evidence of the miracles themselves." (14:11)

"If I had not done among them what no one else did, they would not be guilty of sin. But now they have seen these miracles...." (15:24)

We live in a generation when some very conservative Christians dismiss miracles as unnecessary, since we now have the Bible. Some conclude that miracles and other supernatural gifts have passed away.

On the other hand, those who know their recent church history, know that in the twentieth century hundreds of thousands of people were converted to Christ after they witnessed miracles.

Miracles are valuable in attracting people to Christ, and are clearly a convincing testimony to the validity of Jesus' gospel. However, John makes the point that merely miraculous signs themselves are inadequate to produce a mature faith in Jesus. A mature faith comes from believing Jesus' words and message (4:42, 50, 53). Miracles, however, are an important beginning point for many.

> **Q4. (John 5:36-37) According to John's Gospel, what is the value of miracles? What is the weakness of faith that depends solely on miracles? Why do you think that we don't have more miracles in our day? How much is that dependent upon a congregation's attitude (and unbelief) towards the importance of modern-day miracles?**
> http://www.joyfulheart.com/forums/topic/1439-q4-value-of-miracles/

3. The Father's Testimony (5:37a)

The third witness to Jesus is the Father himself:

"And the Father who sent me has himself testified concerning me." (5:37a)

This may be another reference to God's confirmation through miracles, but it may refer to the Holy Spirit's presence (1:33) and God's voice at Jesus' baptism: "You are my Son, whom I love; with you I am well pleased" (Luke 3:22)

4. The Testimony of the Scriptures (5:37b-40)

A fourth collaborating witness is found in the Scriptures themselves.

"*37b* You have never heard his voice nor seen his form, *38* nor does his word dwell in you, for you do not believe the one he sent. *39* You diligently study the Scriptures because you think that by them you possess eternal life. These are the Scriptures that testify about me, *40* yet you refuse to come to me to have life." (5:37b-40)

What a strong statement about the deadness of mere study of the Scriptures without application of what you read! The Jewish leaders Jesus addresses are spiritually dull:

"You have never heard his voice nor seen his form, nor does his word dwell in you...." (5:37b-38a)

They are unable to hear the voice of God mediated by the Spirit. They haven't seen God physically nor have they grasped him spiritually. Finally, Jesus says, "nor does his word dwell in you." This phrase is an important definition of a disciple. Later, Jesus tells his disciples in his great discourse on the Vine and the Branches and abiding in the Vine:

"If you remain in me and my words remain in you, ask whatever you wish, and it will be given you." (15:7)

As Jeremiah put it:

"When your words came, I ate them;
they were my joy and my heart's delight,
for I bear your name, O LORD God Almighty." (Jeremiah 15:16)

Paul tells us:

"Let the word of Christ dwell in you richly as you teach and admonish one another with all wisdom, and as you sing psalms, hymns and spiritual songs with gratitude in your hearts to God." (Colossians 3:16)

In a related passage to the Ephesians he equates letting the word of Christ dwell in you with being filled with the Spirit (Ephesians 5:19). That was Nicodemus's problem. He wasn't born of the Spirit and consequently couldn't even see or understand the Kingdom of God (3:3).

The Holy Spirit is absolutely necessary for us to understand and apply the Scriptures. As Paul told the Corinthian church:

"The man without the Spirit does not accept the things that come from the Spirit of God, for they are foolishness to him, and he cannot understand them, because they are spiritually discerned." (1 Corinthians 2:14)

Jesus' enemies made the mistake that many religious people do. They mistook *knowing* the Bible with *internalizing* God's words and *doing* what they say.

"You diligently study the Scriptures because you think that by them you possess eternal life." (5:39)

James puts it another way.

"Do not merely listen to the word, and so deceive yourselves. Do what it says." (James 1:22)

In the same way, Jesus said just prior to his Parable of the House Built upon a Rock:

"Why do you call me, 'Lord, Lord,' and do not do what I say? ... The one who hears my words and does not put them into practice is like a man who built a house on the ground without a foundation...." (Luke 6:46, 49a)

What does it mean to have Christ's word dwell in us? It means to internalize its truths so it guides our whole life. We embrace it and put it into practice. Bible study is good. It is important. But even more important is application and obedience!

The Scriptures Testify about Me (5:39b)

Where do the Scriptures testify about Jesus? We aren't given a single list, but we know that after Jesus' resurrection, on the road to Emmaus:

> "Beginning with Moses and all the Prophets, he explained to them what was said in all the Scriptures concerning himself." (Luke 24:27)

Over breakfast beside the Sea of Galilee, he told his disciples:

> "Everything must be fulfilled that is written about me in the Law of Moses, the Prophets and the Psalms." (Luke 24:44b)

Without doubt, you can find references to these Scriptures in the preaching of the apostles in the early chapters of Acts. In addition, Matthew especially is careful to cite the many places that Jesus fulfilled what had been written about him in the Old Testament.

> **Q5. (John 5:39-40) What should be the role of the Scriptures in our lives? How is it possible for a person to be a great student of the Bible, but so lacking in spiritual discernment and lifestyle? How can we keep our churches orthodox but not legalistic and judgmental?**
> **http://www.joyfulheart.com/forums/topic/1440-q5-discernment-and-scripture/**

Seeking Praise from Men (5:41-44)

Jesus has cited his four witnesses. Now he expresses how little value human testimony ("praise from men") is in light of the divine testimony he has cited.

> "[41] I do not accept praise from men, [42] but I know you. I know that you do not have the love of God in your hearts. [43] I have come in my Father's name, and you do not accept me; but if someone else comes in his own name, you will accept him. [44] How can you believe if you accept praise from one another, yet make no effort to obtain the praise that comes from the only God?" (5:41-44)

So often we are more concerned about what people think about us, than what God thinks of us! God help us!

Moses Wrote about Jesus (5:45-47)

The Pharisees prided themselves on being successors to Moses the Lawgiver.

> "[45] But do not think I will accuse you before the Father. Your accuser is Moses, on whom your hopes are set. [46] If you believed Moses, you would believe me, for he wrote about me. [47] But since you do not believe what he wrote, how are you going to believe what I say?" (5:45-47)

The Pharisees have twisted Moses' teachings so that they didn't have to believe that Jesus is the Prophet that would come (Deuteronomy 18:18-19).

Lessons for Disciples

This has been a long discourse. Let's sum up some of the lessons we should learn as disciples.

1.   Jesus is equal with the father, but voluntarily subjects himself to the Father.

2.   Jesus listens to the Father, then does what the Father is doing. In this he is our example of how we should listen and obey (5:19).

3.   Eternal life beings now for those who put their faith in Jesus. Even though we will appear before God's judgment, we will not be condemned (5:24).

4.   Eternal life is found in Christ himself, not in a religion or good works (1 John 5:11-12).

5.   We, like Jesus, are utterly dependent upon the Father; we are not to function independently.

This entire discourse on Life in the Son has been about how Jesus – uniquely – is the bringer of Life with a capital "L." My prayer for you is that your focus is not merely on the Scriptures that point to Jesus, but to trust Jesus himself, that he might bestow upon you his Life that lasts forever.

Prayer

Jesus, let my focus be on You. Yes, help me to understand and know your Word. But even more, let me know You and walk with you. Let your words find a home in my heart. Let them abide in me that I might abide in You. In your holy name, I pray. Amen.

Key Verses

"'My Father is always at his work to this very day, and I, too, am working.' For this reason, the Jews tried all the harder to kill him; not only was he breaking the Sabbath, but he was even calling God his own Father, making himself equal with God." (John 5:17-18, NIV)

"I tell you the truth, whoever hears my word and believes him who sent me has eternal life and will not be condemned; he has crossed over from death to life." (John 5:24, NIV)

"As the Father has life in himself, so he has granted the Son to have life in himself." (5:26, NIV)

"By myself I can do nothing; I judge only as I hear, and my judgment is just, for I seek not to please myself but him who sent me." (John 5:30, NIV)

"You diligently study the Scriptures because you think that by them you possess eternal life. These are the Scriptures that testify about me, yet you refuse to come to me to have life." (John 5:39-40, NIV)

13. Feeding the Five Thousand, Walking on Water (6:1-21)

We sometimes imagine that a cheap, non-polluting *energy source* would be the ultimate achievement for humankind. But in Jesus' day, where most people were subsistence farmers, finding a labor-free, inexhaustible *food supply* would be considered the prize.

And that's the drawing power of Jesus' miracle of the loaves and fishes, feeding 5,000 men, plus women and children. Perhaps that's why it's Jesus' only miracle that appears in all four gospels.

In one sense, however, it is more a lesson for the disciples' and believers' benefit than for the crowds that were fed. Let me explain.

James J. Tissot, 'Miracle of the Loaves and Fishes' (1886-94), gouache on gray wove paper, 7-3/8x11-9/16", Brooklyn Museum, New York.

Crowds Gather (6:1-4)

"¹ Some time after this, Jesus crossed to the far shore of the Sea of Galilee (that is, the Sea of Tiberias), ² and a great crowd of people followed him because they saw the miraculous signs he had performed on the sick. ³ Then Jesus went up on a mountainside and sat down with his disciples. ⁴ The Jewish Passover Feast was near." (6:1-4)

The miracle appears to have occurred on a mountainside above the city of Bethsaida (Luke 9:10) in the area known today as the Golan Heights.[242] Bethsaida had been the home of Philip (12:21), and, at least for a while, of several

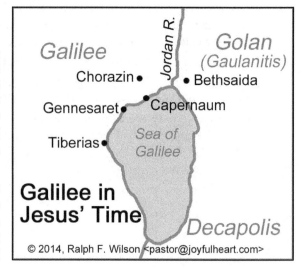

Galilee in Jesus' Time
© 2014, Ralph F. Wilson <pastor@joyfulheart.com>

[242] John doesn't specify the location, but says that it occurred on the "other side" of the Sea of Galilee – a pretty loose designation. "The far shore" (NIV), "the other side" (NRSV, ESV), "over" (KJV) is *peran*, "marker of a position across from something else, with intervening space, on the other side" (BDAG 796, bα). Perhaps Bethsaida was "across" the top of the lake from Capernaum, where Jesus' ministry was centered.

of Jesus' disciples (1:44; Mark 1:29). Bethsaida ("house of fish" or "house of fishermen") is at the northeast end of the Sea of Galilee, on a hill east of where the Jordan River enters the lake. In Old Testament times it had been the capital of the Aramean kingdom of Geshur. In the New Testament era, Herod the Great's son Philip rebuilt the city and named it Julius.[243]

John notes that it is near the time of Passover (6:4) and that there is grass on the mountainside (6:10). He probably mentions Passover because of its association with Moses and the Exodus, which he mentions in his Bread of Life discourse that we'll look at in Lesson 14.

From the Synoptic Gospels, we know that the disciples have just returned from their mission. John the Baptist has just been executed (Matthew 14:13), and that Jesus and his disciples are trying to take a break from the multitudes to a solitary place (Mark 6:31).

They take their accustomed boat (Mark 6:32), push off from the shore, and set sail toward a deserted area near the town of Bethsaida, only a few miles from Capernaum. By taking the boat, they are hoping to discourage the crowds from following them. They are trying to get away.

Involving the Disciples in Feeding (6:5-9)

However, they don't succeed in avoiding the crowds.

"5 When Jesus looked up and saw a great crowd coming toward him, he said to Philip, 'Where shall we buy bread for these people to eat?' 6 He asked this only to test him, for he already had in mind what he was going to do. 7 Philip answered him, 'Eight months' wages would not buy enough bread for each one to have a bite!'" (6:5-7)

Jesus sees the crowds and knows they must be hungry. According to the Synoptic Gospels, he teaches them for a while before the miracle. Now he asks Philip, who is a resident of Bethsaida and who would be familiar with food sources in the area, "Where shall we buy bread for these people to eat." Jesus is testing him.[244] Will Philip look to God to provide? No.

Philip doesn't give a location where they can buy food. Rather, he explains to Jesus how expensive it would be to buy bread for them all – "eight month's wages" (NIV), an approximate equivalent of 200 denarii (ESV). In America and Canada and Australia we would say, "That would take thousands of dollars." In the UK they would say, "That would take thousands of pounds." You substitute your own currency here. The point is, that this is a staggering sum, a sum way beyond what Jesus' band is carrying with them. It is way beyond their means. Philip's comment is probably included to emphasize how impossible it would be to buy a truckload of bread.

In each of the Synoptic Gospels the disciples urge Jesus to send the people away, rather than try to feed them, but Jesus insists: "*You* give them something to eat." He asks them to see what they have in store (Mark 6:38). It's interesting how Jesus seeks to involve his disciples in this feeding, both in finding what they have – and later in distributing the multiplied loaves and fish.

After they've obeyed Jesus, and inventoried their resources, Andrew makes his report. Only John gives this disciple's name and that it is a boy who has the food.

---

[243] Rami Arav, "Bethsaida," in *Jesus & Archaeology*, pp. 145-166.
[244] "Test" (NIV, NRSV, ESV), "prove" (KJV) is *peirazō*, "to endeavor to discover the nature or character of something by testing, try, make trial of, put to the test" (BDAG 792, 2b).

"⁸ Another of his disciples, Andrew, Simon Peter's brother, spoke up, ⁹ 'Here is a boy²⁴⁵ with five small barley loaves and two small fish....'" (6:8-9a)

The poor would eat barley loaves, while those better off would eat bread made from wheat. The fish seemed to be a couple of small dried or preserved fish.²⁴⁶ It's a simple lunch.

"... but how far will they go among so many?" (6:9b)

Again, Andrew emphasizes how tiny their resources are in face of the gargantuan task of Jesus' harebrained idea (so they thought) of feeding the entire crowd.

Huge Task, Tiny Resources

The lesson that Jesus is about to teach his disciples is the lesson of Gideon's army (Judges 6-7). When your resources are tiny compared to the need, you know the victory is God's, not man's.

Only now are the disciples prepared to see what God can accomplish with what they *do* have. At the very least, this is an adventure they will not soon forget.

Here's the sequence so far. They have examined the problem and seen no solution except to send the people away to fend for themselves. Jesus doesn't let them off the hook: "You feed them."

"We can't," they protest.

"What *do* you have?" Jesus asks.

"Five loaves and two fish."

"Give them to me," Jesus says.

Until the disciples are willing to commit what they *do* have to the enterprise, Jesus waits. Their contribution and commitment of it must be part of the solution, however tiny and inadequate.

Q1. (John 6:5-9) Why does Jesus try to get the disciples to own the task of feeding the crowds? What is the significance to the story of the boy's five loaves and two little fish? http://www.joyfulheart.com/forums/topic/1441-q1-involving-disciples/

Seating the Multitude (6:10)

Jesus is undeterred by his disciples' skepticism.

"Jesus said, 'Have the people sit down.' There was plenty of grass in that place, and the men sat down, about five thousand of them." (6:10)

Now Jesus organizes for the miracle that is about to take place. He gets the crowds arranged in an orderly fashion, presumably with paths between groups of fifty. Now the disciples can easily determine how much bread should be brought to each group, and seated, the people won't be pushing and shoving in order to grab at what is being distributed. The distribution channel is in place.

²⁴⁵ "Boy" (NIV, ESV), "lad" (NRSV, KJV) is the double diminutive of *paidarion*, "child," perhaps here "a youth" who is no longer a child, or it could mean, "young slave" (BDAG 748, 1b or 2).
²⁴⁶ "Fish" is *opsarion*, "fish", the double diminutive of *ospon*, originally "cooked food" eaten with bread. Here "fish," especially "dried or preserved fish." (BDAG 746; Brown, John 1:233). The Synoptics use the term *ichthus*, "fish."

There are 5,000 men, but in addition, women and children, probably swelling the number to more than double that. John's observation about "plenty of grass" is an indication of the season, springtime. In the summer, the grass becomes dry and brown. It is the kind of observation you'd expect an eyewitness to make.

Q2. (John 6:10) Why does Jesus have the crowds sit down before feeding them? What is the disciples' role in this? Why would you prepare for a miracle if you don't think it would happen? How ready is your congregation to see miracles take place?
http://www.joyfulheart.com/forums/topic/1442-q2-preparing-for-a-miracle/

Giving Thanks and Distributing (6:11)

"Jesus then took the loaves, gave thanks, and distributed to those who were seated as much as they wanted. He did the same with the fish." (6:11)

Jesus takes the loaves and fish, perhaps placing them in a basket in front of him. Then he lifts his eyes to heaven and "gave thanks." The word is *eucharisteō* (from which we get our English word "Eucharist"), "to express appreciation for benefits or blessings, give thanks, express thanks, render/return thanks."[247] The Jews took meals as an opportunity to offer praise and blessing to God himself. The traditional prayer is: "Blessed are you, Lord our God, King of the world, who has caused bread to come forth out of the earth."[248] Oh, disciple, do you bless God before your meals like Jesus did? If not, why don't you begin today?

The disciples appear to have baskets with them, used both to distribute the food and to collect the leftovers later on. The word is *kophinos*, "basket," probably a large, heavy basket for carrying things.[249] In Josephus' book, *Wars of the Jews*, the word is used for the large baskets soldiers used to carry their equipment and rations.[250] Emmerson says, "The *kophinos* was probably a basket of wickerwork, such as were carried by Jews as food containers, slung on the back by means of a cord handle."[251]

Though we're not told the details, I see Jesus breaking the small barley loaves into one disciple's basket, who goes off and serves a group of 50, while Jesus fills the next disciple's basket. A couple hundred baskets later, and a lot of breaking of fish and bread, each seated group has had its first round of food. Jesus and his disciples may have served them in this way for several hours. Breaking, carrying, distributing, and then back to Jesus for more.

---

[247] *Eucharisteō*, BDAG 415, 2. In the Synoptics, the word is *eulogeō*, from which we get our word "eulogize," the root meaning of which is "speak well of, praise, extol" (BAGD 322). When the Jews prayed before meals, they didn't usually pray, "Thank you for this food that we are about to receive."

[248] For more on this, see my article, "Don't Ask the Blessing, Offer One," *Joyful Heart*, November 15, 1999. (www.joyfulheart.com/holiday/offer-blessing.htm)

[249] *Kophinos*, BAGD 447.

[250] Josephus, *Wars of the Jews*, 3, 5, 5.

[251] Grace I. Emmerson, "Basket," ISBE 1:437-438.

This continued until all had eaten their fill. Then, presumably, Jesus dismissed the crowd and the people began the long walk home, full of food and full of wonder at this Jesus.

> **Q3. (John 6:11) How did Jesus distribute the multiplied loaves and fishes to the multitudes? How do the disciples fit in? How are the baskets used? What impression do you think this is making on the disciples as they work hard during the ongoing miracle?**
> **http://www.joyfulheart.com/forums/topic/1443-q3-the-hands-of-his-disciples/**

Twelve Baskets Left Over (6:12-13)

> "[12] When they had all had enough to eat, he said to his disciples, 'Gather the pieces that are left over. Let nothing be wasted.' [13] So they gathered them and filled twelve baskets with the pieces of the five barley loaves left over by those who had eaten." (6:12-13)

The disciples are very tired by now, but Jesus gives them one further task – to pick up the broken pieces of bread that are scattered over the hillside. When their task is completed, they come back with all twelve baskets full.

Why does Jesus have the tired disciples do this? To make the point to them that God's provision that day has not been merely adequate, but more than enough to meet the need. Weeks later when they are short of food, Jesus reminds them by asking:

> "'When I broke the five loaves for the five thousand, how many basketfuls of pieces did you pick up?' 'Twelve,' they replied." (Mark 8:19)

Each disciple can feel the weight of his basket of bread as he bears it back to Jesus and he will never forget the abundance of that day.

John alone notes Jesus' reason for picking up the remnants: "Let nothing be wasted" (6:12b, NIV) or "lost" (NRSV, ESV, KJV).[252] Though there is abundance, there is no waste. Collecting what was left over at the end of the meal was a Jewish custom.[253]

> **Q4. (John 6:12-13) Why does Jesus have his disciples pick up the left-over pieces? What does this have to do with his attitude towards waste? What does it have to do with his teaching the disciples about abundance?**
> **http://www.joyfulheart.com/forums/topic/1444-q4-left-overs/**

---

[252] The word is *apollymi*, "perish." In the middle voice, it can refer to things, "be lost, pass away, be ruined," of bursting wineskins, transitory beautify of gold, of flowers, of food that spoils (6:27). Also, "to lose something that one already has or be separated from a normal connection, lose, be lost," of falling hair, of wine that has lost its flavor (BDAG 116, 3b).

[253] Carson, *John*, p. 271, cites Strack and Billerback, 4:625-626.

The People See a Prophet and King (6:14-15)

The Feeding of the Five Thousand causes trouble for Jesus.

> "After the people saw the miraculous sign that Jesus did, they began to say, 'Surely this is the Prophet who is to come into the world.'" (6:14)

People are quick to use Jesus for their own ends – as they are today. The people quickly made the connection between Moses who brought manna (food from heaven) and Jesus' miracle. So it is natural that they see Jesus (rightly) as "the Prophet who is to come into the world," as we see elsewhere in John (1:21, 25; 7:40; Acts 3:22; 7:37). It is a reference to Moses' words:

> "The LORD your God will raise up for you a prophet like me from among your own brothers. You must listen to him." (Deuteronomy 18:15)

In Jesus' day, at least in some circles, this Prophet was identified with the Messiah.

Jesus knew the people's hearts. They weren't so interested in who Jesus was, but what he could do for them – provide free food (6:26) or use him to lead a rebellion against the Romans or their Herodian puppet rulers.

> "Jesus, knowing that they intended to come and make him king by force, withdrew again to a mountain by himself." (6:15)

Notice the strong verb used here. "By force" (NIV), "take by force" (NRSV, KJV) is *harpazō*, "snatch, seize," that is, take suddenly and vehemently, or take away. Here it means, "to grab or seize suddenly so as to remove or gain control, snatch/take away."[254] If the crowd used Jesus as a rebellion rallying point – even against his will – it would not only bring swift retaliation from the Romans, but also put an end to Jesus' mission.

Jesus puts an end to their designs by sending the disciples off, dismissing the crowd (Matthew 22:23), and leaving the scene.[255] Then he finds a place of refuge in one of the mountains on the Golan Heights where he can spend time in prayer (Matthew 14:23).

> **Q5. (John 6:14) How does the people's desire to make him king relate to the third temptation Jesus met in the wilderness (Luke 4:9)? What would have happened to God's plan of redemption if Jesus hadn't retreated to the hills on this occasion? Why must we resist giving in to people's plans for our lives?**
> **http://www.joyfulheart.com/forums/topic/1445-q5-peoples-plans-for-jesus/**

Jesus Walks on the Water (6:16-21)

Jesus had probably arranged with his disciples that, if he didn't join them by a particular time, they should disembark and go ahead to Capernaum.

---

[254] *Harpazō*, BDAG 134, 2a.

[255] "Withdrew" (NIV, NRSV, ESV), "departed" (KJV) is *anachōreō*, "to depart from a location," here, "withdraw, retire, take refuge" (BDAG 75, 1b).

"[16] When evening came, his disciples went down to the lake, [17] where they got into a boat and set off across the lake for Capernaum. By now it was dark, and Jesus had not yet joined them." (6:16-17)

What follows is a miracle recorded not only here, but also by Matthew and Mark, though John shapes the retelling for the particular purpose of his Gospel.

"[18] A strong wind was blowing and the waters grew rough. [19] When they had rowed three or three and a half miles, they saw Jesus approaching the boat, walking on the water; and they were terrified. [20] But he said to them, 'It is I; don't be afraid.' [21] Then they were willing to take him into the boat, and immediately the boat reached the shore where they were heading." (6:16-21)

Research on winds around the Sea of Galilee has found that, in addition to the constant westerly wind blowing in from the Mediterranean, in the evening as the land cools compared to the lake temperature, winds would blow from the land toward the lake, combining with the regular katabatic (gravity-driven) winds that blow down the steep slopes surrounding the lake.[256]

Among the disciples were fisherman who were well-aware of this phenomenon. The winds didn't frighten them. Nevertheless, they were fully engaged and rowing hard west towards Capernaum, not making much progress. The boat's sail had been taken in.

What did frighten them, however, was seeing an apparition (who turned out to be Jesus) walking on the water! John doesn't include Matthew's account of Peter trying to walk on water; John's purpose is to bring his readers to believe on Jesus as the Son of God.

The brave fisherman are "terrified."[257] Jesus says to them, "It is I. Don't be afraid." And, at that point, they believe him enough to let this night phantom into their boat.

The text says, "immediately" the boat reached its destination on the shore. Whether because the winds let up, they were close to shore anyway, or another miracle has occurred, we're not sure.

Some Simple Principles of Ministry

As I reflect on the Miracle of the Loaves and Fishes, I ask myself why Jesus performed this miracle. Was it out of compassion? Yes and no. He could have dismissed the people early enough so they could have gotten home in time to get something to eat. But he decided against it. In fact, the miracle caused him trouble before long as we see in 6:15, and raised Messianic expectations that could have quickly derailed Jesus' ministry (6:26).

John includes this miracle to show Jesus' power, help his readers believe in Jesus as the Son of God, and lead into Jesus' discourse on the Bread of Life. But I believe Jesus actually performed this miracle mainly for the disciples' benefit. Jesus could have created bread at the snap of his finger. He didn't need the disciples' pitiful five loaves and two fish. But they – and we – need to learn some very simple principles of ministry.

1.   Our resources are woefully inadequate to meet the need.

---

[256] Arieh Bitan, "Lake Kinneret (Sea of Galilee) and its exceptional wind system," *Boundary-Layer Meteorology*, 21:4 (December 1981), pp 477-487.

[257] "Terrified" (NIV, NRSV), "afraid" (KJV) is *phobeō* (from which we get our words "phobia" and "phobic"), "to be in an apprehensive state, be afraid," the aorist tense is often in the sense of "become frightened" (BDAG 1060, 1a).

2. We are to take inventory and bring what resources we have to Jesus.

3. We place them in his hands to do what he wishes with them, and in the process, release control to him.

4. He in turn blesses them and places them back in our hands, multiplied, more powerful than we could have imagined.

This is a faith process, a faith experience. Too often we are overwhelmed with the vastness of the need and give up. Or we belittle our resources to the point that we never release them to God, but selfishly hang on to them because that is all we know and all we have. We are inadequate, we know, but we refuse to let go.

Or we insist that God perform the task by himself, without us participating in the process even in a tiny way.

We must release our resources to him in trust. Their smallness in our eyes must not be an obstacle. He is teaching us a trust journey, and it must be accompanied by our learning to trust him by doing what he asks, even if we have no idea where he is going with it. If we can learn, if we *will* learn this vital lesson, then we can graduate to the next level.

- It is the lesson of Abraham offering Isaac, his only son.

- It is the lesson of Gideon seeing his small but inadequate army whittled down to a pitiful 300.

- It is the lesson that you and I face more often than we would like to admit.

- It is an essential lesson in the school of discipleship.

But if we will learn to trust, then we will experience the joy of being basket-bearers of Jesus-empowered food to the multitudes. And we'll be there to pick up the left-over pieces and marvel at the weight of his abundance.

It's just a small question – but a vital one for disciples: "How many loaves do you have? Go and see."

Prayer

Lord, too often I block you by my refusal to just trust you and go ahead as you are seeming to direct. How much ministry and blessing do I miss out on, Lord? Too much, I fear. Please forgive me. Help me to count it a joy to be a participant in the great thing you are doing rather than being a mere bystander. Lord, here are my small resources. I offer them to you unconditionally. Do with me as you will – where you will, when you will, with whom you will. In Your holy name, I pray. Amen.

Key Verse

"Another of his disciples, Andrew, Simon Peter's brother, spoke up, [9] 'Here is a boy with five small barley loaves and two small fish, but how far will they go among so many?'" (John 6:8-9, NIV)

14. I Am the Bread of Life (6:22-71)

Jesus has fed the five thousand, with twelve basketfuls of pieces left over. But in John's Gospel this is more than a miracle of compassion for people who are hungry. It is a "miraculous sign" (6:14), *sēmeion*, a sign that points people to see something beyond the miracle itself.

This miracle was a sign pointing to who Jesus is – the Bread of Life that God has sent down to quench our spiritual hunger and give us Life.

In Lesson 13 we examined the Feeding of the 5,000. Now we look at the effect of this miracle on those who had witnessed it. As we'll see, their motives for pursuing Jesus weren't out of spiritual hunger, so much as physical hunger – Jesus as a means to feed them physically.

Looking for Jesus for the Wrong Reasons (6:26)

The day after Jesus fed the 5,000 – and disappeared – people seemed to be frantically looking for him.

James J. Tissot, 'The Gathering of the Manna' (1896-1903), gouache on board, 11-7/16"x 9-5/16", The Jewish Museum, New York

"²² The next day the crowd that had stayed on the opposite shore of the lake realized that only one boat had been there, and that Jesus had not entered it with his disciples, but that they had gone away alone. ²³ Then some boats from Tiberias landed near the place where the people had eaten the bread after the Lord had given thanks. ²⁴ Once the crowd realized that neither Jesus nor his disciples were there, they got into the boats and went to Capernaum in search of Jesus. ²⁵ When they found him on the other side of the lake, they asked him, 'Rabbi, when did you get here?'" (6:21-25)

The Feeding of the Five Thousand appears to have occurred on a mountainside above the city of Bethsaida (Luke 9:10) in the area known today as the Golan Heights. They find Jesus across the top of the lake in Capernaum and ask how he got there. Jesus doesn't answer their question, but goes immediately to the real reason for their quest.

"Jesus answered, 'I tell you the truth, you are looking for me, not because you saw miraculous signs but because you ate the loaves and had your fill.'" (6:26)

There is a difference between faith in Jesus because his miracles point you to him and a desire to have someone meet your physical needs.

The Bread of Life Discourse (6:27-71)

This lesson contains Jesus' lengthy Bread of Life discourse, which can be divided into four general sections:

1. Jesus, the True Manna (6:27-34)
2. Jesus, the Bread of Life (6:35-51)
3. Partaking of the Son of Man (6:52-59)
4. Reactions to Jesus' Teaching (6:60-71)

But Jesus doesn't really use an outline. Rather this is a running dialog between Jesus and his hearers.

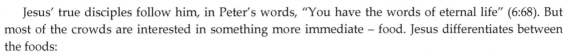

Food that Endures to Eternal Life (6:27)

"Do not work for food that spoils, but for food that endures to eternal life, which the Son of Man will give you. On him God the Father has placed his seal of approval." (6:27)

Jesus' true disciples follow him, in Peter's words, "You have the words of eternal life" (6:68). But most of the crowds are interested in something more immediate – food. Jesus differentiates between the foods:

Food that spoils	Natural food
Food that endures to eternal life	Spiritual food

"Endures" is the common verb *menō*, "remain, stay," here, in the sense of "to continue to exist, remain, last, persist, continue to live."[258] It's the same verb that is key to Jesus' discourse on the Vine and the Branches – the necessity for the branch retaining its connection to the vine – "abide in me, and I in you" (15:4). Food that isn't eaten spoils. But spiritual food, Jesus says, lasts for, endures for (*eis*, "until") eternity.

You'll see several close parallels between the Bread of Life discourse and the Woman at the Well. Jesus is making the same point there as here.

"Everyone who drinks this water will be thirsty again, but whoever drinks the water I give him will never thirst. Indeed, the water I give him will become in him a spring of water welling up to eternal life." (4:13-14)

Living water quenching thirst eternally corresponds to bread of life satisfying spiritual hunger forever.

Jesus uses his title of the Heavenly Man – "the Son of Man" – in making this promise of enduring food.

"Do not work for food that spoils, but for food that endures to eternal life, which the Son of Man will give you. On him God the Father has placed his seal of approval." (6:27)

---

[258] *Menō*, BDAG 631, 2b.

"Placed his seal of approval" (NIV), "set his seal" (NRSV, ESV), "sealed" (KJV) is *sphragizō*, "to mark with a seal as a means of identification, mark, seal."[259] When did this sealing take place? We're not told, but probably at Jesus' baptism, where the dove marked the presence of the Holy Spirit and the Father spoke words of authentication:

> "You are my Son, whom I love; with you I am well pleased." (Luke 3:22)

Or perhaps on the mount of transfiguration, God's words:

> "This is my Son, whom I love; with him I am well pleased. Listen to him!" (Matthew 17:5)

Q1. (John 6:26-27) Why were some of these "believers" following Jesus? What were their selfish motives? For what motives do true disciples seek Jesus?
http://www.joyfulheart.com/forums/topic/1446-q1-believers-motives/

The Work of God – Believe (6:28-29)

Jesus has said:

> "Do not **work**[260] for food that spoils, but for food that endures to eternal life" (6:27)

So the crowd follows up on this idea of working. They wonder what kind of work is necessary to get this everlasting food?

> "28 Then they asked him, 'What must we do to do the **works** God requires?'
> 29 Jesus answered, 'The **work** of God is this: to believe in the one he has sent.'" (6:28-29)

The same verb, *ergazomai*, "to work" (verse 27) occurs in verse 28, along with its corresponding plural of the noun, *ergon*, "works."[261] The Jews were used to the idea of meritorious works that would bring them favor from God. What should we be doing? they ask naively, as if they can perfectly perform what God requires if they just know what it is. Jesus answers with one work – faith, "to believe in the one he has sent" (6:29).

Paul says the same thing in different words as he combats "works righteousness" in his letter to the Galatian church.

> "We know that a person is justified not by the works of the law but through faith in Jesus Christ." (Galatians 2:16a)

Eternal life isn't earned; it is a gift, appropriated by faith – as it simply says in John 3:16.

Q2. (John 6:28-29) What kind of "works" do people sometimes pursue to please God? According to Jesus, what is the most important "work" that God requires of us?
http://www.joyfulheart.com/forums/topic/1447-q2-our-work/

---

[259] *Sphragizō*, BDAG 980, 3.

[260] "Work" (NIV, NRSV), "labor" (KJV) is the common verb *ergazomai*, "to engage in activity that involves effort, work" (BDAG 389, 1).

[261] *Ergon*, "that which displays itself in activity of any kind, deed, action," here, "deed, accomplishment" (BDAG 390, 1cα).

Requiring another Miraculous Sign (6:30-31)

The crowd doesn't seem to have a clue. Jesus has performed many miraculous signs in their presence, most recently feeding 5,000 people.[262] But now they want Jesus to prove by still another sign that they should put their faith in him.

> "30 So they asked him, 'What miraculous sign then will you give that we may see it and believe you? What will you do? 31 Our forefathers ate the manna in the desert; as it is written: "He gave them bread from heaven to eat."'" (6:30-31)

Here's their reasoning – faulty though it might be. Moses told us to expect another Prophet we should believe in (Deuteronomy 18:15-18). You want us to believe in you. Moses fed us with bread. So what miracle will you do to prove you're the Prophet?

The True Bread from Heaven (6:32-34)

First, Jesus corrects them. The verse they quoted doesn't say that Moses fed them, but that God fed them.

> "32 Jesus said to them, 'I tell you the truth, it is not Moses who has given you the bread from heaven, but it is my Father who gives you the true bread from heaven. 33 For the bread of God is he who comes down from heaven and gives life to the world.' 34 'Sir,' they said, 'from now on give us this bread.'" (6:32-34)

Jesus identifies himself as the "true bread" – another use of John's style of using "true" to differentiate from the inferior. The true bread comes down from heaven (like the manna did), but it doesn't spoil quickly like manna did if it wasn't consumed immediately (Exodus 16:20). The true bread doesn't just give physical life, but eternal life.

The crowd responds, "Sir[263], give us this bread always" (6:34, NRSV), but as the dialogue continues, we see that they are too spiritually dull to understand what Jesus is talking about. The woman at the well had responded in similar fashion, "Sir, give me this water so that I won't get thirsty and have to keep coming here to draw water" (4:15). At that point she was as clueless as the crowd is here.

I Am the Bread of Life (6:35-36)

Jesus senses their unbelief.

> "35 Then Jesus declared, 'I am the bread of life. He who comes to me will never go hungry, and he who believes in me will never be thirsty. 36 But as I told you, you have seen me and still you do not believe.'" (6:35-36)

Again, Jesus' words sound much like his promises of living water to the woman at the well (4:13-14). But they don't believe.

---

[262] See Appendix 5. "Signs" in John's Gospel.

[263] "Sir" (NIV, NRSV), "lord" (KJV) is *kyrios*. In the mouths of disciples, it means "Lord/Yahweh," but here it seems to be used in its secular sense, as a title of respect: "one who is in a position of authority, lord, master," as in 12:21 and 20:15 (BDAG 577, 2a).

The "I AM" Passages

"Then Jesus declared, '**I am** the bread of life.'" (John 6:35a)

This is the first of seven "I AM" passages in John, that include two Greek words *egō eimi*, "I am," together with a predicate or object.[264] "I am," of course, is a rather unveiled reference to the name by which God revealed himself to Moses as Yahweh – "I AM THAT I AM" (Exodus 3:14).

In saying "I am" in this way, Jesus is declaring his divinity and oneness with the Father. It is no coincidence that John emphasizes Jesus' "I AM" statements. He wants his readers to believe in Jesus as the Son of God and have eternal life (20:31). See Appendix 4. The 'I Am' Passages in John's Gospel.

A Passage of Promises (6:37-40)

Now we enter a section of the Bread of Life discourse where Jesus speaks in terms that clearly suggest both predestination and the perseverance of the saints, two very controversial doctrines argued over by Calvinists and Arminians. First, let's look at Jesus' assertion that he won't lose any whom the Father sends him. After that, we'll consider the matter of predestination.

How does this idea fit here? Jesus has just offered tremendous promises to a spiritually dull, unbelieving crowd. But Jesus assures them – and the readers – that not all will disbelieve. There will be people the Father sends who will believe and will continue or abide in that faith in spite of the unbelief of this crowd. This isn't about the workers in the harvest! It is the Father's harvest and he will not fail to bring it in.

> "37 All that the Father gives me will come to me, and whoever comes to me I will never drive away. 38 For I have come down from heaven not to do my will but to do the will of him who sent me. 39 And this is the will of him who sent me, that I shall lose none of all that he has given me, but raise them up at the last day. 40 For my Father's will is that everyone who looks to the Son and believes in him shall have eternal life, and I will raise him up at the last day." (6:37-40)

First, those whom the Father gives to Jesus *will* come to him (6:37a), a verse that strongly suggests predestination at work. We'll consider that when we look at 6:44 in a few moments.

Second, Jesus offers assurance. "Whoever comes to me I will never drive away" (6:37b). He is inviting people, not pushing them away.

> "Come to me, all you who are weary and burdened, and I will give you rest." (Matthew 11:28)

Third, Jesus says he will "lose none" the Father has given (6:39), a promise of Jesus' power to protect his disciples. A similar verse, often quoted, follows the analogy of protecting sheep from theft, says, "no one can snatch them out of my hand" (10:28). We'll examine the doctrine of the Perseverance of the Saints further when we discuss 10:28 (Lesson 19); 15:4-5 (Lesson 26); and 17:11-15 (Lesson 29). For the moment, suffice it to say, we can have assurance that Jesus takes care of his own disciples as his charge from the Father. We can trust him to keep us.

Fourth, is a wonderful promise – "Everyone who looks to the Son and believes in him shall have eternal life, and I will raise him up at the last day" (6:40). What we must do is to look at Jesus as our

---

[264] There are more verses in John translated, "I am," but in most cases they don't include the pronoun *egō*, which can be implied by the verb *eimi* itself, since in Greek the distinctive inflection of the verb tells us gender, tense, and voice. When the pronoun appears with the verb, it is emphatic – there to make a point.

Savior – like Jesus' example of the bronze snake in the wilderness (6:14-15; Numbers 21:6-9). If we look with faith, we live!

Fifth, twice Jesus promises to raise believers from the dead at the Last Day. We're talking about resurrection. The Pharisees believed in it, but the Sadducees did not. What is bold and blasphemous (if it weren't true), is that Jesus here claims to be the one to personally raise believers from the dead. Such a claim must have angered Jesus' enemies no end.

What wonderful promises crammed into just four verses!

No One Can Come Unless the Father Draws Him (6:41-47)

Predictably, Jesus' enemies bristle because of his amazing claims. We know his parentage, they say. His claims to be the bread come down from heaven are preposterous!

"41 At this the Jews[265] began to grumble about him because he said, 'I am the bread that came down from heaven.' 42 They said, 'Is this not Jesus, the son of Joseph, whose father and mother we know? How can he now say, "I came down from heaven"?'

43 'Stop grumbling among yourselves,' Jesus answered.

44 'No one can come to me unless the Father who sent me draws him, and I will raise him up at the last day.

45 It is written in the Prophets: 'They will all be taught by God.' Everyone who listens to the Father and learns from him comes to me. 46 No one has seen the Father except the one who is from God; only he has seen the Father. 47 I tell you the truth, he who believes has everlasting life." (6:41-47)

Jesus is recognizing that not everyone can see spiritual things. It is a gift from God (6:44). Certainly, his enemies are blind to who he is, even though they pour over the Scriptures (5:39). In the Synoptic Gospels following the Parable of the Sower, Jesus quotes Isaiah to indicate that the spiritual blindness of some is to be expected.

"You will be ever hearing but never understanding;
you will be ever seeing but never perceiving.
For this people's heart has become calloused;
they hardly hear with their ears,
and they have closed their eyes.
Otherwise they might see with their eyes,
hear with their ears,
understand with their hearts and turn,
and I would heal them." (Matthew 13:14-15)

However, Jesus, says (quoting Isaiah 54:13), "They will all be taught of God" (6:45) Those who truly seek the Father will recognize Jesus as speaking God's truth – and in believing Jesus they will find everlasting life.

---

[265] For John's use of "the Jews" to refer to Jewish leaders, see Appendix 2. 'The Jews' in John's Gospel.

Predestination and Prevenient Grace

We need to look carefully at three verses in Jesus' discourse on the Bread of Life that strongly indicate God's sovereignty.

"All that the Father gives me will come to me." (6:37a)

"No one can come to me unless the Father who sent me draws[266] him." (6:44a)

"No one can come to me unless the Father has enabled[267] him." (6:65b)

In certain corners of the evangelical movement there has been a long-standing insistence that anyone can come to Christ, based on the idea, "whosoever will may come." People must make a decision. They're responsible to respond with faith. It is up to them. That's one side of the coin. And, make no mistake, personal responsibility to obey God has plenty of backing in Scripture.

But the other side of the coin is that God is behind the scenes making it possible for us to come. The truth is that we are not free moral agents in a neutral world. There is an enemy who captures and ensnares many, who blinds the eyes of unbelievers (2 Corinthians 4:4). And there is the Holy Spirit who convicts and draws us (16:8). There is an ongoing spiritual battle for the souls of men and women.

This involves what followers of John Wesley call "prevenient grace" or "preceding grace," God's grace that comes before or precedes our human decision. It exists prior to and without reference to anything humans may have done. Calvinists follow St. Augustine who taught that prevenient grace cannot be resisted – "irresistible grace," the I in the TULIP acronym of 5-point Calvinism. Wesleyan Arminians, on the other hand, believe that prevenient grace enables, but does not ensure, personal acceptance of the gift of salvation.

This involves a whole series of arguments that I don't want to sidetrack us now – I just wanted you to be aware of it. The bottom line is that God is at work in our salvation. Unless the Father draws you, according to 6:44, you won't (or can't) really come to Jesus with your heart. Be thankful! (Matthew 13:16-17).

How do I resolve this? I don't fully. It's a mystery we can't know fully this side of heaven. Our assurance comes from believing the strong promises of God's drawing and keeping. But our preaching comes from obedience to the command to preach the gospel to every creature, regardless of the response (Mark 16:15-16). If we aren't willing to work with that kind of passion, we might become like the hyper-Calvinist who responded to William Carey's passion to bring Christ's gospel to India – "Young man, sit down; when God pleases to convert the heathen, he will do it without your aid and mine." We must be obedient to preach the gospel to all nations and leave the results to God. When we get to heaven the mystery will clear!

---

[266] "Draws" in 6:44 is the verb *helkō*, "to move an object from one area to another in a pulling motion, draw." It can refer to someone who is dragged into court (James 2:6), drawing a sword (John 18:10), or hauling a net (John 21:6, 11). Here it is used figuratively, "to draw a person in the direction of values for inner life, draw, attract."[266] Jesus uses it in this sense when he says, "When I am lifted up from the earth, will draw all men to myself" (12:32).

[267] "Enabled" (NIV), "it is granted" (NRSV, ESV), "given" (KJV) is the perfect passive participle of the common verb *didōmi*, "to give," here, "to grant by formal action, grant, allow" (BDAG 243, 14 or perhaps 17b).

Q3. (John 6:37, 44, 65) What is the significance of Jesus' teaching that only the ones the Father "draws" to him can come to him? In what way does this sound like predestination? How does the Holy Spirit prepare people to put their faith in Christ?
http://www.joyfulheart.com/forums/topic/1448-q3-drawn-by-the-father/

The Bread of Life that Comes Down from Heaven (6:48-51a)

Now Jesus repeats his claim that he is the Bread of Life he had spoken of earlier (6:33, 35).

"48 I am the bread of life. 49 Your forefathers ate the manna in the desert, yet they died. 50 But here is the bread that comes down from heaven, which a man may eat and not die. 51 I am the living bread that came down from heaven. If anyone eats of this bread, he will live forever." (6:48-51a)

"Bread of Life" and "Living Bread" mean bread that brings life, just as "Living Water," in the spiritual sense, means water that brings life. It is not physical life that physical bread and water sustain that he is talking of here, but eternal life. Jesus contrasts himself to the manna that came down from heaven in the wilderness (Exodus 16:13-36). People ate the manna, but eventually died. But those who eat of the Living Bread will have eternal life.

Eat My Flesh (6:51b-52)

Notice that in 6:51b, Jesus switches metaphors, from eating bread that brings life to giving his literal, physical flesh – that is, his body on the cross – to bring life to the whole world, that is redeem it from sin.

"51b This bread is my flesh, which I will give for the life of the world.

52 Then the Jews[268] began to argue sharply among themselves, 'How can this man give us his flesh to eat?'" (6:48-52)

Their question about eating Jesus' flesh, has continued as a controversy to our day, since the following verses use language that reminds Christian readers of partaking of the Lord's Supper, Communion, the Eucharist.

"53 Jesus said to them, 'I tell you the truth, unless you **eat the flesh** of the Son of Man and **drink his blood**, you have no life in you. 54 Whoever **eats my flesh and drinks my blood has eternal life**, and I will raise him up at the last day. 55 For my flesh is real food and my blood is real drink. 56 Whoever **eats my flesh and drinks my blood remains in me**, and I in him. 57 Just as the living Father sent me and I live because of the Father, so the one who **feeds on me** will live because of me. 58 This is the bread that came down from heaven. Your forefathers ate manna and died, but he who feeds on this bread will live forever.'" (John 6:53-58)

---

[268] For John's use of "the Jews" to refer to Jewish leaders, see Appendix 2. 'The Jews' in John's Gospel.

Is Jesus Speaking of the Lord's Supper Here?

The big question is this: Is Jesus speaking about the Lord's Supper in this passage? His audience, remember, is primarily those he is trying to bring to faith in Christ, but John knew that Christians would read these words too – and that they couldn't help but think of the Lord's Supper. What is Jesus saying here? Jesus has been going back and forth between three metaphors:

1. **Manna**, "bread from heaven" (6:31-34, 38, 41-42, 49-50, 58)

2. **Bread of Life**, that is, bread that brings about eternal life (6:35-42, 51, 58)

3. **Flesh and blood** as "food" (6:51b-56)

These metaphors are related in that they all refer to eating and nourishing. These are the elements Jesus uses to weave a beautiful and powerful teaching on faith and eternal life. Of course, he is speaking spiritually here, not physically, following the tradition of Isaiah 55:1-2.

So what does the metaphorical language "eating" the "Bread of Life" mean?

- verse 47: He who believes | has eternal life
- verse 51a: If anyone eats of this (living) bread | he will live forever

It is quite clear that "believing in Jesus" corresponds to "eating the Bread of Life," since these are used as parallel statements in the same context and with the same result – everlasting life. This theme weaves itself through this discourse, and is said first one way and then another throughout the passage (6:39-40, 47, 57, 63, etc.). St. Augustine put it this way: "For to believe on Him is to eat the living bread. He that believes eats; he is sated invisibly...."[269]

> **Q4. (John 6:35-51) What does the metaphor of "eating the Bread of Life" mean in practical terms? To extend the same metaphor, what do you think might be the difference between nibbling the Bread of Life rather than actually making a meal of it?**
> http://www.joyfulheart.com/forums/topic/1449-q4-eating-the-bread-of-life/

Flesh Given for the Life of the World (6:51b)

In verse 51b, Jesus now moves from the analogy of the Bread of Life to a new analogy: the sacrifice of his body on the cross. This is the transition verse:

> "This bread is my flesh, which I will give for the life of the world." (John 6:51b)

Notice the words here that point to a physical sacrifice:

- "Flesh" (*sarx*) here means "physical body."[270]
- "Give, given" (*didōmi*) means "to dedicate oneself for some purpose or cause, give up, sacrifice."[271]
- "For" (*hyper*) means, "in behalf of, for the sake of someone or something."[272]

---

[269] Augustine, *Homilies on John*, 26, 1.
[270] *Sarx*, BDAG 914-916, 2a.
[271] *Didōmi*, BDAG 242, 10.
[272] *Hyper*, BDAG 1030-1031.

The purpose of Jesus' gift of his body is "the life of the world," that is eternal life, the theme Jesus keeps coming back to in this passage.

The Bread of Life Discourse and the Lord's Supper

Each of the Synoptic Gospels includes the Lord's Supper, and what theologians call "the Words of Institution," in some form or another. Here's Matthew's account:

> "26 While they were eating, Jesus took a loaf of bread, and after blessing it he broke it, gave it to the disciples, and said, 'Take, eat; this is my body.' 27 Then he took a cup, and after giving thanks he gave it to them, saying, 'Drink from it, all of you; 28 for this is my blood of the covenant, which is poured out for many for the forgiveness of sins.'" (Matthew 26:26-28)

The Apostle Paul states the Words of Institution in a similar way:

> "23b The Lord Jesus on the night when he was betrayed took a loaf of bread, 24 and when he had given thanks, he broke it and said, 'This is my body that is for you. Do this in remembrance of me.' 25 In the same way he took the cup also, after supper, saying, 'This cup is the new covenant in my blood. Do this, as often as you drink it, in remembrance of me.'" (1 Corinthians 11:23-25)

John, however, is unique in that he does *not* include a description of the Lord's Supper. He records a series of Farewell Discourses given the night Jesus was betrayed (chapters 13-17), but there is no mention of the Lord's Supper there. Why? We're not sure.

But it seems like this is another instance of the Synoptic writers giving the *facts* of an account, while John probes the *meaning* of the account. John assumes that his readers, at least his Christian readers, are familiar with one or more of the Synoptic Gospels. So he is free to take us deeper. Jesus' teaching on the Bread of Life serves as a kind of parallel teaching to the Words of Institution.

Joos van Cleve (Dutch artist, 1485-1540), detail "The Last Supper," oil on wood, 45 x 206 cm, Musée du Louvre, Paris, Predella of "Altarpiece of the Lamentation" (c. 1530).

Literal or Figurative? (6:53-57)

Jesus' metaphor shifted from eating bread to eating flesh. And there is an immediate reaction to Jesus' words, due to a revulsion in Judaism and most other cultures against cannibalism:[273] Instead of backing off when he saw this reaction (6:54), he makes it more specific yet.

---

[273] For Jews to drink blood would have been morally repugnant because of the strong prohibitions against drinking blood (Genesis 9:3; Leviticus 7:26; 17:14; 19:26; Deuteronomy 14:4-5; Acts 15:29). Even the priests who partook of the flesh of the sacrifices in the tabernacle and temple didn't drink the blood. Though Jews could eat the meat of clean animals, to eat human flesh was especially repugnant to them (Talmud, *Chulin* 92b). The only times we hear of it in the Bible are during wartime sieges that mothers might eat their dead infants in order to keep from starving themselves (Leviticus

"[53]Jesus said to them, 'I tell you the truth, unless you eat the flesh of the Son of Man and drink his blood, you have no life in you. [54]Whoever eats my flesh and drinks my blood has eternal life, and I will raise him up at the last day. [55]For my flesh is real food and my blood is real drink. [56]Whoever eats my flesh and drinks my blood remains in me, and I in him. [57]Just as the living Father sent me and I live because of the Father, so the one who feeds on me will live because of me.'" (6:53-57)

Though some believe he is speaking literally of his own flesh and blood in the Eucharist, I see this as an example of Jesus' use of hyperbole to make his point powerful and unforgettable (such as in Matthew 5:29-30; 19:24; Luke 6:41-42; 14:26; 1 Corinthians 9:27).

In my book *Lord's Supper: Meditations for Disciples on the Eucharist or Communion* (JesusWalk, 2011), I consider in greater detail the arguments of Roman Catholics, for example, who take Jesus' words literally with respect to the Eucharist, to the effect that partaking of the Eucharist is essential to obtaining eternal life.

However, I believe this is a continuation and intensification of that same metaphor Jesus was using earlier in the discourse comparing manna to the Bread of Life. That was clearly figurative; it is unlikely that verses 53-57 should be taken literally, especially since Jesus sums up in verse 58 with a clearly figurative idea:

"This is the bread that came down from heaven. Your forefathers ate manna and died, but he who feeds on this bread will live forever." (6:58)

What Does Jesus Mean by Eating His Flesh and Drinking His Blood?

If this is figurative language, as I believe it is, then what is Jesus saying? Observe in 6:53-59 the consequences of eating Jesus' flesh and drinking his blood. Let's look at these verse by verse, examining the consequence as well as similar sayings elsewhere:

Verse 53 – "Having life in oneself." The consequence of believing is to have life in his name, according to 20:31. In 1 John 5:10-12, having life is associated with believing in the Son of God.

Verse 54a – "Has eternal life." Eternal life is the consequence of believing in 6:40a, as well as in 3:15-16; 3:36; 5:24; 1 Timothy 1:16; 1 John 5:13; etc.

Verse 54b – "Resurrection on the last day." Resurrection on the last day is the consequence of believing according to John 6:40b. Jesus also connects believing in him with resurrection and eternal life in the raising of Lazarus (11:25-26).

Verse 56 – "Remains or abides in Jesus." This is also a consequence of believing Jesus' words according to 15:7. His word remaining or abiding in us is connected with eternal life (1 John 2:23-25), being true disciples (8:31-32), and bearing fruit (15:5).

Verse 57 – "Live because of me." Eternal life is the consequence of believing in the "I am the resurrection and the life" passage (11:25-26).

26:29; Deuteronomy 28:53-57; Isaiah 9:20; Lamentations 4:10; Ezekiel 5:10), and then with a sense of repugnance and revulsion.

Verse 58 – "Live forever." This is the consequence of eating of the "living bread" in 6:51b above. It is another way of saying one "has eternal life" (see 6:54a above). In 11:26 Jesus connects believing in him with never dying.

It is clear that the consequences of putting one's faith in Jesus – believing in Jesus – are the same as the consequences of "eating his flesh and drinking his blood." This is a strong, even *extreme*, metaphor for faith.[274] As F.F. Bruce puts it: "To believe in Christ is not only to give credence to what he says; it is to be united to him by faith, to participate in his life."[275]

> **Q5. (John 6:53-59) What is "eating the Bread of Life" a metaphor of? What is "eating Jesus' flesh and drinking his blood" a metaphor of? How are these metaphors similar to each other? Why do you think Jesus used such a vivid and repugnant metaphor?**
> **http://www.joyfulheart.com/forums/topic/1450-q5-eating-flesh-drinking-blood/**

The Vivid Metaphor Causes an Uproar (6:59-66)

The metaphor was so vivid, so extreme, in fact, that it caused an uproar. Many "disciples" left and no longer followed Jesus.

> [59] He said these things while he was teaching in the synagogue at Capernaum. [60] When many of his disciples heard it, they said, 'This teaching is difficult; who can accept it?'

> [61] But Jesus, being aware that his disciples were complaining about it, said to them, 'Does this offend you? [62] Then what if you were to see the Son of Man ascending to where he was before? [63] It is the spirit that gives life; the flesh is useless. The words that I have spoken to you are spirit and life. [64] But among you there are some who do not believe.' For Jesus knew from the first who were the ones that did not believe, and who was the one that would betray him. [65] And he said, 'For this reason I have told you that no one can come to me unless it is granted by the Father.' [66] Because of this many of his disciples turned back and no longer went about with him."

As I reflect on the reaction to Jesus' vivid metaphor, Jesus' response seems very unlike what a modern politician would do. A politician would immediately have his press office issue a statement saying he was misquoted and then detail what he meant to say.

But Jesus' reaction in verses 61-62 to the complaining "disciples" (distinguished from the Twelve in 6:67) is to say, "If this offends you, then you'll be even more offended when I ascend to heaven." Jesus says something curious:

---

[274] Other Bible references to drinking blood are Isaiah 49:26 and Revelation 16:16.

[275] F.F. Bruce, *The Hard Sayings of Jesus* (InterVarsity Press, 1983), p. 21. St. Augustine (354-430 AD) gave guidelines on how to determine whether an expression is to be taken literally or figuratively. On 6:63 he comments: "If the sentence is one of command, either forbidding a crime or vice, or enjoining an act of prudence or benevolence, it is not figurative. If, however, it seems to enjoin a crime or vice, or to forbid an act of prudence or benevolence, it is figurative. 'Except ye eat the flesh of the Son of man,' says Christ, 'and drink His blood, ye have no life in you.' This seems to enjoin a crime or a vice; it is therefore a figure, enjoining that we should have a share in the sufferings of our Lord, and that we should retain a sweet and profitable memory of the fact that His flesh was wounded and crucified for us" (*On Christian Doctrine*, III, 16, 24).

"It is the spirit that gives life; the flesh is useless. The words that I have spoken to you are spirit and life." (6:63)

In other words, Jesus seems to be saying, to take these words literally, as if I was talking about literal bread and flesh, is pointless. I am speaking of spiritual things. The Spirit inspires Jesus' words, and these words, taken in their true sense, bring eternal life to those who believe.[276]

John reminds his readers that Jesus had said not all would believe – and that Jesus knew Judas would betray him in the end, as John quotes Jesus in verses 70-71.

"[70] Jesus answered them, 'Did I not choose you, the twelve? Yet one of you is a devil.' [71] He was speaking of Judas son of Simon Iscariot, for he, though one of the twelve, was going to betray him." (6:70-71)

We would be very upset to lose big numbers from church attendance. But Jesus knew that losing unbelievers from following him was no great loss. In fact, pruning dead limbs back to the living wood helps the health of the tree – and the vine (see chapter 15).

Will You Also Go Away? (6:67-69)

"[67] So Jesus asked the twelve, 'Do you also wish to go away?' [68] Simon Peter answered him, 'Lord, to whom can we go? You have the words of eternal life. [69] We have come to believe and know that you are the Holy One of God.'" (6:67-69)

There are some "hard sayings" in life that cause the faint of heart to let go. There are those who assent to Jesus' words, but when there is a crisis of faith, those who *continue to feed* on Jesus, who continue to believe, who abide in him, they are his true disciples; the others walk away. This entire passage is about Jesus having "the words of eternal life," that is, the words, which, when believed, result in eternal life.

Q6. (John 6:61-66) What was the difference between the Twelve and the crowd of "disciples" that turned away from Jesus? What is the mark of true disciples according to John 8:31-32? http://www.joyfulheart.com/forums/topic/1451-q6-turning-away/

---

[276] There has been lots of controversy about the exact meaning of this verse. The central question is what does "flesh" (*sarx*) refer to? (1) The most natural reference would be back to Jesus' previous paragraph – eating his flesh and drinking his blood. If we take "eating my flesh" figuratively as "believing in Jesus," as I have argued, the meaning would be: The Spirit gives life, believing in me counts for nothing. But that doesn't make any sense. This is rather a contrast between Spirit and flesh. (2) If we take "eating my flesh" literally of the Eucharist, the meaning would be: The Spirit gives life, eating the sacramental flesh counts for nothing. Zwingli argued along this line against Luther's view of the Real Presence. But this assumes that Jesus in this discourse in Capernaum was speaking directly concerning the Lord's Supper which would take place later, an assumption we just don't have evidence to make. (3) More likely then, Jesus is not referring to the flesh of 6:53-56, but rather contrasting flesh and Spirit, much as he did in his discussion with Nicodemus in John 3:6: "That which is born of the flesh is flesh; and that which is born of the Spirit is spirit." In this case "flesh" would mean, "the natural principle in man which cannot give eternal life" (Brown, *John* 1:300). So the meaning of Jesus' words in 6:63 is probably: The Spirit gives life; what man can understand and achieve on his own counts for nothing. The words I have spoken to you – spiritually discerned and believed – bring spiritual life, eternal life.

As indicated earlier, while I don't believe Jesus deliberately gave this teaching with reference to the Sacrament of the Eucharist, I do believe that John, as he composed the Fourth Gospel, included this discourse knowing that his readers would read it with the Lord's Supper in mind. The Bread of Life passage and the Lord's Supper have parallel teachings.

The Lord's Supper deliberately uses elements intended to remind us of Jesus' body and blood: chewy bread to remind us of flesh, red wine to remind us of blood. The act of partaking of the Lord's Supper certainly is one of feeding on Jesus – a physical symbolic act that speaks of a much deeper communion indeed:

- To feed on the Bread of Life is to believe Jesus' words and trust in him as the source of our life.
- To eat Jesus' flesh and blood means to utterly depend upon him and the truths he teaches for sustenance and life itself.

When we partake of the Lord's Supper we are commanded to remember Jesus' death for our sins. Our mind also turns to the Spirit of God who raised him from the dead, the same Spirit that gives spiritual life to us and will ultimately raise our bodies from the dead on the Last Day. The Lord's Supper is an act of remembering, reflecting, believing, trusting – this indeed reenergizes us as food to our souls and life to our faith. As the Anglican service directs as the bread is given to the recipient:

> "Take and eat this in remembrance that Christ died for thee, and feed on him in thy heart by faith, with thanksgiving."

Feeding on Jesus' words and basking in his presence are the essence of trust, of true belief in him. Yes, partake of his body and blood in the Lord's Supper as a sign that you indeed feed on him in your heart – and so grow in your faith. Amen.

Lessons for Disciples

This has been a long and complex lesson. But several lessons stand out for us disciples to ponder and obey.

1. Sometimes people follow Jesus for merely selfish reasons (because Jesus gave them physical bread, for example), but true disciples must look beyond the physical blessings to hunger for spiritual life, eternal life (6:26-27).
2. Eternal life is gained by faith, not by certain works of righteousness (6:28-29).
3. Jesus is the Bread of Life who nourishes people spiritually and gives them eternal life (6:35).
4. We can't come to Jesus independently on our own terms and at our own time. We are only able to come as the Father draws us through prevenient grace – grace that comes prior to our salvation (6:44, also 6:37, 65).
5. Eating the Bread of Life and eating Jesus' flesh/drinking his blood, are vivid metaphors for putting our whole faith in him (6:53-59).
6. Not all who have the name of disciple will continue with Jesus. Those who have only a selfish or surface belief will fall away when Jesus tells them hard sayings or asks difficult things of them (6:61-66).

Prayer

Jesus, please teach me how to feed on you more than I do. I do believe in you; increase my faith, my willingness to obey, and the effectiveness of my ministry on your behalf. In your holy name, I pray. Amen.

Key Verses

This lesson has many quotable verses that are worth memorizing:

"Then they said to him, 'What must we do to perform the works of God?' Jesus answered them, 'This is the work of God, that you believe in him whom he has sent.'" (John 6:28-29, NIV)

"Jesus said to them, 'I am the bread of life. Whoever comes to me will never be hungry, and whoever believes in me will never be thirsty.'" (John 6:35, NIV)

"Everything that the Father gives me will come to me, and anyone who comes to me I will never drive away." (John 6:37, NIV)

"This is indeed the will of my Father, that all who see the Son and believe in him may have eternal life; and I will raise them up on the last day." (John 6:40, NIV)

"No one can come to me unless drawn by the Father who sent me; and I will raise that person up on the last day." (John 6:44, NIV)

"I am the living bread that came down from heaven. Whoever eats of this bread will live forever; and the bread that I will give for the life of the world is my flesh." (John 6:51, NIV)

"Whoever eats my flesh and drinks my blood has eternal life, and I will raise him up at the last day." (John 6:55, NIV)

"The Spirit gives life; the flesh counts for nothing. The words I have spoken to you are spirit and they are life." (John 6:63, NIV)

"Lord, to whom shall we go? You have the words of eternal life. We believe and know that you are the Holy One of God." (John 6:68b, NIV)

15. Streams of Living Water (7:1-52)

When he began his ministry, Jesus had been seen as a popular Galilean teacher, a prophet along the lines of John the Baptist. But the more he taught, the more he healed, the more people he attracted, the more he was suspect by Jewish leaders from Jerusalem. They saw him as a threat to their legalistic form of Judaism, as well as their own authority among the people. And so they plotted how they might kill him. As a result, John tells us, Jesus spent more time in Galilee, away from his enemies in Judea.

This lesson traces an encounter with Jesus' enemies, precipitated by Jesus' sudden appearance at the Feast of Tabernacles in Jerusalem. The controversy swirls around three issues: (1) legalism – Jesus healing on the Sabbath, (2) authority –

The annual Feast of Tabernacles or Booths (Hebrew *Sukkot*) celebrated the Israelites' camping in the Wilderness. To recall this, each family would build a temporary shelter in which to eat. Jesus went up to Jerusalem during this Feast. Artist unknown.

who did he think he was, anyway? and (3) origins – did Jesus meet the birthplace qualifications of the Messiah in the Scripture?

In the midst of the controversy of this chapter, Jesus brings a wonderful prophecy that the Holy Spirit would pour out of those who believe in him like rivers of living water.

Staying away from Judea (7:1)

In John 6, Jesus feeds the 5,000 and then discusses his role as the Bread of Life. He concludes the discourse with how his disciples must eat his flesh and drink his blood. His analogy was so offensive that many of his own disciples left him, and he raised the ire of the Jewish leaders. So John records:

> "After this, Jesus went around in Galilee, purposely staying away from Judea because the Jews[277] there were waiting to take his life[278]." (7:1)

Jesus isn't afraid of death, but to fulfill his Father's mission he has much yet to do, in particular, to train his disciples to carry on his work after his crucifixion and resurrection. So Jesus stays in Galilee, away from his enemies, teaching and working with his disciples.

[277] For John's use of "the Jews" to refer to Jewish leaders, see Appendix 2. 'The Jews' in John's Gospel.
[278] "Take his life" (NIV), "kill" (NRSV, ESV, KJV) is *apokteinō*, literally, "to deprive of life, kill" (BDAG 114, 1a), from *apo-*, "from," indicating separation + *kteino*, "to slay," English "to kill off" so as to put out of the way (*apo*) (Thayer, p. 64, 1).

Feast of Tabernacles or Booths (*Sukkot*, 7:2)

"But when the Jewish Feast of Tabernacles was near...." (7:2)

The annual Feast of Tabernacles or Booths (Hebrew *Sukkot*) celebrates the Israelites' camping in the Wilderness and, later, the harvest that had been gathered in. It was one of the three annual festivals at which the men would gather in Jerusalem for the celebration bringing an offering (Deuteronomy 16:16). We'll look at the Feast of Tabernacles in greater detail in a moment.

His Brothers Didn't Believe in Him (7:2-5)

Jesus' brothers, who were apparently living in Capernaum at this time, urged him to use this occasion to proclaim himself in the capital city of the Jews through miracles.

"² But when the Jewish Feast of Tabernacles was near, ³ Jesus' brothers said to him, 'You ought to leave here and go to Judea, so that your disciples may see the miracles[279] you do. ⁴ No one who wants to become a public figure[280] acts in secret. Since you are doing these things, show yourself to the world.' ⁵ For even his own brothers did not believe in him." (7:2-5)

You can catch in his brothers' words a kind of a patronizing sneer that reveals their unbelief. It's as if they are saying: Since you are such a sensation in Galilee, you ought to proclaim yourself in Jerusalem, too. After all, that's what people do who want to be known by the public. John tells us that his brothers weren't believers at this point – though one of his brothers, James, later became leader of the Jerusalem church and author of the Letter of James!

Q1. (John 7:1-5) Why did Jesus stay in Galilee and avoid Jerusalem? What is the balance between taking precautions to protect yourself and trusting yourself into God's care? http://www.joyfulheart.com/forums/topic/1452-q1-avoiding-jerusalem/

Jesus Goes to the Feast in Secret (7:6-10)

"⁶ Therefore Jesus told them, 'The right time[281] for me has not yet come; for you any time is right. ⁷ The world cannot hate you, but it hates me because I testify that what it does is evil[282]. ⁸ You go to the Feast. I am not yet[283] going up to this Feast, because for me the right time has not yet come.'

[279] "Miracles" (NIV), "works" (NRSV, ESV, KJV) is *ergon*, "deed, accomplishment," specifically, miracles (also in 7:21) (BDAG 390, 1cα).

[280] "Become a public figure" (NIV) is literally, "seeks to be known openly" (ESV). "Public" (NIV), "widely known" (NRSV), "known openly" (KJV, ESV) is *parrēsia*, "openness to the public, in public, publicly" before whom speaking and actions take place (BDAG 781, 2). Also in 7:13, 26; 11:54; and 18:20.

[281] "Right time" (NIV), "time" (NRSV, KJV, ESV), twice in verse 6, once in verse 8, is *kairos*, "a moment or period as especially appropriate; the right, proper, favorable time" (BDAG 497, 1b).

[282] "Evil" is the adjective *ponēros*, "pertaining to being morally or socially worthless, wicked, evil, bad, base, worthless, vicious, degenerate" (BDAG 851, 1aα).

[283] In verse 8, the word "yet" (NIV, KJV, *oupō*, B L T W Θ Ψ p⁶⁶, ⁷⁵) is included in most early manuscripts, but omitted in a few key early manuscripts (NRSV, ESV, *ouk*, Aleph D K). The Editorial Committee of the Greek New Testament omits *oupo* for the "harder reading" of *ouk*, reasoning that "yet" was "introduced at an early date in order to alleviate the inconsistency between vs. 6 and vs. 10" (Metzger, *Textual Commentary*, p. 216).

⁹ Having said this, he stayed in Galilee. ¹⁰ However, after his brothers had left for the Feast, he went also, not publicly²⁸⁴, ²⁸⁵ but in secret²⁸⁶." (7:6-10)

Jesus explains that this is not so simple. His enemies in Jerusalem – Pharisees, teachers of the law, and the high priests – hate him because he has confronted some of their evils, such as their self-serving legalisms, their profaning of the temple by selling sheep and cattle there, their silly rules about keeping the Sabbath. Matthew's Gospel recounts Jesus' confrontation with them, pronouncing seven woes upon them as he exposes their sins. He has publicly called them hypocrites, blind guides, a brood of vipers! (Matthew 23).

For Jesus to enter Jerusalem publicly would be to sign his own death warrant – as he does at the Triumphal Entry that began the last week of his life.

So Jesus *does* attend the Feast of Tabernacles, but goes incognito, without a retinue of disciples to make him obvious, waiting until the right time to make a public statement.

Fear of the Jewish Leaders (7:11-13)

Even though Jesus isn't visible at the Feast, everybody is talking about him.

"¹¹ Now at the Feast the Jews²⁸⁷ were watching for him and asking, 'Where is that man?' ¹² Among the crowds there was widespread whispering about him. Some said, 'He is a good man.' Others replied, 'No, he deceives the people.' ¹³ But no one would say anything publicly²⁸⁸ about him for fear of the Jews." (7:11-13)

This back and forth discussion goes on in whispers. The Jewish leaders have such power in Jerusalem that they can punish those who disagree with them. Later, we read:

"The Jews²⁸⁹ had decided that anyone who acknowledged that Jesus was the Christ would be put out of the synagogue." (9:22)

And they do excommunicate the healed man who was born blind. The Jewish leaders have created a climate of fear in Jerusalem and people fear to cross them.

Learning without Study (7:14-15)

Jesus doesn't reveal himself until this eight-day feast was well underway. Jesus seems to have customarily taught within the temple courts in a covered, shaded colonnade called Solomon's Porch (10:23; cf. Acts 3:11).

---

²⁸⁴ "Publicly" (NIV, NRSV, ESV), "openly" (KJV) is *phanerōs*, "in plain view, openly, publicly" (BDAG 1047, 1).

²⁸⁵ "As it were" (*ōs*, NRSV, KJV) is present in most manuscripts (p⁶⁶, ⁷⁵ B L W etc.), but omitted (NIV, ESV) in a few (Aleph D it cop). The "harder reading" would be to include it, to help explain and soften the text. The Editorial Committee retains it in brackets with a {D} doubtful rating.

²⁸⁶ "Secret" (NIV, NRSV, KJV), "private" (ESV) is *kryptos* (from which we get our word "cryptology"), substantive, "a hidden entity, something hidden," with the preposition en, "in secret, secretly, privately" (BDAG 571, 2b).

²⁸⁷ For John's use of "the Jews" to refer to Jewish leaders, see Appendix 2. 'The Jews' in John's Gospel.

²⁸⁸ "Publicly" (NIV), "openly" (KJV, NRSV, ESV) is *parrēsia*, which we saw in 7:4, "plainly, openly" (BDAG 781, 1).

²⁸⁹ See Appendix 2. 'The Jews' in John's Gospel.

"[14] Not until halfway through the Feast did Jesus go up to the temple courts and begin to teach. [15] The Jews were amazed and asked, 'How did this man get such learning[290] without having studied[291]?'" (7:14-15)

Jesus would have studied Hebrew and the Scriptures as a boy in the school in his local synagogue. But he didn't have advanced teaching gained by becoming a disciple of a famous rabbi or "teacher of the law," such as Paul boasted of: "Under Gamaliel I was thoroughly trained in the law of our fathers" (Acts 22:3). Discipleship to a renowned rabbi was the "seminary training" available in Jesus' day necessary to be considered an "authority."

The Jewish leaders, however, are duly impressed with the profundity of Jesus' teaching – and its influence on the people. They are amazed that he has gained such a depth of understanding without sitting under a famous rabbi.

Excursus on Seminaries and Hearing God's Voice

I want to pause for a moment to discuss the place of Bible schools and seminaries. When I was younger, I was in a church that didn't believe in Bible schools and seminaries to train ministers. Seminaries were called "cemeteries." Ha, ha. As I continued, I saw that ignorance was being glorified and learning was being vilified. That isn't right.

Jesus took much time to train twelve men to be his disciples. They weren't untrained, but instructed in the Scriptures and trained in practical ministry.

Dear friends, we need balance in our learning to be disciples. Much of our spiritual formation is likely to take place in our local congregation, under the care of a pastor or older man or woman. The role of Bible colleges and seminaries is to train us to interpret the Bible accurately, to teach us to ask questions that help us probe further, to gain a more comprehensive understanding about what the Bible teaches concerning God, and to help us to communicate God's Word. We do this under (hopefully) godly professors and teachers. This is important!

However, learning the Bible is different from what is known today as "spiritual formation" – learning to yield our lives to Christ, to hear his voice, to walk with him, to become like him in our character. I once met a person who said, "I'd rather have a verse than a voice." No. One of the essential skills of a Christian is to learn to hear and obey God's voice.

We need the Scriptures to help us understand what God's voice sounds like and to keep us from getting off track. We need the Bible, and we need to learn to walk in the Spirit. The Pharisees were Bible scholars, but they lacked the life of the Spirit. Jesus offered both Bible instruction and an example of how to walk in the Spirit. We too need both careful, godly Bible scholarship *and* we need to learn to walk in the Spirit! That makes for well-rounded, in-it-for-the-long-run disciples. (Thanks for listening to my rant.)

---

[290] "Get/have such learning" (NIV, NRSV), "letters" (KJV) is *gramma*, "letters," plural, "learning, knowledge," literally, "knows his letters." (BDAG 206, 3).

[291] "Studied" (NIV), "been taught" (NRSV), "learned" (KJV) is *manthanō*, "to gain knowledge or skill by instruction, learn" (BDAG 615, 1).

My Teaching Is Not my Own (7:15-17)

"The Jews[292] were amazed and asked, 'How did this man get such learning without having studied?'" (7:15)

Jesus must have heard the Jewish leaders' whispers, because he comments about the teaching that so impresses them.

"Jesus answered, 'My teaching is not my own. It comes from him who sent me.'" (7:16)

Notice Jesus' humility. He *is* a pupil of someone else after all, they think. He admits that he is sharing his mentor's teaching, the rabbi he has studied under. But then Jesus goes one step farther. He declares God to be his mentor, his rabbi, the one who sends him.

"If anyone chooses to do God's will, he will find out whether my teaching comes from God or whether I speak on my own." (7:17)

My teaching comes from God, says Jesus. I bring his message – not the accumulated wisdom of this rabbi or another. I speak directly for God! It is his honor and glory I seek, not my own.

"He who speaks on his own does so to gain honor[293] for himself, but he who works for the honor of the one who sent him is a man of truth; there is nothing false about him." (7:18)

Q2. (John 7:15-17) How were rabbis trained in Jesus' day? How was Jesus trained? How were his disciples trained? What is the value of formal theological training? What is the value of learning to hear and obey the voice of the Spirit?
http://www.joyfulheart.com/forums/topic/1453-q2-training-disciples/

Choosing to Do God's Will (7:17)

How can a person know for sure that Jesus is speaking from God? Let's look again at Jesus' answer:

"If anyone chooses to do God's will, he will find out whether my teaching comes from God or whether I speak on my own." (7:17)

"Chooses" (NIV), "resolves" (NRSV), "will" (KJV, ESV) is *thelō*, "to desire, want," here, "to have something in mind for oneself, of purpose, resolve, will, wish, want, be ready."[294] The phrase is literally, "If anyone's will is to do God's will" (ESV).

This is profound. The only way you'll know if Jesus' teaching is true is to firmly commit yourself to doing God's will wherever that will lead. Later, Jesus said the same thing in different words:

"If you hold to my teaching, you are really my disciples. Then you will know the truth, and the truth will set you free." (8:31-32)

---

[292] For John's use of "the Jews" to refer to Jewish leaders, see Appendix 2. 'The Jews' in John's Gospel.
[293] "Honor" (NIV), "glory" (NRSV, KJV) is *doxa*, "glory," here, "honor as enhancement or recognition of status or performance, fame, recognition, renown, honor, prestige" (BDAG 258, 3). See more in Appendix 6. "Glory" and "Glorify" in John's Gospel.
[294] *Thelō*, BDAG 448, 2.

There are many people who are "always learning and never able to arrive at a knowledge of the truth" (2 Timothy 3:7). They dabble here and then study that – sampling one thing after another. The only way to know Christ – to really know him and know the truth of his teachings – is to experience him yourself, by choosing a path of learning and obedience, the path of a disciple who hungers after the truth and pursues it.

Someone said that the chief obstacle to being a Christian for many is not intellectual but moral. Many people are unwilling to repent of their sins and follow Christ. They love their lifestyle more than finding God. Sad, but true.

Q3. (John 7:17) Can we truly know God's will if we're not really willing to obey the truth we know? Why not?
http://www.joyfulheart.com/forums/topic/1454-q3-obeying-and-knowing/

Inconsistencies with the Sabbath Regulations (7:19-24)

Now Jesus turns the tables on the Jewish rulers by accusing them of not keeping the Mosaic law.

"[19] 'Has not Moses given you the law? Yet not one of you keeps the law. Why are you trying to kill me?'
[20] 'You are demon-possessed,' the crowd answered. 'Who is trying to kill you?'
[21] Jesus said to them, 'I did one miracle, and you are all astonished. [22] Yet, because Moses gave you circumcision (though actually it did not come from Moses, but from the patriarchs), you circumcise a child on the Sabbath. [23] Now if a child can be circumcised on the Sabbath so that the law of Moses may not be broken, why are you angry with me for healing the whole man[295] on the Sabbath? [24] Stop judging by mere appearances, and make a right judgment.'" (7:19-24)

Though they claimed to keep the Sabbath, yet they circumcised on the Sabbath, with the justification that circumcision made the person whole or complete.[296] If making a person whole by circumcision is allowable on the Sabbath day, Jesus argues, then healing and making him whole is also allowable.

Jesus calls on them to stop making picky judgments based on outward appearances[297], and judge the issue fairly.[298]

---

[295] "Healing the whole man" (NIV) or "made a man's whole body well" (ESV) includes several words: *holos*, "whole, entire, complete" (BDAG 704, 1a); and *hygiēs*, "pertaining to being physically well or sound, healthy, sound" (BDAG 1023, 1a).

[296] The rabbis claimed that Abraham was not called *shalame*, complete, or perfect, until he was circumcised, referring to Genesis 17:1 – "...Walk before me and be perfect." Thus, prior to his circumcision, Abraham was evidently lacking perfection.

[297] "Appearance/s" is *opsis*, "external or physical aspect of something, outward appearance, aspect" (BDAG 746, 2).

[298] "Right/righteous" is the adjective *dikaios*, "pertaining to being in accordance with high standards of rectitude, upright, just, fair" (BDAG 246, 1a).

Where Does the Christ Come From? (7:25-29)

John has included the issues of Jesus' authority for his teaching and healing on the Sabbath. Now he touches on a third controversy that surrounded him in Jerusalem – the fact that Jesus grew up in Galilee, while the scriptures said the Messiah would come from Bethlehem in Judea (Micah 5:2). And there was a popular belief that when the Messiah appeared his origins wouldn't be known at all.[299]

> "[25] At that point some of the people of Jerusalem began to ask, 'Isn't this the man they are trying to kill? [26] Here he is, speaking publicly, and they are not saying a word to him. Have the authorities really concluded that he is the Christ? [27] But we know where this man is from; when the Christ comes, no one will know where he is from.'
>
> [28] Then Jesus, still teaching in the temple courts, cried out, 'Yes, you know me, and you know where I am from. I am not here on my own, but he who sent me is true. You do not know him, [29] but I know him because I am from him and he sent me.'" (7:25-29)

As I've mentioned before, John seems to assume that his readers are familiar with the Synoptic Gospels – and both Matthew and Luke make clear that Jesus was born in Bethlehem of Judea in fulfillment of the prophecy. So John's writing is ironic, since he knows that the reader is aware of the truth while Jesus' enemies are bumbling around in the dark.

But Jesus doesn't tell his enemies that he is born in Bethlehem. To do so would argue more strongly that he was the Messiah, charge his ministry with a political threat to Rome, and make it more and more difficult for him to minister in Jerusalem. So Jesus is silent about Bethlehem.

Jesus responds. He "cried out" (NIV, NRSV, KJV), "proclaimed" (ESV), using the word *krazō*, to make a public announcement. He claims once more that He has been sent by God and authorized by him to minister. He also notes that the people "do not know him" (7:28d). Amazing, isn't it, how we can say all sorts of things as if they were true, but don't really know what we're talking about.

Attempts to Arrest Jesus (7:30-32)

Jesus' claims are so bold that the officials try to arrest him. But they can't, because God's timing for his death and glorification have not come yet.

> "At this they tried to seize[300] him, but no one laid a hand on him, because his time[301] had not yet come." (7:30)

The crowd, however, isn't so interested in the controversies about breaking the Sabbath and Jesus' birthplace, but that he is working miracles. They reason, even the Messiah himself can't be expected to do more miracles than Jesus.

> "Still, many in the crowd put their faith in him. They said, 'When the Christ comes, will he do more miraculous signs than this man?'" (7:31)

---

[299] 4 Ezra (= 2 Esdras) 13:52 and Justin Martyr, *Dialogue with Trypho* 8.4.

[300] "Seize" (NIV), "arrest" (NRSV, ESV), "take" (KJV) in verses 30, 32 and 44 is *piazō*, "to seize with intent to overpower or gain control," here, "seize, arrest, take into custody" (BDAG 812, 1).

[301] "Time" (NIV) "hour" is *hōra*, "a point of time as an occasion for an event, time" (BDAG 1103, 3).

The Pharisees and the chief priests (who were Sadducees) are aware of Jesus' growing popularity and decide to do something about it. These two opposing religious parties are united about one thing – Jesus has to go!

> "The Pharisees heard the crowd whispering such things about him. Then the chief priests and the Pharisees sent temple guards to arrest him." (7:32)

Jesus Predicts His Death (7:33-36)

Jesus, realizing that the order has been put out for his arrest, speaks cryptically of his soon departure, speaking of his death. His enemies don't understand what he is saying, but his disciples remember later that he had spoken clearly of his death.

> "[33] Jesus said, 'I am with you for only a short time, and then I go to the one who sent me. [34] You will look for me, but you will not find me; and where I am, you cannot come.'

> [35] The Jews said to one another, 'Where does this man intend to go that we cannot find him? Will he go where our people live scattered[302] among the Greeks[303], and teach the Greeks? [36] What did he mean when he said, 'You will look for me, but you will not find me,' and 'Where I am, you cannot come'?'" (7:33-36)

Culmination of the Feast of Tabernacles (7:37-39)

We come to the culmination of the Feast of Tabernacles and a major proclamation by Jesus:

> "[37] On the last and greatest day of the Feast, Jesus stood and said in a loud voice, 'If anyone is thirsty, let him come to me and drink. [38] Whoever believes in me, as the Scripture has said, streams of living water will flow from within him.' [39] By this he meant the Spirit, whom those who believed in him were later to receive. Up to that time the Spirit had not been given, since Jesus had not yet been glorified." (7:37-39)

Feast of Tabernacles

To understand the significance of Jesus' words on this occasion, we need to review in greater detail the way the Feast of Tabernacles was celebrated annually in Jesus' day in September or early October.

To recall how God had cared for the Israelites as they camped in the Wilderness for forty years, each family would build a temporary shelter in which to eat and sleep during this eight-day festival.

> "Live in booths for seven days ... so your descendants will know that I had the Israelites live in booths when I brought them out of Egypt. I am the LORD your God." (Leviticus 23:42-43)

This was a joy-filled time after the harvest had been gathered, so the festival was sometimes called the Festival of Ingathering, to celebrate God's blessing on the harvest. Moses had directed:

> "Celebrate the Feast of Tabernacles for seven days after you have gathered the produce of your threshing floor and your winepress. Be joyful at your Feast – you, your sons and daughters, your

---

[302] "Scattered" (NIV), "the Dispersion" (NRSV), "the dispersed" (KJV) is *diaspora*, "state or condition of being scattered, dispersion" (BDAG 236, 1).

[303] "Greeks" (NIV, NRSV), "Gentiles" (KJV) is *Hellēn*, "Greek," in the broader sense, all persons who came under the influence of Greek, as distinguished from Israel's, culture, "a gentile, polytheist, Greco-Roman" (BDAG 318, 2a).

menservants and maidservants, and the Levites, the aliens, the fatherless and the widows who live in your towns." (Deuteronomy 16:13-14)

On the first day of the Feast the pilgrims would come to the temple carrying a fruit tree branch in their left hands, and a palm branch in their right hands, with a myrtle and a willow branch on either side of it. There were grand processions of the Levites with the blowing of silver trumpets, and sacrifices on the altar.

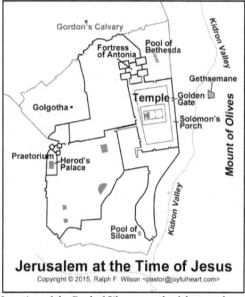

Jerusalem at the Time of Jesus
Copyright © 2015. Ralph F. Wilson <pastor@joyfulheart.com>

Location of the Pool of Siloam, south of the temple.

One daily feature of the Feast was the libations. A priest, accompanied by a joyous procession with music, would go down to the Pool of Siloam, where he would draw water into a golden pitcher. The priest would enter the temple through the Water Gate up to the altar, welcomed by a three-fold blast from the priests' trumpets. Then wine and the water from the golden pitcher would be poured simultaneously upon the altar as a libation, poured out as a sacrifice to the Lord. After this, the temple music began and the antiphonal chanting of the Hallel (Psalms 113-118) would begin. The whole rite echoed the words of the Prophet Isaiah:

> "With joy you will draw water
> from the wells of salvation." (Isaiah 12:3)

> "For I will pour water on the thirsty land,
> and streams on the dry ground;
> I will pour out my Spirit on your offspring,
> and my blessing on your descendants." (Isaiah 44:3)

Indeed, the outpouring of the water in the Feast of Tabernacles was understood by the rabbis and the people as symbolic of the outpouring of the Holy Spirit.[304]

Jesus Cries Out (7:37-39)

We've seen the daily libation during each day of the Feast. But now on the last and greatest day as the Feast culminates[305], Jesus stands up in the temple "cries out" in a loud voice, making a major public proclamation. [306]

> "'If anyone is thirsty, let him come to me and drink. Whoever believes in me, as the Scripture has said, streams of living water will flow from within him.' By this he meant the Spirit, whom those

---

[304] For this Alfred Edersheim (*The Temple and Its Services as They Were at the Time of Christ* (1874), chapter 14) cites Jerusalem Talmud, *Sukkot* Vol. 1, p. 55 *a* (5.1). Also, Edersheim, *Life and Times*, book 4, chapter 7; Morris, John pp. 420-21.

[305] There is some question whether the festival lasted seven days or eight. The last water libation would have occurred on the seventh day. So on the eighth day, if that is what John means here, there was no libation and Jesus offered one (Morris, *John*, p. 421, fn. 74).

[306] "Said in a loud voice" (NIV), "cried out" (NRSV), "cried" (KJV) is *krazō*, "to communicate something in a loud voice, call, call out, cry," indicating Jesus making an important public statement (also at 1:15; 7:28) (BDAG 564, 2a).

who believed in him were later to receive. Up to that time the Spirit had not been given, since Jesus had not yet been glorified.[307] " (7:37-39)

Jesus speaks to the spiritual thirst of the Jewish people, just as he had offered thirst-quenching "living water" to the Samaritan woman (4:10, 13). His words constitute both an invitation and a promise.

1. Invitation. "If anyone is thirsty, let him come to me and drink" (7:37). This turns my mind to several similar invitations in the Bible:

> **"Come, all you who are thirsty,**
> **come to the waters;**
> and you who have no money,
> come, buy and eat!
> Come, buy wine and milk
> without money and without cost.
> Why spend money on what is not bread,
> and your labor on what does not satisfy?
> Listen, listen to me, and eat what is good,
> and your soul will delight in the richest of fare." (Isaiah 55:1-2)

> **"Come to me, all you who are weary and burdened,**
> **and I will give you rest.**
> Take my yoke upon you and learn from me,
> for I am gentle and humble in heart,
> and you will find rest for your souls." (Matthew 11:28-29)

> "The Spirit and the bride say, 'Come!'
> And let him who hears say, 'Come!'
> **Whoever is thirsty, let him come;**
> and whoever wishes,
> let him take the free gift of the water of life." (Revelation 22:17)

What keeps us away from Christ so that we don't eagerly drink of his refreshing, life-giving presence? Answer: our preoccupation with ourselves and our own concerns. Perhaps our creeping secular mindset. Our pride in doing it ourselves and not asking for help. Our spiritual dullness.

Dear friends, how thirsty are you for Christ? Really? I want the same kind of intense thirst that I see in the Apostle Paul:

> **"I want to know Christ** and the power of his resurrection and the fellowship of sharing in his sufferings, becoming like him in his death, and so, somehow, to attain to the resurrection from the dead.... Brothers, I do not consider myself yet to have taken hold of it. **But one thing I do: Forgetting what is behind and straining toward what is ahead, I press on** toward the goal to win the prize for which God has called me heavenward in Christ Jesus." (Philippians 3:10-11, 13-14)

I think of that old Gospel hymn: "Revive us again!" Lord, strip the calluses off my heart and renew in me a strong desire to know you and partake of you in all your fullness! Christ invites us to come to him and drink.

---

[307] See more in Appendix 6. "Glory" and "Glorify" in John's Gospel.

2. Promise. The second part of Jesus' proclamation that day is a promise to those who accept his invitation.

> "38 'Whoever believes in me, as the Scripture has said, streams[308] of living water will flow[309] from within him.' 39 By this he meant the Spirit, whom those who believed in him were later to receive. Up to that time the Spirit had not been given, since Jesus had not yet been glorified." (7:38-39)

The promise is made to "whoever believes in me," literally "the one believing in me." The river flows "from within him" (NIV), "out of his heart" (ESV), "out of his belly" (KJV), phrases that translate the noun *koilia*, which refers to the organs of the abdomen, thought to be the "seat of inward life, of feelings and desires," what we express in English as the functional equivalent of "heart."[310]

The promise is that from within the believer, will flow "rivers/streams of living water." This might seem strange, since we might think of Jesus himself as the source of the water, the life, not the believer. But we see a similar phrase in Jesus' words to the woman at the well:

> "Whoever drinks the water I give him will never thirst. Indeed, the water I give him will become in him a spring of water welling up to eternal life." (4:14)

The river begins as a spring bubbling up and becomes a river flowing out. "Living water," means running water as opposed to still water. But here, Jesus uses "living water" in the sense of water that brings life. A similar figure is seen of the holy city in the last chapter of Revelation:

> "Then the angel showed me **the river of the water of life**, as clear as crystal, flowing from the throne of God and of the Lamb down the middle of the great street of the city. On each side of the river stood the tree of life, bearing twelve crops of fruit, yielding its fruit every month. And the leaves of the tree are for the healing of the nations." (Revelation 22:1-2)

The Holy Spirit within the Believer (7:39)

John explains concerning our text,

> "By this he meant the Spirit, whom those who believed in him were later to receive. Up to that time the Spirit had not been given, since Jesus had not yet been glorified." (7:39)

In John's Gospel we see clearly that Jesus will pour out the Spirit, and the Spirit will reside in each believer individually. Later, we'll come to chapters 14, 15, and 16 where Jesus teaches about the Paraclete, Counselor, Comforter, another name for the Holy Spirit.[311] There, Jesus says:

> "16 And I will ask the Father, and he will give you another Counselor **to be with you forever** – 17 the Spirit of truth. The world cannot accept him, because it neither sees him nor knows him. But you know him, for he lives with you and **will be in you**." (14:16-17)

The Spirit is present in Jesus. But when the Spirit is poured out, he will reside in each believer. That's what it means in Acts where it says, "They saw what seemed to be tongues of fire that separated and came to rest on each of them." (Acts 2:3)

---

[308] "Streams" (NIV), "rivers" (NRSV, KJV) is *potamos*, "river, stream," from which we get our word "hippopotamus" ("horse of the river") (BDAG 856, b).

[309] "Flow" is *rheō*, "to flow with liquid," here in a transferred sense (BDAG 904, a).

[310] *Koilia*, BDAG 550, 3.

[311] For more on this see Appendix 8. The Paraclete.

When Jesus Is Glorified (7:39)

"Up to that time the Spirit had not been given, since Jesus had not yet been glorified." (7: 39b)

In John's Gospel, the term "glorified" often refers to Jesus being crucified, raised from the dead, and being restored to the place of glory that Jesus has had with the Father from before the beginning. Jesus prays in his so-called "high priestly prayer" in chapter 17, on the night before he was crucified:

"And now, Father, glorify me in your presence with the glory I had with you before the world began." (17:5)

We see this expression several other times:

"Only after Jesus was glorified did they realize...." (12:16)

"The hour is come, that the Son of man should be glorified." (12:23)

"Now is the Son of man glorified...." (13:31)

"Father, the time has come. Glorify your Son...." (17:1)

At the end of his ministry, the hour has arrived for him "to leave this world and go to the Father" (13:1).[312] See more in Appendix 6. "Glory" and "Glorify" in John's Gospel.

The Power of the Spirit in Believers (7:39)

Jesus looks forward to his death, but beyond that, to his resurrection, his ascension, and the sending of the Holy Spirit (which we'll read more about in chapters 14-16). The Spirit will come with power. Consider these verses:

"Truly, truly, I say to you, whoever believes in me will also do the works that I do; and greater works than these will he do, **because I am going to the Father**." (14:12, ESV)

"I tell you the truth: It is for your good that I am going away. Unless I go away, the Counselor will not come to you; but **if I go, I will send him to you**." (16:7)

Luke relates some of Jesus' final words to his disciples:

"But **you will receive power when the Holy Spirit comes on you**; and you will be my witnesses in Jerusalem, and in all Judea and Samaria, and to the ends of the earth." (Acts 1:8)

Dear friends, for too long, most Christians haven't exercised this power of the Holy Spirit. But the power is there for us if we seek Him. There's a joyful, upbeat praise chorus from the Jesus Movement that applies this text to our lives:

"There's a river of life flowing out of me,
Makes the lame to walk and the blind to see,
Opens prison doors, sets the captive free.
There's a river of life flowing out of me.
   Spring up a well within my soul,
   Spring up a well that makes me whole...."[313]

---

[312] The Synoptics bring another "hour," the period "when darkness reigns" (Luke 22:53). It began in the Garden of Gethsemane, "Look, the hour is near, and the Son of Man is betrayed into the hands of sinners" (Matthew 26:45).

[313] Betty Carr Pulkingham and L. Casebolt, "There's a River of Life," © 1971, 1975, Celebration.

Isaiah prophesies concerning the time of the Messiah when:

"Each man will be like a shelter from the wind
and a refuge from the storm,
like streams of water in the desert
and the shadow of a great rock in a thirsty land." (Isaiah 32:2)

Lord, let your Spirit pour out of us to help quench the thirst of many people around us who dwell in a dry place!

Q4. (John 7:37-39) In Jesus' teaching on streams of living water from within, whom does he invite to drink? What does he promise to believers? How is this fulfilled at Pentecost rather than immediately after Jesus spoke it? To what degree has this been fulfilled in your life? http://www.joyfulheart.com/forums/topic/1455-q4-streams-within/

Controversy over the Christ Coming from Galilee (7:40-43)

From the high point of Jesus' words about the Spirit, this chapter concludes with a bit more about the controversy Jesus was causing in Jerusalem.

"40 On hearing his words, some of the people said, 'Surely this man is the Prophet.' 41 Others said, 'He is the Christ.' Still others asked, 'How can the Christ come from Galilee? 42 Does not the Scripture say that the Christ will come from David's family and from Bethlehem, the town where David lived?' 43 Thus the people were divided because of Jesus." (7:40-43)

Some people identified him with the Prophet that Moses said would follow him (Deuteronomy 18:15). Others thought he was the Messiah. Apparently, some people in that time saw the Prophet as a Messianic figure, others didn't associate the two.

Those who believed Jesus was the Messiah were confronted with the Scripture text in Micah 5:2 that Christ would come from Bethlehem. John's readers who, we assume, were familiar with the Synoptic Gospels, would sense the irony of the situation. But Jesus doesn't tell them his birthplace, for he doesn't want to be publicly recognized as the Messiah at this point. His hour was not yet.

No One Ever Spoke This Way (7:44-49)

The temple guards sent to arrest Jesus come back empty handed.

"44 Some wanted to seize him, but no one laid a hand on him. 45 Finally the temple guards went back to the chief priests and Pharisees, who asked them, 'Why didn't you bring him in?'

46 'No one ever spoke the way this man does,' the guards declared.

47 'You mean he has deceived you also?' the Pharisees retorted. 48 'Has any of the rulers or of the Pharisees believed in him? 49 No! But this mob that knows nothing of the law – there is a curse on them.'" (7:44-49)

The Pharisees had a low opinion of the common people, since they weren't as scrupulous about keeping every point of the oral law, as the Pharisees did. This is reflected in their characterization of "this mob" – they saw them as rabble.[314]

The irony of the Pharisees question, "Has any of the rulers or of the Pharisees believed in him?" (7:48) is immediately apparent in verse 50, since Nicodemus, a Pharisee and member of the ruling Sanhedrin, is becoming a believer, though not yet open about his faith.

Nicodemus Defends Jesus (7:50-52)

Nicodemus protests this rush to arrest Jesus, since he hasn't been given a hearing, which would be the just thing.

> "⁵⁰ Nicodemus, who had gone to Jesus earlier and who was one of their own number, asked, ⁵¹ 'Does our law condemn anyone without first hearing him to find out what he is doing?' ⁵² They replied, 'Are you from Galilee, too? Look into it, and you will find that a prophet does not come out of Galilee.'" (7:50-52)

The unbelieving Pharisees don't answer Nicodemus. Instead they put him down by saying that he might be from Galilee – certainly an insult coming from a Jerusalem Pharisee. Their mind is made up. They can't see what is staring them in the face – that Jesus is doing miracles by God's power.

Lessons for Disciples

There are a number of lessons here for disciples.

1. Like Jesus, you'll always have people who misinterpret who you are (7:12-13).
2. Jesus was taught by the Father, not by the great rabbis of his day, yet he had a depth and authority that they could only envy. While formal training is good, even more important is an ongoing conversation with the Father that can form you spiritually (7:15-17).
3. We can only know God's will if we're willing to be obedient to Christ's teaching. There is no "theoretical" truth, but only "experiential" knowing of God's will (7:17).
4. Jesus took precautions not to expose himself to dangerous situations, but was unafraid when the Father directed him to go to Jerusalem. The Father protected Jesus from arrest and stoning because it wasn't yet his time (7:1, 30, 44-47).
5. Jesus taught that the Holy Spirit would be like a stream of water flowing from inside a person, but the Holy Spirit wouldn't come until after Jesus' glorification – that is, his crucifixion, resurrection, and ascension (7:37-39).

Prayer

Father, help us to learn both from our brothers and sisters, and from Jesus, how to walk as disciples. Help us to grow deep in you. Let your Spirit flow from deep within us to touch a thirsty world. Fulfill the potential you have for each of us. We pray in Jesus' name. Amen.

---

[314] "Mob" (NIV), "crowd" (NRSV), "people" (KJV) is *ochlos*, "a relatively large number of people gathered together, crowd," here, "a large number of people of relatively low status the (common) people, populace ... rabble" (BDAG 745, 1bα).

Key Verses

"If anyone chooses to do God's will, he will find out whether my teaching comes from God or whether I speak on my own." (John 5:17, NIV)

"Stop judging by mere appearances, and make a right judgment." (John 7:24, NIV)

"'If anyone is thirsty, let him come to me and drink. Whoever believes in me, as the Scripture has said, streams of living water will flow from within him.' By this he meant the Spirit, whom those who believed in him were later to receive. Up to that time the Spirit had not been given, since Jesus had not yet been glorified." (John 7:37-39, NIV)

"'No one ever spoke the way this man does,' the guards declared." (John 7:46, NIV)

16. Jesus and the Adulterous Woman (7:53-8:11)

In the account of Jesus and the woman taken in adultery, we see Jesus' compassion on full public display in the temple. This story is matched only by Jesus' Parable of the Prodigal Son in showcasing God's love and mercy – and the way to salvation.

This passage is also one of the most misinterpreted incidents in the New Testament – and at the same time, wasn't even originally part of the New Testament. Nevertheless, it is worthy of careful examination.

Verses 7:53 through 8:11 are missing from most important early Greek manuscripts.[315] In the ancient manuscripts where the passage appears, it is sometimes placed elsewhere

Liz Lemon Swindle, "He That Is without Sin," copyrighted by the artist. Permission requested.

than its position in John's Gospel in our Bibles.[316] The vocabulary and style are closer to Luke's than John's, and the case against John's authorship seems to be conclusive. Having said that, Metzger concludes:

> "The account has all the earmarks of historical veracity. It is obviously a piece of oral tradition which circulated in certain parts of the Western church and was subsequently incorporated into various manuscripts at various places."[317]

The passage doubtless records an authentic part of Jesus' ministry, and has been loved by Christians throughout the ages. Let's see what the message is for us today.

Teaching in the Temple (7:53-82)

> "[7:53] Then each went to his own home. [8:1] But Jesus went to the Mount of Olives. [2] At dawn he appeared again in the temple courts, where all the people gathered around him, and he sat down to teach them." (7:53-8:2)

---

[315] The passage is missing from p[66,75] Aleph B L N T W etc. and early Greek fathers.

[316] Codex D, etc.

[317] Metzger, *Textual Commentary*, pp. 220-221.

Jesus is in Jerusalem teaching. At night he is on the Mount of Olives, but in the mornings he teaches in the temple (Luke 21:37-38) – probably in the area at the edge of the Court of the Gentiles known as Solomon's Porch, where, after his resurrection, the early church would gather for teaching (John 10:23; Acts 3:11; 5:12).

In our culture public speakers stand to teach, but in Jesus' culture, the rabbi would often sit to teach (Matthew 5:1; 13:2; 15:29; Mark 4:1; 9:35; Luke 5:3; John 6:3).

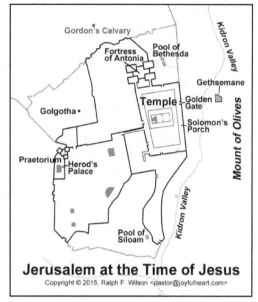

Jerusalem at the Time of Jesus
Copyright © 2015. Ralph F. Wilson <pastor@joyfulheart.com>

The 'No-Win' Trap (8:3-6a)

Jesus has been teaching in the temple, but now his enemies bring a clear challenge, designed to embarrass Jesus and get him in trouble.

"3 The teachers of the law[318] and the Pharisees brought in a woman caught in adultery. They made her stand before the group 4 and said to Jesus, 'Teacher, this woman was caught in the act of adultery. 5 In the Law Moses commanded us to stone such women. Now what do you say?' 6 They were using this question as a trap, in order to have a basis for accusing[319] him." (8:3-6a)

Jesus' opponents often sought to trap him (Mark 3:2; 10:2). This one was similar to his opponents' challenge about whether Jews should pay taxes to Caesar (Matthew 22:15-22). It was a trick, a trap[320] to turn the authorities – and the people – against Jesus. Jesus' enemies had invented a "no win" predicament for him – at least that what they thought. If Jesus were to say the woman *should* be stoned, he would be going contrary to his longstanding reputation for showing mercy to the broken and disreputable. And it could get him in trouble with the Romans, who might view stoning as overstepping the Jews' authority to exercise the death penalty.[321] But if Jesus said she *shouldn't* be stoned, he could be accused of teaching against the Law of Moses and undermining the social order.

Q1. (John 8:3-6) What was the trap Jesus' enemies tried to spring on him with the woman taken in adultery? What might be the consequence if he upheld stoning her? What might be the consequence if he said not to stone her?
http://www.joyfulheart.com/forums/topic/1456-q1-the-trap/

---

[318] "Teachers of the law" (NIV), "scribes" (NRSV, ESV, KJV) is *grammateus*, "specialists in the law of Moses: experts in the law, scholars versed in the law, scribes" (BDAG 206, 2a). Used only once in John. See Appendix 3. Religious Leaders in Jesus' Day.

[319] "Accusing" (NIV) is *katēgoreō*, nearly always as legal technical term, "bring charges" in court (BDAG 533, 1a).

[320] "As a trap" (NIV), "to test" (NRSV, ESV), "tempting" (KJV) is *peirazō*, which we've seen before in 6:6, here in the sense of, "to attempt to entrap through a process of inquiry, test" (BDAG 793, 3).

[321] The right to impose the death penalty had been taken away from the Jewish courts by the Roman authorities about 30 BC (*Sanhedrin* 41a). After this the Sanhedrin would petition the Roman governor to put a person to death (John 18:31; Matthew 27:1), though there are records of mob violence in stoning (Acts 13:28).

Hypocrisy behind the Trap (8:3-6a)

It is clear that this was a "set-up." However, there were some serious legal problems with the Jews' test case:

1. Caught in the act. The accusers were clear that the woman had been caught in the actual act of adultery.[322] This isn't easy to do. Just finding a man and woman in the same room might not be enough. Careful planning must have been done to entrap the couple – and to entrap Jesus. This wasn't an innocent inquiry to a rabbi concerning how to apply the Law of Moses.

2. Only the woman was brought. Where was the man? The Law specifically states:

> "If a man commits adultery with another man's wife – with the wife of his neighbor – both the adulterer and the adulteress must be put to death." (Leviticus 20:10)

There was something fishy about the charge here.

3. Stoning wasn't specified for all cases of adultery. The Law of Moses doesn't specify stoning for all cases of adultery (though it might be implied), but only in the case when a betrothed virgin was caught in adultery, in which case both parties would be stoned (Deuteronomy 22:23-24).

4. Death for adultery was seldom carried out, since the Jews were denied at that time the ability to inflict the death penalty (18:31). In fact, the most common punishment for adultery in Jewish society in Jesus' day was not death, but divorce and financial compensation for the husband from the adulterer himself.[323]

Writing on the Ground (8:6b-8)

The accusers demanded a response, but Jesus didn't answer right away.

> "[6b] But Jesus bent down[324] and started to write on the ground with his finger. [7] When they kept on questioning him, he straightened up[325] and said to them, 'If any one of you is without sin, let him be the first to throw a stone at her.' [8] Again he stooped down and wrote on the ground." (8:6b-8)

There is lots of speculation about what Jesus wrote in the sand covering the bricks that paved the temple courtyard. We don't know. If it had been important to the story, surely we would have been told. Probably, it was a way of letting their specious charge be considered by all – Jesus' audience as well as his opponents. Jesus let the gravity of the situation sink in.

Cast the First Stone (8:7)

Then he straightened up from his writing and spoke a simple sentence:

> "If any one of you is without sin, let him be the first to throw a stone at her." (8:7)

---

[322] "Caught" (NIV, NRSV, ESV), "taken" (KJV) is *katalambanō*, generally, "to seize, lay hold of," of forceful seizure. Here, "to come upon someone, with implication of surprise, catch," of moral authorities, "catch, detect" (BDAG 520, 3a). "Act" is the adjective *autophōros*, "(caught) in the act," from *autos*, "self" + *phōr*, "thief." The word was used first of thieves, and then of other wrongdoers, especially adulterers.

[323] The Mishnah tractate *Sotah* 5:1 seems to take for granted that the punishment for adultery would be divorce.

[324] "Bent/stooped down" in verses 6 and 8 is *kyptō*, "bend (oneself) down" (BDAG 575).

[325] In verses 7 and 10, "straightened up" (NIV, NRSV), "stood up" (ESV), "lifted up himself" (KJV) is *anakyptō*, "to raise oneself up to an erect position, stand erect, straighten oneself" (BDAG 66, 1).

This verse is often pointed to by liberals to invalidate anyone from judging any sin as wrong. Let's carefully consider Jesus' answer.

1. Without sin is *anamartētos*, "without sin," that is, not having sinned.[326] I don't think he means that any person who has ever sinned cannot condemn another person as having broken the law. That would completely overthrow the rule of law. It seems to refer to a witness or judge who has another interest in the matter besides justice for the accused. In many modern courts, a judge who has a personal interest or conflict of interest in a case is required to recuse himself or herself.

This is much like Jesus' teaching in the Sermon on the Mount. Judge not, *until* you have removed the sin from your life that keeps you from seeing another's sin clearly and dispassionately (Matthew 7:1-5).

2. Throw the first stone is a reference to a requirement in the Law of Moses that witnesses be the first to put a person to death.

> "You [who heard his blasphemy] must certainly put him to death. Your hand must be the first in putting him to death, and then the hands of all the people." (Deuteronomy 13:9)

> "6 On the testimony of two or three witnesses a man shall be put to death, but no one shall be put to death on the testimony of only one witness. 7 The hands of the witnesses must be the first in putting him to death, and then the hands of all the people. You must purge the evil from among you." (Deuteronomy 17:6-7)

But the witnesses in this particular case weren't interested in justice being done, but rather in entrapping Jesus. Thus they were tainted witnesses who had an interest in the outcome of the case – and everyone knew it. They weren't without sin!

3. The fine balance Jesus achieved with his simple reply accomplished several things: (1) It upheld the Law of Moses, (2) it required the accusers to take action to carry out the law, (3) it pointed to their culpability as prejudiced, evil witnesses in this case, and (4) it may have prevented a "lynching" in this woman's case. This is a good example of a "word of wisdom" (1 Corinthians 12:8).

Jesus' words have the desired effect. Jesus goes back to writing in the sand, but gradually all the accusers leave.

> "At this,[327] those who heard began to go away[328] one at a time, the older ones first, until only Jesus was left, with the woman still standing there." (8:9)

I don't think the people Jesus had been teaching left, only the woman's accusers, though the text is not clear.

---

[326] *Anamartētos*, BDAG 67.

[327] The KJV, "being convicted by their own conscience," is an explanatory gloss found in some later manuscripts (K boᵖᵗ and the Textus Receptus), but omitted by most (U Γ 28 700 892 101 pm). Metzger gives the text without the gloss an {A} "virtually certain" rating (Metzger, *Textual Commentary*, p. 222).

[328] "Began to go away" (NIV), "went away" (NRSV), "went out" (KJV) is *exerchomai*, "go out," in the imperfect tense, continuing action in the past. The accusers left gradually, over a period of time.

Q2. (John 8:3-8) Why did Jesus insist on unbiased, righteous witnesses casting the first stone? Why is verse 7 so often misused? Does Jesus require sinlessness of those called on to judge? What does he require? How does this compare with Jesus' teaching in Matthew 7:1-5?
http://www.joyfulheart.com/forums/topic/1457-q2-righteous-judges/

Q3. (John 8:3-8) Why do you think Jesus wrote on the ground? Was the content of his writing important to the story? What effect did this have on the situation?
http://www.joyfulheart.com/forums/topic/1458-q3-writing-in-the-dust/

Neither Do I Condemn You (8:10-11)

Now Jesus, who has been writing in the sand, straightens up again.

> "10 Jesus straightened up and asked her, 'Woman, where are they? Has no one condemned you?'
> 11 'No one, sir,' she said.
> 'Then neither do I condemn you,' Jesus declared. 'Go now and leave your life of sin.'" (8:10-11)

The woman, who had been the defendant in a capital case, is now alone in court. Only Jesus, the rabbi who had been asked to settle the case is still present. None of her accusers – and, more important, witnesses against her – are present to testify. The case is thrown out of court for lack of evidence.

"Then neither do I condemn you," says Jesus. According to the Law of Moses, no sentence or condemnation is appropriate without witnesses.

Go and Sin No More (8:11b)

But this doesn't mean that no sin has occurred. The woman knows it and so does Jesus. Jesus is not acting as if her sin is of no consequence, just that it cannot be legally judged without competent witnesses. Rather, here Jesus is taking sin very seriously indeed, just as he did with the man healed at the Pool of Bethesda:

> "Stop sinning or something worse may happen to you." (5:14b)

Here he says to the woman:

> "Go your way, and from now on do not sin again." (8:11b, NRSV)

The core of both these commands is exactly the same in Greek, literally, "sin no longer,"[329]

A Call to Repentance

In both instances, Jesus does not excuse or pass over sin. Rather, he gently calls the sinner to repentance, to change. Sometimes in our day the gospel is presented in such a way that real

---

[329] *Mēketi*, "no longer, not from now on" (BDAG 647, fα). *Mēketi hamartane*, imperative present active of the verb *hamartanō*, "to sin."

repentance from sin doesn't seem to be required. Dear friends, this is not the true gospel! There is no forgiveness, no new birth, no change without repentance. Consider these passages:

> "From that time on Jesus began to preach, '**Repent**, for the kingdom of heaven is near.'" (Matthew 4:17)

> "Unless you **repent**, you too will all perish." (Luke 13:3, 5)

> "There will be more rejoicing in heaven over one sinner who **repents** than over ninety-nine righteous persons who do not need to **repent**." (Luke 15:7)

> "**Repent** and be baptized, every one of you, in the name of Jesus Christ for the forgiveness of your sins. And you will receive the gift of the Holy Spirit." (Acts 2:38)

> "**Repent**, then, and turn to God, so that your sins may be wiped out, that times of refreshing may come from the Lord." (Acts 3:19)

> "In the past God overlooked such ignorance, but now he commands all people everywhere to **repent**." (Acts 17:30)

> "First to those in Damascus, then to those in Jerusalem and in all Judea, and to the Gentiles also, I preached that they should **repent** and turn to God and prove their repentance by their deeds." (Acts 26:20)

Repentance is not a so-called "work of righteousness," it is an act of faith. We believe that Jesus is Lord, and then consequently are sorry for everything we have done that goes contrary to our Lord's way.

Yes, our repentance may be shallow at first, but there we must start. Years ago, Dr. Sam Shoemaker advised people, "Give all you know of yourself to all you know of God." As our knowledge of ourselves and of God increases, then we must give that as well.

Q4. (John 8:10-11) Why didn't Jesus condemn the lady? Was she guilty, do you think? Instead of condemnation, what did Jesus tell her to do? Why is repentance necessary for salvation? What happens to the gospel when we don't emphasize repentance?
http://www.joyfulheart.com/forums/topic/1459-q4-repentance/

When we are called upon to restore a person who has fallen away, Paul tells us to do it both gently and humbly.

> "Brothers, if someone is caught in a sin, you who are spiritual should restore him gently. But watch yourself, or you also may be tempted. Carry each other's burdens, and in this way you will fulfill the law of Christ. If anyone thinks he is something when he is nothing, he deceives himself." (Galatians 6:1-3)

Lessons for Disciples

There are several things we can learn from Jesus' actions and words in this story.

1. When people tried to trap Jesus in words, he relied on the wisdom from God to help him find a "word of wisdom." So can we (1 Corinthians 12:8). Writing quietly on the ground was part of the wisdom Jesus exercised on this occasion.
2. Jesus doesn't require absolute sinlessness of judges and elders. But he does require us to have dealt with our own sins so that we can see clearly and dispassionately. Otherwise we're likely to project our weaknesses and sins upon another person in our judgment. We are to restore a person with gentleness and humility (Galatians 6:1-3)
3. Jesus refuses to condemn the lady because the requirements of the law were not met – not because he is soft on sin.
4. Jesus calls on her to repent and stop sinning. Repentance is vital for salvation.

Prayer

Father, give us wisdom when people try to put us on the spot. Help us to seek our wisdom from you. Help us not to be harsh and judgmental, but gentle and compassionate. Help us to repent from our sins and to support Jesus' call for repentance in his church. In Jesus' holy name, we pray. Amen.

Key Verses

"If any one of you is without sin, let him be the first to throw a stone at her." (John 8:7b, NIV)

"'Then neither do I condemn you,' Jesus declared. 'Go now and leave your life of sin.'" (John 8:11, NIV)

17. Truth that Sets You Free (8:12-59)

As you will recall, the account of the Woman Taken in Adultery (7:53-8:11) isn't in the earliest manuscripts of John's Gospel, so the context of today's lesson goes back to the previous chapter, and continues Jesus' sayings at the Feast of Tabernacles in Jerusalem.

I Am the Light of the World (8:12)

According to Jewish scholar Alfred Edersheim, each night of the Feast of Tabernacles, the Court of Women in the temple would be brilliantly illuminated, hosting celebrations of festive joy that centered around the final harvest and the "days of the Messiah." He notes that the term "light" had special meaning during this festival in relation to the expected Messiah.[330]

It is in this context that Jesus makes the second of his "I am" declarations, "I am the light of the world."[331] We also see several "I am" references in this chapter that don't have an object (such as "light of the world" or "gate for the sheep"), but emphasize Jesus' oneness with the Father.

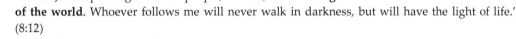

- "I am [he]" (8:24) – unless you believe you'll die in your sins

- "I am [he]" (8:28) – the Son of Man

- "Before Abraham was, I am!" (8:58)

Jesus' enemies were deeply offended that Jesus identified himself so closely with the Father, "making himself equal with God" (5:18). They were correct that this was his intent.

Here, in the midst of the a Feast that emphasizes light and the expected Messiah, Jesus speaks boldly.

William Holman Hunt, "The Light of the World" (1853-54), Keble College, Oxford, and a later copy in St. Paul's Cathedral, London. It illustrates Revelation 3:20 – "Behold, I stand at the door and knock...."

> "When Jesus spoke again to the people, he said, '**I am the light of the world**. Whoever follows me will never walk in darkness, but will have the light of life.'" (8:12)

Light in Messianic Passages

Psalm 118 was read and sung throughout the Feast of Tabernacles, laden with clear messianic allusions.

---

[330] Edersheim, *Life and Times*, Book 4, chapter 8, pp 837ff.
[331] See Appendix 4. The 'I Am' Passages in John's Gospel.

"²² The **stone** the builders rejected
has become the **capstone**;
²³ the LORD has done this,
and it is marvelous in our eyes.
²⁴ This is the day the LORD has made;
let us rejoice and be glad in it.
²⁵ O LORD, save us; [**"Hosanna"**]
O LORD, grant us success.
²⁶ Blessed is he who comes in the name of the LORD.
From the house of the LORD we bless you.
²⁷ The LORD is God,
and **he has made his light shine upon us**.
With boughs in hand,
join in the festal procession up to the horns of the altar. " (Psalm 118:22-27)

Jesus as the Light is an important theme elsewhere in John's Gospel as well.

"In him was life, and that life was the **light of men**. The **light** shines in the darkness, but the darkness has not understood it." (1:4-5)

"The **true light** that gives **light** to every man was coming into the world." (1:9)

"This is the verdict: **Light** has come into the world, but men loved darkness instead of light because their deeds were evil." (3:19)

"As long as it is day, we must do the work of him who sent me. Night is coming, when no one can work. While I am in the world, I am the **light of the world**." (9:4-5)

"You are going to have the **light** just a little while longer. Walk while you have the **light**, before darkness overtakes you. The man who walks in the dark does not know where he is going. **Put your trust in the light** while you have it, so that you may become **sons of light**." (12:34-36a)

In addition, several Messianic prophecies contain the idea of light.

"The people walking in darkness have seen a **great light**;
on those living in the land of the shadow of death a **light has dawned**....
For unto us a child is born." (Isaiah 9:2, 6)

"The **sun of righteousness** will rise with healing in its wings." (Malachi 4:2a)

Simeon's prophecy: "My eyes have seen your salvation ... a **light** for revelation to the Gentiles and for glory to your people Israel." (Luke 2:30-32)

Paul summarizes the law and the prophets as proclaiming:

"... that the Christ would suffer and, as the first to rise from the dead, would proclaim **light** to his own people and to the Gentiles." (Acts 26:23)

Never Walk in Darkness (8:12b)

Jesus makes a promise in our passage:

"I am the light of the world. Whoever follows me will never walk in darkness, but will have the light of life." (8:12)

Those who follow Jesus as a disciple (*akoloutheō*[332]) – and continue to do so (present tense suggesting continued action) – will always have light to guide them. This is similar to Jesus' saying later in this discourse:

> "If you hold to my teaching, you are really my disciples. Then you will know the truth, and the truth will set you free." (John 8:31b-32)

There is no salvation in mere inquiry or intellectual examination of Jesus and his claims. Salvation comes in continuing to follow him, in holding to his teachings.

> "If anyone chooses to do God's will, he will find out whether my teaching comes from God or whether I speak on my own." (7:17)

The assurance comes in following, in embracing, in obeying.

> **Q1. (John 8:12) In what sense is Jesus the Light of the World? What is Jesus' promise concerning light for his followers? Exactly what does that mean for the way you live?**
> **http://www.joyfulheart.com/forums/topic/1460-q1-light-of-the-world/**

The Father's Testimony (8:13-20)

John 8 contains a running dialog between the Pharisees and Jesus where they challenge him and he replies. The Pharisees begin by challenging Jesus' claim to be the light of the world on the grounds that it is just his claim, not backed up by two or three witnesses as would be required in court according to the Mosaic Law.

> "[13] The Pharisees challenged him, 'Here you are, appearing as your own witness; your testimony is not valid.'
> [14] Jesus answered, 'Even if I testify on my own behalf, my testimony is valid, for I know where I came from and where I am going. But you have no idea where I come from or where I am going. [15] You judge by human standards; I pass judgment on no one. [16] But if I do judge, my decisions are right, because I am not alone. I stand with the Father, who sent me. [17] In your own Law it is written that the testimony of two men is valid. [18] I am one who testifies for myself; my other witness is the Father, who sent me.'
> [19] Then they asked him, 'Where is your father?'
> 'You do not know me or my Father,' Jesus replied. 'If you knew me, you would know my Father also.'" (8:13-19)

Notice that their criticism in 8:15 comes from judging Jesus by "human standards" (NIV, NRSV), literally "according to the flesh" (ESV, cf. KJV). It's so easy for our world to judge Jesus according to the world's standards as a good man and founder of a religion, but not to see him as the Son of God, a Savior and Rescuer who would be their Friend. The Pharisees and our world judge that way because they don't know Jesus' origin from the Father. As Paul said,

---

[332] *Akoloutheō*, BDAG 36, 3.

"So from now on we regard no one from a worldly point of view. Though we once regarded Christ in this way, we do so no longer." (2 Corinthians 5:16)

In verse 15b, Jesus says, "I pass judgment on no one" (NIV). We know that he will judge all men on the Last Day (Acts 17:31; 10:42; 5:22; 2 Corinthians 5:10; 2 Timothy 4:1), but for now he does not come to condemn or pass judgment, but to save (3:17; 8:11; 12:47).

Verse 20 highlights the charged atmosphere Jesus faced in the temple from his enemies.

"He spoke these words while teaching in the temple area near the place where the offerings were put.[333] Yet no one seized[334] him, because his time had not yet come." (8:20)

Jesus' claims were interpreted as blasphemy by his enemies – and previously the chief priests and Pharisees had sent temple guards to arrest him (7:30, 32, 44) – but it wasn't his time yet.

You Will Die in Your Sins (8:21-24)

Jesus' conflict with the Pharisees is not just verbal sparring. There are life and death issues at stake. If they don't believe, they will die in their sins.

"[21] Once more Jesus said to them, 'I am going away, and you will look for me, and you will die in your sin. Where I go, you cannot come.'
[22] This made the Jews ask, 'Will he kill himself? Is that why he says, "Where I go, you cannot come"?'" (8:21-22)

Jesus is referring to his crucifixion and exaltation to heaven. Even after his resurrection, most of his enemies didn't believe in him, but continued to seek the Messiah elsewhere – as Jews do today.

"[23] But he continued, 'You are from below; I am from above. You are of this world; I am not of this world. [24] I told you that you would die in your sins; if you do not believe that I am [the one I claim to be][335], you will indeed die in your sins.'" (8:23-24)

Because of their unbelief Jesus says to the Jewish leaders, "You will indeed die in your sins" (8:24b). How sad! The Savior from sin is present and he will die for their sins, but they look elsewhere for salvation.

This afternoon God led me to visit a 94-year-old man I've known for more than 20 years. His parents were devout, his brother attended my church during his lifetime. This man counts himself as a believer. He thinks that he's "a pretty good Christian," and hopes to go to heaven, but hardly ever attends church.

I failed to help him move closer to Jesus, though I tried. I suppose that after 94 years, you have your defenses pretty well built up. But the man's Savior guided me to visit him and speak to him one more time about his relationship with Jesus so that he won't die in his sins.

What does it mean to die in your sins? Paul put it this way to the Ephesian church:

---

[333] The thirteen shofar-chests or offering boxes were probably in the area of the Court of Women, since the women had access to them (Mark 12:41-42).

[334] "Seized" (NIV), "arrested" (NRSV, ESV), "laid hands on" (KJV) is *piazō*, "seize, arrest, take into custody" (BDAG 812, 2a).

[335] *Egō eimi*, "I am," here, as the NIV puts it, "I am [the one I claim to be]." See Appendix 4. The 'I Am' Passages in John's Gospel.

"As for you, you were dead in your transgressions and sins, in which you used to live when you followed the ways of this world.... All of us also lived among them at one time, gratifying the cravings of our sinful nature and following its desires and thoughts. Like the rest, we were by nature objects of wrath." (Ephesians 2:1-3)

Without trusting in Jesus as your Savior, you are "dead in your transgressions and sins," while desperately needing life that comes only from the One who can free you from those sins. To die in our sins means to die without trusting Christ as Savior. To die in our sins means to die without having the guilt of sins removed from us. And on Judgment Day we will have to answer for every one of our sins – unless our names are written in the Grace Book, the Lamb's Book of Life where those who trust in Jesus are recorded (Revelation 21:2; 20:12).

> **Q2. (John 8:21-24) What does it mean to "die in your sins"? What is the consequence of this? How is it possible for Jesus' enemies to be speaking with the Savior from sin without receiving forgiveness from him? They are so close, but so far! Do you know anyone like this?**
> **http://www.joyfulheart.com/forums/topic/1461-q2-die-in-your-sin/**

Sent by the Father (8:25-29)

The dialogue continues.

> "25 'Who are you?' they asked.
> 'Just what I have been claiming all along,' Jesus replied. 26 'I have much to say in judgment of you. But he who sent me is reliable, and what I have heard from him I tell the world.'
> 27 They did not understand that he was telling them about his Father. 28 So Jesus said, 'When you have lifted up the Son of Man, then you will know that I am [the one I claim to be] and that I do nothing on my own but speak just what the Father has taught me.
> 29 The one who sent me is with me; he has not left me alone, for I always do what pleases him.'"
> (8:25-29)

His enemies don't recognize Jesus' relation to the Father. But Jesus tells them that after they have lifted him up on the cross,[336] they will know by his resurrection that he is who he claims, the divine Son of Man, that his words come from the Father.

Notice verse 29, where Jesus acknowledges the Father's presence and power with him. Jesus' heart is to do what pleases the Father; that should be our heart as well!

The Truth Will Set You Free (8:30-32)

Perhaps we were imagining only Jesus verbally sparring with his vocal enemies. But there were many among the listeners to this dialogue who came to faith by what they heard (see also 7:31). For them, Jesus has a promise.

---

[336] The theme of being "lifted up from the earth" is found elsewhere: 3:14 and 12:32-34.

³⁰ Even as he spoke, many put their faith in him. ³¹ To the Jews who had believed him, Jesus said, "If you hold to my teaching, you are really my disciples. ³² Then you will know the truth, and the truth will set you free."

Verse 32 is one of the most often-quoted sayings in the Bible. It adorns many public buildings – on courthouses, universities, even in the lobby of the headquarters of the US Central Intelligence Agency! Most of the time verse 32 is quoted by itself, without the context of verse 31. Verse 31 is the "if clause," while verse 32 is the "then clause," only true when the conditions of the "if clause" are met.

Let's look at what Jesus was saying:

If-clause (verse 31a): "If you hold to my teaching, you are really my disciples." "Teaching" (NIV), is literally "word" (NRSV, KJV), though *logos* here implies more than a single word, but includes one's entire "proclamation, instruction, teaching, message."[337] "Hold to" (NIV), "continue in" (NRSV, KJV), "abide in" (ESV) is the preposition *en*, "in" and the common verb *menō*, "remain, stay." It can be used of a location, "stay," often in the special sense of "to live, dwell, lodge." Here, it is in the transferred sense of someone who does not leave a certain realm or sphere: "remain, continue, abide."[338] It isn't enough to casually peruse Jesus' teachings; we must remain/abide in them, continue to follow them. That is the condition of the if-clause.

Then-clause (verse 31b): "... you are *really* my disciples." A person who continues to believe in Jesus' teachings – not just for a while, but permanently – is a true disciple of Jesus. "Disciple" is *mathētēs*, "learner, pupil, disciple."[339] To be a true disciple, means to be *alēthōs*, that is, "corresponding to what is really so, truly, in truth, really, actually."[340] John often uses this word group to distinguish the true and authentic from the false and inauthentic.[341] A true/actual/real disciple believes for the long run. This theme is found elsewhere.

"... nor does his word (*logos*) **dwell** in you, for you do not believe the one he sent." (John 5:38)

"Anyone who runs ahead and does not **continue** in the teaching of Christ does not have God; whoever **continues** in the teaching (*didachē*) has both the Father and the Son." (2 John 1:9)

"But as for you, **continue** in what you have learned and have become convinced of...." (2 Timothy 3:14)

The context of 8:31-32 speaks of the truth according to Jesus – spiritual truth, not secular truth or natural science. Those who hold to this spiritual truth are Jesus' disciples.

Result-clause (verse 32). "Then[342] you will know the truth, and the truth will set you free." The results of being a true disciple are expressed in the future tense in verse 32. Especially in John's

---

[337] *Logos*, BDAG 600, 1aβ.

[338] *Menō*, BDAG 631, 1bβ.

[339] *Mathētēs*, BDAG 609.

[340] *Alēthōs*, BDAG 44, b.

[341] *Alēthēs*, "true" and *alēthinos*, "authentic" are also in this word group. So Jesus is the "true light" (1:9), the "true bread" (6:32), the "true vine" (15:1). There are "true worshippers" (4:23), a "true Israelite" (1:47), the "true God" (17:3).

[342] The connecting word here is the common conjunction *kai*, "and," though here it serves "to introduce a result that comes from what precedes: and then, and so" (BDAG 495, 1bζ).

Gospel, *alētheia*, "truth," carries the idea of "authenticity, divine reality, revelation."[343] Jesus is the Word, the Logos, the Expression of God himself, the one who speaks the Words of God (1:1).

So the truth of verse 32 is spiritual, God's reality truth, not just human truth. And as we will see in verses 34-36, you will be set free not from ignorance but from sin. Only when we conform our lives with reality, with truth, can we be truly free.

Of course, there is a general sense in which any kind of truth sets a person free from ignorance, from superstitions, from false charges in a court of law. And education's truths can set people free from poverty, perhaps. These are the senses in which the world quotes the phrase. But the sense in which Jesus spoke it – as can be easily demonstrated from the context – is that Jesus' spiritual truth can set people free from sin that otherwise can enslave them, so long as they continue to affirm and live in this truth.

> Q3. (John 8:31-32) What is the mark of a "real" disciple? What does it mean to "continue" in Jesus' word? What truth sets us free? When this is quoted in a secular content, how does its meaning differ from its context here in John's Gospel?
> http://www.joyfulheart.com/forums/topic/1462-q3-continue-in-my-word/

Slaves to Sin (8:33-36)

The world misunderstands the saying, so we shouldn't be surprised if Jesus' opponents misunderstood it too. They took "set free" to mean emancipation from slavery, as the word is often used.[344] They took offense. Though politically under Roman rule, Jews still maintained some freedom under their own kings (Herod's sons) and high priests (appointed by Herod's family). At least, they insist, they aren't *slaves*!

> "They answered him, 'We are Abraham's descendants and have never been slaves of anyone. How can you say that we shall be set free?'" (8:33)

So Jesus explains that he is not talking about political or social slavery, but spiritual slavery.

> "³⁴ Jesus replied, 'I tell you the truth, everyone who sins is a slave to sin. ³⁵ Now a slave has no permanent place in the family, but a son belongs to it forever. ³⁶ So if the Son sets you free, you will be free indeed.'" (8:34-36)

Slavery to sin is a difficult concept for us – mainly because we usually don't understand how trapped we are by our habits, core beliefs, thought patterns, desires, passions, and lifestyles. Remember the verse from Paul that we considered above:

> "As for you, you were dead in your transgressions and sins, in which you used to live when you followed the ways of this world and of the ruler of the kingdom of the air, the spirit who is now at work in those who are disobedient. All of us also lived among them at one time, gratifying the

---

[343] Rudolf Bultmann, *alētheia*, TDNT 1:245.
[344] "Set free" is *eleutheroō*, "to cause someone to be freed from domination, free, set free" (BDAG 317).

cravings of our sinful nature and following its desires and thoughts. Like the rest, we were by nature objects of wrath." (Ephesians 2:1-3)

We thought we did this of our own free will, but our will has become ensnared, trapped in our sin. The sin we may have once committed out of our own (relatively) free will, now enslaves us, making us unable to stop. This is not just a matter of will-power, but is demonic, following "the ruler of the kingdom of the air" (Ephesians 2:1). Paul speaks clearly of this slavery to sin (Romans 6:17-18, 22; 8:2).

Jesus says, "Everyone who sins is a slave to sin" (8:34). That is, he does what his master ("sin") causes him to do. We cannot free and reform ourselves. We need a Savior, a Rescuer to break the power of sin in us. We need the Spirit to deliver us and renew us in the spirit of our minds. We need the Son to set us free and give us a status before God as sons, not slaves (8:35).

> **Q4. (John 8:34-36) How does sinning enslave a person? What is necessary to set a person free from bondage to sin? What part does Jesus' "truth" (8:32) have in this? How does the "Son" set people free? If you find yourself trapped by habitual sin, how can you get free?**
> **http://www.joyfulheart.com/forums/topic/1463-q4-slaves-to-sin/**

Abraham's Children (8:37-41)

Now Jesus questions his opponents' supposed allegiance to Abraham. You aren't acting like Abraham did, Jesus says.

> "37 'I know you are Abraham's descendants. Yet you are ready to kill me, because you have no room for my word. 38 I am telling you what I have seen in the Father's presence, and you do what you have heard from your father.'
> 39 'Abraham is our father,' they answered.
> 'If you were Abraham's children,' said Jesus, 'then you would do the things Abraham did. 40 As it is, you are determined to kill me, a man who has told you the truth that I heard from God. Abraham did not do such things. 41 You are doing the things your own father does.'
> 'We are not illegitimate children,' they protested. 'The only Father we have is God himself.'" (8:37-41)

Abraham was a man of faith. You can only claim to be his spiritual descendants if you do what he did.

A Liar and the Father of Lies (8:42-47)

Now Jesus speaks harshly to his opponents. Abraham was a man of faith. He listened to God. Those who love Abraham's God will recognize the Son when he brings the Father's words.

> "42 Jesus said to them, 'If God were your Father, you would love me, for I came from God and now am here. I have not come on my own; but he sent me. 43 Why is my language not clear to you? Because you are unable to hear what I say.
> 44 You belong to your father, the devil, and you want to carry out your father's desire. He was a murderer from the beginning, not holding to the truth, for there is no truth in him. When he lies, he speaks his native language, for he is a liar and the father of lies.

45 Yet because I tell the truth, you do not believe me! 46 Can any of you prove me guilty of sin? If I am telling the truth, why don't you believe me? 47 He who belongs to God hears what God says. The reason you do not hear is that you do not belong to God.'" (8:42-47)

Rather than being Abraham's children, Jesus says, you are the devil's children, since you act like him – rejecting truth. Their desire to arrest and kill Jesus is an additional indication of their true allegiance to the one who "was a murderer from the beginning."

Just because a person is an adherent of a religion doesn't mean that he belongs to God! Many in church today are *functionally unbelievers*, as sad as that is to say.

> **Q5. (John 8:44) What does this verse teach us about the devil's character? What does this tell us about people who don't always tell the truth? If Jesus is "the Truth" (14:6), what is an habitual liar?**
> **http://www.joyfulheart.com/forums/topic/1464-q5-father-of-lies/**

Believers Never See Death (8:48-51)

Jesus' enemies answer his charge that they are children of the devil with name-calling.

"48 The Jews answered him, 'Aren't we right in saying that you are a Samaritan and demon-possessed?'

49 'I am not possessed by a demon,' said Jesus, 'but I honor my Father and you dishonor me. 50 I am not seeking glory for myself; but there is one who seeks it, and he is the judge.'" (4:48-50)

There are others listening to this exchange, some of whom are being convinced by Jesus (7:31; 8:30), so in verse 51 Jesus speaks again to them.

"I tell you the truth, if anyone keeps my word, he will never see death." (8:51)

Here's another if-then statement like we saw in 8:31.

If-clause. "If anyone keeps my word...." "Keeps" is *tēreō*, "to keep watch over, guard," here in the sense, "to persist in obedience, keep, observe, fulfill, pay attention to," especially of law and teaching.[345] This is similar to the if-clause in 8:31a, "If you hold to/continue in (*menō*) my word...."

Then-clause. "He will never see death." "See" (*theōreō*) is used here figuratively in the sense of "undergo, experience."[346] A similar figurative expression we see is "taste death" in 8:52.[347] This is not physical death Jesus is speaking of, but spiritual death, separation from God. Jesus is speaking in terms of eternal life and eternal death as he does elsewhere:

"He has crossed over from death to life." (5:24)

"I am the resurrection and the life. He who believes in me will live, even though he dies; and whoever lives and believes in me will never die." (11:25-26)

---

345 *Tēreō*, BDAG 1002, 3.

346 *Theōreō*, BDAG 454, 2c.

347 *Geuomai*, "to partake of something by mouth, taste, partake of," here in the figurative sense of, "to experience something cognitively or emotionally, come to know something" (BDAG 195, 2).

What a wonderful promise!

Unbelief (8:52-55)

Ears of faith hear Jesus' promise of eternal life and rejoice. But Jesus' opponents are incensed. They go back to Jesus' assertion that they don't act like their supposed father, Abraham. Abraham died, they say, how can a person not die?

> "[52] At this the Jews exclaimed, 'Now we know that you are demon-possessed! Abraham died and so did the prophets, yet you say that if anyone keeps your word, he will never taste death. [53] Are you greater than our father Abraham? He died, and so did the prophets. Who do you think you are?'
>
> [54] Jesus replied, 'If I glorify myself, my glory means nothing. My Father, whom you claim as your God, is the one who glorifies me. [55] Though you do not know him, I know him. If I said I did not, I would be a liar like you, but I do know him and keep his word.'" (8:52-55)[348]

You claim to know my Father, says Jesus, but you do not.

Before Abraham Was, I Am (8:56-59)

Now Jesus speaks boldly about his pre-existence!

> "[56] 'Your father Abraham rejoiced at the thought of seeing my day; he saw it and was glad.'
>
> [57] 'You are not yet fifty years old,' the Jews said to him, 'and you have seen Abraham!'
>
> [58] 'I tell you the truth,' Jesus answered, 'before Abraham was born, I am!'" (8:56-58)

Jesus' opponents have no idea who Jesus is. Nor do they really know the Father. So to them, Jesus' claim to precede Abraham appears as blasphemy. But, as it turns out, it is the truth. Jesus said, literally,

> "Before Abraham was, I am." (8:58b)

Notice he didn't say, before Abraham "I was" (past tense), which you'd expect him to say, speaking about his pre-existence, but "I am" (present tense). It is clear that Jesus is identifying himself with Yahweh, the great I AM who appeared to Moses at the burning bush.[349] Moses asks God's name.

> "God said to Moses, **'I am who I am.'** He said further, 'Thus you shall say to the Israelites, "**I am** has sent me to you."'" (Exodus 3:13-14)

The context of John 8:58 is time. Jesus is saying that he not only precedes Abraham in time, but he exists timelessly! This takes us back to the very preface to the Gospel of John:

> "In the beginning was the Word, and the Word was with God, and the Word was God. He was in the beginning with God." (1:1-2)

This eternal timelessness of Jesus is expressed in Hebrews:

> "Jesus Christ is the same yesterday and today and forever." (Hebrews 13:8)

And Christ's eternal origins match the timelessness of God the Father in the Book of Revelation.

---

[348] See more in Appendix 6. "Glory" and "Glorify" in John's Gospel.
[349] For more on this see Appendix 4. The "I Am" Passages in John's Gospel.

Father: "... who is and who was and who is to come, and from the seven spirits who are before his throne (Revelation 1:4).

Father: "I am the Alpha and the Omega," says the Lord God, who is and who was and who is to come, the Almighty" (Revelation 1:8).

Christ: "I am the first and the last, and the living one. I was dead, and see, I am alive forever and ever; and I have the keys of Death and of Hades" (Revelation 1:17-18).

Father: "Holy, holy, holy, the Lord God the Almighty, who was and is and is to come" (Revelation 4:8).

Father: "It is done! I am the Alpha and the Omega, the beginning and the end. To the thirsty I will give water as a gift from the spring of the water of life" (Revelation 21:5-6).

Christ: "I am the Alpha and the Omega, the first and the last, the beginning and the end" (Revelation 22:13).

Yes, these are the eternal implications when Jesus said, "Before Abraham was, I am." (8:58b)

Jesus' opponents are spiritually dull, but they are astute enough to grasp the fact that Jesus is making himself equal with God – again. And they respond.

"At this, they picked up stones to stone him, but Jesus hid himself, slipping away[350] from the temple grounds.[351]" (8:59)

It wasn't Jesus' time. Soon, but not yet.

Q6. (John 8:58) What does Jesus' statement, "Before Abraham was, I am," tell us about Jesus? How does this statement relate to John 1:1-5?
http://www.joyfulheart.com/forums/topic/1465-q6-before-abraham-i-am/

Lessons for Disciples

Though much of this passage is a running dialog between Jesus and his enemies, we find a number of lessons that we can apply as disciples.

1. Jesus is the Light of the world, the Light that illuminates our pathway (8:12).

2. Unless people put their trust in Jesus, they will die in their sins, that is, without their sins forgiven. The issues are life and death! (8:24).

3. Real disciples continue in Jesus' teaching and follow it. Only this way can they really know the truth that can set them free from sin (8:31-32).

---

[350] "Hid himself" is *kryptō*, middle voice used in an active sense, "hide" (see also 12:36; BDAG 571, 1a). "Slipping away" (NIV), "went out" (NRSV, KJV) is *exerchomai*, "go out, come out, go away, retire" (BDAG 1aα).

[351] KJV includes at the end of verse 59, "going through the midst of them, and so passed by," but it is not found in the earliest manuscripts.

4. Those who sin are a slave to sin, and need emancipation from slavery from the Son himself – Jesus (8:34-36).

5. Those who love God will also embrace Jesus – if it is truly Yahweh, the God of the Bible, that they love. Otherwise, their love of God is a sham (8:42).

6. The devil is described as a murderer, devoid of real truth. He is liar and the father of those who lie (8:44)

7. Those who follow Jesus' teachings in faith will never see spiritual death (8:51).

8. Jesus' preexistence predates Abraham (8:58).

Prayer

Father, thank you for drawing us to Jesus, who can set us free and keep us free – from sin and from whatever binds us. We are so easily deceived; thank you for putting love for you in our hearts. We do love you! Help us to continue on the path with our Lord. In Jesus' name, we pray. Amen.

Key Verses

"I am the light of the world. Whoever follows me will never walk in darkness, but will have the light of life." (John 8:12, NIV)

"I told you that you would die in your sins; if you do not believe that I am [the one I claim to be], you will indeed die in your sins." (John 8:24, NIV)

"When you have lifted up the Son of Man, then you will know that I am [the one I claim to be] and that I do nothing on my own but speak just what the Father has taught me." (John 8:28, NIV)

"To the Jews who had believed him, Jesus said, 'If you hold to my teaching, you are really my disciples. Then you will know the truth, and the truth will set you free.'" (John 8:31-32, NIV)

"I tell you the truth, everyone who sins is a slave to sin. Now a slave has no permanent place in the family, but a son belongs to it forever. So if the Son sets you free, you will be free indeed." (John 8:34-36, NIV)

"If God were your Father, you would love me, for I came from God and now am here. I have not come on my own; but he sent me." (John 8:42, NIV)

"You belong to your father, the devil, and you want to carry out your father's desire. He was a murderer from the beginning, not holding to the truth, for there is no truth in him. When he lies, he speaks his native language, for he is a liar and the father of lies." (John 8:44, NIV)

"I tell you the truth, if anyone keeps my word, he will never see death." (John 8:51, NIV)

"'I tell you the truth,' Jesus answered, 'before Abraham was born, I am!'" (John 8:58, NIV)

18. Healing Blindness (9:1-41)

John's account of the healing of the man born blind is certainly a sign, for it points to Jesus the Healer and Light of the World. At the same time as it contrasts physical blindness that can be healed, with spiritual blindness that cannot.

Jesus has just left the temple grounds at the conclusion of the Feast of Tabernacles (8:59), if we can assume a continuity between chapters 8 and 9.

The Man Born Blind (9:1)

> "As he went along[352], he saw a man blind[353] from birth.[354]" (9:1)

The blind man may have been in the custom of asking for alms near the gate to the temple (Acts 3:2), so that people in a merciful mood might drop a coin or two in his hands. Almsgiving towards the poor was a command (Deuteronomy 15:8, 11) that would be rewarded by God himself (Matthew 6:2-4).

This man is specifically identified as one who was "blind from birth." How did they know this? We're not sure, but perhaps because of his relatively young age.

Harold Copping (1863-1932), "At the Pool of Siloam" (watercolor illustration)

(His parents were still living, we're told later in the story.) Those nearby who knew the man might have shared this information as well.

Sin and Sickness (9:2-3)

Seeing a young man with no sight caused Jesus' disciples to wonder aloud the cause. Why, Lord? They were curious. They assumed that his blindness was a result of sin, but since he was young, they wondered if it might have been his parents' sin that caused it, not his. So they asked their rabbi – Jesus.

> [2] His disciples asked him, 'Rabbi, who sinned, this man or his parents, that he was born blind?'
> [3] 'Neither this man nor his parents sinned,' said Jesus, 'but this happened so that the work of God might be displayed[355] in his life.'" (9:2-3)

---

[352] "Went along" (NIV), "walked along" (NRSV), "passed by" (ESV, KJV) is *paragō*, either (1) "to move along and so leave a position, go away" or (3) "to go past a reference point, pass by" (BDAG 761, 1 and 3).

[353] "Blind" is *typhlos*, "pertaining to being unable to see, blind" (BDAG 1021, 1a).

[354] "Birth" is *genetē*, "coming into being through birth, birth" (BDAG 193).

[355] "Be displayed" (NIV, ESV), "be revealed" (NRSV), "made manifest" (KJV) is *phaneroō*, here, passive, "become public knowledge, be disclosed, become known" (BDAG 1048, 2aβ).

Jesus' answer makes it clear that in this case his affliction wasn't because of someone's sin, but because God had a larger purpose in it, that "the work of God might be displayed in his life" (9:3).

It is clear in Scripture that sometimes afflictions *do* come as a result of sin (1 Corinthians 11:30; Psalm 38:3; James 5:16). This may have been the case in the man healed at the Pool of Bethesda (John 5:14). But Job's afflictions weren't the result of sin – even though his "friends" were insistent that Job's sin was the cause (Job 1:11-12).

> **Q1. (John 9:1-3) Is sin always the cause of sickness or affliction? What are some of the good results that come out of the sicknesses and afflictions of godly people?**
> **http://www.joyfulheart.com/forums/topic/1466-q1-cause-of-affliction/**

I Am the Light of the World (9:4-5)

Seeing the blind man, Jesus speaks of light and darkness – perhaps with the idea that the eyes are the portals of light to the body (Matthew 6:22-23).

> "[4] As long as it is day, we[356] must do the work of him who sent me. Night is coming, when no one can work. [5] While I am in the world, I am the light of the world." (9:4-5)

Does the phrase "night is coming" forebode the coming of the evil one? I don't think so. If that were the case, the disciples themselves wouldn't be able to work after Jesus left them. It is probably another way of speaking of Jesus death.

Jesus is saying simply that we must do God's works while we have opportunity, because the time will come when we won't be able to do them any longer. It is a word to motivate those of us who feel too busy (or too selfish) to fulfill our calling. Don't put off for later what you can do today!

Spreading Mud on the Man's Eyes (9:6-7)

Now John describes the healing in a few short words.

> "[6] Having said this, he spit on the ground, made some mud with the saliva, and put[357] it on the man's eyes. [7] 'Go,' he told him, 'wash[358] in the Pool of Siloam' (this word means Sent). So the man went and washed, and came home seeing." (9:6-7)

Jesus spits on the ground and makes mud to put on the man's eyes. Then he tells him to wash in the Pool of Siloam where water had just been drawn to celebrate the Feast of Tabernacles (see Lesson 15). The Pool of Siloam (like the Pool of Bethesda) was a Jewish *mikveh*, a bath or pool used for ritual immersion for ceremonial cleansing.

---

[356] KJV "I must do" vs. more recent translations "we must do" is difficult. Metzger (Textual Commentary, p. 227) sees "somewhat superior external support" for "we," and a slightly higher probability that copyists would have altered "we" to "I" than vice versa. The Committee adopts "we" but gives it a {D} "doubtful" rating.

[357] "Put it on" (NIV), "spread" (NRSV), "anointed" (KJV) is *epichriō*, "to apply a viscous substance, anoint, spread/smear (on)," from *epi-*, "upon" + *chriō*, "anoint" (BDAG 387).

[358] "Wash" is *niptō*, "to cleanse with use of water, wash," here, in the middle voice, "wash oneself," also 9:11ab (BDAG 674, 1bα).

Are we to see this as some kind of medicinal poultice applied to heal blindness? Some point to the fact that saliva was thought to possess medicinal qualities in Hellenism and Judaism. Jesus himself uses saliva in two additional healings – of a dumb man (Mark 7:33) and another blind man (Mark 8:23). But beyond those incidents, Jesus isn't depicted as a physician resorting to natural medicines, but as a miracle-worker. Certainly, whatever natural medicinal properties that might be thought to be

in saliva were not believed by the people of Jesus' day to cure a man born blind! Healing a man born blind had never happened in recorded Jewish history!

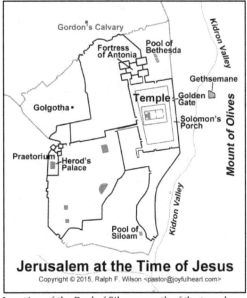

Why does Jesus use saliva and mud on this occasion? Why does he sometimes lay on hands for healing (Luke 4:40; Mark 6:5), and other times just speak the word of command (Matthew 8:5-13) or cast out a demon (Matthew 17:18)? Why does he put his fingers in deaf ears (Mark 7:33)? Why does he encourage his disciples to anoint with oil for healing (Mark 6:13)? We can see no fixed pattern to the forms of Jesus' healing ministry. He listens to the Father (John 5:19, 30), and then acts as he is led. His guidance from the Father is both in his message and the manner in which it is communicated (12:49). Jesus is our example in this. We minister as he leads us.

Location of the Pool of Siloam, south of the temple.

Notice that since the healing wasn't instantaneous, the blind man never actually saw Jesus, but only knew his name (9:11). He went to the Pool of Siloam and washed off the mud "and came home seeing" (9:7b). Perhaps this was a healing in which Jesus sought to have the blind man exercise his own faith in obedience. We see this in the case of healing the ten lepers whom he told to go and show themselves to the priests. We read, "and as they went, they were cleansed" (Luke 17:14).

John indicates the derivation of the name Siloam as meaning "sent." Perhaps he is making the point that the man was healed because he was "sent" to wash in the pool; the healing didn't just happen by itself.

Q2. (John 9:6). Why do you think Jesus healed in different ways? Laying on of hands, command, mud on eyes, fingers in ears, etc.? How much do you think was at his Father's direction (5:19, 30; 12:49). Why is it important to seek God's guidance in *how* we should minister to a person? http://www.joyfulheart.com/forums/topic/1467-q2-methods-of-healing/

The Man Tells His Story to His Neighbors (9:8-12)

The healed man didn't return to where Jesus was, but went home. He must have caused a real stir in his neighborhood!

"⁸ His neighbors and those who had formerly seen him begging asked, 'Isn't this the same man who used to sit and beg?' ⁹ Some claimed that he was. Others said, 'No, he only looks like him.' But he himself insisted, 'I am the man.'
¹⁰ 'How then were your eyes opened?' they demanded.
¹¹ He replied, 'The man they call Jesus made some mud and put it on my eyes. He told me to go to Siloam and wash. So I went and washed, and then I could see.'
¹² 'Where is this man?' they asked him.
'I don't know,' he said." (9:8-12)

The miracle was so great that some of his neighbors didn't believe he could be the same man they saw begging. But he told them, "I am the man," and related the story of how it happened.

The Pharisees Interrogate the Man (9:13-17)

"They brought to the Pharisees the man who had been blind." (9:13)

It wasn't right to hide this miracle of healing, so his neighbors or parents brought him before the local religious authorities – after all, it was a religious healing. There is no indication here that his neighbors were trying to get Jesus in trouble, but just tell others of the wonderful thing God had done.

However, where the neighbors saw a miracle, the Pharisees saw a serious infraction of the Sabbath laws prohibiting kneading and healing on the holy day.

"¹⁴ Now the day on which Jesus had made the mud and opened the man's eyes was a Sabbath. ¹⁵ Therefore the Pharisees also asked him how he had received his sight. 'He put mud on my eyes,' the man replied, 'and I washed, and now I see.'
¹⁶ Some of the Pharisees said, 'This man is not from God, for he does not keep the Sabbath.' But others asked, 'How can a sinner do such miraculous signs?' So they were divided." (9:14-16)

Some of the Pharisees were so focused on the Sabbath infraction that they couldn't see the miracle. But others (apparently a minority, because they didn't prevail) stated the obvious – that a sinner couldn't perform such an amazing healing. Jesus must be from God!

Since they couldn't come to a consensus, they asked the healed man what he thought about the man who healed him.

"Finally they turned again to the blind man, 'What have you to say about him? It was your eyes he opened.'
The man replied, 'He is a prophet.'" (9:17)

The formerly blind man gave his healer the highest office he knew, that of a prophet. But that wasn't what Jesus' enemies wanted to hear.

The Pharisees Interrogate the Parents (9:18-23)

The majority of the Pharisees (now referred to as "the Jews"[359]), didn't believe that such a miracle could have really taken place.

> "[18] The Jews still did not believe that he had been blind and had received his sight until they sent for the man's parents. [19] 'Is this your son?' they asked. 'Is this the one you say was born blind? How is it that now he can see?'
>
> [20] 'We know he is our son,' the parents answered, 'and we know he was born blind.
>
> [21] But how he can see now, or who opened his eyes, we don't know. Ask him. He is of age; he will speak for himself.'
>
> [22] His parents said this because they were afraid of the Jews, for already the Jews had decided that anyone who acknowledged that Jesus was the Christ would be put out of the synagogue. [23] That was why his parents said, 'He is of age; ask him.' (9:18-23)

Notice how careful the parents are! They don't want to cross the dangerous Pharisees. So they affirm that the healed man is their son and was born blind, but offer no opinion on his healer. "Ask him. He will speak for himself."

You would expect most parents to be ecstatic about their blind son being healed. You'd think they'd be ready to tell everyone far and wide this wonderful thing that had happened.

But they are just poor people – so poor that they allowed their son to beg. They know they are no match for the leaders who have already made up their minds to excommunicate anyone who claims Jesus to be the Messiah. So they clam up. They are afraid. What would happen to them if they were excluded from their own religious community and shunned by friends? Don't get involved! Say as little as possible!

The Pharisees Re-Interrogate the Healed Man (9:24-34)

His parents are fearful, but the healed man is not! He may be uneducated, but he is not afraid. The authorities summon him again to appear before them.

> "A second time they summoned the man who had been blind. 'Give glory to God,' they said. 'We know this man is a sinner.'" (9:24)

These are not fair judges seeking truth. They have already reached a conclusion. Now they are seeking evidence so they can accuse their enemy Jesus. They weren't able to stone him in the temple (8:59; cf. 10:31-32). Perhaps they can find cause to indict him for healing on the Sabbath.

"Give glory to God" may mean either, "God deserves the glory for this healing, not Jesus who just put mud on your eyes," or, perhaps, "Know that God sees you, so give him due honor by speaking the truth."[360]

They must have asked the healed man again about his healer. Admit that Jesus is a sinner for healing on the Sabbath! they insist.

> "He replied, 'Whether he is a sinner or not, I don't know. One thing I do know. I was blind but now I see!'" (9:25)

[359] See Appendix 2. "The Jews" in John's Gospel.
[360] See Morris, John, p. 490.

The formerly blind man isn't going to be trapped into saying Jesus is a sinner. He states his testimony, unshakable in its simplicity: "One thing I know. I was blind but now I see."

> "²⁶ Then they asked him, 'What did he do to you? How did he open your eyes?'
> ²⁷ He answered, 'I have told you already and you did not listen. Why do you want to hear it again? Do you want to become his disciples, too?'" (9:26-27)

The Pharisees ask the same questions again, trying to bully the man into saying something against Jesus. But he isn't intimidated. Rather, he has an "attitude." He accuses the Pharisees of not listening the first time and, dripping with sarcasm, suggests that maybe they are inquiring again because of spiritual interest in becoming Jesus' disciples. He knows that they are not impartial judges!

> "²⁸ Then they hurled insults at him and said, 'You are this fellow's disciple! We are disciples of Moses! ²⁹ We know that God spoke to Moses, but as for this fellow, we don't even know where he comes from.'" (9:28-29)

They respond to his sarcasm by insulting their witness. But they say too much: "We don't know where he comes from" (9:29b). That is their problem. They see him as a nobody, an upstart; they are so blind that they are unwilling to see that he has been sent to them by God Himself!

The once-blind man, unlearned but bold, can't resist pointing out their lack of logic – still with great sarcasm.

> "³⁰ The man answered, 'Now that is remarkable![361] You don't know where he comes from, yet he opened my eyes. ³¹ We know that God does not listen to sinners. He listens to the godly man who does his will. ³² Nobody has ever heard of opening the eyes of a man born blind. ³³ If this man were not from God, he could do nothing.'" (9:30-33)

Here's the man's flawless logic:

1. Jesus healed my eyes.
2. God doesn't listen to sinners (so Jesus can't be a sinner).
3. This is an unheard of miracle – opening the eyes of a man born blind – not some common kind of healing that you might explain away.
4. If Jesus isn't from God, he couldn't do such a miracle.
5. (Therefore Jesus is from God!)

They don't attempt to answer his clear logic, rather they pull rank on him. They're the authorities, not he!

> "To this they replied, 'You were steeped in sin at birth; how dare you lecture[362] us!' And they threw him out." (9:34)

They insult him as "steeped in sin at birth" (as proved by his blindness from birth) and unlearned, therefore not qualified to offer an opinion. No matter that the man's opinion makes great sense, while their opinion makes no sense at all.

"They threw him out," probably means they excommunicated him from the synagogue.

---

[361] "Remarkable" (NIV), "astonishing/amazing/marvelous thing" (NRSV, ESV, KJV) is *thaumastos*, "pertaining to being a cause of wonder or worthy of amazement, wonderful, marvelous, remarkable" (BDAG 445).
[362] "Lecture" (NIV), "teach" (NRSV, KJV) is *didaskō*, "to tell someone what to do, tell, instruct" (BDAG 241, 1).

Jesus Reveals Himself to the Healed Man (9:35-38)

The once-blind man has been cut off from his faith because he challenged the bigotry of the Jewish leaders. He is healed now, but alone. He is being persecuted for Jesus' sake, because he will not cooperate with the corrupt leaders who are seeking to destroy his Healer. Jesus seeks him out.

> "[35] Jesus heard that they had thrown him out, and when he found him, he said, 'Do you believe in the Son of Man?'
> [36] 'Who is he, sir?' the man asked. 'Tell me so that I may believe in him.'
> [37] Jesus said, 'You have now seen him; in fact, he is the one speaking with you.'
> [38] Then the man said, 'Lord, I believe,' and he worshiped him." (9:35-38)

The man has been thrown out of his synagogue, but he is more than ready to believe. Jesus finds him and asks him if he believes in "the Son of Man" (a reading that has stronger attestation than "the Son of God" as in the KJV).[363] The man eagerly asks for more information and Jesus identifies himself as the Son of Man. Immediately, the man confesses his faith and kneels or prostrates himself before him in an act of worship.[364]

It's interesting to watch the progression of faith in this once-blind man. He moves from one who hardly knows of Jesus to a worshipper.

1.   "The man called Jesus..." (9:11a).
2.   "He is a prophet" (9:17c).
3.   He is one who does God's will (9:31b).
4.   He worshipped him (9:38b).

Q3. (John 9:35-38) Why did Jesus go looking for the man he had healed? What was the healed man's level of openness? His level of faith? His knowledge? What did he need at this point? What people do you know who are so ready that they just need some guidance in how to believe in Jesus?
http://www.joyfulheart.com/forums/topic/1468-q3-believing-in-jesus/

Judgment on the Spiritually Blind (9:39-41)

The healed man's interview with Jesus is probably private. But later, in public, Jesus reflects on the irony of his role.

> "Jesus said, 'For judgment I have come into this world, so that the blind will see and those who see will become blind.'" (9:39)

---

[363] Most early manuscripts read "Son of Man" (p[66,75] Aleph B L W syr[s] cop[sa,bo,ach,fa]), though some read "Son of God" (A L Θ Ψ *f*[1.13] Byzantine). "The external support for *anthrōpou* is so weighty, and the improbability of *thou* being altered to *anthrōpou* is so great, that the Committee regarded the reading adopted for the text as virtually certain," with an {A} level of certainty (Metzger, *Textual Commentary*, pp. 228-229).

[364] "Worshiped" is *proskyneō*, "to express in attitude or gesture one's complete dependence on or submission to a high authority figure, (fall down and) worship, do obeisance to, prostrate oneself before, do reverence to, welcome respectfully" (BDAG 882, a).

"Judgment" is *krima*. Here it refers to "the judicial decision which consists in the separation of those who are willing to believe from those who are unwilling to do so."[365] By his very presence as Light, Jesus becomes a polarizing figure – attracting those who are seeking God and repelling those who wish retain their own way of life while denying the obvious truth that stares them in the face. Those who turn from the Light are truly blind.

Jesus' words, "So that the blind will see," reflects Isaiah's prophecies that the blind would be healed in the Messianic Age:

> "In that day ... out of gloom and darkness the eyes of the blind will see." (Isaiah 29:18)

> "Then will the eyes of the blind be opened...." (Isaiah 35:5; cf. 42:7)

Indeed, healing the blind was one of the signs of his Messiahship that he communicated to John the Baptist (Matthew 11:4-6).

Because they do not want to believe, the Pharisees and other Jewish leaders become fixed in their blindness. How sad! There are many like them today who are blind to Jesus because they know their lives would need to change if they believed in him. Such people "suppress the truth by their wickedness" (Romans 1:18).

The Pharisees rightly perceived that Jesus' ironic statement was directed at them.

> "[39] Jesus said, 'For judgment I have come into this world, so that the blind will see and those who see will become blind.'
> [40] Some Pharisees who were with him heard him say this and asked, 'What? Are we blind too?'
> [41] Jesus said, 'If you were blind, you would not be guilty of sin; but now that you claim you can see, your guilt remains.'" (9:39-41)

A person who professes ignorance along with a willingness to learn is not guilty. But one who claims to see and is unwilling to learn is indeed guilty. As the writer of Proverbs observed:

> "Do you see a man wise in his own eyes?
> There is more hope for a fool than for him." (Proverbs 26:12)

It is clear from Jesus' words that you and I are responsible for the knowledge we do have and for rightly interpreting what we see. When we turn a blind eye to truth, it is a serious and dangerous action.

Spiritual Blindness Today

One of the paradoxes of John's Gospel is that people see miracles with their own eyes, but don't "connect the dots." Spiritual blindness was present in Jeremiah's day as well as in our own.

> "To whom can I speak and give warning?
> Who will listen to me?
> Their ears are closed so they cannot hear.
> The word of the LORD is offensive to them;
> they find no pleasure in it." (Jeremiah 6:10)

---

[365] *Krima*, BDAG 567, 6.

The Pharisees are a reminder to us that not everyone can "see" and "hear" Jesus. Only those who have eyes to see (Revelation 3:18) and ears to hear (Luke 8:8; 14:35; Mark 8:18; Revelation 2:7, 11). Spiritual blindness is a curse of the devil.

> "The god of this age has blinded the minds of unbelievers, so that they cannot see the light of the gospel of the glory of Christ, who is the image of God." (2 Corinthians 4:4)

But at the same time, according to Jesus, we are responsible for our hard hearts:

> "If you were blind, you would not be guilty of sin; but now that you claim you can see, your guilt remains." (9:41)

God, have mercy on us all!

Q4. (John 9:39-41) Were the Pharisees responsible for their hard hearts and spiritual blindness? According to 2 Corinthians 4:4, what causes spiritual blindness? Was Pharaoh responsible for his hardness of heart? (see Exodus 8:15, 32; 9:34; 10:3; 13:15; 1 Samuel 6:6). http://www.joyfulheart.com/forums/topic/1469-q4-spiritual-blindness/

Lessons for Disciples

The story of the healing of the man born blind has a number of lessons for Jesus' disciples to learn.

1. Sickness and affliction are not necessarily the result of someone's sin. Sometimes it is so that God may be glorified (9:1-3).
2. Jesus' method of healing varied – he didn't always heal the same way (9:6). No doubt he sought the Father about whom he should heal and the particular method in each case (5:19, 30; 12:49).
3. Some people refuse to commit themselves to Christ out of fear of how others might react to it (9:22; cf. 12:42).
4. Some people are just waiting to know how to put their trust in the Lord – like the man who was healed (9:35-38). All they need is some guidance.
5. Some unbelievers are not seeking, but have their minds already made up. They are set in their spiritual blindness (9:39-41).

Prayer

Father, I am grieved at the spiritual blindness I see in some of my loved ones. I pray for them that you will "grant them repentance leading to a knowledge of the truth" (2 Timothy 2:25). Lord, have mercy on our world. Send revival to us and sweep many into your Kingdom, I pray. In Jesus' name. Amen.

Key Verses

> "Neither this man nor his parents sinned," said Jesus, "but this happened so that the work of God might be displayed in his life." (John 9:3, NIV)

"Whether he is a sinner or not, I don't know. One thing I do know. I was blind but now I see!" (John 9:25, NIV)

"Jesus heard that they had thrown him out, and when he found him, he said, 'Do you believe in the Son of Man?' 'Who is he, sir?' the man asked. 'Tell me so that I may believe in him.' Jesus said, 'You have now seen him; in fact, he is the one speaking with you.' Then the man said, 'Lord, I believe,' and he worshiped him." (John 9:35-38, NIV)

"If you were blind, you would not be guilty of sin; but now that you claim you can see, your guilt remains." (John 9:41, NIV)

19. I Am the Good Shepherd (10:1-42)

Throughout the ancient Near East, rulers and leaders were often spoken of as shepherds of their people. In chapter 9, Jesus has just dealt with some of Jerusalem's "shepherds," the scribes and Pharisees and members of the Sanhedrin, who weren't interested at all in the sheep, rather in finding cause to destroy the true Shepherd who *did* care about the flock.

Corrupt Shepherds

In their day, the prophets had castigated such self-serving shepherds. Ezekiel declared the word of Yahweh:

> **"Woe to the shepherds of Israel** who only take care of themselves! Should not shepherds take care of the flock? You eat the curds, clothe yourselves with the wool and slaughter the choice animals, but you do not take care of the flock. You have not strengthened the weak or healed the sick or bound up the injured. You have not brought back the strays or searched for the lost. You have ruled them harshly and brutally. So they were scattered because there was no shepherd, and when they were scattered they became food for all the wild animals.

> ... **I am against the shepherds and will hold them accountable for my flock**. I will remove them from tending the flock.... **I myself will search for my sheep** and look after them. As a shepherd looks after his scattered flock when he is with them, so will I look after my sheep." (Ezekiel 34:2-5, 10-12)

Statue of the Good Shepherd (c. 300-350), marble, 39 inches high. Rome, from Catacomb of Domitilla, Vatican, Museo Pio Cristiano.

Jesus, too, pronounced a series of woes on the religious leaders of his day. Jesus castigated the scribes and Pharisees for their hypocrisy. They (1) prevented the people from entering the Kingdom of God (Luke 11:52); made deceptive oaths (Matthew 23:16); tithed scrupulously, but neglected mercy, justice, and faith (Matthew 23:23-24); took advantage of widows and tricked them out of their houses (Matthew 23:14); looked good on the outside, but were unclean within (Matthew 23:25-27); burdened the people with laws, but wouldn't lift a finger to help them (Luke 11:46); and made a big show of their piety to be praised by men (Matthew 6:1-18). We have seen many occasions in John where they ignored the miracles and those who were healed, but rather sought to kill the miracle-worker. As a result, God's people suffered.

> "When he saw the crowds, he had compassion on them, because they were harassed and helpless, like sheep without a shepherd." (Matthew 9:36)

So as we examine Jesus' discourse on the Good Shepherd, it should be seen in the context of the corrupt shepherds of the nation.

The Form of Jesus' Teaching on the Good Shepherd

Before we begin, however, we need to understand the form of Jesus' teaching. In the Synoptic Gospels we see Jesus often teaching in parables, stories with a spiritual point. But we err if we understand this discourse as the kind of parable we find there.

In verse 10, John describes it as a "figure of speech" (NIV, NRSV, ESV) rather than a "parable" (KJV). The Greek word refers to "a pithy saying ... a brief communication containing truths designed for initiates, veiled saying, figure of speech, in which especially lofty ideas are concealed." [366]

Probably this discourse is best understood as a series of teachings based on analogies from sheep-herding, a practice very familiar to Jesus' hearers. Many of them had cared for the family flock. They knew what was involved. Rather than a single analogy or figure of speech, we see four primary analogies drawn from this pastoral imagery:

1. The sheep-pen (10:1-2).
2. The Shepherd's voice (10:3-5).
3. The Gate or Door of the sheep-pen (10:6-9).
4. The Good Shepherd who lays down his life for the sheep (10:10-18).

The Sheepfold and the Shepherd (10:1-2)

The first analogy Jesus draws from sheep-herding relates to the sheep pen where the sheep are kept at night.

> "[1] I tell you the truth, the man who does not enter the sheep pen by the gate, but climbs in by some other way, is a thief and a robber. [2] The man who enters by the gate is the shepherd of his sheep." (10:1-2)

Jesus has in mind an enclosed pen, open to the sky, with a doorway[367] through which one might enter.[368] Such an enclosure would protect the sheep from straying at night, and from attack by wild animals, such as lions, wolves, and bears, that had threatened sheep in Palestine for centuries.

A pen might have been constructed next to the family's house. But Jesus has in mind a sheep-pen out on the grazing fields some distance from town. Such a pen would likely be made of rocks piled up to make an enclosure; wood is scarce in this hilly, rocky terrain. However, a gate might have been constructed from wood or scrub. Or perhaps the shepherd himself might sleep in the doorway so that no one could get to the sheep except by climbing over his body.

In this first analogy, Jesus speaks of thieves who would try to climb over the fence to steal a sheep. A shepherd or the owner of the sheep would use the gate, which would be closed and guarded; only thieves[369] or bandits[370] would try to get in undetected some other way.[371]

---

[366] *Paroimia*, BDAG 779, 2.

[367] "Gate" (NIV), "door" (KJV) is *thyra*, "door," here, "a passage for entering a structure, entrance, doorway, gate" (BDAG 462, 2b).

[368] "Pen" or "fold" is *aulē*, "an area open to the sky (frequently surrounded by buildings, and in some cases partially by walls), enclosed open space, courtyard," here fold for sheep (BDAG 150, 1), in verses 1 and 16.

The "thieves and robbers" in this analogy are, of course, the religious leaders who take advantage of their positions of trust to ravage God's flock. The identity of the "sheep-pen" isn't as clear. Israel? The church? We're not sure. Making a point with such an analogy doesn't require every element to be identified.

The Sheep Recognize the Shepherd's Voice (10:3-5)

Jesus point is that the legitimate shepherd comes in through the gate and his sheep know him.

"3 The watchman opens the gate for him, and the sheep listen[372] to his voice. He calls[373] his own sheep by name[374] and leads them out. 4 When he has brought out all his own, he goes on ahead of them, and his sheep follow him because they know his voice. 5 But they will never follow a stranger; in fact, they will run away from him because they do not recognize a stranger's voice." (10:3-5)

Verse 3 mentions a gatekeeper.[375] When several flocks would be put in the same pen on a remote sheep-field, one of the shepherds would be assigned as the gatekeeper for his watch. Of course, he would open up for a shepherd whose flock is contained within.

When you have several flocks penned together for the night, the way they get sorted out in the morning is by each sheep recognizing its own shepherd's voice and coming when he calls them out of the pen for another day of grazing. The shepherd might even have a name for every sheep that he might call out if the sheep didn't come when he called the flock. Jesus is referring to the intimate relationship between the shepherd and his own sheep – mutual knowledge.

George Adam Smith, who travelled in the Holy Land at the end of the nineteenth century before its modern development and westernization, relates an incident that illustrates this passage:

"Sometimes we enjoyed our noonday rest beside one of those Judean wells, to which three or four shepherds come down with their flocks. The flocks mixed with each other and we wondered how each shepherd would get his own again. But after the watering and the playing were over, the shepherds one by one went up different sides of the valley, and each called out his peculiar call; and the sheep of each drew out of the crowd to their own shepherd, and the flocks passed away as orderly as they came."[376]

The sheep knows its shepherd's voice.

I believe that one of the neglected, seldom-taught skills necessary to be a disciple, is to learn to discern Jesus' voice. We hear many voices – the pressures of our society's expectations, our family's

---

[369] "Thief" is *kleptēs* (from which we get our word, "kleptomaniac"), "thief" (BDAG 574).

[370] "Robber" (NIV, KJV), "bandit" (NRSV) is *lēstēs*, "robber, highwayman, bandit" (BDAG 594, 1).

[371] "Some other way" is *allachothen*, "from another place" (BDAG 46).

[372] "Listen" (NIV), "hear" (NRSV, KJV) is *akouō*, "hear," but here with the idea of "to give careful attention to, listen to, heed someone"(BDAG 38, 4).

[373] "Calls" is *phōneō*, "to produce a voiced sound/tone, frequently with reference to intensity of tone," here, "to call to oneself, summon" (BDAG 107, 3).

[374] "By name" (*kat' onoma*).

[375] "Watchman" (NIV), "gatekeeper" (NRSV, ESV), "porter" (KJV) is *thyrōros*, "doorkeeper, gatekeeper" (BDAG 462).

[376] George Adam Smith, *The Historical Geography of the Holy Land* (New York: A.C. Armstrong and Son, 1900), p. 312.

desires, and our own selfish desires. It is possible to hear Jesus' voice and distinguish it from the others, but we must make a practice of learning which is which. I don't know any way to learn this without making some mistakes in the process, so it is good to learn this with the help of a more mature Christian brother or sister.

Once we learn to discern Jesus' voice – the leading of the Spirit, same thing – then he can guide us, teach us, and use us much more effectively than before. Read the Book of Acts and look for instances where the Lord speaks to his servants – Peter, Paul, James, Philip. This exercise will demonstrate to you how very important it is to hear Jesus' voice.

> **Q1. (John 10:3-4) What does it mean that Jesus' sheep "know his voice"? How can you discern his voice from your own thoughts and the expectations of others?**
> **http://www.joyfulheart.com/forums/topic/1470-q1-the-shepherds-voice/**

I Am the Gate for the Sheep (10:6-9)

The analogy is confusing to some of Jesus' hearers. So he explains it a bit more, at the same time adding new elements and shifting the analogy some.

> "[6] Jesus used this figure of speech[377], but they did not understand what he was telling them. [7] Therefore Jesus said again, 'I tell you the truth, I am the gate for the sheep. [8] All who ever came before me were thieves and robbers, but the sheep did not listen to them. [9] I am the gate; whoever enters through me will be saved. He will come in and go out, and find pasture[378].'" (10:6-9)

Jesus shifts his analogy from the multiple-flock sheep pen with an assigned gatekeeper to one in which all the sheep in the pen belong to the same shepherd.

In the third of his "I am" declarations, Jesus says in verse 7b, "I am the gate/door for the sheep.[379] Perhaps he is comparing himself to a gate to protect the sheep, swinging open on hinges to let the sheep through. But there is another possibility, illustrated by another story reputedly told by George Adam Smith to commentator G. Campbell Morgan.

> "[Smith] was one day travelling with a guide and came across a shepherd and his sheep. The man showed him the fold into which the sheep were led at night. It consisted of four walls, with a way in. [Smith] said to him, 'That is where they go at night?' 'Yes,' said the shepherd, 'and when they are there, they are perfectly safe.' 'But there is no door,' said [Smith]. 'I am the door,' said the shepherd. '... When the light has gone and all the sheep are inside, I lie in that open space, and no sheep ever goes out but across my body, and no wolf comes in unless he crosses my body; I am the door.'" [380]

---

[377] *Paroimia*, "pithy saying" (BDAG 779, 2).

[378] "Pasture" is *nomē*, generally, "pasturing-place, grazing land, pasturage" (BDAG 675, 1).

[379] See Appendix 4. The "I Am" Passages in John's Gospel.

[380] Morris, *John*, p. 507, n. 30, citing G. Campbell Morgan, *The Gospel According to John* (London and Edinburgh, 1951). In the fuller quote, Smith explains that the shepherd "was not a Christian man, he was not speaking in the language of the New Testament. He was speaking from the Arab shepherd's standpoint."

However we understand Jesus' words, whether as a swinging gate or by his own body, Jesus teaches that he is both the protector (Savior) of the sheep, as well as their point of access to life beyond the fold – pasture, water, life, and ultimately, the Kingdom of God in the presence of the Father.

Abundant Life (10:10)

Now Jesus repeats and amplifies this idea further.

> "The thief comes only to steal and kill and destroy[381]; I have come that they may have life, and have it to the full." (10:10)

Jesus is the sheep herd's protection against thieves – the false Jewish religious leaders, whose only motive is to exploit the sheep for their own benefit. Jesus' motive is for the sheep to have a full life – protection from wolves and thieves, as well as pasture, water to drink, and the shepherd's experienced hands to rescue them and bind up their wounds. The words of the Twenty-Third Psalm come to mind:

> "[1] The LORD is my shepherd;
> I shall not want.
> [2] He makes me lie down in green pastures.
> He leads me beside still waters.
> [3] He restores my soul.
> He leads me in paths of righteousness for his name's sake.
> [4] Even though I walk through the valley of the shadow of death,
> I will fear no evil,
> for you are with me; your rod and your staff,
> they comfort me...." (Psalm 23:1-4, ESV)

Some see the Christian life as no fun, somehow constrained and diminished by the restrictions of Jesus' commands. But true disciples realize that only in Jesus' care can they truly flourish. They are healed within and protected without. They can live life to the full as it was intended to be lived.

In verse 10b, "to the full" (NIV), "abundantly" (NRSV, KJV) is the Greek word *perissos*, "exceeding the usual number or size ... pertaining to being extraordinary in amount, abundant, profuse," here, "going beyond what is necessary."[382]

> **Q2. (John 10:10) What would an "abundant life" look like if you were a sheep with a really good shepherd? In what ways is the Christian life to be an "abundant" life? How does this abundance relate to persecutions and hardships that come to us as Christians. Can the life of a unbeliever be more "abundant," free, and fun?**
>
> **http://www.joyfulheart.com/forums/topic/1471-q2-abundant-life/**

---

[381] "Destroy" is *apollymi*, "ruin, destroy," especially, "put to death" (BDAG 116, 1aα).
[382] *Perissos*, BDAG 805, 2a.

Shepherd Lays Down His Life for the Sheep (10:11-13)

Now Jesus changes the analogy once again. In verse 10a, the threat is thieves who would try to break into the fold. Now the figure turns to a shepherd with his sheep out on the open fields, where the flock is threatened by a wolf, whose strategy is to suddenly attack the flock, which will scatter, then go after the slowest sheep to react – usually the youngest or weakest of the flock.

> "[11] I am the good shepherd. The good shepherd lays down[383] his life for the sheep. [12] The hired hand is not the shepherd who owns the sheep. So when he sees the wolf coming, he abandons[384] the sheep and runs away[385]. Then the wolf attacks[386] the flock and scatters[387] it. [13] The man runs away because he is a hired hand and cares[388] nothing for the sheep." (10:11-13)

A hired hand isn't willing to risk his life fighting off a dangerous animal like a wolf. But the owner of the sheep doesn't run. Rather he stands up to the predator, ready to "lay down his life for the sheep." We think of David as a young shepherd, who explained to Saul, just before going out to defeat Goliath:

> "Your servant has been keeping his father's sheep. When a lion or a bear came and carried off a sheep from the flock, I went after it, struck it and rescued the sheep from its mouth. When it turned on me, I seized it by its hair, struck it and killed it." (1 Samuel 17:34-35)

Of course, when Jesus talks about laying down his life for the sheep, he is not talking merely about taking risks to protect the sheep from predators. This is a thinly veiled reference to his death on the cross, to bear the sins of the sheep, and deliver them from sin and its consequences. We see this especially in verses 17 and 18.

This theme of the shepherd laying down his life for the sheep is repeated five times in this discourse. It is therefore vital for us to grasp its importance.

> "The good shepherd **lays down** his life for the sheep." (10:11)
>
> "I **lay down** my life for the sheep." (10:15)
>
> "I **lay down** my life – only to take it up again. (10:17)
>
> "No one takes it from me, but I **lay it down** of my own accord." (10:18a)
>
> "I have authority to **lay it down** and authority to take it up again." (10:18b)

---

[383] "Lays down" (NIV, NRSV) is *tithēmi*, "put, place," here, in the sense, "lay down or give (up) one's life" (verses 11, 15, 17, and 18). It is a characteristic Johannine expression (also in 13:37-38; 15:13; and 1 John 3:16) (BDAG 1003, 1bβ). In verses 11 and 15 (but not verse 17 and 18), KJV text is "giveth," *didōmi*, "give," supported by p45 Aleph* D. The Editorial Committee prefers *tithēmi*, which they say is characteristically Johannine, while *didōmi* is found in the Synoptic Gospels (Matthew 20:28; Mark 10:45). They give *tithēmi* a {B}"some degree of doubt" rating (Metzger, *Textual Commentary*, p. 230).

[384] "Abandons" (NIV), "leaves" (NRSV, KJV) is *aphiēmi*, here, "to move away, with implication of causing a separation, leave, depart from ... abandon" (BDAG 156, 3a).

[385] "Runs away" (NIV, NRSV), "flees" (ESV, KJV) is *pheugō*, "to seek safety in flight, flee," (BDAG 1052, 1).

[386] "Attacks" (NIV), "snatches" (NRSV), "catcheth" (KJV) is *harpazō*, "snatch, seize," that is, take suddenly and vehemently, "to make off with someone's property by attacking or seizing, steal, carry off, drag away something" (BDAG 134, 1).

[387] "Scatters" is *skorpizō*, "to cause a group or gathering to go in various directions, scatter, disperse" (BDAG 931, 1).

[388] "Care" is *melomai*, "be an object of care, be a cause of concern" (BDAG 628).

Verses 17 and 18ab talk about laying down his life, but verses 11 and 15 give the *reason*: "for the sheep," indicating a sacrifice made on behalf of another.[389]

I Am the Good Shepherd (10:11, 14)

Verses 11 and 14, "I am the Good Shepherd," have the fourth of John's seven "I am" declarations.[390] The "Good Shepherd" is prepared to lay down his life for his sheep. The Greek word for "good" is *kalos*, which may also carry the idea of "beautiful" – the "Beautiful Shepherd" (though that is probably an over-translation).[391] It also carries the ideas of the "Noble Shepherd"[392] – one who stands up for his sheep and does not run away when his life is threatened.

Mutual Knowledge (10:14-15)

"[14] I am the good shepherd; I know[393] my sheep and my sheep know me – [15] just as the Father knows me and I know the Father – and I lay down my life for the sheep." (10:14-15)

Jesus is referring to the mutual, intimate knowledge of the shepherd for the sheep, the shepherd who can call each of them by his or her special name (verse 3). He knows their peculiarities and weaknesses, and accommodates for these as he shepherds them. And in turn, they trust their shepherd because he always looks out for them, rescues them when they get lost or caught in something. He brings them to the best places to graze and water. They can trust him, so when he speaks they listen and follow.

Verse 15a suggests that this intimate knowledge and love between the shepherd and his sheep is a picture of the intimate knowledge, love, and trust between the Son and the Father.

My dear friend, how intimate is your knowledge of your Shepherd? How much do you trust him to lead you better than you can lead yourself? How much do you love him? How much do you listen for his voice, or do you let it be drowned out by the noise of the world? He longs for you to know him and love him as he knows you – and as the Father and Son love each other!

Q3. (John 10:11-15) How does a "good shepherd" differ from what a hired shepherd would do in time of danger? In what way did Jesus the Good Shepherd "lay down his life for the sheep"? http://www.joyfulheart.com/forums/topic/1472-q3-laying-down-his-life/

---

[389] The preposition *hyper* is used with the genitive case: "a marker indicating that an activity or event is in some entity's interest, for, in behalf of, for the sake of someone/something." *Hyper*, BDAG 1030, 1aε).

[390] See Appendix 4. The "I Am" Passages in John's Gospel.

[391] Morris, *John*, p. 509, n. 34, citing Rieu.

[392] Beasley-Murray, *John*, p. 170.

[393] "Know" four times in verses 14 and 15 is the generic word *ginōskō*, "to know," here of persons, "know someone" (BDAG 200, 6aβ).

One Flock and One Shepherd (10:16)

> "I have other sheep that are not of this sheep pen. I must bring[394] them also. They too will listen to my voice, and there shall be one flock and one shepherd." (10:16)

Who are the "other sheep that are not of this sheep pen"? Clearly, these are sheep that are not found in Judaism, but Gentiles who will come to faith in the future. As the Lord told Paul in Corinth about future converts: "I have many people in this city" (Acts 18:10). Verse 16b is a plea for unity between Jewish and Gentile believers. We see the same things in Paul's letter to the Ephesian church:

> "For he himself is our peace, who has made the two one and has destroyed the barrier, the dividing wall of hostility ... to create in himself one new man out of the two, thus making peace" (Ephesians 2:14-15).

Authority to Die, Authority to Rise (10:17-18)

> "17 The reason[395] my Father loves me is that I lay down my life – only to take it up again.[396] 18 No one takes[397] it from me, but I lay it down of my own accord. I have authority to lay it down and authority to take it up again. This command I received from my Father." (10:17-18)

Verse 17 seems strange at first glance, seeming like the Son needed to do something to earn the Father's love. But elsewhere in John we see that that the love between the Father and Son has existed before all time – long before men were created and needed redemption (17:24). The unity of purpose and trust, the love that exists between the Father and Son, makes itself visible in obedience – the Son's obedience to carry out the plan of salvation by going to the cross (10:17-18) and our abiding in the Son (15:9-10).

Verse 18 is fascinating. Jesus doesn't act on his own, but based on the *authority* granted by God. "Authority" (NIV, ESV), "power" (NRSV, KJV), used twice in verse 18, is *exousia*, "a state of control over something, freedom of choice, right", that is, the "right" to act, decide, or dispose of one's property as one wishes.[398] So the Son acts freely, based on his own wishes, which conform exactly to his Father's command.[399] He doesn't die martyr's death – one forced upon him by his enemies (10:18a) – but he dies as a voluntary sacrifice for our sins, according to the plan of salvation of God the Father, fully agreed to by the Son.

Also observe that not only the crucifixion was part of the plan of salvation, but also the resurrection. There is a unity between the two:

> "I have authority to lay it down and authority to take it up again." (10:18b)

---

[394] "Bring" is *agō*, "lead, bring, lead off, lead away" (BDAG 16, 1a).

[395] "For this reason" (NRSV, ESV, NIV), "therefore" (KJV) is *dia touto oti*. The preposition *dia* with the accusative case is "through," here, "therefore, for this reason, (namely) that" (BDAG 225, B2b).

[396] "Take it up" in verses 17 and 18 is *lambanō*, "take, receive," here, "to take into one's possession, take, acquire something" (BDAG 583, 3).

[397] "Takes" in 18a is *airō*, "to take away, remove, or seize control without suggestion of lifting up, take away, remove" (BDAG 28, 3).

[398] *Exousia*, BDAG 352, 1.

[399] "Command/ment" is *entolē*, "mandate, ordinance, command," here perhaps, "an order authorizing a specific action, writ, warrant," (BDAG 340, 1).

Divided Response (10:19-21)

Jesus' words of intimacy with the Father, of laying down his life and taking it up again, provoked a response among the Jewish leaders who heard them. And, interestingly enough, the response varied from one person to another.

> "[19] At these words the Jews were again divided. [20] Many of them said, 'He is demon-possessed and raving mad. Why listen to him?' [21] But others said, 'These are not the sayings of a man possessed by a demon. Can a demon open the eyes of the blind?'" (10:19-21)

Some concluded he was mad, but others weren't so sure. They had seen his miracles and agreed with the man born blind that God didn't listen to sinners (9:31-33) and Nicodemus, who said, "No one can do these signs that you do unless God is with him" (3:2).

The Feast of Dedication (10:22)

In verse 22, John indicates that an interval of time has passed since Jesus' discourse on the Good Shepherd.

> "[22] Then came the Feast of Dedication at Jerusalem. It was winter, [23] and Jesus was in the temple area walking in Solomon's Colonnade[400]." (10:22-23)

Jesus is back in Jerusalem, this time for the Feast of Dedication, known also as the Festival of Lights and Hanukkah (from ḥānak, "to dedicate"). The temple had been desecrated by the Greeks under Antiochus Epiphanes (168 BC), who had ordered an altar to Zeus to be erected in the temple and pigs sacrificed on it. He halted the normal daily sacrifices offered by the Jews for a period of three and a half years. Hanukkah is an eight-day feast was begun in 165 BC by Judas Maccabee and his brothers to celebrate the rededication of the temple and restoration of sacrifices following the desecration (1 Maccabees 4:36-59).

Believe Me for the Miracles (10:24-26)

The context again is a controversy with the Jewish leaders that seems to occur each time he travels to Jerusalem (7:1; 10:40). They are badgering him to declare himself openly as the Messiah – so they can find grounds to accuse him.

> "[24] The Jews gathered around him, saying, 'How long will you keep us in suspense? If you are the Christ, tell us plainly.' [25] Jesus answered, 'I did tell you, but you do not believe. The miracles[401] I do in my Father's name speak for me, [26] but you do not believe because you are not my sheep.'" (10:24-26)

Jesus hasn't declared publically that he is the Christ, the Messiah – though he acknowledged it to the Samaritan woman (4:26) and (perhaps[402]) to the man born blind (9:35-37). But anyone who observed him closely saw miracles done in the Father's name, as well as his messianic references in the

---

[400] Solomon's Colonnade was a covered porch support by columns on the east side of the temple. It is only mentioned here and in Acts 3:11; 5:12, though it is likely that Jesus often taught here when in the temple precincts.

[401] "Miracles" (NIV), "works" (NRSV, KJV) is *ergon*, "deed, accomplishment," speaking of miracles (BDAG 390, 1cα). Used in verses 25, 31, 37, 38.

[402] A better reading of 9:35 is "Son of Man" rather than "Son of God." See my notes on that verse above.

title Son of Man, and his words, such as, "before Abraham was, I am" (8:58). For those who had eyes of faith, such as Jesus' disciples, it was clear. But to unbelieving eyes, nothing he said would convince them of what was plain before them.

> "[25b] The miracles I do in my Father's name speak for me, [26] but you do not believe because you are not my sheep." (10:25b-26)

Some realized that crazy people don't open the eyes of the blind, but many were too spiritually blind to even realize that (10:21).

In verse 25, I would have expected Jesus to say:

- "You are not my sheep because you do not believe." – belief is the reason they're not sheep. But he said rather:
- "You do not believe because you are not my sheep" – not being sheep is the cause of the unbelief.

This and other passages in John suggest that predestination is at work (6:44; 12:37-39). But at the same times as we see predestination, it's clear that those who have become hardened in their unbelief are held fully responsible for their unbelief – they will die in their sin (8:24). Somehow, in a way that we can't understand fully, the grace and sovereignty of God work along with the response of a disciple's faith, as weak as it might be, to bring us to salvation (Ephesians 2:8-9).

In John, we confront the blind unbelief of the Pharisees and Jewish leaders, who see miracles but still want to kill Jesus. In the Synoptic Gospels we see this same truth stated in slightly different ways. Peter's faith that Jesus was "the Christ, the Son of the Living God" wasn't his own deduction, but a gracious revelation from God himself.

> "Blessed are you, Simon son of Jonah, for this was not revealed to you by man, but by my Father in heaven." (Matthew 16:17)

Faith itself is a gift; so is the ability to repent (Ephesians 2:8-9; 2 Timothy 2:25). After telling the Parable of the Sower (Matthew 13:1-11), Jesus explains to his disciples why he speaks in parables.

> "The knowledge of the secrets of the kingdom of heaven has been given to you, but not to them. [12] Whoever has will be given more, and he will have an abundance. Whoever does not have, even what he has will be taken from him. [13] This is why I speak to them in parables:
> Though seeing, they do not see;
> though hearing, they do not hear or understand.
> [14] In them is fulfilled the prophecy of Isaiah:
> 'You will be ever hearing but never understanding;
> you will be ever seeing but never perceiving.
> [15] For this people's heart has become calloused;
> they hardly hear with their ears,
> and they have closed their eyes.
> Otherwise they might see with their eyes,
> hear with their ears,
> understand with their hearts and turn,
> and I would heal them.'"
> (Matthew 13:11-15, quoting Isaiah 6:9-10)

No One Can Snatch My Sheep (10:27-30)

Now Jesus summarizes the special blessings that accrue to being part of Jesus' flock, one of his followers.

> "27 My sheep listen to my voice; I know them, and they follow me. 28 I give them eternal life, and they shall never perish; no one can snatch them out of my hand. 29 My Father, who has given them to me, is greater than all; no one can snatch them out of my Father's hand. 30 I and the Father are one." (10:27-30)

Look at these blessings:

1. Listening to the Shepherd's voice – assurance, direction, and learning. I can hear him speaking to me today, if I'll take time to listen and then obey.
2. Being known by the Shepherd – ultimate significance; the Lord of creation knows and loves me!
3. Following the Shepherd – direction and guidance for my life.
4. The promise of eternal life – stated positively (life forever) and negatively (never perishing).
5. Protection by the Shepherd from this eternal life being snatched away by a predator or thief.

Verse 28 is a wonderful promise that recalls the image of a strong and watchful Shepherd who absolutely will not allow either a predator or thief to snatch any of his sheep! In Greek "no one can snatch...." uses an emphatic double negative (*ou mē*) with the phrase "unto the age" to say "never" in the strongest possible way,[403] emphasizing the absolute impossibility of the enemy being able to snatch us. The sheep can feel secure (3:16; 6:39; 17:12; 18:9).

"Snatch" (NIV, NRSV, ESV), "pluck" (KJV) is *harpazō*, which we saw in 10:12 – "snatch, seize," that is, take suddenly and vehemently, or take away in the sense of "to make off with someone's property by attacking or seizing, steal, carry off, drag away," or similarly, "to grab or seize suddenly so as to remove or gain control, snatch/take away forcefully."[404] As A.T. Robertson puts it, "No wolf, no thief, no bandit, no hireling, no demon, not even the devil can pluck the sheep out of my hand."[405]

This is the same kind of assurance expressed in Psalm 23:4c – "Your rod and your staff, they comfort me."

Then, to emphasize the certainty of his sheep's protection, Jesus mentions his intimate partnership with the Father in this task of protection:

> "29 My Father, who has given them to me, is greater than all; no one can snatch them out of my Father's hand. 30 I and the Father are one." (10:29-30)

When we discuss 15:1-8 (Lesson 26) and 17:11-15 (Lesson 29), we'll examine further the doctrine of the Perseverance of the Saints and the importance of abiding in the vine. Here, of course, Jesus' promises are to those who are his sheep – who listen to his voice and follow him (10:27).

---

[403] This strong phrase is used in 4:14; 8:51-52; 10:28; 11:26; 13:8. "In Johannine usage the term is used formulaically without emphasis on eternity" (*Aiōn*, BDAG 32, 1b).

[404] *Harpazō*, BDAG 134, 2a.

[405] Robertson, *Word Pictures.*

Q4. (John 10:27-30) In the world of shepherds, who would try to "snatch" a sheep? Who would try to "snatch" a Christian if he could? What promise of absolute security are we given? How does that assure you?
http://www.joyfulheart.com/forums/topic/1473-q4-protecting-the-sheep/

Claiming to Be God (10:30-33)

It's hard to imagine a stronger self-declaration of Jesus' divinity.

"I and the Father are one." (10:30)

"One" is *heis*, the Greek number "one." Then it can carry the meaning, "a single person or thing, with focus on quantitative aspect, one."[406] There are two close parallels in John found in Jesus' high-priestly prayer:

"Holy Father, protect them by the power of your name ... so that they may be one as we are one." (17:11)

"... that all of them may be one, Father, just as you are in me and I am in you. May they also be in us so that the world may believe that you have sent me." (17:21)

Elsewhere in John we see very strong assertions of Jesus' divinity, his unity with the Father.

"In the beginning was the Word, and the Word was with God, and the Word was God. He was with God in the beginning." (1:1-2)

"... That all may honor the Son just as they honor the Father. He who does not honor the Son does not honor the Father, who sent him." (5:23)

"Anyone who has seen me has seen the Father. How can you say, 'Show us the Father'? ... It is the Father, living in me, who is doing his work." (14:9-10)

"My Father will love him, and we will come to him and make our home with him." (14:23)

"All that belongs to the Father is mine." (16:15a; cf. 17:10)

Jewish Reaction to Supposed Blasphemy (10:31-33)

The reaction of the Jewish leaders is swift.

"[31] Again the Jews picked up stones to stone him, [32] but Jesus said to them, 'I have shown you many great miracles from the Father. For which of these do you stone me?'
[33] 'We are not stoning you for any of these,' replied the Jews, 'but for blasphemy, because you, a mere man, claim to be God.'" (10:31-33)

They correctly interpret Jesus' words as a claim to be God. Jesus reminds them of his miracles that authenticate his relationship with the Father. But they can't see beyond what they call blasphemy.[407]

---

[406] *Heis*, BDAG 291, 1b.

I Am God's Son (10:34-36)

Now Jesus quotes Psalm 82:6 to them, to demonstrate that the term "gods" could be applied to humans without requiring it to be blasphemy.

"³⁴ Jesus answered them, 'Is it not written in your Law, "I have said you are gods"? ³⁵ If he called them "gods," to whom the word of God came – and the Scripture cannot be broken – ³⁶ what about the one whom the Father set apart as his very own and sent into the world? Why then do you accuse me of blasphemy because I said, "I am God's Son"?'" (10:34-36)

Believe the Miracles (10:37-39)

As inadequate as faith in miracles might be, it is better than no faith at all. So Jesus encourages the Jewish leaders to consider what his miracles say about him.

³⁷ Do not believe me unless I do what my Father does. ³⁸ But if I do it, even though you do not believe me, believe the miracles⁴⁰⁸, that you may know and understand that the Father is in me, and I in the Father." (10:37-38)

The miracles attest to who Jesus is. And if one would ponder them, they might understand that Jesus can do these works of God because he and the Father are intertwined.

But Jesus' enemies would hear none of it.

"Again they tried to seize him, but he escaped their grasp." (10:39)

Here, it sounds like someone may have grabbed him – at least got a hand on him, but couldn't hold on.⁴⁰⁹ Jesus was able to "escape," to walk away.⁴¹⁰ This is only one of several times in John's Gospel where Jesus' enemies try to arrest or stone Jesus, but are not able to (7:30, 32, 44-46; 8:59). We see this same phenomenon in the Synoptic Gospels when people try to stone him in Nazareth (Luke 4:29-30).

Jesus Ministers Across the Jordan (10:40-42)

"⁴⁰ Then Jesus went back across the Jordan to the place where John had been baptizing in the early days. Here he stayed ⁴¹ and many people came to him. They said, 'Though John never performed a miraculous sign, all that John said about this man was true.' ⁴² And in that place many believed in Jesus." (10:40-42)

Jerusalem is a dangerous place for Jesus, so again he retreats to another area to minister (4:3; 7:1; 11:54). There is a time to stand your ground in a dangerous place – and there is a time to make a judicious retreat, since this wasn't Jesus' time to die.

This time Jesus goes across the Jordan River to John the Baptist's old baptizing place. He stays there, ministering there for an extended period of time. The result is that many come to faith in Jesus

---

⁴⁰⁷ *Blasphēmia*, "speech that denigrates or defames, reviling, denigration, disrespect, slander" (BDAG 178, bγ). Here Jesus is accused of words that show disrespect for God by elevating a human to his unapproachable level.

⁴⁰⁸ "Miracles" (NIV), "works" (NRSV, ESV, KJV) in verses 25, 31, and 38 is *ergon*, "deed, accomplishment," referring here to miracles (BDAG 390, 1cα).

⁴⁰⁹ "Escaped their grasp" (NIV) is more literally, "escaped from their hands" (NRSV, ESV, KJV).

⁴¹⁰ "Escaped" is *exerchomai*, "go out from," here, "to get away from or out of a difficult situation" (BDAG 347, 5).

there along the Jordan, as his hearers remember John the Baptist's testimony about him (1:15, 29-34; 3:22-36).

Lessons for Disciples

This passage is rich in lessons for Jesus' disciples.

1. Jesus' sheep know his voice, they know when he speaks to them. We disciples must learn the skill of discerning Jesus' voice from the clutter of voices in our head and in our world (10:3-4).

2. Jesus is the Gate, he provides both protection and freedom of access to find our needs met (10:9).

3. Jesus promises life – eternal life, abundant overflowing life – to his disciples. Despite the hardships of following Jesus, we get to live life to the fullest (10:10).

4. Jesus is the Good Shepherd who is willing to do anything for his sheep. Ultimately, Jesus lays down his life for his sheep, that is, he dies for our sins and is raised to life again (10:14-15).

5. Jesus' "flock" is to consist of both Jews and Gentiles, who will be one with each other (10:16).

6. Jesus and the Father both absolutely protect us from Satan trying to snatch and steal us away from him. We can rest in his strong care over us (10:27-30).

Prayer

Thank you, Lord, that you are a Good Shepherd watching over us, protecting us, meeting our needs, talking to us, and loving us. Thank you for laying down your life for us in the ultimate act of sacrifice. Thank you. In the wonderful and holy name of Jesus we pray. Amen.

Key Verses

"The watchman opens the gate for him, and the sheep listen to his voice. He calls his own sheep by name and leads them out. When he has brought out all his own, he goes on ahead of them, and his sheep follow him because they know his voice." (John 10:3-4, NIV)

"I am the gate; whoever enters through me will be saved. He will come in and go out, and find pasture." (John 10:9, NIV)

"The thief comes only to steal and kill and destroy; I have come that they may have life, and have it to the full." (John 10:10, NIV)

"I am the good shepherd. The good shepherd lays down his life for the sheep." (John 10:11, NIV)

"I am the good shepherd; I know my sheep and my sheep know me – just as the Father knows me and I know the Father – and I lay down my life for the sheep." (John 10:14-15, NIV)

"I have other sheep that are not of this sheep pen. I must bring them also. They too will listen to my voice, and there shall be one flock and one shepherd." (John 10:16, NIV)

"My sheep listen to my voice; I know them, and they follow me. I give them eternal life, and they shall never perish; no one can snatch them out of my hand. My Father, who has given them to me, is greater than all; no one can snatch them out of my Father's hand. I and the Father are one." (John 10:27-30, NIV)

20. I Am the Resurrection and the Life (11:1-54)

The early portion of John's Gospel can be construed as a "Book of Signs" pointing to and revealing that Jesus is indeed the Son of God. The account of the raising of Lazarus is the seventh and final sign that John tells us about.[411]

Moreover, this sign serves as a kind of transition. John portrays it as both the greatest of Jesus' signs, and the one that propels him to his death in Jerusalem, since it serves to harden the resolve of the Jewish religious leaders that Jesus must be killed. One way to analyze John's Gospel demonstrates the pivotal nature of the sign of the raising of Lazarus in John 11.

"The Raising of Lazarus" (6th century), mosaic, Basilica of Sant' Apollinare Nuovo, Ravenna.

1. Prologue (1:1-18)
2. Book of Signs, demonstrating that Jesus is the Son of God (1:19-12:50)
3. Book of Glory, explaining how Jesus is glorified with the Father in his death and resurrection (13:1-20:31)412
4. Epilogue (22:1-25).413

Lazarus Is Sick (11:1-3)

In the Synoptic Gospels we read about Mary and Martha (Luke 10:38-42). Jesus has stayed in their home. Martha resents having to do all the work of entertaining guests while Mary sits at Jesus' feet and listens to his teaching. Now we learn more about these sisters. They live in the village of Bethany, just two miles outside of Jerusalem, either with or close by their brother, who is a special friend of Jesus and his disciples. He is described in verse 3 as "the one you love," using the verb *phileō*, "to have a special interest in someone or something, frequently with focus on close association, have affection for, like, consider someone a friend."[414]

> "¹ Now a man named Lazarus was sick. He was from Bethany, the village of Mary and her sister Martha. ² This Mary, whose brother Lazarus now lay sick, was the same one who poured perfume on the Lord and wiped his feet with her hair. ³ So the sisters sent word to Jesus, 'Lord, the one you love is sick.'" (11:1-3)

---

411 See Appendix 5. "Signs" in John's Gospel.
412 See more in Appendix 6. "Glory" and "Glorify" in John's Gospel.
413 See Brown, *John*, 1:cxxxviii-cxliv.
414 *Phileō*, BDAG 1056, 1a. The word in 12:11 is *philos*, "friend" (BDAG 1059, 2aα).

Lazarus is from the Hebrew *la'zār*, a rabbinic abbreviation of *'el'āzār*, (Eleazar), meaning, "God has helped." Lazarus is sick.[415] We don't know what was wrong with him, but his sisters are worried enough to send a messenger to Jesus, who is ministering east of the Jordan River – about a day's journey away – to let him know that his friend Lazarus is deathly ill.

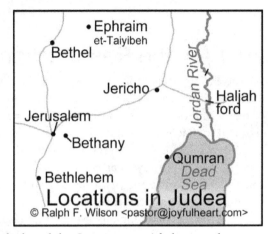

Jesus Delays Coming (11:4-6)

But Jesus doesn't come immediately.

> "[4] When he heard this, Jesus said, 'This sickness will not end in death. No, it is for God's glory so that God's Son may be glorified through it.' [5] Jesus loved Martha and her sister and Lazarus. [6] Yet when he heard that Lazarus was sick, he stayed where he was two more days." (11:4-6)

Jesus hears from the messenger, and then from his Father, and announces:

> "This sickness will not end in death.[416] No, it is for God's glory so that God's Son may be glorified[417] through it." (11:4)

Jesus reveals that the purpose of this sickness will be to glorify God.[418] Similarly, the man born blind was so that "the work of God might be displayed in his life" (9:3). Is all sickness for this purpose? No. The Scriptures show that some sickness is a result of sin (5:14; 1 Corinthians 11:28-30), some for other purposes God has for us (cf. 2 Corinthians 12:7).

Nevertheless, Jesus doesn't immediately rush to Lazarus's bedside, in spite of the fact that John assures us that Jesus loves Lazarus and his family (11:5). Jesus is listening to the Father regarding the timing of his trip. It becomes apparent, when Jesus finally arrives in Bethany, that Lazarus would have already died even if Jesus had left the moment he heard.

The Dangers of Judea (11:7-16)

Finally, after two additional days on the east side of Jordan, Jesus announces his intention to return to Judea. Bethany, the home of Lazarus, is a mere two miles from the center of Judaism in Jerusalem, the center of the enemy camp. So Jesus' statement causes protests from his disciples.

> "[7] Then he said to his disciples, 'Let us go back to Judea.'
>
> [8] 'But Rabbi,' they said, 'a short while ago the Jews tried to stone you, and yet you are going back

---

[415] *Astheneō*, "be weak," here, "to suffer a debilitating illness, be sick" (BDAG 142, 1).

[416] The phrase "sickness ... unto death" (KJV), "end in death" (NIV), "lead to death" (NRSV, ESV) uses the preposition *pros*, of goal, "(aiming) at or (striving) toward," here, of the result that follows a set of circumstances (BDAG 874, 3cγ). The phrase also occurs in 1 John 5:16: "If anyone sees his brother commit a sin that does not lead to death, he should pray and God will give him life..." (1 John 5:16). In 1 John, the sin that leads to death seems to be the brazen and steadfast denial by John's opponents that Jesus Christ is the Son of God.

[417] See more in Appendix 6. "Glory" and "Glorify" in John's Gospel.

[418] See more in Appendix 6. "Glory" and "Glorify" in John's Gospel.

there?'

⁹ Jesus answered, 'Are there not twelve hours of daylight? A man who walks by day will not stumble, for he sees by this world's light. ¹⁰ It is when he walks by night that he stumbles, for he has no light.'" (11:7-10)

Jesus' response about twelve hours of daylight is curious. Twelve hours is another way of saying "a full day." "This world's light" is the sun. You have to get your work done when there's light to see. In other words, we must do what we have to do when we have opportunity, as Jesus also seems to say in 9:4. There is probably a spiritual allusion here too, but we shouldn't make too much out of it.

Now he explains that Lazarus is dead, using the common Jewish euphemism for death as sleep. But the disciples are confused, so Jesus spells it out for them.

"¹¹ After he had said this, he went on to tell them, 'Our friend Lazarus has fallen asleep; but I am going there to wake him up.' ¹² His disciples replied, 'Lord, if he sleeps, he will get better.' ¹³ Jesus had been speaking of his death, but his disciples thought he meant natural sleep. ¹⁴ So then he told them plainly, 'Lazarus is dead, ¹⁵ and for your sake I am glad I was not there, so that you may believe. But let us go to him.'" (11:11-15)

Thomas, called "the Twin," responds with a kind of fatalistic pessimism.

"Then Thomas (called Didymus) said to the rest of the disciples, 'Let us also go, that we may die with him.'" (11:16)

Thomas is usually remembered as "doubting Thomas" (20:25). But this statement shows both loyalty and courage. Later in his life, church tradition tells us that Thomas went to Iraq and India to preach the gospel, landed in Kerala, southwest India, in 52 AD, founded what is known today as the Mar Thoma church, and was martyred in Mylapore, Madras, India. Thomas may have had a rocky start, but he finished well!

Q1. (John 11:16) What does verse 16 teach us about Thomas's character? About his faith?
http://www.joyfulheart.com/forums/topic/1474-q1-faith-of-thomas/

Jesus Arrives in Bethany (11:17-19)

Jesus and his disciples probably take nearly a day's journey trudging up the Jerusalem-Jericho road, rising 3,300 feet from the Jordan Valley to Bethany, just outside of Jerusalem.

"¹⁷ On his arrival, Jesus found that Lazarus had already been in the tomb for four days. ¹⁸ Bethany was less than two miles from Jerusalem, ¹⁹ and many Jews had come to Martha and Mary to comfort[419] them in the loss of their brother." (11:17-19)

Jewish custom was to bury the body immediately, the same day as the death, if possible.[420] So, as we trace back the time – one day for the messenger to get to Jesus, two extra days before leaving, and one

---

[419] "Comfort" in verses 19 and 31 is *paramytheomai*, "console, cheer up." In connection with death and tragic events it carries the idea, "console, comfort" (BDAG 769), from *para-*, "near, beside" + a derivative of *mythos*, "to share a speech, word, saying," then, "to relate a story."

day's travel to get to Bethany – Lazarus was probably dead by the time the messenger arrived to tell the news of his illness to Jesus.

Lazarus's burial for four days had implications as well. Edersheim notes,

> "It was the common Jewish idea that corruption commenced on the fourth day, that the drop of gall, which had fallen from the sword of the Angel and caused death, was then working its effect, and that, as the face changed, the soul took its final leave from the resting-place of the body."[421]

If Jesus had raised Lazarus earlier than four days, it would not be thought to have been as great a miracle as when corruption had begun.

John tells us that "many Jews"[422] had come to comfort Mary and Martha. To visit and sit with the bereaved was considered an extremely important obligation in Judaism.

The fact that many Jews were visiting probably indicates that Lazarus is a prominent person with many friends in Jerusalem. He seems to be a person of some wealth. This explains Mary and Martha's ability to entertain Jesus and his disciples on several occasions, as well as Mary's access to the expensive perfume with which she anointed Jesus (12:3). In addition, his burial in a cave rather than the common burial ground is another sign of means.

The presence of these "many Jews" guarantee that the resurrection to follow will have many prominent witnesses – and that news of it will spread like wildfire in nearby Jerusalem.

Jesus Meets with Martha (11:20-22)

Word travels fast in small towns, too. The house is full of mourners, so Martha comes out to meet Jesus at the edge of town (11:30), a place with more privacy.

> "20 When Martha heard that Jesus was coming, she went out to meet him, but Mary stayed at home. 21 'Lord,' Martha said to Jesus, 'if you had been here, my brother would not have died. 22 But I know that even now God will give you whatever you ask.'" (11:20-22)

Martha voices what everyone must be saying – "If Jesus had been here, he wouldn't have died!" This sentiment is repeated by Mary (11:32) and the crowds (11:37). I don't think Martha or Mary mean it as a criticism, just an observation. They don't blame Jesus, they are only playing the "if only" game that is common when tragedies come. It is an ironic faith statement about Jesus' power to heal. And Martha is undeterred in her faith, despite her brother's death. She has not lost confidence in Jesus.

> "I know that even now God will give you whatever you ask." (11:22)

Her faith is strong, but Martha isn't imagining that Jesus will raise Lazarus from the dead.

I Am the Resurrection and the Life (11:23-27)

Now Jesus mentions resurrection to her.

> "23 Jesus said to her, 'Your brother will rise again.'
> 24 Martha answered, 'I know he will rise again in the resurrection at the last day.'" (11:23-24)

---

[420] Edersheim, *Life and Times*, 4:983, cites Moed K. 28 *a*; comp Sanh. 46 *b*.

[421] Edersheim, *Life and Times*, 4:993, citing Abh. Z. 20 *b*; Ber. R. 100; Vayyik. R. 18.

[422] The term "the Jews" usually refers to Jesus' enemies, but here it probably has its natural meaning, "Judeans," people from Judea. See Appendix 2. "The Jews" in John's Gospel.

Jesus speaks to her about resurrection, with the veiled hint that Lazarus' resurrection may be immediate. But Martha misses it, and sees it as a word of encouragement much like that which friends had spoken to her again and again over the four days since Lazarus' death.

Many Jews in Jesus' day believed in the resurrection of the dead on the Last Day. The Pharisees dogmatically affirmed resurrection in opposition to the Sadducees, who emphatically denied that there was a resurrection to come. Jesus publicly took the Pharisees' position on the fact of the resurrection (Matthew 22:23-34; Luke 14:14). Earlier he had declared:

> "A time is coming when all who are in their graves will hear his voice and come out – those who have done good will rise to live, and those who have done evil will rise to be condemned." (5:28-29)

Indeed, Jesus affirmed that he personally would raise believers up on the Last Day (6:39-40). This expectation of the resurrection on the Last Day is the understanding of the early church as well (Acts 24:15; 1 Corinthians 15; 1 Thessalonians 4:13-18; etc.).

But now, in his fifth of seven "I Am" declarations,[423] Jesus reveals his own central role in resurrection:

> "25 Jesus said to her, 'I am the resurrection and the life. He who believes in me will live, even though he dies; 26 and whoever lives and believes in me will never die." (11:25-26a)

What is Jesus claiming here?

Jesus himself is the resurrection and the life. The Father has bestowed on him the power to have life in himself, and to bestow resurrection life on whomever he will. We saw this previously in his discourse on the divine Son (5:19-47).

> "For just as the Father raises the dead and gives them life, even so the Son gives life to whom he is pleased to give it.... For as the Father has life in himself, so he has granted the Son to have life in himself." (5:21, 26)

But Jesus doesn't just say that he *gives* resurrection and life! He is so closely associated with resurrection and life that he says he *is* the resurrection and life in his own person. The power that will grant resurrection and life on the Last Day is resident within Jesus' person now! (Theologians call this "realized eschatology.") When we believe in Jesus, we are united with him; we are "in him." And so his resurrection power and life power become ours as well. The results are eternal, spelled out in 11:25b-26a.

Resurrection (11:25b)

> "He who believes in me will live, even though he dies." (11:25b)

People who believe in him will live – even though they die (like Lazarus has done). Jesus will raise them from death on the Last Day.

Life (11:26a)

> "... and whoever lives and believes in me will never die." (11:26a)

---

[423] See Appendix 4. The "I Am" Passages in John's Gospel.

People who are alive (spiritually) and believe in him will never die (spiritually) – that is, death will not introduce a break into their relationship with God and their experience of eternal life.

In a few moments, Jesus will demonstrate that he is indeed the Resurrection and the Life as he calls Lazarus from the dead.

> **Q2. (John 11:25-26) In what sense does Jesus embody resurrection? In what sense does he embody life? What is the great promise that he offers us in verses 25 and 26?**
> **http://www.joyfulheart.com/forums/topic/1475-q2-resurrection-and-life/**

Martha's Great Confession (11:26b-27)

Jesus prompts Martha to respond to what he has just said. Her response shows that she may not understand it completely, but she fully believes that Jesus is the Messiah!

"[26b] 'Do you believe this?'
[27] 'Yes, Lord,' she told him, 'I believe that you are the Christ, the Son of God, who was to come into the world.'" (11:26b-27)

Sometimes, based on the account of Martha's busyness in Luke 10:38-42, Martha is seen as less "spiritual" than her sister. But her great confession – given immediately after her brother's death – shows that she is a woman of remarkable faith.

Her confession is similar to the confessions of others that demonstrate what John seeks to show us, "that you may believe that Jesus is the Christ, the Son of God, and that by believing you may have life in his name" (20:31).

John the Baptist: "I have seen and I testify that this is the Son of God." (1:34)

Nathanael: "Rabbi, you are the Son of God; you are the King of Israel." (1:49)

Samaritans: "This man really is the Savior of the world." (4:42)

Peter: "We believe and know that you are the Holy One of God." (6:69)

Thomas: "My Lord and my God!" (20:28)

Martha's confession ranks beside Peter's great confession: "You are the Christ, the Son of the living God" (Matthew 16:16).

It's interesting to see that in John's Gospel, Mary and Martha seem to have a similar portrait as they do in Luke.[424]

	Luke 10:38-42	John 11:20-32
Martha	Activist and busybody.	Rushes to meet Jesus
Mary	Sits at the Lord's feet listening.	Sits quietly at home, then comes and falls at his feet.

---

[424] Brown, *John* 1:433.

Q3. (John 11:27) Based on Luke 10:38-42, what is Martha's reputation compared to that of her sister Mary? What is so amazing about Martha's confession? What does this tell us about her? Which of the sisters seems more spiritual on this day – Martha or Mary?
http://www.joyfulheart.com/forums/topic/1476-q3-marthas-confession/

Mary Goes to Meet with Jesus (11:28-31)

After Martha returns to the house, she speaks to her sister privately.[425]

> [28] And after she had said this, she went back and called her sister Mary aside. 'The Teacher[426] is here,' she said, 'and is asking for you.'
>
> [29] When Mary heard this, she got up quickly and went to him. [30] Now Jesus had not yet entered the village, but was still at the place where Martha had met him. [31] When the Jews who had been with Mary in the house, comforting her, noticed how quickly she got up and went out, they followed her, supposing she was going to the tomb to mourn (*klaiō*) there." (11:28-31)

Now Mary comes – along with the crowd of mourners that has been at the house. They come along to comfort her, thinking that she is going to mourn at the tomb. While Jesus' words to Martha have been private, his words to Mary are heard by all.

Jesus' Anger (11:32-37)

Mary comes to Jesus weeping (11:33), along with her friends. There are strong emotions in Jesus also, but it is difficult to know how to interpret them.

> "[32] When Mary reached the place where Jesus was and saw him, she fell at his feet and said, 'Lord, if you had been here, my brother would not have died.'
>
> [33] When Jesus saw her weeping (*klaiō*), and the Jews who had come along with her also weeping (*klaiō*), he was deeply moved in spirit and troubled. [34] 'Where have you laid him?' he asked. 'Come and see, Lord,' they replied.
>
> [35] Jesus wept (*dakryō*). [36] Then the Jews said, 'See how he loved him!' [37] But some of them said, 'Could not he who opened the eyes of the blind man have kept this man from dying?'
>
> [38] Jesus, once more deeply moved, came to the tomb...." (11:32-38a)

It's not hard to understand the emotions of Mary and the other mourners. Though the burial had probably taken place on the day of Lazarus' death four days prior, the period of mourning was 30 days, with intense mourning for the first three days and first week.[427] The verb used in verses 31 and 33 is *klaiō*, "to cry, wail, lament," of any loud expression of pain or sorrow.[428] While some cultures are quite restrained in their mourning, in the Middle East the norm is loud, unrestrained crying and wailing. Luke's account of the mourning at Jairus' house at the death of his daughter uses an

---

[425] "Called aside" (NIV), "privately" (NRSV, cf. ESV), "secretly" (KJV) is the adverb *lathra*, "(to do something) without others being aware, secretly" (BDAG 581, 1).

[426] *Didaskalos*, probably "rabbi" in Aramaic.

[427] Edersheim, *Life and Times*, 4:989.

[428] Liddell Scott, *Greek-English Lexicon*; cf. BDAG 545, 1; K.H. Rengstorf, TDNT 3:722-726.

additional word to describe mourning practices, *koptō*, "to beat one's breast as an act of mourning, mourn greatly."[429] There the crowd of mourners was described as "aroused, in disorder."[430] Jewish funeral custom dictated that even a poor family was to hire flute players (Matthew 9:23) and a professional wailing woman[431] – and neither Jairus' or Lazarus' family was poor!

All this wailing and clamor of mourning followed Mary from her house to the tomb. Indeed, Mary seemed to be immersed in it herself (11:33). As Jesus had been upset with this sound of unbelief at Jairus' home, so he seems to be here as well.

Two expressions are given in verse 34b that express Jesus' deep feeling:

First, the we see the verb *embrimaomai* with *pneuma* (referring to Jesus' human spirit[432]). Our English versions translate the verb (in verses 33 and 38) as "deeply moved in spirit" (NIV, ESV), "greatly disturbed in spirit" (NRSV), "groaned in the spirit" (KJV),[433] suggesting that Jesus' was feeling compassion and empathy for Mary. However, when *embrimaomai* is used elsewhere in the New Testament and in the Greek Septuagint translation of the Old Testament, it is nearly always in the context of anger.[434] The verb is derived from *en*, "on" + *brimomai*, "snort with anger, to be indignant."[435] It seems clear to me that a better translation of the verb would include the idea of Jesus' anger, such as the ESV's alternate translation, "was indignant."[436]

Second, we see the word "troubled" (NIV, KJV), "deeply moved" (NRSV), "greatly troubled" (ESV), *tarassō*, which means "to shake, stir up," here, by extension, "to cause inward turmoil, stir up, disturb, unsettle, throw into confusion." It is used in our literature of mental and spiritual agitation and confusion.[437] The word is also used when Jesus is speaking of his betrayal: "Jesus was troubled in spirit" (13:21).

Carson suggests the last part of verse 33 should be translated, "he was outraged in spirit, and troubled."[438] I think he's on the right track. The only reason to translate *embrimaomai* as "deeply moved," rather than angry is the difficulty in understanding Jesus' anger here, not the lexical evidence for the word's meaning.

So if Jesus is indignant when Mary and the mourners came to him outside the city, rather than moved with compassion, we wonder: Why is Jesus angry? Several possibilities have been suggested.

---

[429] *Koptō*, BDAG 559.

[430] "Noisy" (NIV), "making a commotion" (NRSV, ESV), "making a noise" (KJV) is *thorybeō*, "disturb, agitate," here, aroused, in disorder" (BDAG 458, 2).

[431] Carson, *John*, p. 415, citing Mishnah *Ketuboth* 4:4.

[432] *Pneuma*, "human spirit, inner emotions, as the source and seat of insight, feeling, and will, generally as the representative part of human inner life" (BDAG 833, 3b).

[433] A recent Greek-English Lexicon softens it to, "feel strongly about something, be deeply moved" (BDAG 322, 3).

[434] Matthew 9:30; Mark 1:43; Mark 14:5; Psalm 7:11; Isaiah 17:13; Lamentation 2:6; Daniel 11:30.

[435] Liddell Scott, *Lexicon*.

[436] So Beasley-Murray, *John*, pp. 192-193; Carson, *John*, p. 415; Barrett, *John*; Kruse, *John*, pp. 253-254; and the early Greek Fathers. Morris (*John*, pp. 555-557) states the evidence for the anger translation, but is ambivalent. Brown (*John* 1:425) sees the basic meaning of *embrimaomai* as implying "an articulate expression of anger."

[437] *Tarassō*, BDAG 991, 2.

[438] Carson, *John*, p. 415.

1.   That Jesus is **angry because a miracle was being forced on him** by the grief of the sisters,[439] but Jesus had already stated his intention to perform a miracle in verse 11.
2.   That Jesus is **angry at the hypocritical mourning of the Jews**, but there's no evidence here to support this.[440]
3.   That Jesus is **angry with himself for not coming sooner**, but this can't be so in light of verses 4-7.
4.   That Jesus is **angry with the sin, sickness, and death** that bring so much sorrow. This is possible, but lacks strong evidence.
5.   That Jesus is **angry at the unbelief** he sees around him (as at Jairus' home, Mark 5:39-40). Despair, "like the rest of men, who have no hope" (1 Thessalonians 4:13), can't be reconciled with faith in the resurrection.

There is a lot of evidence that Jesus is angry at the unbelief of his followers – and the unbelief of the Jewish people in general.[441] When his disciples fail to heal an epileptic boy, Jesus says,

"O unbelieving and perverse generation, how long shall I stay with you? How long shall I put up with you? Bring the boy here to me." (Matthew 17:17)

On the other occasion when Jesus wept (Luke 19:41) his tears were over the obstinate unbelief of the Jews, and the dire consequences thereof. He wanted to gather them to him like a mother gathers her chicks, "but you were not willing" (Luke 13:34b). In John's Gospel we often see Jesus' frustration with unbelief.[442]

"Unless you people see miraculous signs and wonders, you will never believe." (4:48)

Jesus Wept (11:35-37)

"³⁵ Jesus wept (*dakryō*). ³⁶ Then the Jews said, 'See how he loved him!' ³⁷ But some of them said, 'Could not he who opened the eyes of the blind man have kept this man from dying?'" (11:35-37)

Now we come to the shortest verse in the English Bible, "Jesus wept." It's interesting that while the mourners' weeping is expressed by the verb *klaiō*, "weep, wail," Jesus' weeping uses another verb, *dakryō*, "to shed tears, weep," from *dakryon*, "tear."[443] Jesus shed tears. Why?

He isn't weeping because he misses his departed friend Lazarus, as the Jews think (11:36), because he knows that he will momentarily raise him from the dead. If we're correct about the meaning of *embrimaomai* as "to be indignant," then these probably weren't tears of compassion or empathy for the bereaved. They are probably tears at the unbelief he sees around him. Jesus also wept over Jerusalem, when he thought of the devastation that would come to it because of the unbelief of its leaders (Luke 19:41).[444]

As Beasley-Murray comments,

---

[439] Barrett, *John*, p. 399, citing John 2:4; 4:48; 6:26.
[440] Criticisms of the Jews hypocrisy are a focus in the Synoptics, not much in John's Gospel (Carson, *John*, p. 416).
[441] Matthew 6:30 = Luke 12:28; 8:26; 16:8; 17:20; Luke 24:25.
[442] Examples are: John 2:18; 6:36; 12:37-40; 15:24.
[443] *Dakryon* is used only here in the New Testament (BDAG 211).
[444] In Luke 19:41, the verb *klaiō*, "weep, cry, mourn, wail," is used.

"The contrast between the Revealer who brought the word of God and lived by it, and the recipients of it is startlingly exemplified here."[445]

If Jesus weeps over the unbelief of Mary, who sits at his feet and later anoints him with perfume, does he also weep over your unbelief and mine? Does my unbelief move him to tears of grief?[446]

> **Q4. (John 11:32-38) Different writers interpret Jesus' emotions on this occasion differently. Why do *you* think Jesus was "deeply moved"? Why did he weep?**
> **http://www.joyfulheart.com/forums/topic/1477-q4-jesus-wept/**

At the Tomb (11:38)

"Jesus, once more deeply moved, came to the tomb. It was a cave with a stone laid across the entrance." (11:38)

Each town would have its own common burial ground or cemetery where bodies would be buried, wrapped but without coffins. Edersheim tells us that the cemetery would never be closer to the town than 50 cubits, with graves at least a foot and a half apart. But Lazarus is interred in his own private tomb in a cave, perhaps in a garden, protected from depredation by wild animals by a stone across the entrance. It is probably whitewashed as a warning to passers-by that it is a tomb, so they could prevent uncleanness by contact with the dead.

Such a burial cave would have been hollowed out with niches along the sides where bodies of family members would be laid. After a time, the bones would be collected and put into a bone box or chest.[447]

The Raising of Lazarus (11:39-44)

"[39] 'Take away the stone,' he said. 'But, Lord,' said Martha, the sister of the dead man, 'by this time there is a bad odor, for he has been there four days.' [40] Then Jesus said, 'Did I not tell you that if you believed, you would see the glory of God?[448]' [41] So they took away the stone." (11:39-41a)

When Jesus commands the stone to be moved away, one voice is raised in protest, that of Martha, the "practical" sister. "By this time he stinketh" (KJV). By the fourth day, the person was well and truly dead; decomposition had set in.[449] Jesus has said nothing about raising Lazarus as yet. He has only asked where they had laid him. Perhaps Martha thinks Jesus wants to view the corpse of his friend.

---

[445] Beasley-Murray, *John*, p. 193.

[446] Beasley-Murray (*John*, p. 193) cites G. Sass (*Der Auferweckung des Lazarus*, p. 53): "So seen, the anger of Jesus becomes a question to our own faith."

[447] Edersheim, *Life and Times*, 4:987.

[448] See more in Appendix 6. "Glory" and "Glorify" in John's Gospel.

[449] Kruse, *John*, p. 255.

It's fascinating how our unbelief is so quick to correct Jesus' commands. We know better. We have to tell Jesus why he shouldn't do this or that! But if we will trust him, we can "see the glory of God." Lord, I believe. Help my unbelief! (Mark 9:24)

Now Jesus prays. Notice that it's not a petition, but a public glimpse into a running conversation between the Son and the Father. Like the great high-priestly prayer of John 17, it gives us insight into the intimate relationship between them.

> "41b Then Jesus looked up and said, 'Father, I thank you that you have heard me. 42 I knew that you always hear me, but I said this for the benefit of the people standing here, that they may believe that you sent me.'
>
> 43 When he had said this, Jesus called in a loud voice, 'Lazarus, come out!' 44 The dead man came out, his hands and feet wrapped with strips of linen, and a cloth around his face. Jesus said to them, 'Take off the grave clothes and let him go.'" (11:41b-44)

After praying, Jesus speaks a word of command – to a dead man! "Lazarus, come out!" The command consists of a single word in Greek, an adverb of place, *deuro*, functioning as an interjection here, "over here, (come) here, come!"[450] We see the word used as "almost a verb" also in Jesus' call to the rich young ruler, "Come, follow me!"[451]

Lazarus had been accorded Jewish burial customs similar to Jesus' burial by Joseph of Arimathea and Nicodemus:

> "Taking Jesus' body, the two of them wrapped it, with the spices, in [strips of] linen.[452]" (19:40a)

The spices were to lessen the odor of decomposition for a few days. "Strips of linen" in 11:44 is *keiria*, elsewhere used of webbing, belts, mattress suspension, etc. Here, in reference to the preparation of bodies for burial, it means, "binding material."[453] This is the only use of this word in the New Testament. Edersheim calls these bands *Takhrikhin*. Whether this designates a shroud or strips of linen in New Testament times isn't certain.[454]

Imagine the scene, this smelly corpse wrapped in white linen, shuffles and stumbles out of the tomb, hobbled, blind – his face wrapped with a cloth and his hands still tied to his sides by grave wraps. It almost sounds like a horror movie! The crowd is stunned, afraid. No one makes a move to

---

[450] *Deuro*, BDAG 220, 1.

[451] Matthew 19:21; Mark 10:21; Luke 18:22.

[452] *Othonion*, "(linen), cloth, cloth wrapping" is found in John 19:40; 20:5, 6, 7; Luke 24:12. BDAG says, "The applicability of the sense '*bandage*' to our literature is questionable" (BDAG 693).

[453] *Keiria*, BDAG 538.

[454] Edersheim (*Life and Times*, 3:552) describes the preparation of a body for burial in describing the raising of the son of the widow of Nain. "The last sad offices have been rendered to the dead. The body has been laid on the ground; hair and nails have been cut, and the body washed, anointed, and wrapped in the best the widow could procure; for, the ordinance which directed that the dead should be buried in 'wrappings' (*Takhrikhin*), or as they significantly called it, the 'provision for the journey' (*Zevadatha*), of the most inexpensive, linen, is of later date than our period. It is impossible to say, whether the later practice already prevailed, of covering the body with metal, glass, or salt, and laying it either upon earth or salt."

help him. So Jesus has to command them to come forward and assist him: "Unbind[455] him and let[456] him go[457]!"

Finally, some people come forward tentatively to help him. One removes the cloth covering his face. Someone else begins to unwind the linen that has been wrapped around him. And as they do so, this resurrected man appears alive and well. Where there was once inconsolable grief that gave way to fear, now joy and excitement overtakes the crowd. They begin to embrace Lazarus and laugh, leading him back into the town where he is reunited with the rest of his friends. Hallelujah! What a wonderful day!

Brown concludes his comments with the observation, "Thus, in many details, chapter 11 acts out the promise of chapter 5" – "A time is coming when all who are in their graves will hear his voice...." (5:28)[458]

Lazarus' resurrection is a precursor of Jesus' resurrection, who is called "the firstfruits of those who have fallen asleep" (1 Corinthians 15:20). Finally, comes the great resurrection when Christ returns:

> "... In a flash, in the twinkling of an eye, at the last trumpet. For the trumpet will sound, the dead will be raised imperishable, and we will be changed." (1 Corinthians 15:51b-52)

Hallelujah!

Faith and Unbelief (11:45-46)

> "[45] Therefore many of the Jews who had come to visit Mary, and had seen what Jesus did, put their faith in him. [46] But some of them went to the Pharisees and told them what Jesus had done." (11:45-46)

Now, as we have seen before, in the face of a great miracle, many believe, but others are hardened in their unbelief.[459] The same miracle had opposite effects depending upon the heart of the observer.

The Chief Priests and Pharisees Plot to Kill Jesus (11:47-48)

> "[47] Then the chief priests and the Pharisees called a meeting of the Sanhedrin. 'What are we accomplishing?' they asked. 'Here is this man performing many miraculous signs. [48] If we let him go on like this, everyone will believe in him, and then the Romans will come and take away both our place and our nation.'" (11:47-48)

The raising of Lazarus, being so spectacular and taking place so close to Jerusalem, forces the authorities to take some action against Jesus. The high ranking priests[460] tended to be Sadducees,

---

[455] "Take off the grave clothes" (NIV), "unbind" (NRSV, ESV), "loose" (KJV) is *lyō*, literally, "to undo something that is used to tie up or constrain something, loose, untie bonds," then, by extension, "to set free something tied or similarly constrained, set free, loose, untie" (BDAG 606, 2a).

[456] "Let" is *aphiēmi*, to convey a sense of distancing through an allowable margin of freedom, leave it to someone to do something, "let, let go, allow, tolerate" (BDAG 157, 5a).

[457] "Go" is *hypagō*, "go away, withdraw, go," here, "to leave someone's presence, go away," probably here it means, "go home" (BDAG 1028, 1).

[458] Brown, *John*, 1:437.

[459] John 2:23; 7:30-31; 8:30, 59; 10:39, 42; 12:10-11, 42; etc.

opposed by the Pharisees. But in the face of an impending power shift, they are united and call a meeting of the Sanhedrin, the ruling group for the Jews, consisting of 70 members.[461] They say, "If we let him go on like this, everyone will believe in him" (11:48a). Jesus' ministry is having a significant effect in the area.

Notice their reasoning.

1. Power shifts to Jesus, as he rapidly gains popularity with the people.

2. The Romans will view this as a popular unrest or rebellion, and take away the power they had granted to the Sanhedrin and the chief priests to rule under their authority.

3. The Romans will take away "our place," that is, the temple.

4. The Romans will take away "our nation," that is, bring a crackdown where the Romans will rule Palestine directly, not through vassal kings (such as Herod) and the Sanhedrin.

If these leaders believed Jesus were the Messiah, they would have been glad to see him gain power. But they obviously did not. They exaggerated the threat to the temple and the nation, and moved to protect their own positions of power and authority – even if it meant killing a miracle-worker.

Caiaphas Prophesies Jesus' Death on behalf of Israel (11:49-53)

Joseph Caiaphas, son-in-law of Annas[462], a former high priest, filled the office of high priest from 18 to 36 AD. He had been placed in office by Pontius Pilate's predecessor as Roman procurator of Judea, demonstrating that the high priesthood was a political office, not controlled by the Jews themselves during this period, but essentially appointed by the Roman rulers.[463] No wonder the high priestly class felt insecure. The chief priest chaired the meetings of the Sanhedrin.

> "[49] Then one of them, named Caiaphas, who was high priest that year, spoke up, 'You know nothing at all! [50] You do not realize that it is better for you that one man die for the people than that the whole nation perish.' [51] He did not say this on his own, but as high priest that year he prophesied that Jesus would die for the Jewish nation, [52] and not only for that nation but also for the scattered children of God, to bring them together and make them one. [53] So from that day on they plotted to take his life." (11:49-53)

The discussion of what to do seems to be deadlocked. Some acknowledge that Jesus is working miraculous signs. But they're not sure how to stop him. Arrest had been attempted in the past, and failed.

Caiaphas, as chairman, rebukes those who are vacillating. He calls for a desperate measure, the rational and ruthless action to taking Jesus' life. However, to persuade the Sanhedrin, Caiaphas

---

[460] "Chief priests" is *archiereus*. In the singular it might refer to the high priest himself (as in 11:49), but here in the plural, it refers to "a priest of high rank, chief priest," denoting members of the Sanhedrin who belonged to high priestly families, that is, ruling high priests, those who had been deposed, and adult male members of the most prominent priestly families.

[461] For more on the Sanhedrin, see Appendix 3. Religious Leaders in Jesus' Day.

[462] For more on Annas, see on 18:13 (Lesson 30).

[463] Josephus, *Antiquities of the Jews* 18, 2, 2.

couches his move in terms of sacrificing the lesser ("one man") for the greater ("the whole nation") – one man perishing, rather than the Jewish nation. He makes it sound like their patriotic duty! They agree. The die is cast. The Sanhedrin has resolved to take Jesus' life.[464]

Notice John's observation about the prophetic nature of Caiaphas's words:

> "[51] He did not say this on his own, but as high priest that year he prophesied that Jesus would die for the Jewish nation, [52] and not only for that nation but also for the scattered children of God, to bring them together and make them one." (11:51-52)

Caiaphas saw this as a necessary action to protect the Jewish people. But since he was in the holy office of high priest, John says that he speaks prophetically on this occasion. What he proposes is, in reality, Jesus dying as a sacrifice for the sins of the nation and the Diaspora ("the scattered children of God").[465] The result will be to unite the believers around the world and make them one. But John is looking beyond the Jewish Diaspora here, to the Gentiles around the world who will become believers. In John's writings, Jesus is clearly depicted as a world Savior:

> "We know that this man really is the Savior of the world." (4:42)

> "I have other sheep that are not of this sheep pen. I must bring them also. They too will listen to my voice, and there shall be one flock and one shepherd." (10:16)

> "And I, when I am lifted up from the earth, will draw all people to myself." (12:32, ESV)

> "He is the atoning sacrifice for our sins, and not only for ours but also for the sins of the whole world." (1 John 2:2)

> "With your blood you purchased men for God
> from every tribe and language and people and nation." (Revelation 5:9)

We see hints of this in Paul's Letter to the Ephesians of Jesus' mission "to bring them together and make them one" (11:52b):

> "For he himself is our peace, who has **made the two one** and has destroyed the barrier, the dividing wall of hostility, by abolishing in his flesh the law with its commandments and regulations. His purpose was **to create in himself one new man out of the two**, thus making peace, and in this one body to reconcile both of them to God through the cross, by which he put to death their hostility." (Ephesians 2:14-16)

Q5. (John 11:49-53). What did Caiaphas intend to say to the Sanhedrin? What is the prophetic meaning of his statement?
http://www.joyfulheart.com/forums/topic/1478-q5-caiaphas-prophecy/

---

[464] "Plotted" (NIV), "planned" (NRSV), "took counsel together" (KJV) is *bouleuō*, "to reach a decision about a course of action, resolve, decide." *Bouleuō*, BDAG 181, 2.

[465] The verb is *diaskorpizō*, "scatter, disperse," seed, a flock, a people, etc. (BDAG 236, 1). A synonym, *diaspeirō*, "scatter," has a noun form, *diaspora*, from which we get our English word "Diapora." Peter uses the noun to refer to Gentiles: "Peter, an apostle of Jesus Christ, to the strangers scattered throughout Pontus, Galatia, Cappadocia, Asia, and Bithynia..." (1 Peter 1:1). James uses it to refer to the "twelve tribes scattered abroad," which probably also refers to the Gentiles (James 1:1).

Jesus Withdraws to Ephraim (11:54)

Though the Apostle John probably had sources within priestly circles, the Sanhedrin's decision couldn't be kept a secret for long. The word was put out: report Jesus' whereabouts so he can be arrested (11:57)

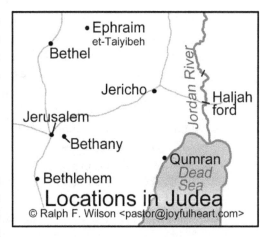

Locations in Judea
© Ralph F. Wilson <pastor@joyfulheart.com>

> "Therefore Jesus no longer moved about publicly among the Jews. Instead he withdrew to a region near the desert, to a village called Ephraim, where he stayed with his disciples." (11:54)

If Jesus' disciples were afraid to come to Jerusalem before the raising of Lazarus (11:7-8, 16), now they are doubly afraid, since this astounding miracle has triggered what amounts to an official warrant for Jesus' arrest (11:57). Prior to this, Jesus and his disciples had been east of the Jordan (10:40), far from Jesus' enemies in Jerusalem. Now, they retire to the village of Ephraim, near the Judean desert. Ephraim is generally identified with the village of et-Taiyibeh, about 13 miles north-northeast of Jerusalem.[466]

Q6. (John 11:54) Why did Jesus withdraw to Ephraim? Does this show fear? What does this teach us about strategic retreat?
http://www.joyfulheart.com/forums/topic/1479-q6-strategic-retreat/

Lessons for Disciples

1. We must do the work God gives us when we have the opportunity, rather than put it off because of our fears (11:9-10).

2. We must have courage to follow Jesus even when it is dangerous or costly to do so. "Doubting" Thomas sets the standard for us here: "Let us also go, that we may die with him" (11:16). We may experience fear, but courage is doing what is needed in spite of our fears.

3. Jesus embodies in his person both Resurrection and Life, and he is the only one who has authority to bring them. Raising Lazarus was an indication of this authority and a precursor of Jesus' resurrection and our own (11:25).

4. Eternal life that Jesus gives begins now and survives physical death (11:26). Those who are alive spiritually and believe will never suffer spiritual death (11:27).

5. Though Martha has a reputation for being less "spiritual" than her sister Mary, she is the one who makes the outstanding confession: "I believe that you are the Christ, the Son of God, who

---

[466] William Ewing and Robert J. Hughes III, "Ephraim," ISBE 2:119; Urban C. Von Wahlde, "Archaeology and John's Gospel," in *Jesus & Archaeology*, p. 571.

was to come into the world" (11:27). Though we are "wired" differently from one another, we can all express faith in the ways God gives us to.

6.   Jesus is angry at and weeps concerning the unbelief of his followers, many of whom have already seen him do marvelous things (11:33-38). We must not give ourselves permission for unbelief or mental reservations if we are to please him.

7.   Like Martha, trying to prevent Jesus from removing the stone for practical reasons, we often explain to God why we shouldn't obey his "obviously" unpractical directions (11:39). Rather, we should obey without complaint. In the words of an old hymn:

> "Trust and obey,
> for there's no other way
> to be happy in Jesus,
> but to trust and obey."[467]

8.   God can speak through the most unlikely people when he wants to, in this case, Caiaphas. He might have been an unbelieving and politically appointed high priest, but God used him in spite of himself (11:49-53).

9.   It is okay to retreat strategically, so long as we are willing to obey at danger to our lives when it is time to do so (11:54)

Prayer

Father, thank you for giving us this glimpse of Jesus' glory in raising Lazarus. We so want your glory to be seen in our world today. Give us faith to believe so that your glory can peek out often. In Jesus' name, we pray. Amen.

Key Verses

"Jesus said to her, 'I am the resurrection and the life. He who believes in me will live, even though he dies; and whoever lives and believes in me will never die. Do you believe this?' 'Yes, Lord,' she told him, 'I believe that you are the Christ, the Son of God, who was to come into the world.'" (John 11:25-27, NIV)

"Jesus wept." (John 11:35, NIV)

"Then Jesus said, 'Did I not tell you that if you believed, you would see the glory of God?'" (John 11:40, NIV)

"Jesus called in a loud voice, 'Lazarus, come out!' The dead man came out, his hands and feet wrapped with strips of linen, and a cloth around his face. Jesus said to them, 'Take off the grave clothes and let him go.'" (John 11:43-44, NIV)

"[Caiaphas] did not say this on his own, but as high priest that year he prophesied that Jesus would die for the Jewish nation, and not only for that nation but also for the scattered children of God, to bring them together and make them one." (John 11:51-52, NIV)

---

[467] Words by John H. Sammis, 1887; music by Daniel B. Towner.

21. Anointing at Bethany and Triumphal Entry (11:55-12:22)

Events are coming to a climax. After the raising of Lazarus and the Sanhedrin's decision to kill Jesus, the Master and his band retreat to the village of Ephraim, about 15 miles north northeast of Jerusalem.

But now Passover is at hand, when devout Jews travel to Jerusalem. Two opposing forces are about to meet – Jesus the Light of the World, and the world leaders who are intent upon extinguishing the Light that exposes the hypocrisy of their religious observances and their Light-blindness.

James J. Tissot, 'Mary Magdalene's Box of Very Precious Ointment' (1886-94), gouache on grey wove paper, 8 x 11.2 in., Brooklyn Museum, New York.

Looking for Jesus to Appear (11:55-57)

"When it was almost time for the Jewish Passover, many went up from the country to Jerusalem for their ceremonial cleansing[468] before the Passover." (11:55)

Prior to Passover, people would come to Jerusalem to purify themselves from an uncleanness. Any kind of ceremonial defilement would make a person ineligible from keeping Passover. Such defilement could be incurred by touching something unclean, such as a dead body, an unclean animal, a grave, etc. (Leviticus 7:20-21; Numbers 9:6-7; 2 Chronicles 30:17). Sepulchers and graves were whitewashed (Matthew 23:27) to identify them so that people wouldn't accidentally touch them at festival time and become ceremonially unclean. Particularly those that lived in the countryside, in contact with Gentiles (and unmarked Gentile graves) would come early for purification.

These purification rituals might take several days (Numbers 19:11-12), so many people would arrive at Jerusalem as much as a week ahead of the festival to wash in a *mikveh* or ritual bath in Jerusalem – such as the Pool of Bethesda or the Pool of Siloam.

During this time prior to Passover and the Feast of Unleavened Bread that followed it, speculation was rampant about Jesus and the Jewish leaders' plan to arrest him.

"[56] They kept looking for Jesus, and as they stood in the temple area they asked one another, 'What do you think? Isn't he coming to the Feast at all?' [57] But the chief priests and Pharisees had

---

[468] "Ceremonial cleansing" (NIV), "to purify" (NRSV, ESV, KJV) is *hagnizō*, "to purify or cleanse and so make acceptable for cultic use, purify," of lustrations and rites of atonement (BDAG 12, 1a).

given orders that if anyone found out where Jesus was, he should report[469] it so that they might arrest him." (11:56-57)

In the face of such a threat, many wondered, would Jesus even come to Jerusalem?

Dinner in Bethany (12:1-2)

Nevertheless, Jesus arrives for a rather public meal in his honor at a home in Bethany, just two miles outside of Jerusalem.

"[1] Six days before the Passover, Jesus arrived at Bethany, where Lazarus lived, whom Jesus had raised from the dead. [2] Here a dinner was given in Jesus' honor. Martha served, while Lazarus was among those reclining at the table with him." (12:1-2)

From John's Gospel we would assume that the meal was held in Lazarus's home. But by comparison with an similar account in Mark 14:3-11 and Matthew 26:6-16, it appears that the home belonged to a man named Simon the Leper.[470] It wouldn't be uncommon (or out of character) for Martha to be enlisted by another household to help serve the meal for Jesus and his disciples – and you'd expect Jesus' prominent friend Lazarus to be a guest at the dinner.

While in modern Western cultures, it's common to sit in chairs around a table, in Jesus' time we see a characteristically Eastern style of dining, with guests arranged around a very low table, reclining[471] on their left arm and supported by divans or cushions, leaving their right hand free to feed themselves. Their feet, sandals removed, would be splayed out behind them, with some space between their feet and the walls so those who are serving the meal can bring the various dishes to the table. This is also the likely arrangement at the Lord's Supper when Jesus washes the feet of the disciples reclining around the table (13:5).

Mary Anoints Jesus' Feet (12:3)

While the men are reclining at the meal, Mary – the one who at another time had "sat at Jesus feet" listening to him teach (Luke 10:39) – anoints Jesus' feet in an extravagant act of devotion.

"Then Mary took about a pint[472] of pure[473] nard, an expensive perfume[474]; she poured[475] it on Jesus' feet and wiped[476] his feet with her hair. And the house was filled with the fragrance of the perfume." (12:3)

---

[469] "Report" (NIV), "let them know" (NRSV, ESV), "shew" (KJV) is mēnyō, "to offer information presumed to be of special interest, inform, make known, reveal" (BDAG 648).

[470] There are four accounts in the Gospels of a woman anointing Jesus with perfume from an alabaster flask, all taking place while Jesus is reclining at a meal. Of these John's account has much in common with the accounts in Mark 14:3-11 and Matthew 26:6-16, such as the timing during holy week prior to Passover, the location in Bethany, and criticism that such an extravagantly expensive perfume should be sold and the proceeds given to the poor. Luke 7:36-50, on the other hand is placed early in Luke's Gospel, far from Holy Week. It relates a dinner in a Pharisee's home and anointing by a notorious sinful woman. It culminates in Jesus' contrasting the host's lack of generous hospitality with the woman's extravagant love, and ends with a parable about forgiveness involving a creditor forgiving the unequal debts of two individuals. Though there are some differences, such as the anointing of the feet in John and the head in Mark/Matthew, I believe these accounts related the same incident, and the Luke 7 incident is separate.

[471] "Reclining" (NIV, ESV), "sat" (KJV) is anakeimai, "lie, recline," here, "reclining at table," the equivalent of "to dine" (BDAG 65, 2).

[472] "Pint" (NIV), "pound" (NRSV, KJV) is litra, "a (Roman) pound" (327.45 grams). Our pound is 453.6 grams.

Nard (sometimes called "spikenard") comes from the spikenard plant (*Nardostachys jatamansi*), native to India's eastern Himalayas, growing from 10,000 to 16,000 feet elevation (3,000 to 5,000 meters). The rhizomes or roots are crushed and distilled into an intensely aromatic, amber-colored essential oil that was a favorite perfume in antiquity. The best spikenard was imported from India in sealed alabaster containers.[477] It was very expensive because of the tedious extraction process as well as the cost of importing it along extensive caravan routes leading west to the Mediterranean. In verse 5, Judas calculates its value as 300 denarii, which, at the wage of about a denarius per day, was nearly one year's wages – a very expensive perfume indeed! This perfume might be worth $30,000 to $50,000 USD in today's currency!

John includes a distinctive detail – also mentioned in 11:2 – that marked this event as quite intimate, indeed, shocking. Respectable women didn't go out in public with their hair down – that was the mark of a loose woman. But Mary had let down her hair and was drying excess perfume from Jesus' feet with her hair!

Mary of Bethany vs. Mary Magdalene

There is a lot of confusion about which Mary anointed Jesus' feet. There are some similarities between this anointing in Bethany and an unnamed sinful woman anointing Jesus' feet in a separate instance in Luke 7:36-50, which took place earlier in Jesus' ministry. Mary Magdalene, a wealthy and devoted disciple from Magdala, on the west coast of the Sea of Galilee, was said to have been delivered from seven demons (Luke 8:2; Mark 16:9). Much later Mary Magdalene was thought to be a sinful woman, since the demonic involvement was assumed to be sexual (thus making her a "sinful woman"), and since her name was Mary (thus confused with Mary of Bethany). The idea that Mary Magdalene was a repentant sinner can be traced back to Ephraim the Syrian in the fourth century, and an influential homily by Pope Gregory I ("the Great") about 591 AD that conflated Mary Magdalene with the "sinful woman" of Luke 7:36-50, as well as Mary of Bethany, a kind of "composite Mary," that was widely accepted by the Roman Catholic Church until modern times.

We must be clear. Mary of Bethany is a devout and upright disciple, not to be confused with the "sinful woman" of Luke 7:36-50, nor with Mary from Magdala.

The House Is Filled with Fragrance (12:3b)

"The house was filled with the fragrance[478] of the perfume." (12:3)

---

[473] "Pure" (NIV), *pistikos*, which probably means, "genuine, unadulterated," from *pistis*, "faithful, trustworthy" (BDAG 818).

[474] "Perfume" (NIV, NRSV, ESV), "ointment" (KJV) is *myron* (a Semitic loanword, related to Arabic *myrr*, from which we get our word "myrrh"), "ointment, perfume" (BDAG 661).

[475] "Poured" (NIV), "anointed" (NRSV, ESV, KJV) is *aleiphō*, literally, "to anoint by applying a liquid such as oil or perfume, anoint" (BDAG 41).

[476] "Wiped" (NIV) is *ekmassō*, "to cause to become dry by wiping with a substance, wipe" (BDAG 306).

[477] R. K. Harrison, "Nard," ISBE 3:491, cites Pliny, *Natural History*, 12, 24-26. Pliny notes that other varieties of spikenard came from Arabia and Syria

[478] "Fragrance" (NIV, NRSV, ESV), "odor" (KJV) is *osmē*, "quality of something that stimulates sense of smell, odor, smell." The term itself does not denote whether it is agreeable or disagreeable (BDAG 729, 1a).

You can imagine the sudden, overpowering fragrance of the perfume filling the room, as Mary broke the seal on the alabaster flask and poured it over Jesus' feet. The whole room was charged with the beautiful aroma. Paul uses this image to elucidate the power of a Christian presence:

> "Thanks be to God, who always leads us in triumphal procession in Christ and through us spreads everywhere the **fragrance** of the knowledge of him. For we are to God the **aroma** of Christ among those who are being saved and those who are perishing." (2 Corinthians 2:14-15)

Mary had performed a beautiful, startling, and extravagant act of worship that was destined to be remembered long after her time (Mark 14:9). The Wise Men believed in extravagant worship, as well:

> "They bowed down and worshiped him. Then they opened their treasures and presented him with gifts of gold and of incense and of myrrh." (Matthew 2:11)

David was a strong believer in worship that was not cheap. Araunah the Jebusite was willing to give for free his threshing floor to David for a place to offer a sacrifice (later the site of the temple), but David refused.

> "I insist on paying you for it. I will not sacrifice to the LORD my God burnt offerings that cost me nothing." (2 Samuel 24:24a)

Giving greatly in worship helps destroy greed's hold over us.

Judas Objects to Wasting Money (12:4-6)

However, not all recognized the beauty of Mary's extravagant act of worship.

> "[4] But one of his disciples, Judas Iscariot, who was later to betray him, objected, [5] 'Why wasn't this perfume sold and the money given to the poor? It was worth a year's wages.' [6] He did not say this because he cared about the poor but because he was a thief; as keeper of the money bag, he used to help himself to what was put into it." (12:4-6)

Why do some people feel they have to exalt themselves by putting someone else down? Judas objects to the extreme extravagance of Mary's gesture – and you might too. How would you react if someone gave a $50,000 gift to your church that would be literally "blown away" by the wind in just a few minutes?[479] You would be outraged – and you would misunderstand Mary's act of worship.

Judas Iscariot's heart isn't pure. John, who knew Judas well, tells us two facts that help us understand him: (1) He is the treasurer for Jesus' mission – he kept the money box. And (2) he makes it a practice to steal[480] from the common fund. We would call that "embezzlement." It reveals a serious character flaw – greed, avarice – which gives us a motive that helps explain why he might betray Jesus to the chief priests for 30 pieces of silver (Matthew 26:15; Luke 22:5).

We are bothered by Mary's $50,000 extravagance for perhaps several reasons:

---

[479] If, in Jesus' day, this perfume represented a year's wages. In 2013 U.S. real (inflation adjusted) median household income was $51,939.

[480] "Help himself" (NIV, ESV), "steal" (NRSV), "bare" (KJV) is the imperfect tense of the verb *bastazō*, "to carry something from a place, carry away, remove," here, with moral implication, "take surreptitiously, pilfer, steal" (BDAG 171, 3b). The imperfect tense indicates continuous action in the past, as a habit or practice.

1. **Value**. If we aren't wealthy, $50,000 seems like a great deal in our own scale of value. But to a rich person with $10 million, $50,000 isn't so valuable. Money is only worth the value you attach to it!

2. **Love**. We don't love Jesus with the intensity that Mary did. Our love is more abstract, theoretical, detached.

3. **Worship**. We don't value worship much, and the worship we do participate in is often formal, unemotional, and sometimes seemingly sterile. Perhaps we value money more than heart worship.

Mary's worship tells us a lot about her – and ourselves! So does Judas' heart.

Jesus Defends Mary's Gracious Act (12:7-8)

Jesus comes to Mary's defense.

> "7 'Leave her alone,' Jesus replied. '[It was intended] that she should save this perfume for the day of my burial.[481] 8 You will always have the poor among you, but you will not always have me.'" (12:7-8)

It's difficult to know exactly how to render verse 7b.[482] It probably means that instead of selling it to help the poor, Mary has kept[483] it for just such a purpose, as the NIV and NRSV translations suggest. Mark's Gospel gives the same idea:

> "She did what she could. She poured perfume on my body beforehand[484] to prepare for my burial." (Mark 14:8)

Jesus is not opposed to alms for the poor – and says that there will always be poor they can give alms to in times to come. But this is a special occasion. If Mary doesn't do this now, the opportunity will be lost forever. Jesus approves!

Just as the fragrance of her act immediately filled the room, so it will eventually fill the world. In Mark's Gospel we read:

> "I tell you the truth, wherever the gospel is preached throughout the world, what she has done will also be told, in memory of her." (Mark 14:9)

---

[481] "Burial" is *entaphiasmos*, "the performance of what is customary for burial, preparation for burial or burial itself" (BDAG 339). Morris (*John*, p. 579, n. 23) says that the word "refers properly not so much to the burial as to the 'laying out' of the corpse, the preparation for burial." The word is also found in Mark 14:8.

[482] The Greek of verse 7b could be taken several ways as the various translations demonstrate. Carson (*John*, pp. 429-430) sees the best alternative as similar to the NRSV translation. He renders it, "[She has done this] in order to keep it for the day of my burial." He notes, "This will make sense only if what Mary has done, in the understood ellipsis, is not the anointing itself, but the keeping of the perfume for just such an occasion rather than selling it and distributing the proceeds to the poor."

[483] "Save" (NIV), "keep" (NRSV, ESV), "hath kept" (KJV) is *tēreō*, "to cause a state, condition, or activity to continue, keep, hold, reserve, preserve someone or something," here, for a definite purpose or a suitable time (BDAG 1002, 1a).

[484] *Prolambanō*, "to do something that involves some element of temporal priority, here, with the temporal force of *pro* felt rather strongly "do something before the usual time, anticipate something" (BDAG 872, 1a).

Q1. (John 12:3-8) Why did Judas object to Mary's extravagant act of devotion? Why did Jesus defend her? Why did Mary do this? What does this teach us about worship? Does your worship tend to be cheap or extravagant? For you, what would be extravagant worship?
http://www.joyfulheart.com/forums/topic/1480-q1-extravagant-worship/

Many Are Trusting Jesus (12:9-11)

Jesus' miracle of the raising of Lazarus is bringing large crowds to Bethany.

"⁹ Meanwhile a large crowd of Jews found out that Jesus was there and came, not only because of him but also to see Lazarus, whom he had raised from the dead. ¹⁰ So the chief priests made plans to kill Lazarus as well, ¹¹ for on account of him many of the Jews were going over[485] to Jesus and putting their faith in him." (12:9-11)

Both verbs in verse 11 are in the imperfect tense, continuing action in the past, indicating and ongoing and growing movement of people in Jerusalem to faith in Jesus. Both Jesus and Lazarus are attracting crowds and inspiring faith. As a result, Lazarus is put on the chief priests' "hit list." No matter that Lazarus is the object of an amazing miracle – he must die. This is evidence of the evil blindness of Jesus' enemies. Paul characterizes this kind of aggressive persecution in his Letter to the Romans:

"The wrath of God is being revealed from heaven against all the godlessness and wickedness of men who suppress[486] the truth by their wickedness, since what may be known about God is plain to them, because God has made it plain to them."(Romans 1:18-19)

They have seen truth staring them in the face, but they cannot endure it because it threatens their lifestyle. Such has been the basis of persecution of faithful Christians ever since.

Triumphal Entry (12:12-18)

The Synoptic Gospels describe the Triumphal Entry in greater detail, explaining how Jesus directed disciples to the young donkey that he would ride into Jerusalem, but John focuses on the procession itself, and what it tells us about who Jesus is.

The procession begins in Bethany, the town where Lazarus, Martha, and Mary live, which is located about 2 miles east of Jerusalem on the eastern slope of the Mount of Olives.[487] The Synoptic Gospels describe Jesus' route as down the Mount of Olives (Luke 19:37), then into the city.

---

[485] "Going over to" (NIV), "deserting" (NRSV), "going away" (ESV), "went away" (KJV) is *hypagō*. The original sense is, "go away, withdraw," but it tends more and more to mean simply "go" in colloquial speech, which I think is the sense here.

[486] "Suppress" (NIV, NRSV, ESV), "hold" (KJV) is *katechō*, "to prevent the doing of something or cause to be ineffective, prevent, hinder, restrain," here, "hold down, suppress something" (BDAG 532, 1b).

[487] It is identified by early Christian tradition with the Palestinian town el-Azariyeh. W. Harold Mare, "Bethany," *New International Dictionary of Bible Archaeology* (Zondervan, 1983), p. 97; Avraham Negev (ed.), *The Archaeological Encyclopedia of the Holy Land* (Revised Edition; Thomas Nelson, 1986), p. 56. The name Bethany means "house of depression, misery, poverty." The site of Bethphage is uncertain.

"¹² The next day the great crowd that had come for the Feast heard that Jesus was on his way to Jerusalem. ¹³ They took palm branches and went out to meet him, shouting, 'Hosanna!' 'Blessed is he who comes in the name of the Lord!' 'Blessed is the King of Israel!'

¹⁴ Jesus found a young donkey and sat upon it, as it is written, ¹⁵ 'Do not be afraid, O Daughter of Zion; see, your king is coming, seated on a donkey's colt.'

¹⁶ At first his disciples did not understand all this. Only after Jesus was glorified[488] did they realize that these things had been written about him and that they had done these things to him.

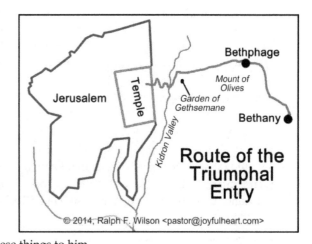

Route of the Triumphal Entry

© 2014, Ralph F. Wilson <pastor@joyfulheart.com>

¹⁷ Now the crowd that was with him when he called Lazarus from the tomb and raised him from the dead continued to spread the word. ¹⁸ Many people, because they had heard that he had given this miraculous sign, went out to meet him.

¹⁹ So the Pharisees said to one another, 'See, this is getting us nowhere. Look how the whole world has gone after him!'" (12:12-19)

In Jerusalem, stories of Jesus' raising of Lazarus have spread from person to person among the pilgrims who have come to the city for Passover. So when word comes that Jesus is coming into the Holy City, crowds go out to meet him (12:17-18).

John says that "they took palm branches[489] and went out to meet him." Mark tells us, "Many people spread their cloaks on the road, while others spread branches they had cut in the fields" (Mark 11:8). Though palms grew especially along the Jordan River, they were also found in the hill country (Judges 4:5; Nehemiah 8:15), and were commonly used during the Feast of Booths (Leviticus 23:40), and in other celebrations of praise (1 Maccabees 13:51; 2 Maccabees 10:7). In Revelation a great multitude stands before the Lamb with palm branches in their hands. The palms are also seen in Psalm 118 that the people were referring to in their shouts:

"With boughs in hand,
join in the festal procession up to the horns of the altar." (Psalm 118:27)

Shouting Praises (12:13b)

"They took palm branches and went out to meet him, shouting, 'Hosanna! Blessed is he who comes in the name of the Lord! Blessed is the King of Israel!'" (12:13b)

---

[488] See more in Appendix 6. "Glory" and "Glorify" in John's Gospel.

[489] "Palm branches" is two words: *baion*, "palm branch" (BDAG 162) and *phoinix*, the *Phoenix dactylifera*, "date-palm, palm tree" (BDAG 1063, 1).

The procession grows and people continue to shout[490] – the imperfect tense of the verb indicates continued action in the past. John records three shouts in particular:

"Hosanna!" means, "Save us!" and comes from Psalm 118:25, where it is a cry to God for help.

"Blessed is he who comes in the name of the Lord!" is found in the following verse, Psalms 118:26.

"Blessed is the King of Israel!" "King of Israel" (also 1:49) is a clear declaration that Jesus is the Messiah. The Synoptics tell of the crowd shouting, "Son of David" (Matthew 21:9), which amounts to the same thing, since the Son of David is the expected Messiah who would be a descendant of David.

Psalm 118 is one of six psalms (113-118) of which the Hallel or "Praise" psalms is composed. The Hallel would be sung by the Jews as a thanksgiving liturgy during the three major religious holidays: Passover, Pentecost, and Tabernacles. As a processional psalm, it was sung outside the temple gates and then continued inside as well. Here are verses 19-29 of Psalm 118, so you can hear the context.

> "Open for me the gates of righteousness;
> I will enter and give thanks to the Lord.
> This is the gate of the Lord
> through which the righteous may enter.
> I will give you thanks, for you answered me;
> you have become my salvation.
>
> **The stone the builders rejected**
> **has become the capstone;**
> the Lord has done this,
> and it is marvelous in our eyes.
>
> This is the day the Lord has made;
> let us rejoice and be glad in it.
>
> O Lord, save us; [literally, **"Hosanna!"**]
> O Lord, grant us success.
> **Blessed is he who comes in the name of the Lord.**
>
> From the house of the Lord we bless you.
>
> The Lord is God,
> and he has made his light shine upon us.
> **With boughs in hand, join in the festal procession**
> **up to the horns of the altar.**
>
> You are my God, and I will give you thanks;
> you are my God, and I will exalt you.
>
> Give thanks to the Lord, for he is good;
> his love endures forever." (Psalm 118:19-29)

Like other Royal Psalms, Psalm 118 was increasingly interpreted as Messianic by late Judaism.[491] Thus, for phrases of this psalm to be applied to Jesus is a recognition by the people that he is the

---

[490] *Kraugazō*, "to utter a loud sound, ordinarily of harsh texture, cry (out)" (BDAG 565). The verb occurs several times in John, here and in 11:43; 18:40; 19:6, 12, 15.

Messiah. This becomes especially apparent in the last of the crowd's continuing chants: "Blessed is the King of Israel!"

Riding on a Young Donkey (12:14-16)

Even Jesus riding into Jerusalem on a young donkey has profound Messianic significance as the fulfillment of prophecy.

> "[14] Jesus found a young donkey[492] and sat upon it, as it is written, [15] 'Do not be afraid, O Daughter of Zion; see, your king is coming, seated on a donkey's colt.[493]'
>
> [16] At first his disciples did not understand all this. Only after Jesus was glorified[494] did they realize that these things had been written about him and that they had done these things to him." (12:14-16)

John is quoting from Zechariah 9:9, a passage that comprises one of the great soprano arias of Handel's *Messiah*:

> "Rejoice greatly, O Daughter of Zion!
> Shout, Daughter of Jerusalem!
> See, your king comes to you,
> righteous and having salvation,
> gentle and riding on a donkey,
> on a colt, the foal of a donkey.
>
> I will take away the chariots from Ephraim
> and the war-horses from Jerusalem,
> and the battle bow will be broken.
> He will proclaim peace to the nations.
> His rule will extend from sea to sea
> and from the River to the ends of the earth." (Zechariah 9:9-10)

The donkey was domesticated in Mesopotamia by the Third Millennium BC and was used as a beast of burden from the patriarchal period. It was renowned for its strength and was the animal normally ridden by nonmilitary personnel (Numbers 22:21; Judges 10:4; 1 Samuel 25:20).[495] The Scriptures indicate that riding a donkey is not at all beneath the dignity of Israel's noblemen and kings (2 Samuel 18:9; 19:26). Indeed, David indicates his choice of Solomon to be king by decreeing that the young man should ride on the king's own mule (1 Kings 1:32-40).

In the Synoptic Gospels, Jesus' instructions are clear that the donkey must be one that has never been ridden (see Numbers 19:2; Deuteronomy 21:3; 1 Samuel 6:7; 2 Samuel 6:3). It is set apart,

---

[491] Hyuk J. Kwon, "Psalm 118 (117 lxx) in Luke-Acts: Application of a 'New Exodus Motif,'" *Verbum et Ecclesia* 30(2), Art. #59, 6 pages. Kwon shows in Tables 1 and 2 Jewish Midrash on the Hallel Psalms and Psalm 118 in particular. Leslie C. Allen, *Psalms 101-150* (Word Biblical Commentary, vol. 21; Word, 1983), p. 125.

[492] "Young donkey/ass" is *onarion*, literally "little donkey," the diminutive of *onos*, "donkey" (BDAG 710).

[493] "Donkey's/ass's colt" is two words: *pōlos*, "young animal, foal" (originally, "colt of a horse") (BDAG 900, 1) and *onos*, "(domesticated) ass, donkey" (male or female) (BDAG 714).

[494] See more in Appendix 6. "Glory" and "Glorify" in John's Gospel.

[495] R.K. Harrison, "Ass," ISBE 1:330.

consecrated for a specific use – for the Master's use. There is a rabbinic tradition that no one should use the animal on which a king rides.[496]

It is fascinating to me that in Zechariah's prophecy, the gentle king who comes into Jerusalem riding a young donkey is the same king who will defeat chariots and war-horses and bring peace to the nations. One of the final scenes of Revelation is a picture of the conquering Christ riding a white war-horse (Revelation 19:11-16), but today he rides a donkey in hope of peace.

When Jesus indicates to his disciples that he should ride on a donkey that no one had ever ridden before, he is initiating a public kingly act. He is revealing openly that he is the Messiah.

> **Q2. (John 12:14-16) What is the prophetic significance of Jesus riding into Jerusalem on a donkey? Why did he do it? What was the effect on the crowds?**
> **http://www.joyfulheart.com/forums/topic/1481-q2-riding-on-a-donkey/**

Continual Praise during the Procession (12:13b)

> "They took palm branches and went out to meet him, shouting, 'Hosanna!' 'Blessed is he who comes in the name of the Lord!' 'Blessed is the King of Israel!'" (12:13b)

It is a day of excitement and jubilation as the King's procession reaches the road's highest point as it crosses the ridge of the Mount of Olives. At this time of year, pilgrims clogging the roads rejoice as they come in sight of the city. And the pilgrims already in Jerusalem, hearing that Jesus is about to enter the city, come out to meet him (12:12, 18). The city is abuzz with the news of Jesus raising Lazarus from the dead, and the pilgrims are eager to see this miracle worker.

As this increasingly large band of "disciples" crosses the ridge and begins its descent into the Kidron Valley the people sing praise from Psalm 118. The sound is increasing. The enthusiasm is building with a carpet of clothing and branches on the road, with singing, and with rejoicing. The Pharisees present in the crowd are scowling. They are deeply offended and can't suppress their disdain. Luke tells us:

> "Some of the Pharisees in the crowd said to Jesus, 'Teacher, rebuke your disciples!'
> 'I tell you,' he replied, 'if they keep quiet, the stones will cry out.'" (Luke 19:39-40)

It Is Time to Be Recognized as Messiah

Up until now Jesus has been very guarded about his identity as Messiah (see, for example, Mark 8:30). Rather than using the term Christ (*christos*, Greek for "anointed one") or Messiah (*māshîah*, Hebrew for "anointed one"), he has usually identified himself as Son of Man. If Jesus had previously acknowledged publicly that he was the Messiah, the political implications would be such that he could not complete his intended ministry of teaching, healing, and proclaiming the Kingdom. But now that ministry is complete.

---

[496] Green, *Luke*, p. 685, fn. 9, mentions Catchpole, "Triumphal Entry," in *Jesus and the Politics of His Day*, edited by Ernst Bammel and C.F.D. Moule (Cambridge University, 1984), p. 324, who cites *Sanh* 2.5.

His claim as King must now be clear. Indeed, this claim of Messiahship, this open acknowledgement of Kingship, seems to precipitate his death. It was certainly on the lips of everyone in Jerusalem that week. Jesus is not crucified for his good works or his miracles. He is killed for his claim to Kingship, to the extent that over his cross is a sign which reads, "King of the Jews" (19:19).

> **Q3. (John 12:12-13) What about the people's praise show they believed Jesus to be the Messiah? On this occasion, why doesn't Jesus shun such an open declaration that he is the Messiah, as he has in the past?**
> http://www.joyfulheart.com/forums/topic/1482-q3-messianic-praise/

> **Q4. If Jesus is your King, what kind of worship is appropriate? What kind of service? What kind of priorities? What kind of obedience? Are you giving Jesus his due as King?**
> http://www.joyfulheart.com/forums/topic/1483-q4-worshiping-the-king/

Witnesses of Lazarus' Resurrection Spread the Word (12:18-19)

This section ends with an ominous note.

> "¹⁸ Many people, because they had heard that he had given this miraculous sign, went out to meet him. ¹⁹ So the Pharisees said to one another, 'See, this is getting us nowhere. Look how the whole world has gone after him!'" (12:17-19)

The Pharisees exaggerate, of course, the way we do when we're frustrated with what's going on. But the Pharisees' conclusion is that half-way measures aren't enough. They must go forward with their plan to kill Jesus. That is the only way to stop him.

The Greeks Ask to See Jesus (12:20-22)

The Pharisees were exaggerating to complain that "the whole world" has gone after him. But in the next verse, John tells us that what they are saying is indeed true![497] The whole world *is* going after him – as evidenced by some Greek-speaking people.

> "²⁰ Now there were some Greeks among those who went up to worship at the Feast. ²¹ They came to Philip, who was from Bethsaida in Galilee, with a request. 'Sir,' they said, 'we would like to see Jesus.' ²² Philip went to tell Andrew; Andrew and Philip in turn told Jesus." (12:20-22)

The "Greeks" were doubtless Greek-speaking Jews from the Jewish Diaspora who had come to the Passover. They came to Philip, who had a Greek name, to ask for an audience with Jesus. We're not told whether or not the Greeks ended up meeting with Jesus.

---

[497] Earlier we see another example of words that can be taken two ways. Caiaphas meant his words one way – "It is better for you that one man die for the people" – but they were actually a prophecy taken another way (11:50).

This coming of the Greeks to see Jesus (12:20-22) may have been a sign of the completion of an era of his ministry to reach out to "the lost sheep of Israel" only (Matthew 10:6; 15:24). The gospel has been declared to the Jews in Palestine. Now is the time for it to be declared in the whole world – which is the thrust of the Great Commission (Matthew 28:19-20; Acts 1:8). This expansion of the gospel mandate beyond the Jews cannot be accomplished by one individual. It can only be adequately accomplished by the Holy Spirit filling the believers and dispersing them throughout the world. As Jesus says later in Holy Week:

"Unless I go away, the Counselor will not come to you; but if I go, I will send him to you." (16:7)

Lessons for Disciples

What are we disciples to make of the anointing and triumphal entry? As I ponder the passages I see several lessons:

1. Mary's act of devotion cost tens of thousands of dollars. Extravagant praise is received by Jesus. Are you ever extravagant in your worship? If so, why? If not, why not?

2. Praise can be received with humility. Jesus did not crave the praise of men, but neither did he silence it. It was fitting. It was appropriate.

3. There is a time to be guarded about who we are in God, and there is a time to be fully open about it. We must not operate out of fear or self-absorption, but be sensitive to what God wants to do and then cooperate with that.

4. And, of course, one of the strongest lessons of this passage is that Jesus *is* King! He *is* the Messiah, the Son of David, and as such, it is fitting that we worship him.

Prayer

Thank you, Jesus, for daring to come as King – even though it cost you dearly. O crucified and risen King, be my King today. In your holy name, I pray. Amen.

Key Verses

"Then Mary took about a pint of pure nard, an expensive perfume; she poured it on Jesus' feet and wiped his feet with her hair. And the house was filled with the fragrance of the perfume." (John 12:3, NIV)

"You will always have the poor among you, but you will not always have me." (John 12:8, NIV)

"They took palm branches and went out to meet him, shouting, 'Hosanna!' 'Blessed is he who comes in the name of the Lord!' 'Blessed is the King of Israel!'" (John 12:13, NIV)

"Jesus found a young donkey and sat upon it, as it is written, 'Do not be afraid, O Daughter of Zion; see, your king is coming, seated on a donkey's colt.'" (John 12:14-15, quoting Zechariah 9:9, NIV)

22. The Hour Has Come to Be Glorified (12:23-50)

This passage chronicles the winding down of Jesus' public ministry. Jesus talks about his death, which he refers to as being "glorified" and "lifted up" and has a final exchange with the Jewish leaders who are intent on discrediting and killing him.

Hour Has Come to Be Glorified (12:23)

"Jesus replied, 'The hour has come for the Son of Man to be glorified.'" (12:23)

"Being glorified" (*doxazō*) seems like a strange way to describe one's death, but we see this idea in the great Suffering Servant passage that begins in Isaiah 52:13 and extends through chapter 53.

"See, my servant will act wisely;
he will be raised and lifted up and highly exalted."
(Isaiah 52:13)

We'll refer to this later in the lesson. For more on this see Appendix 6. "Glory" and "Glorify" in John's Gospel.

Jesus seems to use "being glorified" to refer to his death, resurrection, and ascension.

James J. Tissot, "The Lord's Prayer" (1886-1894), gouache on gray wove paper, 8.5"x6.4", The Brooklyn Museum, New York.

"Up to that time the Spirit had not been given, since Jesus had not yet been **glorified** (*doxazō*)." (7:39b)

"Only after Jesus was **glorified** (*doxazō*) did they realize that these things had been written about him and that they had done these things to him." (12:16b)

"Isaiah said this because he saw Jesus' **glory** (*doxa*) and spoke about him." (12:41)

To the men on the road to Emmaus, Jesus explained the Scriptures and then said:

"Did not the Christ have to suffer these things and then enter his **glory**?" (Luke 24:26)

It's like us humans to think that suffering and pain are bad, and ease is good. But when do we learn the most? When do we make the greatest strides forward? When we're really struggling. We look back at some of those times and marvel how God has helped us. The song "How He Loves," contains the lines:

"When all of a sudden I am unaware of these **afflictions**
Eclipsed by glory and I realize just how beautiful You are,
And how great Your affections are for me."[498]

It's in the afflictions that God's glory shines its brightest. When a lame man walks. When a man born blind sees. It's at times like that the Jesus' glory peeks out for all to see. And on the dark, dark day of the cross, when Jesus says, "It is finished," and breathes his last, his glory blazes out once more as the power of Satan and sin are broken, sin is atoned, and men and women are set free. When, like Moses, we pray, "Show me your glory" (Exodus 33:18), the answer may not be what we anticipated, but when his glory is revealed, it's all worth it.

Kernel of Wheat Dies and Produces Many Seeds (12:24)

Now Jesus begins to explain how his death is the beginning of his glory – as evidenced in the multiplication of one seed to many – but only after death and burial.

"I tell you the truth, unless a kernel of wheat falls to the ground and dies[499], it remains only a single seed. But if it dies, it produces many seeds." (12:24)

Paul repeats this concept in his teaching on the resurrection of the body.

"What you sow does not come to life unless it dies." (1 Corinthians 15:36)

I think Jesus is anticipating the powerful coming of the Holy Spirit that his death, resurrection, and ascension will unleash:

"Unless I go away, the Counselor will not come to you; but if I go, I will send him to you." (16:7)

Then there will be not just a single Man anointed by the Holy Spirit – Jesus – but many, many of his followers all over the world, empowered to advance his Kingdom.

Q1. (John 12:23-24) How can God's glory be revealed even in death? How does the seed illustrate this? How does Jesus' death illustrate this? How does us dying to our old life illustrate this?
http://www.joyfulheart.com/forums/topic/1484-q1-glorified-in-death/

He Who Loves His Life Will Lose It (12:25-26)

Again, Jesus speaks with paradoxes and contrasts.

"The man who loves his life will lose it, while the man who hates his life in this world will keep it for eternal life." (12:25)

"Love" and "hate" are used here as opposites. But "hate" in the New Testament doesn't necessarily carry the visceral emotional content of the concept in English. The lexicographer explains concerning the Greek verb *miseō*:

---

[498] "How He Loves," words and music by John Mark McMillan, © 2005 Integrity's Hosanna! Music.

[499] Of course, from a scientific viewpoint, the seed doesn't die. But from the observation of a farmer – and this audience was made up of people who had experience with subsistence farming – it might well appear like death and burial, and resurrection glory when the seeds appear on the plant.

> "Depending on the context, this verb ranges in meaning from 'disfavor' to 'detest.' The English term 'hate' generally suggests affective connotations that do not always do justice, especially to some Semitic shame-honor oriented use of [the Hebrew equivalent] *shānē'*, (e.g. Deuteronomy 21:15-16) in the sense 'hold in disfavor, be disinclined to, have relatively little regard for.'"[500]

It is also true that Jesus often speaks in hyperbole in order to make his point with greater impact. Nevertheless, the Synoptic Gospels echo this teaching. Twice in Matthew we read the same basic message:

> "Anyone who loves his father or mother more than me is not worthy of me; anyone who loves his son or daughter more than me is not worthy of me; and anyone who does not take his cross and follow me is not worthy of me. Whoever finds his life will lose it, and whoever loses his life for my sake will find it." (Matthew 10:37-39)

> "If anyone would come after me, he must deny himself and take up his cross and follow me. For whoever wants to save his life will lose it, but whoever loses his life for me will find it." (Matthew 16:24-25)

Verse 26 provides a corollary to verse 25.

> "Whoever serves me must follow me; and where I am, my servant also will be. My Father will honor the one who serves me." (12:26)

If Jesus is in a dangerous place – like Jerusalem, or the barrios of the inner city, or on a mission in a Muslim land – his servants, his disciples will be there also. We naturally seek to protect ourselves and our possessions. But that is putting ourselves before Jesus. What he demands is the opposite: to follow him, even when it leads you into danger. Disciples are not wimps or cowards; Jesus calls us to a courageous Christianity. We see this kind of courage modeled in Jesus' words in the next verse:

> "What shall I say? 'Father, save me from this hour'? No, it was for this very reason I came to this hour. Father, glorify your name!" (12:27b-28a)

Jesus sees the danger coming, but refuses to shrink from it. Rather he must do what he is called to do.

The principle of this verse is the bedrock of what it means to be a disciple:

> "The man who loves his life will lose it, while the man who hates his life in this world will keep it for eternal life." (12:25)

For us, the issue is not necessarily danger, but willingness to obey in the small things. For us, the good can easily be the enemy of the best. We are doing things we enjoy, things that are good, things that are not sin. But the still, small voice of the Spirit is saying, stop doing that, stop living there. I've got something better for you. We are confused. There's nothing wrong with what I am doing, Lord. Why should I stop? And we aren't given the reasons. We aren't always to know – until much later, and maybe not even then. But our Lord's way is better. If we let him guide our lives by giving up what he asks of us, and taking on what he shows us, the place he leads us will be the center of his will for us. Not always comfortable. Not necessarily pain free. But the place of an obedient disciple serving Christ as he is leading.

---

[500] *Miseō*, BDAG 652.

Can you do this? This was the issue Jesus faced in the Garden of Gethsemane, and it is our issue today. Not my will, but yours be done. It is the way of Jesus.

Q2. (John 12:25-26) In what way is verse 25 the essence of what it means to be a disciple? In this verse, what does it mean to "love" your life? What does it mean to "hate" your life? How did Jesus live this out in the Garden of Gethsemane?
http://www.joyfulheart.com/forums/topic/1485-q2-loving-your-life/

Father, Glorify Your Name (12:27-30)

"Now my heart is troubled...." (12:27a)

Why is Jesus' heart "troubled"[501]? Is he troubled for himself? Is this what we see in the Garden of Gethsemane, when Jesus asks the Father to remove this cup from him? Probably, given the immediate context. But in the larger context of the Triumphal Entry, Luke 19:41-44 records Jesus weeping over Jerusalem and their fate, since they won't recognize the Messiah who came to them.

Whatever Jesus is troubled by, he doesn't give into the natural human reaction to escape from danger and death. Rather he sees that this is his "time," his "hour" to glorify the Father in his death, resurrection, and ascension. Prior to this, Jesus has slipped away from his enemies and ministered elsewhere to avoid arrest and stoning (7:30; 8:59; 10:31, 39; 11:53-54). Jesus is very aware of timing. Until now, his "time" or "hour" had not yet come (2:4; 7:8; 7:30; 8:20). But now is his time. Now he faces it head on.

"[27] Now my heart is troubled, and what shall I say? 'Father, save me from this hour'? No, it was for this very reason I came to this hour. [28] Father, glorify your name!" (12:27-28a)

Jesus clearly sees his death as glorifying the Father, since, according to the Father's plan, Jesus' sacrificial death is necessary to atone for the sins of the whole world, and redeem men and women to fellowship with their Creator.[502]

"[28] 'Father, glorify your name!' Then a voice came from heaven, 'I have glorified it, and will glorify it again.' [29] The crowd that was there and heard it said it had thundered; others said an angel had spoken to him. [30] Jesus said, 'This voice was for your benefit[503], not mine.'" (12:28-30)

The Father's audible voice confirms Jesus' words to the crowds and disciples who are present on this occasion – though they don't have the spiritual acuity to understand it. This is the third occasion in Jesus' ministry where the audible voice of God is heard (though the only one recorded by John) – first, at his baptism (Matthew 3:17) and second, at his transfiguration (Matthew 17:5). The crowds don't know what to make of it. But Jesus is clear: the voice isn't for his benefit. His communion with the Father is such that he knows this already.

---

[501] "Troubled" is *tarassō*, which we saw in 11:33 at Lazarus's tomb. It means, "to cause inward turmoil, stir up, disturb, unsettle, throw into confusion" (BDAG 991, 2).

[502] John 1:29; 11:51-42; 1 John 2:2; 4:10; Romans 3:25; 1 Peter 2:24; 3:18.

[503] This is the preposition *dia* with the accusative: "the reason why something happens, results, exists: because of, for the sake of" (BDAG 225, B2a).

Casting Out the Prince of This World (12:31)

> "Now is the time for judgment on this world; now the prince of this world will be driven out." (12:31)

Here's a paradox. Jesus is speaking of his own death and at the same time he is saying that by condemning Jesus to death on the cross, the world itself is being judged. They have received a sentence of condemnation (*krisis*).[504] The world thinks it is passing judgment on Jesus, but the cross passes judgment on them, for when they reject the Son, they reject the Father who sent him. As Jesus said earlier in John's Gospel:

> "Whoever believes in him is not condemned, but whoever does not believe stands condemned[505] already because he has not believed in the name of God's one and only Son." (3:18)

Indeed, the Holy Spirit will "convict the world ... in regard to judgment (*krisis*) because the prince of this world now stands condemned (*krinō*)" (16:8, 11).

The devil is prince of "all the kingdoms of the world and their splendor" (Matthew 4:8-10). The "prince of this world" is mentioned one more time in John:

> "... The prince of this world is coming. He has no hold on me...." (14:30)

In 2 Corinthians 4:4 Satan is called "the god of this world." This coming of the "prince of this world" culminates in Jesus' arrest in the Garden of Gethsemane, when Jesus tells his captors, "This is your hour – when darkness reigns" (Luke 22:53). But this reign of darkness is short-lived! Hallelujah!

Our text says:

> "Now the prince of this world will be driven out." (12:31b)

The verb "driven out" (NIV, NRSV), "cast out" (ESV, KJV) is *ekballō*, "to throw out," here, "force to leave, drive out, expel."[506] The verb is followed by the adverb *exō*, "out," pertaining to a position outside an area or limits, as result of an action.[507] It gives the sense of thrown *completely* out!

What does this mean? We can't be sure, but several passages shed some light on the question. The first is Jesus' words after seventy-two disciples return from a mission:

> "The seventy-two returned with joy and said, 'Lord, even the demons submit to us in your name.' He replied, '**I saw Satan fall like lightning from heaven**. I have given you authority to trample on snakes and scorpions and to overcome all the power of the enemy; nothing will harm you.'" (Luke 10:17-19)

> "And having disarmed the powers and authorities, he made a public spectacle of them, **triumphing over them** by the cross." (Colossians 2:15)

> "He ... shared in their humanity so that **by his death he might destroy him** who holds the power of death – that is, the devil." (Hebrews 2:14)

---

[504] *Krisis*, "legal process of judgment, judging, judgment." The word often means "judgment that goes against a person, condemnation, and the sentence that follows" (BDAG 569, 1aβ).

[505] "Condemned" in 3:18 is *krinō*, the verb form of *krisis*. The basic meaning is "to set apart so as to distinguish, separate." Here, the sense is, "to engage in a judicial process, judge, decide, hale before a court, condemn, also hand over for judicial punishment," frequently as a legal technical term. (BDAG 568, 5bα).

[506] *Ekballō*, BDAG 299, 1.

[507] *Exō*, BDAG 354, 2a.

"The reason the Son of God appeared was **to destroy the devil's work.**" (1 John 3:8b)

The final passage is a vision in the Book of Revelation about the fall of Satan.

"⁷ And there was war in heaven. Michael and his angels fought against the dragon, and the dragon and his angels fought back. ⁸ But he was not strong enough, and they **lost their place in heaven**. ⁹ The great dragon was **hurled down** – that ancient serpent called the devil, or Satan, who leads the whole world astray. He was hurled to the earth, and his angels with him.
¹⁰ Then I heard a loud voice in heaven say:
'Now have come the salvation and the power
and the kingdom of our God,
and the authority of his Christ.
For the accuser of our brothers,
who accuses them before our God day and night,
has been **hurled down**.[508]
¹¹ They overcame him by the blood of the Lamb
and by the word of their testimony;
they did not love their lives so much as to shrink from death.
¹² Therefore rejoice, you heavens and you who dwell in them!
But woe to the earth and the sea,
because the devil has gone down to you!
He is filled with fury, because he knows that his time is short.'" (Revelation 12:7-12)

I wish we understood more about the present state of Satan and his angels. Much of what we think we know is speculative, deduced by reading between the lines and trying to piece together clues from various parts of the Bible to create a comprehensive picture. What we do know at the very least, however, are these truths:

1. Jesus won profound and decisive victories over Satan during his temptations in the wilderness before his ministry, during his ministry in "binding the strong man and plundering his goods" (Luke 11:20-22), and through his death, resurrection, and ascension.
2. Satan's power is broken. The key battle has been won, but Satan is still dangerous. He is still considered "the god of this world" (2 Corinthians 4:4) and the world is still under his control (1 John 5:19).
3. Through the Holy Spirit, Christians have power over Satan and demons (Luke 10:17-19; Mark 16:17). Greater is the Spirit in us than Satan, demons, and the antichrist (1 John 4:4).
4. The final battle where Satan's hold on this world is completely broken will take place in the Last Days at the coming of Christ (Revelation 20:10).

Son of Man Will Be Lifted Up (12:32-34)

Now we consider Jesus' declarations about being lifted up.

"³² 'But I, when I am lifted up from the earth, will draw all men to myself.'
³³ He said this to show the kind of death he was going to die. ³⁴ The crowd spoke up, 'We have

---

[508] In Revelation 12:9-10, "Hurled down" (NIV), "thrown down" (NRSV, ESV), "cast out" (KJV) is the verb *ballō*, "to cause to move from one location to another through use of forceful motion, throw" (BDAG 163, 1b).

heard from the Law that the Christ will remain forever, so how can you say, "The Son of Man must be lifted up"? Who is this "Son of Man"?'" (12:31-34)

Jesus' insight comes from the great Suffering Servant passage in Isaiah 52:13-53:12. This passage begins with these words:

> "See, my servant will act wisely;
> he will be raised and lifted up (*hypsoō*) and highly[509] exalted (*doxazō*)."
> (Isaiah 52:13)[510]

I have indicated in parentheses the Greek words used in the Septuagint translation of the Old Testament. They are the same as the words in John's Gospel where Jesus describes his being "lifted up" and his "glorification."

While Jesus' words about being lifted up refer initially to his being lifted up on the cross (12:32-33), his words seem to have a triple meaning – (1) being lifted up on the cross, (2) being raised or lifted up from the grave, and (3) being lifted up to heaven in the ascension. Here are the three passages on "lifting up" in John's Gospel, all using the verb *hypsoō*, "to lift up spatially, lift up, raise high."[511]

> "Just as Moses **lifted up** the snake in the desert, so the Son of Man must be **lifted up** (*hypsoō*), that everyone who believes in him may have eternal life." (3:14-15)

> "When you have **lifted up** the Son of Man, then you will know that I am [the one I claim to be] and that I do nothing on my own but speak just what the Father has taught me." (8:28)

> "'But I, when I am **lifted up** from the earth, will draw all men to myself.' He said this to show the kind of death he was going to die." (12:32-33)

So John speaks of Jesus' glorification and being lifted up in a way that includes the crucifixion, resurrection, and ascension as a single event.

Q3. (John 12:32-33) What does Jesus mean when he talks about being "lifted up." Do you think Jesus means being "lifted up" literally or figuratively or both? "Extra credit": How does this phrase relate to Isaiah 52:13? How does it relate to Philippians 2:8-9?
http://www.joyfulheart.com/forums/topic/1486-q3-lifted-up/

Sons of Light (12:35-36)

> "[35] Then Jesus told them, 'You are going to have the light just a little while longer. Walk while you have the light, before darkness overtakes you. The man who walks in the dark does not know where he is going. [36] Put your trust in the light while you have it, so that you may become sons of light.' When he had finished speaking, Jesus left and hid himself from them." (12:35-36)

---

[509] *Sphodra*, "very much, exceedingly" (Liddell-Scott, *Lexicon*).

[510] Paul says something similar: "Therefore God exalted him to the highest place (*hyperypsoō*) and gave him the name that is above every name...." (Philippians 2:9). *Hyperypsoō* means, "to raise to a high point of honor, raise, exalt" (BDAG 1034, 1).

[511] *Hypsoō*, BDAG 1046, 2.

Here, Jesus isn't talking about daylight fading, but the crucifixion of the Light of the World that is coming soon. Jesus says,

"Put your trust in the light while you have it, so that you may become sons of light." (12:36a)

Jesus is saying to the crowd listening to him: Put your trust in me now, while I'm still here. This way you will be "sons of light," that is, people who take on the nature of light themselves, by their faith in and emulation of me – in the way that Jesus had said to his disciples, "You are the light of the world..." (Matthew 5:14-16).

Isaiah's Prophecy of Blind Eyes (12:37-41)

In each of the Gospels, but especially in John's Gospel, we see the terrible irony of people seeing powerful miracles, but reacting to them in different ways, depending upon the openness of their hearts. John comments on this, quoting a passage from Isaiah 6:10, also quoted in the Synoptics (Matthew 13:11-17; Mark 4:12; Luke 8:10) and Acts 28:26.

"37 Even after Jesus had done all these miraculous signs in their presence, they still would not believe in him. 38 This was to fulfill the word of Isaiah the prophet:

'Lord, who has believed our message
and to whom has the arm of the Lord been revealed?' [Quoting Isaiah 53:1]

39 For this reason they could not believe, because, as Isaiah says elsewhere:

40 'He has blinded their eyes and deadened their hearts,
so they can neither see with their eyes,
nor understand with their hearts,
nor turn – and I would heal them.' [quoting Isaiah 6:10]

41 Isaiah said this because he saw Jesus' glory and spoke about him." (12:37-41)

Isaiah's task is to preach God's word as a faithful witness, knowing that his preaching will have the effect of hardening the hearts of those who have set their hearts against God. In the same way, Jesus' teaching and miracles have a hardening effect on those who resist God.

Q4. (John 12:37-41) In what way does declaring truth to resistant people harden them further? How can a person (or a Pharisee) see a miracle and become even more determined to resist Jesus? How do you understand this paradox?
http://www.joyfulheart.com/forums/topic/1487-q4-hardened-hearts/

Loved Men's Praise More than God's (12:42-43)

Many rejected Jesus, but many believed in him.

"⁴² Yet at the same time many even among the leaders believed[512] in him. But because of the Pharisees they would not confess[513] their faith for fear they would be put out of the synagogue; ⁴³ for they loved praise from men more than praise from God." (12:42-43)

To be a believer in Jerusalem at that time was difficult. Jesus' enemies were prominent Pharisees, influential in the city's synagogues. They had let it be known that any believers in Jesus as the Messiah would be excommunicated from membership in their neighborhood synagogue, their primary religious and social community. The adjective *aposynagōgos* means, "expelled from the synagogue, excluded, put under a curse/ban."[514]

John explores various kinds of belief in this Gospel.

1. Belief resulting from miracles that goes no further.
2. Belief in Jesus that isn't confessed openly because of fear (as in this passage).
3. Belief in Jesus that may have started with miracles, but continues to open, confessing faith and following (the faith of the disciples, of Mary and Martha, the man born blind, etc.).

At times in church history, believers have been threatened with death unless they recant. All of the eleven apostles, except John himself, were martyred for their faith. In later Roman persecutions, many caved into the pressure, but some, such as St. Polycarp of Smyrna (69 to 155-160 AD), refused to recant.

"Eighty and six years have I served Him, and He never did me any injury: how then can I blaspheme my King and my Savior?"[515]

But here, John is talking about social pressure – excommunication from the synagogue – not physical punishment or execution. And John – who himself was exiled for his faith to the island of Patmos (Revelation 1:9) – is critical to those whose faith isn't strong enough to stand during persecution.

"... For they loved praise from men more than praise from God." (12:43)

"Praise" (NIV, KJV), "glory" (NRSV, ESV) is noun is *doxa*, "glory." Here it refers to "honor as enhancement or recognition of status or performance, fame, recognition, renown, honor, prestige."[516] In our passage, John has been talking about Jesus being "glorified" by his death. But many so-called believers shun true "glorification" from God, in exchange for approval by or glory from their peers. Not a good trade!

In his Parable of the Sower or Soils, Jesus referred to such fair-weather believers with the figure of seeds sown on rocky soil.

---

[512] "Believed" is in the Aorist tense, action at a past point of time.

[513] "Confess" is in the Imperfect tense, continued action in the past.

[514] *Aposynagōgos*, BDAG 123. The word is used three times in John – 9:22; 12:42; and 16:2.

[515] *Martyrdom of Polycarp*, 9. A recent article in *Christianity Today* pondered whether the church in the Middle East might become extinct, due to intense persecution from radical Islam. The author traces church history to examine other times when the church has responded to such persecution, such as in Japan and China in previous centuries. The church in situations like this often goes underground, with clandestine meetings, etc., with believers who are hidden, but believing – "crypto-Christians" (Philip Jenkins, "On the Edge of Extinction," *Christianity Today*, November 2014, pp. 36-42).

[516] *Doxa*, BDAG 257, 3.

"The one who received the seed that fell on rocky places is the man who hears the word and at once receives it with joy. But since he has no root, he lasts only a short time. When trouble or persecution comes because of the word, he quickly falls away." (Matthew 13:20-21)

Were they "true believers"? Some debate this. But we know they didn't persevere to bear fruit. Sad!

Dear friend, are you afraid to be open about your faith in Christ because some people in your circle of friends might criticize or reject you? Christ is calling you to the faithfulness of a true believer!

Q5. (John 12:42-43) When we are quiet about our relationship to God out of fear that people will criticize us, what does this say about our priorities? About whether we are true disciples? When Peter denied knowing Jesus in the High Priest's courtyard, what was the effect in his life? http://www.joyfulheart.com/forums/topic/1488-q5-praise-of-men/

The Believer Sees the One Who Sent Me (12:44-46)

In the last few verses of chapter 12, Jesus speaks encouragement to those who hear and believe (verses 44-46), as well as a warning to those who hear but do not follow Jesus' teaching (verses 47-50).

Jesus begins by clarifying what belief or faith entails. He cries out these words in a loud voice:[517]

"Then Jesus cried out, 'When a man believes in me, he does not believe in me only, but in the one who sent me.'" (12:44)

For Jesus there is no separation between belief in the Son and belief in the Father. If people really know the Father they will recognize and welcome the Son. To his enemies, the Pharisees, he said:

"You do not know me or my Father.... If you knew me, you would know my Father also." (8:19)

Jesus continues:

"When he looks at me, he sees the one who sent me." (12:44)

What an amazing statement. Later Jesus clarifies it to Philip, who asks Jesus to show them the Father: "Anyone who has seen me has seen the Father" (John 14:19).

The question for us today is, if someone looks at you, will he see the One you believe in? If not, why not? To be disciplers, people who disciple others, we must have a life in which Christ is visible and a life worth imitating. As Paul taught:

"Follow my example[518], as I follow the example of Christ." (1 Corinthians 11:1; cf. 4:16)

Jesus concludes this section with another reference to himself as the "Light of the World" (8:12):

"I have come into the world as a light, so that no one who believes in me should stay in darkness." (12:46)

---

[517] *Krazō*, "to communicate something in a loud voice, call, call out, cry" (BDAG 564, 2a). Jesus also calls out loudly at the Feast of Tabernacles: "If anyone is thirsty, let him come to me and drink" (7:37).

[518] "Follow my example" (NIV) is more literally, "imitate me" (NRSV, ESV), "be followers of me" (KJV) is the verb *ginomai*, "become, be" and the noun *mimētēs*, "imitator" (BDAG 652, a).

This is a theme developed earlier in this Gospel (1:4-5; 3:19; 8:12; 9:5). The Apostle John carries this idea into his First Epistle as well:

> "But if we walk in the light, as he is in the light, we have fellowship with one another, and the blood of Jesus, his Son, purifies us from all sin." (1 John 1:7)

People have a choice whether or not they wish to "stay[519] in darkness" (12:45). When we move into the light – and then walk or conduct our lives there, then we live in his light. That is, we make a life practice of following the teachings of the One in whom we believe. Those who claim to believe, but refuse to walk in Jesus' teachings, deceive themselves if they think they are really Christ's followers (1 John 1:6).

The Unbeliever Will Be Judged by My Words (12:47-50)

Now Jesus turns from the blessings of the believer to warn those who hear – and even understand – but don't follow Jesus' teachings.

> "[47] As for the person who hears my words but does not keep them, I do not judge him. For I did not come to judge the world, but to save it. [48] There is a judge for the one who rejects me and does not accept my words; that very word which I spoke will condemn him at the last day." (12:47-48)

These people hear and seem to understand. The verb "hears" is *akouō* with the genitive object: "to hear," usually to hear with appreciation and understanding.[520] But they don't go the next step of keeping Jesus' message or teaching.[521] "Keep" (NIV, NRSV, ESV) in verse 47 is found in all the earlier manuscripts, in contrast to the KJV's "believe," which is found only in late manuscripts. The verb is *phylassō*, "watch, guard." Here it has the meaning, "to continue to keep a law or commandment from being broken, observe, follow."[522] We're not under Jesus' words as a law, whereby if we keep them we are saved. Rather, we keep Jesus' words and observe his teachings as an indicator that we actually believe in him. Jesus said something similar in his Parable of the Wise and Foolish Builders:

> "Everyone who hears these words of mine and does not put them into practice is like a foolish man who built his house on sand." (Matthew 7:26)

There is a pitfall that those of us who attend church can easily fall into – of thinking that *familiarity* with Jesus' words is the same as *keeping* them! Jesus' brother James notes:

> "Do not merely listen to the word, and so deceive yourselves. Do what it says." (James 1:22)

Jesus says about a person who hears but doesn't follow:

> "I do not judge him. For I did not come to judge the world, but to save it." (12:47b)

Some people imagine that if they do something bad God will strike them down with a bolt of lightning: active judgment. I didn't come to judge, Jesus says, but to save! When his disciples want to call down fire on a Samaritan village that wouldn't receive Jesus, he rebukes them. In some

---

[519] "Stay" (NIV), "remain" (NRSV, ESV), "abide" (KJV) is *menō*, in transferred sense, "of someone who does not leave a certain realm or sphere: remain, continue, abide" (BDAG 631, 1aβ).

[520] Morris, *John*, p. 608, n. 120, cf. also p. 318, n. 76; Brown, *John* 1:491; BDAG 37, definitions 7 or 1bγ.

[521] "Words" is the plural of *rhēma*, "that which is said, word, saying, expression, or statement of any kind" BDAG 905, 1).

[522] *Phylassō*, BDAG 1068, 5a.

manuscripts he says, "The Son of man did not come to destroy men's lives, but to save them" (Luke 9:56, NKJV). Jesus is criticized for associating with tax collectors and sinners without telling them how bad they are. His reply is:

> "It is not the healthy who need a doctor, but the sick. But go and learn what this means: 'I desire mercy, not sacrifice.' For I have not come to call the righteous, but sinners." (Matthew 9:12-13)

Jesus didn't come with an impatient judgmental spirit, but a spirit of love, mercy, and patience (2 Peter 3:9).

But those who don't follow his teachings don't get off scot-free. Though they are not subject to immediate judgment, nevertheless they will be held responsible for Jesus' words, for they are the Father's words.

> "[48] There is a judge for the one who rejects me and does not accept my words; that very word which I spoke will condemn him at the last day. [49] For I did not speak of my own accord, but the Father who sent me commanded me what to say and how to say it. [50] I know that his command leads to eternal life. So whatever I say is just what the Father has told me to say." (12:48-50)

Q6. (John 12:47-49) In what way can judging people get in the way of saving them? How did Jesus deal with this in his own ministry? What will it take for us to lose our stiffness and judgmental demeanor so that we might be able to be Jesus' agents of salvation?
http://www.joyfulheart.com/forums/topic/1489-q6-judging-and-resucing/

Jesus is fulfilling the description of the prophet predicted in Deuteronomy:

> "I will raise up for them a prophet like you from among their brothers; I will put my words in his mouth, and he will tell them everything I command him." (Deuteronomy 18:18)

While the NIV of verse 49 reads, "what to say and how to say it,"[523] it is probably better to render the verbs as synonyms, that the Father tells Jesus "what to say (*eipon*[524]) and what to speak (*laleō*[525])" (NRSV, ESV, cf. KJV).[526] That being said, it is true that God can guide us in both the words to say and how to say it, whether as a parable or a saying or a rebuke (12:49). Recently, God gave me a rebuke for a group I was speaking to – and told me to deliver this message on my knees, so that they might be more inclined to receive it. God wants to – and is able to – guide us in not just *what*, but *how* to say it, if we'll seek him for this wisdom.

---

[523] Supported without much comment by Brown, *John* 1:489, and Carson, *John*, p. 452.

[524] *Eipon*, used as the second aorist of *legō*, "say, tell" (BDAG 286, 1a).

[525] *Laleō*. In older Greek it referred to small talk, but in the New Testament it is becoming the equivalent to *legō*, with the meaning, "to utter words, talk, speak" (BDAG 582, 2aβ).

[526] The verbs are synonyms that are difficult to differentiate here. So Morris, *John*, p. 609. Barrett (*John*, p. 435) sees the use of synonyms as characteristic of John's style.

Lessons for Disciples

1. God's glory can reveal itself even in death, as expressed in the parable of the seed that dies and is buried (12:23-24).

2. We disciples must not hang onto our lives, but surrender them to God, otherwise we'll lose them (12:25-26). This willingness to surrender our lives to obey Christ is at the very basis of what it means to be a disciple. Jesus gave us an example of the surrender of our wills in the Garden of Gethsemane.

3. Jesus sees his death – "being lifted up from the earth" – as the precursor of being exalted by the Father and glorified, as prophesied in Isaiah 52:13 (12:32-34).

4. We must recognize, as Jesus did, that sharing truth with people who resist God has the effect of hardening already hard hearts even further. The same miracle or teaching can cause one person to believe and another to become harder in unbelief (12:37-41).

5. Failure to publicly side with Jesus out of fear of people's criticism, shows that we care more about the praise of men than of God (12:42-43).

6. Like Jesus, we are effective only when people can clearly see God in us (12:44).

7. Jesus didn't come to judge people, but to save them. We need to dispense with our judgmental attitude and adopt Jesus' mission strategy. People who reject the truths of God that we share with them will be judged by those very words on Judgment Day unless they repent – though judgment isn't our goal (12:47-49).

Prayer

Father, teach us to find the glory in laying down our lives before you in trust and obedience. We often don't trust you enough to surrender to you. Forgive us. Help us grow, Lord. Help us become like our Master Jesus. In his holy name, we pray. Amen.

Key Verses

"The hour has come for the Son of Man to be glorified. I tell you the truth, unless a kernel of wheat falls to the ground and dies, it remains only a single seed. But if it dies, it produces many seeds." (John 12:23-24, NIV)

"The man who loves his life will lose it, while the man who hates his life in this world will keep it for eternal life." (John 12:25, NIV)

"Now my heart is troubled, and what shall I say? 'Father, save me from this hour'? No, it was for this very reason I came to this hour. [28] Father, glorify your name!" (John 12:27-28a, NIV)

"'But I, when I am lifted up from the earth, will draw all men to myself.' He said this to show the kind of death he was going to die." (John 12:32-33, NIV)

"Many even among the leaders believed in him. But because of the Pharisees they would not confess their faith for fear they would be put out of the synagogue; for they loved praise from men more than praise from God." (John 12:42-43, NIV)

"When a man believes in me, he does not believe in me only, but in the one who sent me. When he looks at me, he sees the one who sent me." (John 12:44P-45, NIV)

"As for the person who hears my words but does not keep them, I do not judge him. For I did not come to judge the world, but to save it. There is a judge for the one who rejects me and does not accept my words; that very word which I spoke will condemn him at the last day." (John 12:47-48, NIV)

"For I did not speak of my own accord, but the Father who sent me commanded me what to say and how to say it." (John 12:49, NIV)

Section III. The Farewell Discourses (13:1 – 17:26)

If the type of Jesus' teaching most featured in the Synoptic Gospels is the parable, then in John it is the discourse. In the first part of John – sometimes known as "The Book of Signs" – these discourses mainly follow signs, that is, miracles intended to point to Jesus as the Christ. The second part of John – sometimes known as "The Book of Glory" – begins with a series of Farewell Discourses that talk about a New Commandment, Christ the Way, the coming of the Holy Spirit, Jesus' going to the Father, the True Vine, capped by Jesus' High Priestly prayer.

The genre of Farewell Discourses is seen elsewhere the final words or testaments of famous men in the Hellenistic world, but especially in the Bible – Jacob's last words to his sons (Genesis 49), Joshua's final words to Israel (Joshua 22-24), and David's address to Solomon (1 Chronicles 28-29).

Duccio di Buoninsegna, "Christ Taking Leave of His Disciples" panel from the Maesta Altarpiece (1308–1311), Museo dell'Opera Metropolitana del Duomo, Siena, Italy.

Two important questions have been raised about Jesus' Farewell Discourses. First, where do they begin? Some believe they begin them at 14:1, where Jesus begins to talk of his leaving the disciples. Others see the beginning at 13:31, where Jesus speaks of a "new commandment," to love one another.[527] I've begun this section when Jesus and his disciples had a meal in the Upper Room, following the close of Jesus' public ministry.[528]

A second important question is whether these discourses were completed in the Upper Room or perhaps elsewhere, because of Jesus' words, "Come now; let us leave" at the end of chapter 14. We'll consider that question in Lesson 25.

---

[527] So Carson, *John*, pp. 476-477.
[528] So Morris, *John*, pp. 610-611.

23. Washing the Disciples' Feet, Love One Another (13:1-38)

I suppose that the account of Jesus washing his disciples feet is one that comes to mind perhaps more than any other of Jesus' acts – with the exception of the cross. Humble service! It is so important, and yet so difficult to perform consistently from the heart!

Though parables as "stories with a point" are not prominent in John as in the Synoptics, John's Gospel does include parables, in particular, the acted parable of washing the disciples' feet.

Timing of the Footwashing (13:1a)

"It was just before the Passover Feast... The evening meal[529] was being served...." (13:1a, 2a)

There is difficulty dating Jesus' betrayal and crucifixion in John's Gospel because of differences from the Synoptic accounts.[530]

Ford Madox Brown (British Pre-Raphaelite painter, (1821-93), 'Jesus Washing Peter's Feet' (1852-56), oil on canvas, 1167 x 133 mm, Tate Gallery, London.

But the footwashing described here apparently took place the same night as the Last Supper, since the incident of Jesus predicting Peter's betrayal (tied to the Last Supper in the Synoptics) takes place during what seems to be the same evening. John doesn't include any mention of the Last Supper, since he assumes that his readers are acquainted with one or more of the Synoptic Gospels that were circulating among the churches by the late first century. Instead, he relates another teaching from that night that the Synoptic Gospels omit. For further information, see Appendix 7. The Chronology of Holy Week in John's Gospel.

[529] "Evening meal" (NIV), "supper" (NRSV, ESV, KJV) is *deipnon*, "the main meal of the day." It can refer to an everyday meal, or of a formal meal with guests, "feast, dinner" (BDAG 215, bα).

[530] At first glance, John seems to place Jesus' crucifixion on Passover itself, rather than the Last Supper as a Passover Meal as the Synoptics do. The issues are complex, but the difficulties can probably be resolved either by assuming a different calendar system used in John from the Synoptics, or care in interpreting the verses that regard dating. (For more details, see Appendix 7. The Chronology of Holy Week in John's Gospel.)

Prologue to the Footwashing (1:1-3)

Up to this point, John has related Jesus' public ministry of signs and discourses. Again and again we see Jesus saying something like, "My hour has not yet come" (2:4; 7:6, 8, 30; 8:20;). But now the situation changes; Jesus knows that the hour is upon him, the time has come.

> "¹ It was just before the Passover Feast. Jesus knew that the time had come for him to leave this world and go to the Father. Having loved his own who were in the world, he now showed them the full extent of his love. ² The evening meal was being served, and the devil had already prompted Judas Iscariot, son of Simon, to betray Jesus. ³ Jesus knew that the Father had put all things under his power, and that he had come from God and was returning to God...." (13:1-3)

John makes two assertions to introduce this transition in his Gospel.

1. Jesus knows that his time had come to be crucified – that he has come from God and is returning to God.

2. Jesus knows that Judas will betray him, but it is under the Father's rule.

Knowing these two facts would cause you and me to panic, but Jesus acts deliberately in full assurance that this night will play out precisely according to his Father's will.

The Setting of the Last Supper

Peter and John had been tasked with securing a room in Jerusalem and preparing for the meal (Luke 22:7-13). The remaining disciples now enter with Jesus. They are arranged around a very low table, reclining on their left arms and supported by divans or cushions, leaving their right hands free to feed themselves. Their feet, sandals removed, are splayed out behind them, with some space between their feet and the walls so those serving the meal can bring the various dishes to the table.

This traditional Passover would be like the twenty or thirty Passovers each of them had experienced before, except that, instead of gathering with their extended families, they gather tonight as a spiritual family of Jesus' followers.

Who Is the Greatest? (Luke 22:24-27)

We know from Luke's Gospel that even at this holy meal, there is an undercurrent of unrest among the disciples.

> "A dispute arose among them as to which of them was considered to be greatest." (Luke 22:24)

This wasn't the first time the subject had come up, but here it is again at this most holy meal – perhaps sparked by the seating arrangements at this meal, with John on Jesus' right, and perhaps Judas to his left (John 13:23-26). Jesus uses this dispute as a "teachable moment."

Washing the Disciples' Feet (13:4-5)

It is at this point, I believe that Jesus gets up from the table to perform an outrageous act of humility – Jesus, the One they believe to be the Christ, the Messiah, their Rabbi (Hebrew "great one"), their Teacher ("Master," KJV).

"⁴ ... He[531] got up from the meal, took off his outer clothing and wrapped a towel around his waist.
⁵ After that, he poured water into a basin and began to wash his disciples' feet, drying[532] them with the towel that was wrapped around him." (13:4-5)

Since feet clad only in sandals tend to get dusty on the unpaved roads of Palestine, it was customary for a host to provide a basin of water so guests could wash their own feet.[533] Washing someone else's feet was a task reserved for the most menial of servants. A Jewish commentary on the Book of Exodus suggests that Jewish slaves could not be required to wash the feet of others, that it was so demeaning it should be reserved for Gentile slaves or for women, children, or pupils.[534] A wife might wash a husband's feet; a child might wash a parent's feet. Rarely a disciple might honor a distinguished rabbi by washing his feet. But for a superior to wash an inferior's feet was unheard of! It was never ever done!

But Jesus does it. John describes the scene. Jesus takes off his outer clothing[535], and wraps[536] a towel[537] about his waist – typical servant attire (Luke 12:37; 17:8[538]). His disciples are dressed in their best for the Passover Meal while Jesus looks like a servant. It is humiliating for the disciples.

But Jesus goes further. He pours some water into a basin[539] and proceeds to gently wash the feet of the disciples, whose feet are splayed out as they recline around the table.

If you've ever participated in a footwashing service, you know that most people's feet aren't soft and pretty – especially older people whose toes have been broken numerous times and whose feet are often bony and calloused. These disciples are relatively young, but have spent their lives in sandals or bare feet, and have suffered many minor injuries – not to mention the dust of the day.

Jesus takes the feet of each disciple in his hands, washes them gently, then dries them with the towel that is around his waist. Finishing, he goes to the next and to the next. I imagine that the room is absolutely still, except for softly spoken encouragements of love from the Master. His disciples don't know what to say. It is painful for them to see him like this. To submit to this intimate service from him. It is awkward in the extreme!

Simon Peter's Objection (13:6-9)

But when he comes to Peter, the bold fisherman can't stop himself from protesting.

---

[531] "So" in the NIV is not in the Greek text.

[532] "Dry" (NIV), "wipe" (NRSV, ESV, KJV) is *ekmasso*, "to cause to become dry by wiping with a substance, wipe" (BDAG 306).

[533] Brown, *John* 2:564.

[534] *Mekhilta* §1 on Exodus 21:2.

[535] "Outer clothing/garments" (NIV, ESV), "outer robe" (NRSV), "garments" is *himation*, "a piece of clothing," here, of outer clothing, "cloak, robe" (BDAG 475, 2).

[536] "Wrapped around ... waist" (NIV), "girded" (KJV) is *diazōnnymi*, "tie around" (BDAG 228), from *dia* + *zōnnymi*, "gird," in verses 4 and 5.

[537] "Towel" is *lention*, "linen cloth, towel" (BDAG 592), in verses 4 and 5.

[538] In both these verses the servant "girds himself" (*perizōnnymi*, from *peri-*, "all around" + *zōnnymi*, "gird") as Jesus did.

[539] "Basin" is *niptēr*, "(wash) basin" (BDAG 674), from the verb *niptō*, "to wash," used in this verse.

> "[6] He came to Simon Peter, who said to him, 'Lord, are you going to wash my feet?'
>
> [7] Jesus replied, 'You do not realize[540] now what I am doing, but later you will understand.[541]'" (13:6-7)

Peter and Jesus have so much history together. Peter has confessed him as "the Christ, the Son of the living God."[542] Jesus had called him to fish for men alongside him.[543] Jesus caught him when he started to sink,[544] rebuked him and the other disciples numerous times, called him a friend,[545] invited him out of the band of twelve to be a witness to his transfiguration[546] and the raising of Jairus' daughter.[547]

Peter loves this man, and he can't stand this, so he blurts out, "Lord, are you going to wash my feet?" I can't stand seeing you like a menial servant! It offends my sense of rightness and order! And I don't deserve it from you!

Jesus gently replies that later he'll understand why this is necessary. But Peter will have none of it.

> " 'No,' said Peter, 'you shall never wash my feet.'" (13:8a)

The Greek here is extremely strong, literally, "not ever unto the age," the double negative *ou mē*, with the idea of "to eternity, eternally, in perpetuity"[548] tacked on for good measure.

Washed by Jesus (13:8b-10a)

Jesus' response is equally strong:

> "[8b] Jesus answered, 'Unless I wash[549] you, you have no part[550] with me.'
>
> [9] 'Then, Lord,' Simon Peter replied, 'not just my feet but my hands and my head as well!'" (13:6-9)

Jesus insists that he must wash Peter. But here, Jesus moves in meaning from physical footwashing to spiritual cleansing from sin that is absolutely necessary for any person to have fellowship with Christ the Lord, symbolized here by footwashing and elsewhere by baptism (Acts 22:16; Titus 3:5; 1 Corinthians 6:11; Ephesians 5:26).

Peter's response is immediate: Then wash me from head to toe!

> "Jesus answered, 'A person who has had a bath[551] needs only to wash his feet[552]; his whole body is clean[553].'" (13:10a)

---

[540] "Know" (NIV) is *eidō*, "realize" (NIV), "know" (NRSV, KJV), "understand" (ESV), here in the sense of, "to grasp the meaning of something, understand, recognize, come to know, experience" (BDAG 694, 4).

[541] "Understand" (NIV), *ginōskō*, "know," here, "to grasp the significance or meaning of something, understand, comprehend" (BDAG 200, 3).

[542] Matthew 16:13.

[543] Matthew 4:19.

[544] Matthew 14:31.

[545] Luke 12:4; John 15:14-15; 21:15.

[546] Matthew 17:1.

[547] Luke 8:51.

[548] *Aiōn*, BDAG 32, 1b.

[549] "Wash" is *niptō*, "to cleanse with use of water, wash" (BDAG 674, 1a).

[550] "Part" (NIV, KJV), "share" (NRSV, ESV) is *meros*, "share," here, "have a place with someone" (BDAG 634, 2). Robertson (*Word Studies*) comments, "Jesus does not make foot-washing essential to spiritual fellowship, but simply tests Peter's real pride and mock-humility by this symbol of fellowship."

What does Jesus mean by this? Jesus is using the analogy of taking a bath vs. footwashing and salvation. It is necessary for every believer to experience full salvation and cleansing from sin (depicted by taking a bath). After that, all that is necessary is washing away the occasional dust of the road, the sins that we commit day by day. John wrote about this in his First Epistle.

> "If we claim to be without sin, we deceive ourselves and the truth is not in us. If we confess our sins, he is faithful and just and will forgive us our sins and purify us from all unrighteousness." (1 John 1:8-9)

> "My dear children, I write this to you so that you will not sin. But if anybody does sin, we have one who speaks to the Father in our defense – Jesus Christ, the Righteous One. He is the atoning sacrifice for our sins, and not only for ours but also for the sins of the whole world." (1 John 2:1-2)

Sometimes, like Peter, we resist this frequent need for cleansing – whether out of false pride or a sense of unworthiness or vulnerability We don't want to let the Holy One this close, this intimate. And so we resist him. How foolish of us! He knows us and our sins and wants to restore to us his full cleansing and fellowship. And we must let him!

> **Q1. (John 13:10) Jesus seems to speak to Peter in symbolic language here. In what sense does a "full bath" represent baptism? If this is so, then what kind of needed cleansing does "footwashing" symbolize?**
> http://www.joyfulheart.com/forums/topic/1490-q1-cleansing/

The Betrayer (13:10b-11)

Now, on this night in which he was betrayed, Jesus extends this teaching to inform his disciples that he knew Judas would betray him. Judas is the exception in this band of cleansed men.

> "'And you are clean[554], though not every one of you.' [11] For he knew who was going to betray[555] him, and that was why he said not every one was clean." (13:10-11)

John will return to Judas' evil role that night in verses 21-30.

---

[551] "Had a bath/has bathed" (NIV, NRSV, ESV), "is washed" (KJV) is *louō*, "to use water to cleanse a body of physical impurity, wash, as a rule of the whole body, bathe " (BDAG 603, 1b).

[552] There is some confusion with 13:10a in the manuscripts. A number omit the words "except for his feet," but Metzger concludes that the words "except for his feet" "may have been omitted accidentally (or even deliberately because of the difficulty of reconciling them with the following declaration, 'his whole body is clean'), a majority of the committee considered it safer to retain them on the basis of the preponderant weight of external attestation" (Metzger, *Textual Commentary*, p. 240).

[553] "His whole body is clean" (NIV) is more literally, "entirely/completely clean" (NRSV, ESV), "clean every whit" (KJV). There are two words, the adjective *katharos*, "pertaining to being clean or free of adulterating matter, clean, pure" (BDAG 489, 1); and *holos*, "pertaining to being complete in extent, whole, entire, complete" (BDAG 704, 1bγ).

[554] *Katharos*, "clean," here in the sense of, "pertaining to being free from moral guilt, pure, free from sin" (BDAG 489, 3a).

[555] "Betray" is *paradidōmi*, "hand over, turn over, give up a person," as a technical term of police and courts 'hand over into [the] custody [of]'" (BDAG 762, 1b).

Rabbi and Lord (13:12-13)

The acted parable is over. Now Jesus takes a few minutes to explain part of its meaning to the disciples.

"¹² When he had finished washing their feet, he put on his clothes and returned[556] to his place. 'Do you understand what I have done for you?' he asked them. ¹³ 'You call me "Teacher" and "Lord," and rightly so, for that is what I am.'" (13:12-13)

Jesus acknowledges their feelings of inappropriateness at such an exalted figure as Jesus humbling himself so. They think of him as Rabbi and Lord – and appropriately so[557], "for that is what I am," Jesus says.

Rabbi. The word translated, "teacher" (NIV, NRSV, ESV), "master" (KJV) corresponds to the title of Rabbi.[558] Ordination at the completion of one's studies gave a person the exclusive right to be called Rabbi. In Jesus' time, well-known Jerusalem rabbis or "teachers of the law" were surrounded by their devoted disciples. Disciples treated their rabbis with great deference. When a famous rabbi passed by in the streets, people stood. They were offered the best seats at banquets. They were addressed as Rabbi ("great one"), Master, Father. From Jesus' time, we hear the names of great rabbis Hillel, Shammai, and Gamaliel.[559] The apostle Paul was a trained rabbi, which opened doors for him in synagogues across the Mediterranean.[560] Unlike the rabbis, however, Jesus spoke with authority, not quoting the wise words of previous rabbis, but accurately transmitting the teaching of his Father. Yes, Jesus was rightly called Rabbi – ordained, not by men, but by his Father.

Lord. But Jesus is more than their Rabbi. He is their Lord, the One to whom they belong and owe obedience. The Greek word is *kyrios*, generally, "lord, master." It can refer to "one who is in charge by virtue of possession, owner," then, "one who is in a position of authority, lord, master."[561] But even more significantly, the Greek word *kyrios* was used in the Septuagint to translate the divine name Yahweh, spoken when it was read aloud by Jews as *Adonai* (Hebrew for "Lord"). Thus, the title "Lord" in our verse takes on associations of divinity.

Jesus is Rabbi, teaching the Father's words. And Jesus is Lord, one with the Father. The Logos or Word who was with God in the beginning is God (1:1-3).

An Example of Humble Service (13:14-17)

Jesus has established his right to be served. Now he takes that right and turns it on its head.

"¹⁴ Now that I, your Lord and Teacher, have washed your feet, you also should wash one another's feet. ¹⁵ I have set you an example[562] that you should do as I have done for you. ¹⁶ I tell you

---

[556] "Returned to his place" (NIV) is *anapiptō*, "to recline on a couch to eat, lie down, recline" (BDAG 70, 1).

[557] "Rightly so" (NIV), "you are right" (NRSV, ESV), "say well" (KJV) is *kalōs*, "pertaining to being in accord with a standard, rightly, correctly" (BDAG 505, 4b).

[558] *Didaskalos*, BDAG 241.

[559] E. Lohse, *rhabbi*, TDNT 6:961-965. Jeremias, *Jerusalem*, pp. 233-245.

[560] Paul was trained "at the feet of Gamaliel" (Acts 22:3), an honored "teacher of the law" (Acts 5:34).

[561] *Kyrios*, BDAG 578.

[562] "Example" is *hypodeigma*, "an example of behavior used for purposes of moral instruction, example, model, pattern" (BDAG 1037, 1).

the truth, no servant[563] is greater than his master[564], nor is a messenger[565] greater than the one who sent him. [17] Now that you know these things, you will be blessed[566] if you do them." (13:14-17)

If Jesus the Lord and Rabbi sets an example of humbling himself to serve, how much more should we, his disciples, do so, rather than touting our own self-importance. In Mark's Gospel Jesus taught his disciples:

> "Whoever wants to become great among you must be your servant, and whoever wants to be first must be slave of all. For even the Son of Man did not come to be served, but to serve, and to give his life as a ransom for many." (Mark 10:43-45)

Q2. (John 13:14-15) Why do you think Jesus went to such an extent to break all social norms in washing his disciples feet? What value did he establish in his Kingdom by this dramatic act? How are we to live this out in the Christian community?
http://www.joyfulheart.com/forums/topic/1491-q2-humble-service/

To Be Seen by Men

How much we like titles and adulation. How much we like the best seat, the corner office, the designated parking space. It makes us feel important, significant, powerful. It feeds our pride. Even before this night, Jesus had taught his disciples the danger of pride – using the Pharisees as his prime example.

> "[5] Everything they do is done for men to see: They make their phylacteries wide and the tassels on their garments long; [6] they love the place of honor at banquets and the most important seats in the synagogues; [7] they love to be greeted in the marketplaces and to have men call them 'Rabbi.' [8] But you are not to be called 'Rabbi,' for you have only one Master and you are all brothers. [9] And do not call anyone on earth 'father,' for you have one Father, and he is in heaven. [10] Nor are you to be called 'teacher,' for you have one Teacher, the Christ. [11] The greatest among you will be your servant. [12] For whoever exalts himself will be humbled, and whoever humbles himself will be exalted." (Matthew 23:5-12)

Luke tells us that on the occasion of the Last Supper, Jesus corrected their arguments about who was greatest:

Luke tells us:

> "[25] Jesus said to them, 'The kings of the Gentiles lord it over them; and those who exercise authority over them call themselves Benefactors. [26] But you are not to be like that. Instead, the greatest among you should be like the youngest, and the one who rules like the one who serves. [27] For who

---

[563] "Servant" is *doulos*, "male slave as an entity in a socioeconomic context, slave" (BDAG 259, 1).

[564] "Master" (NIV, NRSV, ESV), "lord" (KJV) is *kyrios*, "one who is in charge by virtue of possession, owner (BDAG 572, II, 1b).

[565] "Messenger" (NIV, NRSV, ESV), "he that is sent" (KJV) is *apostolos*, "of messengers without extraordinary status, delegate, envoy, messenger" (BDAG 122, 1).

[566] "Blessed" (NIV, NRSV, ESV), "happy" (KJV) is *makarios*, "pertaining to being especially favored, blessed, fortunate, happy, privileged," here, "privileged recipient of divine favor" (BDAG 611, 2a).

is greater, the one who is at the table or the one who serves? Is it not the one who is at the table? But I am among you as one who serves.'" (Luke 22:25-27)

Our culture expects Great Men to exalt themselves and allow others to serve and exalt them. But in the Kingdom of God it is different. Here the greatest serves the least, with Jesus leading the way.

The year 2013 saw the election of Argentine Cardinal Bergoglio as Pope of the Roman Catholic Church. Though a Jesuit, he took the name Francis I after St. Francis of Assisi, who had revolutionized the church of the thirteenth century by his humility and refreshingly simple obedience to the commands of Christ. Pope Francis, known in Buenos Aires for living simply and taking the bus to work, brought the same kind of humility to Rome. He insisted on paying his hotel bill, declined to wear red papal shoes in favor of priestly black, and refused to live in the lush papal apartment in favor of a two-room guest-house on the Vatican grounds. His first act as Pope was to kneel before the people gathered in St. Peter's square and ask people to pray for him. Setting an example of simple, humble living is gradually changing a tradition-bound, hierarchical religious organization into one that focuses more directly on Christ's mission. Pray for our Roman Catholic brothers and sisters – and our own congregations where pastors and leaders too often get away from simple lives of humility.

When we exalt others – or allow others to exalt us – we go contrary to Jesus' remarkable example and express teaching.

> **Q3. (Luke 22:25-27) In the world, Great Men have others serve them and exalt them with great titles. How is the Kingdom of God to be different than that? How has Roman Catholic Pope Francis I set an example of humility before his flock?**
> **http://www.joyfulheart.com/forums/topic/1492-q3-humble-leaders/**

Washing One Another's Feet (13:14)

> "Now that I, your Lord and Teacher, have washed your feet, you also should wash one another's feet." (13:14)

What does Jesus' instruction mean? It means to serve others humbly, rather than expecting them to wait on us.

In one church where I served on the staff, the senior pastor always made it a point to help at potlucks, to be the last one to fill his plate, and to lead in clean-up. He set the example for others to follow.

It also means to have the humility to clean up after people whose lives have been trashed by their sins, as well as brothers and sisters who have fallen into some sin or another. Paul wrote,

> "Brothers, if someone is caught in a sin, you who are spiritual should restore him gently. But watch yourself, or you also may be tempted. Carry each other's burdens, and in this way you will fulfill the law of Christ." (Galatians 6:1-2)

If we feel we are too good to deal with the messy people and difficult situations, we must remember that our Lord wasn't. He took upon himself all our messy, disgusting sins and bore them on the cross that we might be made whole! Humility and love, service and the cross. Living like this is living the Good News!

One of You Will Betray Me (13:18-30)

John had mentioned Jesus' betrayer in verses 2 and 10-11. But now Jesus reveals to his disciples the terrible fact that he will be betrayed by one of them around the table, one who has shared his bread, one who been included in the trusted circle of his disciples.

> "I am not referring to all of you; I know those I have chosen. But this is to fulfill the scripture: 'He who shares my bread has lifted up his heel against me.'" (13:18)

Jesus is quoting from the Psalms, where David recounts being surrounded by enemies, but not overcome.

> "Even my close friend, whom I trusted,
> he who shared my bread,
> has lifted up his heel against me." (Psalm 41:9)

Jesus continues.

> "[19] I am telling you now before it happens, so that when it does happen you will believe that I am He. [20] I tell you the truth, whoever accepts anyone I send accepts me; and whoever accepts me accepts the one who sent me." (13:19-20)

Jesus doesn't want the fact of his betrayal to crush his disciples' faith. So he tells them ahead of time so that they know that this is part of God's plan, prophesied ahead of time, that is working to its final completion.

In verse 20 Jesus is underscoring his own solidarity with the apostles, the sent ones, the ones he is sending. They, too, will experience rejection, betrayal, and death on his account – and the joy of seeing people come to faith.[567]

Now Jesus tells them outright of his impending betrayal.

> "[21] After he had said this, Jesus was troubled[568] in spirit and testified, 'I tell you the truth, one of you is going to betray me.' [22] His disciples stared at one another, at a loss to know which of them he meant." (13:21-22)

They are stunned. In Matthew we read,

> "They were very sad and began to say to him one after the other, 'Surely not I, Lord?'" (Matthew 26:22)

They have no idea who Jesus is talking about. Jesus knows. Judas knows. But no one else has a clue. Judas has hidden his duplicity well.

But Peter wants to know who it is.

> "[23] One of them, the disciple whom Jesus loved, was reclining next to him. [24] Simon Peter motioned to this disciple and said, 'Ask him which one he means.' [25] Leaning back against Jesus, he

---

[567] This solidarity of the master and disciples is also found in Matthew 10:40-42; 25:40; Mark 9:37 = Luke 9:48; Luke 10:16.

[568] *Tarassō*, "to cause inward turmoil, stir up, disturb, unsettle, throw into confusion," of Jesus, "troubled, agitated" (BDAG 990, 2).

asked him, 'Lord, who is it?' [26] Jesus answered, 'It is the one to whom I will give this piece of bread when I have dipped it in the dish.' Then, dipping the piece of bread, he gave it to Judas Iscariot, son of Simon. [27] As soon as Judas took the bread, Satan entered into him." (13:23-27a)

John seems to be seated to Jesus' right, reclining on his left elbow. He leans back and whispers to Jesus and Jesus answers him.

Jesus tears off a small piece of bread (what the KJV terms a "sop")[569], dips[570] it in the common pot from which they are eating, and hands it to Judas, probably reclining just to Jesus' left.

"As soon as Judas took the bread, Satan entered into him." (13:27a)

Satan has already "prompted"[571] Judas to betray Jesus (13:2). Luke says that prior to making an agreement with the chief priests to betray Jesus, "Satan entered Judas" (Luke 22:3). But here, at the Last Supper, in the intimacy of receiving bread from his Master, Judas could have broken down and confessed his evil plot. But he didn't. He received the bread from his Master with a straight face. He had determined to go through with it. His love for Jesus was a sham, and his betrayal was later sealed with a sign of affection for the one he was betraying, a kiss.

Was Judas Demon-Possessed?

Was Judas demon-possessed? Demon-possessed implies that a person's will is entirely taken over by a demonic power. My own mental model is not either-or, but one of degrees – demonic influence, temptation, habitual sin, then oppression, and at the far end of the scale, possession, where the demonic power entirely controls the will.

We know from 12:6 that Judas was tempted with money, that as treasurer of Jesus' band, he stole from the money box. Though in recent years some have tried to paint Judas in a more sympathetic light, it's pretty clear that the temptation of 30 pieces of silver played a large role in motivating him to betray Jesus. Greed. Perhaps Judas could see that Jesus wouldn't be able to escape the plots of the chief priests and the Pharisees anyway, so why not profit on the inevitable?

When we sin, we open ourselves to greater temptation. We becomes slaves of sin in the sense that we "obey" its temptations more and more frequently (8:34; Romans 7:12, 25). We get stronger by saying "no" to temptation. We get weaker by saying "yes." Judas had opened himself to the sin of greed and its hold grew stronger and stronger in him.

But our text says,

"As soon as Judas took the bread, Satan entered into him." (13:27a)

The common verb *eiserchomai* means, "to move into a space, enter," here it is used in the sense of "enter into someone."[572] The verb is used of evil spirits entering people (Mark 9:25; Luke 8:30) and animals (Mark 5:12 = Luke 8:32), as well as Satan entering into Judas (Luke 22:3 and John 13:27). So the

---

[569] "Piece/morsel of bread" (NIV, NRSV, ESV), "sop" (KJV) is *psōmion*, "(small) piece/bit of bread," the diminutive of *pōmos*, "morsel" (BDAG 1100).

[570] "Dip" is *baptō*, "to dip something in a liquid, dip, dip in" (BDAG 160), a derivative of *baptizō*, from which we get our word "baptize."

[571] "Prompted" (NIV), "put it into the heart" (NRSV, ESV, KJV) refers to the devil's temptation.

[572] *Eiserchomai*, BDAG 294, 1bγ.

Scripture indicates some level of demon-possession of Judas. But it is not against his will; it exploits his existing weakness for greed. Can Judas resist it? I suppose so, but Scripture indicates that he did not; the foreknowledge of prophesy tells us that he would not. Certainly, he is held responsible for his actions; he is not innocent. Matthew's witness to the Last Supper includes Jesus' words:

> "The Son of Man will go just as it is written about him. But woe to that man who betrays the Son of Man! It would be better for him if he had not been born." (Matthew 26:24)

Judas Went Out. It Was Night (13:27b-30)

After Jesus hands Judas the bread, Jesus tells him to get on with the betrayal. And Judas does – knowing full well that Jesus knows of his betrayal.

> "[27b] 'What you are about to do, do quickly,' Jesus told him, [28] but no one at the meal understood why Jesus said this to him. [29] Since Judas had charge of the money, some thought Jesus was telling him to buy what was needed for the Feast, or to give something to the poor. [30] As soon as Judas had taken the bread, he went out. And it was night."

Judas took the bread and immediately went out.[573] John's observation, "and it was night," is pregnant with meaning. Judas had made his decision and entered into outer darkness. John has constantly come back to the theme of the conflict between light and darkness (1:3-5; 3:19-20; 8:12; 12:35-40, 46). Judas has chosen the dark of night to carry out his evil deeds. But this isn't the last word. "The light shines in the darkness, and the darkness has not overcome it" (1:5, ESV).

> **Q4. (John 13:27-30) Judas gave into his temptation to greed by stealing from the mission's money bag. How does habitual sin tend to open us to greater influence from Satan in our lives? How did Judas eating Jesus' bread illustrate the magnitude of his betrayal?**
> **http://www.joyfulheart.com/forums/topic/1493-q4-sin-and-betrayal/**

Now Is the Son of Man Glorified (13:31-33)

> "[31] When he was gone, Jesus said, 'Now is the Son of Man glorified and God is glorified in him. [32] If God is glorified in him, God will glorify the Son in himself, and will glorify him at once. My children, I will be with you only a little longer. You will look for me, and just as I told the Jews[574], so I tell you now: Where I am going, you cannot come." (13:31-33)

With Judas gone, Jesus explains that his death will result in his glory. In the Synoptic Gospels, Jesus three times tells the disciples that he will be betrayed, crucified, and rise from the dead (Matthew 16:21; 17:22; 20:18). By this time in the Last Supper, they have partaken of the Bread and the Wine, where Jesus has spoke of the breaking of his body and the shedding of his blood. John's readers know this. But what John believes they need to understand in addition, is that Jesus' death ends not in

---

[573] "As soon as" (NIV), "immediately" (NRSV, ESV, KJV) is the adverb *euthys*, "immediately, at once" (BDAG 406, 1).
[574] John 8:21-22.

tragedy, but in glory. For more on this theme, see Appendix 6. "Glory" and "Glorify" in John's Gospel. John develops this theme further in the great High Priestly prayer in John 17.

A New Command: Love One Another (13:34-35)

The Last Supper has been a time of incredible teachings, no doubt more than the disciples could absorb and process at one time:

1. Humble service vs. self-exaltation
2. Jesus' betrayal by one of his own disciples.
3. His body as broken bread, his blood as poured out wine.
4. The glory of his death, and, in a moment,
5. The prediction that Peter himself will disown him this very night.

But now we reach perhaps the apex of Jesus' teaching, in what he calls "a new command," circling back to his acted parable of humble service towards one another at the beginning chapter 13:

> "34 'A new command I give you: Love one another. As I have loved you, so[575] you must love one another. 35 By this all men will know that you are my disciples, if you love one another.'" (13:34-35)

It is so important, it is repeated in 15:12 and again in 15:17. In verses 34 and 35, we find a number of elements:

1. Love as a command.
2. Love as a *new* command.
3. Jesus' love as the standard and source.
4. Love as an indicator of discipleship.

In a real sense, love has been Jesus' theme throughout his ministry. When asked what was the greatest command in the Bible, Jesus points to two:

> "'Love the Lord your God with all your heart and with all your soul and with all your mind.' This is the first and greatest commandment. And the second is like it: 'Love your neighbor as yourself.' All the Law and the Prophets hang on these two commandments." (Matthew 22:35-40)

The idea of love isn't new to Judaism. Indeed Jesus quotes from the Pentateuch itself to establish these two commandments. When someone asks, "Who is my neighbor?" Jesus responds with the Parable of the Good Samaritan, with the point that the neighbor to love is one who is in need, not just one's close friends (Luke 10:29-37).

Love as a Command

We might think of love as a spontaneous, voluntary expression of care and concern for another's welfare. Can love be commanded? I suppose it can. By framing it as a commandment, Jesus puts at the very top of what it means to live as his disciple. It is not a lifestyle *suggestion*, it is a lifestyle *requirement*.

---

[575] Verse 34b, "As I have loved you," begins with the adverb *kathōs*, often translated as an adverb of comparison or degree. But it can also indicate cause: "since, in so far as" (*Kathōs*, BDAG 494, 3).

Love as a *New* Command

Jesus speaks of this as a "new command." In what sense is it "new"? Loving one's neighbor as oneself is an old command (Leviticus 19:18). Some have suggested that it is new in the sense that loving one's neighbor has been elevated to be second only to loving God. Others see the newness in the new standard, to love as Jesus loves us, rather than as we love ourselves.[576] But probably the idea of newness comes from the *New Covenant* instituted at the Last Supper that night (1 Corinthians 11:25; Luke 22:20; Jeremiah 31:31-34),[577] with "the new order that both mandates and exemplifies."[578]

Indeed, this "new command" is "the Law of the new order."[579] Paul calls it "the law of Christ" (Galatians 6:2), the "fulfillment of the Law" (Romans 13:9-10). James calls it "the royal law" (James 2:8). It is no exaggeration to say that love is the theme of the entire New Testament.

Jesus' Love Is the Standard and Source

These verses also teach that Jesus' love for us is the standard and source of our love. Too often I have heard the humanistic truism that "you have to love yourself before you can love others." Yes, in a sense it is true, but it is at best the love-yourself mantra of pop psychology. It is not what Jesus teaches. What Jesus teaches is that the extent of his love for us – laying down his life for us – is to be the standard by which our love is measured. And that is a high standard indeed!

Our love is a result of his love:

"We love because he first loved us." (1 John 4:19)

There is a sense in which Jesus is both the standard and the source of our love. We imitate his love:

"Be imitators of God, therefore, as dearly loved children and live a life of love, just as Christ loved us and gave himself up for us as a fragrant offering and sacrifice to God." (Ephesians 5:1-2)

Q5. (John 13:34) Why is love exalted to the level of a command? How does love characterize Jesus' life? In what way does love fulfill the law and the prophets?
http://www.joyfulheart.com/forums/topic/1494-q5-the-love-command/

Love Is an Indicator of Discipleship

Finally, Jesus teaches that love for one another is an indicator that we are truly disciples of Jesus.

"By this all men will know that you are my disciples, if you love one another." (13:35)

Some people measure discipleship by purity of doctrine, precise orthodoxy. But the indicator here is love for one another. Indeed, in his First Epistle, John states that this kind of love is an essential indicator of true love for God (1 John 2:9; 4:8, 19-21). It's absence is a red flag that a person's faith is

---

[576] So Carson, *John*, p. 484; Morris, *John*, p. 633.
[577] Brown, *John* 2:613-614.
[578] Carson, *John*, p. 484.
[579] Beasley-Murray, *John*, p. 247.

suspect. Again and again we are exhorted to have "love for the brothers" (Romans 12:10; Hebrews 13:1; 1 Peter 1:22).

> Q6. (John 13:35) In what sense is love for one another an indicator to all of our status (or lack of status) as Jesus' disciples? Why do we sometimes avoid living in an intimate Christian community in favor of only a large-meeting expression of our faith? Why is it so difficult to love people in an intimate Christian community? How does your church or group measure up by the indicator of love for one another? How do you measure up?
> http://www.joyfulheart.com/forums/topic/1495-q6-indicator-of-discipleship/

Before the Rooster Crows You Will Disown Me (13:36-38)

This passage ends with Jesus' prediction of Peter's denial. Jesus had been saying, "Where I am going, you cannot come." (13:33). Peter picks up on that and asks where Jesus is going.

> "Simon Peter asked him, 'Lord, where are you going?' Jesus replied, 'Where I am going, you cannot follow now, but you will follow later.'" (13:36)

But Peter is unwilling to accept "No" for an answer.

> "[37] Peter asked, 'Lord, why can't I follow you now? I will lay down my life for you.'
> [38] Then Jesus answered, 'Will you really lay down your life for me? I tell you the truth, before the rooster crows, you will disown me three times!'" (13:37-38)

When we come to the point of full surrender to Christ, we say things like, "I will lay down my life for you," as Peter did. But lest we become too impressed with the fullness of our surrender, we must be aware of our own brokenness and weakness. Surrender is the beginning. But standing under pressure is the test of that surrender. Thank God for his understanding and his mercy towards our sometimes pathetic protestations of faithfulness.

All four Gospels contain this prediction of Peter disowning Jesus three times before the cock crows (Matthew 26:34; Mark 14:30; Luke 22:34). But only John records Jesus restoring Peter to his mission, when after the resurrection, Jesus asks Peter three times, "Do you love me?", hears three times Peter's assurance of his love, and three times restores him to his ministry: "Feed my lambs" (21:15-27). Thank God for mercy.

Lessons for Disciples

The intimate occasion of the Last Supper has a number of lessons for us who seek to follow Jesus as his disciples. Among these are:

1. Contrary to all social conventions, Jesus washed the disciples' feet in order to teach them that humble service is of highest value in the New Order that he is bringing. We are called to self-humbling in order to serve (13:14-15).
2. Just as we need a full bath (baptism) to be clean all over, we need to seek forgiveness through confession of sins day by day (footwashing) to keep us in fellowship with Christ (13:10).

3. Sin in us can fester and, if not dealt with, can increase Satan's ability to influence our lives (12:6; 13:2, 26-30).

4. Love for other disciples is an indicator that we are Jesus' disciples (13:35).

5. Love is the characteristic command of the New Covenant (13:34).

Prayer

Jesus, thank you for setting the example of humbling yourself to serve. We need to see that. I need to see that. Help me to love like you do. Teach me, guide me, and forgive me when I fall short. In your holy name, I pray. Amen.

Key Verses

"Now that I, your Lord and Teacher, have washed your feet, you also should wash one another's feet. I have set you an example that you should do as I have done for you." (John 13:14-15, NIV)

"A new command I give you: Love one another. As I have loved you, so you must love one another. By this all men will know that you are my disciples, if you love one another." (John 13:34-35)

24. I Am the Way, the Truth, and the Life (14:1-14)

As we continue the Farewell Discourses, Jesus seeks to comfort his disciples.

They knew the threat to Jesus when they came to Jerusalem for Passover this time (11:7, 16). Now in Jerusalem, Jesus has been teaching, then hiding from his enemies because his hour was not yet (12:36). Prior to this, Jesus has told his disciples three times that he would be betrayed and crucified (Matthew 16:21; 17:22; 20:18-19). (They didn't remember until later that on each of those occasions he also told them he would rise from the dead.)

On this very evening he has delivered to them three pieces of shocking news:

Robert Zünd, "The Road to Emmaus" (1877), oil on canvas, 119.5 x 158.5 cm., Kuntzmuzeum St. Gallen, Switzerland.

1. One of his own disciples will betray him (13:21).

2. He is leaving them – and they can't follow now (13:33, 36; 16:6).

3. Peter himself will deny him three times – tonight! (13:38).

Jesus has been their life for these last three years. They have left family and jobs – everything – to follow him and assist him on his mission. And now he is leaving? He is the one they believe to be the Messiah, the Son of God. How can his enemies win? They are confused, discouraged. So Jesus speaks much-needed words of comfort to these men whom he loves.

Do Not Let Your Hearts Be Troubled (14:4a)

Jesus says to them,

"Do not let your hearts be troubled." (14:1a)

They are "troubled" – and with good reason! Jesus, too is "troubled" as events rush toward their culmination (12:27; 13:21). The word "troubled" is *tarassō*, "stir/shake up," figuratively, "to cause inward turmoil, stir up, disturb, unsettle, throw into confusion."[580] We'll see the word once again in this chapter:

"Peace I leave with you; my peace I give you. I do not give to you as the world gives. Do not let your hearts be troubled and do not be afraid." (14:27)

In the Garden of Gethsemane a few hours from now Jesus is still deeply troubled.

---

[580] *Tarassō*, BDAG 990, 2.

"He began to be sorrowful[581] and troubled[582]. Then he said to them, 'My soul is overwhelmed with sorrow to the point of death. Stay here and keep watch with me.'" (Matthew 26:37-38)

Luke tells us about the physical manifestations of this stress he was under.

"And being in anguish[583], he prayed more earnestly, and his sweat was like drops of blood falling to the ground.[584]" (Luke 22:44)

Nevertheless, he comforts them with the comfort he has from the Father. He tells them what he knows to be true, even though in his humanness he too is under great stress.

Trust in God; Trust Also in Me (14:1b)

"Do not let your hearts be troubled. Trust in God; trust also in me." (14:1)

Verse 1b can be translated in different ways:
- "Trust in God; trust also in me" (NIV, NRSV, RSV, ESV; both verbs imperatives)
- "Ye believe in God, believe also in me" (KJV, NKJV, first verb indicative, second imperative)

The form of the verbs in Greek in this verse can be taken as *either* indicative *or* imperative (command), though nearly all modern translations take them both as commands. Either way, Jesus is saying that they should believe in him in the same way they believe in God. Again, in a few verses, he will equate seeing him as seeing the Father (14:6-11). As Carson says, these verses "assume a formidably high Christology."[585]

Jesus is comforting his disciples, Don't be afraid, it's going to be okay. You can trust both the Father and me.

In My Father's House Are Many Rooms (14:2)

Now he explains one of the reasons they can trust him.

"In my Father's house are many rooms; if it were not so, I would have told you. I am going there to prepare a place for you." (14:2)

"In my Father's house...." The word is *oikia*, "a structure used as a dwelling, house."[586] Sometimes when "the house of the Lord" is mentioned in the Bible, it refers to the tabernacle and later the temple in Jerusalem (2:16).[587] But here Jesus is talking about God's heavenly dwelling, as Paul put it, "a house

---

[581] *Lypeō*, "be sad, be distressed, grieve" (BDAG 604, 2b).

[582] "Troubled" (NIV, ESV), "distressed" (NRSV), "very heavy" (KJV), is *adēmoneō*, "be in anxiety, be distressed, troubled" (BDAG 19), from a, "not" + *dēmos*, "at home," thus uncomfortable.

[583] *Agōnia*, "apprehensiveness of mind, esp. when faced with impending ills, distress, anguish" (BDAG 17).

[584] Whether this was profuse sweat dripping off him or broken capillaries that tinged his sweat with blood, we aren't sure. Whichever it was, it indicates severe stress.

[585] Carson, *John*, p. 488.

[586] *Oikia*, BDAG 695, 1b.

[587] For example, Exodus 23:19; Judges 19:18; Psalm 27:4; etc.

(*oikia*) not made with hands, eternal in the heavens" (2 Corinthians 5:1).[588] This passage is often read at funerals – and rightly so!

Every time I see this verse, I think of a wonderful Negro spiritual:

"Come and go with me to my Father's house,
To my Father's house, to my Father's house,
Come and go with me to my Father's house,
There is joy, joy, joy!

Jesus will be there, in my Father's house....

There'll be no crying there, in my Father's house...." (etc.)

And in the Father's house, Jesus says, there will be many rooms. "Rooms" (NIV, ESV), "dwelling places" (NRSV), "mansions" (KJV) is *monē*, "a place in which one stays, dwelling(-place), room, abode."[589]

Jesus says he is going there to "prepare a place[590] for us." "Prepare" is *hetoimazō*, "to cause to be ready, put/keep in readiness, prepare."[591] I can remember going to my grandparents' home, with a guestroom all prepared for my brother and me, clean sheets, etc. But Jesus is going away not just to freshen up rooms for us in heaven, he is also going to prepare the "way" so we can get to heaven at all, as we'll see in verse 6 – dying on the cross so that our sins might be forgiven, rising from the dead so we might have assurance of life forever.

Q1. (John 14:2) What is the "Father's House"? What does verse 2 tell us about what Jesus will do, and what is provided for us? How does that comfort us?
http://www.joyfulheart.com/forums/topic/1496-q1-the-fathers-house/

Coming Again to Take Us with Him (14:3)

Jesus explains that he isn't just leaving, but he is coming back.

"And if I go and prepare a place for you, I will come back and take you to be with me[592] that you also may be where I am." (14:3)

How should we understand this coming back, literally "again coming[593]"? Which coming does this refer to? There are several possibilities.

---

[588] The writer of Hebrews refers to it as the City of God (Hebrews 9:21, 24; 11:10, 16; 12:22; 13:14).

[589] *Monē*, BDAG 658, 2. From *menō*, "continue, abide, stay."

[590] "Place" is *topos*, from which we get our English words "topography, topographical, topical." *Topos* refers to "an area of any size, generally specified as a place of habitation, here, "an abode: place, room," to live, stay, sit, etc. (BDAG 1011, 1e).

[591] *Hetoimazō*, BDAG 440, a.

[592] The phrase "take you to be with me" carries the idea in Greek idiom, "I will take you with me to my home" (Beasley-Murray, *John*, p. 250; Kruse, *John*, p. 297). "Take you" (NIV, NRSV, ESV), "receive you" (KJV) is *paralambanō*, "to take into close association, take (to oneself), take with/along" (BDAG 767, 1).

[593] "Again" is *palin*, "pertaining to return to a position or state, back" (BDAG 752, 1a). "Coming" is the very common verb *erchomai*, "come."

1. Jesus' appearances after his resurrection (16:16, 19-22; 20:19-29).
2. Jesus' coming through his Holy Spirit sent after his ascension (John 14:16-19).
3. Jesus' presence with believers at the present time (Matthew 18:20; 28:20; etc.), especially his coming to believers at the hour of their death to take them to heaven.[594]
4. Jesus' eschatological Second Coming at the end of the age, (21:22-23; 1 John 3:2, 1 Thessalonians 4:16-17; etc.).

Sometimes John speaks ambiguously, with sayings that can be taken in different ways. However, while we know that each of these four comings are real, probably John has Jesus' Second Coming most in mind here.[595]

The Place Jesus Is Going (14:4-5)

Jesus concludes his "going to prepare a place for you" saying with these words:

"You know the **way** to the place where I am going." (14:4)

But by subsequent statements, it is clear that the disciples do *not* know what he is talking about. This verse transitions us to Jesus' statement that he himself is the Way.

"Thomas said to him, 'Lord, we don't know where you are going, so how can we know the **way**?'" (14:5)

Thomas doesn't know where Jesus is going. Jesus has said they can't go with him now (13:33, 36). So the way to this unknown place is a mystery.

Where is Jesus going? He is "returning to God" (13:3), "going to the Father" (14:13; 16:10, 17), he is going to "my Father's house" (14:2). Is this heaven? Probably. The danger of calling it "heaven," however, is that the word "heaven" is encumbered by a great deal of popular mythology – St. Peter at the pearly gates, streets of gold, white robes, clouds, and harps. Many of these images come from highly symbolic language in the Book of Revelation expressing the glory and greatness of God's Presence, of the Holy City. But at best, this is symbolic language trying to express in *physical* terminology something that is a *spiritual* reality. What do we know for sure about its exact characteristics? Some things. For example, it is a place of joy and life, where God will wipe every tear from our eyes (Revelation 7:17; 21:4). In John 14, Jesus tells us that "in the Father's house" is a place for us in the presence of Jesus and the Father. This doesn't answer all our questions, but it is enough.

The Way, the Truth, and the Life (14:6)

Jesus and Thomas have dialoged about the way to the Father's house.

"⁴ ....'You know the **way** to the place where I am going.' ⁵ Thomas said to him, 'Lord, we don't know where you are going, so how can we know the **way**?'" (14:4-5)

Now comes one of the key declarations of the Gospels.

---

[594] 2 Corinthians 5:1 suggests that through death, Christians are taken to the Father's house.

[595] This position is argued strongly by Beasley-Murray, *John*, pp. 250-251. The various possibilities are reviewed by Brown, John 2:624-627, with his conclusion that the primary idea is the parousia. So Kruse, *John*, pp. 296-297; Carson, *John*, pp. 488-490; Morris, *John*, pp. 639-640.

"⁶ Jesus answered, 'I am the **way** and the truth and the life. No one comes to the Father except through me.'" (14:6)

This is the sixth of seven "I am" declarations in John's Gospel, where Jesus uses the divine "I Am" in combination with a descriptor.[596] Just what does Jesus mean by these three descriptors – the way, the truth, and the life?

The Way (14:6a)

First, Jesus declares that he himself is the Way, the "road, highway"[597] to the Father's presence, the Father's house – heaven, if you will.

This shouldn't surprise us. Jesus' characteristic call is, "Follow me!" As we follow him and are obedient to what he teaches us, then he will lead us all the way to the Father's presence.

This phrase, "The Way," is used several places in the Scriptures.

- Isaiah looks forward to "a highway... [that] will be called the Way of Holiness" (Isaiah 35:8).
- Paul testifies that he persecuted "the followers of this Way" (Acts 22:4).
- Paul tells us, "Through him we both have access to the Father by one Spirit" (Ephesians 2:18).
- The writer of Hebrews speaks of "a new and living way" that gives us access into God's very presence (Hebrews 10:19-20).
- Jesus spoke of himself as "the gate" through which his sheep enter into salvation (John 10:9).

To say that Jesus is "the Way" is to affirm that he is the path to God.

The Truth (14:6b)

Second, Jesus declares himself to be "the Truth." In John's Gospel the noun "truth" (*alētheia*) appears 25 times, compared to once in Matthew and three times each in Mark and Luke. Especially in John's Gospel, *alētheia*, "truth," carries the idea of "authenticity, divine reality, revelation."[598] Jesus is the Word, the Logos, the exact Expression of God himself, the one who speaks the Words of God (1:1).

When the so-called "reality" of this dark world system is confronted with the intense Light of truth and revelation, God's reality, there is dissonance. And it is God's reality that prevails and gives freedom. Jesus, who is "full of grace and truth" (1:14, 18), is the embodiment of what is true in this world and the next. His words are true, and therefore must be believed and obeyed. Jesus says,

"If you hold to my teaching, you are really my disciples. Then you will know the truth, and the truth will set you free." (8:31-32)

When we embrace distortions and outright lies about the meaning of life, we lose freedom. Only when we conform our lives with reality, with truth, can we be truly free. When Jesus says "I am ... the truth," it is an powerful, exclusive statement.

---

[596] See Appendix 4. The "I Am" Passages in John's Gospel.
[597] *Hodos*, BDAG 691, 3a.
[598] Rudolf Bultmann, *alētheia*, TDNT 1:245.

In our day we have largely displaced Jesus' teachings with political correctness, the wisdom of our commercialized world, street smarts, and lessons from the "school of hard knocks." But Jesus is the Truth; his Word is Truth; he speaks to us the words of the Father.

> "The Word" – the clear and accurate expression of the Father – "became flesh and dwelt among us ... full of grace and truth." (1:14a; cf. 1:17)

The Life (14:6c)

Finally, Jesus declares that he is the Life. John's Gospel overflows with this theme. Jesus brings eternal life. In fact, he is the very source of life – both physical life as Co-Creator, but eternal life as well.

> "Through him all things were made; without him nothing was made that has been made. In him was life, and that life was the light of men." (1:3-4)

In a number of places in this Gospel, Jesus asserts his authority to give life.

> "For just as the Father raises the dead and gives them life, even so the Son **gives life** to whom he is pleased to give it." (5:21)

> "As the Father has life in himself, so he has granted the Son to have **life in himself**." (5:26)

> "The bread of God is he who comes down from heaven and **gives life** to the world." (6:33)

> "Just as the living Father sent me and I live because of the Father, so the one who feeds on me will **live because of me**." (6:57)

> Simon Peter: "Lord, to whom shall we go? You have the **words of eternal life**." (6:68)

> "I give them **eternal life**, and they shall never perish." (10:28a)

> "I am the **resurrection and the life**." (11:25a)

> "And this is the testimony: God has given us eternal life, and **this life is in his Son**. He who has the Son has life; he who does not have the Son of God does not have life." (1 John 5:11-12)

Jesus is the Way to God, the Truth from God, and our Source of Life. It is all found in Christ.

Thomas à Kempis (1380-1471), a German priest who wrote *The Imitation of Christ*, put it well:

> "Follow me. I am the way and the truth and the life. Without the way there is no going; without the truth there is no knowing; without the life there is no living. I am the way which you must follow; the truth which you must believe; the life for which you must hope. I am the inviolable way, the infallible truth, the never-ending life. I am the straightest way; the sovereign truth; life true, life blessed, life uncreated. If you abide in my way you shall know the truth, and the truth shall make you free, and you shall attain life everlasting."[599]

Q2. (John 14:6) In what sense is Jesus the Way to God? What does it mean to "follow Jesus"? In what sense is Jesus in himself God's Truth? What are the implications of this for us and our world? In what sense is Jesus God's Life? How does this affect us and those we speak to about him?
http://www.joyfulheart.com/forums/topic/1497-q2-way-truth-and-life/

[599] Thomas à Kempis, *The Imitation of Christ*, 56, 1.

The Exclusivity of Jesus' Path (14:6d)

What makes this wonderful statement controversial in our pluralistic society is that Jesus' declaration claims exclusivity – and this offends non-Christians.

> "I am the way and the truth and the life. No one comes to the Father except[600] through[601] me." (14:6)

The reason Jesus is the exclusive way to God is because he is the Unique Son, the Only-Begotten, the Co-Creator, the only one who has been given the authority to have life in himself. And he speaks the Father's words, the Father's message.

> "The words I say to you are not just my own. Rather, it is the Father, living in me, who is doing his work." (14:10)

In fact, Jesus and the Father are one (10:30; 17:22). To hear one is to hear the other.

Other parts of the New Testament echo this exclusivity of Jesus as the only Way to God, for example:

> "No one knows the Father except the Son and those to whom the Son chooses to reveal him." (Matthew 11:27b)

> "Salvation is found in no one else, for there is no other name under heaven given to men by which we must be saved." (Acts 4:12)

Unbelievers hold the philosophy that "all roads lead to Rome," that we all worship the same God, etc. In solidarity with them, some liberal Christians have come to see the declaration of Jesus as the exclusive Way to God as intolerant and bigoted.

But Jesus himself said,

> "Enter through the narrow gate. For wide is the gate and broad is the road that leads to destruction, and many enter through it. But small is the gate and narrow the road that leads to life, and only a few find it." (Matthew 7:13-14)

Jesus is that Narrow Gate. Jesus is that Narrow Road or Way. Exclusively! To get to our destination, the Father's House, we must follow him and him only.

What About Those Who Have Never Heard?

What about those who have not heard of Jesus? If any are saved, it can only be through Jesus' sacrifice on the cross.

> "He is the atoning sacrifice for our sins, and not only for ours but also for the sins of the whole world." (1 John 2:2)

We know that the Old Testament saints will be saved – their forgiveness was contingent upon what Jesus would do on the cross. What about those in our own time who die never hearing Jesus' name or the gospel? There's a lot we don't know. Paul hints that Gentiles who embrace the light they

---

[600] "Except" (NIV, NRSV, ESV), "but" (KJV) is *ei mē* after a negative, "but," "except, if not," mostly without a verb (BDAG 278, 6iα), used in the same way as Greek *plēn*.

[601] "Through" (NIV, NRSV, ESV), "by" (KJV) is the preposition *dia*, here, a "marker of personal agency, 'through, by' (BDAG 225, 4bβ).

have, might be saved (Romans 2:14-16). We know that those who love God, will embrace Jesus and his Word when they encounter him (8:42).

We know that God is loving and just. And that Jesus died for the sins of the whole world. Thus no one can be saved but "through" Jesus. And we know that our Great Commission is to preach the Good News until Christ returns (Matthew 28:19-20; Mark 16:15-16; Luke 24:47; Acts 1:8). It is vital. It is important. The salvation of people depend upon them hearing the gospel (Romans 10:14). How does this all work together? We don't fully know.

But if we back off from the exclusivity of Jesus as the only Way to God in the name of tolerance, or solidarity with all the peoples of the world, or for any other reason, we are not being faithful to Jesus' own teaching about himself.

> **Q3. (John 14:6d) Is it intolerant to believe that no one comes to God except through Jesus? How does Jesus' death and resurrection atone for the sins of the Old Testament saints? Why are some Christians uncomfortable with the statement that "No one comes to the Father but by me"?**
> http://www.joyfulheart.com/forums/topic/1498-q3-exclusivity-of-jesus-way/

Show Us the Father (14:7-11)

Thomas had asked, "Lord, we don't know where you are going, so how can we know the way?" (14:5), but he voiced the confusion felt by all the disciples. Now Jesus rebukes Thomas.

> "If you really knew me, you would know my Father as well. From now on, you do know him and have seen him." (14:7)

The grammar of verse 7a implies that Thomas should have known Jesus better.[602] Jesus responds by affirming that to know him is to know his Father. But such a thought is so different from the normal monotheism of Judaism, that it doesn't seem to register with Philip.

> "Philip said, 'Lord, show us the Father and that will be enough for us.'" (14:8)

Jesus responds with a rebuke that is amazing in its clear explanation of Jesus' oneness with the Father.

> "Jesus answered: 'Don't you know me, Philip, even after I have been among you such a long time? Anyone who has seen me has seen the Father. How can you say, "Show us the Father"?'" (14:9)

This goes back to the Prologue to John's Gospel.

> "In the beginning was the Word, and the Word was with God, and the Word was God. He was with God in the beginning. Through him all things were made; without him nothing was made that has been made." (1:1-3)

Jesus is the Word, the Logos, the clear expression of the Father's words. Now Jesus continues his explanation to Philip.

---

[602] "Really knew" (NIV), "know" (NRSV), "had known" (ESV, KJV) is the Perfect tense of *ginōskō*, "to know," suggesting something that began in the past and continues to the present.

"¹⁰ Don't you believe that I am in the Father, and that the Father is in me? The words I say to you are not just my own. Rather, it is the Father, living in me, who is doing his work. ¹¹ Believe me when I say that I am in the Father and the Father is in me; or at least believe on the evidence⁶⁰³ of the miracles⁶⁰⁴ themselves.'" (14:10-11)

It is best to believe in Jesus because you know and believe his words. But if that's too much for you, Jesus tells Philip, believe for the sake of the miracles you have seen me do (also 5:36; 10:37-38). They are evidence that the Father is working through me.

> **Q4. (John 14:1b, 6-11) In what sense is trusting Jesus the same as trusting God? How accurately does Jesus portray God's actions and words? What does it mean that Jesus and the Father are one (John 10:30)?**
> http://www.joyfulheart.com/forums/topic/1499-q4-i-and-the-father-are-one/

Greater Things Will You Do (14:12)

"I tell you the truth, anyone who has faith in me will do what (*ergon*) I have been doing. He will do even greater things than these, because I am going to the Father." (14:12)

The objects of this promise are "anyone who has faith in me" – believers. The verb translated "has faith" (NIV), "believes" (NRSV, ESV, KJV) is *pisteuō*, "to entrust oneself to an entity in complete confidence, believe (in), trust." This is much more than intellectual assent. It implies total commitment to the one who is trusted.⁶⁰⁵

This verse raises three important questions:
1. What does Jesus going to the Father have to do with us doing greater works than Jesus?
2. What are the "works" Jesus has been doing?
3. How could there be any greater works than Jesus has done?

Let's examine these issues one by one.

First, what does Jesus going to the Father have to do with this? Immediately following 14:12 is Jesus' promise to send the Spirit in verses 15 and 16.

"¹⁵ If you love me, you will obey what I command. ¹⁶ And I will ask the Father, and he will give you another Counselor to be with you forever – ¹⁷ the Spirit of truth." (14:15-17a).

"Unless I go away, the Counselor will not come to you; but if I go, I will send him to you." (16:7)

We'll discuss this in greater depth in lessons to come, but the point here is that the believers' ability to do "greater works" is enabled by the Holy Spirit who will be poured out on them.

---

⁶⁰³ "Evidence" (NIV), "because of" (NRSV), "on account of" (ESV), "for [their] sake" (KJV) is *dia*, "marker of something constituting cause, "the reason why something happens, results, exists: because of, for the sake of" (BDAG 225, 2a).
⁶⁰⁴ "Miracles" (NIV), "works" (NRSV, ESV, KJV) is *ergon*.
⁶⁰⁵ *Pisteuō*, BDAG 817, 2aβ.

Second, what are the "works" Jesus is referring to? In verse 12, "what" (NIV), "works" (NRSV, ESV, KJV) is *ergon*, "deed, accomplishment," of the deeds of God, specifically, miracles.[606] Of course, "works" could refer to anything Jesus did or accomplished, but the immediate context for "works" is verse 11 where Jesus challenges his disciples to believe on the basis of his "works," if nothing else. The word here clearly is referring to miracles. Carson says, "Jesus 'works' may include more than his miracles; they never exclude them."[607]

Third, how could we have the nerve to believe we could do anything greater than Jesus Christ the Lord? It sounds presumptuous – except that Jesus promised it! "Greater" is the comparative of the adjective *megas*, "great," exceeding a standard involving related objects.[608] Are our works to be greater in quantity, quality, intensity, importance, or spectacularity? Jesus isn't specific.

We have the example of Elisha who received a "double portion" of Elijah's spirit (2 Kings 2:9), and seemed to do greater miracles than Elijah had.

Certainly, when the power of the Holy Spirit rests on thousands of believers, together they can do a greater quantity of miracles than one man. It's hard to believe, however, that we could do miracles greater than Jesus' raising of the dead, feeding the 5,000, etc.

Jesus' words and deeds were somewhat veiled. They weren't fully understood during his lifetime, not until after his death and resurrection. But by means of Jesus' death and resurrection he ushered in an age of clarity and power.[609] After Pentecost, three thousand are swept into the Kingdom in a single day. Persecution scattered believers all over the known world resulting in a mushrooming growth of the church in the first century.

Many quarters of the church today believe that this verse isn't for them, that the age of miracles is past. But there is no scriptural warrant to believe that. It is merely a convenient excuse for unbelief. God, let us see a return to the age of miracles and a great moving of the Spirit in our churches, in our regions! Forgive us for our complacency and unbelief!

Q5. (John 14:8) What happens after Jesus' "glorification" that enables believers to do greater things than Jesus? Is this promise limited to the apostles? Why are Christians today uncomfortable with this promise?
http://www.joyfulheart.com/forums/topic/1500-q5-greater-works/

Ask Anything in My Name (14:13-14)

Our lesson closes with an amazing promise of answered prayer.

"¹³ And I will do whatever you ask in my name, so that the Son may bring glory to the Father. ¹⁴ You may ask me for anything in my name, and I will do it." (14:13-14)

---

[606] *Ergon*, BDAG 390, 1cα.
[607] Carson, *John*, p. 495.
[608] *Megas*, BDAG 623.
[609] Carson, *John*, pp. 495-496.

Following the parameters given in verse 12, the promise is made to "those who believe." Let's examine what the promises in verse 13 and 14 entail.

"Those who believe...." This is a promise made to all believers. Elsewhere, Jesus said,

> "If you believe, you will receive whatever you ask for in prayer." (Matthew 21:22)

"Whatever you ask" / "anything." Jesus doesn't limit this promise to certain kinds of requests only. It is open-ended. The only requirements seem to be faith (verse 12), "in Jesus' name," and that will bring glory to the Father. There are no limits to prayer!

Notice that in verse 14, Jesus is clear that we may ask him, pray to him, not just to the Father.

"In my name." The phrase "in my name" occurs seven times in John, all in these Farwell Discourses – 14:13, 14, 26; 15:16; 16:23, 24, 26. In the ancient world, a name stood for one's whole personality, it expressed in some way the whole person. To pray in the name of Jesus is to pray in accordance with all the name stands for,[610] as commissioned and authorized by him.[611] Hawthorne puts it this way:

> "To pray in the name of Jesus, to ask anything in His name, is not merely to add to one's prayers a meaningless formula, but it is to ask something from God as Christ's representatives on earth, in His mission and stead, in His spirit, and with His aim."[612]

In law we have the concept of "power of attorney," a written authorization to represent or act on another's behalf in private affairs, business, or some other legal matter. When my mother was in her nineties, she gave me power of attorney to act for her in financial affairs and make health decisions on her behalf. Later, when she suffered from dementia, I made decisions concerning her care without even consulting her. However, I felt bound as her son to act in what I felt was her best interest. I was her advocate with her caregivers to make sure she got the very best care. When I needed to make a financial transaction, I could present the power of attorney and act as if I were she.

Praying in Jesus' name is something like that. Jesus has given us his name to act on behalf of his kingdom. When people hear us, they are hearing Jesus through us, and are responsible to act on the information, as if it were given directly to them by Jesus itself. It is an awesome responsibility. As we act in the Spirit, Jesus even gives the church power to forgive sins in his name (20:23), which we'll discuss in Lesson 33). Jesus gives his servants power to heal and cast out demons on his name (Mark 9:37, 39; 16:17).

Jesus' name is not just a formula for prayer. It is a privilege given to Jesus' disciples by their Master. Unbelievers may try to act in Jesus' name, but the power of his name is given only to those who believe in him (Acts 19:13-16).

According to US law, a power of attorney can be used against the grantor's will. Not so with Jesus' name. Prayer in Jesus' name is similar to prayer in accordance must be in accordance with God's will.

> "If you remain in me and my words remain in you, ask whatever you wish, and it will be given you." (15:7)

---

[610] Morris, *John*, p. 646.

[611] Hans Bietenhard, "Name," NIDNTT, 2:654.

[612] Gerald F. Hawthorne, "Name," ISBE 3:483.

"This is the confidence we have in approaching God: that if we ask anything according to his will, he hears us. And if we know that he hears us – whatever we ask – we know that we have what we asked of him." (1 John 5:14-15)

Prayer is never intended to cajole God into giving in to our desires. Rather, prayer is about seeking him and his will with the intent of seeing his will to come to pass in our lives. That doesn't mean that we have to always pray tentatively. Seek him, find the will of God and then pray it boldly before the Father, in the name of Jesus.

Purpose: Glory. "So that the Son may bring glory to the Father." God is glorified when his children begin to ask the Father for Kingdom projects, as the Son is teaching them. Selfish prayers bring no glory at all. But prayers prayed in Jesus' name, careful to be according to God's will, bring great glory to the Father. Part of the Lord's Prayer is to pray,

"Thy kingdom come,
Thy will be done
on earth,
as it is in heaven."

Q6. (John 14:13-14) What does it mean to pray "in Jesus' name"? What happens to prayers that are out of his will and purposes? Are there any practical limits to this promise of answered prayer.
http://www.joyfulheart.com/forums/topic/1501-q6-in-jesus-name/

Lessons for Disciples

This continuation of the Farewell Discourses contains a number of radical lessons for Jesus' disciples to grasp – some quite contrary to our world culture, and even our church cultures.

1. Jesus tells us to trust in him in the same way that we trust in the Father (14:1). This is because Jesus and the Father are one (10:30). To see and hear Jesus is to see and hear the Father (14:7-11).

2. Jesus promises us that he has a place, a room for us in the Father's House, in heaven (14:2).

3. Jesus promises us that he will return, certainly being with us in Spirit (Matthew 18:20; 28:20), but especially in his Second Coming at the close of the age (21:22-23; 1 John 3:2; etc.) (14:3).

4. Jesus is the Way, Path, and Road to God. By following him and his narrow path, we will arrive at the right destination (14:6a).

5. Jesus is the Truth. He embodies truth and declares God's reality in a world that is enamored with its own distortions and wisdom (14:6b).

6. Jesus is the Life and Lifegiver. True and eternal life is found only in him. (14:6c).

7. Jesus is the exclusive Way to God; people can't get to God unless they go through Jesus (14:6d).

8. Jesus promises that those believe in him will do even greater miracles than he did, because the Holy Spirit is being sent to them (14:12).

9. Jesus promises to answer any prayers that are made in his name, that are according to his will and purpose (14:13-14).

Prayer

Father, thank you for the great comfort of this passage. Thank you for Jesus – our Way, our Truth, and our Life. Thank you for the promise of you working through us and answering prayer. Thank you for the promise of a place in the Father's House for each of us. In your holy name, we pray. Amen.

Key Verses

"In my Father's house are many rooms; if it were not so, I would have told you. I am going there to prepare a place for you. And if I go and prepare a place for you, I will come back and take you to be with me that you also may be where I am." (John 14:2-3, NIV)

"I am the way and the truth and the life. No one comes to the Father except through me." (John 14:6, NIV)

"Anyone who has seen me has seen the Father." (John 14:9b, NIV)

"Believe me when I say that I am in the Father and the Father is in me; or at least believe on the evidence of the miracles themselves." (John 14:11, NIV)

"I tell you the truth, anyone who has faith in me will do what I have been doing. He will do even greater things than these, because I am going to the Father." (John 14:12, NIV)

"And I will do whatever you ask in my name, so that the Son may bring glory to the Father. You may ask me for anything in my name, and I will do it." (John 14:13-14, NIV)

25. I Will Give You Another Counselor (14:15-31)

Earlier in chapter 14, Jesus has been comforting his disciples, explaining that he is the way, the truth, and the life, and also his intimate relationship with the Father.

Now Jesus begins teaching his disciples about the Holy Spirit, the "Paraclete," who will come to take his place when he goes to the Father. Over chapters 14, 15, and 16, we see Jesus' fullest teaching about the Holy Spirit.

We'll be taking our time as we study this passage so we can understand exactly what Jesus is saying about the Holy Spirit. In addition, this lesson introduces an important theme that connects love for Jesus with obeying his commandments.

Gian Lorenzo Bernini, "Holy Spirit," oval stained glass window, part of the massive Chair of St. Pater (1647-1653), behind the altar at St. Peter's Basilica, Vatican.

The Spirit as "Paraclete" (14:15-17)

This lesson begins with the verse

"If you love me, you will obey what I command." (14:15)

However, we'll consider verse 15 with verses 21-25 below. Here, let's focus on the nature of the Paraclete in verses 16 and 17.

"16 And I will ask the Father, and he will give you another Counselor (*paraklētos*) to be with you forever – 17 the Spirit of truth. The world cannot accept[613] him, because it neither sees[614] him nor knows[615] him. But you know him, for he lives with you and will be in you." (14:16-17)

What is this *paraklētos*, identified with the Holy Spirit in verse 17, and mentioned elsewhere in these Farewell Discourses at 14:26; 15:26; and 16:7. The word is variously translated as the "Comforter" (KJV), "Counselor" (NIV, RSV), "Advocate" (NRSV), "Helper" (ESV, NASB). The reason for the wide variety of translations is that the Greek adjective *paraklētos* can't be easy translated into English with a single word that adequately covers its breadth of meaning.

Paraklētos is an adjective formed from the verb *parakaleō*, which has the basic meaning, "call to one's side" for help. But the verb *parakaleō* has a variety of extended meanings that complicate our understanding of the exact force of the noun in our passage. It can mean "to urge strongly, appeal to,

---

[613] "Accept" (NIV), "receive" (NRSV, ESV, KJV) is the common verb *lambanō*, "receive," here figuratively, "to accept as true, receive something," or perhaps, "to enter into a close relationship, receive, make one's own, apprehend/comprehend" mentally or spiritually (BDAG 584, 7 or 8).

[614] "Sees" is *theōreō*, "see," with the sense of "to come to the understanding of something, notice, perceive, observe, find" (BDAG 454, 2b).

[615] "Knows" is *ginōskō*, "know," probably with the sense, "to indicate that one does know, acknowledge, recognize as that which one is or claims to be" (BDAG 200, 7).

urge, exhort, encourage," and "to make a strong request for something, request, implore, entreat," then "comfort, encourage, cheer up," and perhaps "be friendly to, speak to in a friendly manner."[616]

Commentators seem to be agreed that *paraklētos* is passive in form, "called to the side of" for the purpose of helping, "called to one's aid," in a court of justice, and used as a substantive, "legal assistant, advocate."[617]

The translation "Comforter" comes from Wycliffe's translation into English (1392), which drew perhaps upon "comfort's" etymological sense (Latin, *con*, "with" + *fortis*, "strong"). In this sense it might denote "Strengthener," "Helper" (ESV). In Greek, the word can have the idea of one who provides help as a legal advocate, particularly an advocate for the defense (used of Jesus in 1 John 2:1). Another approach to understanding *paraklētos* might be as "Friend," as in a Friend at court. For more, see Appendix 8. The Paraclete.[618] Because different translations use different terms, I'll be using the term Paraclete in these lessons to avoid confusion.

Another Paraclete in Addition to Jesus (14:16-17)

Jesus' statement in verse 16 about the Father sending "*another*[619] Counselor (*paraklētos*)" is intriguing. This implies that the disciples already have a Paraclete to help them, and that the Holy Spirit is another Paraclete in addition. Jesus is saying that at present he is their Paraclete – the one the Father has sent to help them. In verse 17b, Jesus tells his disciples that they, unlike the world, are already familiar with this Paraclete:

"... For he lives with you and will be in you."

Jesus seems to be saying that in his own Person they have experienced the Paraclete living or abiding[620] "with them"[621] or at their side. But, when the Father sends the Holy Spirit, this Paraclete will be (future tense[622]) within them.[623] Thus the Trinity is indwelling the believer, through the Spirit!

Jesus has been their Paraclete, Helper, Friend thus far, but the Holy Spirit will replace Jesus as an interior presence, always with them, to guide and instruct them.

---

[616] *Parakaleō*, BDAG 764-765.

[617] Liddell-Scott, *Greek-English Lexicon*.

[618] In addition, see Leon Morris, "Additional Note F: The Paraclete," *John*, pp. 662-666; and M.M.B. Turner, "Holy Spirit," DJG, pp. 349-351.

[619] "Another" is *allos*, "other, another" (BDAG 46-47).

[620] "Lives" (NIV), "abides" (NRSV), "dwells" (ESV, KJV) is *menō* in the present tense, "remain, stay," in transferred sense, "of someone who does not leave a certain realm or sphere: remain, continue, abide" (BDAG 631, 1aβ). It is possible that *menei*, present tense, could be accented as *meneî* making it future tense (which wouldn't show up in the manuscripts), but the present tense is more likely (Morris, *John*, p. 650, fn. 49).

[621] "With" is the preposition *para* with the dative, "marker of nearness in space, at/by (the side of), beside, near, with" (BDAG 757, 1).

[622] "Will/shall be" is *eimi*, "to be," in the future tense. Most ancient manuscripts show this as the future tense *estai*, except a few as present tense, *estin* – p[75] B D* W it. The future is likely here.

[623] "In" is the preposition *en*, "in," here, a "marker of close association within a limit, in" (BDAG 328, 4c).

Q1. (John 14:15-17) What do you think is the best way to describe the *Paraklētos* that Jesus sends? In what sense is the Holy Spirit "another" Paraclete? Who was the initial Paraclete? In what way can the Holy Spirit replace him?
http://www.joyfulheart.com/forums/topic/1502-q1-another-paraclete/

I Will Come to You (14:18-20)

"[18] I will not leave you as orphans; I will come to you. [19] Before long, the world will not see me anymore, but you will see me. Because I live, you also will live. [20] On that day you will realize that I am in my Father, and you are in me, and I am in you." (14:18-20)

When Jesus said he was going away and would be crucified, his disciples were shocked. Now Jesus assures them by explaining that he won't leave them "desolate" (RSV), literally, "orphaned" (NRSV), a word sometimes used to describe the state of disciples at the death of their rabbi.[624]

Rather than leave them desolate, Jesus says, "I will come to you." The question is: When and how will Jesus come to them? Commentators are divided here.

1. **Second Coming**. Jesus will come at the end of the age, which seems to be what is meant in 14:3. This view was held by the Latin Fathers.

2. **Post-Resurrection Appearances**. Jesus will appear to them after his resurrection. This would accord with the phrase "before long" or "in a little while"[625] – though Jesus describes his Second Coming as "soon" elsewhere (Revelation 22:7, 12, 20). It also is supported by the phrase "the world will not see me anymore." Jesus appeared to his disciples after his resurrection, not to unbelievers (Acts 10:40-41). The connection of "because I live, you also will live" with the resurrection seems obvious.[626] Such an interpretation seems to accord with the passage conceptually closest to it in 16:16-30. This view was generally held by the Eastern Fathers.[627]

3. **Coming of the Holy Spirit**. Jesus is speaking of a more continued presence – "I shall not leave you orphans" (14:18). His words in verses 18-20 imply a permanence. In addition, these verses appear immediately following a promise of the Paraclete in verses 16-17 and are shortly followed by another reference to the Paraclete in verses 25 and 26. Indeed, Jesus tells his disciples, "Lo, I am with you always, to the close of the age" (Matthew 28:20b). Our passage also talks about the mutual indwelling of the Father and Jesus in us (verse 20). In verse 23, Jesus promises obedient believers that he and the

---

[624] "Orphans" (NIV, ESV), "orphaned" (NRSV), "desolate" (RSV), "comfortless" (KJV) is *orphanos* (from which we get our English word "orphan"), "pertaining to being deprived of parents, without parents, orphan," then, by extension, "pertaining to being without the aid and comfort of one who serves as associate and friend, orphaned" (BDAG 725, 2). Disciples of a rabbi (Strack and Billerbeck 2:562) – and disciples of Socrates (*Phaedo* 116A) – were said to be "orphaned" at the death of their mentor (Brown, *John* 2:640).

[625] "Before long" (NIV), "in a little while" (NRSV, ESV, KJV) is two words, *eti*, "yet" and *micros*, "small," here, and in 16:16-19, of time, this combination = "soon" (*micros*, BDAG 651, 1dβ).

[626] Morris, *John*, p. 650-651; Beasley-Murray, *John*, pp. 258-259.

[627] Carson (*John*, p. 501-502) argues that "a concatenation of small clues drives the reader to the conclusion that Jesus is referring to his departure in death and his return after his resurrection." Kruse (*John*, pp. 306-308) also sees this passage as a reference to the coming of the Holy Spirit.

Father, "will come to him and make our home with him" (14:23) – a spiritual, not a physical reality. Brown examines the parallels between verses 15-17 and verses 18-21, and concludes,

> "Such parallelism is John's way of telling the reader that the presence of Jesus after his return to the Father is accomplished in and through the Paraclete. Not two presences but the same presence is involved."[628]

Devout Christians disagree on the exact interpretation of verses 15-17. I think a good case can be made for 2 and 3. For me, arguments for Jesus coming to his disciples in the Holy Spirit seem more compelling than the other possibilities. But, since John is known for his double meanings, it's possible that here Jesus is referring to *both* his coming to them following the resurrection *and* by the Holy Spirit.

Loving Jesus Means Obeying His Commandments (14:15, 21-25)

Now we consider a theme concerning obeying Jesus' commandments found twice in our lesson.

> "If you love me, you will obey what I command." (14:15)

> "21 Whoever has my commands and obeys them, he is the one who loves me. He who loves me will be loved by my Father, and I too will love him and show myself to him.
> 22 Then Judas (not Judas Iscariot) said, 'But, Lord, why do you intend to show yourself to us and not to the world?'
> 23 Jesus replied, 'If anyone loves me, he will obey my teaching. My Father will love him, and we will come to him and make our home with him. 24 He who does not love me will not obey my teaching. These words you hear are not my own; they belong to the Father who sent me. 25 All this I have spoken while still with you.'" (14:21-25)

The key verb is "obey" (NIV), "keep" (NRSV, ESV, KJV), *tēreō*, "keep watch over, guard," here with the extended sense, "to persist in obedience, keep, observe, fulfill, pay attention to," especially of law and teaching.[629,630] The key noun, translated "what I command" (NIV), "commandments" (NRSV, ESV, KJV) is *entolē*, "a mandate or ordinance, command."[631] This theme tying love and obedience is found throughout the Johannine books of the Bible,[632] but less often in the Synoptic Gospels.[633]

What commands is Jesus referring to? In the Synoptic Gospels, Jesus discusses keeping the Mosaic Law and interpreting it properly, correcting some of the Pharisees' distortions. Jesus sums up the law and the prophets in the two great commandments – to love God and love one's neighbor (Matthew 22:36-40). In John's Gospel, of course, just prior to this, Jesus had given a very clear command:

---

[628] Brown, *John* 2:644-646.

[629] *Tēreō*, BDAG 1002, 3.

[630] Most modern translations rely on ancient texts that show this verb in the future tense, though the KJV translates it as an imperative. Future tense (B L Ψ etc.; NIV, NRSV, RSV, ESV, NASB) was preferred by a majority of the Committee, because it accords better with the future tense in verse 16, though the imperative is well supported (A D K W X Δ Θ Π f1 f13 Byz; KJV). Brown, *John* 2:638 translates it in the imperative and says it accords well with verses 15 and 16.

[631] *Entolē*, BDAG 340, 2aGimmel, δ. Used in John 13:34; 14:15, 21; 15:10a, 12; 1 John 2:3-4.

[632] John 8:51-52; 14:15, 21, 23-24; 15:10ab, 20ab; 17:6; 1 John 2:3-5; 3:22, 24; 5:3; Revelation 1:3; 2:26; 3:3, 8, 10; 12:17; 14:12; 22:7. Beyond these passages, the idea of loving Jesus is surprisingly infrequent in the New Testament. It is found with *agapoō* in 8:42; 21:15-17; Ephesians 6:24; 1 Peter 1:8; and with *phileō* in 16:27; 21:17; Matthew 10:37; 1 Corinthians 16:22.

[633] Cf. Luke 11.28; Matthew 10:37.

"A new command I give you: Love one another. As I have loved you, so you must love one another. By this all men will know that you are my disciples, if you love one another." (13:34-35)

When Jesus gives what are called commands, they refer to love. The bulk of Jesus' teaching and ministry concerns aren't couched in terms of "commandments," but as a way of life. To summarize, Jesus teaches his disciples:

- Who he is,
- The meaning of his crucifixion and resurrection,
- Being set free and born by the Spirit,
- Loving one's enemies,
- Forgiveness,
- Humble service,
- Worship from the heart rather than mere outward observance,
- Faith, prayer, and obedience to the Father's direction,
- Healing the sick,
- Commitment to him despite persecution,
- Ministry to the lost,
- The coming Holy Spirit, and
- Final judgment and reward at his return.

As the disciples incorporate this lifestyle and these values into their lives, they are able to carry on his mission and pass it on to others. In the Great Commission Jesus tells us to make disciples, "teaching them to obey (*tēreō*, "keep, observe") everything I have commanded you" (Matthew 28:20). We don't teach a set of commands, a code of law, so much as values and a way of life.

Even though the Christian faith isn't characterized by obeying a set of commands, you and I know that it is clearly possible to live in such a way that displeases God, that is the opposite of what Christ teaches us: sexual immorality, deceit, stealing, selfishness, exploitation of others, etc. But the Christian life doesn't consist in what we *don't* do, what we avoid, but in the positive ways we begin to incorporate Jesus' way of life into our world.

What strikes me is that in these verses is the close relationship between love and obedience. Love seems like a relationship word, while obedience sometimes comes about by other motives than love. We can obey out of fear of getting caught and being punished. We can obey out of hope for advancement and favor. We can obey out of a sense of moral uprightness (which could edge into self-righteousness) without any real love for Jesus. We see this in the Pharisees' observance of the oral law.

But Jesus says that if we love him, we will obey or keep his commandments, his teachings. A quotation attributed to St. Augustine puts it this way:

"Love God and do whatever you please, for the soul trained in love to God will do nothing to offend the One who is Beloved."[634]

If we love someone, we don't have difficulty doing the things we know they want. Keeping Jesus' teachings can be one clear evidence of our love.

---

[634] I have searched diligently for the source of this quotation, but have come up dry. A similar thought, however, is found in Augustine's *Homilies on 1 John*, 7.8.

In Jesus' Parable of the Sheep and the Goats, he recognizes people who keep his teachings:

> "For I was hungry and you gave me something to eat, I was thirsty and you gave me something to drink, I was a stranger and you invited me in, I needed clothes and you clothed me, I was sick and you looked after me, I was in prison and you came to visit me.... I tell you the truth, whatever you did for one of the least of these brothers of mine, you did for me." (Matthew 25:35-36, 40)

Does this mean that we are saved by works rather than faith? No, but the way we live reflects our love and our faith. Jesus' brother James writes:

> "As the body without the spirit is dead, so faith without deeds is dead." (James 2:26)

Love and obedience go hand in hand. Does obeying Jesus' commands introduce a new legalism in the place of grace? No. But just as loving one another is one indicator of being a disciple (13:35), observing Jesus' teachings in the way we live our lives is an indicator of our love for him.

The Gospel of John concludes with this same theme, linking love for Jesus with faithful service.

> "Jesus said to Simon Peter, 'Simon son of John, do you love me more than these?' He said to him, 'Yes, Lord; you know that I love you.' Jesus said to him, 'Feed my lambs.'" (John 21:15)

Q2. (John 14:15, 21-25) How is obedience to Jesus linked to loving him? When Jesus emphasizes obedience, what keeps this from being the heavy burden of a new legalism? Can we love Jesus and *not* obey him? If so, how?
http://www.joyfulheart.com/forums/topic/1503-q2-linking-love-to-obedience/

The Paraclete as Teacher (14:25-26)

Now Jesus returns to explain more about the Paraclete who will be sent to his disciples.

> "25 All this I have spoken while still with you. 26 But the Counselor, the Holy Spirit, whom the Father will send in my name, will teach you all things and will remind you of everything I have said to you." (14:25-26)

In these two verses, Jesus reveals several things about the Paraclete.

1. The Paraclete is sent by Father in name of Jesus. (For more on this see Appendix 9. The Sending of the Holy Spirit.) "In the name of" may suggest that the Spirit is Jesus' personal emissary.[635]

2. The Paraclete refers specifically to the Holy Spirit. This verse makes it explicit.

3. The Paraclete will teach (*didaskō*) the disciples all things.

4. The Paraclete will remind[636] the disciples of what Jesus taught. We probably shouldn't separate reminding and teaching as two *separate* functions. Reminding is part of the teaching function.

---

[635] Carson, *John*, p. 505.

[636] "Remind" (NIV, NRSV), "bring to your remembrance" (RSV, ESV, KJV) is the verb *hypomimnēskō*, "to put another in mind of something, remind," from *mimnēskomai*, "to recall information from memory, remember, recollect, remind

5.   The Paraclete is spoken of in personal terms (14:26). We'll discuss this below in 15:26 (Lesson 27), and in Appendix 8. The Paraclete.

Jesus has been the disciples' rabbi and teacher. Now the Holy Spirit will take over that function. The disciples often misunderstood what Jesus had said and done. When the Holy Spirit comes he will help them remember – so they can understand and interpret correctly for the church – what Jesus had taught them. Now they'll be assessing Jesus' words in the light of his crucifixion, resurrection, and ascension. Evangelicals believe that the Holy Spirit superintended the development of apostolic doctrine so that it properly interpreted Jesus' own teaching (2:17, 22; 12:16).

The Holy Spirit doesn't bring a new revelation (16:13). Rather he represents Jesus and makes Jesus' teaching clear.

> **Q3. (John 14:25-26). What do we learn about the Paraclete in verses 25 and 26? Who is he? Why is his teaching/reminding role important to the apostles?**
> **http://www.joyfulheart.com/forums/topic/1504-q3-he-will-teach-you/**

My Peace I Give You (14:27)

The chapter began with Jesus' comfort: "Let not your hearts be troubled..." (14:1)

> "Peace I leave[637] with you; my peace I give you. I do not give to you as the world gives. Do not let your hearts be troubled and do not be afraid." (14:27)

I am going, says Jesus, but my *shalom*, my peace, I leave with you. Peace, in the Hebrew sense of *shalom*, is a broad word that implies general well-being, welfare, blessing.[638] Our English word "peace," on the other hand is generally applied to the absence of conflict. Among Jews, *shalom* was and is used as a greeting. But Jesus means something more, something deeper than a well-wisher's friendly words.

Jesus' peace is not like worldly peace. Later in the Farewell Discourse, Jesus tells us that peace is found "in me" (16:33). It is not absence of conflict (Matthew 10:34). Indeed, all but one of Jesus' apostles would suffer violent death as a martyr. Jesus' peace is a state of peace and goodwill with the King of Kings; it is "peace with God through our Lord Jesus Christ" (Romans 5:1; Acts 10:36; vs. Luke 19:41-42). It is also wholeness, the health that Jesus offered the woman healed from a hemorrhage,

---

oneself." I don't see much influence on the meaning of the word from the prefix *hypo-*. In classical Greek, *hypomimnēskō* denoted, "put one in mind or remind one of" as well as, "bring to one's mind, mention, suggest" (Liddell-Scott, *Greek-English Lexicon*). The word is also used at Luke 22:61; 2 Timothy 2;14; Titus 3:1; 2 Peter 1:12; 3 John 10; and Jude 5. The noun form *hypomnēsis* is used at 2 Peter 1:13; 3:1; 2 Timothy 1;5.

[637] "Leave" is *aphiēmi*, "to cause someone to undergo separation," here in the sense, "to have something continue or remain in a place, leave standing/lying" (BDAG 156, 4).

[638] "Peace" is *eirēnē*, "a state of concord, peace, harmony," between governments and in personal relationships. Then, "a state of well-being, peace," corresponding to the Hebrew *shalom*, "welfare, health." The farewell greeting, "go in peace," is approximately equivalent to "keep well." According to the prophets, peace will be an essential characteristic of the messianic kingdom. So Christian thought frequently regards peace as nearly synonymous with messianic salvation (*eirēnē*, BDAG 288).

"Daughter, your faith has healed you. Go in peace" (Luke 8:48). Jesus' peace is a promise that he is with us forever – "Surely I am with you always, to the very end of the age" (Matthew 28:20b).

This peace of the Messiah was promised centuries before by the prophet Isaiah.

> "He will be called Wonderful Counselor, Mighty God,
> Everlasting Father, Prince of Peace.
> Of the increase of his government and peace there will be no end." (Isaiah 9:6b-7a)

When Messiah reigns on the Last Day, his peace will reign over all and bring pervasive change, and will include absence of conflict throughout his realm.

> "The wolf will live with the lamb,
> the leopard will lie down with the goat,
> the calf and the lion and the yearling together;
> and a little child will lead them.
> The cow will feed with the bear,
> their young will lie down together,
> and the lion will eat straw like the ox.
> The infant will play near the hole of the cobra,
> and the young child put his hand into the viper's nest.
> They will neither harm nor destroy on all my holy mountain,
> for the earth will be full of the knowledge of the LORD
> as the waters cover the sea." (Isaiah 11:6-9)

Q4. (John 14:27) If it doesn't mean cessation of conflict in our everyday lives, what then is the peace that Jesus offers us now?
http://www.joyfulheart.com/forums/topic/1505-q4-jesus-peace/

Going Away and Coming Back (14:28-29)

"[28] You heard me say, 'I am going away and I am coming back to you.' If you loved me, you would be glad that I am going to the Father, for the Father is greater than I. [29] I have told you now before it happens, so that when it does happen you will believe." (14:28-29)

Some have claimed that the statement, "the Father is greater than I," proves that Jesus didn't claim divinity or equality with God. Not at all. It does show subordination to the Father, which we see elsewhere (5:19; 14:31; Luke 22:42; 1 Corinthians 3:23; 11:3; 15:27-29). But subordination does not imply inferiority of person. As theologians put it, the Son is subordinate functionally, but not ontologically (based on being or existence). Carson points out, if he were to say, "'Her Majesty Queen Elizabeth the Second is greater than I,' no one would take this to mean that she is more of a human being than I."[639]

The Prince of this World (14:30-31a)

Now Jesus reminds them that his time is short.

[639] Carson, *John*, p. 507.

"³⁰ I will not speak with you much longer, for the prince of this world is coming. He has no hold on me, ³¹ but the world must learn that I love the Father and that I do exactly what my Father has commanded me." (14:30-31a)

In these two verses we learn three things.

1. "The prince of this world," Satan, still has power in this world, even though at some point "he will be driven out" (12:31).

2. Satan has no hold on Jesus, no secret power, no sin to accuse him of. "No hold on me" (NIV), "no power over me" (NRSV), "no claim on me" (ESV), "hath nothing in me" (KJV), is literally, "in me he does not have anything (*ouden*)."

3. Jesus' obedience to the Father shows his love. This is part of the "glory" of the cross. This demonstrates the love within the Godhead that has existed before the beginning.

People become subject to blackmail when someone knows a naughty secret from their past, and threatens to expose them unless they do or pay whatever the blackmailer requires. But Satan can find nothing in Jesus to use as leverage. He has nothing on Jesus.

> **Q5. (John 14:30-31a) How does Satan take advantage of our previous sins to control us or make us fearful? In verse 31, how does Jesus stay free from bondage to Satan? How can we free ourselves from bondage to Satan and fear of exposure?**
> **http://www.joyfulheart.com/forums/topic/1506-q5-bondage-to-satan/**

Let Us Leave (14:31b)

The final verse in the chapter is curious:

> "Come now; let us leave." (14:31b)

Since the Farewell Discourses continue for several more chapters, they may have been delivered elsewhere than at the Upper Room -- on the road to the Mount of Olives, perhaps. However, later we read:

> "When he had finished praying, Jesus left with his disciples and crossed the Kidron Valley. On the other side there was an olive grove, and he and his disciples went into it." (18:1)

So where Jesus was during the later part of the Farewell Discourses remains somewhat of a mystery.

Lessons for Disciples

We disciples can learn a number of things from the passage we've been studying:

1. The Father will send us the Holy Spirit, called the "Paraclete," who is a Helper, Advocate, Encourager, and Friend who comes alongside us to help us (14:15-17).

2. The Paraclete is in some aspects a replacement for Jesus, who had come alongside the disciples to help them (14:16).

3. Jesus promises to come to his disciples, though it's not clear whether this refers to Jesus' post-resurrection appearances or to his presence in the Holy Spirit (14:18-20).

4. Love for Jesus will show up in willing obedience to his commands, especially his command to love one another. Lack of obedience indicates lack of love, though this is not intended to become a new legalism (14:15, 21-25).
5. The Paraclete, the Holy Spirit, is sent by the Father in Jesus' name (14:26).
6. The Paraclete will instruct the disciples and remind them of what Jesus taught (14:26).
7. Jesus offers his peace – peace with God – though not yet a lack of conflict in the world (14:27).
8. Jesus says the Father is greater than he – in role and power, but not greater in divinity or in person (14:28).
9. Satan, the "prince of this world," will wreak havoc in the world, but he has no power over Jesus, and doesn't need to have power over us either (14:30-31).

Prayer

Father, thank you for sending us the Holy Spirit. It seems like we have so much to learn about who he is and how to listen to him. Please help us to learn to walk in the presence and the power of the Spirit in our world. We have no power of ourselves, but in You we can overcome the world! In Jesus' name, we pray. Amen.

Key Verses

"If you love me, you will obey what I command." (John 14:15, NIV)

"I will ask the Father, and he will give you another Counselor to be with you forever – the Spirit of truth... You know him, for he lives with you and will be in you." (John 14:16-17)

"On that day you will realize that I am in my Father, and you are in me, and I am in you." (John 14:20, NIV)

"If anyone loves me, he will obey my teaching. My Father will love him, and we will come to him and make our home with him." (John 14:23, NIV)

"The Counselor, the Holy Spirit, whom the Father will send in my name, will teach you all things and will remind you of everything I have said to you." (John 14:26, NIV)

"Peace I leave with you; my peace I give you. I do not give to you as the world gives. Do not let your hearts be troubled and do not be afraid." (John 14:27, NIV)

"I will not speak with you much longer, for the prince of this world is coming. He has no hold on me." (John 14:30, NIV)

26. Abiding in the Vine (15:1-17)

John's Gospel is full of rich nuggets of truth that teach us about our Father, Jesus, salvation, eternal life, and the Holy Spirit. This lesson helps us explore the dynamic relationship between a disciple and his Lord.

Jesus' teaching on the vine and the branches isn't like most of the parables in the Synoptic Gospels, which are usually stories with one or more spiritual points. Here, as in Jesus' discourse on the Good Shepherd (10:1-18), we see an *extended metaphor*. Jesus draws our attention to a fruitful vine and then provides two primary applications for us to learn from – pruning the branches and abiding in the vine. These 17 verses aren't long, but contain some of the most important and beloved passages in the Bible about the disciple's love relationship with Jesus.

Icon of Christ the True Vine (late 20th century), Dormition Convent, Parnes, Greece, based on an early 15th century by Angelos Akotantos at Malles, Hierapetra.

I Am the Vine (15:1)

In verse 1, Jesus introduces the metaphor.

"I am the true vine, and my Father is the gardener." (15:1)

The vine[640] was one of the quintessential plants of Israel representing national peace and prosperity – "every man under his vine and fig tree."[641]

Moreover, the vineyard is often used to identify Israel herself, referred to by the prophets as "my vineyard" (Isaiah 3:14). In the Song of the Vineyard (Isaiah 5:1-7), the vineyard is the "house of Israel" that yields only the bad fruit of injustice and oppression. But in Day of the Messiah, this vineyard will flourish:

"In that day—Sing about a fruitful vineyard:
I, the LORD, watch over it;
I water it continually.
I guard it day and night
so that no one may harm it." (Isaiah 27:2-3)

The Psalms, Ezekiel, Jeremiah, Hosea, and Micah all use the figure of Israel as the Lord's vineyard.[642] Jesus himself carried on this identification of Israel as God's vineyard in his Parable of the Tenants

---

[640] "Vine" is *ampelos*, "vine, grapevine" (BDAG 54, a).

[641] 1 Kings 4:25; 2 Kings 18:31; Zechariah 3:10; Micah 4:4.

[642] Psalm 80:8-16; Ezekiel 15:1-8; 17:1-21; 19:10-14; Jeremiah 2:21; 12:10; Hosea 10:1-2; Micah 7:1.

(Matthew 21:33-44; Mark 12:1-12; Luke 20:9-19) and Parable of the Workers in the Vineyard (Matthew 20:1-16).

So for Jesus to say, "I am the true vine" (in the seventh and last of Jesus' "I AM" sayings"[643]), we see an announcement that, as the Messiah, he now becomes the true Israel, the true locus for God's people. When you think about it, it is an astounding revelation!

> "I am the true vine, and my Father is the gardener." (15:1)

The nation is epitomized in the nation's true King, Jesus.

If Jesus is the true vine, then his Father is the vinedresser[644], the one who tenderly cares for the vine, cutting and pruning so that it produces the maximum amount of fruit possible.

Pruning and Cutting (15:2-3)

> "[2] He cuts off every branch in me that bears no fruit, while every branch that does bear fruit he prunes so that it will be even more fruitful. [3] You are already clean because of the word I have spoken to you." (15:2-3)

Since there are several vineyards within one quarter mile of my house, with the owner a personal friend, I've had considerable opportunity over the years to observe the cycles of pruning, growth, and harvest.

A grapevine consists of the woody trunk with one or more cordons, woody extensions of the trunk that remain from year to year. Together, the trunk and cordons are what Jesus refers to as the "vine." The fruitfulness comes from the canes, shoots, or spurs that grow from these woody cordons.

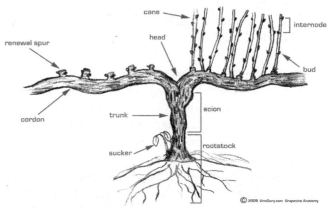

Grapevine Terminology. Diagram © 2009, VinoDiary.com. Used by permission.

These canes, shoots, or spurs Jesus is calling the "branches."[645] The fruit forms from buds on the new canes. The old canes do not produce again.

Pruning takes experience and skill. After the harvest, winter comes when the leaves fall off and the vine goes dormant. During this time, before the new buds of spring, the pruning takes place. Our text discusses two operations – (1) removing unfruitful branches, and (2) pruning the fruitful ones.

The vinedresser looks for any shoots that didn't bear fruit the previous season, due to disease or damage of one kind or another. These he cuts off[646] entirely so that the energy of the plant is not wasted on unfruitful or diseased branches, but can go into branches that do bear fruit.

---

[643] See Appendix 4. The "I Am" Passages in John's Gospel.

[644] "Gardener" (NIV), "vinegrower" (NRSV), "vinedresser" (ESV, RSV), "husbandman" (KJV) is geōrgos, generally, one who is occupied in agriculture or gardening, "farmer," then, "one who does agricultural work on a contractual basis, vine-dresser, tenant farmer" (BDAG 196, 2). This is a compound noun, from ge, "land" + ergon, "worker."

[645] "Branch" is klēma, "branch," especially of a vine (BDAG 547).

The fruitful branches are pruned back to the first two nodes on the old shoot to form new canes for next year's growth. Without pruning, the fruit for the new season will be dramatically diminished, and the vine will begin to grow wild, producing some grapes, but making it hard for the plant to get enough light and making it difficult to harvest what few grapes are produced. Pruning shocks the plant, to be sure, but in the hands of a skillful vinedresser, the vine remains healthy and produces maximum fruit year after year.

What does "cutting off every branch in me that bears no fruit (15:2a)" refer to? Since Jesus the True Vine represents true Israel, the Father is pruning off those who rebel against the Messiah. We see this expressed in the Parable of the Tenants who refused to pay rent to the owner of the vineyard. Jesus concludes the parable with the words:

> "Therefore I tell you that the kingdom of God will be taken away from you and given to a people who will produce its fruit." (Matthew 21:43)

After getting rid of the dead wood, the vinedresser gets down to the exacting work of pruning each shoot or branch. The purposes of pruning are to:

- Stimulate growth,
- Allow the vinedresser to shape the vine,
- Produce maximum yield without breaking the branches with too many clusters for them to bear,
- Protect against mildew,
- Produce better quality wine, with more highly concentrated and flavorful grapes.

Of course, the Father does pruning in our lives, too, so that you and I will become healthy and bear much spiritual fruit. When I had an Internet marketing business, I tried to practice the principle to cut off each year the least cost-effective part of my business, the bottom 10%, so I could free up time and resources for new opportunities.

You may be spending lots of time in activities that are fruitless. I can remember God telling me when I was in college to throw away my cherished notebook of folk music so I could concentrate on music that honored him. Sometimes we suffer losses and grieve about them, but find that God is redirecting and healing us. We can trust the Vinedresser and must be obedient, if we want his skill to make us whole and fruitful.

Churches, too, need pruning. How many activities are continued because "we've always done that," long past the time when they are effective in advancing the Kingdom? Sometimes people need to be removed from leadership and others moved into leadership. Some churches suffer severe injury because they tolerate the unspiritual control and direction of "big givers," but are too weak to say, "No." Pruning is needed. Some churches experience a painful time when a number of members leave over some issue. But when this loss is surrendered to God and forgiveness is sought, this "pruning"

---

[646] "Cuts off" (NIV), "removes" (NRSV), "takes away" (ESV, KJV) is *airō*, "lift up," here, "to take away, remove, or seize control" without suggestion of lifting up, "take away, remove" (BDAG 29, 3). Some writers have suggested that *airō* should be rendered "lifted up" rather than "take away." That fruitless branches are lifted up from the ground so they can be exposed to the sun and will begin to bear fruit. However, there is no evidence that this was the practice of viticulture, ancient or modern (Carson, *John*, p. 518). It is an attempt to avoid the concept that unfruitful Christians are "cut off." But, as I explain in the text, Jesus has in mind the nation of Israel being cut off for unfruitfulness.

can become the impetus for new growth. Trust the Vinedresser and be obedient. Don't prune rashly, but seek his season and his way.

> **Q1. (John 15:2) How does judicious pruning benefit a grapevine? What happens to productivity and health when a vine is left unpruned? What does God use to prune our lives? What does God use to prune our congregations? Why do we resist pruning? What can we do so that the eventual pruning isn't as severe?**
> http://www.joyfulheart.com/forums/topic/1507-q1-benefits-of-pruning/

Cleansed by the Word (15:3)

Now we come to a curious verse.

> "² He cuts off every branch in me that bears no fruit, while every branch that does bear fruit he prunes (*katharizō*) so that it will be even more fruitful. ³ You are already clean (*katharizō*) because of the word I have spoken to you." (15:2-3)

Notice that the Greek word *katharizō*, "to clean, cleanse," can also be translated "prune" (NIV, NRSV, ESV), "purge" (KJV), that is, cleanse the vine. Jesus' Word is a cause of that moral and spiritual cleansing.[647]

Jesus is speaking to his disciples. The effect of obedience and "holding to" Jesus' teaching is freedom from the slavery to sin, and separation from evil (8:31-34). God's Word, when received, has a washing, cleansing, pruning, faith-producing effect on us:

> "Christ loved the church and gave himself up for her to make her holy, **cleansing her by the washing with water through the word**, and to present her to himself as a radiant church, without stain or wrinkle or any other blemish, but holy and blameless." (Ephesians 5:25b-27)

> "**Sanctify them by the truth**; your word is truth." (John 17:17)

> "Now that you have **purified yourselves by obeying the truth** so that you have sincere love for your brothers, love one another deeply, from the heart. For you have been born again, not of perishable seed, but of imperishable, through **the living and enduring word of God**." (1 Peter 1:22-23)

> "He chose to give us birth through the **word of truth**, that we might be a kind of firstfruits of all he created." (James 1:18)

> **Q2. (John 15:2b) How are we pruned or cleansed by exposure to and obedience to Jesus' words? According to John 8:31-32, how does obeying Jesus' teaching bring cleansing and freedom from sin?**
> http://www.joyfulheart.com/forums/topic/1508-q2-cleansed-by-the-word/

---

[647] The preposition *dia* with the accusative is a "marker of something constituting cause" (BDAG 225, B2a).

Remaining, Abiding in the Vine (15:4-5)

Jesus has considered the metaphor of pruning the vine. Now he looks at the metaphor of abiding in the vine.

"4 Remain in me, and I will remain in you. No branch can bear fruit by itself; it must remain in the vine. Neither can you bear fruit unless you remain in me. 5 I am the vine; you are the branches. If a man remains in me and I in him, he will bear much fruit; apart from me you can do nothing." (15:4-5)

"Remain" (NIV), "abide" (NRSV, ESV, KJV) is *menō*, "remain, stay." It can be used of a location, "stay," often in the special sense of "to live, dwell, lodge." Here, it is in the transferred sense of someone who does not leave a certain realm or sphere: "remain, continue, abide."[648] We observed this word previously –

"If you **abide** in my word, you are truly my disciples, and you will know the truth, and the truth will set you free." (8:31-32, ESV)

To "abide" means that we "hold to" (NIV) or "continue in" (NRSV, KJV) Jesus' teaching (cf. John 5:38; 2 John 9). This is the opposite of running hot for a short period of time, and then coasting. Those who abide in Jesus' word don't give up under persecution or allow their fruitfulness to be choked by the "weeds" of worldly pressures (to use the vocabulary of Jesus' Parable of the Sower, Matthew 13:1-8, 18-23). Rather they produce a harvest of 30-fold, 60-fold, or 100-fold. Jesus taught that believers will continue in the faith (Matthew 24:13; Mark 13:3; Luke 8:15). The Apostle Paul also taught that salvation is contingent upon believers continuing or persevering in their faith (Colossians 1:23, *epimenō*[649]; 1 Corinthians 15:2, *katechō*[650], 2 Timothy 3:14, *menō*; see Hebrews 3:6; cf. 10:39).

I. Howard Marshall says:

"The element of trust and commitment in faith is particularly emphasized and expressed in John by the use of the verb 'to abide' (*menō*), which might almost be said to be the Johannine equivalent for 'to persevere.'"[651]

Wayne Grudem begins his statement of the doctrine of the Perseverance of the Saints in this way:

"The perseverance of the saints means that all those who are truly born again will be kept by God's power and will persevere as Christians until the end of their lives...."[652]

But "abiding" extends beyond continuing in faith. In this metaphor of the vine and the branches, "abiding" refers to being intimately connected to and receiving nourishment from the vine. Look at the passage again.

---

[648] *Menō*, BDAG 631, 1bβ.

[649] *Epimenō*, "to continue in an activity or state, continue, persist (in), persevere," from *epi-*, "continuance, rest, influence upon or over" + *menō*, "remain, stay, persist" (BDAG 375, 2).

[650] *Katechō*, "to adhere firmly to traditions, convictions, or beliefs, hold to, hold fast" (BDAG 533, 2a).

[651] I. Howard Marshall, *Kept by the Power of God* (Bethany Fellowship, 1969), p. 183.

[652] Grudem, *Systematic Theology*, p. 788. Grudem completes his definition, with these words "... and that only those who persevere until the end have been truly born again." While Calvinists and Arminians disagree on whether a truly born again person can lose his or her salvation, both agree that the true saints are those who persevere in their faith.

> "⁴ Remain in me, and I will remain in you. No branch can bear fruit by itself; it must remain in the vine. Neither can you bear fruit unless you remain in me. ⁵ I am the vine; you are the branches. If a man remains in me and I in him, he will bear much fruit; apart from me you can do nothing." (15:4-5)

What, then does "abiding" entail? We're not talking about belief as intellectual assent, but belief as embracing, clinging to, and continuing to receive spiritual sustenance from. As we've seen in John (14:15, 21-25) and see later in this lesson (15:9-10) discipleship also involves obedience as an expression of our love for him.

In the face of the clear teaching of John 15, some Christians have an extremely sloppy understanding of the doctrine of the Perseverance of the Saints, asserting that saving faith need not be an enduring faith, one that perseveres.[653] You'll find further discussion of the doctrine of the Perseverance of the Saints in 10:28 (Lesson 19) and 17:11-15 (Lesson 29).

Mutual Indwelling (15:5b)

Abiding also involves a person who

"... **remains** (*menō*) **in me and I in him.**" (15:5b)

This phrase intrigues me, since Jesus also speaks about his relationship with the Father the same way in a number of places in John's Gospel:

"Whoever eats my flesh and drinks my blood **remains** (*menō*) **in me, and I in him.**" (6:56)

"Believe the miracles, that you may know and understand that **the Father is in me, and I in the Father.**" (10:38)

"Don't you believe that **I am in the Father, and that the Father is in me?** The words I say to you are not just my own. Rather, it is **the Father, living in me**, who is doing his work." (14:10)

"On that day you will realize that **I am in my Father, and you are in me, and I am in you.**" (14:20)

"If anyone loves me, he will obey my teaching. My Father will love him, and **we will come to him and make our home** (*monē*) **with him.**" (14:23)

"... that all of them may be one, Father, **just as you are in me and I am in you.**... I have given them the glory that you gave me, that they may be one as we are one: **I in them and you in me.**" (17:21-23)

"... that the love you have for me may be in them and that **I myself may be in them.**" (17:26)

This mutual indwelling is part of the Father's relationship with the Son. The Father and Son are the exemplars of what our relationship is to be with Jesus – constant living together, sharing a deepening relationship of love and (on our part) obedience.

---

[653] Charles Stanley's book *Eternal Security: Can You Be Sure?* (Oliver Nelson, 1990) has a chapter entitled, "For Those Who Stop Believing" (chapter 8). There he says, "The Bible clearly teaches that God's love for his people is of such magnitude that even those who walk away from the faith have not the slightest chance of slipping from his hand" (p. 74). He supports this from Ephesians 2:8-9, noting that faith itself is a gift, and God has a "strict no-return policy" (p. 81). He says, "You and I are not saved because we have an enduring faith. We are saved because *at a moment in time* we expressed faith in our enduring Lord" (p. 80). I understand (but disagree with) Stanley's logic. I have serious problems when I compare Stanley's teaching to Jesus' teaching about abiding in the vine in John 15:1-8.

This idea, of course, of being indwelt by Jesus and his Spirit is found throughout the New Testament. Jesus promises:

"I am with you always, to the very end of the age." (Matthew 28:20)

Paul says the same thing, but in more theological language. Here are just three examples:

"For in Christ all the fullness of the Deity lives in bodily form, and you have been given fullness in Christ...." (Colossians 2:9-10)

"I have been crucified with Christ and I no longer live, but Christ lives in me. The life I live in the body, I live by faith in the Son of God, who loved me and gave himself for me." (Galatians 2:20)

"You, however, are controlled ... by the Spirit, if the Spirit of God lives[654] in you. And if anyone does not have the Spirit of Christ, he does not belong to Christ." (Romans 8:9)

What are we to make of this? What are we do about it? Let's not take for granted that the Father, Son, and Holy Spirit live within us – and we in them. This is your opportunity and mine to really get to know God intimately, to become his Friend. We talk about a "personal relationship with Jesus Christ." What can you and I do to develop this relationship in a personal, on-going manner? To *know* God! To abide in Him!

> **Q3. (John 15:4-5) What does it mean "to abide"? What is the doctrine of the Perseverance of the Saints? How do these verses support it? What does abiding have to do with "mutual indwelling," of a "personal relationship"? How well are you abiding?**
> **http://www.joyfulheart.com/forums/topic/1509-q3-abiding-and-indwelling/**

Apart from Me You Can Do Nothing (15:4-6)

Abiding also involves utter dependence upon Jesus the Vine. If we branches don't continue intimately connected to the vine, our "sap" is cut off. We wither and whatever fruit might have been in the process of ripening becomes like dry raisins rather than lush grapes full of juice.

"[4] Remain in me, and I will remain in you. No branch can bear fruit by itself; it must remain in the vine. Neither can you bear fruit unless you remain in me. [5] I am the vine; you are the branches. If a man remains in me and I in him, he will bear much fruit; apart[655] from me you can do nothing. [6] If anyone does not remain in me, he is like a branch that is thrown away and withers; such branches are picked up, thrown into the fire and burned." (15:4-6)

Jesus observes that the branch must remain connected to the vine to produce any fruit. But we've seen this kind of language before. Jesus taught this truth again and again to his disciples:

"I tell you the truth, the Son can do nothing by himself; he can do only what he sees his Father doing, because whatever the Father does the Son also does." (5:19)

---

[654] *Oikeō*, "to live, dwell."

[655] "Apart from" (NIV, NRSV, ESV), "without" (KJV) is *chōris*, an adverb, here used as a preposition, "pertaining to the absence or lack of something, without, apart from, independent(ly of)" (BDAG 1095, 2aα).

> "By myself I can do nothing; I judge only as I hear, and my judgment is just, for I seek not to please myself but him who sent me." (5:30)

> "I do nothing on my own but speak just what the Father has taught me." (8:28b)

> "I did not speak of my own accord, but the Father who sent me commanded me what to say and how to say it." (12:49)

> "It is the Father, living in me, who is doing his work." (14:10b)

The truth is underscored by the man healed from blindness:

> "If this man were not from God, he could do nothing." (9:33)

There's something that perhaps we don't like about this. It diminishes Jesus' independence, we think. And perhaps we resent the statement, "apart from me you can do nothing," because it diminishes our *own* sense of independence. Part of our old nature loves the lines in William Ernest Henley's poem "Invictus" that read:

> "I am the master of my fate,
> I am the captain of my soul."

Something in our old nature wants to cry: I will be dependent upon no man – nor upon God!

But the path of the Master is a different path than self-determination. It is a path of listening and obeying, of observing and following. Jesus walked this path before us, doing exactly what he saw the Father doing. Now he beckons us to follow him in this same way. It is the path of a disciple following a Master, a Son following a Father. And it requires from us a humility that fully believes that apart from him we can do nothing.

Oh, we can do things by ourselves. We expend great human effort in doing so. But the things that last, that count for eternity, these we cannot do without his leading and his power. The older and wiser man or woman knows something that the young do not always grasp. Paul put it this way:

> "His work will be shown for what it is, because the Day will bring it to light. It will be revealed with fire, and the fire will test the quality of each man's work. If what he has built survives, he will receive his reward. If it is burned up, he will suffer loss; he himself will be saved, but only as one escaping through the flames." (1 Corinthians 3:13-15)

Do you want your life to count for something? Then live your life abiding with Jesus, and with his direction and power accomplish something that lasts. Paul wrote:

> "I can do everything through him who gives me strength." (Philippians 4:13)

> "I have been crucified with Christ and I no longer live, but Christ lives in me. The life I live in the body, I live by faith in the Son of God, who loved me and gave himself for me." (Galatians 2:20)

Q4. (John 15:4-6) Unbelievers can do many things. So what does Jesus mean when he says, "Apart from me you can do nothing"? What is the value of things done without Christ? What is the final end of things done without Christ?
http://www.joyfulheart.com/forums/topic/1510-q4-do-nothing-alone/

Withered Branches (15:6)

Jesus returns to the analogy of the vine as he describes withered branches.

> "If anyone does not remain in me, he is like a branch that is thrown away and withers[656]; such branches are picked up, thrown into the fire and burned." (15:6)

I live on a property with hundreds of trees. Not infrequently, as I walk around the property, I'll see a tree with a branch that is dry and brown. It may be diseased. It may have broken from high wind. Its vital connection with the trunk, however, has been severed, and the life from the sap no longer flows into the branch, bringing life. The leaves turn brown, the wood becomes brittle. It is dead. When I get around to it, I need to pull it into a pile and burn it – or grind it into wood chips with a chipper.

Jesus uses this analogy to impress on us the vital importance of staying connected to him, of abiding, continuing in him. To remain, to abide is a command (verse 4), not just an automatic condition. That means that we must do something to obey the command – not a work of righteousness in order to be saved, but active faith.

> "The work of God is this: to believe in the one he has sent." (6:29)

When Jesus talks here about withered branches being burned, is he talking about backslidden Christians or apostate Christians? Probably not directly. I think he is talking about the Jewish nation, God's vineyard, whose leaders had rejected their Messiah, the True Vine.

Bearing Much Fruit (15:7-8)

Jesus has explained the negative consequence of not abiding in him (verse 6). Now he points to the positive benefits of abiding (verses 7 and 8).

> "[7] If you remain (*menō*) in me and my words remain (*menō*) in you, ask whatever you wish, and it will be given you. [8] This is to my Father's glory, that you bear much fruit, showing[657] yourselves to be my disciples." (15:7-8)

"My words abide in you" means that we continue to obey his teachings and therefore receive Christ's wisdom.

> "If you hold to (*menō*) my teaching, you are really my disciples. Then you will know the truth, and the truth will set you free." (8:31b-32)

If we abide in Christ and in obedience to his teachings, they we can ask anything in prayer and he'll give it to us. Why? Because we'll be praying according to his will and leading! We'll be requesting things that will expand his kingdom, not just selfish requests.

> "Dear friends, if our hearts do not condemn us, we have confidence before God and receive from him anything we ask, because we obey his commands and do what pleases him." (1 John 3:21-22)

> "This is the confidence we have in approaching God: that if we ask anything according to his will, he hears us." (1 John 5:14)

---

[656] "Withers" is *xērainō*, "to stop a flow (such as sap or other liquid) in something and so cause dryness, to dry, dry up." It also can refer to paralysis, "to become dry to the point of being immobilized, be paralyzed," (BDAG 684, 1).

[657] "Showing yourself" (NIV) and "so prove" (ESV) is not in the actual Greek text, which is more literally, "that you bear much fruit and be my disciples." (NRSV margin).

As he gives us answers to our prayers, that is where the fruit-bearing will take place. Notice another indicator here of being a disciple of Jesus. True disciples bear fruit – much fruit, "fruit that will last" (15:16c). And this abundance of fruit brings glory to God the Father. As Jesus says in Matthew:

> "Let your light shine before men, that they may see your good deeds and praise your Father in heaven." (Matthew 5:16)

What Fruit Does Jesus Expect from Us?

So what exactly does Jesus mean by "bear much fruit"? The word *karpos* means fruit, then, "result, outcome, product."[658] To find out what this result is we can do a brief survey of *karpos* in the New Testament. Fruit applies to a new way of life, one's actions, to a way of living.

Fruit can be positive or negative (Romans 6:21-22). False prophets can be identified by their "fruit" (Matthew 7:15b-16a). Both Jesus and John the Baptist demanded repentance. John the Baptist commanded the Pharisees and Sadducees who came to his meetings, "Produce fruit in keeping with repentance" (Matthew 3:8). Concerning the whole Jewish nation that rejected him, Jesus said, "I tell you that the kingdom of God will be taken away from you and given to a people who will produce its fruit" (Matthew 21:43).

A number of verses identify fruit with righteous living (Philippians 1:11; James 3:18; Hebrews 12:11). Some passages spell out what this kind of living looks like:

> "Live as children of light (for the **fruit** of the light consists in all goodness, righteousness and truth)." (Ephesians 5:8b-9)

> "But the **fruit** of the Spirit is love, joy, peace, patience, kindness, goodness, faithfulness, gentleness and self-control." (Galatians 5:22-23a)

> "But the wisdom that comes from heaven is first of all pure; then peace-loving, considerate, submissive, full of mercy and good fruit, impartial and sincere." (James 3:17)

This kind of righteous living is what grows on a tree watered by the Holy Spirit.

In addition to speaking of the fruit of righteousness, Paul speaks of fruit as people won to Christ on his mission (Romans 1:13; 15:28; Philippians 1:22). Especially in the case of people with an apostolic or evangelistic gift, such as his Twelve Apostles, one's righteous character would also be accompanied by people being won to Christ. The same might be true of a person with the spiritual gift of teaching. The fruit would be people who learn the gospel from this teaching. Using our God-given gifts will produce results!

Abiding in Christ produces the fruit of righteous character – especially of love – and influence of this character that brings glory to God.

Q5. (John 15:7-8) The fruit from branches connected to a vine is the grape. What is the nature of the fruit that comes from being connected to Jesus? Is it accurate to define fruit as "souls saved"? What is the danger in this definition?
http://www.joyfulheart.com/forums/topic/1511-q5-fruit/

---

[658] *Karpos*, BDAG 510, 1b.

Obeying and Abiding in Jesus' Love (15:9-11)

John has a way of weaving themes in and out of Jesus' discourses – both in John's Gospel and in the First Epistle of John. So we shouldn't be surprised that this discourse on abiding should come back to the love and obedience that we saw earlier.

> "9 As the Father has loved me, so have I loved you. Now remain (*menō*) in my love. 10 If you obey my commands, you will remain (*menō*) in my love, just as I have obeyed my Father's commands and remain (*menō*) in his love. 11 I have told you this so that my joy may be in you and that your joy may be complete." (15:9-11)

The key verb is "obey" (NIV), "keep" (NRSV, ESV, KJV), *tēreō*, "keep watch over, guard," here with the extended sense, "to persist in obedience, keep, observe, fulfill, pay attention to," especially of law and teaching.[659] The key noun, translated "what I command" (NIV), "commandments" (NRSV, ESV, KJV) is *entolē*, "a mandate or ordinance, command."[660] This theme tying love and obedience is found throughout the Johannine books of the Bible,[661] and occasionally in the Synoptic Gospels.[662] Earlier we read:

> "If you love me, you will obey what I command." (14:15, also 14:21-25)

Some Christians have confused obedience with a kind of legalism that moves away from God's grace, his unmerited favor, to a place of earning favor with God by strict obedience as the Pharisees tried to do. This isn't what Jesus is saying. Rather, he is explaining that obedience is the natural result of love. If you love someone, you try to do what pleases that person.

Think of a disobedient child. Perhaps he loves his parents, but he has a poor way of showing it. They love him, but instead of being able to relax with him, they always have to maintain discipline. Only with children who are obedient can the parents relax in their joy with them. And this joy is what Jesus wants us to experience.

> "I have told you this so that my joy may be in you and that your joy may be complete." (15:11)

As we'll see in verses 14 and 15, Jesus desires to move his disciples from the place of servants, who obey because they have to, to friends, who obey because they want to.

Obedience from the heart, the cessation of rebellion, enables free-flowing fellowship. As John says in his First Epistle:

> "If we walk in the light, as he is in the light, we have fellowship with one another, and the blood of Jesus, his Son, purifies us from all sin." (1 John 1:7)

Q6. (John 15:9-11) How are obedience and joy linked? Is obedience an obstacle to a joyful relationship between you and the Lord?
http://www.joyfulheart.com/forums/topic/1512-q6-obedience-and-joy/

---

[659] *Tēreō*, BDAG 1002, 3.

[660] *Entolē*, BDAG 340, 2aGimmel, δ. Used in John 13:34; 14:15, 21; 15:10a, 12; 1 John 2:3-4.

[661] John 8:51-52; 14:15, 21, 23-24; 15:10ab, 20ab; 17:6; 1 John 2:3-5; 3:22, 24; 5:3; Revelation 1:3; 2:26; 3:3, 8, 10; 12:17; 14:12; 22:7. Beyond these passages, the idea of loving Jesus is surprisingly infrequent in the New Testament. It is found with *agapoō* in 8:42; 21:15-17; Ephesians 6:24; 1 Peter 1:8; and with *phileō* in 16:27; 21:17; Matthew 10:37; 1 Corinthians 16:22.

[662] Cf. Luke 11:28; Matthew 10:37.

Friends of Jesus (15:12-15)

Jesus comes back to his themes of love (13:34-35) and laying down one's life for the sheep (10:11, 15b), and then introduces the idea of friendship.

> "12 My command is this: Love each other as I have loved you. 13 Greater love has no one than this, that he lay down his life for his friends." (15:12-13)

"Friends" is *philos*, which we saw in 11:11 regarding Lazarus. It means, "pertaining to having a special interest in someone, beloved, dear, loving, kindly disposed, devoted," then as a substantive, "one who is on intimate terms or in close association with another, friend."[663] In a general sense, Jesus is called "a friend of tax collectors and sinners" (Luke 7:34b). In another place he refers to his disciples as "my friends" (Luke 12:4a).

Jesus shows his ultimate love by laying down his life for those loves. Amazingly, Paul reminds us, "While we were yet sinners, Christ died for us" (Romans 5:8).

Now Jesus takes this concept of friendship a step further.

> "14 You are my friends if you do what I command. 15 I no longer call you servants, because a servant does not know his master's business.[664] Instead, I have called you friends, for everything that I learned from my Father I have made known to you." (15:14-15)

Don't take verse 14 like you can earn friendship by being good. That's not the point. Jesus is saying that you doing what he commands is an indication that you love him. Servants obey because they have to. Friends obey because they want to.

If you go to work at a shoe store, you are taught how to fit shoes to people's feet. But if you are the owner's son, then you are taught every aspect of the shoe business. And, dear friends, Jesus' family business is the Kingdom of God.

Jesus' friends have the privilege of sitting down with the Master and understanding his Kingdom. Yes, he is King, but he is inviting them to share in his Kingdom, to be part of his administration, to "rule and reign with Christ" (2 Timothy 2:12; Revelation 5:10; 20:4). The Twelve became the foundation for the Church that mushroomed in the first century and beyond.

In teaching his disciples all about his Kingdom over three years, Jesus is explaining the inner workings, the philosophy behind his Kingdom, how to heal, how to pray, how to trust, how to undergo and understand persecution. Jesus spoke in parables to the crowds, which included his enemies, "but when he was alone with his own disciples, he explained everything" (Mark 4:34).

You are Jesus' friend. You get to share in his joy and plans for the future. You get to be a participant in advancing his kingdom. What a wonderful privilege. Value it!

Q7. (John 15:12-15) What is required to be counted a "friend of Jesus"? What privileges do "friends" enjoy according to verse 15? What happens when we take for granted this privilege? http://www.joyfulheart.com/forums/topic/1513-q7-friends-of-jesus/

---

[663] *Philos*, BDAG 1058-1059, 2aα.

[664] "His master's business" (NIV) is more literally, "what his master is doing" (ESV).

Chosen and Appointed to Bear Fruit (15:16-17)

Now, as he concludes this part of the Farewell Discourses, Jesus reminds his disciples that they didn't become Friends by their own choice or hard work. He chose them!

> "[16] You did not choose[665] me, but I chose you and appointed[666] you to go and bear fruit – fruit that will last (*menō*). Then the Father will give you whatever you ask in my name. [17] This is my command: Love each other." (15:16-17)

Jesus sums up in verses 16-17. He reminds them of answered prayer (15:17; 16:23, 26) and his command to love one another (13:34; 15:12), which he had developed earlier in the Farewell Discourses. In Lesson 28 (16:25-28), we'll discuss Jesus' comment here that the Father will answer prayer made in Jesus' name.

Notice that Jesus adds the element of election in verse 16 – God's choice and God's appointment. Popular evangelical terminology tends to cloud this point of election. We speak of "accepting Christ," of "receiving Christ," of "being born again," as if it were our choice. We come back here to the mystery of predestination that we discussed at 6:37-44 (Lesson 14). Surely we must "accept" Christ, we must "receive" him, and we must be "born again." But we don't initiate this. He does. And we must respond to our destiny, unless we are fools who resist Christ and finally turn from him.

Certainly, Jesus chose, commissioned, and appointed the Twelve. But the Great Commission extends not just to them, but to all whom they lead to the Master, to the third and fourth generation of Christ followers, on and on until Christ returns. Until then you and I are appointed to "go and bear fruit – fruit that will last."

Come soon, Lord Jesus!

Lessons for Disciples

This has been a very rich passage, replete with important lessons for Jesus' disciples:

1. Messiah Jesus becomes the New Israel, the true vine from which all believers draw their life (15:1).

2. God's "pruning" or correction/discipline is necessary so that our lives become more like Christ's and bear the fruit of his character (15:2).

3. Listening to and obeying Jesus' words has a cleansing effect on our lives (15:3).

4. An intimate and continuing connection of faith in and obedience to Jesus is necessary so that our lives bear fruit in his character (15:4).

5. We dwell in Christ and he dwells in us – a mutual indwelling. We are not alone! (15:5).

---

[665] "Choose/chose" is *eklegomai*, "to make a choice in accordance with significant preference, select someone/something for oneself" (BDAG 305, 2a). See 13:18; 15:19.

[666] "Appointed" (NIV, NRSV, ESV), "ordained" (KJV) is the extremely common verb *tithēmi*, "put, place," here with the specific meaning, "to assign to some task or function, appoint, assign" (BDAG 1004, 3a). It is also used in this sense in Acts 13:47; 1 Timothy 2:7; 2 Timothy 1:11-12.

6. When we try to accomplish spiritual work in our own strength the result is small. We can do nothing that has a lasting result without relying on Jesus' strength through us. We must practice dependence on him, not independence from him (15:5a).

7. One of the blessings of abiding in Christ and letting his words and character infuse us, is answered prayer, since we'll be much more likely to be praying according to his will (15:7).

8. The fruit Jesus grows in us consists of godly character, as well as effectiveness of whatever mission he calls us to (15:8).

9. Abiding in Christ means loving him, which results in willing obedience to his commands (15:10).

10. Jesus doesn't want us to operate as unthinking servants, but as friends, willing and knowledgeable participants in growing his Kingdom (15:14-15).

11. We've been chosen by God and appointed to produce lasting fruit for his Kingdom (15:16).

Prayer

Father, thank you for including us in your vine. Help us to accept your pruning with trust. Help us to rely on Jesus so that we bear his fruit and so glorify you. Thank you for the immense privilege of being Jesus' friends. In his holy name, we pray. Amen.

Key Verses

"I am the true vine, and my Father is the gardener." (John 15:1, NIV)

"He cuts off every branch in me that bears no fruit, while every branch that does bear fruit he prunes so that it will be even more fruitful." (John 15:2, NIV)

"Remain in me, and I will remain in you. No branch can bear fruit by itself; it must remain in the vine. Neither can you bear fruit unless you remain in me." (John 15:4, NIV)

"I am the vine; you are the branches. If a man remains in me and I in him, he will bear much fruit; apart from me you can do nothing. If anyone does not remain in me, he is like a branch that is thrown away and withers; such branches are picked up, thrown into the fire and burned." (John 15:5-6, NIV)

"If you remain in me and my words remain in you, ask whatever you wish, and it will be given you. This is to my Father's glory, that you bear much fruit, showing yourselves to be my disciples." (John 15:7-8, NIV)

"My command is this: Love each other as I have loved you. Greater love has no one than this, that he lay down his life for his friends." (John 15:12-13, NIV)

"You are my friends if you do what I command. I no longer call you servants, because a servant does not know his master's business. Instead, I have called you friends, for everything that I learned from my Father I have made known to you." (John 15:14-15, NIV)

"You did not choose me, but I chose you and appointed you to go and bear fruit – fruit that will last. Then the Father will give you whatever you ask in my name." (John 15:16, NIV)

27. The Spirit of Truth (15:18-16:11)

In this part of the Farewell Discourses, Jesus prepares his disciples for the persecution that they will surely face after his departure. In addition he explains more about how the Paraclete, the Holy Spirit will help them in Jesus' absence.

The entire thought runs from 15:18 through 16:32. But because of the richness of these chapters, we'll break this lesson arbitrarily into two parts so you can consider it carefully.

We'll spend most of our time in these two lessons examining what Jesus teaches about the Holy Spirit.

The World Will Hate You (15:18-21a)

> "¹⁸ If the world hates you, keep in mind that it hated me first. ¹⁹ If you belonged to the world, it would love you as its own. As it is, you do not belong to the world, but I have chosen you out of the world. That is why the world hates you." (15:18-19)

"Pentecost," stained glass window, St Aloysius' Catholic Church, Somers Town, London. Photo: Fr. Francis Lew, O.P. Used by permission.

Many people become Christians today who aren't aware that they'll be hated by some for their faith. Jesus was loved by some and hated by others. We'll be hated by some for the same reasons.

Difference. Jesus chooses "out of the world," the *kosmos*. The Greek word here has the connotation, "the world, and everything that belongs to it, appears as that which is hostile to God, that is, lost in sin, wholly at odds with anything divine, ruined and depraved."[667] From elementary school through adulthood, people tend to bully and persecute those who are different from them. Yes, it's perverse, but it is true. The Pharisees hated Jesus because he broke their cherished (but misguided) rules concerning the Sabbath.

Contrast. Closely related is the contrast in morals and values between disciples and people who have adopted the relative standards of society. If your values become honesty and putting in your full work day in a culture where people take sick days when they're not sick and come in late, you'll make others angry because your good behavior highlights their bad behavior. If Christians challenge society in issues such as abortion, it tends to focus on the evil of others. People often deride Christians as being "holier than thou," but the problem is often that believers are becoming through Christ's power, "blameless and pure ... without fault in a crooked and depraved generation," people who "shine like

---

[667] *Kosmos*, BDAG 562, 7b.

stars in the universe" (Philippians 2:15). When we refuse to go along with others' sins, we make them look bad. Jesus' humility and purity stood in sharp relief to the Pharisees' legalism and self-serving attitude, and they hated him for it.

Control. People, particularly leaders, often hate what they can't control. Jesus represented a threat to the Jewish leaders' authority because he was attracting more and more followers, thus reducing their influence. When worldly people find that Christians can't be seduced and controlled by money, sex, and power, they sense a loss of power themselves. Christians are viewed as "loose cannons" and are hated for it.

Jesus continues,

> "[20] Remember the words I spoke to you: 'No servant is greater than his master.' If they persecuted me, they will persecute you also. If they obeyed my teaching, they will obey yours also. [21] They will treat you this way because of my name[668], for they do not know the One who sent me." (15:20-21a)

Being a follower of Christ isn't "safe." Jesus reminds us that they will treat us the same way as they treated him. Yes, some will come to faith and have their lives transformed, but others will hate and persecute us, to one degree or another.

In most Western countries, the persecution usually takes the form of social ostracism. But in countries with majority Hindu or Muslim populations, persecution can include loss of jobs, burning of churches, and even "honor killing" of those who convert to Christ.

Jesus is trying to prepare his disciples then – and now – so we won't be surprised when we see persecution. Rather we will remember that he told us it would be this way, so we won't be tempted to fall away (16:1).

Q1. (John 15:18-21a) Why are Christians persecuted even if they haven't hurt others? What about a faithful Christian's life threatens non-Christians? Why does Jesus warn his disciples that persecution will come? What happens to our testimony if we give in under mild persecution? What does it say to persecutors when we don't react to their persecution? Do they see us as weak or as strong?
http://www.joyfulheart.com/forums/topic/1514-q1-persecution/

Hate the Son, Hate the Father (15:22-25)

> "[22] If I had not come and spoken to them, they would not be guilty of sin. Now, however, they have no excuse for their sin. [23] He who hates me hates my Father as well. [24] If I had not done among them what no one else did, they would not be guilty of sin. But now they have seen these

---

[668] "Because of my name" (NIV), "for my name's sake" (KJV) uses the preposition *dia* with the accusative case, "the reason why something happens, results, exists, because of, for the sake of" (BDAG 225, B2a); and the noun *onoma*, "name." Here, *onoma* substitutes for the Jesus himself = "because of me."

miracles, and yet they have hated both me and my Father. ²⁵ But this is to fulfill what is written in their Law: 'They hated me without reason. ⁶⁶⁹'" (15:22-25)

People sin whether or not they know the full truth. The Pentateuch talks about "unintentional sin," that is, transgressing laws that people don't know about.⁶⁷⁰ Western culture in our day, for example, thinks nothing of a couple living together without being married, though it is contrary to the Bible. Some of my ancestors were slaveholders. Probably all of our ancestors who fought in wars raped the women when they conquered a city. The sin was "unintentional"; the culture of the time wasn't particularly aware that it was sinful. Nevertheless, even people who don't know God's laws commonly go contrary to their consciences, and thus sin against what they believe to be right (Romans 2:12-16).

In verse 24, Jesus isn't saying that the Pharisees have no sin at all. Rather, if Jesus had not come they wouldn't be guilty of the terrible sin of rejecting Jesus the Messiah. But since Jesus worked miracles in their midst, they are held responsible to conclude that Jesus is the Messiah. The truth is, since Jesus represents the Father's words and deeds with extreme accuracy, it is a fallacy to say that they love God, but hate Jesus. If they hate Jesus, then they certainly don't know or love his Father!

More about the Paraclete (15:26-27)

Now we come to one of the Paraclete passages that instructs us about the Holy Spirit. (For more on these teachings, see Appendix 8. The Paraclete.)

"²⁶ When the Counselor comes, whom I will send to you from the Father, the Spirit of truth who goes out from the Father, he will testify about me. ²⁷ And you also must testify, for you have been with me from the beginning." (15:26-27)

This passage teaches us several things about the Holy Spirit.

1. Jesus will send him from the Father.
2. He is called the "Spirit of truth" (also 14:17 and 16:13).
3. He is spoken of as a person (14:26; 15:16, 26).
4. He will testify or witness concerning Jesus.

Points 1 and 2 we've discussed above in 14:15-17 and 14:25-26 (Lesson 25), and in Appendix 9 The Sending of the Holy Spirit. But points 3 and 4 are new teachings on the Holy Spirit that we need to discuss.

The Holy Spirit is a Person (14:26; 15:16, 26)

In many languages (Spanish, French, German, etc. – including Greek), words have masculine, feminine, or neuter genders or inflections that have no real counterpart in English.⁶⁷¹ While the "Spirit" is often referred to by a neuter Greek pronoun, since the *pneuma* has a neuter gender in Greek (such as

---

⁶⁶⁹ "Let not those who hate me without reason maliciously wink the eye...." (Psalm 35:19). "More in number than the hairs of my head are those who hate me without cause" (Psalm 69:4).
⁶⁷⁰ Leviticus 4:2, 13, 22, 27; 5:18; Numbers 15:24-29.
⁶⁷¹ Though in English we sometimes refer to ships with a feminine gender as "her sails."

in 14:17, 26; 15:26), on several occasions Jesus uses the masculine pronoun, apparently to emphasize the Spirit's personhood. Observe these verses.

> "But the Counselor, the Holy Spirit (neuter noun), whom (neuter pronoun) the Father will send in my name, **he** (masculine pronoun) will teach you all things and will remind you of everything I have said to you." (14:26)

> "When the Counselor comes, whom I will send to you from the Father, the Spirit (neuter noun) of truth who (neuter pronoun) goes out from the Father, **he** (masculine pronoun) will testify about me." (15:26)

> "When **he** (masculine pronoun), the Spirit (neuter noun) of truth, comes, he (no pronoun in Greek) will guide you into all truth." (16:13a)

C.K. Barrett observes, "The Spirit is thought of in personal terms."[672]

I emphasize the Holy Spirit's divinity and personal nature because some groups specifically deny that the Holy Spirit is a divine being. The Jehovah's Witness *New World Translation*, for example, sometimes even omits the word "Spirit" and substitutes the phrase "God's active force" in its place (hardly a faithful translation!), a phrase that strips away any sense of personhood.[673]

There is solid biblical evidence that points to a conclusion that the Holy Spirit is a distinct person in his own right and performs functions we attribute to personhood. The Holy Spirit appoints missionaries (Acts 13:2; 20:28), he leads and directs them in their ministry (Acts 8:29; 10:19-20; 16:6-7; 1 Corinthians 2:13), he speaks through the prophets (Acts 1:16; 1 Peter 1:11-12; 2 Peter 1:21), he corrects (John 16:8), comforts (Acts 9:31), helps us in our infirmities (Romans 8:26), teaches (John 14:26; 1 Corinthians 12:3), guides (John 16:13), sanctifies (Romans 15:16; 1 Corinthians 6:11), testifies of Christ (John 15:26), glorifies Christ (John 16:14), has a power of his own (Romans 15:13), searches all things (Romans 11:33-34; 1 Corinthians 2:10-11), works according to his own will (1 Corinthians 12:11), dwells with saints (John 14:17), can be grieved (Ephesians 4:30), can be resisted (Acts 7:51), and can be tempted (Acts 5:9). These are functions we attribute to persons, not to impersonal forces. John sees the Holy Spirit as a Person, sent by the Father to replace Jesus' physical presence to be the Paraclete with his disciples.

The personal nature of the Spirit is confirmed in the foundational creeds of the Church. The Nicene Creed uses personal terms to explain our belief in the Spirit.

> "And [we believe] in the Holy Spirit, the Lord and Giver of life, who proceeds from the Father, who with the Father and the Son together is worshiped and glorified, who spoke by the prophets."[674]

---

[672] Barrett, *John*, p. 482, commenting on John 15:26. See also George Eldon Ladd, *A Theology of the New Testament* (Eerdmans, 1974), p. 295.

[673] See Ron Rhodes, *Reasoning from the Scriptures with the Jehovah's Witnesses* (Harvest House, 1993), chapter 8. Citing the New World Translation of Genesis 1:2.

[674] This is the revised version of the original Nicene Creed (325 AD), which was adopted at the First Council of Constantinople (381 AD).

Q2. (John 14:26; 15:26; 16:13a) Why do we believe that the Holy Spirit is not an impersonal force or power, but a Person? What kinds of functions that we attribute to persons does the Holy Spirit do? Why is it so easy to refer to the Spirit as "it" rather than "Him"?
http://www.joyfulheart.com/forums/topic/1515-q2-the-spirit-as-a-person/

The Spirit Testifies Concerning Jesus (15:26-27)

"²⁶ When the Counselor comes, whom I will send to you from the Father, the Spirit of truth who goes out from the Father, he will **testify** about[675] me. ²⁷ And you also must **testify**, for you have been with me from the beginning." (15:26-27)

The Spirit's function of testifying about Jesus is closely related to reminding the disciples what Jesus taught (14:26b). Since the word *paraklētos* has a legal flavor,[676] it is particularly appropriate alongside another word from the legal realm, *martyreō*, "to confirm or attest something on the basis of personal knowledge or belief, bear witness, be a witness, offer testimony."[677] The Spirit presents Christ's case for him before the believers and the world.[678]

Elsewhere, Jesus told his disciples not to worry about what to say when they are brought into court.

"Do not worry about how you will defend yourselves or what you will say, for the Holy Spirit will teach you at that time what you should say." (Luke 12:11b-12)

The Paraclete will serve as your legal advisor as needed when you are persecuted.

In verse 27, Jesus reminds the original apostles that they must testify also, to tell what they know from personal experience (21:24; Luke 24:48) – which the apostles certainly did.[679] Though we are not eyewitnesses of the historical Jesus, we too must bear witness of what Jesus has done in our lives.

Q3. (John 15:26-27) What does it mean to "testify"? In what way does the Spirit testify about Jesus? Can you testify from personal knowledge about Jesus, or only the apostles who were eyewitnesses?
http://www.joyfulheart.com/forums/topic/1516-q3-testifying/

---

[675] "About" (NIV, ESV), "on my behalf" (NRSV), "of" (KJV) is the preposition *peri* with the genitive case, "about, concerning." *Peri* with the genitive denotes "the object or person to which (whom) an activity or especially inward process refers or relates" (BDAG 797, 1a).

[676] See Appendix 8. The Paraclete.

[677] *Martyreō*, from the legal sphere (BDAG 612, 1aα). "In John, witness is especially the witness that is given, not specifically to the facts of Jesus' history, but to the person of Jesus." H. Strathmann, *martyr, ktl.*, TDNT 4:474-514.

[678] Morris, *John*, p. 684.

[679] Acts 1:8, 21-22; 3:15; 4:33; 10:39-42; 18:5; 23:11; 1 Peter 5:1; 2 Peter 1:16-18; Revelation 1:9.

Don't Go Astray When They Persecute You (16:1-4)

In a similar way as in 15:18-21a, Jesus continues to prepare his disciples for persecution.

> "¹ All this I have told you so that you will not go astray. ² They will put you out of the synagogue; in fact, a time is coming when anyone who kills you will think he is offering a service to God. ³ They will do such things because they have not known the Father or me. ⁴ I have told you this, so that when the time comes you will remember that I warned you. I did not tell you this at first because I was with you." (16:1-4)

Jesus' intent is to keep his disciples from falling away in time of persecution (16:1). "Go astray" (NIV), "keep you from stumbling" (NRSV), "keep you from falling away" (ESV), "be offended" (KJV) is the verb *skandalizō*, "to cause to be brought to a downfall, cause to sin."[680] *Skandalizō* is also used in the Parable of the Sower, where Jesus warned that those whose seed fell on rocky ground that these "surface believers" would fall away in time of persecution (Matthew 13:5, 20-21).

Jesus hadn't spent a lot of time preparing them for persecution previously, because at that point he personally bore the brunt of the persecution. But with him gone, they will face the persecution head on, relying on the Paraclete to help them.

It Is Good that I Go Away (16:5-7)

> "⁵ Now I am going to him who sent me, yet none of you asks me, 'Where are you going?'" (16:5)

Technically, Peter had asked this, but his question was really, "*Why* are you going?" and wasn't really a serious inquiry about *where* Jesus was going (13:36). Peter seemed interested only in the consequence for him and the other disciples, not for Jesus.

> "⁶ Because I have said these things, you are filled with grief. ⁷ But I tell you the truth: It is for your good that I am going away. Unless I go away, the Counselor will not come to you; but if I go, I will send[681] him to you." (16:6-7)

The disciples are confused and grieving to hear about Jesus' imminent departure. But Jesus tries to console them with the truth that this will be for their own good.[682] In what way does this benefit Jesus' disciples? In at least two ways:

1. Jesus' going to the cross and being raised from the dead is God's plan for their redemption, and that of the whole world, though this is unspoken here.
2. The Holy Spirit will be poured out on them after Jesus' crucifixion, resurrection, and ascension.

Though the disciples didn't understand until later, God's timing in sending the Spirit was much-anticipated, even in the times of the prophets, but according to God's schedule, Jesus must be

---

[680] *Skandalizō*, BDAG 926, 1a. The sin may consist in a breach of the moral law, in unbelief, or in the acceptance of false teachings. Originally, the word has the idea of striking or catching in a trap or snare, later it can have the meaning "offense, reason for punishment." In the New Testament the noun *skandalon* is an obstacle to faith and hence a cause of falling and destruction (G. Stählin, *skandalon, ktl.*, TDNT 7:339-358).

[681] See Appendix 9. The Sending of the Holy Spirit.

[682] "Good" (NIV), "advantage" (NRSV, ESV), "expedient" (KJV) is *sympherō*, "to be advantageous, help, confer a benefit, be profitable/useful," here impersonal, "something is good (for someone), something is useful or helpful." (BDAG 960, 2a).

"glorified" first. As John had commented on Jesus' prophecy of the Spirit as a spring of living water, welling up in them:

> "Up to that time the Spirit had not been given, since Jesus had not yet been glorified." (7:39)

The Holy Spirit will not only guide, encourage, teach, and remind them, as Jesus had done, but he will also empower them.

> "I tell you the truth, anyone who has faith in me will do what I have been doing. He will do even greater things than these, because I am going to the Father." (14:12)

After the resurrection, Jesus tells his disciples:

> "I am going to send you what my Father has promised; but stay in the city until you have been clothed with power from on high." (Luke 24:49)

> "You will receive power when the Holy Spirit comes on you; and you will be my witnesses in Jerusalem, and in all Judea and Samaria, and to the ends of the earth." (Acts 1:8)

Q4. (John 16:5-7; 14:12) What benefit is there to the disciples that Jesus goes away? What promise do we have in John 14:12 concerning the Spirit's power in believers?
http://www.joyfulheart.com/forums/topic/1517-q4-blessing-of-jesus-departure/

The Paraclete Will Convict the World (16:8)

So far, Jesus has told his disciples how the Paraclete, the Holy Spirit, will benefit them. But now he explains how the Holy Spirit will affect the world.

> "When he comes, he will convict the world of guilt in regard to sin and righteousness and judgment." (16:8)

The role of the Holy Spirit convicting sinners is clear. "Convict of guilt" (NIV), "convict" (ESV, NKJV), "prove wrong" (NRSV), "convince" (RSV), "reprove" (KJV) is the verb *elenchō*, "to bring a person to the point of recognizing wrongdoing, convict, convince someone of something, point something out to someone."[683] The word occurs 18 times in the New Testament, in each instance having to do with showing someone his sin, usually as a summons to repentance.[684]

Oswald Chambers wrote,

> "Conviction of sin is one of the rarest things that ever strikes a man. It is the threshold of an understanding of God. Jesus Christ said that when the Holy Spirit came He would convict of sin, and when the Holy Spirit rouses the conscience and brings him into the presence of God, it is not his relationship with men that bothers him, but his relationship with God."[685]

In what ways does the Holy Spirit bring conviction, according to Scripture?

---

[683] *Elenchō*, BDAG 315, 2. The focus in classical Greek is on "putting to shame, treating with contempt, cross-examining, accusing, bringing to the test, proving, refuting" (Carson, *John*, p. 534).
[684] Carson, *John*, p. 534, citing Friedrich Büschel, *elenchō, ktl.*, TDNT 2:473-474.
[685] Oswald Chambers (1874-1917), *My Utmost for His Highest*, devotion for December 7.

Miracles. One way conviction came in Jesus' ministry and the early church's evangelism was through the miracle power of the Holy Spirit that brought a glimpse of God's immense power and holiness. After witnessing the miraculous catch of fish, for example, Peter falls to his knees and exclaims: "Go away from me, Lord; I am a sinful man!" (Luke 5:8). This was true in Paul's ministry as well.

> "My message and my preaching were not with wise and persuasive words, but with a demonstration of the Spirit's power, so that your faith might not rest on men's wisdom, but on God's power." (1 Corinthians 2:4-5)

> "For we know, brothers loved by God, that he has chosen you, because our gospel came to you not simply with words, but also with power, with the Holy Spirit and with deep conviction[686]." (1 Thessalonians 1:4-5a)

Dear friends, in our day we need the miracle power of the Holy Spirit, for it is one way that he convicts people of their sins and of Christ's power. If you've read reports of world evangelism, you probably are aware that one of the causes of the spread of evangelical Christianity in Latin America and the growth of the church in China is signs and wonders. If you aren't aware of this, you need to research this yourself.

Prophetic words. A second way we see conviction coming in the New Testament is through a prophetic word.

> "But if an unbeliever or someone who does not understand comes in while everybody is prophesying, he will be convinced by all that he is a sinner and will be judged by all, 25 and the secrets of his heart will be laid bare. So he will fall down and worship God, exclaiming, 'God is really among you!'" (1 Corinthians 14:24-25)

If we avoid spiritual gifts because they might be controversial, we cripple the evangelistic power of the church.

Preaching and Testimony. A third way the Spirit brings conviction is by taking a sermon, lesson, or an individual's testimony and convincing a person of the truth of it in their heart of hearts. For example, after Peter's sermon on the Day of Pentecost, "they were cut to the heart and said to Peter and the other apostles, 'Brothers, what shall we do?'" (Acts 2:37). When we preach out of our mind, we have little power. But when we preach relying on the Holy Spirit to take our words and use them, we have great power.

Our righteous lives. A fourth way that the Holy Spirit uses to convict people is through our righteous lives. Peter tells us:

> "Live such good lives among the pagans that, though they accuse you of doing wrong, they may see your good deeds and glorify God on the day he visits us." (1 Peter 2:12)

Peter exhorts Christian wives:

> "Be submissive to your husbands so that, if any of them do not believe the word, they may be won over without words by the behavior of their wives, when they see the purity and reverence of your lives." (1 Peter 3:1-2)

---

[686] *Plērophoria*, "state of complete certainty, full assurance, certainty" BDAG 827).

Instruction and prayer. A fifth way mentioned in the New Testament that the Holy Spirit brings conviction is through patient instruction with prayer. Paul counsels Timothy concerning the role of a servant of God.

> "Those who oppose him he must gently instruct, in the hope that God will grant them repentance leading them to a knowledge of the truth, and that they will come to their senses and escape from the trap of the devil, who has taken them captive to do his will." (2 Timothy 2:25-26)

Notice the importance of God's intervention, which is necessary because:

> "The god of this age has blinded the minds of unbelievers, so that they cannot see the light of the gospel of the glory of Christ, who is the image of God." (2 Corinthians 4:4)

Evangelism is not only declaring the word, but also earnestly praying for the salvation of unbelievers, for God to intervene and open their blind eyes and deaf ears (Acts 26:18). Both are vital! This is a spiritual battle. In a number places were are told to pray for the lost and for ministry to them (e.g., Romans 10:1; 1 Timothy 2:1-6; Colossians 4:3; Ephesians 6:19-20; 1 John 5:13-15).

Q5. (John 16:8) Through what means does the Holy Spirit convict unbelievers? Is it our job as preachers or lay Christians to convict unbelievers or backslidden people? If not, why not? What damage do we inflict on people when we try to do the Holy Spirit's job?
http://www.joyfulheart.com/forums/topic/1518-q5-convicting-the-world/

Conviction of Sin, Righteousness, and Judgment (16:8-11)

> "8 When he comes, he will convict the world of guilt in regard to sin and righteousness and judgment: 9 in regard to sin, because men do not believe in me; 10 in regard to righteousness, because I am going to the Father, where you can see me no longer; 11 and in regard to judgment, because the prince of this world now stands condemned." (16:8-11)

Because of the compressed explanations of the Spirit's convicting power in verses 9-11, it is sometimes difficult to arrive at an exact interpretation of them. Here's the sense I make of them:

Sin[687]. The Spirit will convict unbelievers of sin – graciously – so that they might recognize their need and turn to Christ.

Righteousness. The Spirit will convict the world of its false self-righteousness, because when Jesus goes to the Father. He sends the Spirit who empowers thousands of disciples to follow Jesus and, by their lives and faith in the Righteous One, they convict the world of its empty righteousness.

Judgment[688]. The Spirit will convict the world of its spiritual blindness and false judgments of Jesus, since the chief slanderer of Jesus, "the prince of this world," has himself been judged and stands condemned[689] by the triumph of the cross.[690]

---

[687] "Sin" is *hamartia*, "a departure from either human or divine standards of uprightness, sin" (BDAG 50, 1a).
[688] "Judgment" is *krisis*, legal process of judgment, judging, judgment," here, "judgment that goes against a person, condemnation, and the sentence that follows" (BDAG 569, 1aβ).

We need to stop here, though there is no natural break. We'll pick up Jesus' teaching on the Holy Spirit in the next lesson.

Lessons for Disciples

But there is much to ponder in these verses. Here are some lessons for us disciples to grasp and incorporate into our own lives.

1. We will be persecuted by the "world" because we are different. Our righteous lives make sinners feel uncomfortable, and people can't control us.

2. When people hate or reject Jesus, they also hate and reject his Father, for Jesus accurately portrays the Father's words and actions.

3. Jesus speaks of the Holy Spirit as a person. In the New Testament, the Spirit's actions and functions are those we would ascribe to a person.

4. From his personal experience, the Spirit "testifies" about Jesus. We are to testify about Jesus also from our experience of him.

5. Jesus tells us not to fall away when we suffer severe persecution. We should expect it (16:1-4)

6. The Holy Spirit's coming is contingent upon Jesus going to the Father. Even though Jesus won't be with us in person, the Spirit's presence is for our good, and will empower us to continue Jesus' ministry.

7. The Holy Spirit will convict or convince the world through miracles, prophetic words, preaching and testimonies, our faithful lives, and instruction and prayer.

Prayer

Father, help us to get acquainted with the person of the Holy Spirit. Help us to enjoy his fellowship and learn to hear his voice. Thank you for the power and joy of your Spirit. In Jesus' name, we pray. Amen.

Key Verses

"No servant is greater than his master. If they persecuted me, they will persecute you also. If they obeyed my teaching, they will obey yours also." (John 15:20, NIV)

"When the Counselor comes, whom I will send to you from the Father, the Spirit of truth who goes out from the Father, he will testify about me." (John 15:26, NIV)

"I tell you the truth: It is for your good that I am going away. Unless I go away, the Counselor will not come to you; but if I go, I will send him to you." (John 16:7, NIV)

"When he comes, he will convict the world of guilt in regard to sin and righteousness and judgment." (John 16:8, NIV)

---

[689] "Stands condemned" (NIV), "condemned" (NRSV), "judged" (ESV, KJV) is *krinō*, "to engage in a judicial process, judge, decide, hale before a court, condemn," also "hand over for judicial punishment," frequently as a legal technical term (BDAG 569, 5bα).

[690] I am following, for the most part, Carson, *John*, pp. 536-537. Of course, there are many different interpretation of these cryptic verses.

28. The Spirit Will Guide You (16:12-33)

In Jesus' Farewell Discourses on the Holy Spirit, there's too much material to cover in one lesson, so we arbitrarily ended the previous lesson at 16:11, though there's no natural break there. We pick up Jesus' teaching on the Spirit's role of guiding us into all truth in 16:12.

The Spirit Will Guide You into All Truth (16:12-13a)

By now, Jesus' disciples are on emotional overload. They are confused, frightened, and not in a state to comprehend the truths Jesus is teaching them. So Jesus promises that the Spirit will explain all to them in due time.

> "[12] I have much more to say to you, more than you can now bear[691]. [13] But when he, the Spirit of truth, comes, he will guide you into all truth." (16:12-13a)

Holy Trinity, stained glass, Our Lady of Fatima Catholic Church, Wilton, Connecticut. The window shows the hand to represent the Father, the Chi-Rho symbol to represent Christ, and the Holy Spirit as a dove.

Before we examine that explanatory role of the Spirit in verses 13-15, let's look carefully at verse 13a. Observe that the "he[692]" in Greek is a masculine pronoun referring to *pnuema*, "Spirit," which is a neuter gender noun. As I explained in the previous lesson, it is clear that Jesus is making a point that we should think of the Holy Spirit in personal terms.

In verse 13a, Jesus promises his disciples that the "Spirit of truth" will guide them into all truth. "Guide" is *hodēgeō*. Literally, it means, "to assist in reaching a desired destination, lead, guide." Here it is used figuratively, "to assist someone in acquiring information or knowledge, lead, guide, conduct."[693]

I believe that in this verse Jesus is speaking to his (now) Eleven Apostles, who will lay the teaching foundation within the first-century church that will soon be formed. Though the Spirit can guide us into truth today, it is usually rather arrogant to presume that our interpretation is the only correct interpretation, that the whole Church over two thousand years since Pentecost is wrong. We must seek the Spirit's guidance with great humility and desire to learn. Spiritual truths must be spiritually discerned through the action of the Holy Spirit (1 Corinthians 2:12-14).

---

[691] "Bear" is *bastazō*, literally, "to sustain a burden, carry, bear." Figuratively, "be able to bear up under especially trying or oppressive circumstances bear, endure" (BDAG 171, 2bβ).

[692] "He" (NIV) is the masculine, nominative of *ekeinos*, "that person, that thing, that," especially in John, referring back to and resuming a word immediately preceding, oft. weakened to "he, she, it" (BDAG 302, aβ).

[693] *Hodēgeō*, BDAG 690, 2. It is an old verb, from the noun *hodos*, "way" and *hēgeomai*, "to lead."

The Spirit Will Speak What He Hears (16:13b-15)

The Spirit, Jesus explains to us, won't be teaching us new doctrines. Rather he will be reminding his disciples of what Jesus has already taught them (14:26). The Spirit will listen to Jesus and relay this to us, just as Jesus listened to the Father and relayed that to his disciples (5:30), and only spoke what the Father told him to say (12:49).

> "13b He will not speak on his own; he will speak only what he hears, and he will tell[694] you what is yet to come. 14 He will bring glory to me by taking from what is mine and making it known to you. 15 All that belongs to the Father is mine. That is why I said the Spirit will take from what is mine and make it known to you." (16:13b-15)

Both Jesus and the Spirit will speak the Father's Words to us. We don't have the task of the first apostles who helped lay the doctrinal foundation of the Church, but we still seek to understand the Word of God accurately. I encourage you to call on the Holy Spirit, the Reminder, the Explainer, the Guide into all truth, to assist you to understand accurately the Father's words to your heart. Bible study should not be merely an intellectual exegetical exercise, but at the same time a heart seeking for truth.

> **Q1. (John 16:12-15) In what sense does the Holy Spirit guide us into all truth. Does this promise apply only to the apostolic age to lay the foundations of the faith? In what sense does it apply to us today?**
> http://www.joyfulheart.com/forums/topic/1519-q1-guide-to-truth/

In a Little While (16:17-19)

Now Jesus goes back to a theme we've seen before.

> "In a little while you will see me no more, and then after a little while you will see me." (16:16)

Jesus had made these kinds of cryptic statements in 7:33; 12:35; 13:33; 14:19; 16:10. Jesus' disciples are understandably confused and begin to talk about it to each other.

> "17 Some of his disciples said to one another, 'What does he mean by saying, "In a little while you will see me no more, and then after a little while you will see me," and "Because I am going to the Father"?' 18 They kept asking, 'What does he mean by "a little while"? We don't understand what he is saying.'
> 19 Jesus saw that they wanted to ask him about this, so he said to them, 'Are you asking one another what I meant when I said, "In a little while you will see me no more, and then after a little while you will see me"'"? (16:17-19)

---

[694] "Tell" (NIV) in verse 13b and "make known" (NIV) in verse 14 and 15, "declare" (NRSV, ESV), "shew" (KJV), is *anangellō*, literally, "to carry back information, report," then, generally, "to provide information, disclose, announce, proclaim, teach" (BDAG 59, 2), from *ana-*, "back, again" + *angellō*, "announce," *angelia*, "message." Our word "evangel" and "evangelism," tell good news, come from the same root.

Your Grief Will Turn to Joy (16:20-22)

Now Jesus speaks a word of comfort, as he did in 14:1.

> "20 I tell you the truth, you will weep and mourn while the world rejoices. You will grieve, but your grief will turn to joy. 21 A woman giving birth to a child has pain because her time has come; but when her baby is born she forgets the anguish because of her joy that a child is born into the world. 22 So with you: Now is your time of grief, but I will see you again and you will rejoice, and no one will take away your joy." (16:20-22)

Your grief will be deep. The "world," Jesus speaks of is all that is hostile to God in the *kosmos*, as well as the "prince of this world" (12:31; 16:11). But soon your grief will turn to joy that cannot be taken away.

Jesus is referring to the joy they'll experience when they see him raised from the dead in his resurrection glory. And the lasting joy they will have in the risen Christ long after his ascension. Nearly all these disciples were martyred for their faith, but even through the pain of that, they clung to their joy in their resurrected Lord. Because of this they were unstoppable.

Praying to the Father in Jesus' Name (16:23-24)

Jesus goes again to the theme of answered prayer that he has addressed several times in these Farewell Discourses (14:13-14; 15:7, 16).

> "23 In that day you will no longer ask me anything. I tell you the truth, my Father will give you whatever you ask in my name. 24 Until now you have not asked for anything in my name. Ask and you will receive, and your joy will be complete." (16:23-24)

We discussed prayer in Jesus' name in Lesson 24 on 14:13-14. Remember that in Hebrew thought, one's name stands for that person. To pray in Jesus' name means to pray with his commission, his authority – and in his will. It has similarities to our "power of attorney." Notice the progression in these verses concerning whom we are to ask.

Ask Jesus. "And I will do whatever you ask in my name.... You may ask me for anything in my name, and I will do it." (14:13-14)

Ask? "If you remain in me and my words remain in you, ask whatever you wish, and it will be given you." (15:7)

Father. "Then the Father will give you whatever you ask in my name." (15:16b)

Father. "My Father will give you whatever you ask in my name." (16:23b)

Jesus' primary teaching seems to be that we are to ask the Father in his name. Jesus certainly addressed his prayers to the Father. But in 14:14, Jesus says his disciples can ask *him* for anything, though in 16:23, Jesus, looking forward to the period after his resurrection, says, "In that day you will no longer ask me anything," but rather speak directly to the Father in his name.

Is it wrong to pray to Jesus? No. We see a number of examples of prayer to Jesus. People asked Jesus for healing during his ministry; that is prayer, of course. But after Jesus' resurrection, churches "call on the name of our Lord Jesus Christ" (1 Corinthians 1:2). We see prayers to Jesus from Stephen (Acts 7:59), at Paul's conversion (Acts 9:6; 10-11), the last prayer in the Bible (Revelation 22:20; 1

Corinthians 16:22), and elsewhere (2 Corinthians 12:8; 1 Thessalonians 3:11-13; etc.). The normal pattern is prayer to the Father, but prayer to Jesus is all right also.

Can we pray to the Holy Spirit? Is it wrong to say, "Come, Holy Spirit" or "Holy Spirit, fall upon us"? I think we can. We are called into the fellowship of the Spirit (2 Corinthians 13:14). After all, we believe that the Holy Spirit is God, a divine person, one of the Trinity, as we discussed above in 14:16-17. Nevertheless, the normal pattern of prayer taught us by Jesus is to prayer to the Father in Jesus' name.

Ask and You Will Receive (16:24)

> "Until now you have not asked for anything in my name. Ask and you will receive, and your joy will be complete." (16:24)

Jesus is inviting his disciples to embark on the joyful adventure of prayer, of asking and receiving. We read something similar in the Sermon on the Mount:

> "Ask and it will be given to you; seek and you will find; knock and the door will be opened to you. For everyone who asks receives; he who seeks finds; and to him who knocks, the door will be opened." (Matthew 7:7-8)

You Will Ask the Father Directly in My Name (16:25-28)

Jesus continues his teaching on prayer.

> 25 "Though I have been speaking figuratively, a time is coming when I will no longer use this kind of language but will tell you plainly about my Father. 26 In that day you will ask in my name. I am not saying that I will ask the Father on your behalf. 27 No, the Father himself loves you because you have loved me and have believed that I came from God. 28 I came from the Father and entered the world; now I am leaving the world and going back to the Father." (16:25-28)

Francisco de Zurbaran (1598-1664), 'St. Francis in Meditation' (1635-39), oil on canvas. National Gallery, London, 162 x 137 cm.

Jesus is saying in verse 26 that they don't have to pray to Jesus as a Mediator for them. Why? Because the Father himself knows them and loves them. So they can pray directly to the Father in Jesus' name.

Is Jesus still our Mediator? Yes, in the sense that he brought us to God through his redemption on the cross (1 Timothy 2:5; Hebrews 12:24). But now he is saying that once his atonement has been made, they can access the Father directly.

Yes, we need him, but no longer to bring us into the Father's presence – that work has been completed on the cross; the veil of the temple separating the holy place from the holy of holies has been rent (Mark 15:38). The way is open to the Father (Hebrews 10:19-20; 4:16). Nevertheless, we read that both Jesus and the Spirit continue to intercede for us before God's throne (Romans 8:26-27, 34; Hebrews 7:25; 1 John 2:1).

Verse 26 is a significant teaching that concerns our Roman Catholic and Eastern Orthodox brothers and sisters who have a long-standing tradition of praying to various saints who will intercede for them before God. The reasoning sometimes is that, because of a saint's great piety, God will listen to the saints and answer their prayers for their sake, even when God might not listen to us and answer our prayers.

The problem arises when prayer to the saints becomes our normal prayer life, rather than an occasional exception. When devotion focuses on one of the worthy saints, it can sometimes take away from the devotion that we offer to God. The one to whom we pray is the one with whom we build a relationship, an attachment. So it is important that we follow Jesus' teaching here as our normal pattern of prayer – prayer to the Father in Jesus' name. Remember, "the Father himself loves you."

Dear friend. The Father loves you yourself, and you have the marvelous privilege to appear before him in Jesus' name and by Jesus' death for you and his cleansing of you to make you holy in God's sight. You don't need others to use their influence to persuade him to act on your behalf. Pray boldly as best as you can discern his will, then leave it in his hands. He will answer you. That's what Jesus is saying.

> "Let us then approach the throne of grace with confidence, so that we may receive mercy and find grace to help us in our time of need." (Hebrews 4:16)

Q2. (John 16:23-28) What does it mean to pray to the Father "in Jesus' name"? Is it okay to pray to Jesus and to the Holy Spirit? Why or why not? Is it scriptural to pray to a saint to intercede for us? Why are we allowed to pray to the Father directly?
http://www.joyfulheart.com/forums/topic/1520-q2-prayer-to-the-father/

The Disciples' Faltering Faith (16:29-32)

Jesus' disciples are relieved that he is now speaking to them in words that can understand.

> "29 Then Jesus' disciples said, 'Now you are speaking clearly and without figures of speech. 30 Now we can see that you know all things and that you do not even need to have anyone ask you questions. This makes us believe that you came from God.'
>
> 31 'You believe at last!' Jesus answered. 32 'But a time is coming, and has come, when you will be scattered, each to his own home. You will leave me all alone. Yet I am not alone, for my Father is with me.'" (16:29-32)

As I consider these verses, it seems that Jesus' statement in verse 31 is tinged with irony: "You believe at last!" -- yet Jesus continues to explain how they will be scattered at his crucifixion. The disciples' belief is still weak.

I like verse 32 especially:

> "You will leave me all alone. Yet I am not alone, for my Father is with me." (16:32b)

In life's circumstances, we are sometimes afflicted with loneliness. But Jesus gives us a pattern to follow. "I am not alone, for my Father is with me." He *values* the fellowship of his disciples (Matthew 26:38), but his relationship with his Father is strong and deep, so that he is not *dependent* upon others. This challenges me to deepen my relationship with my Father. I am not alone; my Father is with me. As David observed:

> "If I say, 'Surely the darkness will hide me
> and the light become night around me,'
> even the darkness will not be dark to you;
> the night will shine like the day,
> for darkness is as light to you." (Psalm 139:11-12)

Q3. (John 16:32) Jesus said that he is not alone, that the Father is always with him. What does this mean to us when we are lonely? What should we do to deepen our fellowship with the ever-present Father so that we aren't as lonely?
http://www.joyfulheart.com/forums/topic/1521-q3-never-alone/

I Have Overcome the World (16:33)

Jesus has spoken to his disciples to prepare them for what is to come – his violent death, separation, the Holy Spirit's coming, and strong hope for the future.

> "I have told you these things, so that in me you may have peace. In this world you will have trouble. But take heart! I have overcome the world." (16:33)

Our primary peace is in Jesus, not in gentle circumstances. In the world we have "trouble" (NIV), "persecution" (NRSV), "tribulation" (ESV, KJV). The word is *thlipsis*, literally, "pressing, pressure." Here it is used metaphorically in the sense of "trouble that inflicts distress, oppression, affliction, tribulation."[695] Jesus acknowledges and understands the trouble we face, even though others might not. As the Negro spiritual puts it,

> "Nobody knows the trouble I see,
> Nobody knows but Jesus...."

But Jesus says that in the midst of this trouble that we should "take heart" (NIV, ESV), "take courage" (NRSV), "be of good cheer" (KJV). The word is *tharseō*, "to be firm or resolute in the face of danger or adverse circumstances, be enheartened, be courageous," from *tharos*, "courage" in the face of fear.[696] And what is the basis of our courage? The knowledge that Jesus has "overcome" (NIV, ESV, KJV), "conquered" (NRSV) the world. The verb *nikaō* is often used in the context of a court battle, military campaign, or athletic competition: "to win in the face of obstacles, be victor, conquer, overcome, prevail." Here it means, "to overcome, vanquish someone."[697]

---

[695] *Thlipsis*, BDAG 457, 1.
[696] *Tharseō*, BDAG 444. Also in Matthew 9:2, 22; Mark 10:9.
[697] *Nikaō*, BDAG 673, 2a.

In the wilderness, Jesus stood against all of Satan's temptations. On the cross, Jesus bore all of the sin and degradation of mankind, and was raised from the dead in spite of it all. He now reigns at the right hand of the Father and intercedes for us. He has sent his Holy Spirit to be with us. We are not alone! We can have courage in our troubles because we know this.

"See, the Lion of the tribe of Judah, the Root of David, has **triumphed**." (Revelation 5:5)

Because Jesus overcomes, we too can overcome. Many times in the Book of Revelation we read promises addressed to the "Overcomers" (Revelation 2:7, 11, 17, 26, etc.).

"To **him who overcomes**, I will give the right to sit with me on my throne, just as **I overcame** and sat down with my Father on his throne." (Revelation 3:21)

"**They overcame him** by the blood of the Lamb and by the word of their testimony; they did not love their lives so much as to shrink from death." (Revelation 12:11)

"You, dear children, are from God and **have overcome them**, because the one who is in you is greater than the one who is in the world." (1 John 4:4)

"Everyone born of God **overcomes the world**. This is the victory that has overcome the world, even our faith. Who is it that **overcomes the world**? Only he who believes that Jesus is the Son of God." (1 John 5:4-5)

Yes, to overcome the world we will need courage. Jesus has won the decisive battle. But we are involved, after all, with mop-up battles in a spiritual war. So, my dear friends, take courage and put away your fear.

"Put on the full armor of God so that you can take your stand against the devil's schemes." (Ephesians 6:11)

Stand in His strength, by the power of His Spirit, and you shall overcome!

Q4. (John 16:33) In what sense has Jesus "overcome" the world? In what sense can we "overcome" the world? Can we overcome Satan even though we are martyred in the process? (see Revelation 12:11)
http://www.joyfulheart.com/forums/topic/1522-q4-overcoming-the-world/

Lessons for Disciples

Here are lessons that we disciples need to internalize and apply in our lives.

1. As we listen, the Holy Spirit will guide us into all truth (16:13).
2. Just like Jesus accurately told the disciples what the Father was saying, so the Holy Spirit will take Jesus' words and accurately communicate them to us as his present-day disciples (16:15).
3. Jesus teaches us that we can pray directly to the Father in Jesus' name. While it is not wrong to pray to Jesus or to the Holy Spirit, the normal pattern is to pray to the Father directly, for he cares for us and knows us intimately (16:23-24).

4. The implications of this are that we don't need to go to the Father through an intermediary, such as a saint or even Jesus. We can go to the Father directly in Jesus' name (16:23-24).
5. Just like Jesus was not alone because of the Father's presence, so we can develop such a fellowship with God that we don't have to be tormented by loneliness (16:23).
6. Just as Jesus has overcome the world, so he strengthens us to overcome as well (16:33).

Prayer

Father, I ask you to guide me and my brothers and sisters into all your truth. Open up our hearts. Remove our prejudices and shallow interpretations. And speak to our hearts so that we might possess and embody your Holy Words. In Jesus' name, we pray. Amen.

Key Verses

"When he, the Spirit of truth, comes, he will guide you into all truth." (John 16:13a, NIV)

"The Spirit will take from what is mine and make it known to you." (John 16:15b, NIV)

"In that day you will no longer ask me anything. I tell you the truth, my Father will give you whatever you ask in my name. Until now you have not asked for anything in my name. Ask and you will receive, and your joy will be complete." (John 16:23-24, NIV)

"In that day you will ask in my name. I am not saying that I will ask the Father on your behalf. No, the Father himself loves you...." (John 16:26-27a)

"You will leave me all alone. Yet I am not alone, for my Father is with me." (John 16:32b)

"I have told you these things, so that in me you may have peace. In this world you will have trouble. But take heart! I have overcome the world." (John 16:33, NIV)

29. Jesus' Prayer for His Disciples (17:1-26)

Ever since the fifth century, Jesus' prayer in chapter 17 has been referred to as Jesus' High Priestly Prayer, praying for others as a mediator, in a priestly way (Hebrews 8:34; Hebrews 4:14-15; 7:25; 1 John 2:1).[698] Carson notes that "prayers of one sort or another were frequently associated with 'farewell discourses' in the ancient world, both in Jewish and Hellenistic literature"[699] such as Genesis 49 and Deuteronomy 32-33.

Ian McKillop, "Jesus' High Priestly Prayer," Gethsemane series. Permission requested.

Though we call it a prayer, it is obvious that the content of this prayer has the disciples who heard it in mind,[700] and so it is at the same time a petition, a proclamation, and a revelation.

The outline of the prayer is straightforward:

1. Prayer for himself (17:1-5),
2. Prayer for his disciples (17:6-19), and
3. Prayer for future believers (17:20-26).

However, the prayer is not simple to analyze, since themes weave in and out, themes drawn from the entire Gospel that now find their fulfillment in Jesus' glorification that is imminent. Themes include: obedience, glorification of the Father, revelation of God, choosing the disciples out of the world, unity modeled on the Father and Son, and their final destiny in the presence of Father and Son.

Remarkably, the prayer not gloomy, but breathes a kind of "triumphant expectation" of what will occur when Jesus' mission is completed and his disciples begin their mission.

Glorify Your Son (17:1-2)

Jesus begins the prayer talking with the Father about his "glorification" – crucifixion, resurrection, and ascension. (For more on "glorify," see Appendix 6. "Glory" and "Glorify" in John's Gospel.)

"¹ After Jesus said this, he looked toward heaven and prayed: 'Father, the time[701] has come. Glorify your Son, that your Son may glorify you. ² For you granted him authority over all people that he might give eternal life to all those you have given him.'" (17:1-2)

This High Priestly Prayer has glory woven throughout it (verses 1, 4, 5, 10, 22, and 24).

---

[698] Brown (*John* 2:747) cites a reference in Cyril of Alexandria (*Commentary on John* 9.8), and later by Lutheran theologian David Chytraus (1531-1600).

[699] Carson, *John*, pp. 550-551.

[700] We see this in Jesus' prayer at Lazarus' tomb also: "... I said this for the benefit of the people standing here, that they may believe that you sent me" (11:42).

[701] "Time" (NIV), "hour" (NRSV, ESV, KJV) is *hōra*, "a point of time as an occasion for an event, time" (BDAG 1103, 3). Except for 7:6, 8, John seems to use *hōra* instead of *kairos* to refer to the time of his crucifixion.

The reference to Jesus being given authority[702] over all people recalls the familiar Son of Man passage:

> "And to him was **given dominion** and glory and a kingdom, that **all peoples**, nations, and languages should serve him....[703]" (Daniel 7:14)

Jesus has spoken previously of his authority to grant eternal life:

> "For just as the Father raises the dead and gives them life, even so the Son gives life to whom he is pleased to give it.... For as the Father has life in himself, so he has granted the Son to have life in himself. And he has given him authority to judge because he is the Son of Man." (5:21, 26-27)

Eternal Life – to Know You (17:3)

Verse 3 is somewhat of a definition of eternal life.

> "Now this is eternal life: that they may know you, the only true God, and Jesus Christ[704], whom you have sent." (17:3)

We might think of eternal life as life with no end, but it's clear that just existence isn't the point. The "life" comes from a never-ending relationship with God and his Son – "knowing" them. The prophets foresaw this:

> "No longer will a man teach his neighbor,
> or a man his brother, saying, 'Know the LORD,'
> because **they will all know me**,
> from the least of them to the greatest." (Jeremiah 31:34)

> "The earth will be full of **the knowledge of the LORD**
> as the waters cover the sea." (Isaiah 11:9; also Habakkuk 2:14)

Jesus and the prophets are not just saying that everyone will know *about* him, but that they will *know him intimately*. Paul is willing to count every other thing as dung, garbage, "that I may know him" (Philippians 3:10). If this personal relationship between God's people and him is our destiny, now is the time to explore and deepen this relationship.

> **Q1. (John 17:3) If the average person were to define the words "eternal life," what would they say? Does Jesus define eternal life in terms of duration of time? What is the key element of his definition? How are you doing at present in Jesus' definition of eternal life.**
> **http://www.joyfulheart.com/forums/topic/1523-q1-knowing-god/**

---

[702] "Authority" (NIV, NRSV, ESV), "power" (KJV) is *exousia*, here, "the right to control or command, authority, absolute power, warrant" (BDAG 353, 3).

[703] The Greek words in John differ from those in the Septuagint translation of Daniel 7:14, however. John has to grant "authority" (*exousia*), instead of "dominion" (*archē*). John has *sarx*, "all people/flesh" vs. *laos*.

[704] The title "Jesus Christ" appears only twice in John, here and "grace and truth came through Jesus Christ" (1:17).

Completing the Father's Mission (17:4)

"I have brought you glory on earth by **completing** (*teleioō*[705]) the work you gave me to do." (17:4)

Jesus is now in the "home stretch." During the years of his earthly ministry, he has been doing the Father's work. Now it is coming to its culmination and completion with the cross and resurrection – and the redemption the cross will bring. Completion of the Father's mission has been foremost on his mind -- to glorify the Father on earth by making sure that the Father's plan for salvation is accomplished, finished, completed.

"My food is to do the will of him who sent me and to **finish** (*teleioō*) his work." (4:34)

"The very work that the Father has given me to **finish** (*teleioō*)...." (5:36)

Finally, at the cross, Jesus' last words concern the completion of this mission:

"Jesus said, '**It is finished** (*teleō*[706]).' With that, he bowed his head and gave up his spirit." (19:30)

Q2. (John 17:4) What was the "work" the Father gave Jesus to do? How did it bring glory to the Father? What is the "work" the Father has given *you* to do? In what ways are you bringing glory to the Father in this?
http://www.joyfulheart.com/forums/topic/1524-q2-completing-the-work/

Pre-existent Glory (17:4-5)

"[4] I have brought you glory on earth by completing the work you gave me to do. [5] And now, Father, glorify me in your presence with the glory I had with you before the world began." (17:4-5)

We look at the cross and see anguish, pain, and Jesus being crushed under the weight of the sins of multiplied billions of men and women. But Jesus sees the cross as bringing glory to the Father on earth. It is the glory of the Son's obedience and the Father's divine love that brings redemption to humanity, but at a staggering cost.

Now Jesus looks forward to glory in the Father's presence, the glory he left when he "emptied himself" and became a man (Philippians 2:7). What is this glory that preceded Jesus' earthly mission, that he alludes to again in verse 24? John's Gospel begins:

"In the beginning was the Word, and the Word was with God, and the Word was God. He was with God in the beginning. Through him all things were made; without him nothing was made that has been made." (1:1-3)

---

[705] "Completing" (NIV), "finishing/finished" (NRSV, KJV), "having accomplished" (ESV) is *teleioō*, "to complete an activity, complete, bring to an end, finish, accomplish" (BDAG 996, 1). Robertson calls it an "old verb from *teleios* (perfect)" (*Word Studies*).

[706] *Teleō*, "to complete an activity or process, bring to an end, finish, complete something" (BDAG 997, 1). Delling says, "The verbs *teleō* and *teleioō* coincide in the NT especially in the sense 'to carry through, to complete.' Whereas that is the chief meaning of *teleō*, the thought of totality is stronger in the case of *teleioō*. The findings suggest for *teleō* the meanings of *telos*, 'goal, issue, end,' and for *teleioō* those of *teleios*, 'whole, complete, perfect'" (Gerhard Delling, *telos, ktl.*, TDNT 8:84).

Paul speaks of this pre-existent glory in superlative terms – glory that Jesus again receives when he leaves this earth to ascend to the Father.

> "He is **the image of the invisible God**, the **firstborn** over all creation. For **by him all things were created**: things in heaven and on earth, visible and invisible, whether thrones or powers or rulers or authorities; all things were created by him and for him. [17] He is **before all things**, and **in him all things hold together**. And he is the **head of the body**, the church; he is **the beginning** and the **firstborn from among the dead**, so that in everything he might have the **supremacy**." (Colossians 1:15-18)

The writer of Hebrews says,

> "The Son is **the radiance of God's glory** and the **exact representation of his being**, sustaining all things by his powerful word. After he had provided purification for sins, he sat down at the right hand of the Majesty in heaven." (Hebrews 1:3)

Later, John the Apostle has a vision of Christ in heaven as a Lamb before the throne, receiving the praise due his name.

> "... The four living creatures and the twenty-four elders fell down before the Lamb. Each one had a harp and they were holding golden bowls full of incense, which are the prayers of the saints. And they sang a new song: 'You are worthy....'
>
> Then I looked and heard the voice of many angels, numbering thousands upon thousands, and ten thousand times ten thousand. They encircled the throne and the living creatures and the elders. In a loud voice they sang:
>
>> 'Worthy is the Lamb, who was slain,
>> to receive power and wealth and wisdom
>> and strength and honor and glory and praise!'
>
> Then I heard every creature in heaven and on earth and under the earth and on the sea, and all that is in them, singing:
>
>> 'To him who sits on the throne and to the Lamb
>> be praise and honor and glory and power,
>> for ever and ever!'" (Revelation 5:8-9a, 11-13)

On earth, people saw the carpenter-turned-preacher. They saw a man who walked the dusty roads of Palestine, speaking in its villages, healing its sick and casting out demons. They saw their leaders pour abuse on him, and finally have him executed in great shame and disgrace. But near the end of this prayer, Jesus asks the Father, that his disciples might glimpse him in his true glory:

> "Father, I want those you have given me to be with me where I am, and to see my glory, the glory you have given me because you loved me before the creation of the world." (17:24)

Father, lift our eyes above this earth to see our Lord's present glory, "glory as the only Son of the Father, full of grace and truth" (1:14). I think of that Messianic Psalm that was put to music in Handel's Messiah:

> "Lift up your heads, O you gates;
> be lifted up, you ancient doors,
> that the King of glory may come in.

Who is this King of glory?
The LORD strong and mighty,
the LORD mighty in battle.
Lift up your heads, O you gates;
lift them up, you ancient doors,
that the King of glory may come in.
Who is he, this King of glory?
The LORD Almighty – he is the King of glory." (Psalm 24:7-10)

Q3. (John 17:4-5) What was Jesus' preexistent glory like? What was his glory like during his earthly ministry? How did his glory peek through? What is his glory like now in the presence of his Father? Why do you think Jesus wants his disciples to see him in this glory (verse 24)? http://www.joyfulheart.com/forums/topic/1525-q3-preexistent-glory/

I Have Revealed You to the Ones You Gave Me (17:6-8)

Jesus has prayed that he might glorify the Father by his own mission. Now he turns to the second part of this prayer and talks to his Father about his disciples.

> "I have revealed you to those whom you gave me out of the world. They were yours; you gave them to me and they have obeyed your word." (17:6)

Notice how Jesus speaks of his disciples: They were the Father's, given to Jesus out of the world. They weren't the fruit of Jesus' recruiting prowess, but the Father's chosen gifts to his Son.

> "7 Now they know that everything you have given me comes from you. 8 For I gave them the words you gave me and they accepted them. They knew with certainty that I came from you, and they believed that you sent me." (17:7-8)

Prior to his redemptive work on the cross, Jesus labored to reveal the Father to his disciples in word and deed. Jesus accurately communicates the Father's message to them (12:49; 14:10; 15:15), and they receive it for what it is – the Father's own words. They believe that the Father is in Jesus, and Jesus is in the Father, that Jesus is The Word, the Logos (1:1-2).

Sometimes I wonder about the arrogance of us preachers who feel free to bring our own message and "slant" to our congregations. My brothers and sisters, our charge is not to bring our opinions, but to communicate Jesus' message with accuracy, just as Jesus spoke his Father's words with accuracy. We are not independent pundits, but on-message spokesman for the Messiah!

I Am Praying for Them (17:9-10)

Jesus prays for his disciples in a number of places in the Gospels: 14:16; 16:26-27; Luke 22:32; Hebrews 7:25; etc. "Pray" in verse 9 is *erōtaō*, "to ask," here, "to ask for something, ask, request."[707]

---

[707] *Erōtaō*, BDAG 395, 2. It is used in common speech, but also in prayer at in verse 20, as well as 16:26; Luke 3:48; 1 John 5:16.

"⁹ I pray for them. I am not praying for the world, but for those you have given me, for they are yours. ¹⁰ All I have is yours, and all you have is mine. And glory has come to me through them." (17:9-10)

God loves the whole world (3:16). Jesus died for the sins of the whole world (1:19; 4:42; 1 John 2:2). He came as a light to the world (3:19; 9:5; 12:46; 17:21), to give life to the world (6:33, 51), and to save the world (12:47). But here he prays for his tiny band, those whom the Father has given him, the first recruits in what will become a mighty army of the Redeemed.

Jesus is not selfish or possessive of those the Father has given him. Jesus realizes that he shares everything with the Father; they co-possess everything. And there is a sense in which we are co-heirs in this way, as well, as we are one with Christ and the Father.

> "**All things are yours**, whether Paul or Apollos or Cephas or the world or life or death or the present or the future – all are yours, and you are of Christ, and Christ is of God." (1 Corinthians 3:21b-23)

> "Now if we are children, then we are heirs – **heirs** of God and **co-heirs** with Christ, if indeed we share in his sufferings in order that we may also **share in his glory**." (Romans 8:17)

Q4. (John 17:6-10) In what sense do the Son and the Father "co-possess" everything? What does that say about their relationship with each other? In what sense do we "co-possess" everything with the Father and Son? How should that affect our values? The way we live?
http://www.joyfulheart.com/forums/topic/1526-q4-co-possessing/

The Father Protects His Children Forever (17:11-15)

Jesus is leaving the dangerous world that has marked him as an enemy, but his disciples remain and need protection.

> "¹¹ I will remain[708] in the world no longer, but they are still in the world, and I am coming to you. Holy Father, protect (*tēreō*) them by the power of your name – the name you gave me – so that they may be one as we are one. ¹² While I was with them, I protected (*tēreō*) them and kept them safe (*phylassō*) by that name you gave me. None has been lost except the one doomed to destruction so that Scripture would be fulfilled.

> ¹³ I am coming to you now, but I say these things while I am still in the world, so that they may have the full measure of my joy within them. ¹⁴ I have given them your word and the world has hated them, for they are not of the world any more than I am of the world. ¹⁵ My prayer is not that you take them out of the world but that you protect (*tēreō*) them from the evil one." (17:11-15)

Three Greek words describe this keeping and protecting power of the Father.

1. "Protect" (NIV, NRSV) in verses 11 and 12, **"keep"** (ESV, KJV) is the verb *tēreō*, "guard, keep," here, "to cause a state, condition, or activity to continue, keep, hold, reserve, preserve someone or

---

[708] "Remain" (NIV) is not in the Greek text of verse 11. A more literal translation would be, "I am no longer in the world" (ESV).

something," specifically, "keep someone (unharmed) by or through something."[709] This is close in meaning to a second word used here: *phylassō*.

2. "Kept them safe" (NIV), **"guarded"** (NRSV, ESV), **"kept"** (KJV) is *phylassō*, "to carry out sentinel functions, watch, guard," here, "to protect by taking careful measures, guard, protect."[710] We see these two words used in New Testament passages which teach us about the Father's protection for his children, especially from Satan's attacks.

> "... The One who was born of God **keeps him safe** (*tēreō*), and the evil one cannot harm him." (1 John 5:18)

> "May your whole spirit, soul and body be **kept** (*tēreō*) blameless at the coming of our Lord Jesus Christ." (1 Thessalonians 5:23)

> "To those who have been called, who are loved by God the Father and **kept** (*tēreō*) by Jesus Christ...." (Jude 1)

> "... Who by God's power are being **guarded** (*phroureō*[711]) through faith for a salvation ready to be revealed in the last time." (1 Peter 1:5)

> "To him who is able to **keep** (*phylassō*) you from falling and to present you before his glorious presence without fault and with great joy...." (Jude 24)

> "But the Lord is faithful, and he will strengthen and **protect** (*phylassō*) you from the evil one." (2 Thessalonians 3:3)

3. Not "lost," the third word shows the result of God's guarding. The verb is *apollymi*, "to cause or experience destruction," here, "perish, be ruined, die," especially of eternal death.[712] We've seen this word twice before as part of powerful promises of salvation.

> "For God so loved the world that he gave his one and only Son, that whoever believes in him shall not perish (*apollymi*) but have eternal life." (3:16)

> "I give them eternal life, and they shall never perish (*apollymi*); no one can snatch them out of my hand." (10:28)

Everyone is on the road to hell, to "perishing" (Matthew 7:13-14; Luke 13:23-24). But those who put their faith in Jesus are saved from this destruction. For those who have heard about Jesus' salvation, hell is clearly their own fault.

> "They perish (*apollymi*) because they refused to love the truth and so be saved." (2 Thessalonians 2:10b)

The idea of hell is difficult for us. We don't like it. But it is clear in Scripture, and if we try to remove it from Christian doctrine or hush it up because it is unpopular, we aren't declaring the whole gospel of salvation.

John has some of the strongest promises of protection in the Bible – but notice that the promises are made toward believers – not to those who once believed but no longer do so – but to those who

[709] *Tēreō*, BDAG 1002, 2b.
[710] *Phylassō*, BDAG 1068, 2b.
[711] *Phroureō*, "to provide security, guard, protect, keep" (BDAG 1067, 3).
[712] *Apollymi*, BDAG 116, 1bα.

continue to believe, those who abide (15:1-8). You'll find further discussion of the doctrine of the Perseverance of the Saints in 10:28 (Lesson 19) and 15:4-5 (Lesson 26).

None Was Lost Except Judas (17:12b)

Now let's go back to verse 12b, where Jesus qualifies his protection of those the Father gave him.

"None has been lost except the one doomed to destruction so that Scripture would be fulfilled." (17:12b)

In John's Gospel, Jesus is very clear that he lost none that the Father gave him (6:49; 18:9). He provides complete protection. Absolutely no one can snatch one of his sheep (10:28-29). So it is important for John to explain that Judas is the exception.

Judas betrayal had been prophesied long before (13:18). John makes it clear that Jesus knew from the beginning that Judas would betray him (6:64, 70-71; 13:11). It's not entirely clear that Judas was ever a true believer, even though Jesus chose him to be an apostle. In John's Gospel we see a differentiation between disciples who believe primarily because of the miracles, but don't go further (2:23-25; 6:26; 12:42), disciples who leave because they are offended by Jesus' teaching (6:60-62, 66), and those who follow Jesus out of a deeper trust, in spite of persecution (6:68-69; 8:30-31). Perhaps Judas was a disciple who possessed an initial belief, but, like many, didn't go deeper (Matthew 13:1-9, 18-23). For more on Judas' betrayal, see 13:18-30 (Lesson 23) and 18:2-5 (Lesson 30).

In the World but Not *of* the World (17:13-16)

In our passage we see a clear distinction between "in the world" and "of the world."

"[13] I am coming to you now, but I say these things while I am still **in the world**, so that they may have the full measure of my joy within them. [14] I have given them your word and the world has hated them, for they are not **of the world** any more than I am **of the world**. [15] My prayer is not that you take them **out of the world** but that you protect them from the evil one. [16] They are not **of the world**, even as I am not **of it**." (17:13-16)

The "world" (*kosmos*) here refers to "the system of human existence in its many aspects" that is hostile to God – lost in sin, wholly at odds with anything divine, ruined and depraved.[713] In his First Epistle, John defines what he means by "the world":

"For everything in the world – the cravings of sinful man, the lust of his eyes and the boasting of what he has and does – comes not from the Father but from the world." (1 John 2:16)

Various prepositions in our passage serve to define a person's relationship to the world.

- **"In the world"** (17:13)[714] – physically located in the world and surrounded by its people.
- **"Of the world"** (17:14)[715] – belonging to, arising from, originating from the world (8:23; 5:19).
- **"Out of the world"** (17:5)[716] – removing disciples from being physically located in the sphere of the world.

---

[713] *Kosmos*, BDAG 562, 7b.

[714] The preposition is *en*, "marker of a position defined as being in a location, "in, among" (BDAG 326, 1a).

[715] The preposition is *ek*, here marker denoting origin, cause, motive, reason, "from, of" (BDAG 296, 3b).

Though we disciples are in the world, surrounded by an environment that is often hostile to Jesus and his disciples, we aren't part of the world system. In reality, we are no longer citizens of the world, but citizens of Jesus' Kingdom. We are resident aliens. As a 1950s gospel song puts it:

> "This world is not my home, I'm just a-passing through...."[717]

We are in the world – Jesus wants us here to represent him and his Kingdom – but we are not to adopt its value system and lifestyle. Paul writes,

> "Do not conform any longer to **the pattern of this world**, but be transformed by the renewing of your mind. Then you will be able to test and approve what God's will is – his good, pleasing and perfect will." (Romans 12:2)

The Holy Spirit allows us to continue here without caving into the pressure to conform.

> "You, dear children, are from God and have overcome them, because the one who is in you is greater than **the one who is in the world**." (1 John 4:4)

Q5. (John 17:15-16) Is God's desire to immediately extract us from the earth, or to leave us here? How is it possible to be "in" the world, but not "of" it, or contaminated by it? How do we achieve this?
http://www.joyfulheart.com/forums/topic/1527-q5-not-of-the-world/

Sanctify Them by the Truth (17:17-19)

> "[17] Sanctify them by the truth; your word is truth. [18] As you sent me into the world, I have sent them into the world. [19] For them I sanctify myself, that they too may be truly sanctified." (17:17-19)

"To sanctify" is an Old Testament concept from the Hebrew verb *qādash*, "be hallowed, holy, sanctified." The root idea seems to be "set apart, separated" from a common use to a sacred use, to become the exclusive property of the King, the Holy God.[718]

How are people sanctified or made holy? Several times in the New Testament we see the power of God's Word to cleanse and empower Christ's disciples:

> "If you **hold to my teaching**, you are really my disciples. Then you will know the truth, and the **truth** will set you free." (8:31-32)

> "You are already **clean** because of the **word** I have spoken to you." (15:3)

---

[716] The same preposition *ek* is used, but with the verb *airō*, "take." It is clear the preposition is used as marker denoting separation, "from, out of, away from" (BDAG 295, 1a).

[717] "This World Is Not My Home," words and music by Albert E. Brumley, © 1952, Acclaim Music.

[718] Francis Brown, S.R. Driver, and Charles A. Briggs (eds.), *A Hebrew and English Lexicon of the Old Testament* (Oxford: Clarendon Press, 1907) *Qādash*, p. 872. "Sanctify" is *hagiazō*, "consecrate, sanctify" by contact with what is holy. To include a person in the inner circle of what is holy, in both cultic and moral associations of the word, "consecrate, dedicate, sanctify." BDAG 10, 2.

"Christ loved the church and gave himself up for her to **make her holy**, cleansing her by the washing with water through the **word**...." (Ephesians 5:25b-26)

"Now that you have **purified** yourselves by **obeying the truth**...." (1 Peter 1:22)

Jesus, the Word, the Logos, the Message of God has come and Jesus' disciples have received him and his message as from God. This in itself has set them apart from the world, sanctified, set apart, with the mission of taking Jesus' message to the world. In the same way Jesus is set apart to complete his own mission, to redeem mankind for God.

When we read the Word, our thoughts begin to conform to God's thoughts. This Word is one of the most important means of changing our minds and hearts, of sanctifying us – both making us like Jesus, and helping us adopt his mission to the world.

That All of Them May Be One (17:20-23)

Now Jesus' prayer focus shifts from his disciples, to those whom his disciples will bring to faith in him.

"20 My prayer is not for them alone. I pray also for those who will believe in me through their message, 21 that all of them may be one, Father, just as you are in me and I am in you. May they also be in us so that the world may believe that you have sent me. 22 I have given them the glory that you gave me, that they may be one as we are one: 23 I in them and you in me. May they be brought to complete unity to let the world know that you sent me and have loved them even as you have loved me." (17:20-23)

Jesus' burden is the perfect unity of his people. "Brought to complete unity" (NIV), "become completely/perfectly one" (NRSV, ESV), "be made perfect in one" (KJV), is literally, "become perfected into one." Jesus prays that the unity will be perfected.[719]

God knows that we see a lot of imperfect unity. Often various Christian denominations feel superior to others. There is misunderstanding and resentment and pride and hurt. Within a city, smaller congregations sometimes act as if they're in competition with the larger churches. Within congregations there are sometimes factions, resentments that can have gone unresolved and unforgiven for decades. Oneness. Unity. That is what Jesus prays for.

I don't think that Jesus' burden is organizational unity – one single large denomination of Christian churches. But love between the churches and groups that exist. Love that covers a multitude of sins. Love that bridges divisions. Love that overlooks differences due to centuries-old traditions. Love that unites in Christ.

Jesus gives his relationship with the Father as our example of unity.

"... That all of them may be one, Father, just as you are in me and I am in you. May they also be in us so that the world may believe that you have sent me." (17:21)

As we are "in" the Father and Son, we will naturally be unified with brothers and sisters who also love the Father and Son.

---

[719] The verb is the perfect passive participle of *teleioō*, "to overcome or supplant an imperfect state of things by one that is free from objection, bring to an end, bring to its goal/accomplishment," here, "make perfect" (BDAG 996, 2cα). The noun is the number "one," *heis*, that is used several times in this passage.

Twice in this passage Jesus ties Christian unity with evangelism:

"...**so that the world may believe** that you have sent me." (17:21b)

"May they be brought to complete unity **to let the world know** that you sent me and have loved them even as you have loved me." (17:23)

This is similar to what Jesus said earlier:

"By this **all men will know** that you are my disciples, if you love one another." (13:35)

Unity, of course, is dependent upon mutual love for each other. And that love more than anything is to be the mark of Jesus' disciples.

Verse 22 talks about Christ's glory upon his disciples:

"I have given them the glory that you gave me, that they may be one as we are one." (17:22)

In what sense did Jesus give his disciples his glory? This is difficult. Morris sees this as teaching them "to follow the path of lowly service, culminating in the cross."[720] Certainly Jesus taught them to walk sensitive to the Father's voice, obeying the Father in everything, and so completing his work. Carson sees this transmission of glory in the sense of Jesus completing his task of revealing the Father to them.[721] The source of Jesus' glory is knowing and fellowship with the Father. He has shared that with his disciples to the extent that he can say, "If you have seen me you have seen the Father." The glory of the knowledge of God will be complete when we are in his presence face-to-face.

> **Q6. (John 17:11b, 20-21) Why is unity between Christians so important? What is the model Jesus gives of this unity in verse 21a? What effect does true Christian unity have on our witness to the world?**
> http://www.joyfulheart.com/forums/topic/1528-q6-unity/

May They See the Glory You Have Given Me (17:24)

Now Jesus comes around again to the recurring theme of glory.

"Father, I want those you have given me to be with me where I am, and to see my glory, the glory you have given me because you loved me before the creation[722] of the world." (17:24)

Jesus mentioned this at the beginning of this prayer in verse 5 above, where we discussed Jesus' pre-existent glory.

"And now, Father, glorify me in your presence with the glory I had with you before the world began." (17:5)

---

[720] Morris, *John*, pp. 734-735.

[721] Carson, *John*, p. 568-569.

[722] "Creation" (NIV), "foundation" (NRSV, ESV, KJV) is *katabolē*, "the act of laying something down, with implication of providing a base for something, foundation" (BDAG 515, 1). We see this phrase "from the foundation of the world" a number of times in the New Testament indicating that God has long had a loving relationship with Jesus, and planned, through him, to save the world through his death on the cross: Matthew 13:35; 25:34; Luke 11:50; Ephesians 1:4; Hebrews 4:3; 9:26; 1 Peter 1:20; Revelation 13:8; 17:8.

How much Jesus must have missed the glory of his former fellowship with the Father! Yes, being able to talk on the telephone and Skype are good when you're separated from loved ones geographically, but there's something special about being in the same room and sharing your thoughts in person.

It's very difficult for us to understand what it cost Jesus to leave heaven and enter our fallen world.

> "Who, being in very nature God,
> did not consider equality with God something to be grasped,
> but made himself nothing,
> taking the very nature of a servant,
> being made in human likeness." (Philippians 2:6-7)

Missionaries often experience severe "culture shock" when they leave their own culture to live in another land. To what do we compare the glorious Son, waited on hand and foot by angels, leaving the Father's presence to enter our world filled with struggle and sorrow, hate and pain? Love sent him. But now, longing for the Father is calling him home. He can hardly wait!

That Your Love and I May Be in Them (17:25-26)

Now Jesus concludes his prayer.

> "25 Righteous Father, though the world does not know you, I know you, and they know that you have sent me. 26 I have made you known to them, and will continue to make you known in order that the love you have for me may be in them and that I myself may be in them." (17:25-26)

In verse 11 he calls on his "holy Father," emphasizing the Father's holiness. Here, he calls on his "righteous Father," the one whose very character is the standard of righteousness. He is the righteous and holy Father whom the world does not know. The world has created their own gods or version of God, but they don't know the "true God" (verse 3) nor the Christ whom he has sent.

But his disciples now know the Father, because Jesus, the Word, the Logos, the very expression of God has made him known to them. And Jesus will continue this mission of revelation.

Making the Father known through Jesus his Son, that is our mission too. Why? So that those who don't know the Father can experience this love that sent Jesus to earth and back -- love that is the central reality of the Kingdom of God, the mark of Jesus' disciples, and the essential element of the unity we have with other believers.

Lessons for Disciples

Jesus' prayer has much to teach us disciples:

1. The essence of eternal life is not in its duration, but in its "life" – knowing the Father and the Son (17:3).
2. We need to understand Jesus, not just as the earthly Man, but the glorified Son of God in the presence of the Father in heaven. Only then will we grasp his true nature (17:4-5).
3. Just as the Son and the Father "co-possess" all things, so we "co-possess" all things with them (17:6-10).

4. God's desire is not to extract us from earth, but to leave us here – protected by the power of Jesus' name – so that we might carry out his work here, but remain uncontaminated by the world's value system and lifestyle (17:15-16).

5. We are set apart and cleansed by exposure to and obedience to Jesus' words and truth (17:17).

6. Jesus' desire is unity between all who believe in him – a unity patterned after the unity between the Father and Son. This unity serves as a proof to the world of Jesus' divinity (17:11b, 20-21).

7. Jesus desires us to see him in the glory the Father has given him from before time (17:24).

Prayer

Father, sometimes we feel so earth-bound, so worldly! I pray that you would cut the fetters that bind us to the world system that is at enmity with you. Help us to long for the glory of your presence. Give us more longing to be with you than to live a long life here. Transform our minds and value systems. But while we're here, I pray that you help us to share your love and glory with others, and especially that we may be at one with our brothers and sisters! In Jesus' name, we pray. Amen.

Key Verses

"Now this is eternal life: that they may know you, the only true God, and Jesus Christ, whom you have sent." (John 17:3, NIV)

"I have brought you glory on earth by completing the work you gave me to do. And now, Father, glorify me in your presence with the glory I had with you before the world began." (John 17:4-5, NIV)

"Holy Father, protect them by the power of your name – the name you gave me – so that they may be one as we are one." (John 17:11b, NIV)

"My prayer is not that you take them out of the world but that you protect them from the evil one. They are not of the world, even as I am not of it." (John 17:15-16, NIV)

"Sanctify them by the truth; your word is truth." (John 17:17, NIV)

"My prayer is not for them alone. I pray also for those who will believe in me through their message, that all of them may be one, Father, just as you are in me and I am in you. May they also be in us so that the world may believe that you have sent me." (John 17:20-21, NIV)

"I have given them the glory that you gave me, that they may be one as we are one: I in them and you in me. May they be brought to complete unity to let the world know that you sent me and have loved them even as you have loved me." (John 17:22-23, NIV)

"Father, I want those you have given me to be with me where I am, and to see my glory, the glory you have given me because you loved me before the creation of the world." (John 17:24, NIV)

Section IV. The Crucifixion and Resurrection (20:31)

Now John's Gospel turns from the Farewell Discourses and Jesus' prayer for his disciples to Christ's Passion. The word "passion" comes by way of Middle English and Anglo-French, from Late Latin *passion, passio*, "suffering." So Christ's Passion means Christ's suffering.

Protestants sometimes pride themselves on the Empty Cross that emphasizes the resurrected Christ, rather than the Crucifix that emphasizes the suffering of Christ, now past. But I think there is value in both. There is value in contemplating the sufferings of Christ on our behalf. If you are near a Catholic church or retreat center, take some time to walk and pray the 14 Stations of the Cross and meditate on what Christ suffered for you.

Or meditate on my virtual "Stations of the Cross for Protestants and Catholics" (www.joyfulheart.com/stations-of-the-cross).

In the next several lessons we'll explore Christ's sufferings and his resurrection.

Matthias Grünewald, 'Die Kreuzigung Christi' (1523-1524), Tauberbischofsheimer Altar, 193 x 151 cm. Kunsthalle, Karlsruhe, Germany.

30. Jesus' Arrest and Trial (18:1-19:16)
31. Jesus' Death and Burial (19:17-42)
32. Jesus Appears to Mary Magdalene (20:1-18)
33. As the Father Sent Me, So I Send You (20:19-31)

Then we'll conclude John's Gospel with the Epilogue, Lesson 34. Feed My Sheep (21:1-25).

The observant reader will notice various differences between John's account of Jesus' passion and resurrection and those in the Synoptic Gospels. Since these lessons tend to be more devotional than analytical in nature, I refer you to Appendix 10. Harmony between John and the Synoptic Gospels, and an introduction to the New Testament to study the complex Synoptic Problem. We'll only make passing reference to it in these lessons.

30. Jesus' Arrest and Trial (18:1-19:16)

In John's Gospel we move from Jesus' High Priestly Prayer directly to the Garden of Gethsemane. You'll observe some different emphases between John's Gospel and the Synoptics regarding Jesus' trails, crucifixion, and resurrection. For example, we see that John has truncated his account of Jesus' various trials to suit his purpose. We'll only give the differences a passing mention in these lessons.[723]

As you read John's account, you'll become aware that none of these events take Jesus by surprise. He knows what will happen. Though he is the one arrested, tried, and ultimately crucified, he is no martyr. He is clearly in charge. Earlier, Jesus had said:

> "The reason my Father loves me is that I lay down my life – only to take it up again. No one takes it from me, but I lay it down of my own accord. I have authority to lay it down and authority to take it up again. This command I received from my Father." (10:17-18)

I beg your indulgence, for in this lesson I spend considerable time explaining each detail of John's account so that we can understand the crass injustice, gross brutality, and deep humiliation that Jesus endured for us.

Hans Holbein (the younger), detail of 'The Passion' Altarpiece (1524-25), oil on limewood, Kunstmuseum, Öffentliche Kunstsammlung, Basel, Switzerland.

Betrayal in Gethsemane (18:1-3)

Exactly where Jesus completed his Farewell Discourses and High Priestly Prayer isn't certain from Jesus' earlier words, "Come now, let us leave" (14:31b), during his Farewell Discourses. They must have taken place in the city – perhaps the Upper Room, since 18:1 has Jesus "going out" with his disciples, crossing the Kidron brook, and arriving on the slope of the Mount of Olives.

> "When he had finished praying, Jesus left[724] with his disciples and crossed the Kidron Valley. On the other side there was an olive grove, and he and his disciples went into it." (18:1)

[723] For more detail, see Appendix 10. Harmony between John and the Synoptic Gospels, and a full Introduction to the New Testament.

[724] *Exerchomai*, "to move out of or away from an area, go out, come out, go away, retire" (BDAG 347, 1aα Gimmel).

On the slopes of the Mount of Olives is an "olive grove" or "garden"[725], which is referred to in Matthew and Mark as Gethsemane (Hebrew for "olive press"). It may have been a walled garden, since Jesus and his disciples are said to go into it (verse 1) and out of it (verse 4). Luke tells us that during Holy Week, Jesus and his disciples have repeatedly spent the night[726] on the Mount of Olives (Luke 21:37; 22:39).

Location of the Garden of Gethsemane east of Jerusalem.

Because the location and times were predictable and free of crowds, this is the spot Judas chose to betray Jesus.

> "2 Now Judas, who betrayed him, knew the place, because Jesus had often met[727] there with his disciples. 3 So Judas came to the grove[728], guiding a detachment of soldiers and some officials from the chief priests and Pharisees. They were carrying torches, lanterns and weapons." (18:2-3)

This detachment of soldiers appears to be Roman, due to the Roman military technical terms used in the text to refer to the detachment (*speira*[729]) and its commander (*chiliarchos*, 18:12). They were accompanied by "officials from the chief priests and Pharisees." The officials included temple guards (*hypēretēs*[730]) who had been sent to arrest Jesus earlier – and failed (7:32, 45-46).

While the Synoptics speak of an armed "crowd" (Matthew 26:47), John's details indicate that Roman soldiers were present also. Due to the throngs of people in Jerusalem during Passover, the Romans transferred auxiliary troops (usually garrisoned in Caesarea) to the Fortress of Antonia adjacent to the Temple. They were there to prevent mob riots and incipient rebellion at this volatile festival. Apparently, the Romans had been asked to send some soldiers to assist in this arrest to insure overwhelming odds. Starting a riot or a fight with Jesus' disciples wouldn't have served the chief

---

[725] "Olive grove" (NIV) or "garden" (NRSV, ESV, KJV) is *kēpos*, "garden," here, 18:26 and 19:41 (BDAG 542).

[726] *Aulizomai*, "to have a temporary sleeping arrangement, spend the night." The word originally meant spending the night in the *aulē*, in the open air, then also of temporary lodging, with context indicating whether outdoors ('bivouac') or indoors (BDAG 151, 1).

[727] "Met" (NIV, NRSV, ESV), "resorted" (KJV) is *synagō*, passive, "be gathered or brought together" or "gather, come together, assemble" (BDAG 962, 1). We get our word "synagogue" from this verb.

[728] In Greek this is the adverb *ekei*, "there, in that place."

[729] "Detachment/band of soldiers" (NIV, NRSV, ESV) is *speira*, a military technical term, "cohort," the tenth part of a legion. The *speira* normally had 600 men, but the number varied (BDAG 936). To arrest Jesus, however, they probably took a much smaller detachment.

[730] "Officials" (NIV), "police" (NRSV), "officers" (ESV, KJV) is *hypēretēs*, here, and in verses 12, 22, and 19:6, frequently as technical term for a governmental or other official, "one who functions as a helper, frequently in a subordinate capacity, helper, assistant" (BDAG 1035).

priests' purposes. But, even though Roman soldiers were present, the arrest was clearly made by the chief priests' officers, since Jesus was taken to the high priest's residence (19:12), not a Roman facility.

I Am He! (18:4-9)

Jesus is no victim. Instead of slipping away as he had done on previous occasions when it wasn't his time (7:30; 8:59; 10:39; Luke 4:29-30), Jesus "went out" and confronted the soldiers and temple officers.

> "4 Jesus, knowing all that was going to happen to him, went out and asked them, 'Who is it you want?' 5 'Jesus of Nazareth,' they replied. 'I am he,' Jesus said. (And Judas the traitor[731] was standing there with them.) 6 When Jesus said, 'I am he,' they drew back and fell to the ground." (18:4-6)

James J. Tissot, 'The Guards Falling Backwards' (1884-1896), gouache on grey wove paper, 7-13/16 x 10-3/8 in, Brooklyn Museum, New York.

Notice Jesus' reply to those who demand Jesus of Nazareth: literally, "I am" (*egō eimi*), words that reflect Yahweh's self-revelation as the Great "I AM." (For more on this, see Appendix 4. The "I Am" Passages in John's Gospel.) The effect on those who come to arrest him is remarkable – and two-fold: They

1. Drew back, physically retreated,[732] and
2. Fell to the ground.[733]

Some scholars have tried to find natural explanations for the soldiers falling down. Since those in front backed up into them, they suggest, it caused row after row of soldiers to fall down. If that were the case, John would have ignored this detail. But he shares it so that we might see the awesome Shekinah glory of God upon Jesus.

How do we explain this falling incident? In the Bible, people fall when the Holy Spirit or the power of God comes upon them (Numbers 11:25-26; 1 Samuel 10:11; 19:20-24; 1 Kings 8:10-11; 2 Chronicles 5:14; Matthew 28:4; Acts 9:3). This incident in the Garden of Gethsemane should probably be understood in this category. Pentecostals and Charismatics sometimes observe a phenomenon they refer to as "being slain in the Spirit" or "falling under the power." Clearly, the soldiers are overwhelmed by the presence of God.

---

[731] "Traitor" (NIV), "who betrayed him" (NRSV, ESV, KJV) is *paradidōmi*, here, "hand over, turn over, give up a person" (as a technical term of police and courts 'hand over into [the] custody [of]') (BDAG 762, 1b).

[732] "Drew back" (NIV, ESV), "stepped back" (NRSV), "went backward" (KJV) is the verb *aperchomai*, "go," here, "draw back" a short distance (BDAG 102, 1b) and a prepositional phrase with the adverb *opisō*, "marker of a position in back of something, behind" (BDAG 716, 1aα).

[733] "Fell to the ground" is the verb *piptō*, "fall, fall to the ground, fall down (violently)" (BDAG 815, 1aαℵ); and the adverb *chamai*, "pertaining to location on the ground as objective of movement, "to/on the ground" (BDAG 1076, 2).

"⁷ Again he asked them, 'Who is it you want?' And they said, 'Jesus of Nazareth.' ⁸ 'I told you that I am he,' Jesus answered. 'If you are looking for me, then let these men go.⁷³⁴' ⁹ This happened so that the words he had spoken would be fulfilled: 'I have not lost one of those you gave me.'" (18:7-9)

Jesus' promise to protect his disciples (6:39) is primarily spiritual, but his requesting that they be let go is symbolic of that care.

Peter Cuts Off the High Priest's Servant's Ear (18:10-11)

Luke's Gospel tells us that as part of the Upper Room discourse, Jesus had instructed his disciples to now carry more on their mission trips than he had previously allowed them. He encouraged them to take a purse, a bag, "and if you don't have a sword, sell your cloak and buy one" (Luke 22:36). The disciples then produced two swords, one of which was in Peter's possession. John explains:

"¹⁰ Then Simon Peter, who had a sword⁷³⁵, drew it and struck the high priest's servant, cutting off his right ear. (The servant's name was Malchus.⁷³⁶) ¹¹ Jesus commanded Peter, 'Put your sword away! Shall I not drink the cup the Father has given me?'" (18:10-11)

Jesus rebukes Peter, and, Luke tells us, "touched the man's ear and healed him" (Luke 22:51). He actually performs a miracle before the arresting officers and they arrest him anyway!

Jesus doesn't need to be defended – he has legions of angels at his beck and call (Matthew 26:53). Peter's defense, heroic though it is in the face of overwhelming force, is intended to prevent Jesus from "drinking the cup" that the Father has given him, that is, the destiny or mission that he has fully accepted from his Father earlier that night after agonizing in the Garden – "Not my will, but yours be done" (Luke 22:42). Throughout John's Gospel we've seen references leading up to this "hour," this destiny. Jesus will not be denied his glory and the Father's plan of salvation by Peter's clumsy swordplay.

> **Q1. (John 18:1-11) What do you think caused the soldiers to fall back in the Garden (18:6)? Why does John tell us this detail? Why does Jesus rebuke Peter for defending him with a sword (18:11)? Jesus is facing forces sent by hell. Why doesn't he resist?**
> **http://www.joyfulheart.com/forums/topic/1529-q1-peters-sword/**

Arrested and Brought to Annas (18:12-14)

"¹² Then the detachment of soldiers with its commander⁷³⁷ and the Jewish officials arrested Jesus. They bound him ¹³ and brought him first to Annas, who was the father-in-law of Caiaphas, the

---

⁷³⁴ "Let ... go" is the verb *aphiēmi*, "allow," and the infinitive of *hypagō*, "to leave someone's presence, go away" (BDAG 1028, 1).

⁷³⁵ Peter's sword (*machaira*) was "a relatively short sword, dagger, or other sharp instrument (BDAG, 622, 1).

⁷³⁶ Only John tells us the servant's name, Malchus, perhaps because of John's more intimate knowledge of the high priest's household. For a depiction of this scene, read my short story, "Malchus, the Slave Whose Ear Was Cut Off" (www.joyfulheart.com/easter/malchus.htm).

high priest that year. [14] Caiaphas was the one who had advised the Jews that it would be good if one man died for the people." (18:12-14)

Modern-day readers are surprised that Jesus isn't brought before the ruling high priest rather than his father-in-law. But that's because we don't understand the intricacies of Jewish history and the politics of this period.

Annas had been appointed high priest in 7 AD by Quirinius, governor of Syria, and deposed by Valerius Gratus in 15 AD. But though he no longer had official power, he still commanded great influence as the patriarch of his family. Annas belonged to the Sadducean aristocracy, and, like others of that class, he seems to have been arrogant, astute, ambitious, and enormously wealthy.

Gerrrit van Honthorst, 'Christ before the High Priest Annas' (c. 1617), National Gallery, London.

His influence with Rome and power behind the scenes of Judaism are demonstrated by the fact that, over several decades, Annas saw to it that five sons and one son-in-law were appointed high priest. Annas wielded the power of high priest during this period; Caiaphas merely held the title and served as chairman of the Sanhedrin. So the soldiers bound Jesus and brought him first before Annas.

Peter's First Betrayal (18:15-18)

"[15] Simon Peter and another disciple were following Jesus. Because this disciple was known to the high priest, he went with Jesus into the high priest's courtyard, [16] but Peter had to wait outside at the door. The other disciple, who was known to the high priest, came back, spoke to the girl on duty there[738] and brought Peter in." (18:15-16)

Exactly what courtyard[739] Peter and the other disciple enter isn't certain. Do Annas and Caiaphas live in the same palace? How far is it from there to the meeting place of the Sanhedrin in the temple, presumably where the trial takes place later? We're not sure. But the meeting with Annas couldn't have been in the temple grounds, since a servant girl[740] is the doorkeeper here, not a Levite.

---

[737] "Commander" (NIV), "officer" (NRSV), "captain" (ESV, KJV) is *chiliarchos*, literally, "leader of a thousand soldiers," then also = the Roman "military tribune," the commander of a cohort, about 600 men, roughly equivalent to major or colonel (BDAG 1084).

[738] *Thyrōros*, "Doorkeeper, gatekeeper" (BDAG 462), in verses 16 and 17. Here the noun has a feminine article, indicating a female doorkeeper.

[739] "Courtyard" (NIV, NRSV, ESV), "palace" (KJV) is *aulē*, "an area open to the sky, frequently surrounded by buildings, and in some cases partially by walls, enclosed open space, courtyard," though it could refer to a dwelling complex, "palace" (BDAG 150, 1 and 2b), though here it is obviously a courtyard, since the soldiers are warming themselves at a fire there.

[740] "Girl" (NIV), "woman" (NRSV), "servant girl" (ESV), "damsel" (KJV) is *paidiskē*, the diminutive of *pais*, "girl," in the New Testament, always of the slave class, "female slave" (BDAG 749).

It is clear that Peter and the "other disciple" gain entrance into the courtyard because the "other disciple" is "known to the high priest."[741] To gain immediate entry means that the "other disciple" was recognized on sight and admitted without question. Who is this "other disciple"? Though he isn't named, some believe that this is John, the Beloved Disciple, though we can't be sure.[742]

Immediately, the girl at the door questions Peter.

"17 'You are not one of his disciples, are you?' the girl at the door asked Peter. He replied, 'I am not.' 18 It was cold, and the servants and officials stood around a fire they had made to keep warm. Peter also was standing with them, warming himself." (18:17-18)

John describes the scene with Peter standing around in the same vicinity as the "officers" (*hypēretēs*), a brave but foolish place to hang out, as we see in verse 26.

Annas Questions Jesus (18:19-24)

Inside, Annas is interrogating Jesus.

"19 Meanwhile, the high priest questioned[743] Jesus about his disciples and his teaching.
20 'I have spoken openly to the world,' Jesus replied. 'I always taught in synagogues or at the temple, where all the Jews come together. I said nothing in secret. 21 Why question me? Ask those who heard me. Surely they know what I said.'" (18:19-21)

Annas has two questions. First, about Jesus' disciples. How many were there? Were they likely to resist or rebel at Jesus' arrest? And, second, about the content of Jesus' teaching. Jesus assures Annas that what he said to his disciples privately[744] is the same thing that he taught publically.

Then Jesus questions Annas. Why is Annas interrogating the accused? According to Jewish law, an accusation must be substantiated by credible witnesses, not by questioning the accused.[745] True, this seems to be an informal interrogation, not a trial. But for this "impertinence" Jesus is slapped in the face.

"22 When Jesus said this, one of the officials nearby struck him in the face.[746] 'Is this the way you answer the high priest?' he demanded.
23 'If I said something wrong,' Jesus replied, 'testify as to what is wrong. But if I spoke the truth, why did you strike me?'" (18:22-23)

---

[741] "Known" in verses 15 and 16 is the adjective *gnōstos*, with the dative case, "pertaining to being familiar or known: known," here, "acquaintance, friend, intimate" (BDAG 204, 1b).

[742] John's Gospel does seem to have insider knowledge concerning the high priest's dealings (11:49-52), the name of the high priest's servant (18:10), etc. There are late Christian writings that identify this person with John, but too late to have historical value. If the "other disciple" is John, son of Zebedee, how would a fisherman's family in Galilee personally know a wealthy Sadducee of a powerful family in Jerusalem? However, there is some indication John's family may have had priestly connections (Morris, *John*, p. 752, fn. 32). We can only speculate.

[743] "Questioned" (NIV, NRSV, ESV), "asked" (KJV) is *erōtaō*, "to put a query to someone, ask, ask a question" (BDAG 395, 1).

[744] "Secret" is the adjective *kryptos*, "hidden, secret," here as a substantive, "a hidden place" (BDAG 670, 2b).

[745] Morris, *John*, p. 755.

[746] "Struck in/on the face" (NIV, NRSV), "struck with his hand" (ESV), "struck with the palm of his hand" (KJV) is two words, *didōmi*, "give" and *rhapisma*, "a blow on the face with someone's hand, a slap in the face" (BDAG 904, 2).

Jesus refuses to be intimidated. He defends his statement and calls on the official to "testify," that is, to "furnish proof"[747] that Jesus said something improper. Jesus demands to be treated according to Jewish law.

Annas apparently concludes that he won't get any more out of Jesus, and sends him on.

"Then Annas sent him, still bound, to Caiaphas the high priest." (18:24)

Where Jesus was sent isn't clear. As mentioned, Caiaphas, the reigning high priest, may have lived in the same palace as Annas, and this seems to be where Peter's denials took place.

But the Synoptics indicate that soon, "when day came" (Luke 22:66), Jesus was brought before the Sanhedrin, usually which met in the temple, with Caiaphas as moderator of the assembly. Many have questioned the legality of these proceedings, but John doesn't linger here.[748]

Peter's Second and Third Denials (18:25-27)

Instead, he relates Peter's second and third denials.

"[25] As Simon Peter stood warming himself, he was asked, 'You are not one of his disciples, are you?' He denied[749] it, saying, 'I am not.' [26] One of the high priest's servants, a relative[750] of the man whose ear Peter had cut off, challenged him, 'Didn't I see you with him in the olive grove?' [27] Again Peter denied it, and at that moment a rooster began to crow." (18:25-27)

Why is Peter there in the high priest's courtyard? Clearly this is an act of bravery, to be right in the enemy's camp and in danger of being recognized. Perhaps he is there to observe what is happening and help Jesus if he sees an opportunity. Perhaps he sees himself as a spy who is operating incognito, unwilling to disclose his true identity so he retains freedom to act later. We don't know.

However, we do know that at the cock's crow, "the Lord turned and looked at Peter" (Luke 22:61) and that Peter "went out and wept bitterly" (Luke 22:62). Peter is crushed as he realizes the depth to which he has fallen. He hasn't been a spy, but a traitor. Perhaps he remembers Jesus' words:

"I tell you, whoever acknowledges me before men,
the Son of Man will also acknowledge him before the angels of God.
But he who disowns me before men
will be disowned before the angels of God." (Luke 12:8-9)

John, however, tells us how Peter was later reinstated by Jesus in spite of his sin (21:15-17) – a big encouragement to those of us who have sinned against Jesus.

---

[747] "Testify" is *martyreō*. Here, "testify to the wrong" is the equivalent of "furnish proof" (BDAG 618, 1aα).

[748] To read my exposition of Luke's account of Jesus' trial before Caiaphas and the Sanhedrin: "Before the Sanhedrin (Luke 22:63-71)," Lesson 102 of my *JesusWalk: Discipleship Lessons from Luke's Gospel* (JesusWalk, 2010). www.jesuswalk.com/lessons/22_63-71.htm

[749] "Denied" is *arneomai*, "to disclaim association with a pers. or event, deny, repudiate, disown someone" (verbally or nonverbally), here and at 13:38 and 8:27 (BDAG 132, 3b).

[750] "Relative" (NIV, NRSV, ESV), "kinsman" (KJV) is *syngenēs*, "belonging to the same extended family or clan, related, akin to" (BDAG 950).

Q2. (John 18:17-18, 25-27) What have been Peter's acts of courage at the arrest and in the high priest's courtyard? Why do you think he ends up denying Jesus? How would you rebuke Peter according to Galatians 6:1b? Has your courage failed lately? What should you do about it? http://www.joyfulheart.com/forums/topic/1530-q2-courage-fails/

Jesus Taken to Pilate's Palace (18:28)

John skips Jesus' early-morning trial before the Sanhedrin that is detailed in the Synoptics, probably because he knows his readers are familiar with that part of the story. Rather, he spends more time giving unique material about Jesus' trial before Pilate that isn't contained in the Synoptics.

> "²⁸ Then the Jews led Jesus from Caiaphas to the palace of the Roman governor. By now it was early morning, and to avoid ceremonial uncleanness[751] the Jews did not enter the palace; they wanted to be able to eat the Passover." (18:28)

It was still very early.[752] The Jews knew that to get Jesus crucified that day, they would have to work fast, since many Roman officials began the day very early in the morning and finished by 10 or 11 am.[753]

For strict Jews, to enter the house of a Gentile would mean incurring ritual defilement that would require waiting and washing themselves, perhaps for several days, depending upon the type of defilement. It is deeply ironic that these Jewish leaders are concerned about ritual defilement and Passover, but not the guilt of seeking the execution of the true Passover Lamb.

The reference to wanting to "eat the Passover" raises again the question of what day Jesus' trial took place – the day after Passover or on Passover itself. Here, it is likely that John is using "Passover" to refer to the entire festival, not just the actual Day of Passover.[754] For more on this problem, see Appendix 7. The Chronology of Holy Week in John's Gospel.

The next question this verse raises is Pilate's location while in Jerusalem. *Praitōrion* refers to the governor's official residence.[755] The governor's normal residence was in the Roman provincial capital of Caesarea, on the coast. However, Pilate would come to Jerusalem several times a year, especially when there was a threat of an uprising from the crowds that filled the city at feasts such as at Passover.

---

[751] "Ceremonial uncleanness" (NIV), "ritual defilement" (NRSV), "be defiled" (ESV, KJV) is the verb *miainō*, originally, "to stain," here, "to cause something to be ritually impure, stain, defile" (BDAG 650, 1).

[752] "Early morning" (NIV, ESV), "early" (KJV) is *prōia*, "early part of the daylight period, (early) morning" (BDAG 892).

[753] Carson, *John*, p. 588, citing A.N. Sherwin-White, *Roman Society and Roman Law in the New Testament* (Oxford, 1963) p. 45.

[754] Carson, *John*, pp. 588-590. It is possible to interpret "eat the Passover" to refer, not to the Passover Meal itself, but the *hagigah*, the feast-offering offered on the morning of the first full paschal day (Numbers 28:18-19). We know that "the Passover" could refer to the combined feast of the paschal meal itself plus the ensuing Feast of Unleavened Bread, as in Luke 22:1.

[755] "Palace of the Roman governor" (NIV), "Pilate's headquarters" (NRSV), "governor's headquarters" (ESV), "hall of judgment" (KJV), is *praitōrion*, a transliteration of the Latin *praetorium*. The word originally referred to the praetor's tent in camp, along with its surroundings, but the course of its history the word also came to designate the governor's official residence (BDAG 859).

Where did Pilate stay when in Jerusalem? The traditional location of the praetorium is the Fortress of Antonia on the East Hill of the city, a Hasmonean castle that was refurbished by Herod the Great in 37-35 BC and used as his palace for twelve years. It now housed a garrison of Roman troops that, since the fortress was directly adjacent to the temple, could easily quell any disturbances that might take place in the temple.

However, it is likely that, when in Jerusalem, Pilate took up residence in the more sumptuous Herod's Palace, on the West Hill, dominating the whole city. This more grandiose structure had been built by Herod the Great and became his palace in 23 BC.[756]

The Jewish Leaders Accuse Jesus (18:29-32)

Pilate accommodates Jewish scruples here. Since they won't enter his palace for fear of defilement, he will come out to them. While it might appear that Pilate has all the power of Rome behind him, to do his job (and remain in power), he must accommodate himself to the local leaders and they to him. It is a delicate balance that neither he nor the Jewish rulers (11:48) want to upset.

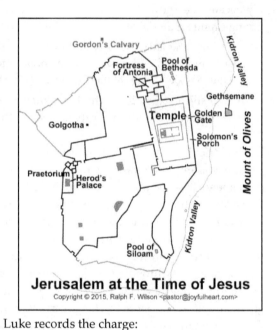

Jerusalem at the Time of Jesus
Copyright © 2015. Ralph F. Wilson <pastor@joyfulheart.com>

> "²⁹ So Pilate came out to them and asked, 'What charges[757] are you bringing against this man?'
> ³⁰ 'If he were not a criminal,' they replied, 'we would not have handed him over to you.'" (18:29-30)

According to procedure, Pilate asks the Jewish leaders for the formal charge against the prisoner. While John doesn't repeat the charge, it is clear as the narrative unfolds that Jesus is being accused of claiming to be king of the Jews (18:33; 19:12, 14-15, 19). Luke records the charge:

> "We have found this man subverting[758] our nation. He opposes payment of taxes to Caesar and claims to be Christ, a king.... He stirs up the people, teaching throughout all Judea, from Galilee even to this place." (Luke 23:2, 5)

Though the Jewish leaders have condemned Jesus for a theological reason – blasphemy (19:7) -- their charge in a Roman court must be political. So they accuse Jesus of being a revolutionary who is

---

[756] Urban C. von Wahlde, in *Jesus and Archaeology*, pp. 572-573; Brown, *John* 2:845; Brown, *Death* 1:705-710. Mark 15:16 identifies the praetorium by the noun *aulē*, "palace, courtyard," the Greek word used by Josephus to designate Herod's place, but never the Fortress of Antonia.

[757] "Charges" (NIV), "accusation" (NRSV, ESV, KJV) is *katēgoria* (from which we get our word "category"), "accusation" (BDAG 533), an "old word for 'formal charge'" (Robertson, *Word Studies*). Also found in 1 Timothy 5:19; Titus 1:6. The word is derived from *kata*, "against" + *agora*, "marketplace, court, assembly," to speak against in court, in the assembly.

[758] "Subverting" (NIV), "perverting" (NRSV, KJV), "misleading" (ESV) is *diastrephō*, "to cause to be distorted, deform," then "make crooked, pervert." Here it has the sense, "to cause to be uncertain about a belief or to believe something different, mislead" (BDAG 237, 3).

stirring up the populace to rebel against Rome – a dangerous man who is a threat to Roman sovereignty.

None of this is new to Pilate. Earlier, the chief priests had requested a contingent of soldiers from Pilate to arrest Jesus (18:3), so they must have made an accusation at that time to warrant their request. But at his arrest in the Garden of Gethsemane, Jesus hadn't acted like a rebel, and that too must have come to Pilate's ears.

The Jewish leaders seek to justify their charge:

"'If he were not a criminal,' they replied, 'we would not have handed him over to you.'" (18:30)

They charge him with being a "criminal" (NIV, NRSV), "doing evil" (ESV), "malefactor" (KJV). The word is *kakopoios*, from *kakos*, "bad, evil" + *poieō*, "to do."[759] It is ironic how, over the centuries, Christ's followers who seek to do good are accused of evil by the evil-doers they put to shame by their good deeds!

Pilate isn't convinced by the Jewish leaders' protestations.

"[31] Pilate said, 'Take him yourselves and judge him by your own law.'
'But we have no right to execute[760] anyone,' the Jews objected. [32] This happened so that the words Jesus had spoken indicating the kind of death he was going to die would be fulfilled." (18:31-32)

Pilate has dealt with these leaders before. They are trying to manipulate him to do their bidding, to accomplish their purposes, so Pilate throws it back at them: "Judge him by your own law. Don't bother me with trivialities!" He is taunting them with their powerlessness.

Roman policy was to let local courts and customs deal with most civil and criminal matters, except those that threatened Roman interests. However, in 6 AD the right to inflict capital punishment had been withdrawn from the Jews and given to the governor exclusively – except for punishment of pagans who enter into the holy temple.[761] Nevertheless, mob actions, such as the stoning of Stephen (Acts 7:58) sometimes occurred.

And so the true reason they have brought him to Pilate comes out – they want nothing less than the death penalty, and can't inflict it without Pilate's cooperation! Moreover, the Jews want Jesus crucified so that he and his followers will be utterly disgraced according to the Law of Moses (Deuteronomy 2:23). But John tells us that crucifixion was necessary to fulfill Jesus own words (verse 32):

"Just as Moses lifted up the snake in the desert, so the Son of Man must be lifted up." (3:14)

"'But I, when I am lifted up from the earth, will draw all men to myself.' He said this to show the kind of death he was going to die." (12:32-33)

"We are going up to Jerusalem, and the Son of Man will be betrayed to the chief priests and the teachers of the law. They will condemn him to death and will turn him over to the Gentiles to be mocked and flogged and crucified. On the third day he will be raised to life!" (Matthew 20:18-19)

---

[759] *Kakopoios*, "pertaining to doing evil, evil doer, criminal" (BDAG 501).

[760] "Execute" (NIV), "put to death" (NRSV, ESV, KJV) is *apokteinō*, literally, "to deprive of life, kill" (BDAG 114, 1a).

[761] Some have disputed the truth of verse 31, but we see evidence of it in Josephus, Wars of the Jews, 2.8.1 and *j. Sanhedrin* 1:1; 7:2.

Pilate Interrogates Jesus (18:33-35)

Pilate knows he cannot dismiss the Jewish leaders' demand so easily, so he leaves them to interrogate Jesus privately.

"³³ Pilate then went back inside the palace, summoned⁷⁶² Jesus and asked him, 'Are you the king of the Jews?'

³⁴ 'Is that your own idea⁷⁶³,' Jesus asked, 'or did others talk to you about me?'" (18:33-34)

How Jesus will answer Pilate's question depends on whether Pilate has a personal interest or is just dealing with the chief priests' accusations. Pilate's answer indicates that it is the latter.

"'Am I a Jew?' Pilate replied. 'It was your people⁷⁶⁴ and your chief priests who handed you over to me. What is it you have done?⁷⁶⁵'" (18:35)

Pilate is trying to cut through the politics of all this. "What have you done to get the high priests so mad at you?" he is asking.

My Kingdom Is Not of this World (18:36-37a)

Now Jesus replies to Pilate's first question, about whether he is the king of the Jews.

"³⁶ Jesus said, 'My kingdom⁷⁶⁶ is not of this world. If it were, my servants⁷⁶⁷ would fight to prevent my arrest by the Jews. But now my kingdom is from another place.'

³⁷ 'You are a king, then!' said Pilate.

Jesus answered, 'You are right in saying I am a king. In fact, for this reason I was born, and for this I came into the world, to testify⁷⁶⁸ to the truth. Everyone on the side of truth⁷⁶⁹ listens⁷⁷⁰ to me⁷⁷¹.'

³⁸ 'What is truth?' Pilate asked." (18:36-38a)

To the Jews' accusation that he is a dangerous rebel who claims to be king of the Jews, Jesus acknowledges his kingship. First he describes his kingdom negatively: that he is not a political king. A political king's followers would have defended him from arrest and put up armed resistance. Jesus, a

---

⁷⁶² "Summoned" (NIV, NRSV), "called" (ESV, KJV) is *phōneō*, "call, address," here, "to call to oneself, summon someone" (BDAG 1071, 3).

⁷⁶³ "Your own idea" (NIV) is a paraphrase. More literally, Jesus asks, "Do you say this from/of yourself?"

⁷⁶⁴ "People" (NIV), "nation" (NRSV, ESV, KJV) is *ethnos*, "a body of persons united by kinship, culture, and common traditions, nation, people" (BDAG 276, 1).

⁷⁶⁵ "Have done" is the Aorist tense of *poieō*, "do, make."

⁷⁶⁶ "Kingdom" is *basileia*, the act of ruling, generally, "kingship, royal power, royal rule ... especially of God's rule," the royal reign of God (usually rendered 'kingdom of God') (BDAG 168, 1b).

⁷⁶⁷ "Servants" is *hypēretēs*, which we saw earlier in 18:3, 12, 22, a technical term for a governmental or other official, "one who functions as a helper, frequently in a subordinate capacity, helper, assistant," here, of a king's retinue (BDAG 1035).

⁷⁶⁸ "Testify" (NIV, NRSV), "bear witness" (ESV, KJV) is *martyreō*, "to confirm or attest something on the basis of personal knowledge or belief, bear witness, be a witness." (BDAG 618, 1).

⁷⁶⁹ "On the side of truth" (NIV), "belongs to the truth" (NRSV), is literally, "of the truth" (ESV, KJV).

⁷⁷⁰ "Listens to me" (NIV) is the verb *akouō*, "hear," here, "to pay attention to by listening, listen to someone/something," with the implication that one's words are heeded and obeyed (BDAG 38, 5).

⁷⁷¹ The phrase "to me" (NIV), "to my voice" (NRSV, ESV, KJV) uses the noun *phōnē*, "the faculty of utterance, voice," (BDAG 1071, 2a). The same phrase is found in Jesus' teaching on the Good Shepherd: "My sheep listen to my voice; I know them, and they follow me" (John 10:27; also 10:16).

rebel? He even healed an ear severed in violence by one of his misguided disciples! No, he is not a rebel king, a threat to Rome.

Jesus explains: "But now my kingdom is from another place" (18:36b) – literally, "not from here" (NRSV). It doesn't arise from the world.

Pilate wants to follow up. Clearly, Jesus is acknowledging some kind of kingship. Pilate observes, "You are a king, then!"

Jesus' answer is difficult to translate into English with clarity:

"You are right in saying I am a king" (NIV)
"You say that I am a king" (literal: NRSV, ESV, KJV)

Jesus isn't denying his kingship, but he is saying something like "'King' is your word, not mine."[772] So, even though Jesus' statement is reluctant or leads to circumlocution, it is unambiguously affirmative, as is rendered by the NIV. In the Synoptics we see a similar answer:

"You say so." (Matthew 27:11; Mark 15:2; Luke 23:3; NRSV, KJV)

Jesus doesn't deny, but affirms Pilate's words in a qualified manner, meaning something like, "Yes, but those aren't the words I would have chosen."

Q3. (John 18:29-35) What do you think the Jewish leaders charged Jesus with before Pilate? If true, why would that be taken seriously by the Romans? What kind of king does Jesus say he is? Where is the source of his kingship, according to Jesus? What is the danger to our gospel message when we politicize Christian causes?
http://www.joyfulheart.com/forums/topic/1531-q3-king-of-the-jews/

King of Truth (18:37b-38a)

Now Jesus explains in positive terms what his kingship entails – a king who testifies to the truth he has personally seen in his Father's House.

[37] 'You are a king, then!' said Pilate.
Jesus answered, 'You are right in saying I am a king. In fact, for this reason I was born, and for this I came into the world, to testify to the truth. Everyone on the side of truth listens to me.'
[38] 'What is truth?' Pilate asked." (18:37-38a)

John brings together in verse 37b two themes that have been interwoven throughout John's Gospel:

1. Testifying, bearing witness. The verb is *martyreō*, which we have seen many times[773]: "to confirm or attest something on the basis of personal knowledge or belief, bear witness, be a witness."[774]

---

[772] C.H. Dodd, *Historical Tradition in the Fourth Gospel* (Cambridge University Press, 1963), p. 99; cited by Carson *John*, p. 594.

[773] John testifies to Jesus (1:7, 15, 34; 3:26, 28; 5:33) and Jesus himself testifies to what things are like in the presence of God (3:11, 26), to what is evil (7:7) and concerning his mission (8:14, 18). The Father testifies concerning Jesus (5:37; 8:18), the Scriptures testify about Jesus (5:39). And the Holy Spirit *will* testify about Jesus (15:26-27).

[774] *Martyreō*, BDAG 618, 1.

2. Truth. The noun is *alētheia*, "the content of what is true, truth" as opposed to falsehood, then "an actual event or state, reality."[775] Throughout John we see references to truth and the divine reality that Jesus reveals directly from the Father.[776] Beyond that, Jesus constantly talks of the "true" (*alēthinos*) or genuine item, the thing that exhibits reality and is not a half-truth or a lie.[777] Often, Jesus prefaces his solemn statements with the phrase, "Truly, truly (*amēn amēn*[778]) I say to you."[779]

So when Jesus says to Pilate, "I came into the world to testify to the truth" (18:37), he is not saying idle words. Throughout his ministry he has been pointing to the Father's truth, the Father's reality. But sadly, his testimony has been largely ignored. To Nicodemus he said sadly:

> "I tell you the truth, we speak of what we know, and we testify to what we have seen, but still you people do not accept our testimony." (3:11)

To Pilate, Jesus gives the same bold challenge concerning the truth he represents and teaches – truth directly from the Father!

> "37d Everyone on the side of truth listens[780] to me[781].'
> 38 'What is truth?' Pilate asked." (18:37d-38a)

Pilate, if you were "on the side of truth" (NIV), that is, "of the truth" (ESV, KJV), then you would listen to my words, and like my sheep, "hear my voice" and "follow me" (10:27). But because Pilate is "of the world," he doesn't care about the search for truth. Like so many in our world today,

> "The god of this world has blinded the minds of the unbelievers, to keep them from seeing the light of the gospel of the glory of Christ, who is the image of God." (2 Corinthians 4:4, ESV)

Pilate is a politician, all about power, caught up with the values of this world system. Later, about him and all the rest of us, John writes:

> "If anyone loves the world, the love of the Father is not in him. For everything in the world – the cravings of sinful man, the lust of his eyes and the boasting of what he has and does – comes not from the Father but from the world." (1 John 2:15b-16)

---

[775] *Alētheia*, BDAG 42, 2 and 3.

[776] Jesus is said to be "full of grace and truth (1:14, 17). Worship of the Father must be in "in spirit and in truth" (4:23-24). "The truth shall set you free" (8:32). Jesus reveals the truth (8:40, 45, 46), while the devil has "no truth in him" (8:44). Jesus is in himself "the Way, the Truth, and the Life" (14:6). He will send the "Spirit of truth" (14:17; 15:26; 16:13), who will guide his disciples into all truth. Jesus' followers are sanctified by words of truth (17:17-18).

[777] The "true light" (1:9), a "true Israelite" (1:47), "true worshippers" (4:23), true witness (5:31-32), "true bread" (6:32), the true Father (7:28; 8:26), true judgments (8:16), true testimonies (8:17; 19:35; 21:24), the "true vine" (15:1), and "the only true God" (17:3).

[778] *Amēn*, strong affirmation of what is stated, here, as an asseverative particle: "truly," meaning "I assure you that, I solemnly tell you" (BDAG 53, 1b). Asseverative in English means, "to declare seriously or positively; affirm." *Amēn* is transliterated from the Hebrew *'amen*, "verily, truly, amen," from the verb *'āman*, "to confirm, support, uphold, be established, faithful, certain" (Jack B. Scott, TWOT #116).

[779] John 1:51; 3:3, 5, 11; 5:19, 24, 25; 6:26, 32, 47, 53; 8:34, 51, 58; 10:1, 7; 12:24; 13:16, 20, 21; 14:12; 16:20, 23; 21:18.

[780] "Listens to me" (NIV) is the verb *akouō*, "hear," here, "to pay attention to by listening, listen to someone/something," with the implication that one's words are heeded and obeyed (BDAG 38, 5).

[781] The phrase "to me" (NIV), "to my voice" (NRSV, ESV, KJV) uses the noun *phōnē*, "the faculty of utterance, voice," (BDAG 1071, 2a). The same phrase is found in Jesus' teaching on the Good Shepherd: "My sheep listen to my voice; I know them, and they follow me" (John 10:27; also 10:16).

Pilate is blind, cynical, and clueless. Jesus speaks to him passionately of truth, and Pilate questions coldly, "What is truth?" To him, everything is relative. When truth is constantly sacrificed on the altar of expediency, one's conscience is seared, deadened. Pilate has the only True One looking him in the eye – the Son of God himself – and Pilate can neither perceive this nor care. How very sad!

> **Q4. (John 18:37-38) Jesus presents himself as the King of Truth, with a mission to testify to the truth. What is the danger when we disciples declare the gospel is absolutely true? How do cynics like Pilate or people in our post-modern age react? If people reject the truth we bring, what is the next step for us?**
> http://www.joyfulheart.com/forums/topic/1532-q4-king-of-truth/

Release Barabbas! (18:38b-40)

As Roman procurator, Pilate is committed to justice, which would require him to release Jesus. But as a politician, he is committed to keeping the peace – and his job! Rome expects him to keep his province peaceful, to diffuse dissent that could become ugly, and, if necessary, to put down rebellion ruthlessly.[782]

Pilate sees a possible solution designed to secure Jesus' release – and shift blame from himself. The plan is to induce the *people* to release Jesus in the traditional holiday prisoner release. Pilate introduces Jesus as "the king of the Jews" to appeal to the crowd's nationalism.

> "[38b] With this he went out again to the Jews and said, 'I find no basis for a charge against him.
> [39] But it is your custom for me to release to you one prisoner at the time of the Passover. Do you want me to release "the king of the Jews"?'
> [40] They shouted back, 'No, not him! Give us Barabbas!' Now Barabbas had taken part in a rebellion." (18:38b-40)

We don't know much about this local custom of releasing a prisoner at Passover; it is mentioned only in the New Testament Gospels. But it sounds like a way for Rome to garner some goodwill at a time when so many Jews are gathered in Jerusalem for the Feast.

Pilate's plan backfires, however. The Jewish leaders have salted the crowd with their own supporters, so that Pilate's condescending "king of the Jews" phrase doesn't have its desired effect. Instead, the crowd insists on the release of Barabbas, a true revolutionary.

Barabbas's name could mean "son of the father" or perhaps "son of the teacher, the Rabbi." He was a real criminal. John describes him with the noun *lēstēs*, the word for "robber, highwayman, bandit" or a "revolutionary, insurrectionist, guerrilla."[783] He is a "notorious[784] prisoner" (Matthew 27:16) who has

---

[782] Luke's Gospel adds at this point an account of Pilate realizing that Jesus was from Galilee. Ah-ha! A chance to pass the burden to Herod Agrippa, a vassal king appointed by the Romans to administer Galilee. So Pilate sends Jesus to Herod, who is also in the city for Passover – probably in the same palace where Pilate is staying. But the wily Herod sends him back to Pilate; he doesn't want to incur the wrath of the high priests either! (Luke 23:5-12).

[783] *Lēstēs*, BDAG 594, 1 and 2.

[784] "Notorious" (NIV, NRSV, ESV), "notable" (KJV) is *episēmos*, "prominent," here in a negative sense, "notorious" (BDAG 378, 2).

participated in a recent uprising[785] in Jerusalem (Mark 15:7; Luke 23:19), and, in the process, has committed murder (Luke 23:19; Acts 3:14). He is exactly the *opposite* kind of person that Pilate wants to release back into the population. Barabbas is a troublemaker, a threat, an enemy of Rome. Clearly, the Jewish authorities are trying to flaunt *their* power over Pilate in demanding Barabbas – and, they wanted to force Pilate to execute Jesus.

Jesus Is Flogged (19:1)

"Then Pilate took Jesus and had him flogged[786]." (19:1)

Pilate now tries Plan B to release Jesus – to gain sympathy for Jesus with the crowd by flogging and humiliating him. Pilate plans to punish Jesus severely to mollify the Jewish leaders, and then let him go in the interests of justice (Luke 23:13-16). He hopes that the Jews will have mercy on one of their own, especially one who is represented as "the king of Jews," when they see the results of flogging, and recognize that their own nation and people are being punished in the person of this "king." At least, that's a positive take on Pilate's reason for the flogging.[787]

In the ancient world, flogging was common – and brutal.[788] If there was ever a "norm" for the barbaric practice of crucifixion among the Romans – and practices varied widely in the first century – it usually began with a flogging using a scourge tipped with glass or metal (Matthew 27:26; Mark 15:15). Some men were flayed to the bone. In others the flogging was so severe that it bit down to deep veins and arteries, even disemboweling the victim.[789] Flogging killed some men outright, before their crucifixion could be carried out.[790] We know that Jesus received a very severe flogging prior to his crucifixion, making it difficult for him to carry his cross and greatly hastening his death.

Jesus Is Mocked (19:2-3)

After the scourging came the mocking, also inside the praetorium (19:4). The Roman soldiers have no love for the Jews, whom they count as enemies. They take this opportunity to show their hatred for the Jews by pouring ridicule on their "king."

"[2] The soldiers twisted together a crown of thorns and put it on his head. They clothed him in a purple robe [3] and went up to him again and again, saying, 'Hail, king of the Jews!' And they struck him in the face." (19:2-3)

---

[785] *Stasis*, "movement toward a (new) state of affairs, uprising, riot, revolt, rebellion" (BDAG 340, 2).

[786] "Flogged" (NIV, NRSV, ESV), "scourged" (KJV) is *mastigoō*, "to beat with a whip or lash, whip, flog, scourge" (BDAG 626, 1a).

[787] So Carson, *John*, p. 596.

[788] The Romans administered flogging in three forms: (1) *Fustigatio*, a less severe beating for minor offences. (2) *Flagellatio*, a brutal flogging administered to criminals for more serious offences. (3) *Verberatio*, the most extreme scourging associated with other punishments, especially crucifixion. Based on Pilate's desire to release Jesus, it is possible that he received the lesser *fustigatio* flogging at this point, and then, after the sentence of crucifixion was given, received the most brutal *verberatio* flogging (Carson, *John*, p. 597, following A. N. Sherwin-White, *Roman Society and Roman Law in the New Testament* (Oxford University Press, 1963), pp. 27-28).

[789] Morris, *John*, p. 790, fn. 2.

[790] Martin Hengel, *Crucifixion in the Ancient World and the Folly of the Message of the Cross* by (translated from the 1976 German edition by John Bowden; Fortress Press/SCM Press, 1977), p. 29, fn. 21, includes half a page of references.

We see four kinds of abuse of the Son of God that followed the scourging: (1) a crown of th
a robe to dress him as a king and mock him and all the Jews, (3) insults, and (4) blows.

The **crown of thorns** is probably designed to mimic the laurel or oak-leaf plaited crowns ;
to victors in a contest, or worn by honored individuals and Roman emperors. It may have been woven
from the common thornbush *Poterium spinosium*, or perhaps acanthus.[791] This crown isn't meant to
honor Jesus but to mock him and the Jews he represents, and to inflict scalp wounds that will bleed
profusely.

The **purple robe**[792] is the *chlamys* or the red military cloak or mantle worn by Roman soldiers
(Matthew 27:28).[793] The costume includes a staff in his right hand to indicate a scepter (Matthew 27:29).

The **mocking** involves the soldiers repeatedly[794] calling to him (sometimes kneeling, Matthew
27:29), saying, "Hail, king of the Jews." The irony of the situation is that Jesus *is* the King of the Jews,
and not only the Jews, but King of all kings and Lord of all lords. He is King of the Universe, but in
their racial bigotry and cruelty the Roman soldiers cannot perceive it.[795]

The **striking** involves blows to the face[796] (19:3). Matthew and Mark tell us they also spat on him
and struck[797] his head with a stalk or staff.[798] Each blow would drive the crown of thorns deeper into
his scalp.

This abuse reminds me of Isaiah's prophecy of what would happen to the Suffering Servant:

"He was despised and rejected by men,
a man of sorrows,
and familiar with suffering.
Like one from whom men hide their faces he was despised,
and we esteemed him not....
But he was pierced for our transgressions,
he was crushed for our iniquities;
the punishment that brought us peace was upon him,
and by his wounds we are healed." (Isaiah 53:2, 5)

Why does Jesus allow this to happen to him? The brutality, the mocking? I think of the writer of
Hebrews, who calls us to perseverance in the face of persecution:

---

[791] "Thorns" is *akantha* (from which we get our plant name "acanthus"), "thorn-plant" (BDAG 34). Speculations about the
type of crown and material made of can be found in Brown, John 2:875. Some see this as the "radiant corona" or "sun
crown" that served as a ruler's adornment in many of the coins in Jesus' time, perhaps made from the cruel spikes at the
base of a palm branch (Morris, John, pp. 790-791, n. 3). However, since the text uses the verb *plekō*, "to plait, braid,
weave, together" (Thayer, p. 516; BDAG 824), I think that the wreath-type crown is more likely.

[792] *Himation*, "piece of clothing," here, of outer clothing, "cloak, robe" (BDAG 475, 2).

[793] *Chlamys*, BDAG 1085.

[794] The verb is in the imperfect tense, continued action in past time.

[795] Compare this to Nathanael's confession and insight: "Rabbi, you are the Son of God; you are the King of Israel" (1:49).
Earlier, prior to Jesus' trial before the Sanhedrin, soldiers mocked and insulted him as well (Luke 22:63-65).

[796] The verb is *rhapisma*, which we saw when Jesus was before the high priest, "a blow on the face with someone's hand, a
slap in the face" (BDAG 904, 2).

[797] *Typtō*, "to inflict a blow, strike, beat, wound" (BDAG 1020, 1a).

[798] *Kalamos*, "stalk, staff" (BDAG 502, 2).

"Let us fix our eyes on Jesus, the Author and Perfecter of our faith, who **for the joy set before him endured the cross, scorning its shame**, and sat down at the right hand of the throne of God. Consider him who endured such opposition from sinful men, so that you will not grow weary and lose heart." (Hebrews 12:2-3)

Jesus is determined to complete the task the Father gave him, to redeem the world by taking our sins upon him on the cross!

Crucify Him! (19:4-6)

Jesus is now a bloody mess, still dressed in the filthy robe over his lacerated back, with blood streaming down his face from the crown of thorns. Pilate seems to be hoping that this punishment will be considered sufficient to satisfy the Jewish leaders. He is wrong.

"⁴ Once more Pilate came out and said to the Jews, 'Look, I am bringing him out to you to let you know that I find no basis for a charge against him.' ⁵ When Jesus came out wearing the crown of thorns and the purple robe, Pilate said to them, 'Here is the man!' ⁶ As soon as the chief priests and their officials saw him, they shouted, 'Crucify! Crucify!'" (19:4-6a)

Pilate again declares Jesus innocent of fomenting a rebellion with himself as king. Pilate points to Jesus, parodied as king as the soldiers have dressed him, and declares, "Here is the man!" (NIV, NRSV) or "Behold, the man!" (ESV, KJV), Latin, *ecce homo*. Pilate could have meant, "Look at the poor fellow," or perhaps, "See how ridiculous your claim is that he is the king of the Jews." But likely, John intends the reader to see this as a reference to Jesus as *the* Man, recalling his self-designation, Son of Man. Paul develops the idea of Jesus as the archetypical Man, the Last or Second Adam (1 Corinthians 15:45-49; Romans 5:15).

"There is one God and one mediator between God and men, **the man Christ Jesus**, who gave himself as a ransom for all...." (1 Timothy 2:5-6a)

"The chief priests and their officials" shout "Crucify! Crucify!" and others, following them, take up the shout. Pilate fears that the scene might degenerate into a riot.

"But Pilate answered, 'You take him and crucify him. As for me, I find no basis for a charge against him.'" (19:6b)

Pilate continues to maintain Jesus' innocence. His statement, "You take him and crucify him," is a jab at the Jews' impotence; Pilate has no intention of letting the Jews undertake a crucifixion; that is the exclusively Roman punishment.

Q5. (John 19:1-6) Why do you think Pilate maintains Jesus' innocence and then has him brutally scourged? Why does Jesus allow himself to be brutally scourged and then mocked? (see Hebrews 12:2) How much persecution are you willing to endure to accomplish the mission the Father has given you?
http://www.joyfulheart.com/forums/topic/1533-q5-scourging/

He Claims to be the Son of God (19:7-11)

Now the Jewish leaders introduce the real reason they want Jesus crucified. It is not political ("king of the Jews") like their first charge; it is theological ("Son of God").

> "The Jews insisted, 'We have a law, and according to that law he must die, because he claimed to be the Son of God.'" (19:7)

The term "son of God" in the Old Testament is sometimes used to describe angelic beings and Israel's kings (2 Samuel 7:14-16; Psalm 89:24, 28-37). The king is God's agent who exercises God's authority on earth. The title "Son of God" does not seem to be a common title for the Messiah in intertestamental Judaism.[799] But in the Gospels we see the term used in tandem with Messianic terms in the mouths of Nathanael (1:49), Martha (11:27), Peter (Matthew 16:16), and the high priest (Matthew 26:63). In John's Gospel, the term "Son of God" is often used in the sense of divine Sonship, the Son who was preexistent with the Father.[800] This kind of equality with God is what the Jews (rightly) accused him of (5:18), and on this occasion, are accusing him before Pilate (19:7).

However, in Pilate's ears, the term "Son of God" is alarming. Greek and Roman mythologies had many divine beings that went around as men. Pilate is now afraid that he has offended a god. He withdraws and continues to interrogate the bloody Jesus.

> "[8] When Pilate heard this, he was even more afraid, [9] and he went back inside the palace. 'Where do you come from?' he asked Jesus, but Jesus gave him no answer.
> [10] 'Do you refuse to speak to me?' Pilate said. 'Don't you realize I have power either to free you or to crucify you?'
> [11] Jesus answered, 'You would have no power over me if it were not given to you from above. Therefore the one who handed me over to you is guilty of a greater sin.'" (19:7-11)

Jesus refuses to answer further questions about where he comes from, fulfilling a theme emphasized in the Synoptic Gospels[801] in fulfillment of Isaiah's prophecy of the Suffering Servant:

> "He was oppressed and afflicted,
> yet he **did not open his mouth**;
> he was led like a lamb to the slaughter,
> and as a sheep before her shearers is **silent**,
> so **he did not open his mouth**." (Isaiah 53:7)

Pilate is mystified. Why isn't Jesus pleading for mercy from the only one who can save him from crucifixion – the Roman governor? Jesus breaks his silence to remind this proud man of the real source of his power – God!

> "You would have no power over me if it were not given to you from above. Therefore the one who handed me over to you is guilty of a greater sin." (19:11)

Isn't Pilate guilty of sin in ultimately crucifying Jesus? Yes. He is blind, arrogant, and self-serving. But at least he sees Jesus as innocent of the charges made against him and seeks several ways to

---

[799] Adam Winn, "Son of God," DJG[2], pp. 886-887.
[800] John 1:18; 3:18; 5:25; 6:69; 10:36; 11:4, 27; 20:1; cf. Luke 1:35.
[801] Matthew 26:63; 27:13-14; Mark 14:61; 15:4-5; Luke 23:9; Acts 8:32; 1 Peter 2:23.

release him. The Jewish leaders are clearly more to blame, since they have seen and heard of Jesus' miracles and yet seek to kill him.

Jesus is the bloodied prisoner, yet he is comforting the heathen governor and talking to him about his lesser sin. Amazing!

The Jewish Leaders Threaten Pilate with Reporting Him to the Emperor (19:12)

Pilate doesn't know what to say. He continues to try to set Jesus free. But when the Jewish leaders threaten to report Pilate to Caesar for being lenient with a self-proclaimed king, Pilate's will buckles.

> "From then on, Pilate tried to set Jesus free, but the Jews kept shouting, 'If you let this man go, you are no friend of Caesar. Anyone who claims to be a king opposes Caesar.'" (19:12)

The term "friend of Caesar" refers to a loyal supporter of Rome. The Jews threaten to contact the notoriously suspicious Emperor Tiberius with the claim that Pilate doesn't suppress treason, and allows to live a person who claims to be a king in opposition to Caesar's reign. Since the Jews had communicated to the emperor their displeasure with him previously, Pilate knows that this is not an idle threat.

In the writings of first century Hellenistic Jewish philosopher Philo, we find a description of Pilate's potential problems with Rome. Regarding a different occasion, Philo, writes,

> "[Pilate] feared that if they actually sent an embassy, they would also expose the rest of his conduct as governor by stating in full the briberies, the insults, the outrages and wanton injuries, the executions without trial constantly repeated, the ceaseless and supremely grievous cruelty."[802]

Even though Philo has likely overstated this, it is clear that Pilate doesn't want an investigation into the conduct of his governorship. Pilate capitulates.

To illustrate Pilate's precarious position, we learn that in AD 37, Tiberius orders Pilate back to Rome after he harshly suppresses a Samaritan uprising. Pilate is replaced by Marcellus.[803]

Pilate Takes the Judge's Seat (19:13-14a)

Pilate's mind is made up. So long as he can defend an innocent man without being in personal danger, he is willing to. But now the Jewish leaders' threats hit home.

> "13 When Pilate heard this, he brought Jesus out and sat down on the judge's seat at a place known as the Stone Pavement (which in Aramaic is Gabbatha). 14 It was the day of Preparation of Passover Week, about the sixth hour.
> 'Here is your king,' Pilate said to the Jews.
> 15 But they shouted, 'Take him away! Take him away! Crucify him!'" (19:13-15)

"Judge's seat/bench" (NIV, NRSV), "judgment seat" (ESV, KJV) is *bēma*, "a dais or platform that required steps to ascend, tribunal," a platform on which the governor sat with his clerks and advisors.[804] The word has the special meaning, "judicial bench."[805]

---

[802] Philo, *Embassy to Gaius*, 302, as quoted in Morris, *John*, p. 799, fn. 27.
[803] Josephus, *Antiquities*, 18.4.1-2.
[804] Carson, *John*, p. 607.

This place of judgment was at a location known at the time as the "Stone[s?] "paved with blocks of stone, stone pavement or mosaic."[806] Gabbatha, the Aramaic n[ame?] means "height" or "raised place," perhaps because Herod's Palace was built on bedroc[k] hill in Jerusalem.[807]

John gives the time of the sentence as "about the sixth hour," which would be, measuring t[he?] from sunrise to sundown, about noon. This is an apparent discrepancy with Mark's report that [Jesus?] was crucified at "the third hour" (about 9 am; Mark 15:25). There have been various approaches [to?] resolve the problem, none completely convincing.[808] Morris concludes,

> "In neither Mark nor John is the hour to be regarded as more than an approximation. People in antiquity did not have clocks or watches, and the reckoning of time was always very approximate."[809]

The reference to the day of Preparation is ambiguous. I take it to mean the preparation for Sabbath on Friday night, a special Sabbath since it fell during the Feasts of Passover and Unleavened Bread. See Appendix 7. The Chronology of Holy Week in John's Gospel.

The Leaders Again Demand Jesus' Crucifixion (19:14b-16)

Now seated on the official place of judgment, Pilate presents Jesus, knowing what the result will be.

> "[14b] 'Here is your king,' Pilate said to the Jews.
> [15] But they shouted, 'Take him away! Take him away! Crucify him!'"
> "'Shall I crucify your king?' Pilate asked.
> 'We have no king but Caesar,' the chief priests answered.
> [16] Finally Pilate handed him over to them to be crucified. So the soldiers took charge of Jesus."
> (19:15b-16)

At the end, Pilate wins from the chief priests a hypocritical confession, "We have no king but Caesar," but it is hollow and everyone knows it. What is sad and ironic is that the chief priests reject the true King of Israel and claim a false pagan to be king over them.

Pilate "handed him over,"[810] that is, conceded to their wishes. He gives the order for Jesus to be crucified, and the Roman soldiers take over from there.

---

[805] *Bēma*, BDAG 175, 3. Josephus tells us of an incident that sounds quite similar that took place some 30 years later when the Roman prefect Florus was in Jerusalem. "Florus then took up residence at the palace, and on the following day, having had the *bēma* put in place in front of the building, took his seat. The chief priests, the nobles, and the most eminent citizens then coming forward, stood before the *bēma*..." (Josephus, *Wars of the Jews*, 2.14.8, 66 AD, translated by Urban C. von Wahlde, "Archaeology and John's Gospel," in *Jesus and Archaeology*, p. 574).

[806] *Lithostrōtos*, BDAG 596. Though a 3,000 square foot stone paved area has been found at the Fortress of Antonia, this comes from the second century AD, and thus couldn't be the pavement spoken of in this verse (von Wahlde, *Jesus and Archaeology*, pp. 574-575, fn. 156).

[807] Von Wahlde, *Jesus and Archaeology*, pp. 573-575.

[808] For details of the approaches, see Carson, *John*, p. 604-605; and Morris, *John*, pp. 800-801.

[809] Morris, *John*, p. 801.

[810] "Handed over" (NIV, NRSV), "delivered" (ESV, KJV) is *paradidōmi*, which we've seen before: "hand over, turn over, give up a person," as a technical term of police and courts, "hand over into [the] custody [of]" (BDAG 762, 1b).

late fear when the Jewish leaders report that Jesus claimed to be
ite fear when the Jewish leaders threaten to report him to Caesar?
rs control you and keep you from serving Jesus fully? What
our life?

rums/topic/1534-q6-pilates-fear/

Pavement," an area
ame for this place,
on the highest
he hours
Jesus

ıt Jesus' arrest and trial. But here are some lessons for us disciples to

1. Jesus is ... m in this account. He is the master of the arrest in the Garden as well as of the conversation with Pilate. He willingly lays down his life for our sins.

2. Peter has the courage to wield a sword at Jesus' arrest and be in the high priest's inner courtyard where there are people who may have seen him in the Garden. But his courage fails and he denies Jesus. I think the lesson for disciples is to realize our own weakness, and not rely on our own bluster for strength, but in humility rely on the Lord (18:17-18, 25-27).

3. Jesus clearly comes with a spiritual kingdom, not a political kingdom. When we politicize Christian causes, we seriously confuse the world about what we stand for – a spiritual message, rather than a temporal message (18:36-37).

4. Jesus presents himself as the King of Truth, with a mission to testify to the truth. When cynics like Pilate and post-modern relativists hear this, they often deflect it with relativism. Even though we know this will happen we, like Jesus, must still testify to the truth. Some will listen (18:37-38).

5. Jesus is scourged brutally and then mocked mercilessly as the King of the Jews, which he actually is! Jesus put up with this because he had a higher mission, to endure the cross (19:1-6).

6. Pilate wants to avoid crucifying Jesus and tries several times to release him because he believes Jesus is unjustly charged.

7. The Jewish leaders then try to manipulate Pilate with fear – fear of punishing a Son of God, and the greater fear of being reported to Caesar for being soft on revolutionaries. Ultimately, the fear of losing his job wins out. We disciples should analyze our fears to make sure fear isn't controlling us rather than faith.

Prayer

Father, it is heartbreaking to realize the mocking, brutal torture, and crass injustice that Jesus had to endure for us. He is King, yet no one can see it! We are not worthy of such a King who gives his all and suffers humiliation that we might be saved. Thank you for your amazing grace to us! In Jesus' name, we pray. Amen.

Key Verses

"When Jesus said, 'I am he,' they drew back and fell to the ground." (John 18:6, NIV)

"Jesus commanded Peter, 'Put your sword away! Shall I not drink the cup the Father has given me?'" (John 18:11, NIV)

"My kingdom is not of this world. If it were, my servants would fight to prevent my arrest by the Jews. But now my kingdom is from another place." (John 18:36, NIV)

"You are right in saying I am a king. In fact, for this reason I was born, and for this I came into the world, to testify to the truth. Everyone on the side of truth listens to me." (John 18:37)

"You would have no power over me if it were not given to you from above. Therefore the one who handed me over to you is guilty of a greater sin." (John 19:11, NIV)

31. Jesus' Death and Burial (19:17-42)

A great deal of posturing went on between the Jewish leaders and the Roman governor. But in the end the Jewish leaders had their way, and Jesus was on his way to be crucified.

> "¹⁶ Finally Pilate handed him over to them to be crucified. So the soldiers took charge of Jesus. ¹⁷ Carrying his own cross, he went out to the place of the Skull (which in Aramaic is called Golgotha). ¹⁸ Here they crucified him, and with him two others – one on each side and Jesus in the middle." (19:16-18)

Crucifixion in the Ancient World

The cross in Jesus' time was an instrument of torture and execution, pure and simple. There wasn't a figurative use of "cross" as a "burden" or "trial" in those days. Death on the cross was shameful, excruciating, and often protracted. An ancient Greek poem describes it this way:

> "Punished with limbs outstretched,
> they see the stake as their fate;
> they are fastened (and) nailed to it in the most bitter torment,
> evil food for birds of prey and grim pickings for dogs."⁸¹¹

Thomas Eakins (American painter, 1844-1916), "The Crucifixion" (1880), Oil on canvas, 96 x 54 inches, Philadelphia Museum of Art.

From the third century BC onwards there is evidence of the use of the Latin word *crux* as a vulgar taunt among the lower classes, found on the lips of slaves and prostitutes, the English equivalent of which might be "gallows-bird" or "hang-dog."⁸¹² Martin Hengel affirms that the attitude of people of the ancient world was not casual or a matter of indifference. "It was an utterly offensive affair, 'obscene' in the original sense of the word."⁸¹³

There was no "norm" for execution on the cross, though it often included flogging beforehand, the victim carrying the beam to the place of execution, being nailed to it with outstretched arms, raised up, and seated on a small wooden peg. Seneca indicates there were many variations:

> "I see crosses there, not just of one kind but made in many different ways: some have their victims with head down to the ground; some impale their private parts; others stretch out their arms on the gibbet."⁸¹⁴

⁸¹¹ Psuedo-Manetho, *Apotelesmatica* 4:198ff, cited by Martin Hengel, (translator John Bowden), *Crucifixion in the Ancient World and the Folly of the Message of the Cross* (German edition 1976; English edition: Fortress Press/SCM Press, 1977), p. 9.
⁸¹² Hengel, *Crucifixion*, pp. 9-10.
⁸¹³ Hengel, *Crucifixion*, p. 22.
⁸¹⁴ Seneca, *Dialogue* 6 (*De consolatione ad Marciam*) 20.3. Cited by Hengel, p. 25.

In Jesus' day it was customary for the criminal under the sentence of death to carry his cross out to the place of execution. Typically, the cross consisted of two parts:

1. **The cross-beam or horizontal member** (Latin *patibulum*[815]) on which the arms would be stretched out and attached. This was the part of the cross that the condemned man would typically carry to the execution site.[816] Often the cross piece was carried behind the nape of the neck like a yoke, with the condemned man's arms pulled back and hooked over it,[817] perhaps tied to it so it wouldn't fall off.

2. **The vertical post or stake** (Latin *stipes, staticulum*) that would be sunk in the earth and remain in place at the execution site.[818] The Greek word for cross is *stauros*, originally "an upright pointed stake or pale," such as might be used in constructing a palisade. Later the word *stauros* came to refer to any part of the cross, whether the upright, or cross-piece.[819]

And so Jesus begins to carry or drag the beam from the Roman praetorium where he had been flogged, along the Via Dolorosa to his execution outside the walls. Jesus the carpenter has felled trees and fashioned many a beam, and borne them on his shoulders to a new house or remodeling project in Nazareth. But now he must carry the heavy beam on shoulders lacerated by the Roman scourge, greatly weakened from loss of blood. Seneca describes the "swelling with ugly welts on the shoulders and chest" that would result from the scourging.[820] While John doesn't relate the incident, Jesus must have staggered and fallen, unable to continue. Matthew and Luke tell us that Simon of Cyrene is seized from the crowd of onlookers and forced to carry the beam behind Jesus (Matthew 15:21; Luke 23:26).

The Place of the Skull (19:17)

The destination of this mournful procession is outside Jerusalem:

"[17] Carrying his own cross, he went out to the place of the Skull (which in Aramaic is called Golgotha). [18] Here they crucified him, and with him two others – one on each side and Jesus in the middle." (19:17-18)

The "place of the Skull (*kranion*)" is "Golgotha" in Aramaic. The term evokes the haunting specter of death. The KJV uses the term "Calvary" to describe the place, from the Vulgate's Latin word *calvaria*, "skull."

---

[815] Latin *patibulum* also refers to a bar for closing a door or a sail yardarm (Brown, *Death* 2:913).

[816] The Roman playwright Platus (c. 254-184 BC) refers to carrying the *patibulum* in some of his plays (*Miles Gloriosus*, Acts 2, 4; *Mostellaria* 56-67; *Carbonaria*, fragment 1. However, the references aren't completely clear.

[817] Brown, *Death* 2:913.

[818] Johannes Schneider, *saturos, ktl.*, TDNT 7:572-584, esp. 573.

[819] *Stauros*, BAGD 764-765. TDNT 7:572. The Jehovah's Witness' contention that Jesus died on an impaling stake shows a narrowness in interpreting the ancient evidence. While men were impaled on impaling stakes in ancient times, it is clear that Jesus is nailed to the cross and left to die. The shape of the *stauros* varied greatly. It could be a single upright post, or with a cross-piece added, either to the top in a T shape (L. *crux commissa*), or with intersecting beams of equal length (L. *crux immissa*).

[820] Seneca, *Epistle 101 to Lucilius*, quoted in Hengel, pp. 30-31.

There is disagreement about the site of Golgotha. Scriptures indicate that it was outside the city (Hebrews 13:12) but close to it (John 19:20), probably along some public thoroughfare (Matthew 27:39), as well as being visible from afar (Mark 15:40; Luke 23:49). Two possible locations have been considered.

Jerusalem at the Time of Jesus
Copyright © 2015, Ralph F. Wilson <pastor@joyfulheart.com>

1. **Church of the Holy Sepulcher.** A site within the Church of the Holy Sepulcher is not too far from the supposed site of Jesus' tomb. This site has the support of church tradition going back to Eusebius in the fourth century.[821] According to archeological studies in the 1960s, the location would have been well outside the city walls according to Josephus' description of the city's fortifications. Prior to the city's expansion it was a quarry into which a number of tombs had been cut.[822] This site is widely accepted as the correct site of both Golgotha and the tomb.[823]

1. **"Gordon's Calvary."** A prominent, rounded, grassy hill above the so-called "Grotto of Jeremiah," northeast of the modern Damascus Gate. It sometimes called "Gordon's Calvary," after famous British General Charles George Gordon (1833-1885), an early advocate of the site. Though it has some resemblance to a skull, the "eyeholes" and rounded top are due to artificial excavations going back a couple of centuries and are not ancient.[824] This isn't likely to be the correct location.

Though we think of Golgotha as on a hill, the text doesn't tell us that. Only the ability to see it from afar suggests a hill. The exact location isn't important, however; what happened there is of vital importance.

They Crucified Him (19:18)

The Gospel writers don't dwell on the gruesome execution, they say simply "they crucified him," Greek *stauroō*, "nail to the cross, crucify."[825] Hegel says,

---

[821] Eusebius, *Vita Constantini* iii.26.

[822] Joel B. Green, "Death of Jesus," DJG, pp. 146-163, in particular, p. 150.

[823] Urban C. von Wahlde ("Archaeology and John's Gospel," in *Jesus and Archaeology*, pp. 576-582) lays out the most recent archaeological information supporting this location.

[824] David F. Payne, "Golgotha," ISBE 2:523-524. Edersheim, *Life and Times* 2:585-586, describes it and suggests that this was the actual location.

[825] *Stauroō*, BAGD 765.

"In Roman times not only was it the rule to nail the victim by both hands and feet, but that the flogging which was a stereotyped part of the punishment would make the blood flow in streams."[826]

It is certain that Jesus' hands and feet were nailed to the cross,[827] though the nails did not usually kill the condemned person. These wounds bled little. Most of the blood loss would be from the scourging administered before the crucifixion. That Jesus died within six hours on the cross is a testimony to the severity of the scourging administered by Pilate's soldiers before he was sent to Golgotha.

Death would come only slowly to most of the crucified, usually only after several days. Death resulted either from shock or "a painful process of asphyxiation as the muscles used in breathing suffered increasing fatigue."[828] Imagine your body hanging from the arms for days at a time. To take a breath you'd have to raise your chest by pulling on your arms and pushing with your legs. Eventually, slowly, a condemned man became too weak to breathe.

Along with the Criminals (19:18)

"Here they crucified him, and with him two others – one on each side and Jesus in the middle." (19:18)

Jesus is crucified alongside common criminals.[829] Jesus has suffered the final shame, something we might equate with death in the electric chair or gas chamber. Paul writes, "He humbled himself and became obedient to death – even death on a cross!" (Philippians 2:8). The writer of Hebrews says, he "endured the cross, scorning its shame" (Hebrews 12:2). He did it for us. Eight centuries before, Isaiah had prophesied of the Suffering Servant,

"He poured out his life unto death,
and was numbered with the transgressors.
For he bore the sin of many,
and made intercession for the transgressors." (Isaiah 53:12)

James and John had asked for the places at his right and at his left – in his glory (Mark 10:37). But as Jesus is "glorified" in death, at his left and right are robbers, common thieves (Matthew 27:38; Mark 15:27). And now he makes intercession for the transgressors. Luke tells us that one of these thieves came to faith on the cross (Luke 23:39-43).

Jesus of Nazareth, King of the Jews (19:19-22)

Carson tells us that it was the custom for the crime for which a person was sentenced to crucifixion to be written on a table or placard and hung around his neck or carried before him on the way to the

---

[826] Hengel, *Crucifixion*, pp. 31-32.
[827] "Look at my hands and my feet. It is I myself!" Luke 24:39; also John 20:25; Acts 2:23; Colossians 2:14.
[828] Green, DJG, p. 147.
[829] Luke 23:33 – *kakourgos*, "criminal, evil-doer, one who commits gross misdeeds and serious crimes" (BAGD 398). Matthew 27:38; Mark 15:27 – *lēstēs*, "robber, highwayman, bandit" (BDAG 594, 1). Luke's account tells us that one of these put his faith in Christ (Luke 23:40-43).

place of execution. Then it was often fastened to the cross.[830] The purpose of the placard was to publicize to the populace that this kind of crime will result in such a punishment.

> "[19] Pilate had a notice[831] prepared and fastened to the cross. It read: JESUS OF NAZARETH, THE KING OF THE JEWS. [20] Many of the Jews read this sign, for the place where Jesus was crucified was near the city, and the sign was written in Aramaic, Latin and Greek.
> [21] The chief priests of the Jews protested to Pilate, 'Do not write "The King of the Jews," but that this man claimed to be king of the Jews.'
> [22] Pilate answered, 'What I have written, I have written.'" (19:19-22)

The placard tells the reason for Jesus' crucifixion for the world to see. He *is* the King of the Jews, and for this he has been crucified. He is the king the Jewish leaders rejected, but remains the King, the Messiah, nevertheless.

The chief priests don't like the inscription, since it implies that this Jesus *was* the king of the Jews. They want the wording softened to Jesus' claim only. But Pilate refuses. He is angry that he has been manipulated into this crucifixion, and wants to rub it in that he is crucifying the Jew's king to humiliate them, knowing that it will anger the leaders.

But it is part of Jesus' glory. The King who dies for the sins of his people, lifted up, glorified, ready to draw all to himself.

The Soldiers Divide Jesus' Garments (19:23-24)

While in the Praetorium, Jesus had been dressed in the mocking clothes of royalty, he comes to Golgotha in his own clothing. It was the custom that the soldiers would be given the clothing of the crucified.

> "[23] When the soldiers crucified Jesus, they took his clothes, dividing them into four shares, one for each of them, with the undergarment remaining. This garment was seamless, woven in one piece from top to bottom. [24] 'Let's not tear it," they said to one another. "Let's decide by lot who will get it.' This happened that the scripture might be fulfilled which said, 'They divided my garments among them and cast lots for my clothing.' So this is what the soldiers did." (19:23-24)

John mentions this incident because it clearly fulfills Scripture (Psalm 22:18), underscoring the fact that Jesus' death is not a tragic martyrdom, but that it was prophesied long ago and takes place according to God's plan.

It is likely that Jesus was crucified completely naked – considered extremely shameful to the Jews – which seems to have been the normal practice of Roman crucifixion.[832] Indeed, that is the way he is depicted in an early portrayal of the crucified Jesus,[833] though later depictions portray Jesus with a loincloth.

---

[830] Carson, *John*, p. 610.

[831] "Notice" (NIV), "inscription" (NRSV, ESV), "title" (KJV) is *titlos*, "inscription, notice" (BDAG 1009). The technical Roman term *titulus*, "a placard or notice." Used for a bill or notice of sale affixed to a house (*Vincent's Word Studies*).

[832] Artemidorus Daldianus, *Oneirokritika* 2:53 (second century).

[833] A tiny second century carving on a jasper gem (Brown, *Death* 2:947).

The four soldiers on the crucifixion detail divide up his clothing. But Jesus' seamless *chitōn*, a long garment worn next to the skin, would be ruined if divided, so they cast lots for it. Apparently, such a garment was not really a luxury item, for it could be woven by a craftsman with no exceptional skill.[834]

The prophetic Psalm 22 gives us some idea of what Jesus felt:

> "I am poured out like water,
> and all my bones are out of joint.
> My heart has turned to wax;
> it has melted away within me.
> My strength is dried up like a potsherd,
> and my tongue sticks to the roof of my mouth;
> you lay me in the dust of death.
> Dogs have surrounded me;
> a band of evil men has encircled me,
> they have **pierced my hands and my feet**.
> I can count all my bones;
> people stare and gloat over me.
> **They divide my garments among them**
> **and cast lots for my clothing**. Psalm 22:14-18

O Lord, what have we done to humiliate you so?

Q1. (John 19:23-24; Psalm 22:14-18) In what ways did Jesus fulfill Psalm 22:14-18? What does the Psalms passage tell us about how Jesus felt on the cross?
http://www.joyfulheart.com/forums/topic/1535-q1-agony-in-the-psalms/

Woman, Behold Your Son (19:25-27)

Now we come to the third of the Seven Last Words of Christ on the cross.[835]

> "25 Near the cross of Jesus stood his mother, his mother's sister, Mary the wife of Clopas, and Mary Magdalene. 26 When Jesus saw his mother there, and the disciple whom he loved standing nearby, he said to his mother, 'Dear woman, here is your son,' 27 and to the disciple, 'Here is your mother.' From that time on, this disciple took her into his home." (19:25-27)

---

[834] Brown (*Death* 2:956) cites H. Th. Braun, *Fleur bleue, Revue des industries du lin* (1951), pp. 21-28, 45-53.

[835] The Seven Last Words are: (1) "Father, forgive them" (Luke 23:34); (2) "This day you will be with me in paradise" (Luke 23:43; (3) "Woman, behold your son" (John 19:26-27); (4) "My God, why have You forsaken me?" (Mark 15:34); (5) "I thirst" (John 19:28); (6) "It is finished" (John 19:30); and "Father, into your hands I commit my spirit" (Luke 23:46). I've written a book that details each of these words: *Seven Last Words of Christ from the Cross* (JesusWalk, 2009). http:www.jesuswalk.com/books/7-last-words.htm

Jesus' Mother at the Foot of the Cross

Of the four gospel writers, John is the only one who records Mary's presence at the cross. But it would be expected that Jesus' mother be in Jerusalem at Passover – after all, we read, "Every year his parents went to Jerusalem for the Feast of the Passover" (Luke 2:41). Probably, after Joseph's death – presumed to have taken place before Jesus began his ministry – Mary would come up to Jerusalem for the Feast with friends and relatives.

Her son is in trouble – arrested, tried, condemned, and now dying. Surely, Mary's place is close to her son. And so Simeon's prophecy given at Jesus' dedication comes to pass:

> "And a sword will pierce your own soul too." (Luke 2:35b)

She is near him now, but her heart is broken. She is consoled by friends.

James J. Tissot, "Mater Dolorosa, Sorrowful Mother" (1889-1896), opaque watercolor, Brooklyn Museum, NYC

The Identity of the Other Women

Just who are these friends? Verse 25 seems to include Mary plus three other women.[836] These are probably the same women who appear in the Synoptic Gospels. In addition to Mary, Jesus' mother, the women at the cross are:

Mary Magdalene who is mentioned consistently in all three gospels.

Mary (the wife) of Clopas, who seems to correspond easily to "Mary the mother of James the younger and of Joses (Joseph)" (Mark 15:40; Matthew 27:56). She is probably "the other Mary" who was with Mary Magdalene at the tomb Friday night and on Sunday morning (Matthew 27:61; 28:1).[837]

The third woman, **Jesus' mother's sister**, may well be **Salome**, who is the **mother of James and John**, the sons of Zebedee.[838] Then James and John would be Jesus' cousins. This would make sense. James and John are part of Jesus' inner circle with Peter. It also explains why their mother might presume to ask that her sons sit on Jesus' right and left in his kingdom (Matthew 20:20-21). She had been rebuked by Jesus on that occasion, but here she is at the foot of the cross consoling Mary, Jesus' mother, her sister.

---

[836] Some commentators see this as two or three women, but these explanations of the sentence don't make as much sense.

[837] An early church tradition mentioned by Chrysostom (347-407 AD) identifies Alphaeus, the father of an apostle named James (Matthew 10:3), with this Clopas, father of "James the Less," though this is uncertain. A.W. Fortune, "Alphaeus," ISBE 1:100. Tradition also sees this Alphaeus / Clopas as the brother of St. Joseph (Eusebius, *Church History*, 3.11.2; cf. "Clopas," ISBE 1:724). See also R. Laird Harris, "James (2)," ISBE 2:958-959.

[838] See Kathleen E. Corley, "Salome," ISBE 4:286; Beasley-Murray, *John*, p. 348.

They are there with "the disciple whom he loved," probably John the disciple identified as the author of the Gospel of John (John 21:24).

Woman, Here Is Your Son

"[26b] He said to his mother, 'Dear woman, here is your son,' [27] and to the disciple, 'Here is your mother.' From that time on, this disciple took her into his home." (John 19:26b-27)

Jesus' Third Word from the cross to this small band of faithful friends huddled below is fascinating for all it implies.

James J. Tissot, "*Sabat Mater* (Woman Behold your Son)" (1886-1894), opaque watercolor, Brooklyn Museum.

First, Jesus addresses his mother not as "Mother," but as "woman," translated appropriately as "dear woman" by the NIV. We might sense a coldness in the term as used in our culture, but in Jesus' culture it was perfectly proper for a man to address a woman this way – but still strange for a son to a mother.[839] The reason for this more formal address is probably that Jesus intends his words to be understood as a formal testamentary disposition under Jewish family law.[840]

As Mary's firstborn, Jesus is legally responsible for her welfare to ensure that she has a place to live and food to eat during her widowhood. Jesus entrusts his mother to John's care and John takes this commission seriously:

"From that time on, this disciple took her into his home."[841] (John 19:27b)

Q2. (John 19:26-27) What is Jesus' mother Mary feeling at the cross? Why does Jesus give John responsibility to care for his mother? What does this say about Jesus' values?
http://www.joyfulheart.com/forums/topic/1536-q2-caring-for-mother/

I Am Thirsty (19:28-30a)

Now we hear Jesus utter the fifth of the Seven Last Words from the cross.

"[28] Later, knowing that all was now completed, and so that the Scripture would be fulfilled, Jesus said, 'I am thirsty.' [29] A jar of wine vinegar was there, so they soaked a sponge in it, put the

---

[839] Brown, *Death of the Messiah*, p. 1020. He notes that the word is not found elsewhere for a son addressing his mother (citing P. Benoit, *Jesus and the Gospel* (Herder, 1973), p. 86).

[840] Beasley-Murray, *John*, p. 349. We see somewhat similar formula-like language in the Book of Tobit, part of the Apocrypha that appears in Catholic, Orthodox, and Anglican Bibles. When Tobit is engaged to Sarah, Tobit is told: "Take your kinswoman; from now on you are her brother and she is your sister. She is given to you from today and forever" (Tobit 7:11, NRSV).

[841] While the bulk of church tradition considers Mary's grave to have been in the Valley of Kidron near Jerusalem some later sources write that she died in Ephesus where John was residing (Barnabas Meistermann, "Tomb of the Blessed Virgin Mary," *The Catholic Encyclopedia* (vol. 14; Robert Appleton Company, 1912)).

sponge on a stalk of the hyssop plant, and lifted it to Jesus' lips. [30] When he had received the drink, Jesus said, 'It is finished.'" (19:28-30a)

It has become hard for Jesus to even get a breath. Hung from his arms, he must pull himself up each time he wants to breathe. His shoulders ache, his mouth is parched. He is exhausted. And yet he does not want to die without a final word. He asks for something to drink to wet his lips for this final effort.

The Fulfillment of Scripture

"Knowing that all was now completed, and so that the Scripture would be fulfilled...." (John 19:28a)

What Scripture was fulfilled here? A psalm of lamentation, written by David, seems to have been fulfilled literally in Jesus:

"They put **gall**[842] in my food
and **gave me vinegar**[843] **for my thirst**." (Psalm 69:21)

Offering of Wine Vinegar (Posca)

The Roman soldier pushes a sponge on a reed up to Jesus' lips. James J. Tissot, "I Thirst" (1886-1894), opaque watercolor, Brooklyn Museum.

Jesus had been offered bitter wine just before being crucified, perhaps as an intoxicant to dull the pain (Matthew 27:34; Mark 15:23). Now he is offered something to quench his thirst after hanging on the cross for some time.

"A jar of wine vinegar was there, so they soaked a sponge in it, put the sponge on a stalk of the hyssop plant, and lifted it to Jesus' lips." (John 19:29)

Wine vinegar (*oxos*) doesn't have any alcohol left, but is sour wine that has turned to vinegar. What is a container of wine vinegar doing on Golgotha that day? It is posca, a drink popular with soldiers of the Roman army, made by diluting sour wine vinegar with water. It was inexpensive, considered more thirst quenching than water alone, prevented scurvy, killed harmful bacteria in the water, and the vinegary taste made bad smelling water more palatable. All over the empire, posca was the soldier's drink of choice. The soldiers had brought posca to sustain them during their crucifixion duty. They weren't getting drunk on it, just using it to quench their own thirst.

The Sponge

When Jesus indicates his thirst, the soldiers use a sponge to give him posca. Sponges were part of a Roman soldier's kit, widely used in ancient times to line and pad a soldier's helmet. Soldiers also used

[842] "Gall" (Hebrew *rōʾsh*, Greek Septuagint *cholē*) probably refers to a Babylonian plant name which originally meant "head" of some kind of plant. It comes to mean "poison" and "poisonous" and occurs twelve times in the OT. In Psalm 69:21 it is used figuratively as "bitter herbs" (TWOT #2098).
[843] Vinegar (Hebrew *ḥōmeṣ*) comes from *ḥāmēṣ*, "be sour, be leavened" (TWOT #679b).

sponges as drinking vessels.[844] A soldier wasn't required to share his drink with the criminals under his care. But on this occasion a soldier has seen Jesus dying unlike any other criminal he had ever seen. No cursing, no blaming, no anger. Perhaps it had impressed the soldier with something like Peter's words:

> "'He committed no sin,
> and no deceit was found in his mouth.'
> When they hurled their insults at him,
> he did not retaliate;
> when he suffered, he made no threats.
> Instead, he entrusted himself
> to him who judges justly." (1 Peter 2:22-23)

Peter concludes this passage with something, however, that the soldier did not yet know, echoing the words of the Suffering Servant passage of Isaiah 53:

> "He himself bore our sins in his body on the tree, so that we might die to sins and live for righteousness; by his wounds you have been healed." (1 Peter 2:24)

The posca offered by a soldier on his sponge that day is an act of mercy to the One who is bringing God's mercy to all humankind.

John makes a point of specifying the hyssop plant, a small bush with blue flowers and highly aromatic leaves,[845] whereas the Synoptic Gospels refer to it as a "stick" (NIV, NRSV) or "reed" (KJV, RSV).[846] Hyssop was used to sprinkle blood on the doorposts and lintels on the first Passover (Exodus 12:22). It was associated with purification and sacrifices in the tabernacle (Leviticus 14:4, 6; Numbers 19:6, 18). No doubt John had this in mind when he recorded this.

Receiving the Posca

John tells us that Jesus actually drank some of the vinegary posca from the sponge.[847]

> "When he had received the drink, Jesus said, 'It is finished.' With that, he bowed his head and gave up his spirit." (John 19:30)

For a few seconds, at least, Jesus sucks the posca from the sponge. He doesn't drink long enough to slake what must have been moderate to severe dehydration from loss of blood, exposure to the elements, and the necessity of gasping for breath through his mouth. The end is near. So he drinks only enough to moisten his parched throat so that his last words of triumph might be heard across the expanse of Golgotha.

---

[844] Thomas F. Johnson, "Sponge," ISBE 4:605. Sponges were also carried by Roman soldiers to use the way we use toilet paper.

[845] *Hyssōpos*, BDAG 104.

[846] *Kalamos*, "1. reed, 2. stalk, staff" (BDAG 502; Matthew 27:48; Mark 15:36). This sometimes causes confusion, our dramatic depictions of the cross usually picture Jesus elevated far above the onlookers. However, most likely his cross was much shorter. All that was necessary was to have the feet elevated high enough so they didn't touch the ground. We have some reports of the feet of crucified criminals being ravaged by dogs. A common guess is that Jesus' cross stood some 7 feet high (Brown, *Death*, pp. 948-949).

[847] "Received" (*lambanō*) carries the idea "to take into one's possession, take, acquire" (BDAG 583, 3).

Finished (19:30)

John records the sixth of the Seven Last Words of Christ from the cross.

> "When he had received the drink, Jesus said, 'It is finished.' With that, he bowed his head and gave up his spirit." (19:30)

"It is finished." The word is *teleō*, "to complete an activity or process, bring to an end, finish, complete something."[848] It is part of a word group that derives from the same Greek root, *telos*, which means "end" – primarily a termination point, then by extension, the end to which all things relate, the aim, the purpose.[849] We find a related verb in John's Gospel – *teleioō*, "to complete an activity, complete, bring to an end, finish, accomplish."[850] When we look back at these two verbs in John's Gospel we begin to see the importance of Jesus' sixth word at the cross.

> "'My food,' said Jesus, 'is to do the will of him who sent me and **to finish** (*teleioō*) **his work.'**" (4:34)

> "The very **work that the Father has given me to finish** (*teleioō*), and which I am doing, testifies that the Father has sent me." (5:36)

> "I have brought you glory on earth by **completing** (*teleioō*) **the work** you gave me to do." (17:4)

> "Later, knowing that **all was now completed** (*teleō*), and so that the Scripture would be fulfilled (*teleioō*), Jesus said, 'I am thirsty.'" (19:28)

What mission has Jesus completed? Why did he come? The beginning chapters of John's Gospel reveal his mission. Jesus came to:

- **Bring eternal life**: "In him was life, and that life was the light of men." (1:4)
- **Bring grace and truth**: "The Word became flesh and made his dwelling among us. We have seen his glory, the glory of the One and Only, who came from the Father, full of grace and truth." (1:14)
- **Reveal the Father and the Father's glory**: "No one has ever seen God, but God the One and Only, who is at the Father's side, has made him known." (1:18)
- **Die as a sacrifice for our sins**. "Behold, the Lamb of God, who takes away the sin of the world!" (1:29)

Jesus has done what he has been sent to do. He has taught truth using the very words of the Father. He has revealed the glory of the Father through his miracles. He has words of eternal life. He has borne the sins of all the world upon him on the cross. And now it is finished. The verb form is *tetelestai* in the perfect tense, that is, a tense that emphasizes the present and ongoing result of a completed action.

In the last couple of centuries, scholars have found thousands of papyrus scraps, many of them mundane commercial documents in which we find this word. Moulton and Milligan pored over many of these receipts and contracts to better understand New Testament Greek. They observed that receipts

---

[848] *Teleō*, BDAG 997, 1. It is part of a word group that has the idea of completion, coming to perfection.

[849] *Telos*, Thayer.
[850] *Teleioō*, BDAG 996, 1.

are often introduced by the phrase *tetelestai*, usually written in an abbreviated manner indicating that the bill had been paid in full.[851] The obligation has been completed. The debt has been paid off. *Tetelestai* – it is finished.

Christ's redemption is finished and complete forever. As the writer of Hebrews put it:

"[Christ] has appeared once for all at the end of the ages to do away with sin by the sacrifice of himself." (Hebrews 9:26)

It is finished! It is complete!

A Cry of Victory

It is clear from Matthew and Mark that just before Jesus breathes his last, he "cried out again in a loud voice" (Matthew 27:50, cf. Mark 15:37). John gives us the content of this loud cry: "It is finished!"

Those who are defeated go out with a whimper, but the victor announces his victory loudly and broadly: "It is finished!" The victory shout of Jesus echoes across the hills and valleys of Jerusalem and Judea, and to the world beyond. It is finished!

The Announcement of Obedience Fulfilled

It is a cry of accomplishment, but it is also an announcement of obedience fulfilled. This shout began in the painful will of the Father – the cup, the baptism, the suffering, the cross. "It is finished" announces the full obedience of the One who, though equal with God:

"... Made himself nothing,
taking the very nature of a servant,
being made in human likeness.
And being found in appearance as a man,
he humbled himself
and became obedient to death
– even death on a cross!
Therefore God exalted him
  to the highest place
and gave him the name
that is above every name,
that at the name of Jesus
every knee should bow,
in heaven and on earth and under the earth,
and every tongue confess
that Jesus Christ is Lord,
to the glory of God the Father."
(Philippians 2:7-11)

---

[851] J.H. Moulton and G. Milligan, *Vocabulary of the Greek Text: Illustrated edition the Papyri and Other Non-Literary Sources* (Eerdmans, 1957), p. 630, under *teleō*.

The ability to say, "It is finished" to the Father's commission is not the beginning of some kind of "glory road," but the end. It is the final culmination of a life of obedience, humility, and suffering that now ushers in a new era.

Q3. (John 19:30) When Jesus says, "It is finished," what does he mean? What mission(s) had the Father given him. In what way did he complete them?
http://www.joyfulheart.com/forums/topic/1537-q3-it-is-finished/

The Soldiers Pierce Jesus Side (19:31-34)

The normal Roman practice was to leave the body of those crucified to be eaten by vultures. However, the next day was a special Sabbath.

> "Now it was the day of Preparation, and the next day was to be a special Sabbath. Because the Jews did not want the bodies left on the crosses during the Sabbath, they asked Pilate to have the legs broken and the bodies taken down." (19:31)

Because it was the day before Sabbath – a special Sabbath[852] at that, the one occurring during the Feasts of Passover and Unleavened Bread and because the second paschal day was devoted to the very important sheaf offering (Leviticus 23:11) – the Jewish leaders asked that the bodies be taken down so they wouldn't cause desecration according to the Pentateuch:

> "If a man guilty of a capital offense is put to death and his body is hung on a tree, you must not leave his body on the tree overnight. Be sure to bury him that same day, because anyone who is hung on a tree is under God's curse. You must not desecrate the land the LORD your God is giving you as an inheritance." (Deuteronomy 21:22-23)

Pilate, granted their request, for not to do so would enflame them unnecessarily.

> "The soldiers therefore came and broke the legs of the first man who had been crucified with Jesus, and then those of the other." (19:31)

A crucified man was hanging by his arms, so each breath was an act that would require pulling on his arms and pushing up with his feet so that his lungs expand enough to fill with air. Eventually, slowly, a condemned man became too weak to breathe. But death could be hastened by breaking the criminal's legs. No longer able to push up without excruciating pain, the criminal would quickly die of asphyxiation.

It was common throughout the Roman empire, if a quick death were sought, to smash[853] the legs with an iron club, an act called in Latin *crurifragium.*

---

[852] "Special Sabbath" (NIV), "Sabbath of great solemnity" (NRSV), "that Sabbath was a high day" (ESV, KJV) uses the words *hēmera,* "day" and *megas,* "large, great," here, of things, "great, sublime, important" (BDAG 624, 4b). See Appendix 7. The Chronology of Holy Week in John's Gospel.

[853] "Broken" is *katagnymi,* "break" (BDAG 515), from *kata-* + *rhegnumi,* "rend in pieces, crack apart."

"33 But when they came to Jesus and found that he was already dead, they did not break his legs.
34 Instead, one of the soldiers pierced Jesus' side with a spear, bringing a sudden flow of blood and water." (19:33-34)

To verify that Jesus was indeed dead, one of the soldiers pierces[854] his side[855] with his spear.[856] When he does so, blood and water sudden flow out, indicating to the soldier that Jesus is already dead. What this indicates physiologically is debated. It may have been from fluid gathering around the heart and lungs. Theologians have tried to show the water and blood had some kind of symbolic meaning (such as of baptism and the Lord's Supper), but none of these are convincing to me. This detail has been memorialized in some lines of the old hymn, "Rock of Ages:

> "... Let the water and the blood
> from thy riven side which flowed,
> be of sin the double cure;
> save from wrath and make me pure."[857]

The significance for us is the assurance that Jesus actually died. He did not just *appear* to die; he *actually* died. Thus the resurrection is a full-blown miracle, not a fortunate resuscitation.

Eyewitness Testimony (19:35-37)

At this point John, or perhaps an editor, verifies that this account is given by an eyewitness and is thus reliable.

"35 The man who saw it has given testimony, and his testimony is true. He knows that he tells the truth, and he testifies so that you also may believe. 36 These things happened so that the scripture would be fulfilled: 'Not one of his bones will be broken,' 37 and, as another scripture says, 'They will look on the one they have pierced.'" (19:35-37)

Verses 36 and 37 refer to several Old Testament passages:

"[The Passover lamb] must be eaten inside one house; take none of the meat outside the house. Do not break any of the bones." (Exodus 12:46; cf. Numbers 9:12a)

"He protects all [a righteous man's] bones,
not one of them will be broken." (Psalm 34:20)

"And I will pour out on the house of David and the inhabitants of Jerusalem a spirit of grace and supplication. They will look on me, the one they have pierced, and they will mourn for him as one mourns for an only child, and grieve bitterly for him as one grieves for a firstborn son." (Zechariah 12:10)

---

[854] "Pierced" is *nyssō*, "to penetrate with a pointed instrument, ordinarily not a violent or deep piercing, prick, stab" (BDAG 682, 1). The Septuagint of Zechariah 12:12 uses *ekkenteō*, "pierce" (BDAG 303), also used in the quotation of this verse in verse 37 of this passage, and in Revelation 1:7.

[855] "Side" is *pleura* (from which we get our word "pleurisy"), "side" (BDAG 824).

[856] "Spear" is *lonchē*, "spear, lance" (BDAG 601). There is a fourth century legend that the soldier who pierced Jesus' side was a centurion named Longinus. The spear was the Roman *pilium*, a javelin about 6 feet (2 meters) long with an iron shank on a wooden shaft.

[857] Augustus M. Toplady, "Rock of Ages" (1763).

Q4. (John 19:31-37) Why do you think Jesus died in such a relatively short time? What does the water and blood flowing from Jesus' side indicate? How did it fulfill Scripture?
http://www.joyfulheart.com/forums/topic/1538-q4-water-and-blood/

Joseph of Arimathea and Nicodemus Step Forward (19:38-39a)

It is over. Jesus has breathed his last. Now his friends and disciples work quickly to see to an honorable burial before nightfall and the Sabbath that begins Friday night at sundown.

As mentioned, the normal Roman practice was to leave the carcasses of executed criminals on their crosses for weeks. In other times, the bodies of executed criminals were handed over to the next of kin – except in the case of those convicted of sedition.[858] However, leaving bodies on the crosses offended Jewish sensibilities and law (Deuteronomy 21:22-23), so the Jews would normally bury crucified criminals in a special burial site.[859] Criminals would not be allowed a proper burial in a family tomb.

> "Later, Joseph of Arimathea asked Pilate for the body of Jesus. Now Joseph was a disciple of Jesus, but secretly because he feared the Jews. With Pilate's permission,[860] he came and took the body away." (19:38)

Joseph of Arimathea is a highly-placed friend who cares deeply for Jesus. He is from the town of Arimathea, just north of Jerusalem.[861] He is a "prominent member" of the Sanhedrin (Mark 15:43) who hadn't gone along with the plot against Jesus (Luke 23:50-51). We don't know if he has ever talked to Jesus one-on-one. He is a "secret"[862] discile (19:38), one who is "waiting[863] for the Kingdom of God" (Luke 23:51). But he is a believer; he is a disciple. Often, secret believers burrow deeper in a time of crisis, but sometimes they rise to the occasion to do what is required.

Joseph chooses this moment to make his allegiance clear at whatever personal risk to his reputation and his future. Joseph requests Jesus' body to be given to him for burial, and because of his position, Pilate both receives him and grants his request. Mark notes that "he went boldly[864]" (Mark 15:43)

> "He was accompanied by Nicodemus, the man who earlier had visited Jesus at night." (19:39a)

Joseph of Arimathea is joined in this act of mercy by Nicodemus, another member of the Sanhedrin. He had originally come to Jesus by night to learn from him (3:1-10). Later, he had publicly

---

[858] See Brown, *Death* 2:1207-1209.

[859] Josephus, *Antiquities* 5.1.14; War 4.5.2; 3.8.5.

[860] "With permission" (NIV), "gave permission" (NRSV, ESV), "gave leave" (KJV) is *epitrepō*, "to allow someone to do something, allow, permit" (BDAG 385, 1).

[861] Arimathea is identified with Ramathaim-zophim (1 Samuel 1:1), modern Rentis, just north of Jerusalem (Marshall, *Luke*, p. 879).

[862] "Secretly" is perfect passive of *kryptō* (from which we get our words, "crypt" and "cryptology"), "of states or conditions withdraw from sight or knowledge, hide, keep secret" (BDAG 572, 1b).

[863] "Waiting" is the Greek verb *prosdechomai*, "to look forward to, wait for" (BDAG 877, 2b). The word is used early in Luke's Gospel to describe godly people who don't yet participate in the Kingdom, but are eagerly awaiting it – Simeon (2:25), Anna (2:38), etc.

[864] *Tolmaō*, "to show boldness or resolution in the face of danger, opposition, or a problem, dare, bring oneself to (do something)" (BDAG 1010, b).

questioned the Sanhedrin's prejudicial condemnation of Jesus without a hearing (17:50-52), and is probably suspected now of being a sympathizer.

Both Joseph and Nicodemus are wealthy men. Joseph of Arimathea owns a private tomb, newly hewn out of rock in a garden near Golgotha (Matthew 27:60). In this family tomb, never used, Joseph makes a place for the Master. For his part, Nicodemus purchases expensive preparations for the burial.

Jesus' Body Is Prepared for Burial (19:38-40)

"[39b] Nicodemus brought a mixture[865] of myrrh[866] and aloes[867], about seventy-five pounds.[868] [40] Taking Jesus' body, the two of them wrapped it, with the spices, in strips of linen. This was in accordance with Jewish burial customs." (19:38-40)

Myrrh and aloes were used to reduce the smell of the decaying body. Seventy-five pounds suggests a quantity that might be used at a royal burial. The compound was inserted in the wrappings as they wrapped each limb and the body with linen.

The Synoptic Gospels tell us that some female disciples accompanied the men bearing the body to the tomb, so they knew the location (Luke 23:55). Marshall observes, "It is improbable in eastern conditions that women would have come afterwards to perform rites on a body that had not already had some kind of anointing to preserve it."[869] The women brought additional spices to complete the body's preparation on Sunday morning.

Jesus Is Laid in a Garden Tomb (19:41-42)

"[41] At the place where Jesus was crucified, there was a garden[870], and in the garden a new tomb[871], in which no one had ever been laid. [42] Because it was the Jewish day of Preparation and since the tomb was nearby, they laid Jesus there." (19:41-42)

Like the location of Golgotha (see above), the location of the garden tomb has also been disputed. While tourists to Jerusalem are sometimes shown a site elsewhere, there is strong evidence that the tomb now covered by the Church of the Holy Sepulcher is the correct location of Jesus' burial, not far from Golgotha, also found within this ancient church.[872]

---

[865] "Mixture" is *migma*, "mixture, compound" (BDAG 650).

[866] "Myrrh" is *smyrna*, "the resinous gum of the bush *Balsamodendron myrrha*, myrrh" (BDAG 933).

[867] Aloes is *aloē*, "aloes," here probably referring to the strong aromatic, quick-drying juice of the *Aloe vera* or *Aloe succotrina*" (BDAG 48).

[868] "Seventy-five pounds" (NIV, ESV), "a hundred pounds" (NRSV, KJV) is, in Greek, one hundred *litra*, "a (Roman) pound" (327.45 grams). An international or United States customary pound is 453.592 grams.

[869] Marshall, *Luke*, p. 880. He cites Josephus, *Antiquities* 17:199; *Wars* 1:673, but acknowledges that these references don't attest a second anointing.

[870] "Garden" is *kēpos*, "garden" (BDAG 542), also used at 18:1, 26 and Luke 13:19.

[871] "Tomb" (NIV, NRSV, ESV), "sepulcher" (KJV) is *mnēmeion*, literally, "token of remembrance," here "grave, tomb" (BDAG 655). Also at 11:17, 31; 12:17 (of Lazarus' tomb), and 19:42; 20:1-4, 6, 8, 11ab; (of Jesus' tomb).

[872] For an authoritative overview of the issues, see Urban C. von Wahlde, "Archaeology and John's Gospel," in *Jesus and Archaeology*, pp. 576-585.

It is not a natural cave, but one which has been "hewn in rock" (Luke 23:53).[873] It is found in a garden. Green describes the type of tomb alluded to in this passage:

> "... Fashioned by quarrying into the side of a rock face. Such a tomb might have included a fore-court before a cave, the mouth of which could be covered by a large, disk-shaped stone set in a groove cut in the rock beneath. The entrance would lead into the burial chamber with a stone step and central pit of sufficient height to allow persons to stand in order to prepare a corpse for internment on one of the stone benches carved into the rock along the sides of the chamber.... The body was placed on a sand-covered stone bench; after a twelve-month period of decomposition, the bones were collected and placed in an ossuary."[874]

Tombs of this type might contain 8 niches (3 on each side, two on the end), or 13 niches (4 on each side, 3 at the end, and one on each side of the entrance).[875]

That Jesus is buried in a brand new tomb reflects the great esteem in which Joseph holds Jesus. It also counteracts any suggestion that when Jesus' body is missing on resurrection morning that the women mistake it for another burial.

Q5. (John 19:38-42) Who were Joseph of Arimathea and Nicodemus? Was it good that they were "secret disciples"? What risk did they incur by participating in Jesus' burial? Why is the burial account important to Jesus' story? To our understanding of who Jesus is?
http://www.joyfulheart.com/forums/topic/1539-q5-secret-disciples/

Lessons for Disciples

It's hard to know what more to say about Jesus' crucifixion and resurrection. The lessons are many, and as you meditate on it you are overwhelmed with the utter sadness that Jesus' family and close friends must have felt. But it was an indispensible part of Jesus' journey.

Here are just some of the lessons we disciples can glean from this account.

1. Jesus had been brutally beaten, so he died relatively quickly on the cross. He did this for you and me (19:33)
2. The placard over Jesus' cross declared his true title, "King of the Jews." He was openly the suffering Messiah (19:19-21).
3. Jesus' death fulfilled a number of Old Testament passages, one after another. John seems to refer specifically to Psalm 22:18; Psalm 69:7; Exodus 12:46; Psalm 34:20; Zechariah 12:10; but many others were also fulfilled.
4. Even as he is dying an excruciating death, Jesus' compassion for his mother shows through. Responsibility for our families must be a high value for us disciples (19:26-27).

---

[873] Greek *laxeutos*. Marshall, *Luke*, p. 880, who indicates that it does not mean "built with hewn stones," as demonstrated by Deuteronomy 4:49 LXX.

[874] Green, *Luke*, p. 830, fn. 7.

[875] Edersheim, *Life and Times* 2:318.

5. Jesus said, "It is finished," and completed his mission. We, too, must complete the tasks that the Father has given us with the same dogged persistence as our Master (19:30).

6. Jesus truly died. This has been questioned by modern unbelievers who have supposed that he just fainted and then revived in the tomb. The soldiers who dealt in death knew he was dead, but verified it by inflicting what would have been a mortal wound had he still been alive. The Docetists believed that Jesus only seemed to be human. But John makes it clear that the "Word became flesh" (1:14) and truly died the death of a human.

7. The redemptive significance of Jesus death is only touched on in John's Gospel, referring to Jesus as "the Lamb of God who takes away the sin of the world"(1:29). The doctrine of redemption is developed primarily in the preaching of the early church (Book of Acts), and in the letters of Paul, Peter, and John. John later says, for example: "The blood of Jesus, his Son, purifies us from all sin" (1 John 1:7b), and "He is the atoning sacrifice for our sins, and not only for ours but also for the sins of the whole world" (1 John 2:2).

8. There is a time for us to publicly identify ourselves with Jesus, even though fear might have prevented it in the past. Both Joseph of Arimathea and Nicodemus put their lives and reputations on the line as they assist Jesus (19:38-39).

9. Everything we have is to be put at Jesus' disposal. Joseph is wealthy and has a brand new tomb. He is honored for Jesus to be placed there. Nicodemus no doubt paid for expensive burial ointments out of his own finances. So did the women. Even in death, his disciples bestow on him an extravagant love. Our possessions are to be used for our Lord's glory.

10. Jesus' death and burial are carefully documented. Jesus was actually dead. Jesus' disciples are sure of it. They have seen the soldiers finally pierce his side so that water and blood run out (John 19:33-34). They have handled his lifeless corpse. They have anointed it and wrapped it carefully and laid it in a tomb blocked by a heavy stone. The Gospel writers give us this detail so that we can know with certainty that Jesus' resurrection is no error, no mistaken identity, no fluke. The resurrection is one of the central Christian beliefs and it is solid.

Prayer

Father, it grieves me anew as I recall in detail my Lord's suffering for me. Thank you for my salvation, that my sins were on him and have been forgiven. Help my life to be so purified that it might in some small way be worthy of the Son of God. In Jesus' mighty name, I pray. Amen.

Key Verses

"Pilate had a notice prepared and fastened to the cross. It read: JESUS OF NAZARETH, THE KING OF THE JEWS." (John 19:19, NIV)

"This happened that the scripture might be fulfilled which said, 'They divided my garments among them and cast lots for my clothing.'" (John 19:24, NIV)

"When Jesus saw his mother there, and the disciple whom he loved standing nearby, he said to his mother, 'Dear woman, here is your son,' and to the disciple, 'Here is your mother.' From that time on, this disciple took her into his home." (John 19:26-27, NIV)

"When he had received the drink, Jesus said, 'It is finished.' With that, he bowed his head and gave up his spirit." (John 19:30, NIV)

"When they came to Jesus and found that he was already dead, they did not break his legs. Instead, one of the soldiers pierced Jesus' side with a spear, bringing a sudden flow of blood and water." (John 19:33-34, NIV)

"These things happened so that the scripture would be fulfilled: 'Not one of his bones will be broken,' and, as another scripture says, 'They will look on the one they have pierced.'" (John 19:36-37, NIV)

"At the place where Jesus was crucified, there was a garden, and in the garden a new tomb, in which no one had ever been laid. Because it was the Jewish day of Preparation and since the tomb was nearby, they laid Jesus there." (John 19:41-42, NIV)

32. Jesus Appears to Mary Magdalene (20:1-18)

How do you talk matter-of-factly about an event so mind-boggling as the raising of a person from the dead, the Resurrection of Jesus Christ? Hollywood would use special effects to impact the viewer. Novelists would employ powerful prose. But the Scripture just tells the story of the disciples, both male and female, as they discover this unexpected and life-jolting joy. And the Scripture tells it simply, clearly, and convincingly.

The historicity of the Resurrection is crucial to the Christian faith. Our own eternal future hinges on this question. Paul writes:

> "And if Christ has not been raised, our preaching is useless and so is your faith. More than that, we are then found to be false witnesses about God, for we have testified about God that he raised Christ from the dead... If Christ has not been raised, your faith is futile; you are still in your sins.... If only for this life we have hope in Christ, we are to be pitied more than all men." (1 Corinthians 15:14-15, 17, 19)

Piero della Francesca (1420-1492),"Resurrection" (1463-65), Mural in fresco and tempera, 225 x 200 cm, Pinacoteca Comunale, Sansepolcro, Italy.

Each of the Gospel writers adds specific details to the story of the resurrection. Occasionally, it is hard to understand just how all these details fit together, though it is possible to harmonize them. (See Appendix 11. A Possible Harmonization of the Resurrection Accounts.) However, we're studying John's account, so I won't try to weave in everything included in the Synoptic Gospels. For example, John doesn't mention the Roman soldiers who guard the tomb (Matthew 27:62-66; 28:11-15) or the women who accompany Mary Magdalene to the tomb. We'll focus on John's telling of the story.

The Disciples' Emotional State

But before we can understand the impact of the resurrection on the disciples, we need to assess their emotional state. Jesus has been tortured, crucified, and succumbed to the agony of the cross with an early death. The death of the bandits crucified on each side must be hastened by having their legs broken, but not Jesus. When a soldier pierces his side to confirm his death, water and blood flow out.

The body is taken down, Mary his mother probably embraces him one last time and then the body is carried in a large shroud to the nearby burial place. The women follow, and perhaps help as Joseph of Arimathea and Nicodemus fold myrrh and aloes into the grave wrappings. Then the men together put their shoulders to the heavy stone and with all their might roll it into place, where it stops with a clunk. The grave is shut.

With heavy hearts the women follow the men into the city as Sabbath night falls, lit by the full moon of Passover. Saturday seems to take forever to be over, as the disciples go through the motions of the day. They are deeply depressed. Hope is gone and replaced by fear. Are they thinking of resurrection? No! They have seen their Messiah and Lord die a horrible death. It is over. Their dream of a glorious kingdom is gone. They walk as dead men.

That night they furtively bar the doors of the place they are staying against the soldiers who may well come for them as well. They are exhausted, but sleep doesn't come easily. They toss and turn until the wee hours of the morning when they fall into a fitful sleep. That is their emotional state – all of them.

But early – very early – on Sunday morning, Mary Magdalene and some other women rise and go to the tomb to complete the hurried burial. And that is when all glory begins to break loose in their lives. Not easily, but Jesus gradually pries loose their faith so they can see his glory, the resurrection glory of the Only-Begotten of the Father.

Mary from Magdala

At this point John introduces an important member of Jesus' ministry team, a woman, who is the first witness to the risen Christ. Let me fill in some details about her life taken from Luke's Gospel:

> "The Twelve were with him and also some women who had been cured of evil spirits and diseases: Mary (called Magdalene) from whom seven demons had come out; [3] Joanna the wife of Cuza, the manager of Herod's household; Susanna; and many others. These women were helping to support them out of their own means." (Luke 8:1b-3)

Mary is from Magdala, which was probably on the western shore of the Sea of Galilee, the modern Migdal (meaning "watchtower"), about three miles northeast of Tiberias along the coast.[876] It was a strongly Hellenized town with an important dried-fish industry. Josephus refers to it by its Greek name Tarichaea, meaning "drying and salting." Archaeological digs in the early 1970s revealed a small 26.5 x 23.5 foot synagogue from New Testament times, and confirmed its urban character.[877] Rabbis criticized the immorality of its inhabitants.[878] It was a prosperous city that by AD 60-70 had a hippodrome (stadium for horse races) and 40,000 inhabitants.[879]

Mary is from a wealthy family, since she helped support Jesus and his disciples from her personal fortune.

---

[876] Green, *Luke*, p. 320.

[877] Avraham Negev (ed.), "Magdala, Migdal Nunayah, Taricheae," *The Archaeological Encyclopedia of the Holy Land* (Revised Edition; Thomas Nelson, 1986), pp. 225-226. Edersheim, *Life and Times* 1:571 cites Midrash on Eccl. x. 8., ed. Warsh, p. 102b. Edersheim, *Life and Times* 1:572, suggests that it might be a suitable location for a dyeworks using shell-fish that abound in these waters for the purple and scarlet dye, but gives no evidence that that such an industry actually existed here.

[878] Rainer D. Riesner, "Archeology and Geography," DJG, pp. 37-38, citing Strack and Billerback, I, 1047. Edersheim, *Life and Times* 1:571 cites *Jer. Taan.* u. s.; *Midrash on Lam* ii. 2., ed. Warsh. p. 67b middle.

[879] Josephus, *Wars of the Jews*, ii, 21,3-4. During the rebellion against Rome, Taricheae was fortified, and finally taken by Vespasian.

Mary was troubled, and had been healed by Jesus from seven demons which he had cast out of her. Some paint Mary as a prostitute or loose woman, but the New Testament clearly distinguishes the demonized from sinners and prostitutes. How this demonic activity manifested itself, we don't know. Perhaps in some kind of mental illness or self-destructive behavior. As mentioned in Lesson 21 (12:3) above, later writings conflated the sinful woman that anointed Jesus feet in Luke 7:36-50, with Mary of Bethany and Mary Magdalene. But nowhere are we told that Mary Magdalene was a sinful woman.

Mary is single. We are not told anything about her husband, as we would have been if she were married. She was either unmarried, or, more likely, a widow.

Mary is devoted to Jesus. She traveled with his party throughout Galilee, and was with him in Jerusalem at his crucifixion and resurrection. She was one of those who followed Jesus because her life had been so remarkably changed by his healing power.

Women's place in Judaism was in submission to the patriarchal or father-led power structure. Many rabbis, at least, had a misogynist view of women. There are, however, indications of a place for women in Judaism, especially, evidence that some women held the office of ruler or president of synagogues.[880]

However, the way Jesus treats women, ministers to their needs, and allows them to travel as a regular part of his team is unparalleled in ancient history. Jesus strongly denounced sexual immorality, adultery, and lust (Matthew 15:19; 5:28), and commanded an adulteress to "go and sin no more" (John 8:11). But there is no indication that within his band there is any sexual immorality whatsoever.

I have little doubt that the women who have been healed by Jesus and travel with him play an important part in ministering to the throngs of suffering women who come to him. I would expect they do a lot of encouraging, counseling, and instruction with those of their gender, as part of Jesus' ministry team.

But this woman, Mary Magdalene, has the immense privilege of being the first to see the resurrected Christ.

Q1. (John 20:1; Luke 8:1-3) What do we know about Mary Magdalene? Why do you think a woman was given the honor of seeing the risen Christ first?
http://www.joyfulheart.com/forums/topic/1540-q1-mary-magdalene/

woman first to sin [handwritten]

Mary Magdalene Sees the Tomb Is Open (20:1-2)

"¹ Early on the first day of the week, while it was still dark, Mary Magdalene went to the tomb and saw that the stone had been removed from the entrance. ² So she came running to Simon Peter and the other disciple, the one Jesus loved, and said, 'They have taken the Lord out of the tomb, and we don't know where they have put him!'" (20:1-2)

---

[880] David M. Scholer, "Women," DJG, p. 881, citing Kraemer. See B. Brooten, *Women Leaders in the Ancient Synagogue* (Chico: Scholars, 1982). See Ross S. Kraemer, "Sampler of Inscriptions Documenting Jews and Judaism in the Greco-Roman Diaspora," University of Pennsylvania, 1995.

The first day of the week for Jews, of course, was the day after the Sabbath – Sunday. This is the third day since Jesus' burial.[881] Mary Magdalene begins her trek to the garden tomb very early, before it is light. We know from the Synoptic Gospels that other women accompanied her (24:9-10), but John focuses on Mary Magdalene's experience of the resurrection. She knows the correct location of the tomb, since Mark specifically tells us,

"Mary Magdalene and Mary the mother of Joses saw where he was laid" (Mark 15:47).

When Mary Magdalene arrives she sees that the stone that closed the entrance to the tomb has been removed, leaving a gaping hole in the side of the cliff. She is shocked and imagines a grave robbery.

She runs to where Peter and John are staying with the breathless message: "They have taken the Lord out of the tomb, and we don't know where they have put him!" (20:2). Note that the reference to "we" in verse 2 implies that Mary had been accompanied to the tomb by other women.

Grave Clothes Neatly Folded (20:3-7)

John's Gospel certainly reads like an eyewitness account.

"[3] So Peter and the other disciple started for the tomb. [4] Both were running, but the other disciple outran[882] Peter and reached the tomb first. [5] He bent over[883] and looked in at the strips of linen lying there but did not go in. [6] Then Simon Peter, who was behind him, arrived and went into the tomb. He saw the strips of linen lying there, [7] as well as the burial cloth that had been around Jesus' head. The cloth was folded up by itself, separate from the linen."(20:3-7)

Eugène Burnand (French painter, 1850-1921) "The Disciples Peter and John Running to the Sepulcher on the Morning of the Resurrection" (1898), Paris, Musée d'Orsay.

To understand what Peter and John are seeing, it helps to review Jewish burial practices. "Strips of linen" (NIV), "linen wrappings" (NRSV),

[881] While modern westerners might measure days in 24-hour periods, the Jews measured time differently, counting each portion of a day as a whole day. The Greek adjective used in Luke 24:7 is *tritos*, "third in a series" (BDAG 1016). Looking forward, the third day would be the day after tomorrow. Looking backward, it would be the day before yesterday. This is the third day counting parts of three days – Friday, Saturday, and Sunday. Even though Jesus refers to his entombment as a sign such as Jonah (Luke 11:29-30; Matthew 12:39-40), this is a minor parable, not an historical statement. It does not require us to believe, against the clear evidence of all four Gospels, that Jesus remained in the grave for three days and nights (Jonah 1:17). The rabbis said, "A day and a night make an 'Onah and a part of an 'Onah is the whole"; and again, "The part of a day is as the whole day" (Strack and Billerback, I, p. 649, cited in fn. 101 by Leon Morris, *The Gospel According to Matthew* (Eerdmans, 1992), p. 325-326). Morris notes: "Matthew elsewhere speaks of Jesus as rising 'on the third day' (16:21) and 'after three days' (27:63); there is no reason to think that he sees any difference between these expressions."

[882] "Outran" is *protrechō*, "run ahead" (BDAG 889).

[883] "Bent over and looked in" (NIV, NRSV), "stooping to look in" (ESV), "stooping down and looking in" (KJV) is *parakyptō*, "to bend over for the purpose of looking, with focus on satisfying one's curiosity, take a look," here 20:11 and Luke 24:12 (BDAG 767, 1).

"linen cloths" (ESV), "linen clothes" (KJV) is the Greek noun *othonion*, "(linen) cloth, cloth wrapping." There is some debate between the translation of strips of linen (NIV) or larger cloth wrappings.[884] The raising of Lazarus gives us some idea of burial customs in Palestine at that time (John 11:44, Lesson 20). Sanders and Bastin describe the practice.

> "The corpse would have been placed on a strip of linen, wide and long enough to envelop it completely. The feet would be placed at one end, and the cloth would then be drawn over the head to the feet, the feet would be bound at the ankles, and the arms secured to the body with linen bandages...."[885]

The "burial cloth" (NIV), "cloth" (NRSV), "face cloth" (ESV), "napkin" (KJV) [886] that had been on Jesus' head was folded separately. Ladd says that this was a separate piece of cloth that was wrapped over the head and under the chin to prevent the jaw from sagging.[887]

The Witness of the Grave Clothes

Luke mentions Peter seeing "strips of linen lying by themselves" (Luke 24:12) and John tells of "the strips of linen lying there" (20:6) – not scattered about the tomb but lying together! The presence of the grave clothes neatly folded on the shelf are mute testimony that Jesus' body had slipped free of the grave clothes without disturbing them whatsoever. Church Father Chrysostom observed,

> "If anyone had removed the body, he would not have stripped it first, nor would he have taken the trouble to remove and roll up the napkin and put it in a place by itself."[888]

As Peter and John survey the scene, it becomes pretty clear that the body wasn't stolen. The modern theory that Jesus had been in a coma and somehow revived in the cool of the tomb meets its match as well. If Jesus had revived, he would have had to unwind the grave shroud in order to walk free.

As Michael Perry puts it,

> "It seems to be the evangelist's intention to suggest that Peter saw the grave clothes like a chrysalis out of which the risen body of the Lord had emerged."[889]

---

[884] *Othonion*, BDAG 693. The term *keiria*, "binding material," used to describe Lazarus' grave wrappings, may refer to some kind of webbing (BDAG 538). Barrett (*John*, p. 404) sees the meaning "bandage" attested in the papyri, and observes that "such winding strips that seem to have been in use in Jewish practice." He sees *othonion* as "a linen bandage, such as might be used for wrapping a corpse" (*John*, p. 559), and cites Moulton and Milligan for the phrase *othonia euona*, "fine linen wrappings for a mummy." Brown, *John* 2:941-942, contains an extended note designed to defend the idea that the Shroud of Turin (a linen sheet 14 feet long and 4 feet wide) could have been described by *othonia*, rather than the modern interpretation of "linen strips" or "bandages." He says there is no evidence that Jews wrapped their corpses with bands or strips similar to those used for Egyptian mummies. "Granted the obscurity of the term," he concludes, "we had best translate it vaguely as 'cloth wrappings.'" Danker observes concerning the word *othonion*, "The applicability of the sense 'bandage' in our literature is questionable" (BDAG 693).

[885] J.N. Sanders and B.A. Mastin, *A Commentary on the Gospel According to St. John* (Black's NT Commentary, 1968), p. 276, cited by Beasley-Murray, *Word Biblical Commentary: John*, p. 195.

[886] "Burial cloth" (NIV), "cloth" (NRSV), "face cloth" (ESV), "napkin" (KJV) is *soudarion*, "face-cloth" for wiping perspiration, corresponding somewhat to our "handkerchief," probably simply, "a cloth " (BDAG 934).

[887] Ladd, *Resurrection*, p. 94.

[888] Chrysostom, *In Jo. Hom.* 85.4 quoted in Beasley-Murray, *John*, p. 372.

[889] S.H. Hooke, *The Resurrection of Christ* (London: Darton, Longman and Todd, 1967), p. 79, cited by Ladd, *Resurrection*, p. 94.

Belief in Christ's Resurrection (20:8-10)

> "[8] Finally the other disciple, who had reached the tomb first, also went inside. He saw and believed. [9] (They still did not understand from Scripture that Jesus had to rise from the dead.) [10] Then the disciples went back to their homes...." (20:8-10)

Something remarkable has taken place. John believes at this point, but Peter can't quite fathom what is happening. He goes away "wondering to himself what had happened" (Luke 24:12b).[890] He is amazed, but not believing that Jesus is raised from the dead. Not yet.

It is hard for us to understand why the disciples can be so dense as to ignore Jesus' clear foretelling that he would be raised from the dead, outlined in the Synoptic Gospels. Jesus gave three clear predictions of his resurrection.

> **Caesarea Philippi**: From that time on Jesus began to explain to his disciples that he must go to Jerusalem and suffer many things at the hands of the elders, chief priests and teachers of the law, and that he must be killed and **on the third day be raised to life**." (Matthew 16:21)

> **Galilee**: "The Son of Man is going to be betrayed into the hands of men. They will kill him, and **on the third day he will be raised to life**." (Matthew 17:22-23)

> **Going up to Jerusalem**: "The Son of Man will be betrayed to the chief priests and the teachers of the law. They will condemn him to death and will turn him over to the Gentiles to be mocked and flogged and crucified. **On the third day he will be raised to life!**" (Matthew 20:17-19)

In John's Gospel, Jesus has repeatedly hinted that they will see him again (16:16, 22). And after the death of Lazarus, Jesus tells Mary:

> "I am the resurrection and the life. He who believes in me will live, even though he dies; and whoever lives and believes in me will never die." (John 11:25-26)

But the thought of Jesus' death and leaving them is so overwhelming that they don't listen to the resurrection part. They have seen Jesus raise people from the dead, but the idea of Jesus' resurrection wasn't yet part of their understanding. We can criticize the disciples for their dullness, but, dear friends, we too are dull sometimes about things too amazing for us to grasp at this point in our lives and experience.

> **Q2. (John 20:3-9) What is the significance of the presence and position of the grave clothes in the tomb? Why do you think it was difficult at this time for Peter to believe that Jesus was raised from the dead?**
> http://www.joyfulheart.com/forums/topic/1541-q2-grave-clothes/

Two Angels Appear to Mary Magdalene (20:10-13)

In John's account, the disciples return to where they are staying, but Mary remains.

---

[890] "Wondering" (NIV, KJV), "amazed" (NRSV), "marveling" (ESV) is the Greek verb *thaumazō*, "to be extraordinarily impressed or disturbed by something, admire, wonder at" (BDAG 444-445).

"10 Then the disciples went back to their homes, 11 but Mary stood outside the tomb crying. As she wept, she bent over to look into the tomb 12 and saw two angels in white, seated where Jesus' body had been, one at the head and the other at the foot. 13 They asked her, 'Woman, why are you crying?'
'They have taken my Lord away,' she said, 'and I don't know where they have put him.'" (20:10-13)

The words translated "crying" and "weeping/wept" in verse 11 are the same word in Greek, *klaiō*, which we examined in the account of the raising of Lazarus in Lesson 20, "to cry, wail, lament," of any loud expression of pain or sorrow.[891] Mary is weeping loudly and without restraint because she believes that Jesus' body has been stolen.

As she weeps, she leans down and looks into the tomb again. Now on the shelf where Jesus' body had been laid are two angels sitting, dressed in white. They ask her why she is weeping. She answers:

"They have taken my Lord away, and I don't know where they have put him." (20:13b).

Mary doesn't seem surprised by their presence in the tomb. That she seems to be in shock is evidenced by the strangeness of her conversation with the angels and the supposed gardener in verse 15.

Jesus Appears to Mary Magdalene (20:14-16)

She has been peering into the tomb, conversing with angels. Now she straightens up and sees someone nearby.

"14 At this, she turned around and saw Jesus standing there, but she did not realize that it was Jesus.
15 'Woman,' he said, 'why are you crying? Who is it you are looking for?'
Thinking he was the gardener, she said, 'Sir, if you have carried him away, tell me where you have put him, and I will get him.'
16 Jesus said to her, 'Mary.'
She turned toward him and cried out in Aramaic, 'Rabboni!' (which means Teacher)." (20:14-16)

Mary, still overcome by grief and wailing, now glances back and sees someone behind her. It is Jesus, but she doesn't recognize him. On other occasions, too, Jesus isn't immediately recognized after his resurrection – by the men on the road to Emmaus (Luke 24:16; Mark 16:12), and on the beach at the Sea of Galilee (John 21:4).

She tells the supposed gardener that if he knows where Jesus' body is, she will arrange to have people fetch it and provide for reburial. After all, she is a woman of some means (Luke 8:2-3).

Jesus speaks to Mary gently.

"'Woman,' he said, 'why are you crying? Who is it you are looking for?'" (20:15a).

In our culture, to address a person as "woman" seems harsh, but in Jesus' culture, it was perfectly proper for a man to address a woman this way.[892] Jesus asks her about her grief, but, of course, he

---

[891] Liddell Scott, *Greek-English Lexicon*; cf. BDAG 545, 1; K.H. Rengstorf, TDNT 3:722-726.
[892] Brown, *Death of the Messiah*, p. 1020. He notes that the word is not found elsewhere for a son addressing his mother (citing P. Benoit, *Jesus and the Gospel* (Herder, 1973), p. 86). We see this expression elsewhere in John, with Jesus

knows why she is weeping. He just wants to get her attention, for her to snap out of her grief and look at him. She is still facing away towards the tomb. She tells him, "Sir, if you have carried him away…", without identifying who she is talking about. She is overwhelmed with grief and hardly functioning. When she finishes her sentence. Jesus speaks one word, her name: "Mary." She suddenly recognizes his voice and turns to face him:

> "She turned toward him and cried out in Aramaic, 'Rabboni!' (which means Teacher)." (20:16b)

Rabboni is Aramaic for "my lord, my master,"[893] literally "my rabbi." While it doesn't mean "teacher" specifically, it is the term used to convey respect and obedience by disciples towards the rabbi or teacher they followed. Hebrew rab denotes one who holds an exalted position, for example, an official.[894]

I Have Seen the Lord (20:17-18)

Now Jesus gives Mary a gentle rebuke.

> "Jesus said, 'Do not hold on to me, for I have not yet returned to the Father.'" (20:17a)

"Hold on" is haptō, generally, "touch, take hold of, hold." It could mean simply touch – "Don't touch me." But we know that Jesus invited the disciples (Luke 24:40[895]) and doubting Thomas (20:27) to touch him, so that isn't likely the sense. Here it probably has the connotation, "cling to." Jesus is saying, "Stop clinging to me!"[896]

Mary had seen her Master die a most horrible death. She had watched as he was taken down from the cross and placed in a tomb. She had seen the great stone rolled in place to seal the doorway. And then she has thought that his body has been stolen by grave robbers. Now that she has found him again, she cannot stop holding him, overcome by emotion. But she can't hold on forever.

How often we want to cling to Jesus as Mary Magdalene did, or build shrines to commemorate great occasions, as did Peter on the Mount of Transfiguration (Mark 9:5). Our life is not in just the high points, but in the entire journey, and he calls us forward. It is enough to know that he is always with us and we with him – and always will be!

Jesus interrupts her fervent embrace to tell her that he has a mission – to return to his Father – and Mary has a mission as well.

> "Go instead to my brothers and tell them, 'I am returning to my Father and your Father, to my God and your God.'" (20:17b)

And so Mary hurries back into the city – probably running – brimming over with wonderful news.

> "Mary Magdalene went to the disciples with the news: 'I have seen the Lord!' And she told them that he had said these things to her." (20:18)

---

speaking to his mother (2:4), to the Samaritan woman (4:21), and to the woman taken in adultery (8:10). The angels also address Mary Magdalene as "woman" (21:13). See also Luke 13:12 = Matthew 15:28; Luke 22:52.

[893] Rhabboni, BDAG 902.

[894] Rhabboni is an alternate form of rhabbi and doesn't differ significantly (Eduard Lohse, TDNT 6:961-965).

[895] Luke uses the verb psēlaphaō, "to touch by feeling and handling, touch, handle" (BDAG 1097-1098, 1).

[896] Haptō, BDAG 126, 2b. See the discussion of possible meanings in Carson, John, pp. 641-643. He notes, "This verse belongs to a handful of the most difficult passages in the New Testament."

Mark tells us of their reaction.

> "He appeared first to Mary Magdalene, out of whom he had driven seven demons. She went and told those who had been with him and who were mourning and weeping. When they heard that Jesus was alive and that she had seen him, they did not believe it." (Mark 16:9b-11)

Q3. (John 20:14-18) What has been Mary's emotional state prior to recognizing Jesus? Why does Jesus tell her not to "hold on" to him? What is the mission he gives her?
http://www.joyfulheart.com/forums/topic/1542-q3-holding-on/

Q4. (John 20:1-18) What are the evidences for the resurrection presented in this passage? Why is the truth of the resurrection so important as an indispensable foundation stone of the Christian faith? What does Jesus' resurrection mean to *your* outlook on life?
http://www.joyfulheart.com/forums/topic/1543-q4-resurrection/

Lessons for Disciples

What are we as disciples to learn from this passage? Several things:

1. Jesus dies, is buried, and is raised from the dead in history, in real-time. This is not portrayed as a myth but as an historical event.
2. The neatness and position of the graveclothes attest that his body was not stolen, nor that he unwrapped himself (20:4)
3. Mary Magdalene, before any man, is given the privilege of seeing the risen Christ. That should tell us something about the place of women in Jesus' kingdom.
4. The discovery of the empty tomb is not a case of mistaken identity, since the women were witnesses to Jesus' burial.
5. The fact of the empty tomb and the presence of the graveclothes are attested by Peter – and John – before they are convinced that Jesus has actually been raised from the dead.

My dear friends, John's testimony – and the testimony of each of the Gospel writers – is that Jesus is not dead. He is risen. The historical fact of the resurrection is the foundation stone of the Christian faith. Years later, the Apostle Paul declares the same truth:

> "For what I received I passed on to you as of first importance: that Christ died for our sins according to the Scriptures, that he was buried, that he was raised on the third day according to the Scriptures." (1 Corinthians 15:3-4)

Prayer

Father, thank you for the fact that Christ is risen! It is wonderful news! Help us to put each and every aspect in our lives in that perspective. In Jesus' name, we pray. Amen.

Key Verses

"Simon Peter ... arrived and went into the tomb. He saw the strips of linen lying there, as well as the burial cloth that had been around Jesus' head. The cloth was folded up by itself, separate from the linen." (John 20:6-7)

"Do not hold on to me, for I have not yet returned to the Father. Go instead to my brothers and tell them, 'I am returning to my Father and your Father, to my God and your God.'" (John 20:17)

"Mary Magdalene went to the disciples with the news: 'I have seen the Lord!' (John 20:18a)

33. As the Father Sent Me, So I Send You (20:19-31)

The disciples' sprint to the grave to witness the orderly grave clothes and Mary's experience of the risen Christ begin the first day of the week. But this Resurrection Day concludes with Jesus ministering hope and vision to his dear disciples behind closed doors.

While Jesus' appearance to Mary is intended to help the reader grasp the truth of the resurrection, John's account of Jesus' Upper Room appearances are designed to help the reader grasp the implications of the resurrection for the future.

Caravaggio, 'The Incredulity of Saint Thomas' (c. 1601–1602), oil on canvas, 42 x 57 inches, Sanssouci Palace, Potsdam, Berlin, Germany.

Jesus Appears to Ten Disciples (20:19)

"19 On the evening of that first day of the week, when the disciples were together, with the doors locked for fear of the Jews, Jesus came and stood among them and said, 'Peace be with you!'" (20:19)

We're not sure where the disciples were staying at this point in the feast, but it may have been the same "Upper Room" in Jerusalem where the disciples stayed until Pentecost, fifty days after Passover (Acts 1:13). Since the fourth century, the traditional site of the Cenacle (from Latin *cena*, "dinner") or Upper Room has been venerated in the southwest corner of Jerusalem.

Because of their fear of arrest by the Jewish authorities[897], the disciples had locked the door. Though simple keyed locks had been known for 2,000 years, verse 19 probably indicates merely barring the door from the inside to prevent it from being forced open.[898]

By Sunday evening, the apostles had begun to receive reports of Jesus-sightings. They knew that Jesus had appeared to Mary Magdalene. Jesus had appeared to Peter (Luke 24:34). The disciples Jesus had appeared to on the road to Emmaus had also reported in (Luke 24:33). But the door was still locked.

---

[897] "Fear of the Jews" (20:19) is mentioned three times in John, here and 7:13 and 12:42.

[898] "Locked" (NIV, NRSV, ESV), "shut" (KJV) here and in verse 26 is *kleiō*, "to prevent passage at an opening, shut, lock, bar" (BDAG 546, 1a); William S. LaSor, "Locks and Keys," ISBE 3:149.

Now Jesus appears to the assembled disciples – though Thomas is absent on this occasion.

> "[19b] Jesus came and stood among them and said, 'Peace be with you!'[20] After he said this, he showed them his hands and side. The disciples were overjoyed[899] when they saw the Lord." (20:19b-20)

Luke adds a few details about this meeting.

> "[36] While they were still talking about this, Jesus himself stood among them and said to them, 'Peace be with you.' [37] They were startled[900] and frightened[901], thinking they saw a ghost.[902]
>
> [38] He said to them, 'Why are you troubled[903], and why do doubts[904] rise in your minds? [39] Look at my hands and my feet. It is I myself! Touch me and see; a ghost does not have flesh and bones, as you see I have.' [40] When he had said this, he showed[905] them his hands and feet." (Luke 24:36-40)

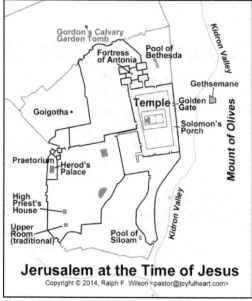

Jerusalem at the Time of Jesus
Copyright © 2014, Ralph F. Wilson <pastor@joyfulheart.com>

The traditional site of the Cenacle or Upper Room is in the southwest corner of the city.

Jesus comforts and assures them in several ways. First, he comes with the words, "Peace be with you." *Shalom* was the standard Hebrew greeting, offering to the hearer wishes of peace, prosperity, completeness, welfare. But I think Jesus' words offer two more thoughts: (1) "I come in peace!" to calm their very understandable fears, and (2) "True peace with God is yours through the forgiveness of sins." Jesus came with the full blessing of multiplied peace.

Second, since they think he must be a ghost or spirit, he demonstrates his physical reality by showing them his wounds from the crucifixion, and in Luke's account invites them to touch him. [906] In 1919, Edward Shillito wrote a poem entitled "Jesus of the Scars." A couple of lines give the idea.

> "... Our wounds are hurting us; where is the balm?
> Lord, Jesus, by Thy Scars, we claim Thy grace."

---

[899] "Overjoyed" (NIV), "rejoiced" (NRSV, KJV), "were glad" (ESV) is *chairō*, "to be in a state of happiness and well-being, rejoice, be glad" (BDAG 1074-1075, 1).

[900] "Startled" (NIV) or "terrified" (KJV) is the Greek verb *ptoeō*, "be terrified, be alarmed, frightened, startled" (BDAG 895).

[901] "Frightened" is the Greek adjective *emphobos*, "pertaining to being in a state of fear, afraid, startled, terrified" (BDAG 326).

[902] "Ghost" (NIV, NRSV) or "spirit" (ESV, KJV) is *pneuma*, "an independent non-corporeal being, in contrast to a being that can be perceived by the physical senses, spirit, ghost."

[903] Greek *tarassō*, "be troubled, frightened, terrified" from the idea of "stir up, disturb, unsettle" (BDAG 990).

[904] Greek noun *dialogismos*, "reasoning that gives rise to uncertainty, doubt" (BDAG 232-233).

[905] *Deiknymi*, "to exhibit something that can be apprehended by one or more of the senses, point out, show, make known" (BDAG 214).

[906] "Touch" (NIV) or "handle" (KJV) *psēlaphaō*, "to touch by feeling and handling" (BDAG 1097-1098).

Jesus gained credibility by revealing the scars from his horrible torture. There is a sense in which we gain credibility with those who are seeking authenticity when we have the transparency to reveal our personal scars as well as the healing that God has done in our lives. Jesus' body is not just some kind of vision or hologram, but a phenomenon that can be touched with the hands and probed with the fingers. Jesus' resurrected body has substance.

Third, in Luke's account, Jesus eats in their presence.

> "And while they still did not believe it because of joy and amazement, he asked them, 'Do you have anything here to eat?' They gave him a piece of broiled fish, and he took it and ate it in their presence." (Luke 24:41-43)

This third proof of Jesus' corporal presence is in eating something – something presumably a spirit or ghost would not be able to do.

What We Learn about Jesus' Resurrected Body

Was Jesus raised *bodily* from the dead? That is, was his resurrection body the same physical body as before? The answer is yes, but more. The Gospels give us several characteristics of Jesus' resurrection body:

- Jesus described it as flesh and bones (Luke 24:39c).
- He could eat (Luke 24:42-43; Acts 1:4).
- His body could be touched and handled by others (Matthew 28:9; Luke 24:39b).
- He could walk and talk (Luke 24:15), even cook (John 21:9), just as a normal human body.
- Yet Jesus' wounds were still visible in his resurrected body (Luke 24:39-40; John 20:20, 25-27).
- Jesus could be recognized by others – but only when he wanted to be. The timber of his voice remained the same (Matthew 28:9; Luke 24:16, 31; John 20:14-16, 20; 21:4, 12).
- Jesus could enter locked doors (John 20:19, 26), disappear (Luke 24:31), and appear (Luke 24:36) at will.

To summarize, Jesus' resurrected body:

- **Has definite physical aspects** – flesh, bones, the ability to eat food, converse intelligently, and walk for miles on a road.
- **Has continuity with the previous body before death.** Jesus' wounds in his hands, feet, and side are still clearly visible, and probably still open rather than healed over. The Gospel writers are making utterly clear the nature of a real body, not just the appearance or vision that is not physical or corporeal.
- **Is not bound to the physical sphere** – it can appear and disappear at will, and walk through locked doors. While Jesus' body can relate to the physical world, it is not bound by space and time.

Jesus' resurrection body is clearly one that has continuity with the old, but includes new powers and abilities. We don't know a lot more about Jesus' resurrected body than this. But we have a promise that when Christ returns our earthly remains will be resurrected in the same way he was (1 Corinthians 15:51-52; 1 Thessalonians 4:14-17). And the Apostle John promises:

"We know that when he appears, we shall be like him, for we shall see him as he is." (1 John 3:2b)

Q1. (John 20:19-20) What do we know about the relationship of Jesus' physical body to his spiritual body? Was Jesus' resurrected *bodily*? How is his body similar to his physical body? How is it different?
http://www.joyfulheart.com/forums/topic/1544-q1-bodily-resurrection/

As the Father Sent Me, So I Send You (20:21)

John includes elements in the Upper Room account that aren't mentioned in the Synoptic Gospels. The first is Jesus' commission.

"Again Jesus said, 'Peace be with you! As the Father has sent (*apostellō*[907]) me, I am sending (*pempō*[908]) you.'" (20:21)

Curiously, two different Greek words are used in verse 21, but their meanings are quite similar. Use of synonyms merely for the sake of variation is part of John's style.

In John's Gospel, Jesus has placed considerable stress on the fact that he has been sent by his Father. Thirty-eight times we read about "him who sent me."[909] It is a constant theme. The implications for Jesus are clear. He does not come as an independent agent with his own message. He doesn't ad lib. Rather, he only says what the Father tells him to say (5:19, 30). He stays "on message" throughout his entire time on earth. Jesus said:

"[16] **My teaching is not my own. It comes from him who sent me.** [17] If anyone chooses to do God's will, he will find out whether my teaching comes from God or whether I speak on my own. [18] **He who speaks on his own does so to gain honor for himself, but he who works for the honor of the one who sent him is a man of truth**; there is nothing false about him." (7:16-18)

Jesus' mission of redemption is not something we are to duplicate. His role as the Son of God to redeem the world to himself on the cross is a once-for-all event. Nevertheless, we share his mission to spread word of his redemption throughout the world.

It is important to recognize, however, that we are sent in the same way Jesus was sent. We are under orders just as Jesus was; we bring another's message, and are charged to bring it accurately and clearly. Sometimes we're tempted to water down parts of the message that are difficult for the world to receive. Yes, we must communicate the Word in ways that are clear to our own culture, but we do not have freedom to alter the message to make it more palatable. It is not our message, it is his.

---

[907] "Sent" (NIV) is *apostellō*, "to dispatch someone for the achievement of some objective, send away/out" (BDAG 121, 1c).

[908] "Sending/send" is *pempō*, "to dispatch someone, whether human or transcendent being, usually for purposes of communication, send someone." The idea of moving from one place to another, which is inherent in 'sending', can retreat into the background, so that *pempō* takes on the meaning, "instruct, commission, appoint" (BDAG 794, 1).

[909] Jesus says that he is sent by the Father in John 3:34; 4:34; 5:23-24, 30, 36-38; 6:29, 38-39, 44, 57; 7:16, 28-29, 33; 8:16, 18, 26, 29, 42; 9:4; 10:36; 11:42; 12:44-45, 49; 13:30; 14:24; 15:21; 16:5; 17:3, 8, 18, 21, 23, 25; 20:21.

The Father sent Jesus. Now Jesus sends us on this holy relay team. And we are to pass on this responsibility to those who follow us.

> "As you sent me into the world, I have sent them into the world." (17:18)

As Paul put it,

> "We speak as men approved by God to be **entrusted**[910] with the gospel. We are not trying to please men but God, who tests our hearts." (1 Thessalonians 2:4)

> "And the things you have heard me say in the presence of many witnesses **entrust**[911] to reliable men who will also be qualified to teach others." (2 Timothy 2:2)

The Great Commission

John's Gospel talks specifically about the sending. Each of the Synoptic Gospels further details the Great Commission:

> "Go into all the world and preach the good news to all creation." (Mark 16:15)

> "Go and make disciples of all nations, baptizing them in the name of the Father and of the Son and of the Holy Spirit, and teaching them to obey everything I have commanded you." (Matthew 28:19-20)

Q2. (John 20:21) What is the relationship between the way the Father sent Jesus and how Jesus sends us? How careful are you to listen and get directions from Jesus in serving the Lord?
http://www.joyfulheart.com/forums/topic/1545-q2-sent-as-jesus/

Power and the Holy Spirit (20:21-22)

Now we move to Jesus' next directive:

> "[21] 'Peace be with you! As the Father has sent me, I am sending you.' [22] And with that he breathed on them and said, 'Receive the Holy Spirit.'" (20:21-22)

Luke's Gospel and Acts connect the sending of the Holy Spirit with the disciples' commission to declare the gospel.

> "Repentance and forgiveness of sins will be preached in his name to all nations, beginning at Jerusalem. You are witnesses of these things. I am going to send you what my Father has promised; but stay in the city until you have been **clothed with power** from on high." (Luke 24:47-49)

> "But you will receive **power** when the **Holy Spirit** comes on you; and you will be my witnesses in Jerusalem, and in all Judea and Samaria, and to the ends of the earth." (Acts 1:8)

---

[910] "Entrust" (NIV), "put in trust" (KJV) is *pisteuō*, "believe," here, to believe in someone enough that you "entrust something to someone" (BDAG 818, 3). See Galatians 2:7; 1 Timothy 1:11; Titus 1:3.

[911] "Entrust" (NIV, NRSV, ESV), "commit" (KJV) is *paratithēmi*, "to entrust for safekeeping, give over, entrust, commend" (BDAG 772, 3a).

It is clear that the disciples must receive the Holy Spirit, the Paraclete, in order to have the power to accomplish Jesus' mission. They are not to attempt to accomplish their sending on their own power; rather they are to wait for his power.

Receive the Holy Spirit (21:22)

But this word in the Upper Room is difficult to understand:

"He breathed on them and said, 'Receive the Holy Spirit.'" (21:22)

We ask, What is the significance of Jesus breathing on them? And when do they receive the Spirit? On that occasion before Jesus' ascension, or at Pentecost as described in the Book of Acts, or both?

First, Jesus breathed or blew upon[912] his disciples. No doubt this is symbolic of the Holy Spirit, since the word for "spirit, breath, wind" are all the same word – and this is true in both Hebrew (*ruach*) and in Greek (*pneuma*). The idea of giving life through breathing upon a person comes from the Old Testament (Genesis 2:7; Ezekiel 37:9).

In verse 22, Jesus commands his disciples to "receive the Holy Spirit." "Receive" is the very common verb *lambanō*, "take, grasp, receive," here probably, "to take into one's possession, take, acquire."[913] In the Book of Acts, "receive" is often used in the context of the initial experience of the Holy Spirit – at Pentecost (Acts 2:38), at Samaria (8:15), at Caesarea (Acts 10:47), and at Ephesus (Acts 19:2).

But in John's Gospel, when do the disciples receive the Spirit? There are several interpretations that have been put forward.

1.   Some sort of actual impartation of the Spirit took place, perhaps a preliminary enduement.
2.   This verse is John's Pentecost, the promised endowment of the Spirit.
3.   It is a symbolic promise of the gift of the Spirit to be given later at Pentecost.

I think in light of the historic coming of the Holy Spirit on the Day of Pentecost recorded in Acts 2, and Jesus' statements that the Spirit comes only when Jesus has gone (16:7), that the least confusing explanation of verse 22 is the third possibility. Jesus breathing on the disciples is some kind of proleptic or anticipatory symbol of a future act.[914] Just as footwashing was symbolic of cleansing from sin that had not yet taken place (13:8), so Jesus breathing on his disciples is symbolic of the coming of the Holy Spirit on Pentecost.

> **Q3. (John 20:22) Why do you think Jesus commissioning the disciples (verse 21) is so closely linked with his giving the Holy Spirit (verse 22)? (See Acts 1:4, 8) Why is Jesus sending the Holy Spirit? Why do you think the work of the Holy Spirit tends to be neglected and misunderstood in our day?**
> **http://www.joyfulheart.com/forums/topic/1546-q3-receive-the-holy-spirit/**

---

[912] "Breathed" is *emphysaō*, "to blow on someone" (BDAG 326, 1), from *en-*, "on" + *physaō*, "to blow."
[913] *Lambanō*, BDAG 583, 3.
[914] Carson (*John*, pp. 649-655) argues convincingly for this interpretation over several pages.

Power to Forgive Sins (20:23)

If verse 22 is difficult to grasp, so is verse 23.

"If you forgive anyone his sins, they are forgiven; if you do not forgive them, they are not forgiven." (20:23)

Reception of the Holy Spirit in verse 22 seems to be linked to forgiveness of sins in verse 23; the disciples can forgive sins because they are filled with the Holy Spirit.

But what does this mean? In what way do believers have the power to forgive sins? All sins, or just some sins?

In Matthew's Gospel, Jesus indicates that amazing power is granted to Jesus' disciples.

"I will give you the keys of the kingdom of heaven; whatever you bind on earth will be bound in heaven, and whatever you loose on earth will be loosed in heaven." (Matthew 16:19)

"I tell you the truth, whatever you bind on earth will be bound in heaven, and whatever you loose on earth will be loosed in heaven. Again, I tell you that if two of you on earth agree about anything you ask for, it will be done for you by my Father in heaven. For where two or three come together in my name, there am I with them." (Matthew 18:18-20)

In these passages, the metaphor of keys could apply to control of provisions,[915] or to admission to or exclusion from the Kingdom. The metaphor of binding and loosing was used by the rabbis for declaring something forbidden or permitted, so this metaphor seems to refer to the regulation of conduct.[916]

Later in the epistles, James and John connect intercessory prayer with forgiveness of sins.

"And the prayer offered in faith will make the sick person well; the Lord will raise him up. If he has sinned, he will be forgiven. Therefore confess your sins to each other and pray for each other so that you may be healed. The prayer of a righteous man is powerful and effective." (James 5:15-16)

"If anyone sees his brother commit a sin that does not lead to death, he should pray and God will give him life. I refer to those whose sin does not lead to death. There is a sin that leads to death. I am not saying that he should pray about that." (1 John 5:16)

How shall we understand this? Historically we see different understandings about whether a pronouncement of absolution is:

1. Conferring forgiveness upon a person.
2. Declaring the forgiveness brought about by Christ's redemption.

Conferring. The Roman Catholic Church, as well as Eastern Orthodox, Anglican, and some Lutheran[917] churches, teach that the Church through her priests (unworthy though they are) can grant

---

[915] R.T. France, *The Gospel of Matthew* (New International Commentary on the New Testament; Eerdmans, 2007), p. 625. The key conveys the ideas of access and admission: "To the angel of the church in Philadelphia write: These are the words of him who is holy and true, who holds the key of David. What he opens no one can shut, and what he shuts no one can open." Revelation 3:7

[916] Leon Morris, *The Gospel According to Matthew* (Pillar New Testament Commentary; Eerdmans, 1992), pp. 425-427.

[917] *Augsburg Confession*, Articles 11, 12, 25. Luther's *Larger Catechism*, 2, III.

absolution from sin, where there is true repentance and sincere confession. For example, after hearing a confession, a Roman Catholic priest will say:

> "God, the Father of mercies, through the death and resurrection of his Son has reconciled the world to himself and sent the Holy Spirit among us for the forgiveness of sins; through the ministry of the Church may God give you pardon and peace, and **I absolve you from your sins in the name of the Father, and of the Son, and of the Holy Spirit."**

Declaring. During the Reformation, many Protestants rebelled against what they perceived to be abuses of the power of absolution, for example, granting absolution to those who went on the Crusades, selling indulgences, and excommunication of individuals for political reasons. Many reformers argued that only God can forgive sins, that there is no mediator except Christ (1 Timothy 2:5), and that the power of the church to forgive sin is *to declare* through the gospel that God forgives sins through Jesus' death on the cross.[918] I grew up in the Presbyterian Church, which would include in its worship service a prayer of confession followed by this assurance of pardon:

> "Almighty God, who freely pardons all who repent and turn to Him, now fulfill in every contrite heart the promise of redeeming grace; remitting all our sins, and cleansing from an evil conscience; through the perfect sacrifice of Christ Jesus our Lord. Amen."[919]

However, you interpret Jesus' words, whether forgiveness is by conferring or declaring, or a combination of both, we have strong assurance of forgiveness from the Lord himself. The Apostle John, late in his life, wrote:

> "If we confess our sins, he is faithful and just and will forgive us our sins and purify us from all unrighteousness." (1 John 1:9)

> "My dear children, I write this to you so that you will not sin. But if anybody does sin, we have one who speaks to the Father in our defense – Jesus Christ, the Righteous One. He is the atoning sacrifice for our sins, and not only for ours but also for the sins of the whole world." (1 John 2:1-2)

Note: Christians disagree about the power to forgive sins, so be kind and loving in your responses, even if you disagree with another participant.

Q4. (John 20:23) In what sense does the Church have the power to forgive sins? Do we (or the church's authorized representatives) confer forgiveness or declare it? Or both?
http://www.joyfulheart.com/forums/topic/1547-q4-forgiving-sins/

---

[918] Resources for this section are from: Wikipedia article on "Absolution"; William Cecil Gibbon Proctor, "Absolution," Walter A. Elwell (editor), *Evangelical Dictionary of Theology* (Baker, 1984), pp. 7-8.

[919] *Book of Common Worship* (Philadelphia: Board of Christian Education of the Presbyterian Church USA, 1946), p. 12. See the *Second Helvetic Confession*, 14. Westminster Confession of Faith (1646), 30: "To these [church] officers the keys of the Kingdom of Heaven are committed, by virtue whereof they have power respectively to retain and remit sins, to shut that kingdom against the impenitent, both by the word and censures; and to open it unto penitent sinners, by the ministry of the gospel, and by absolution from censures, as occasion shall require."

Thomas Refuses to Believe (20:24-25)

> "24 Now Thomas (called Didymus), one of the Twelve, was not with the disciples when Jesus
> came. 25 So the other disciples told him, 'We have seen the Lord!' But he said to them, 'Unless I see
> the nail marks in his hands and put my finger where the nails were, and put my hand into his
> side, I will not believe it.'" (20:24-25)

Thomas – always referred to as "the twin[920]" in John – gained a reputation as "doubting Thomas"
from this account. John's purpose in relating the story seems to be to set up the blessing for those who
believe even when they don't see (verse 29).

For some reason Thomas wasn't with the other disciples at Jesus' first Sunday night appearance.
And he is particularly obstinate when he hears the others' testimony that Jesus has indeed been raised.
His statement is what we might characterize as both crude and disrespectful. He sounds like a lot of
agnostics I've talked to.

> "Unless I see the nail marks[921] in his hands and put[922] my finger where the nails were, and put my
> hand into his side, I will not believe it." (20:25b)

Thomas concludes his rant with a very strong statement that he won't believe – emphasized by a
Greek double negative.[923]

Trust but Verify

Thomas's philosophy seems to be, "seeing is believing." I need to personally verify the truth of
things if I am to believe them. When US President Ronald Reagan was negotiating with the Soviet
Union about nuclear arms in the mid-1980s, he learned a Russian proverb, "Trust, but verify" (*doveryai
no proveryai*) that he then used extensively in developing treaties that included monitoring of a
country's compliance with the terms of a treaty.

Sometimes we fear for our children's safety because they haven't developed critical thinking that
teaches them to question things that seem to good to be true. It makes them vulnerable to people who
would harm them.

I had a friend who fell for the Nigerian scam, which ended up costing him and his wife their life
savings. In business we are taught to perform "due diligence," an investigation of a business or person
before signing a contract. When making big decisions, this is wise.

I've found that this is important in spiritual things as well. I've heard preachers say a lot of things –
some of which don't accurately reflect what the Scripture teaches. I've learned to look it up myself in
the Bible, to check the context of the passage, to see if an interpretation will hold up to scrutiny. This is
careful interpretation.

---

[920] *Didymus* means "twin." Used also to describe Thomas in 11:16 and 21:2.

[921] "Mark" (NIV, NRSV, ESV), "print" (KJV) is *typos*, "a mark made as the result of a blow or pressure, mark, trace"
(BDAG 1019, 1).

[922] "Put" (NIV) is *ballō*, "throw, cast," here, "to put or place something in a location, put, place, apply, lay, bring" (BDAG
163, 3b). Used in verse 25 twice and once in verse 27.

[923] "Not" (NIV, NRSV, KJV), "never" (ESV) is *ou mē*, a marker of reinforced negation. In combination with *ou*, *mē* has the
effect of strengthening the negation" (BDAG 646, 4aα).

However, there are some things we can't investigate thoroughly. History, for example. We can't go back and view a video recording of Jesus teaching in the temple. Nor can we see a video of Napoleon's defeat at the Battle of Waterloo in 1815. So we test historical events by examining and weighing sources, eyewitness accounts, indirect witnesses, plausibility, results of an event, etc.

I've heard some people talk about a "leap of faith." A more considered approach to faith might be resting on the "preponderance of the evidence," a legal concept.

If you're wondering about the truth of Christianity, be assured that our faith can bear careful examination. Many books are available to help you examine the sources and consider the credibility of a Christian world view in comparison with competing world views.[924]

But Thomas was particularly obstinate. He had heard eyewitness testimony from people he had worked closely with over a three year period. He had heard Jesus' own predictions of his resurrection, and was, no doubt, reminded of them by the other disciples. And he had the evidence of the graveclothes and the empty tomb. Thomas was not willing to accept the preponderance of the evidence, and he stated his doubts in the most graphic terms.

My Lord and My God (20:26-28)

Jesus loves Thomas – and challenges Thomas's adamant unbelief.

> "[26] A week[925] later his disciples were in the house again, and Thomas was with them. Though the doors were locked, Jesus came and stood among them and said, 'Peace be with you!'
> [27] Then he said to Thomas, 'Put your finger here; see my hands. Reach out your hand and put it into my side. Stop doubting[926] and believe.[927] [28] Thomas said to him, 'My Lord and my God!'" (20:26-28)

Would Jesus challenge your faith? Have you been doubting, even after examining the preponderance of the evidence? There is a time to stop studying and commit yourself to a conclusion. There is a time to put your faith fully in Jesus Christ, the Risen Lord.

Notice Thomas's reaction. He no longer needs to put his hands in Jesus' wounds. Rather he speaks words of faith: "My Lord and my God!"

Is Jesus actually God? Or some kind of lesser god? Or only the son of God in a lesser sense? If Thomas had misunderstood Jesus' divinity, surely Jesus would have corrected him at this point and John would have recorded it. But letting his words stand helps us clarify this issue: Jesus IS God, fully God! And Thomas's use of the word "Lord" probably reflects the Hebrew *Adonai*, which was used as a substitute for Yahweh when Jews read the Old Testament Scriptures. Thomas is saying that Jesus is both Yahweh (the specific name for the God of the Old Testament) and God himself!

---

[924] Some books I recommend include C.S. Lewis, *Mere Christianity* (1941-1943); Lee Strobel, *The Case for Christ* (1998); and Ravi Zacharias, *Jesus Among Other Gods* (2000, 2002). There are many excellent Christian apologists. I've found helpful Peter Kreeft and Ronald K. Tacelli, *Handbook of Christian Apologetics* (1994), among others.

[925] "Week" (NIV, NRSV) is actually "eight days" (ESV, KJV).

[926] "Doubting/doubt" (NIV, NRSV), "disbelieve" (ESV), "be faithless" (KJV) is the adjective *apistos*, "without faith, disbelieving, unbelieving" (BDAG 104, 2).

[927] "Believe/believing" is the adjective *pistos*, "pertaining to being trusting, trusting, cherishing faith/trust" (BDAG 821, 2).

The rest of the story church tradition tells us is that Thomas preached in present-day Iraq and Iran. Then he went to India in 52 AD to found a church that still exists today. He was martyred in Mylapore, India, in 72 AD. He had a strong faith!

Appearances of the Risen Christ

John records specific post-resurrection appearances. But the New Testament includes a number of other appearances of the Risen Christ:

- Mary Magdalene saw him first and spoke to him (Mark 16:9, longer ending; John 20:16).
- Other women also saw him and touched him (Matthew 28:9).
- Jesus appeared to Peter and the other apostles (Luke 24:34; 1 Corinthians 15:5; Mark 16:14 longer ending; Luke 24:36).
- Jesus appeared to Thomas (John 20:26-28).
- Later, Jesus appeared to more than 500 people at one time (1 Corinthians 15:6).

The disciples who were in deep depression after his crucifixion were finally convinced that he had indeed risen from the dead. Paul sums up for us the faith of the first century church:

> "For what I received I passed on to you as of first importance: that Christ died for our sins according to the Scriptures, that he was buried, that he was raised on the third day according to the Scriptures, and that he appeared to Peter, and then to the Twelve. After that, he appeared to more than five hundred of the brothers at the same time, most of whom are still living, though some have fallen asleep. Then he appeared to James, then to all the apostles, and last of all he appeared to me also...." (1 Corinthians 15:3-8)

Blessed Are Those Who Have Not Seen, Yet Believe (20:29)

Jesus concludes his words to Thomas with a general statement that touches you and me.

> "Then Jesus told him, 'Because you have seen me, you have believed; blessed are those who have not seen and yet have believed.'" (20:29)

Thomas had the privilege of seeing Jesus with his own eyes, a privilege denied to those of us born twenty-one centuries later. Thomas's belief is understandable. But there is a special blessing for those of us who have examined the evidence, believed, and encountered the Risen Christ ourselves.

> **Q5. (John 20:24-29) Why do you think Thomas is so stubborn about believing that Jesus was raised from the dead? How do you think he felt when Jesus appeared before him? What was Thomas's confession in verse 28? What is Jesus' blessing offered to future believers?**
> **http://www.joyfulheart.com/forums/topic/1548-q5-thomass-confession/**

The Purpose of John's Gospel: That You May Believe (20:30-31)

John has pointed us to the blessedness of belief for those of us who haven't seen Jesus. Now he states the purpose of his Gospel, which I have quoted numerous times in this study.

"[30] Jesus did many other miraculous signs in the presence of his disciples, which are not recorded in this book. [31] But these are written that you may believe that Jesus is the Christ, the Son of God, and that by believing you may have life in his name." (20:30-31)

John explains that he was very selective in what he included in his Gospel. We believe that his readers were familiar with one or more of the Synoptic Gospels, so he wasn't required to repeat all the incidents included there. John concludes the book with the acknowledgement:

"Jesus did many other things as well. If every one of them were written down, I suppose that even the whole world would not have room for the books that would be written." (21:25)

There is a two-fold purpose that guides John in selecting materials for this Gospel:

1. That you may believe, and
2. That you may have life.

The belief John strives for is not just a general openness, but very specific: "that Jesus is the Christ, the Son of God." Christ, of course, means the same thing as Messiah. Jesus is the Son of David, promised for nearly one thousand years and pointed to by many prophets. He is the Promised One. And he is the Son of God. This is more than "son of God" in the sense of being Israel's king. It is clear that Jesus' relationship as a Son to the Father is one of equality and shared divinity.

Notice how John differentiates between belief and life. Belief is not life in itself, but it opens up the door to the eternal life that flows from relationship with the Father, Son, and Spirit – a life of joy and fellowship, now and forever. Amen.

Q6. (John 20:30-31) How did John decide what to include in his Gospel and what to leave out? What is the purpose of his Gospel? John differentiates in verse 31b between believing and having life. Why?
http://www.joyfulheart.com/forums/topic/1549-q6-belief-and-life/

Lessons for Disciples

This passage gives us disciples a number of things to ponder.

1. Jesus' resurrection body has continuity with his physical body, so that we can say he was raised from the dead bodily. But it is not bound to the physical sphere; it can appear, disappear, and walk through locked doors. (20:19-20).
2. Jesus' disciples are sent in the same way Jesus was sent by the Father – with a mission to accomplish, to do and say particular things. We are to communicate his message clearly to our generation, not add to it or take away from it (20:21).
3. Jesus links his sending and commissioning his disciples to the bestowal of the Holy Spirit. This is because the power of the Holy Spirit is indispensible for us to be able to spread his gospel with power (20:21-22; see Acts 1:4, 8).
4. Jesus gives his disciples (and through them to the Church) the awesome responsibility to forgive sins. Christians disagree about whether this authority is to actually confer for-

giveness, or to declare God's forgiveness, or both. The authority to forgive sins is very much connected to both the Great Commission and the sending of the Holy Spirit (20:23).

5. Reflecting on Thomas's adamant refusal to believe: We need to balance critical thinking that comes with experience, with the realization that God's power can act in ways outside of our experience.

6. Thomas's confession is a powerful statement declaring Jesus to be God himself (20:28).

7. Jesus extends a blessing to those who believe in him without confirming his resurrection with their own eyes (20:29). We must do this by relying on a preponderance of the evidence, as well as through the revelation of Jesus by the Holy Spirit.

8. The guiding purpose of John's Gospel is to help readers both believe (intellectual) and find life (spiritual) in Jesus Christ (20:30-31). The intellect is not enough. We must put our trust in Jesus and experience him personally.

Prayer

Lord, there are several things that seem a mystery to us about your appearances to your disciples. However, we ask you to send your Holy Spirit to us again and again so that we are filled to overflowing. Send us to fulfill your mission in our world that sins might be forgiven through the amazing power of grace released by your resurrection. And help us to believe in you. In your holy name, we pray. Amen.

Key Verses

"Jesus said to them again, 'Peace be with you. As the Father has sent me, even so I am sending you.'" (John 20:21, NIV)

"And when he had said this, he breathed on them and said to them, 'Receive the Holy Spirit.'" (John 20:22, NIV)

"If you forgive the sins of any, they are forgiven them; if you withhold forgiveness from any, it is withheld." (John 20:23, NIV)

"Thomas answered him, 'My Lord and my God!'" (John 20:28, NIV).

"Have you believed because you have seen me? Blessed are those who have not seen and yet have believed." (John 20:29, NIV)

"Now Jesus did many other signs in the presence of the disciples, which are not written in this book; but these are written so that you may believe that Jesus is the Christ, the Son of God, and that by believing you may have life in his name." (John 20:30-31, NIV)

Section V. Epilogue (21:1-25)

The Gospel is almost finished. There remains a scene on the beach at Galilee.

Many commentators believe that this was not part of the Gospel as it was first written, that it was written later -- and surely the final sentences, verses 24 and 25 were written by an editor, not John. The reasons that some see chapter 21 as an addition are two-fold:

James J. Tissot, 'Jesus Christ Appears on the Shore of Lake Tiberias' (1884-96), gouache on gray wove paper, 5-7/8" x 9-1/16", Brooklyn Museum, New York.

1. John 20:30-31 explaining the purpose of the Gospel, seem like the closing words. They wrap up the Gospel rather neatly.

2. The reason for the addition, it is suggested, is to correct a misperception that John wouldn't die before Jesus comes (verses 22-23), and thus protect the church when the Apostle John eventually did die.

However, it's not that simple. Many others observe that:

1. There is no break in style between the first 20 chapters and chapter 21.

2. No ancient manuscript whosoever contains John's Gospel without chapter 21.

My own tentative conclusion is that all of chapter 21 – except perhaps verses 24 and 25 -- were written by John himself. The reason for the seeming break between the chapters is primarily the time that followed by a few days or weeks the events of Holy Week that occupied chapters 13 through 20 of the Gospel, though they may have been written later.

34. Feed My Sheep (21:1-25)

John's Gospel closes with a scene on the Sea of Galilee that underscores Jesus' resurrection, the importance of the disciples' ongoing mission to shepherd God's sheep, and the eventual deaths of Peter and John.

Peter and Other Disciples Go Fishing in Galilee (21:1-3)

James J. Tissot, 'The Second Miraculous Draft of Fish' (1884-96), gouache on gray wove paper, 6-1/8" x 10", Brooklyn Museum, New York.

"¹ Afterward Jesus appeared again to his disciples, by the Sea of Tiberias.[928] It happened this way: ² Simon Peter, Thomas (called Didymus), Nathanael[929] from Cana in Galilee, the sons of Zebedee, and two other disciples were together. ³ 'I'm going out to fish,' Simon Peter told them, and they said, 'We'll go with you.' So they went out and got into the boat, but that night they caught nothing." (21:1-3)

Concerning this incident that occurred prior to Pentecost, many sermons have been preached blaming Peter and the apostles for turning back to their old ways, for fishing once more on Lake Galilee. But there's no criticism in this passage or chiding by Jesus. Disciples and their families need to eat. And doing together what they had done for years must have brought some comfort and order to this otherwise turbulent time.

According to Matthew's and Mark's account of resurrection morning, an angel at the empty tomb had directed the women,

"Go quickly and tell his disciples: 'He has risen from the dead and is going ahead of you into Galilee. There you will see him.' Now I have told you." (Matthew 28:7; cf. Mark 16:7)

Then Jesus himself appears to the women with the command:

---

[928] The Sea of Galilee is known by different names in the Bible. Galilee is the name of the district. Gennesaret is the fertile plain at the north end of the lake (1 Maccabees 11:67; Luke 5:1; Josephus). Tiberias (6:1; 21:1) is Herod's capital city on the west shore. In the Old Testament it is known as the Sea of Chinnereth or Chinneroth (Numbers 34:11; Joshua 13:27; 12:3), after an ancient Canaanite town on the northwest shore (William W. Bueler, "Galilee, Sea of," ISBE 2:391-392).

[929] Nathanael, mentioned here and in 1:45-49, seems to be one of the apostles, or very closely associated with them. Since the ninth century, it has been proposed that Nathanael is the Bartholomew mentioned in the Synoptic Gospels, because: (1) John doesn't mention a Bartholomew, (2) Bartholomew is coupled with Philip in the Synoptic lists of the apostles, and (3) Bartholomew is mentioned immediately after Thomas here and in Acts 1:13. However, Church Fathers Chrysostom and Augustine saw him as a disciple outside the circle of the Twelve. We can't be sure (Victor R. Gordon, "Nathanael," ISBE 3:492).

"Do not be afraid. Go and tell my brothers to go to Galilee; there they will see me." (Matthew 28:10)

So it is entirely possible that the disciples are in Galilee in obedience to the angel's command. But they must have returned to Jerusalem later, since we know that Jesus' final ascension forty days after his resurrection (Acts 1:3) took place in the area around Jerusalem (Acts 1:4-8).

Peter and at least some of the disciples are in Galilee, probably home in Capernaum (Matthew 4:13; Mark 1:29) where their boats were pulled onshore during the day. So one evening, Peter says to his comrades, "I'm going out to fish."[930]

Throw Your Net on the Right Side of the Boat (21:4-8)

The disciples fish all night, but as dawn is approaching, they haven't caught anything. It isn't completely light and mist is probably rising from the water, making it difficult to recognize the figure onshore who is hailing them from the beach.

> "⁴ Early in the morning, Jesus stood on the shore, but the disciples did not realize that it was Jesus.
> ⁵ He called out to them, 'Friends, haven't you any fish?'
> 'No,' they answered.
> ⁶ He said, 'Throw your net on the right side of the boat and you will find some.'" (21:4-6a)

Though they haven't recognized him yet, Jesus addresses his disciples with a very intimate term. "Friends" (NIV), "children" (NRSV, ESV, KJV) is *paidion*, a diminutive of *pais*, "child, servant," that refers to a very young child up to seven years old.[931] It is probably an equivalent of a colloquial expression, "boys" or "guys," or perhaps the English term, "lads."[932] Earlier in John's Gospel, Jesus addressed his disciples with a synonym, *technion*, "my children" (13:33),[933] though these expressions seem rare outside the New Testament.[934]

> "⁶ He said, 'Throw your net on the right side of the boat and you will find some.' When they did, they were unable to haul the net in because of the large number of fish. ⁷ Then the disciple whom Jesus loved said to Peter, 'It is the Lord!'
> As soon as Simon Peter heard him say, 'It is the Lord,' he wrapped his outer garment around him (for he had taken it off) and jumped into the water. ⁸ The other disciples followed in the boat, towing the net full of fish, for they were not far from shore, about a hundred yards." (21:6-8)

It may sound strange to us that these professional fishermen would heed the directions of an unknown person on the shore. Of course, rod-and-reel fishermen in our day receive all sorts of suggestions from others on where to cast their hook, on where the fish are biting. But the disciples follow the suggestion. What do they have to lose?

---

[930] The verb is *halieuō*, "to fish," used only here in the New Testament (BDAG 44), from *halieus*, "sailor, fisherman," from *hals*, "salt" (BDAG 44), probably because the Greeks were saltwater fishermen and sailors.

[931] Here *paidion* is used "as a form of familiar address on the part of a respected person, who feels himself on terms of fatherly intimacy with those whom he addresses (BDAG 749, 3b).

[932] Carson, *John*, p. 670. Robertson, *Word Pictures*.

[933] In John's First Epistle, the apostle uses *paidion* to address his readers: "little children" (1 John 2:18). A similar term is used elsewhere in First John as well as in John 13:33 – *technion*, a diminutive of *teknon*, "child," which could be rendered, "little child" (1 John 2:1, 12, 28; 3:7, 18; 4:4; 5:21). Paul uses it in Galatians 4:19 (BDAG 994).

[934] Morris, *John*, p. 862.

Instantly their nets are hit by a large school of fish that just "happen" to be swimming on the right side of the boat.

Suddenly all hands are working with all their might to pull the heavy net on board. It is so heavy that they're not able to, so instead, they pull the heavy net to shore to land this amazing catch. Once ashore, they count 153 fish – to them an amazingly large number for a single net of fish.

This miracle is similar, but with different details, [935] to a miracle that took place when the disciples had just met Jesus, recorded by Luke. Jesus has been teaching from Peter's boat.

> "4 When he had finished speaking, he said to Simon, 'Put out into deep water, and let down the nets for a catch.'
> 5 Simon answered, 'Master, we've worked hard all night and haven't caught anything. But because you say so, I will let down the nets.' 6 When they had done so, they caught such a large number of fish that their nets began to break. 7 So they signaled their partners in the other boat to come and help them, and they came and filled both boats so full that they began to sink.
> 8 When Simon Peter saw this, he fell at Jesus' knees and said, 'Go away from me, Lord; I am a sinful man!' 9 For he and all his companions were astonished at the catch of fish they had taken,
> 10 and so were James and John, the sons of Zebedee, Simon's partners.
> Then Jesus said to Simon, 'Don't be afraid; from now on you will catch men.'
> 11 So they pulled their boats up on shore, left everything and followed him." (Luke 5:4-11)

In Luke's account, Peter recognizes Jesus' holiness with awe, and the men are told they will catch men hereafter. In John's account, John recognizes it is the Risen Christ, Peter swims ashore, and is recommissioned, this time using the analogy "feed my sheep," rather the earlier analogy to be "fishers of men."

By relating this post-resurrection incident of the miraculous catch, perhaps John is indicating that now the disciples have come full circle. They first committed their lives to Christ after another miraculous catch. And now at the end they recommit themselves to the Risen Christ after a similar miracle.

I don't think John intended it this way, but, in a sense, this is a story about laboring in vain, and then listening to and heeding Jesus' command, and then seeing results far above our own abilities. It is an illustration of the power of the Spirit. The life of a disciple is to be lived in tandem with Jesus, listening, obeying, and seeing his works accomplished far beyond our abilities.

Q1. (John 21:4-8) Why did Jesus tell the disciples to cast their net on the right side of the boat? Why did the disciples obey? What was the result? What impression did it make on the disciples?
http://www.joyfulheart.com/forums/topic/1550-q1-finding-fish/

---

[935] The differences between the miracles are that: (1) In the early incident the nets began to break, here they held, but barely (21:11). (2) In Luke's account, they transferred the fish from the nets into two boats, while here they dragged the net ashore. (3) Luke's account takes place early in Jesus' ministry, while John's account takes place at the end. (4) In Luke's account Jesus directs them to put their nets out, while in John's account their nets seem to be out, but are to be put to the other side of the boat. Brown (*John* 2:1089-1091) sees John's and Luke's accounts as different traditions of the same event, but I disagree.

Peter Swims Ashore (21:7b)

While in Luke's account, Peter wants to get away from this holy Jesus, here, Peter can't wait to get to him, once John calls out that it is Jesus.

> "As soon as Simon Peter heard him say, 'It is the Lord,' he wrapped his outer garment around him (for he had taken it off) and jumped into the water." (21:7b)

We might strip to swim ashore, but Peter is stripped for work and is a strong swimmer. He probably isn't completely naked (which would have been offensive to Jewish sensibilities), but wears only minimal clothing on board so as not to impede his work. Peter grabs his outer garment[936], girds it about him, tucking it up so it won't prevent him from swimming[937], jumps in, and swims the 100 yards or so to the place where he can wade the rest of the way. These details are the sign of an eyewitness account. Peter can't wait to get ashore to be with Jesus. He probably wants to be appropriately dressed out of respect as he greets Jesus face to face.

Fish on the Fire (21:8-11)

> "⁸ The other disciples followed in the boat, towing the net full of fish, for they were not far from shore, about a hundred yards. ⁹ When they landed, they saw a fire of burning coals[938] there with fish on it, and some bread. (21:8-9)

Jesus has come prepared with some bread from town as well as a fish. He has a fire going, perhaps from firewood along the beach, and has begun to cook the fish, in anticipation of having breakfast with his disciples. Jesus is their host once again, though he invites them to bring a few of the fish from their amazing catch to supplement the breakfast.

> "¹⁰ Jesus said to them, 'Bring some of the fish you have just caught.' ¹¹ Simon Peter climbed aboard and dragged the net ashore. It was full of large fish, 153, but even with so many the net was not torn." (21:10-11)

Peter's colleagues have now rowed the boat ashore, dragging the net behind them. Now Peter climbs aboard the boat and lends his strength to pull the heavy net across the shallow rocks onto the shore – without tearing the net in the process.

The number 153 has inspired many, many attempts to find a spiritual meaning in the number, but none of these explanations has proved convincing. It appears to be an eyewitness detail to emphasize the great number of fish caught, without any intended deeper meaning. John specifies that these were "large fish," not tiny ones!

---

[936] "Outer garment" (NIV, ESV), "some clothes" (NRSV), "fisher's coat" (KJV) is *ependytēs*, "a garment put on over another garment, outer garment, coat" (BDAG 361).

[937] "Wrapped" (NIV), "put on" (NRSV, ESV), "girt" (KJV) is *diazōnnymi*, "tie around" (BDAG 228), used in 13:4-5 of the towel Jesus tied around himself when washing the disciples' feet. It is possible that Jesus is already wearing the outer garment loosely already and now cinches it up. Brown (*John* 2:1072) pictures it: "Clad only in his fisherman's smock, Peter tucks it into his cincture so that he can swim more easily, and dives into the water."

[938] "Fire of burning coals" (NIV, cf. KJV), "charcoal fire" (NRSV, ESV) is *anthrakia* (from which we get our term "anthracite" coal), "a charcoal fire" (BDAG 80), also at 18:18.

Jesus Offers the Disciples Breakfast (21:12-14)

Now Jesus speaks again to the disciples.

> "[12] Jesus said to them, 'Come and have breakfast[939].' None of the disciples dared ask him, 'Who are you?' They knew it was the Lord. [13] Jesus came, took the bread and gave it to them, and did the same with the fish. [14] This was now the third time Jesus appeared to his disciples after he was raised from the dead." (21:12-14)

Jesus calls them to have some breakfast, but no one dares[940] to ask him who he is. They know, and they also know that to ask him a stupid question is to invite a rebuke from the Master (for example, 4:27; 14:5-9; Mark 7:18; 8:17; 8:33; 9:32; 16:14). Jesus taking the bread and fish and giving it to them is quite reminiscent of the Feeding of the Five Thousand (6:11). There he was the host to thousands, but here and at the Last Supper he is host to his beloved team of men.

John counts this as Jesus' third post-resurrection appearance to his disciples as a group – twice in the Upper Room (20:19-23 and 20:26-29) and here.

James J. Tissot, "Feed My Lambs" (1884-96), gouache on gray wove paper, 9-5/8" x 6-3/8", Brooklyn Museum, New York.

Q2. (John 21:7-14) What does Jesus preparing breakfast for the disciples say about his love for them? His provision? What does Peter's early morning swim say about his love for Jesus?
http://www.joyfulheart.com/forums/topic/1551-q2-breakfast/

Peter, Do You Love Me? Feed My Sheep (21:15-17)

In the Upper Room, Luke tells us that Jesus had the following conversation with Peter.

> "'Simon, Simon, Satan has asked to sift you as wheat. But I have prayed for you, Simon, that your faith may not fail. And when you have turned back, strengthen your brothers.'
> But he replied, 'Lord, I am ready to go with you to prison and to death.'
> [34] Jesus answered, 'I tell you, Peter, before the rooster crows today, you will deny three times that you know me.'" (Luke 22:31-34)

Peter boasts of his reliability in front of the disciples, then fails miserably. Now he must be restored to ministry among them, but Jesus requires Peter to humble himself. Jesus pointedly asks Peter if – after all that has ensued – he still thinks that he loves Jesus more than the other disciples do.

---

[939] "Have breakfast" (NIV, NRSV, ESV), "dine" (KJV) is the verb *aristaō*. Since the time of Hippocrates, it has meant "eat breakfast," though it can also refer to any meal or any type of food (BDAG 131, 1).

[940] "Dared" (NIV), "durst" (KJV) is *tolmaō*, "dare, have the courage, be brave enough" (BDAG 1010, aα).

"¹⁵ When they had finished eating, Jesus said to Simon Peter, 'Simon son of John, do you truly love me more than these?'

'Yes, Lord,' he said, 'you know that I love you.'

Jesus said, 'Feed my lambs.'

¹⁶ Again Jesus said, 'Simon son of John, do you truly love me?'

He answered, 'Yes, Lord, you know that I love you.'

Jesus said, 'Take care of my sheep.'

¹⁷ The third time he said to him, 'Simon son of John, do you love me?'

Peter was hurt because Jesus asked him the third time, 'Do you love me?' He said, 'Lord, you know all things; you know that I love you.'

Jesus said, 'Feed my sheep.'" (21:15-17)

Courageous Peter cuts off the ear of Malchus the high priest's servant (18:10), but after Jesus' arrest, he is overcome by fear and denies three times that he even knows Jesus (chapter 18). Though he is still the de facto leader of the disciples (20:2), runs to the tomb on resurrection morning (20:3-8), and has had a private post-resurrection meeting with Jesus himself (Luke 24:34; 1 Corinthians 15:5), Peter still feels worthless and humiliated. He who was once given the keys to the kingdom feels unworthy of any honor. And he is under a cloud in the view of the other apostles.

He has denied Jesus three times. Now Jesus renews his "call to preach" three times – "Feed my sheep." Jesus assures Peter that he has been restored to the ministry of caring for God's flock. What a wonderful example of grace! [941]

Much has been made out of the variations in Jesus' words to Peter in verses 15-17:

1.	"Do you truly love (*agapaō*) me more than these?"	"You know that I love (*phileō*) you."	"Feed (*boskō*) my lambs (*arnion*)."
2.	"Do you truly love (*agapaō*) me?"	"You know that I love (*phileō*) you."	"Take care of (*poimainō*) my sheep (*probaton*)."
3.	"Do you love (*phileō*) me?"	"You know that I love (*phileō*) you."	"Feed (*boskō*) my sheep (*probaton*)."

Because John varies his words, some people see a subtle interplay between Jesus asking whether Peter loves him with agape love (*agapaō*[942]), while Peter can only answer that he loves with filial love (*phileō*[943]). I don't believe that Jesus intended this. After all, it reflects the subtlety of two *Greek* words, not *Aramaic* words. John's style is known for using synonyms for the sake of variety. It is clear in verses 15-17 that he varies the words he uses for sheep (*probaton*[944]) and lambs (*arnion*[945]) and to

---

[941] See my short story, "Feed My Sheep" joyfulheart.com/easter/feed-sheep.htm

[942] *Agapaō* (which the NIV translates "truly love") is the word most often used in the New Testament for self-giving love. It is seldom found in classical Greek, and was given its unique content as God-like, unselfish love by its use in the New Testament Scriptures.

[943] *Phileō* (which the NIV translates "love") is the word commonly used for love for one's family or friends: "have affection for, like, consider someone a friend." But it is also used for the type of love the Father has for the Son (5:20) and his disciples (16:27) (BDAG 1056, 1).

[944] *Probaton*, "sheep," is used of cattle or small cattle in Greek, but not in the New Testament, where it is only used of sheep (BDAG 866).

[945] *Arnion* "little lamb," is the diminutive of *arēn*, "lamb" under a year old (Liddell-Scott). Danker says *arnion* can refer to "a sheep of any age, sheep, lamb" (BDAG 133).

shepherd (*poimainō*[946]) and to feed (*boskō*[947]). He doesn't intend for us to make anything of this variation. The variation is only to keep it from being repetitive and boring. The same is true of the variation between *agapaō* and *phileō*.[948]

> **Q3. (John 21:15-17) Why does Jesus repeat the question and the assurance three times? What does this teach us about God repeating the lessons he wants us to learn? What does it say about God's mercy and willingness to restore sinners to ministry?**
> **http://www.joyfulheart.com/forums/topic/1552-q3-feed-my-sheep/**

Jesus Prophesies Peter's Death (21:18-19)

Now Jesus gives a prophecy of Peter's death.

> "Truly, truly, I say to you, when you were younger, you used to gird yourself and walk wherever you wished; but when you grow old, you will stretch out your hands and someone else will gird you, and bring you where you do not wish to go. [19] Now this He said, signifying by what kind of death he would glorify God. And when He had spoken this, He said to him, 'Follow Me!'" (21:18-19, NASB)

I believe the NIV and ESV over-translate *zōnnymi* / *zōnnuō* as "dressed/dress," where the basic meaning is probably intended: "gird someone[949]." The NRSV's "fasten your own belt" is better, and the NASB/KJV "gird" is best, because when *zōnnymi* / *zōnnuō* is used in the second half of the verse, it probably means being tied to the cross-beam (as we'll discuss below), not having to be dressed as a feeble old man.

Notice John's explanation of the prophecy in the verse 19.

> "Jesus said this to indicate the kind of death by which Peter would glorify God." (21:19)

It is possible that Jesus is referring to a proverb or aphorism popular in his day that compares the freedom of youth with the restrictions of old age (though we have no examples of such a proverb available to us today[950]). But by adding the phase, "you will stretch out your hands," he shifts the saying to a prophecy of Peter's crucifixion.

The phrase, "you will stretch out[951] your hands" makes no sense if Jesus is talking about a feeble old man. But it makes lots of sense when we realize that the language of stretching out one's hands

---

[946] *Poimainō* means "to herd, act as a shepherd." Here it is used figuratively of people: "to watch out for other people, to shepherd," of activity that protects, rules, governs, fosters (BDAG 842, 2aα).

[947] *Boskō*, "feed" means specifically, "to tend to the needs of animals, herd, tend," probably linguistically related to *bous*, "ox, head of cattle, cow"(BDAG 181, 1).

[948] That the use of *agapaō* and *phileō* here is merely stylistic variation is argued effectively by Brown, *John* 2:1102-1103; Carson, *John*, pp. 676-678; Morris, *John*, pp. 872-874.

[949] *Zōnnymi* / *zōnnuō* BDAG 431), the imperfect active of customary action (Robertson, *Word Pictures*).

[950] So Rudolf Bultmann, *The Gospel of John* (Oxford: Blackwell, 1971), pp. 713-714; cited by Beasley-Murray, *John*, p. 408.

[951] "Stretch out/forth" is *ekteinō*, "to cause an object to extend to its full length in space, stretch out," here, of one who is crucified (BDAG 309, 1).

was widely used in the ancient world to refer to crucifixion.[952] Early church writers indicate that Peter died in Rome by crucifixion in 64 AD at the time of the great fire.[953]

When you put together the reference to crucifixion with being girded or tied by another, you realize that this prophecy probably refers to the common Roman practice of tying the cross-piece onto the condemned's man's shoulders prior to the crucifixion, and then, carrying the cross-piece, led to the place of crucifixion. This seems to be how John understood the prophecy, which had already taken place by the time John's Gospel was written.

Now that we've interpreted the prophecy, I want to draw your attention to two additional elements in verse 19.

First, John says that the prophecy signifies by what kind of death he would "glorify God." Since when does death "glorify God"? You'll remember a number of times Jesus connected his death with being glorified (See Appendix 6. "Glory" and "Glorify" in John's Gospel). A century ago the idea of a "good death" was a popular concept. The ideal would be to die at home, able to spend time with friends and relatives during the last days, and pass on with a testimony of God's goodness on your lips. When I read verse 19, I wonder how my life – and eventual death – will "glorify God." I want my life to count. And I pray that at my death people will continue to see consistency in my faith.

Second, Jesus concludes this word about Peter's death with the familiar words, "Follow me" (21:19), followed a few sentences later by the statement, "You must follow me" (21:22). The words have been used to call Jesus' disciples (Mark 1:17; 2:14; 8:34; 10:21; John 1:23; 10:27). But why does Jesus say these words on this occasion? I think John is looking back to a conversation Peter had with Jesus at the Last Supper.

> "³⁶ Simon Peter asked him, 'Lord, where are you going?'
> Jesus replied, 'Where I am going, you cannot **follow** now, but **you will follow later**.'
> ³⁷ Peter asked, 'Lord, why can't I **follow** you now? I will lay down my life for you.'
> ³⁸ Then Jesus answered, 'Will you really lay down your life for me? I tell you the truth, before the rooster crows, you will disown me three times!'" (13:36-38)

The disciples are confused. Where is Jesus going? Why can't they follow him now? Because he is going to the cross. Peter can't follow immediately, "but you will follow later" (13:36b). In John 21:19 and 22, Jesus is saying to Peter: You must follow me to the cross, not immediately, but later. That is the way you will die.

---

[952] Carson, *John*, p. 679, cites E. Haenchen, translated by R.W. Funk, *Commentary on the Gospel of John* (1984), 2:226-227) for a comprehensive listing of references. This language, for example, occurs in the so-called *Epistle of Barnabas* 12.4 (80-120 AD); Justin Martyr, *First Apology* 90 (155-157 AD); and the apocryphal *Acts of Peter* 38. Secular writers, too, attest this usage, for example Epictetus: "You have stretched yourself in the manner of those crucified" (*Discourses* 3, 26, 22).

[953] In the late first century, Clement of Rome indicates that Peter was martyred (Corinthians 5). About 195 AD Tertullian says, "How happy is its church, on which apostles poured forth all their doctrine along with their blood! where Peter endures a passion like his Lord's, where Paul wins his crown in a death like John's [i.e., beheaded]..." (*Against Heretics*, 36). About 203-204 AD Tertullian says, "Then is Peter girt by another, when he is made fast to the cross" (*Scorpiace* 15), referring to our passage. Eusebius confirms that Peter was crucified under Nero (*Church History* 2.25.5). Later, the apocryphal *Acts of Peter* (150-200 AD) indicates that Peter was crucified upside down (*Acts of Peter*, 35-38).

Q4. (John 21:18-19) What does death have to do with glorifying God? How will your life and death bring glory or credit to God? What does this passage teach us about God's fore-knowledge?
http://www.joyfulheart.com/forums/topic/1553-q4-glory-in-death/

Jesus Predicts John's Long Life (21:20-23)

By this time, Peter and Jesus are walking together, probably along the beach. But John is right behind them listening.

> "20 Peter turned and saw that the disciple whom Jesus loved was following them. (This was the one who had leaned back against Jesus at the supper and had said, 'Lord, who is going to betray you?') 21 When Peter saw him, he asked, 'Lord, what about him?' 22 Jesus answered, 'If I want him to remain alive until I return, what is that to you? You must follow me.' 23 Because of this, the rumor spread among the brothers that this disciple would not die. But Jesus did not say that he would not die; he only said, 'If I want him to remain alive until I return, what is that to you?'" (21:20-23)

As mentioned in the Introduction above, much has been written about who the author of John really is. It is clear that this Beloved Disciple was close to Jesus (13:23, 24), trusted by Jesus with the care of his mother (19:26-27), was the only disciple who remained at the cross when Jesus died (19:34-35), the disciple who raced Peter to the tomb (20:2-5, 8), and the one who recognized Jesus on the shore after the resurrection (21:7). It is the Beloved Disciple who Jesus hinted might outlive St. Peter (21:20-23). Of course, the term "the disciple that Jesus loved," is a strange way to indentify oneself. But it is also a strange way to identify someone else! There are clear evidences of eyewitness testimony, and much more. As mentioned above, I take the Beloved Disciple, the author of John's Gospel, to be John the Apostle, son of Zebedee.

Peter asks Jesus how John will die, and Jesus effectively tells him, "It's none of your business." Jesus says cryptically, "If I want him to remain alive until I return, what is that to you? You must follow me," that is, to the cross (21:21).

John (or one of his close disciples who edited the Gospel) takes pains to quash a rumor that John wouldn't die. John emphasizes that Jesus' statement was a hypothetical ("if"), not an actual prediction. This was important, since John's Gospel was written towards the end of a long life. John didn't want people to be upset when he died, thinking that Jesus' prediction didn't come true.

The Written Testimony of an Eyewitness (21:24-25)

And now we come to the end of the Gospel.

> "24 This is the disciple who testifies to these things and who wrote them down. We know that his testimony is true. 25 Jesus did many other things as well. If every one of them were written down, I suppose that even the whole world would not have room for the books that would be written." (21:24-25)

The "we" of verse 24 indicates that these two verses were not written by John himself, but are an attestation that John personally wrote the Gospel and they know from him personally that his "testimony" is true. Verse 25 explains that John's Gospel isn't a comprehensive recording of all of Jesus' acts and teachings. In a similar way, we were told at the end of chapter 20 of the reason for John's selection of events and teachings:

> "These are written that you may believe that Jesus is the Christ, the Son of God, and that by believing you may have life in his name." (20:31)

Selections were made with one purpose in mind: to help people believe in Jesus and experience his life. The Gospel concludes with the author (or editor) musing – with a bit of understandable exaggeration:

> "Jesus did many other things as well. If every one of them were written down, I suppose that even the whole world would not have room for the books that would be written." (21:25)

But perhaps it's not so much of an exaggeration after all. Luke's Gospel covers "all that Jesus *began* to do and to teach" (Acts 1:1), but Jesus *continues* to do and teach through his apostles, and pastors, and Sunday school teachers, and people who love him even now. The living Christ is alive today continuing to write His story through our lives day by day.

Lessons for Disciples

I see a number of lessons for us disciples in this final chapter of John's Gospel.

1. Jesus may have performed the miraculous catch of fish to catch the disciples' attention. But there's more to it. Part depends on our perspective. We can be toiling away for hours, where just a few feet away is the Lord's provision, if we'll just listen and shift our focus.
2. Jesus anticipates meeting with his disciples by fixing breakfast. It shows love and compassion – as well as a desire to spend time with us. I think there's a lesson here about spending time with Jesus each day (21:7-14).
3. This passage is also a reminder of Jesus the Provider, who supplied bread and fish to 5,000 people and to this band of men. He will provide for you!
4. Peter's eagerness to come to Jesus is surely an example for us to emulate. It shows his deep love (21:7b).
5. The story of Jesus restoring Peter by asking him to reaffirm his love even to the point of offending him, reminds us of the importance of repeated lessons, when we think to ourselves that we learned it the first time (21:15-17).
6. The lesson is clear that Jesus can restore us to ministry and good reputation in his kingdom even after grievous sin. His grace is abundant to sinners who repent! (21:15-17).
7. We see that Jesus knows our futures and can reveal some of that when it suits his purposes. Our lives are under his watchful care, the One who knows the end from the beginning (21:18-19).
8. It's easy to misunderstand Jesus, and then repeat an error so many times that we believe it is true (like the mistake that John would live until Jesus returned). It behooves us to carefully study what the Scripture *actually* says, not what people say it says. The Bereans, we read,

were of noble character because they "examined the Scriptures every day to see if what Paul said was true" (Acts 17:11).

I want to say a final word to you, one who has studied John's Gospel along with me. We've been on a journey together and it has been good. Keep following the Master! Amen.

Prayer

Lord Jesus, I've had such a good time studying John's Gospel after all these months. I'm going to miss it. And so will my sisters and brothers who have been studying with me. Thank you for teaching us. Thank you for the depth of your Word. Thank you for teaching us about glory and life and abiding – and all the other themes of this Gospel. It has been rich! I pray that I will learn to incorporate in my life more fully a dependence upon you, a tender ear to discern your voice, and courage to obey you. In Jesus' name, we pray. Amen.

Key Verses

"When they had finished eating, Jesus said to Simon Peter, 'Simon son of John, do you truly love me more than these?' 'Yes, Lord,' he said, 'you know that I love you.' Jesus said, 'Feed my lambs.'" (John 21:15, NIV)

"Jesus did many other things as well. If every one of them were written down, I suppose that even the whole world would not have room for the books that would be written." (John 21:1-25, NIV)

Appendices

Appendix 1. Participant Handout Guides

If you are working with a class or small group, feel free to duplicate the following handouts at no additional charge. If you'd like to print 8-1/2" x 11" or A4 size pages, you can download the free Participant Guide handout sheets at:

www.jesuswalk.com/john/john-lesson-handouts.pdf

Discussion Questions

You'll typically find 3 to 6 questions for each lesson, depending on the topics in each lesson. Each question may include several sub-questions. These are designed to get group members engaged in discussion of the key points of the passage. If you're running short of time, feel free to skip questions or portions of questions.

Suggestions for Classes and Groups

Individuals who are studying online can probably complete one full lesson per week, though they'll need to be diligent to do so. But many of the chapters just have too much material for a one hour class discussion. The notes show how a class or group might divide the material into about 17 classes. (Sorry it couldn't be shorter, but this is a long and rich book!)

Because of the length of the these handouts – and to keep down the page count so we can keep the book price lower – they are being made available at no cost online.

Appendix 2. "The Jews" in John's Gospel

James J. Tissot, "A Typical Jew of Jerusalem (1886-7/89), ink on paper 7x4.75 in., Brooklyn Museum, New York

The Synoptic Gospels use the term "the Jews" rarely, and usually in the phrase "King of the Jews." However, John's Gospel uses it 70 times. The adjective *Ioudaios* is literally, "Judean." While in our day, "Jews" generally refers to all those whose faith adheres to the Mosaic tradition, John seems to use it to describe Jews of the Judean area – speaking from the perspective of a Galilean. While occasionally John uses the term in a positive sense (4:22; 11:19), usually he uses the term to refer to the Jewish leaders from Judea who are hostile to Jesus.

In our ears, John's use of the term "the Jews" may sound even anti-Semitic, but it's not. John himself and Jesus his Lord were Jews. However, at the time John was writing his Gospel in the early 90s AD, there was a movement among the Jewish leaders, following the fall of Jerusalem in 70 AD, to reconstitute the Sanhedrin at Jamnia.[954] Around that time, a benediction was developed in Jamnia designed to force Jewish Christians out of the synagogues. The benediction, to be recited by all attendees, contained a curse of heretics, and in some cases, Christians in particular.

In this context it is no wonder that John's use of the term "Jews" referred primarily to the Jewish leaders hostile to Jesus.[955]

---

[954] Present-day Yavne is south of Tel Aviv and north of Ashdod, about 4 miles inland.

[955] Beasley-Murray, *John*, p. 20; Morris, *John*, pp. 130-131; *Ioudaios*, BDAG 478, 2c and d.

Appendix 3. Religious Leaders in Jesus' Day

The religious leaders of Jesus' day mentioned in the Gospels can be confusing, since some of the terms are overlapping. For example, a scribe could be either a Pharisee or a Sadducee, and the word "scribes" is synonymous with other terms such as "teachers of the law" and "lawyers." Hopefully the following will clarify these in your mind.

James J. Tissot, detail of 'Conspiracy of the Jews' (1886-94), gouache on grey wove paper, 9-3/8 x 7-1/4, Brooklyn Museum, New York.

Pharisees

"Pharisees" belonged to a lay movement or party that defined righteousness as observing every detail of traditional rules designed to serve as a "hedge" or "fence" around the commandments. If one kept the traditions, he would not then transgress the law itself. The Pharisees were relatively small in number, but had great influence in first century Judaism. They believed in angels and in the resurrection of the dead at the end of the age, in contrast to the Sadducees. As strict observers of the traditional, oral law they are somewhat akin to modern-day Hasidic Jews.[956]

High Priests

High priests were powerful figures in first century Jerusalem. The high priests (there were several in Jesus' day who had short tenure) had a vested interest in the religious status quo, and probably gained financially from money-changing and sales of sacrifices in the temple. Since in Jesus' day the high priest was appointed by Herod, and served at the pleasure of the Roman Governor, the high priests were often closely aligned with Roman interests.[957]

Sadducees

"Sadducees" were a group closely identified with the priestly aristocracy. They rejected the oral law or "traditions of the elders" held by the Pharisees, and held rather to the Torah itself. They denied the resurrection, and perhaps angels or spirits.[958] Most of Jesus' conflicts were with the Pharisees rather than the Sadducees.

Scribes

"Scribes" (KJV) or "teachers of the law" (NIV) translates Greek *grammateus* – "a class of professional exponents and teachers of the law" who might belong to either the Sadducee party or the

[956] Stephen Westerholm, "Pharisees," DJG, 609-614.
[957] Bruce D. Chilton, "Judaism," DJG 402-405.
[958] Rudolf Meyer, *Saddoukaios*, TDNT 7:35-54.

Pharisee party. While any male Jew could read the scripture in the synagogue and give an interpretation of the scripture, scribes were respected teachers who often had pupils who studied the law with them. Scribes were often poor and depended upon gifts from their students, funds from the distribution to the poor, or the Temple treasury. It was considered meritorious to show hospitality to a scribe, to give him a share of one's property, or to run his business for him.[959] In some ways, Jesus would have been classified in his day as a scribe, with students who leave their families to study with him. But he didn't teach like the scribes, appealing to tradition; rather he spoke authoritatively from God himself. "Teachers of the law" (NIV) or "doctors of the law" (KJV). Greek *nomodidaskalos*, another word for "scribe" in Luke 5:17.[960] "Lawyers" (KJV) or "experts in the law" (NIV), Greek *nomikos*, is another word for "scribe."[961]

"**Rabbi**" (KJV and NIV), a Hebrew/Aramaic word, is a respectful form of address for all teachers that means, literally, "great one." In Jesus' day it was not yet a fixed title for academically schooled, ordained scribes as it became later, and is in our day.[962]

"**Teacher**" (NIV) or "master" (KJV), Greek *didaskalos*, usually translates the Hebrew/Aramaic word *rabbi*.[963]

The Sanhedrin in Jesus' Day

Where it was possible, the Romans would have had a provincial governor who represented Roman authority, but sought to keep in place the local kingdoms and administrative systems that were native to a country (client kingdoms or vassals) – unless a province was so rebellious that the Romans had to rule directly. The Romans had ruled Israel since 36 BC, recognizing Herod the Great as King of the Jews. After Herod's death his kingdom was divided into four tetrarchies, each ruled by one of his sons. During Jesus' time, Herod Antipas was tetrarch[964] over Galilee, who beheaded John the Baptist, and before whom Jesus appeared at his trial.

While the Romans and Herodian kings held civil power, the Jewish Sanhedrin acted as a ruling body for the Jewish people, both at the local level (a "lesser Sanhedrin" which consisted of 23 members in every town that had at least 120 adult male Jews) and the national level (the "Great Sanhedrin"). The latter consisted of 71 members, following the pattern of 70 elders plus Moses (Exodus 24:1; Numbers 11:16, 24-25), though lesser decisions could be made by a panel of 23 members. In Jesus' day, the Great Sanhedrin functioned as both a supreme court, as well as legislature, and met in The Hall of Hewn Stones on the temple mount. In Jesus' day, the Great Sanhedrin was made up of members of the nobility (Sadducees, both priestly and lay), and scholars in the law (mainly Pharisees).[965]

---

[959] Graham H. Twelftree, "Scribes," DJG 732-735.

[960] Ibid., DJG 734.

[961] Ibid.

[962] Rainer Riesner, "Teacher," DJG 807.

[963] DJG 732. "Master" (NIV and KJV), Greek *epistatēs*, a more general term for a supervisory or official person appears rarely and only in Luke's Gospel (DJG 807).

[964] A tetrarch is the governor over a fourth part of a province.

[965] William J. Moulder, "Sanhedrin," ISBE 4:332-334.

Appendix 4. The "I Am" Passages in John's Gospel

John's Gospel includes a number of passages that include two Greek words together, *egō eimi*, "I am."[966] When these words are used emphatically, "I am" is a rather unveiled reference to the name by which God revealed himself to Moses as Yahweh – "I AM THAT I AM" (Exodus 3:14). In saying "I am" in this way, Jesus is declaring his divinity and oneness with the Father.

Here are the "I AM" passages found in John that include a predicate:

1. "I am the bread of life" (6:35, 48, 51).
2. "I am the light of the world (8:12, cf. 9:5).
3. "I am the gate for the sheep" (10:7, 9).
4. "I am the good shepherd" (10:11, 14).
5. "I am the resurrection and the life" (11:25).
6. "I am the way, the truth, and the life" (14:6).
7. "I am the vine" (15:1, 5)

Edward Burne-Jones, "Good Shepherd" stained glass window (1895), Harris Manchester College, Oxford.

Elsewhere in John we see "I am" in clauses structured a bit differently.

- "I am [he]" – Jesus of Nazareth (18:5, 6).
- "I am [he]" (8:24) – unless you believe you'll die in your sins.
- "I am [he]" (8:28) – the Son of Man.
- "Before Abraham was, I am!" (8:58).
- "I am he" (13:19) – the one referred to in Psalm 41:9.

In the Garden of Gethsemane, when the soldiers come looking for Jesus of Nazareth, he answers, "I am" (*egō eimi*) (18:5-6, 8).

It is no coincidence that John emphasizes Jesus' "I AM" statements. He wants his readers to believe in Jesus as the Son of God and have eternal life (20:31).

---

[966] There are more verses in John translated, "I am," but in most cases they don't include the pronoun *egō*, which can be implied by the verb *eimi* itself, since in Greek the distinctive inflection of the verb tells us gender, tense, and voice. When the pronoun appears with the verb, it is emphatic – there to make a point.

Appendix 5. "Signs" in John's Gospel

One of the characteristic words for miracle or healing in John's Gospel is "sign." The term "miraculous signs" (NIV), "signs" (NRSV), "miracles" (KJV) is the plural of *sēmeion*, "a sign or distinguishing mark whereby something is known, sign, token, indication." Here, "an event that is an indication or confirmation of intervention by transcendent powers, miracle, portent."[967] For John, these wonders are not just miracles, but signs that point to who Jesus actually is. In the first such instance, the changing of the water into wine, a "sign" had two functions:

Detail of "Jesus Heals a Blind Man," stained glass window, All Saints Church, Rickling, Essex, UK.

1. **Reveals his glory**.

2. **Inspires faith**. The miracles inspired faith in those who believe in him, but in his enemies they inspired only a determination to eliminate him. Of course, this faith inspired by miracles isn't a mature faith and is sometimes fickle, but it is a beginning, which will hopefully grow into a fuller faith based on who Jesus is.

Toward the end of his Gospel, John explains,

"[30] Jesus did many other miraculous signs in the presence of his disciples, which are not recorded in this book. [31] But these are written that you may believe that Jesus is the Christ, the Son of God, and that by believing you may have life in his name." (20:30-31)

Sēmeion is used in John a number of times (2:11, 18; 4:54; 6:2, 14, 26, 30; 7:31; 9:16; 10:41; 11:47; 12:18, 37; 20:30). In the early part of his Gospel, John numbers two of his signs (2:11; 4:54). If you were to number all the signs about which John gives considerable space, you could come up with Seven Signs:

1. Changing the Water into Wine (2:1-11)

2. Healing of the Nobleman's Son (4:46-54)

3. Healing at the Pool of Bethesda (5:1-9)

4. Feeding the Multitude (6:1-14)

5. Walking on the Water (6:15-25)

6. Healing the Man Born Blind (9:1-8)

7. Raising Lazarus from the Dead (11:1-46)

---

[967] *Sēmeion*, BDAG 920, 2aα.

Appendix 6. "Glory" and "Glorify" in John's Gospel

One of the major themes in John's Gospel is "glory" and "glorification." The Synoptic Gospels (especially Luke) feature the angel's glorious announcement of Jesus' birth, the glory of the transfiguration, and the Son of Man coming in glory. But John's Gospel develops themes of glory and glorification in much greater depth.

Throughout the Old Testament we read about the "glory of God," which was sometimes manifested in fire and brightness, what the Jews called the "Shekinah," the dwelling or settling of the divine presence. In Hebrew "glory" is *kāḇôḏ*, from *kāḇēḏ*—"to be heavy," hence "wealth, honor, dignity, power," etc. In the New Testament, *kāḇôḏ* is translated by *doxa*, "reputation."

God's glory is seen through his actions.

'Jesus in His Glory' (c. 1898), stained glass, San Francisco Columbarium, San Francisco, California

> "The heavens declare the glory of God;
> the skies proclaim the work of his hands." (Psalm 19:1)

Glory in the Exodus

The concept of glory is first developed in Exodus. God reveals his glory and enhances his reputation in his defeat of Pharaoh in Egypt (Exodus 14:4, 17-18) and in other marvelous deeds (Exodus 15:11). When the Israelites grumble about not having food, God not only provides food, but "they looked toward the desert, and there was the glory of the LORD appearing in the cloud" (Exodus 16:10). The glory appeared as both a cloud and fire:

> "The glory of the LORD settled on Mount Sinai. For six days the cloud covered the mountain... To the Israelites the glory of the LORD looked like a consuming fire on top of the mountain." (Exodus 24:16-17)

One day, Moses asked Yahweh,

> "'Now show me your glory.'
> Then the LORD said, "There is a place near me where you may stand on a rock. 22 When my glory passes by, I will put you in a cleft in the rock and cover you with my hand until I have passed by. 23 Then I will remove my hand and you will see my back; but my face must not be seen." (Exodus 33:18, 21-23)

Moses himself was changed by communing with God.

"When Moses came down from Mount Sinai ... he was not aware that his face was radiant[968] because he had spoken with the LORD. When Aaron and all the Israelites saw Moses, his face was radiant, and they were afraid to come near him." (Exodus 34:29-30)

Paul uses this as an analogy of communing with God and being changed by it.

"And we all, with unveiled face, beholding the glory of the Lord, are being transformed into the same image from one degree of glory to another. For this comes from the Lord who is the Spirit." (2 Corinthians 3:18, ESV)

To the people of Israel, Yahweh's glory sometimes manifested himself over the tabernacle in the wilderness by a pillar of cloud by day and a pillar of fire by night (Exodus 13:21). Yahweh is the epitome of light itself.

"You are clothed with splendor and majesty.
He wraps himself in light as with a garment." (Psalm 104:1b-2a)

"His splendor was like the sunrise;
rays flashed from his hand,
where his power was hidden." (Habakkuk 3:4)

"He ... dwells in unapproachable light." (1 Timothy 6:16)[969]

The Asaph compares glory with the presence of God where we will go when we die.

"You guide me with your counsel,
and afterward you will receive me to glory." (Psalm 73:24)

The Jews call this dwelling presence of God the "Shekinah glory," from the Hebrew root *shakan*, "settle, inhabit, dwell," and is seen in the noun, *mishkān*, "dwelling place, tabernacle."[970] We see this idea of Shekinah reflected in the Gospel of John.

"The Word became flesh and made his dwelling among us. We have seen his glory, the glory of the One and Only, who came from the Father, full of grace and truth." (1:14)

John had seen that very Shekinah glory upon Jesus during the transfiguration, and, with Peter and James, "were eyewitnesses of his majesty" (2 Peter 1:16-18).

"After six days Jesus took with him Peter, James and John the brother of James, and led them up a high mountain by themselves. There he was transfigured before them. His face shone like the sun, and his clothes became as white as the light." (Matthew 17:1-2)

The New Testament uses the same concept in Greek as Hebrew *kāḇôḏ*. The words are based on the Greek root *doxa*, from which we get our word, "doxology," a liturgical expression of praise to God.

Doxa (noun), "the condition of being bright or shining, brightness, splendor, radiance" and the idea, "honor as enhancement or recognition of status or performance, fame, recognition, renown, honor, prestige."[971]

---

[968] The radiant glory of God was upon Moses. "Radiant" (NIV), "shone" (NRSV, ESV, KJV) is *qāran*, "shine" (TWOT 816).
[969] Also Exodus 34:29; Revelation 22:5; 1 John 1:5; etc.
[970] Willem A. van Gemeren, "Shekinah," ISBE 4:466-468. R. K. Harrison, "Glory," ISBE 2:477-483.
[971] *Doxa*, BDAG 257-258, 1 and 3.

Doxazō (verb), "to influence one's opinion about another so as to enhance the latter's reputation, praise, honor, extol" and "to cause to have splendid greatness, clothe in splendor, glorify," of the glory that comes in the next life.[972]

Now that we've explored the concept of glory in the Old Testament and considered the Greek words in the New Testament, we're ready to consider glory in John's Gospel.[973]

Jesus' Glory as the One and Only Son

The Prologue to John's Gospel speaks of Jesus as Light, evoking the Shekinah glory of God who "dwells in unapproachable light" (1 Timothy 6:16).

> "In him was life, and that life was the **light** of men. The **light** shines in the darkness, but the darkness has not understood (or overcome) it." (1:4-5)

Later in the first chapter we learn that the Father's only Son displays the Father's glory here on earth.

> "The Word became flesh and made his dwelling among us. We have seen his **glory**, the **glory** of the One and Only, who came from the Father, full of grace and truth." (1:14)

Jesus' Glory in His Signs

Jesus' glory is intended to spill out and be revealed by means of the miraculous signs that he performs. They are sign-posts that point to who he is – the Son of God.

> Of the changing of water into wine at Cana: "This, the first of his miraculous signs, Jesus performed at Cana in Galilee. He thus revealed his **glory**, and his disciples put their faith in him." (2:11)

> Upon hearing of Lazarus' illness: "When he heard this, Jesus said, 'This sickness will not end in death. No, it is for God's **glory** so that God's Son may be **glorified** through it.'" (11:4)

> At the tomb of Lazarus: "Did I not tell you that if you believed, you would see the **glory** of God?" (11:40)

The Father as the Source of the Son's Glory

Jesus plainly acknowledges that his glory comes directly from his Father, a fact that he does not hide from those who listen to his teachings.

> To his opponents, the Jewish leaders: "I honor my Father and you dishonor me. I am not seeking **glory** for myself; but there is one who seeks it, and he is the judge." (8:49-50)

> "If I glorify myself, my **glory** means nothing. My Father, whom you claim as your God, is the one who **glorifies** me." (8:54)

> Nearing Holy Week as Jesus talks about his resurrection: "'Father, **glorify** your name!' Then a voice came from heaven, 'I have **glorified** it, and will **glorify** it again.' The crowd that was there and heard it said it had thundered; others said an angel had spoken to him." (12:28-29)

---

[972] *Doxazō*, BDAG 258, 1 and 2.

[973] Andreas J. Köstenberger provides a helpful outline of the ways in which John treats the subject of glory. "The Glory of God in John's Gospel and Revelation," in Christopher W. Morgan and Robert A. Peterson (editors), *The Glory of God*, Theology in Community, Vol. 2 (Wheaton: Crossway, 2010), pp. 107-126.

Of the Holy Spirit, the Paraclete: "He will bring **glory** to me by taking from what is mine and making it known to you." (16:14)

The High Priestly Prayer in John 17: "After Jesus said this, he looked toward heaven and prayed: 'Father, the time has come. **Glorify** your Son, that your Son may **glorify** you.'" (17:1)

"I have brought you **glory** on earth by completing the work you gave me to do. ⁵ And now, Father, **glorify** me in your presence with the **glory** I had with you before the world began." (17:4-5)

Glory is particularly associated with the Son of Man because of the passage in Daniel: "One like a son of man ... was given authority, glory and sovereign power" (Daniel 7:13-14). We see this theme especially in the Synoptic Gospels:

"For the Son of Man is going to come in his Father's glory with his angels...." (Matthew 16:27)

"They will see the Son of Man coming on the clouds of the sky, with power and great glory." (Matthew 24:30b)

"When the Son of Man comes in his glory, and all the angels with him, he will sit on his throne in heavenly glory." (Matthew 25:31)

This is probably what James and John were referring to when they asked: "Let one of us sit at your right and the other at your left in your glory" (Mark 10:37).

But we also see the theme of the glory of the Son of Man in John's Gospel:

"When [Judas] was gone, Jesus said, 'Now is the Son of Man **glorified**[974] and God is **glorified** in him. If God is **glorified** in him, God will **glorify** the Son in himself, and will **glorify** him at once.'" (13:31-32)

So it begins.

Jesus' Glory at the Cross

The cross especially – along with his subsequent resurrection and ascension – are seen as the means of his glorification. Probably Jesus knew this from a verse from the great Suffering Servant passage from Isaiah that combines his suffering with his glory. In the Greek Septuagint translation it uses the same Greek words that John is using to express the concept.

"See, my servant will act wisely;
he will be raised and lifted up (*hypsoō*) and highly[975] exalted (*doxazō*)."
(Isaiah 52:13)[976]

Jesus echoed these words in his three statements about being lifted up:

"Just as Moses lifted up (*hypsoō*) the snake in the desert, so the Son of Man must be lifted up (*hypsoō*), that everyone who believes in him may have eternal life." (3:14-15)

---

[974] Glory is particularly associated with the Son of Man because of the passage in Daniel: "One like a son of man ... was given authority, glory and sovereign power" (Daniel 7:13-14).

[975] *Sphodra*, "very much, exceedingly" (Liddell-Scott, *Lexicon*).

[976] Paul says something similar: "Therefore God exalted him to the highest place (*hyperypsoō*) and gave him the name that is above every name...." (Philippians 2:9). *Hyperypsoō* means, "to raise to a high point of honor, raise, exalt" (BDAG 1034, 1).

"When you have lifted up (*hypsoō*) the Son of Man, then you will know that I am [the one I claim to be] and that I do nothing on my own but speak just what the Father has taught me." (8:28)

"'But I, when I am lifted up (*hypsoō*) from the earth, will draw all men to myself.' He said this to show the kind of death he was going to die." (12:32-33)

John speaks of Jesus' glorification in a way that includes the crucifixion, resurrection, and ascension as a single event.

"Up to that time the Spirit had not been given, since Jesus had not yet been **glorified** (*doxazō*)." (7:39b)

"Only after Jesus was **glorified** (*doxazō*) did they realize that these things had been written about him and that they had done these things to him." (12:16b)

"Isaiah said this because he saw Jesus' **glory** (*doxa*) and spoke about him." (12:41)

To the men on the road to Emmaus, Jesus explained the Scriptures and then said:

"Did not the Christ have to suffer these things and then enter his glory?" (Luke 24:26)

Glory Is Brought to Jesus through His Followers

To the Father: "All I have is yours, and all you have is mine. And **glory** has come to me through them." (17:10)

"I have given them the **glory** that you gave me, that they may be one as we are one." (17:22)

"Father, I want those you have given me to be with me where I am, and to see my **glory**, the **glory** you have given me because you loved me before the creation of the world." (17:24)

Jesus and His Disciples Bring Glory to the Father

Jesus instructs his disciples that by his life and death he is bringing glory to the Father, and they are to do likewise.

"When [Judas] was gone, Jesus said, 'Now is the Son of Man **glorified** and God is **glorified** in him. If God is **glorified** in him, God will **glorify** the Son in himself, and will **glorify** him at once.'" (13:31-32)

"And I will do whatever you ask in my name, so that the Son may bring **glory** to the Father." (14:13)

"This is to my Father's **glory**, that you bear much fruit, showing yourselves to be my disciples." (15:8)[977]

The High Priestly Prayer in John 17: "After Jesus said this, he looked toward heaven and prayed: 'Father, the time has come. **Glorify** your Son, that your Son may **glorify** you.'" (17:1)

"I have brought you **glory** on earth by completing the work you gave me to do. And now, Father, **glorify** me in your presence with the **glory** I had with you before the world began." (17:4-5)

"Jesus said this to indicate the kind of death by which Peter would **glorify** God." (21:19)

---

[977] We see something similar in Matthew: "Let your light shine before others, so that they may see your good works and give glory (*doxazō*) to your Father who is in heaven" (Matthew 5:16).

Appendix 7. The Chronology of Holy Week in John's Gospel

It is difficult to reconcile the chronology of Holy Week as recorded in John's Gospel with the Synoptic Gospels.

- **The Synoptic Gospels** seem to clearly place the Last Supper as a Passover Meal on Thursday night (Mark 14:12; Luke 22:15).

- **John's Gospel** – to many scholars – puts the Last Supper on Wednesday night, the day before Passover, due to seven verses: John 13:1, 27; 18:28; 19:14, 31, 36, 42.

Harry Anderson (1906-1996), 'Last Supper,' oil on canvas.

There are several ways commentators have dealt with this seeming lack of harmony.

1. Accept John's chronology as true, dismissing the Synoptic dating as self-contradictory.
2. Accept the Synoptic chronology as true, dismissing John's dating as an historical anomaly in order to gain a theological point of Jesus being the true paschal lamb.[978]

Neither of these approaches are acceptable to most evangelicals, who hold to the historical accuracy of the New Testament. Which leaves us two other explanations.

3. Accept both as possible due to disputes in calendars in the first century.
4. Accept the Synoptic chronology as correct, but assert that John's Gospel, rightly interpreted, doesn't contradict this chronology.

We'll consider the arguments for these last two explanations for this difficult question, though it is important to understand that these are *possible* explanations only. We shouldn't be dogmatic on this point. For details, see the commentaries.

For a guide to harmonizing the events of Holy Week between John and the Synoptics, see below Appendix 10. Harmony between John and the Synoptic Gospels.

---

[978] This seems to be the conclusion of the extensive discussion in Joachim Jeremias, Arnold Erhardt (translator), *The Eucharistic Words of Jesus* (Oxford: Basil Blackwell, 1935, 1949; translated 1955), pp. 1-60.

Calendars in the First Century

Essentially, this approach holds that there was some dispute among the Jews concerning the calendar, and that John and the Synoptics are using different calendars. With this approach, Marshall concludes that Jesus held a Passover meal earlier than the official Jewish date, and that he was able to do so as a result of calendar differences among the Jews. John makes use of a different calendar than the Synoptic writers to make the point that Jesus was crucified at the very time the Passover victims were slain in the temple. There is evidence of a calendar dispute between the Pharisees and Sadducees. As well there is evidence of a priestly calendar that we see in the Book of Jubilees, and the more usual one.[979]

Interpreting Carefully the Relevant Verses in John

Another approach to harmonization involves a careful interpretation of the seven verses on which John's chronology hinges. Here is how Carson interprets these verses.[980]

13:1 "It was just before the Passover Feast. Jesus knew that the time had come for him to leave this world and go to the Father." (Prior to Jesus washing the disciples' feet.) Taking this verse as the heading to chapters 13-17, would lead one to assume that the meal they're about to partake of is not the Passover meal. But if you take 13:1 to refer to the footwashing only, then the footwashing is placed before the Passover meal about to begin.[981]

13:27-29 "As soon as Judas took the bread, Satan entered into him. "What you are about to do, do quickly." ... Some thought Jesus was telling him to buy what was needed for the Feast, or to give something to the poor." (After Jesus washed the disciples' feet.) Some take this command to go out into the night to do something as evidence that this preceded the Passover meal, but this isn't convincing. "The Feast" could well refer to the Feast of Unleavened Bread that was about to begin.[982]

18:28 "Then the Jews led Jesus from Caiaphas to the palace of the Roman governor. By now it was early morning, and to avoid ceremonial uncleanness the Jews did not enter the palace; they wanted to be able to eat the Passover." One can interpret "eat the Passover" to refer, not to the Passover Meal itself, but the *hagigah*, the feast-offering offered on the morning of the first full paschal day (Numbers 28:18-19). We know that "the Passover" could refer to the combined feast of the paschal meal itself plus the ensuing Feast of Unleavened Bread, as in Luke 22:1.[983]

19:14 "It was the day of Preparation of Passover Week, about the sixth hour. 'Here is your king,' Pilate said to the Jews." (During Jesus' trial before Pilate). "Day of Preparation" is ambiguous. It could

---

[979] I. Howard Marshall (*Last Supper and Lord's Supper* (Eerdmans, 1980), pp. 57-75) considers various approaches in length, and concludes that different calendars is the best approach to harmonization. Also Morris, *John*, "Additional Note H: Last Supper and Passover," pp. 774-786.

[980] Beasley-Murray (*John*, pp. 225) discusses the problems and shows interest in Bultmann's harmonization along the lines of Carson's, but sees the need for "further patient investigation of the traditions behind the Last Supper...."

[981] Carson, *John*, pp. 460-461.

[982] Carson, *John* p. 475.

[983] Carson, *John*, pp. 588-590.

refer to the day before Passover. But it could also refer to the usual sense of Preparation (*paraskeuē*) Friday, preparing for Sabbath which begins Friday night. This interpretation would allow for Passover on a Thursday night, and Jesus' crucifixion on Friday.[984]

19:31 "Now it was the day of Preparation, and the next day was to be a special Sabbath. Because the Jews did not want the bodies left on the crosses during the Sabbath, they asked Pilate to have the legs broken and the bodies taken down." (After Jesus' death, when the soldiers pierced him in the side.) A "special Sabbath" would refer to Saturday, the day after Jesus' crucifixion, which was not only a Sabbath, but special because the second paschal day was devoted to the very important sheaf offering (Leviticus 23:11).[985]

19:36 "These things happened so that the scripture would be fulfilled: 'Not one of his bones will be broken.'" (After Jesus' death, when the soldiers pierced him in the side.) John's emphasis is that Jesus is the Passover Lamb. The quotation could be either from Exodus 12:46 or Numbers 9:12, regarding the Passover lamb. But it could also refer to Psalm 34:20 describing God's care for the righteous man (cf. Luke 23:47). This verse isn't decisive for the chronology of Holy Week.[986]

19:42 "Because it was the Jewish day of Preparation and since the tomb was nearby, they laid Jesus there." This would refer to the same day of Preparation as in 19:31, commented on above.

Harmonization of John and the Synoptics is not without its problems. But to those of us who believe in the accuracy and historicity of the New Testament, it is important.

Note: Each Easter season I have people e-mail me to attack my traditional chronology of Holy Week, with the Lord's Supper/Passover on Thursday night and the crucifixion on Friday. But I don't think the alternative chronology they offer is nearly as convincing!

[984] Carson, *John*, pp. 603-604.
[985] Carson, *John*, p. 622-623.
[986] Carson, *John*, p. 627.

Appendix 8. The Paraclete

In Jesus' clearest teaching on the coming Holy Spirit, he refers four times specifically, to the Paraclete -- 14:15-17; 25-26; 15:26; 16:5-15 -- and several other times to the Holy Spirit in related contexts.

Translating *Paraklētos*

Paraklētos is variously translated as the "Comforter" (KJV), "Counselor" (NIV, RSV), "Advocate" (NRSV), "Helper" (ESV). It can't be easy translated into English with a word that adequately covers its breadth of meaning.

Paraklētos is an adjective formed from the verb *parakaleō*, that has the basic meaning, "call to one's side" for help. But the verb *parakaleō* has a variety of extended meanings that complicate our understanding of the exact force of the noun in our passage – "to urge strongly, appeal to, urge, exhort, encourage," and "to make a

Louis Tiffany, Holy Spirit or Dove Window (1895-1900), First Presbyterian Church of Springfield, Illinois.

strong request for something, request, implore, entreat," then "comfort, encourage, cheer up," and perhaps "be friendly to, speak to in a friendly manner." [987]

Commentators seem to be agreed that *paraklētos* is passive in form, "called to the side of" for the purpose of helping, "called to one's aid," in a court of justice. As a substantive it means, "legal assistant, advocate." [988]

The translation "Comforter" comes from Wycliffe's translation into English (1392), which drew perhaps upon "comfort's" etymological sense (Latin, *con*, "with" + *fortis*, "strong"). In this sense it might denote "Strengthener," "Helper" (ESV). In Greek, the word can have the idea of one who provides help as a legal advocate, but more an advocate for the defense. Another approach might be "Friend," as in a Friend at court.

In the New Testament, the word is found only in the Johannine literature and is used twice of Christ, who pleads his people's cause before the Father (1 John 2:1), and, by implication, of the Holy Spirit as "another *paraklētos*" (besides Jesus). Elsewhere, *paraklētos* is used of the Holy Spirit (14:16), "the Spirit of truth" (15:26). [989]

---

[987] *Parakaleō*, BDAG 764-765.

[988] Liddell-Scott, *Greek-English Lexicon*.

[989] This appendix draws upon Leon Morris, "Additional Note F: The Paraclete," *John*, pp. 662-666; M.M.B. Turner, "Holy Spirit," DJG, pp. 349-351.

Another Paraclete in Addition to Jesus (14:16-17)

Jesus says that the Father will send "another[990] Counselor (*paraklētos*)." This implies that the disciples already have a Paraclete to help them, and that the Holy Spirit is another Paraclete in addition. Jesus is saying that at present he is their Paraclete – the one the Father has sent to help them. Jesus tells his disciples that they, unlike the world, are already familiar with this Paraclete:

"... For he lives with you and will be in you." (14:17b)

Jesus seems to be saying that in his own Person, they have experienced the Paraclete living or abiding[991] "with them"[992] or at their side. But, when the Father sends the Holy Spirit, this Paraclete will be (future tense[993]) within them.[994]

Jesus has been their Paraclete, Helper, Friend thus far, but the Holy Spirit will replace Jesus as an interior presence, always with them, to guide and instruct them.

The role of the Paraclete in relation to the disciples mirrors Jesus' role with them when he was on earth.[995]

Paraclete	Jesus
Spirit of truth (14:17; 16:13)	The Truth (14:6)
Holy Spirit (14:16)	Holy One of God (6:69)
Known by disciples (14:17)	14:7, 9
Guide into way of truth (16:13)	The Way, the Truth (14:6)
Teaches (14:26)	6:59; 7:14, 18; 8:20
Declares what is to come (16:14)	4:25-26
Bears witness (15:26-27)	8:14
Glorifies Jesus (16:14)	Glorifies the Father (8:28; 12:27-28; 14:13; 17:4)
World cannot accept (14:17)	Evil men do not accept (5:43; 12:48)
World does not see (14:17)	Men soon lose sight of (16:16)
World does not know or recognize (14:17)	Men do not know Jesus (16:3; cf. 7:28; 8:14, 19; 14:7)
Bears witness to the world's hate (15:26; cf. 15:18-25)	Bears witness against the world (7:7)

[990] "Another" is *allos*, "other, another" (BDAG 46-47).

[991] "Lives" (NIV), "abides" (NRSV), "dwells" (ESV, KJV) is *menō* in the present tense, "remain, stay," in transferred sense, "of someone who does not leave a certain realm or sphere: remain, continue, abide" (BDAG 631, 1aβ). It is possible that *menei*, present tense, could be accented as *meneî* making it future tense (which wouldn't show up in the manuscripts), but the present tense is more likely (Morris, *John*, p. 650, fn. 49).

[992] "With" is the preposition *para* with the dative, "marker of nearness in space, at/by (the side of), beside, near, with" (BDAG 757, 1).

[993] "Will/shall be" is *eimi*, "to be," in the future tense. Most ancient manuscripts show this as the future tense *estai*, except a few as present tense, *estin* – p[75] B D* W it. The future is likely here.

[994] "In" is the preposition *en*, "in," here, a "marker of close association within a limit, in" (BDAG 328, 4c).

[995] This chart draws upon Brown, *John* 2:1135-36, Appendix V: The Paraclete.

The Paraclete as a Person (14:26; 15:16, 26)

In many languages (Spanish, French, German, etc. – including Greek), words have masculine, feminine, or neuter genders or inflections that have no real counterpart in English.[996] While the "Spirit" is often referred to by a neuter Greek pronoun, since the *pneuma* has a neuter gender in Greek (such as in 14:17, 26; 15:26), on several occasions Jesus uses the masculine pronoun, apparently to emphasize the Spirit's personhood. Observe these verses.

> "But the Counselor, the Holy Spirit (neuter noun), whom (neuter pronoun) the Father will send in my name, **he** (masculine pronoun) will teach you all things and will remind you of everything I have said to you." (14:26)

> "When the Counselor comes, whom I will send to you from the Father, the Spirit (neuter noun) of truth who (neuter pronoun) goes out from the Father, **he** (masculine pronoun) will testify about me. (15:26)

> "When **he** (masculine pronoun), the Spirit (neuter noun) of truth, comes, he (no pronoun in Greek) will guide you into all truth." (16:13a)

C.K. Barrett observes, "The Spirit is thought of in personal terms."[997]

There is solid biblical evidence that points to a conclusion that the Holy Spirit is a distinct person in his own right and performs functions we attribute to personhood. The Holy Spirit appoints missionaries (Acts 13:2; 20:28), he leads and directs them in their ministry (Acts 8:29; 10:19-20; 16:6-7; 1 Corinthians 2:13), he speaks through the prophets (Acts 1:16; 1 Peter 1:11-12; 2 Peter 1:21), he corrects (John 16:8), comforts (Acts 9:31), helps us in our infirmities (Romans 8:26), teaches (John 14:26; 1 Corinthians 12:3), guides (John 16:13), sanctifies (Romans 15:16; 1 Corinthians 6:11), testifies of Christ (John 15:26), glorifies Christ (John 16:14), has a power of his own (Romans 15:13), searches all things (Romans 11:33-34; 1 Corinthians 2:10-11), works according to his own will (1 Corinthians 12:11), dwells with saints (John 14:17), can be grieved (Ephesians 4:30), can be resisted (Acts 7:51), and can be tempted (Acts 5:9). These are functions we attribute to persons, not to impersonal forces. John sees the Holy Spirit as a Person, sent by the Father to replace Jesus' physical presence as the Paraclete with them.

The personal nature of the Spirit is confirmed in the foundational creeds of the Church. The Nicene Creed uses personal terms to explain our belief in the Spirit.

> "And [we believe] in the Holy Spirit, the Lord and Giver of life, who proceeds from the Father, who with the Father and the Son together is worshiped and glorified, who spoke by the prophets."[998]

---

[996] Though in English we sometimes refer to ships with a feminine gender as "her sails."

[997] Barrett, *John*, p. 482, commenting on John 15:26. See also George Eldon Ladd, *A Theology of the New Testament* (Eerdmans, 1974), p. 295.

[998] This is the revised version of the original Nicene Creed (325 AD), which was adopted at the First Council of Constantinople (381 AD).

The Paraclete as Teacher, Reminder, Witness, and Guide to Truth

One of the important roles of the Paraclete is to guide Jesus' disciples as they remember and then begin to understand what Jesus' taught them while on earth. Various Paraclete passages describe these roles of Teacher, Reminder, Witness, and Guide to truth.

The Paraclete will teach (*didaskō*) the disciples all things (14:25-26). He will also remind[999] the disciples of what Jesus taught. We probably shouldn't divide reminding and teaching as two *separate* functions. Reminding is part of the teaching function.

The Paraclete also testifies about Jesus (15:26). Since the word *paraklētos* has a legal flavor, it is particularly appropriate alongside another word from the legal realm, *martyreō*, "to confirm or attest something on the basis of personal knowledge or belief, bear witness, be a witness, offer testimony."[1000] The Spirit presents Christ's case for him before the believers and the world.[1001]

Elsewhere, Jesus told his disciples not to worry about what to say when they are brought into court (Luke 12:11b-12). The Paraclete serves as the believers' legal advisor as needed when they are persecuted.

In verse 16:13a, Jesus promises his disciples that the "Spirit of truth" will guide them into all truth. "Guide" is *hodēgeō*. Literally, it means, "to assist in reaching a desired destination, lead, guide." Here it is used figuratively, "to assist someone in acquiring information or knowledge, lead, guide, conduct."[1002] The Paraclete isn't said here to bring a new revelation (16:13). Rather he represents Jesus and makes Jesus' teaching clear.

Jesus has been the disciples' rabbi and teacher. Now the Holy Spirit will take over that function. The disciples often misunderstood what Jesus had said and done. When the Holy Spirit comes, he will help them remember so they can understand and interpret correctly for the church what Jesus had taught them. Now they'll be assessing Jesus' words in the light of his crucifixion, resurrection, and ascension. Evangelicals believe that the Holy Spirit superintended the development of apostolic doctrine so that it properly interpreted Jesus' own teaching (2:17, 22; 12:16).

In our day, we must seek the Spirit's guidance with great humility and desire to learn. Spiritual truths must be spiritually discerned through the action of the Holy Spirit (1 Corinthians 2:12-14).

The Holy Spirit as Empowerer (14:12 and 16:7)

The Holy Spirit would not only guide, encourage, teach, and remind them, as Jesus had done, but he will also empower them.

---

[999] "Remind" (NIV, NRSV), "bring to your remembrance" (RSV, ESV, KJV) is the verb *hypomimnēskō*, "to put another in mind of something, remind," from *mimnēskomai*, "to recall information from memory, remember, recollect, remind oneself." I don't see much influence on the meaning of the word from the prefix *hypo-*. In classical Greek, *hypomimnēskō* denoted, "put one in mind or remind one of" as well as, "bring to one's mind, mention, suggest" (Liddell-Scott, *Greek-English Lexicon*). The word is also used at Luke 22:61; 2 Timothy 2:14; Titus 3:1; 2 Peter 1:12; 3 John 10; and Jude 5. The noun form *hypomnēsis* is used at 2 Peter 1:13; 3:1; 2 Timothy 1:5.

[1000] *Martyreō*, from the legal sphere (BDAG 612, 1aα). "In John, witness is especially the witness that is given, not specifically to the facts of Jesus' history, but to the person of Jesus." H. Strathmann, *martyr, ktl.*, TDNT 4:474-514.

[1001] Morris, *John*, p. 684.

[1002] *Hodge*, BDAG 690, 2. It is an old verb, from the noun *hoods*, "way" and *hēgeomai*, "to lead."

> "I tell you the truth, anyone who has faith in me will do what I have been doing. He will do even greater things than these, because I am going to the Father." (14:12)

After the resurrection, Jesus tells his disciples:

> "I am going to send you what my Father has promised; but stay in the city until you have been clothed with power from on high." (Luke 24:49)

> "You will receive power when the Holy Spirit comes on you; and you will be my witnesses in Jerusalem, and in all Judea and Samaria, and to the ends of the earth." (Acts 1:8)

This is part of the meaning of 16:17 where Jesus says, "It is for your good that I am going away." The Spirit is the power behind the various kinds of spiritual gifts given to the Church (1 Corinthians 12, etc.),

The Paraclete as Convictor of the World (16:8-11)

So far, Jesus had told his disciples how the Paraclete, the Holy Spirit, will benefit them. Now he explains how the Holy Spirit will affect the world.

> "When he comes, he will convict the world of guilt in regard to sin and righteousness and judgment." (16:8)

The role of the Holy Spirit convicting sinners is clear. "Convict of guilt" (NIV), "convict" (ESV, NKJV), "prove wrong" (NRSV), "convince" (RSV), "reprove" (KJV) is the verb *elenchō*, "to bring a person to the point of recognizing wrongdoing, convict, convince someone of something, point something out to someone."[1003] The word occurs 18 times in the New Testament, in each instance having to do with showing someone his sin, usually as a summons to repentance.[1004]

The Spirit As Christ's Voice to Us (16:13b-15)

The Spirit, Jesus explains to us, will listen to Jesus and relay this to us, just as Jesus listened to the Father and relayed that to his disciples (5:30), and only spoke what the Father told him to say (12:49).

> "13b He will not speak on his own; he will speak only what he hears, and he will tell[1005] you what is yet to come. 14 He will bring glory to me by taking from what is mine and making it known to you. 15 All that belongs to the Father is mine. That is why I said the Spirit will take from what is mine and make it known to you." (16:13b-15)

Both Jesus and the Spirit will speak the Father's words to us. We don't have the task of the first apostles who helped lay the doctrinal foundation of the Church, but we still seek to understand the Word of God accurately. We also need the Spirit's guidance as we seek him on how to minister and

---

[1003] *Elenchō*, BDAG 315, 2. The focus in classical Greek is on "putting to shame, treating with contempt, cross-examining, accusing, bringing to the test, proving, refuting" (Carson, *John*, p. 534).

[1004] Carson, *John*, p. 534, citing Friedrich Büschel, *elenchō, ktl.*, TDNT 2:473-474.

[1005] "Tell" (NIV) in verse 13b and "make known" (NIV) in verse 14 and 15, "declare" (NRSV, ESV), "shew" (KJV), is *anangellō*, literally, "to carry back information, report," then, generally, "to provide information, disclose, announce, proclaim, teach" (BDAG 59, 2), from *ana-*, "back, again" + *angellō*, "announce," *angelia*, "message." Our word "evangel" and "evangelism," tell good news, come from the same root.

what to say to people. The Spirit serves as our conduit into the very mind of Christ (1 Corinthians 2:10-16). With the Spirit living within us we are truly blessed.

Appendix 9. The Sending of the Holy Spirit

In the Farewell Discourses, Jesus is clear that the Holy Spirit, the Paraclete, will be sent after his death, resurrection, and ascension. One of the questions that has divided Christians historically is who will send the Spirit – the Father or Jesus. Look at the passages in question:

Paolo Veronese (Calairi, 1528-1588), 'The Eternal Father' (oil on canvas), Hospital Tavera, Toledo, Spain.

> "And I will ask the Father, and **he will give you another Counselor**...." (14:16)

> "But the Counselor, the Holy Spirit, whom **the Father will send in my name**...." (14:26a)

> "When the Counselor comes, whom **I will send to you from the Father**, the Spirit of truth who goes out from the Father...." (15:26)

> "Unless I go away, the Counselor will not come to you; but if I go, **I will send him** to you." (16:7b)

In a related passage from Luke, Jesus says at his ascension:

> "I am going to send you what my Father has promised...." (Luke 24:49)

There is no real conflict, since Jesus and the Father are one in purpose and action. It is common to attribute an action to the authorizing authority, not to those who implement the action. For example, Herod Antipas beheaded John the Baptist – that is, he authorized it, but he didn't perform the act itself (Mark 6:16). It is said that Solomon built the temple, but didn't do the labor himself (1 Kings 6:2).

As simple as this might seem, this issue has divided the Western Church from the Eastern Church for nearly two thousand years. The issue involves the term *filoque*, Latin for "and (from) the Son."

The original Greek version of the Nicene Creed, adopted by the Council of Nicea in 325 AD, and amended by the Council of Constantinople in 381 AD reads:

> "And [we believe] in the Holy Ghost, the Lord and Giver-of-Life,
> **who proceeds[1006] from the Father**,
> who with the Father and the Son together is worshipped and glorified...."

However, the Western version, used in the West since the sixth century, and adopted by the Pope in 1014 AD (without agreement by the Eastern Church), reads:

> "And [we believe] in the Holy Spirit, the Lord, the giver of life,
> **who proceeds from the Father *and the Son*,**
> who with the Father and the Son is adored and glorified...."

[1006] The word "proceeds" or "proceedeth" in the Nicene Creed is taken from John 15:26, and is a translation of the Greek verb *ekporeuomai*, "to come forth from, come/go out, proceed" (BDAG 308, 2).

In other words, the Western version says the Holy Spirit comes forth from the Father *and the Son*, while the Eastern version affirms only that the Holy Spirit comes forth from the Father.

Though the issue of papal primacy and stubborn pride are the main cause for the schism between the Eastern and Western Churches in 1054 AD, the issue of the *filoque* has contributed to the conflict, and is an obstacle to modern attempts at reunification.

Appendix 10. Harmony between John and the Synoptic Gospels

Anyone who takes time to compare the accounts of Jesus' Passion and Resurrection will notice differences between John's Gospel and the Synoptic Gospels – Matthew, Mark, and Luke. For most of Jesus' life, John and the Synoptics rarely coincide, because John, for the most part, describes different incidents and teachings. But when we get to the Last Supper, Jesus' arrest, trial, crucifixion, burial, and resurrection we see differences.

Most of these differences can be attributed to John's different style and eyewitness perspective. After all, by the time John's Gospel was written in the 90s AD, the Synoptic Gospels had been circulating throughout the churches for at least twenty years. John felt no need to repeat what had been recorded already. But he did feel a need to paint a picture of Jesus with an evangelistic purpose:

Jacob Jordaens, "The Four Evangelists" (1625–1630), Louvre Museum, Paris.

> "Jesus did many other miraculous signs in the presence of his disciples, which are not recorded in this book. But these are written that you may believe that Jesus is the Christ, the Son of God, and that by believing you may have life in his name." (20:30-31)

To do this John was very selective about the material he chose to include and leave out. If an incident or detail didn't fit his purpose, it wasn't included. So we shouldn't be surprised by the differences.

However, we are surprised that in some cases the details seem to differ, or the order of events varies. Reasons for these differences are several. One important factor is that first century standards of historical accuracy are very different from our own. What was common and expected in the first century is different from what we expect of historians in our own time, so it's important to judge the gospel writers by the standards of their own age rather than ours.

One particular challenge in harmonizing John and the Synoptic Gospels is that day upon which Jesus partook of the Last Supper with his disciples, and was crucified. This is discussed above in Appendix 7. The Chronology of Holy Week in John's Gospel.

The study of the differences between the Gospels, especially between John and the Synoptics, is known as "the Synoptic Problem," and is the subject of many, many books. Much of what has resulted is multiplied speculation. In this volume, my purpose is primarily to develop disciples who will follow Jesus their Master. So I'm not spending a great deal of time on the Synoptic Problem. For more on this topic, consult an introduction to the New Testament.

However, some may find a tentative harmony of John's Gospel and the Synoptic Gospels to be useful. Just realize that this harmony – and, indeed, any harmony of the Gospels – is speculative.

Devout students of the Bible will disagree about the details. And that's okay. This is a brief harmony I found on the Internet.

Harmony of the Events of Holy Week

Day	Event	Matt	Mark	Luke	John
Fri/Sat	Jesus arrives in Bethany				12:1
	Mary anoints Jesus				12:2–8
	Crowd comes to see Jesus				12:9–11
Sunday	Triumphal entry into Jerusalem	21:1–11	11:1–10	19:28–44	12:12–18
	Some Greeks seek Jesus				12:20–36
	Enters temple		11:11		
	Returns to Bethany	21:17	11:11		
Monday	Jesus curses the fig tree	21:18–19	11:12–14		
	Clears the temple	21:12–13	11:15–17	19:45–46	
	Returns to Bethany with the Twelve		11:19		
Tuesday	Disciples see the withered fig tree on the return to Jerusalem	21:20–22	11:20–21		
	Temple controversies in Jerusalem	21:23–23:39	11:27–12:44	20:1–21:4	
	Olivet Discourse on the return to Bethany	24:1–25:46	13:1–37	21:5–36	
Wednesday	Jesus continues daily teaching in the temple			21:37–38	
	Sanhedrin plots to kill Jesus	26:3–5	14:1–2	22:1–2	
Wed/Thur	Preparations for the Passover	26:17–19	14:12–16	22:7–13	
Thursday	Passover meal/Last Supper	26:20–35	14:17–26	22:14–30	
	Upper Room Discourse				13:1–17:26
	Jesus prays in Gethsemane	26:36–46	14:32–42	22:39–46	
Friday	Betrayal and arrest (after midnight?)	26:47–56	14:43–52	22:47–53	18:2–12
	Jewish trial:				
	—before Annas				18:13–24

Day	Event	Matt	Mark	Luke	John
	—before Caiaphas and part of the Sanhedrin	26:57–75	14:53–72	22:54–65	18:19–24
	—before full Sanhedrin (after sunrise?)	27:1–2	15:1	22:66–71	
	Roman trials:				
	—before Pilate	27:2–14	15:2–5	23:1–5	
	—before Herod			23:6–12	
	—before Pilate	27:15–26	15:6–15	23:13–25	18:28–19:16
	Crucifixion (approx. 9:00 a.m. to 3:00 p.m.)	27:27–54	15:16–39	23:26–49	19:16–37
	Burial (evening)	27:57–61	15:42–47	23:50–54	19:38–42
Sunday	Empty-tomb witnesses	28:1–8	16:1–8	24:1–12	
	Resurrection appearances	28:9–20	16:9–20	24:13–53	20:1–21:25

Appendix 11. A Possible Harmonization of the Resurrection Accounts

The gospel accounts are similar, but each is different.

First of all, it's pretty clear that Mark 16:9-19, the so-called longer ending of Mark, wasn't part of the original gospel, that ended – at least the surviving edition that we have – with verse 8. Perhaps the last page was lost. Verses 9-19 were added by the early church because it seemed strange that Mark ended abruptly as it did. Not that these verses are misleading, but they aren't part of the original gospel.

When you compare each of the stories, you can find a number of differences. For example:

Matthias Grünwald, 'Resurrection' (1512-1516), 106x112-1/2 in. The Isenheim Alterpiece (Diptych), Musee d'Unterlinden, Colmar.

1. *Women.* In the Synoptic Gospels, Mary Magdalene and other women go to the tomb. In John's account, Mary Magdalene goes alone.

2. *Appearance to the women.* In Matthew 28:9, Jesus appears to the women before they tell the disciples. In John 20:13-17, Jesus appears to Mary Magdalene (also in the longer ending of Mark) – *after* she reports to the disciples. In Mark, the women tell no one of what they had seen.

3. *Number of angels.* In Matthew and Mark one angel appears; in Luke and John there are two angels.

4. *Purpose of the women's visit.* In Matthew, they go to look at the tomb. In Mark and Luke, they bring spices to anoint Jesus' body. In John the anointing took place on Friday night and no purpose for Mary's visit is given.

5. *Grave clothes.* In Matthew and Mark, Jesus is wrapped in a large linen shroud (*sidrōn*). In John 19:40; 20:5-7 and Luke 24:12, Jesus is wrapped in strips of linen (*othonion*). See the discussion below.

6. *Location.* In Matthew and Mark, Jesus' resurrection appearances are in Galilee, while Luke only records appearances in the vicinity of Jerusalem.[1]

My point isn't to try to pick apart the account or cause you to disbelieve it. But to stimulate you to see what's there. Most of these differences are minor and can be explained or harmonized rather easily.

Eyewitness Accounts

A more troubling question is if eyewitnesses can't seem to get their stories straight, whether we can believe the story or not. When you think about it, you realize that these very differences validate the authenticity of the story.

Whenever you have eyewitnesses testify to any event that they all see, there'll be minor points of difference in what they saw and how they perceived the event. If all the eyewitnesses agree in every detail, a good investigator begins to suspect collusion between the witnesses before testifying.

The Church has been aware of these minor differences in the resurrection accounts for many centuries. Some might express concern with how this might affect our doctrine of the authority of scripture (2 Timothy 3:16). But surely our understanding of the inspiration of scripture must be large enough to encompass the gospel accounts as we find them. Rather than seeing these accounts as evidence of error, the Church has viewed them as evidence of authenticity, representing various eyewitness traditions that are remarkably united on the main points.

Points of Agreement

In the big, important things we see five main points of agreement. They include:

1. Jesus was dead and buried.

2. The disciples were not prepared for Jesus' death. They were overcome with confusion.

3. The tomb was found on Easter morning to be empty. But this in itself didn't inspire faith. Mary thought the body was stolen.

4. The disciples encountered a number of experiences that they took to be appearances of Jesus risen from the dead.

5. The disciples proclaimed the resurrection of Jesus in Jerusalem, near where he had been buried.[1007]

My Biblical exegesis professor at Fuller Theological Seminary, George Eldon Ladd, didn't really recommend a harmonization approach to the resurrection accounts. However, to answer his own question of whether the accounts *could* be harmonized, he worked out the following harmonization, he said, for his own amusement.[1008] Later he found a nearly identical harmonization by Michael C. Perry. Here is George Ladd's approach to a harmonization:

1. The earthquake and removal of stone occurs before dawn.

2. A group of four women come early to the tomb, wondering who will move the stone. As they approach, they are amazed to see that the stone has been rolled away.

3. Mary rushes off to tell Peter and John that the body of Jesus has been stolen (John 20:2).

4. The other women stay in the garden. They enter the tomb and are met by two angels, who tell them to carry the word of the resurrection to the disciples.[1009]

[1007] Ladd, Eldon Ladd, *I Believe in the Resurrection* (Eerdmans, 1975), pp. 93.

[1008] Ladd, *Resurrection*, pp. 91-93.

[1009] Ladd says, "The problem of a young man of Mark 16:5, two men of Luke 24:4, angels of Luke 24:23, is one of the ordinary Synoptic divergencies – of detail" (*Resurrection*, p. 92).

5. The women rush away from the garden, filled with mingled emotions of fear and joy, speaking to no one about the vision of the angels at the empty tomb (Mark 16:8).

6. Later in the day, Jesus met them. (Matthew 28:9 does not say that this meeting occurred in the garden.) They had to run away from the tomb. Jesus tells them to bear the word to the disciples; they depart to find the disciples, who are not together but scattered (Matthew 26:56).

7. Peter and John, having been informed by Mary, come to the tomb after the women have left. They see the clothes; vague comprehension dawns on John. they rush off to gather the disciples.

8. Mary returns to the tomb after Peter and John have left; they had run to the tomb (John 20:4), leaving Mary behind. She still thinks the body has been stolen. She is weeping outside the tomb, knowing nothing of the experience of the women she had left in the garden. She sees the two angels, then Jesus (John 20:11-17).[1010]

9. After the first shock of amazement had worn off, the women find some of the disciples; the disciples cannot believe the fanciful story (Luke 24:11).

10. The disciples have gathered together.

11. Mary arrives and tells her experience (John 20:18).

12. That afternoon, the walk to Emmaus.

13. Sometime that afternoon, an appearance to Peter (Luke 24:34).

14. That evening, the disciples are all together in the closed room. They had been scattered, but the testimony of the women, of Peter and John, then of Mary, serves to bring them all together. Thomas was absent.

15. A second appearance to the eleven, including Thomas.

16. Galilee (Matthew 28:16). The appearance by Tiberias (John 21) and to the 500 brethren (1 Corinthians 15:6).

17. Return to Jerusalem; the final appearance and ascension.

Ladd concludes,

"This harmonization does not mean that the author intends to suggest that the events actually happened in this order. We cannot know."[1011]

[1010] Ladd notes that Mark's longer ending, 16:9 here, is not original (*Resurrection*, p. 92).
[1011] Ladd, *Resurrection*, p. 93.

CPSIA information can be obtained
at www.ICGtesting.com
Printed in the USA
BVHW062213071021
618308BV00002B/13

9 780996 202503